# Globalisation, Migration and Health
*Challenges and Opportunities*

# Globalisation, Migration and Health
## *Challenges and Opportunities*

Edited by

## Andre M N Renzaho
University of Western Sydney, Australia

Imperial College Press

*Published by*

Imperial College Press
57 Shelton Street
Covent Garden
London WC2H 9HE

*Distributed by*

World Scientific Publishing Co. Pte. Ltd.
5 Toh Tuck Link, Singapore 596224
*USA office:* 27 Warren Street, Suite 401-402, Hackensack, NJ 07601
*UK office:* 57 Shelton Street, Covent Garden, London WC2H 9HE

**Library of Congress Cataloging-in-Publication Data**
Names: Renzaho, Andre M. N., author.
Title: Globalisation, migration and health : challenges and opportunities / Andre M.N. Renzaho,
 (Humanitarian and Development Studies, University of Western Sydney, Australia).
Description: New Jersey : Imperial College Press, 2016. |
 Includes bibliographical references and index.
Identifiers: LCCN 2015035385 | ISBN 9781783268887 (alk. paper)
Subjects: LCSH: Public health--International cooperation. | Human beings--Migrations--
 Health aspects. | Medical policy--Cross-cultural aspects.
Classification: LCC RA441 .R46 2016 | DDC 362.1--dc23
LC record available at http://lccn.loc.gov/2015035385

**British Library Cataloguing-in-Publication Data**
A catalogue record for this book is available from the British Library.

Copyright © 2016 by Imperial College Press

*All rights reserved. This book, or parts thereof, may not be reproduced in any form or by any means, electronic or mechanical, including photocopying, recording or any information storage and retrieval system now known or to be invented, without written permission from the Publisher.*

For photocopying of material in this volume, please pay a copying fee through the Copyright Clearance Center, Inc., 222 Rosewood Drive, Danvers, MA 01923, USA. In this case permission to photocopy is not required from the publisher.

In-house Editors: Mary Simpson/Nisha Rahul

Typeset by Stallion Press
Email: enquiries@stallionpress.com

Printed in Singapore by Mainland Press Pte Ltd.

*For…*

*My late mother Pilcherie Mutarataza and father Francois Renzaho. Without you I will not be where and who I am today. You inspired me, shaped my education, and provided me love, encouragement, and support throughout my life.
Requiescat In Pace!*

*Without forgetting people fleeing famine and political upheaval, victims of poverty and deprivation*

# About the book editor

Professor André M.N. Renzaho holds a PhD degree in Public Health from Deakin University (awarded in April 2005) and a Master of Public Health degree from the University of Melbourne (awarded in September 2000, with distinction). He is an ARC Future Fellow and Professor of Humanitarian and Development Studies at the University of Western Sydney (UWS). He joined UWS in 2015 and prior to that he was the Director of Migration, Social Disadvantage, and Health Programmes within the Global Society Unit, the Department of Epidemiology & Preventive Medicine at Monash University. He is internationally renowned for his work in public health in complex humanitarian emergencies and among migrants from developing to developed countries. He has more than 20 years of professional experience in cultural studies, migration and health, especially with respect to forced migration such as natural disasters and complex (protracted) humanitarian emergencies, as well as voluntary migration focusing on the epidemiology of non-chronic diseases and their determinants among migrant populations in developed countries. From 2003 to 2006, he oversaw the evaluation of more than 40 AusAID NGO Cooperation Programmes with World Vision Australia covering Sub-Saharan Africa, Eastern Europe, the Middle East, Latin America, the Pacific, and Asia; and acted as the Technical Director of the Impact Assessment of Australian Aid for the

Bougainville Infrastructure. From 1992 to 1997, he worked with a number of non-government organizations and United Nations agencies including working with Care Australia, Concern Worldwide, Médecins Sans Frontières (MSF), the United Nations High Commission for Refugees (UNHCR), and the United Nations Children's Fund (UNICEF). Professor Renzaho has undertaken research in humanitarian aid and development assistance in developing countries. His recent work in this field includes being the chief lead investigator for the study on Buruli ulcer in Ghana (2005), mortality, nutrition, and food security study in Vanuatu (2004) and during the emergency in Mozambique (2004) and Lesotho (2005), the anthropological aspects of HIV/AIDS in Tanzania and Malawi (2005; 2006), maternal and child health study in Laos (2005), the evaluation of the emergency response and disaster mitigation initiatives in Kenya, Rwanda, Uganda and D.R. Congo (2005), the evaluation of child sponsorship programmes in Ecuador (2006), the evaluation of AusAID support for child nutrition (2013), and the evaluation of the 'Urban Programme on Livelihoods and Income Fortification and Socio-civic Transformation for the Youth in Kampala, Uganda' (2014). He also undertakes consultancy work for State and Commonwealth Governments in Australia and has been a member of a number of governmental and non-governmental Boards, Committees, Expert Panels, and Taskforces.

# Contributors

**Dr Chuck Hui, MD FRCPC,** is a paediatric infectious diseases consultant at the Children's Hospital of Eastern Ontario and an Associate Professor of paediatrics at the University of Ottawa, Ottawa, Canada. An active clinician teacher, he is actively involved in knowledge synthesis and translation of issues pertaining to children and youth that are new to Canada. He has worked with national societies, governments and intergovernmental organisations on migrant child health issues.

**Professor David Mellor, PhD,** is a Professor in the School of Psychology, and Associate Dean (International) for the Faculty of Health at Deakin University, Australia. Professor Mellor teaches into the postgraduate professional programmes in Psychology, and supervises higher degree research students. He has strong research partnerships in Malaysia, China and Chile, and holds honorary visiting professor positions at the Universidad de La Frontera in Temuco (Chile) and Shanghai Mental Health Center-Jiao Tong University.

**Dr Doug Gruner, MD,** is a family physician and Assistant Professor at the University of Ottawa and works at the Bruyere Family Health Center as a clinician, educator and researcher. His area of research involves introducing Global Health and Refugee Medicine to medical students through e-learning.

His interest in refugee health took root after his work in East Timor with the International Committee of the Red Cross and the many refugees he treated while there. He has also worked internationally in Asia, South America and Africa. He became involved in advocacy work in Canada after government cuts to Interim Federal Health in 2012 and is a founding member of the Canadian Doctors for Refugee Care (CDRC).

**Ms Emily Hadgkiss, MPH,** is a public health researcher based in Melbourne, Australia. Her research into asylum seeker health and wellbeing in Australia informed her Public Health Master's thesis and a scoping study for the Social Justice Through Health programme at St Vincent's Health Australia.

**Dr Fabien Schneider, MPH,** is a medical humanitarian programme coordinator at Médecins Sans Frontières (MSF). He has been working with MSF for the past 14 years. He carried out field missions as Nurse, Field Coordinator, Emergency Coordinator, Medical Coordinator and Country Director. He joined the MSF headquarters in Switzerland in 2009 as Programme Manager. He moved to Canada in 2012 to join the MSF Canada office to develop new projects supporting the MSF operation on the field.

**Dr Ilmiye Secer, PhD,** is a lecturer in the Department of Psychology, Eastern Mediterranean University, North Cyprus. She teaches the undergraduate and postgraduate programmes and her research interests are in examining the psychological wellbeing of migrants and the process of acculturation. She also conducts research in the area of cognitive psychology and bilingualism among younger and older adults.

**Professor John Toumbourou, PhD,** is the Chair in Health Psychology within the School of Psychology and Director of Prevention Science in the Centre for Social and Early Emotional Development at Deakin University. He is a prominent social advocate in areas related to child and adolescent mental health promotion and the prevention of alcohol and drug problems, and has been influential internationally and nationally in assisting the development of research and practice in the fields of prevention science and health psychology.

**Mr Joseph Kamara, MICD,** is a Regional Manager for East and West Africa Portfolio at World Vision Australia. He holds a Master's degree in International and Community Development from Deakin University in

Melbourne, Australia and a Bachelor of Development studies from Makerere University in Kampala, Uganda. He has experience of working in various countries and contexts in Africa and Asia, and previously led World Visions' humanitarian responses in Uganda and Mozambique.

**Professor Kevin Dunn, PhD,** is Dean of the School of Social Sciences and Psychology and Professor of Human Geography and Urban Studies at the University of Western Sydney. His areas of research include the geographies of racism, immigration and settlement, Islam in Australia, and local government and multiculturalism. Recent books include *Landscapes: Ways of Imagining the World*, and his recent articles are published in *Analyses of Social Issues and Public Policy, Race and Class, Ethnicities, The Australian Geographer, Studia Islamika, Journal of Intercultural Studies* and the *Australian Journal of Social Issues*. He is a Fellow of the New South Wales Geographical Society and Vice President.

**A/Professor Kevin Pottie, MD,** is an Associate Professor at the Departments of Family Medicine and Epidemiology & Community Medicine, and scientist at the Bruyere Research Institute, University of Ottawa, Canada. In 2011, he published an internationally unique evidence-based migrant health guideline series covering infectious diseases, mental health, and women and child health. In 2013, he won an outstanding national leadership award for contributions to minority and under-served populations

**Dr Lata Satyen, PhD,** is a lecturer in the School of Psychology at Deakin University and a registered psychologist. She teaches across the undergraduate and postgraduate programmes and supervises higher degrees by research students. She conducts research in the area of migrant wellbeing and family violence. Lata assists women from culturally and linguistically diverse communities at various levels in her capacity as a pro bono psychologist. She especially assists migrant women in critical and non-critical situations of family violence.

**Dr Matin Ghayour-Minaie, PhD,** is a research fellow at Deakin University, School of Psychology. She is a skilled social researcher with expertise in health service consulting and family interventions. Her areas of interest include parenting, alcohol and drug use problems and early prevention, adolescence mental health and transition to young adulthood. She is experienced at conducting evaluation projects within the Prevention Science Group and working with families and communities, and specifically working with migrants and refugees.

**Dr Mary Lou de Leon Siantz, PhD,** is a Professor in the Betty Irene Moore School of Nursing and Founding Director of the University of California Davis Center for Multicultural Perspectives on Science. She is internationally known for her research on population health focused on the impact of migration on the risk, protective factors, and resilience of Latino migrant and immigrant families and children.

**Dr Naomi Priest, PhD,** is a Fellow, Australian Centre for Applied Social Research Methods, Research School of Social Sciences, Australian National University. She is also a visiting scientist at Harvard T.H. Chan School of Public Health. She conducts research on the determinants of child health inequalities with a focus on the contribution of discrimination and racism, ethnic/racial socialisation and how children develop racial/ethnic attitudes, and anti-racism and prejudice reduction interventions among children and youth.

**Dr Olta Gishti, PhD,** is a postdoc researcher at the Generation R Study, Erasmus University Medical Center, Rotterdam, the Netherlands. Her work consists of studying several exposures during foetal life and early childhood that might influence health outcomes in later childhood. Recently, she has also studied the ethnic differences in childhood cardiovascular risk factors and its determinants.

**Dr Paul Herfs, PhD,** is a senior researcher at the European Research Centre on Migration and Ethnic Relations of Utrecht University in the Netherlands. He has been closely involved in the integration of International Medical Graduates (IMG) in Dutch health care as many foreign doctors are confronted with non-recognition of their medical degrees.

**Ms Rosalie Atie, BA Hons,** has been a research assistant with the Challenging Racism Project and associated projects at the University of Western Sydney since 2011. These projects include a partnership project with NSW Police on the effects of NSW Police community engagement counter-radicalisation model, a partnership project with the Islamic

Sciences and Research Academy on the Ordinariness of Australian Muslims, an ARC-funded study on ethnic discrimination in the private rental housing market, and an ARC-funded project on cyber-racism and community resilience. She is currently undertaking a PhD at the University of Western Sydney on the poetics, performatives and politics of slam poetry in Western Sydney.

**Dr Sheila Cyril, MPH,** is a Research Fellow in the Department of Epidemiology and Preventive Medicine within the School of Public Health and Preventive Medicine, Monash University, Melbourne, Australia. She is currently managing a study involving the engagement of migrants, new arrivals and ethnic minorities in obesity prevention programmes in Victoria.

**Professor Yin Paradies, PhD,** is Deputy Director (Research) of the Alfred Deakin Institute for Citizenship and Globalisation and Professor of Race Relations at Deakin University. He conducts interdisciplinary research on the health, social and economic effects of racism as well as anti-racism theory, policy and practice.

# Acknowledgements

Since becoming an academic in 2007, it has become clear to me that it is important to balance family and academic life. In order to become successful, you need a strong and supportive family and I have been fortunate to have one. I would like to acknowledge the support, advice and encouragement of my wife Dr Catherine Renzaho, who not only is a loving and supportive partner, but has also been a great mentor who has invested a significant portion of her time to help me develop personally and professionally. Despite having had to work hard and to look after our three children, she always found a way of creating space for me to allow me to complete my writing while also providing professional advice and encouragement, and ultimately the moral support required to complete such a monumental task. I thank our three children, Didier, Daniel and Mireille for being great children and being accommodating, and for their patience and tolerance during my research endeavours. They are the best children to have around me during my writing retreats, fun to be with, happy and loving. They are my rock, motivators and inspiration: hence I dedicate this book to them. With admiration, gratitude and affection, my thanks go to my family back in the Democratic Republic of Congo (formerly Zaire) and my wife's family in Australia for their moral support and encouragement.

I would like to acknowledge Dr Sheila Cyril for help in coordinating the book write-up, chasing contributors and helping them get their endnotes and bibliography in order, and for making sure we are on track. I acknowledge the efforts of the many reviewers who commented on various book chapters. In particular, I would like to thank the following: Dr Apostolos Veizis, Director of Medical Operational Support, Aurélie Ponthieu, Humanitarian Adviser on Displacement, and Dr Ioanna Kotsioni, Migration Advisor from Médecins Sans Frontières for reviewing earlier drafts of the chapter on asylum seekers in Greece, Professor Li Ling, Director of Sun Yat-sen Center for Migrant Health Policy and Professor of School of Public Health at Sun Yat-sen University for her thorough review of the chapter on China, and Professor Mike Toole, Deputy Director, Burnet Institute, for reviewing the chapter on internally displaced people. I thank all contributors for their dedication and for making this book a reality. Their contribution provides a blend of knowledge and skills that typify the complexity of globalisation and migration, hence making this book a great asset to policy makers, programme managers and the community as a whole. This book constitutes one of the expected research outputs for my Future Fellowship ((FT110100345), hence I would like to acknowledge the funding and support by the Australian Research Council. Finally, thank you goes to my colleagues at the University of Western Sydney for providing me with a pleasant and good working environment, which afforded me much needed time to complete this book.

# Foreword

**Professor Fethi Mansouri**

UNESCO Chair, Cultural Diversity and Social Justice
(Deakin University)

Back in 2000 prominent German sociologist Ulrick Beck published an important volume 'What is Globalisation?' in which the central question was the nature of globalisation and its various implications for how societies and international relations are going to be organised and regulated. The volume was timely not only because it came out at the turn of the new millennium but also because debates and discussions pertaining to globalisation have been increasing in volume but decreasing in conceptual precision and intellectual clarity. Indeed, one might still ask the same question today almost 15 years since that publication came to light, and in many ways the answers provided by Beck would still hold sway.

Contrary to popular belief, globalisation is not a new modernist phenomenon since we know that trade routes connecting different countries, indeed continents, existed for thousands of years. People were moving between different regions for millennia in search of new products as was the case with the spice route connecting Asia to the Middle East and North Africa, new trade opportunities as was the case for Europeans exploring markets globally, and in some cases people moved transnationally in order to engage in intercultural and educational exchanges as was the case during the height of the Islamic empire in Moorish Spain. But it is equally true that globalisation accelerated during the second half of the twentieth century thanks to an explosion in communication technologies and significant advancements in transportation systems.

The implications of this new more pronounced surge of globalisation is an increased level of human mobility that engendered new forms of diversity in many societies that were previously exposed in limited ways to migration waves. That migration accelerated during the twentieth century and especially post the Second World War is not a surprising fact. What is surprising, however, is the various policy responses that receiving countries have erected to manage the consequent cultural, social, and demographic manifestations. From assimilationism to multiculturalism, and to the more recent emphasis on civic and social cohesion, migrants had to endure not only the stressors of cultural adaptation but also the challenges of local integration and social acceptance within social milieus that were not always very welcoming. These challenges have and continue to engender serious health outcomes at both the mental as well as the more general health levels.

This book, *Globalisation, Migration and Health*, tries to provide diverse empirical insights from different case studies to allow for a more nuanced reflection on the complex relationship between human mobility in all its forms and health outcomes in all their complexities. Professor Andre Renzaho is to be commended for undertaking this task and bringing together a number of researchers and research teams to share their research on the multiple manifestations of migrant health, ranging from racism to infectious diseases to obesity and its negative impact on individuals and communities. This book will be useful to those with a keen interest in examining different appraisals of migration and its health impacts, less on the basis of rhetorical claims and counter-claims and more in the context of robust methodological and conceptual approaches. The significant empirical evidence presented in this volume should be the basis for future debates and possibly new policies addressing the significant challenge that is migrant health.

# Contents

*About the book editor*   vii
*Contributors*   ix
*Acknowledgements*   xv
*Foreword*   xvii

Chapter 1   Globalisation, migration and health: an introduction   1
*André M.N. Renzaho*

**Section 1:**   **Forced and Voluntary Migration: Patterns of Internal and International Migration, Burden of Diseases and Policy Response**   31

Chapter 2   Forced internal displacement: pattern, health impacts and policy response   33
*André M.N. Renzaho*

Chapter 3   The social and health dimensions of refugees and complex humanitarian emergencies   73
*Joseph Kamara and André M.N. Renzaho*

Chapter 4   Health, social and economic impact of voluntary migration   123
*André M.N. Renzaho*

| | | |
|---|---|---|
| **Section 2:** | **Case Studies — Asylum Seekers, Healthy Migrant Effect, and Access and Utilisation of Health Services** | 205 |
| Chapter 5 | Invisible and suffering: prolonged and systematic detention of asylum seekers living in substandard conditions in Greece<br>*Sheila Cyril and André M.N. Renzaho* | 207 |
| Chapter 6 | The health status, service needs and barriers to accessing care for detention and community-based asylum seekers in Australia<br>*Emily Hadgkiss and André M.N. Renzaho* | 255 |
| Chapter 7 | Women, children and men trapped in unsafe corridors<br>*Kevin Pottie, Chuck Hui and Fabien Schneider* | 291 |
| Chapter 8 | Migration and health effects in the Netherlands<br>*Paul Herfs and Olta Gishti* | 305 |
| Chapter 9 | Health equity: evidence-based guidelines, e-learning and physician advocacy for migrant populations in Canada<br>*Kevin Pottie and Doug Gruner* | 329 |
| Chapter 10 | Hispanic immigration and the epidemiological paradox<br>*Mary Lou de Leon Siantz* | 345 |
| Chapter 11 | Migration and the healthy migrant effect in Australia: current knowledge, gaps and opportunity for future research<br>*André M.N. Renzaho* | 363 |
| Chapter 12 | The social dimensions of internal migration and health in China<br>*André M.N. Renzaho* | 391 |

| | | |
|---|---|---|
| Chapter 13 | Migration challenges and health policy in South Korea<br>*André M.N. Renzaho* | 427 |
| Chapter 14 | Migrant health in the workplace: a multi-country comparison<br>*Lata Satyen, John W Toumbourou, David Mellor, Ilmiye Secer and Matin Ghayour-Minaie* | 479 |
| Chapter 15 | The morbid effects associated with racism experienced by immigrants: findings from Australia<br>*Kevin Dunn, Yin Paradies, Rosalie Atie and Naomi Priest* | 509 |
| **Section 3:** | **Conclusion** | 533 |
| Chapter 16 | Globalisation and migration: reflections, policy directions and conclusion<br>*André M.N. Renzaho* | 535 |
| *Index* | | 553 |

# Chapter 1

# Globalisation, migration and health: an introduction

Professor André M.N. Renzaho

## Globalisation and international migration

The concept of globalisation took place between 1870 and 1914 (Bayly, 2004). It was only popularised in the late 1970s and coincided with the technological revolution and the rise in digital technology use that started to peak at that time. The World Bank has defined globalisation as *"the growing interdependence of countries resulting from their increased economic integration via trade, foreign investment, foreign aid, and international migration of people and ideas"* (Soubbotina, 2004, p. 83). The process of globalisation has gone through three phases (Table 1). The technological revolution and the rise in digital use were seen as a pathway to facilitate trade and financial transactions worldwide. However, it is worth noting that as early as 1962 McLuhan (1962; 1965) introduced the 'global village' theory to acknowledge the global integration of citizens facilitated by electronic media in terms of the world economy, politics, culture, and communication, leading to a collective identity. In this sense, globalisation is conceived as nothing more than a global integration resulting from a global interchange of views, financial trades and flows, commodities, and other socio-cultural, economic, and political aspects shaping the lives of people worldwide.

Table 1: Waves and steps of globalisation

| Period | Characteristics |
|---|---|
| Wave 1:<br>1870–1940s | • Near doubling of exports relative to world GDP<br>• Near tripling of foreign investment relative to the GDP of developing countries<br>• Significant north–south international migration with 10% of the world's population moving from Europe to the New World<br>• Significant international movement of Chinese and Indians to occupy the less populated neighbouring countries<br>• The First World War<br>• The Great Depression<br>• The Second World War<br>• Establishment of the General Agreement on Tariffs and Trade (GATT) |
| Wave 2:<br>1950s–1980s | • Growth of trade and investment flows, mostly in developed countries such as Europe, North America, and Japan<br>• Birth of multilateral agreements on trade liberalisation under the auspices of the GATT between developed countries<br>• Developing countries' primary role limited to goods exporters, a role that isolated these countries from international capital flows<br>• Convergence of per capita incomes between the richer and poorer members of the Organization for Economic Cooperation and Development<br>• The widening of the per capita income gap between the developed and the developing countries<br>• Proliferation of multilateral organisations, e.g. World Bank, the International Monetary Fund, United Nations High Commission or for Refugees, etc. |
| Wave 3:<br>1990s–onward | • Technological advances and growth of the technological industry<br>• Lower transportation, communication, and computation costs<br>• Improved and efficient production cost<br>• Internationalisation of firms in developing countries due to cheap labour<br>• Increased liberalisation of trade and capital markets with more governments lowering import tariffs and minimising non-tariff barriers (e.g. import quotas, export restraints, and legal prohibitions), hence jeopardising the protection of their economies from foreign competition and influence<br>• Birth of the World Trade Organization<br>• Promotion of a global free trade in place of protectionism<br>• Emergence of the so-called 'new globalisers', i.e. characterised by the doubling of the ratio of trade (exports plus imports) to gross domestic product in 24 developing countries |

*Source*: Table constructed by the author — data and information summarised from texts in Chapter 12 of Soubbotina's (2004) book.

Such a broad view attracted many criticisms in the early 1990s, leading researchers to label the concept of globalisation as a discursively constructed myth (Bairoch and Kozul-Wright, 1996; Du Toit and Ewert, 2002; Ferguson, 1992; Geo-JaJa and Zajda, 2015; Holton, 1997). According to Ferguson (1992), globalisation is more about global capitalism and imperialism characterised by seven myths: 'big is better', 'more is better', 'time and space have disappeared', 'global cultural homogeneity', 'saving planet earth', 'democracy for export via American televisions', and 'the New World Order'.

Sceptics of globalisation argue that it is harmful and geared towards promoting industrialised countries' dominance and control or exploitation of low- and middle-income countries (Haque et al., 2015; Ibarra and Carlos, 2015; Zoomers, 2010). They also note that globalisation not only undermines democracy but also produces artificial cultural homogenisation while increasingly destroying the environment (Ferguson, 1992; Kellner, 2002; Perraton et al., 1997). Proponents of globalisation, however, argue that it stimulates the economy by promoting political democratisation and cultural exchange, and by opening a new and exciting world of opportunities (Kellner, 2002; Perraton et al., 1997). As Kellner (2002) emphatically noted, whether viewed negatively or positively, globalisation is inevitable and beyond human control. Therefore, globalisation should be taken seriously.

In 2000, the International Monetary Fund (IMF) identified five main pillars of globalisation: (1) trade, (2) capital movements, (3) international migration for better employment opportunities, (4) technology and knowledge exchange and dissemination, and (5) broader cultural, political and environmental dimensions (International Monetary Fund Staff, 2000). For example, there is an interaction between advances in telecommunication and transportation infrastructure and how they relate to the five dimensions of globalisation. It has been argued that improved telecommunication and transportation infrastructures have resulted in four different outcomes related to the human–environment interaction: substitution (by decreasing the number of trips), complementarity (by stimulating travel and transportation demand), efficiency (by making transportation systems more efficient) and indirect effect such as its impact on the use of land (Kobayashi *et al.*, 2006). The benefits include interdependence of economic and cultural activities with business activities reaching out to remote areas, making the distance and geography less important through technical interaction and increased migration (Kobayashi *et al.*, 2006). Therefore, there is a strong dynamic relationship between globalisation and internal and international migration. The liberal capitalism based on free economies supports free movement of people, the consequence of which includes the internationalisation of domestic markets in terms of production, distribution and consumption. It is this expanded market economy and integrated world trade that has facilitated the increase in human migration with most migration occurring between low- and middle-income countries (Li, 2008).

## International migration theories

However, migration is a complex phenomenon which may involve people movement within a state and between international borders. Therefore, the expanded market economies and integration of trade alone cannot explain human migration. While it is difficult to pinpoint a migration theory that could explain why people migrate, over the years some migration theories have been proposed but none of them is widely accepted by researchers as the best at explaining the migration phenomenon. In fact there has been a call for the development of a comprehensive or general migration theory since the 1960s (de Haas, 2008; Lee, 1966; Massey *et al.*, 1993; Zelinsky, 1971). Nevertheless, theories to explain international migration have been biased towards why and how do people migrate at the expense of theories examining how migrants cope with their new environment.

### Theories related to why and how people migrate

**Laws of migration theory:** In his 1885 paper on the laws of migration in the *Journal of the Statistical Society of London*, Ernest Ravenstein, a migration theorist, wrote an extensive essay using data from the 1871 census to trace the extent of migration throughout the United Kingdom. His essay was triggered by Dr William Farr's earlier remarks that migration appeared to go on without any definite law (Ravenstein, 1885). Ravenstein presented some fascinating findings to justify his 'Laws of Migration', and these findings were later confirmed in a follow-up study in 1889 (Ravenstein, 1889). His findings suggest that migration was influenced by three major factors: distance, population density, and levels of industrial revolution. Ravenstein also noted that the movements of migrants were generally governed by business considerations. Ravenstein's research was the first study to shed light on the pull–push factors of migration and has formed the basis for most modern research on migration. In summarising his findings, he proposed seven laws and these are as follows (Ravenstein, 1885; 1989):

1. **Migration and the urban–rural divide**, i.e. there are differences between urban and rural residents in their propensity to migrate with people born in towns and cities less likely to migrate than those in rural areas. A city or town that is on the boundary of a regional or rural area will attract migrants from those remote areas with the main effect being the depopulation of some rural regions.
2. **The effect of distance**: There is a relationship between migration and distance to be travelled, and the concentration of migrants in certain areas will grow less as the distance to be travelled from that area increases (e.g. an inverse relationship between the volume of migration and the distance to be travelled).
3. **Migration by stages**, i.e. migration occurs in multiple stages, that is, people tend to move to rapidly urbanising cities in search of better opportunities and the gaps left in rural areas are filled up by migrants. Those relocating to cities do not travel there from their homes, rather they reached their destination by stages.
4. **Female migration**, i.e. females are more migratory than males, and predominate among short-journey migrants.
5. **Migration stream dynamics**, i.e. every main current of migration leads to a compensating counter-current, and the process of dispersion is the inverse of that of absorption and has similar features.
6. **The effect of industrial revolution on long-distance migration**, i.e. there is a positive relationship between an increase in migration and an

increase in the means of transportation and industrial development (e.g. manufactures and commerce), and in the case of long-distance migrants gives preference to the great centres of commerce and industry.
7. **Migration for economic motives**, i.e. strong desire inherent in most men to better themselves in material respects.

**Push–pull theory:** It has been proposed that to better conceptualise international migration beyond a pure economic argument, attention needs to be paid to wider social, cultural and political aspects that affects peoples' lives and inform their choices of whether or not to migrate (Table 2). A case in point is the brain drain, which is a result of 'push' factors (failing to return to home countries after training abroad) and 'pull' factors (driving health workers out of their home countries) (Kirigia *et al.*, 2006; Renzaho, 2007a). However, pull and push factors do not act in isolation and vary from one country to another, the outcome of which could lead to eight different types of migration (Castles, 2000).

1. **Temporary labour migrants**, which they also refer to as 'guest-workers' or 'overseas contract workers': people migrating for a limited period in order to work and to send money home (remittances).
2. **Highly skilled and business migrants,** people with qualifications and skills moving within the internal labour markets of transnational corporations and international organisations and between international borders.
3. **Irregular or undocumented or illegal migrants**, people entering a country without the necessary permits usually in search of a job.
4. **Refugees**, persons meeting the criteria of the 1951 United Nations Convention relating to the Status of Refugees and its 1967 protocol, that is, who is outside her or his country of nationality and unwilling or being unable to return for fear of persecution on account of race, religion, nationality, membership of a particular social group, or political opinion.
5. **Asylum seekers**, people who cross borders looking for protection from persecution but whose application for a legal status has not been approved.
6. **Forced migration**, people who are affected by man-made or natural catastrophes or development projects (such as new roads or factories)

Table 2:  Pull and push factors associated with international migration

| Push factors | Pull factors |
| --- | --- |
| **Job security** | |
| • No jobs available<br>• Lack of promotion<br>• Lack of job opportunities/career development<br>• Risk of losing jobs due to lack of funds | • Jobs available<br>• Colleagues, friends, and recruiters telling them about opportunities<br>• Increased promotion opportunities<br>• Fairness and transparency in granting promotion |
| **Working conditions** | |
| • Deteriorating work environment<br>• Poor working conditions and facilities<br>• Violence at workplace and low remuneration<br>• Inadequate medicine and equipment<br>• Lack of research and health facilities<br>• Inability to treat patients appropriately<br>• For nurses, unhappiness with prevalent social attitudes towards the profession<br>• Significant stress, overtime, and generally poor conditions of service resulting in fatigue and burnout<br>• Unsustainable and stressful patient–health care provider ratios, compromising the quality of care<br>• Poor intellectual stimulation | • Satisfaction of practicing medicine and nursing as trained and capable of doing<br>• Reasonable workload and conditions of work<br>• Better working conditions and remuneration<br>• Safer working environment |
| **Economic considerations** | |
| • Disarray in severely economically depressed countries<br>• Low salaries<br>• Inability to accrue savings<br>• Non-payment of salaries, housing allowance, pension<br>• Poor health systems<br>• Poor economy: high inflation<br>• Lack of funding opportunities<br>• Famine and agricultural decline<br>• Environmental degradation | • Search for improved living conditions<br>• Higher pay (and opportunities for remittances)<br>• Reasonable remuneration — able to save money<br>• Recruiters actively sourcing workers internationally with promise of high income and good benefits<br>• Better health and research facilities<br>• Increased economic opportunities<br>• Arable land |

(*Continued*)

Table 2: (Continued)

| Push factors | Pull factors |
|---|---|
| **Political considerations** | |
| • Political, racial, ethnic upheaval<br>• Gender discrimination<br>• Political and religious persecution<br>• Insecurity, wars, and ethnic conflicts<br>• Government training health workers for international export<br>• Limits on personal freedom | • OECD countries wealthy, stable, and democratic<br>• Political and religious freedom<br>• Absence of corruption<br>• Ethnic ties |
| **Physical security** | |
| • Criminality<br>• Gender-based violence<br>• Exposure to HIV — risk of infection through treatment of patients<br>• Natural disasters: droughts, floods, tsunamis | • Safe country<br>• Safe working environment<br>• Appropriate medical equipment to prevent HIV infection |
| **Quality of life** | |
| • Poor accommodation<br>• Lack of transport to go to work<br>• Inability to live a decent life<br>• Poor environmental planning: overpopulation | • Multiethnic and tolerant of diversity<br>• Good quality of life<br>• Family reunion |
| **Education** | |
| • Diminishing quality of education for children | • Greater opportunities for children — good education and ability for them to earn a decent living |

*Source:* Extracted from Packer *et al.* (2009). Expanded using information from Kirigia *et al.* (2006), Pang *et al.* (2002) and Renzaho (2007a).

and have to move from where they live, encompassing refugees, internally displaced people, and asylum seekers.

7. **Family members (or family reunion or family reunification migrants)**, people granted entry based on family ties in the host country.
8. **Return migrants**, people returning to their country of origin after living in another country.

**Theories of international migration perpetuation and reciprocity:** Theories of international migration perpetuation encompasses transnational migration theory, migrations systems theory, and the network hypothesis of social capital theory.

- **Transnational migration theory:** Castles (2008) notes that transnational migration has been facilitated by improvements in transport and communication technologies, the consequence of which has been across-borders' long-term economic, social, cultural and political links. Therefore, the transnational communities (or diasporas) become important social actors. According to Fouron and Schiller (2001), the transnational migration theory refers to "*a process of movement and settlement across international borders in which individuals maintain or build multiple networks of connection to their country of origin while at the same time settling in a new country*" p. 60. However, the theory has received much criticism for many reasons: lack of clarity in defining its scope of study and what it is and is not (Upegui-Hernandez, 2014). In the transnational movements, it is difficult to differentiate the diaspora and transnational communities such as entrepreneurial diasporas, the religious diasporas, the political diasporas, labour diasporas, trade diasporas, or cultural diasporas (Cohen, 2008; McCabe *et al.*, 2005; Sheffer, 2003), and the premise that migrants and their families maintain ties with their home countries is contentious as it is not supported by studies on the bi-dimensional acculturation models (Berry, 1997; Deaux, 2000; Renzaho *et al.*, 2008; Upegui-Hernandez, 2014).

- **Migration systems theory:** According to de Haas (2008), migration systems theory refers to a two-way reciprocal and dynamic interaction between migration and development with significant migration-related changes in the social, cultural, economic, and institutional conditions in both the sending and receiving countries. The theory takes into account the wide contexts by permitting the examination of the interaction between events and circumstances in the wider world and the migrant's individual situation. Such interactions occur at three different levels of both sending and receiving ends: the macrostructure (the nation's and world's economic and political state; migration control and management policies and laws, and globalisation), microstructure (e.g. migrant's own social networks of friends and family community links in destination country, information available to migrants), and meso-structure (migrant agents, organisation recruiting migrants, or people smugglers) (de Haas, 2008; Keeley, 2009). Therefore, the migration systems theory represents "*a set of places linked by flows and counterflows of people, goods, services, and information, which tend to facilitate further exchange, including migration between the places*"(De Haas and Vezzoli, 2010; p. 2). Implicit in this definition is that the core tenet of the migration systems theory is the feedback mechanisms that perpetuate migration processes. As Mabogunje (1970) summed it up,

> "*A system may be defined as a complex of interacting elements, together with their attributes and relationships. One of the major tasks in conceptualizing a phenomenon as a system, therefore, is to identify the basic interacting elements, their attributes, and their relationships. Once this is done, it soon becomes obvious that the system operates not in a void but in a special environment ... favorable or positive feedback will encourage migration and will produce situations of almost organized migratory flows from particular villages to particular cities. In other words, the existence of information in the system encourages greater deviation from the most probable or random state... A system at any given time is not determined so much by initial conditions as by the nature of the process, or the system parameters.*" *(pp. 4, 13 and 15)*

However, the networks of relationships between people in sending and receiving countries can grow and be sustained over time, leading to the '*cumulative Causation of migration*'. That is, when people or a community draw extensively from the accumulation of social capital in the migrant diaspora and family members and friends in the destination country, and use such social capital to gain entry into the country, hence perpetuating the circle of migration (Liang, 2014; Massey, 1990; Massey *et al.*, 1994).

- **The network hypothesis of social capital theory or migration network theory:** The migration systems theory differs from the migration network theory in that the latter focuses mainly on the vital role played by personal relations between migrants and non-migrants as well as the way this social capital facilitates, perpetuates and transforms migration (de Haas, 2008). Therefore, grounded with the social capital theory, the network hypothesis refers to migration-enhancing resources that individuals or groups accrue as a result of having access to migrant networks developed through acquaintances, memberships, and social institutions and use such resources to improve or maintain their position in society (Bourdieu, 1986; Coleman, 1988; Palloni et al., 2001). According to Palloni and colleagues (2001), *migrants networks encompass "interpersonal ties that connect migrants former migrants, and non-migrants to one another through relations of kinship, friendship, and shared community origin"* (p. 1263). These network connections make international migration a perpetual movement of people within and between borders in that the increased likelihood of migration is closely linked with reduced costs and risks of movement that the networks provide and increased net returns associated with migration (e.g. access to finance through remittances) (Palloni et al., 2001). Hence network ties have been identified as a source of migration capital (Massey et al., 1987; Taylor, 1987). In an empirical study testing whether the network hypothesis of social capital theory can be confirmed, Palloni and colleagues (2001) estimated the effects of family network ties on individual migration using a robust multi-state hazard model, controlling for conditions that influence migration risks for all family members. They found social capital distributed among community and household members were strongly associated with the likelihood of out-migration. Their findings confirmed and validated the network hypothesis and their role in international migration. Some scholars such as Ibarra and Carlos (2015) have argued that the social capital theory can only explain how people come to emigrate and how they reach their destination, but it is not adequate enough to explain why people emigrate, as it fails to fully consider the impact of migration policy, capitalist and neoliberal practices, and trade practices on the migration process and people involved in migration.

**Neoclassical economics theory:** Born in 1900, the theory provides both macro and micro frameworks. As a macro theory, it conceptualises migration at the country level as a movement of individuals due to differences between countries (e.g. low- vs. high-income countries) in the supply and demand for labour, characterised by regional differentials in wages (e.g. low-wage, labour-surplus in the country of origin) and employment (high-wage or labour scarcity in the country of destination) conditions (Borjas, 1989; Hicks, 1932; Lewis, 1954; Massey *et al.*, 1993; Todaro and Smith, 2006). As a micro theory, it is closely associated with the human capital theory, and conceptualises migration at the individual level (Sjaadstad, 1962). Most importantly, the theory at the micro level conceptualises migration as the movement of individuals for income maximisation, based on individual rational choices depending on their demographic (e.g. age, gender) and socio-economic (e.g. occupation, educational attainment, or labour market status) characteristics (Bauer and Zimmermann, 1999; Ben-Gad, 2004; Borjas, 1987, 1989; Ibarra and Carlos, 2015; Piore, 2002; Sjaadstad, 1962). That is, because the maximisation of the human capital return is the main objective for emigrating, factors that will make the difference in the decisions between individuals within the same sending country are grouped into two domains: perceived return to human capital in receiving countries and the cost associated with emigrating. Therefore, the likelihood of emigrating increases with the perceived higher return to human capital in receiving countries and lower migration-related cost. This implies that the decision to migrate involves a cost–benefit analysis at the individual level and the best option must meet the financial and legal constraints that is associated with the international migration process (Borjas, 1989, 2008).

The main feature of the neoclassical theory is the so-called 'factor price equalisation'. That is, increased migration leads to a growing convergence between wages in the sending and receiving countries in the long run, hence removing the incentives for migrating (Borjas, 1989; Massey *et al.*, 1987). In the equilibrium model of migration, as people migrate for income maximisation, in the high-wage, labour-scarce regions or countries, the labour force increases and wages fall. In contrast, the labour force in the low-wage, labour-surplus regions or countries decreases while wages increase, and hence over time the net labour migration and net capital flows becomes zero (Borjas, 1989; Massey *et al.*, 1987; Thompson, 1997; Wood, 1982). The neoclassical economics theory provides a framework for identifying hypotheses to be tested in terms of the causes and effects of migration, but it has received many criticisms including its methodological individualism (e.g. seeking to explain socio-economic and migration-related factors at the level of the individual agent), methodological instrumentalism (e.g. characterising behaviours as preference-driven or for maximising preference-satisfaction), and methodological equilibration which is impossible to achieve or substantiate in real-world markets as microeconomic models rarely capture markets' realities (Arnsperger and Varoufakis, 2006; Lavoie, 1992; Rochon, 1999). With its emphasis on the individual 'rational' choice as the major determinant of emigration, most researchers point out that such a stance ignores external forces that shape the structural context of migration (Ibarra and Carlos, 2015). For example, the theory fails to account for the fact that the lack of capital and insurance are a reality in most low- and middle-income countries, hence making it difficult for marginalised groups to access financial services and capital (de Haas, 2008; Schiff 1994). Similarly, in a study analysing earnings of immigrants in the USA, Borjas (1987) found that the differences of earnings between immigrants from different home countries but with the same measurable skills are expected to differ due to the endogeneity of the migration decision, and differences in earnings are mainly attributable to socio-political and economic conditions of origin at the time of migration. The study also found that factors that negatively impacted on the migration rate into the USA at the time included the distance between the country of origin and the USA and the country of origin's economic position with the emigration rate found to be lower for countries with high levels of gross national product per capita (Borjas, 1987). These findings robustly suggest that it is not the poorest individuals who emigrate or send labour, which are the two fundamental tenets of theory.

**The new economics of migration theory:** It differs from the neoclassical migration theory. While both consider migration within the process of economic development and labour dynamics, the new economics of migration theory considers the decision to migrate to be beyond just income maximisation and labour markets. It proposes that there are other factors in the decision-making including how to minimise risks at household level such as the risk to family income, and how to overcome constraints on family production activities (Massey *et al.*, 1993).

Therefore, it is not the isolated individual actors that make the migration decisions, rather such decisions involve the extended family units to maximise income but not at the expense of the risks and constraints. That is, before migrating, individuals and their extended family units assess the costs and benefits that migration brings with it and use the net return as the weighting to make a final decision. The risk and benefits associated with migration take into account not just the migrating individual, but also their families, the household, and their communities, and migration decisions are heavily influenced by a set of factors and conditions in the home country that affect the family units including the risk of losing family income and market failures (labour, insurance and credit markets) (Massey *et al.*, 1993; Stark, 2003). In his study to test whether migration between locations is compatible with a zero expected differential in net earnings between locations, Stark (2003) found that in the absence of an expected net earnings differential, "*migration occurs in an individual context (a taste for migration, return migration), in a familial context (diversification of earnings), and in a communal context (aversion to relative deprivation)*" (p. 13). In discussing his findings, the author noted that factors that facilitate migration include culture (e.g. a society without a culture of migration will produce less migration than a society with such a culture), economic means (e.g. work outside the home that provides a higher purchasing power of earnings at family level will shorten the duration of migration), marriage (e.g. conducive to, rather than hindering, migration), and diversity of income (e.g. a community with higher yet heterogeneous incomes will produce more migration than a community with low but uniform incomes). However, the theory suffers from three limitations: (1) it is difficult to establish the dynamics of the extended family units making migration decisions; (2) it focuses and emphasises dynamics in the sending countries while downplaying dynamics in receiving countries; and (3) it is difficult to isolate the effect of income, employment, and trade policies with market imperfections and distortions.

**Dual labour market theory/the segmented labour market:** Its tenet is the coexistence of a bifurcated occupational structure and a dual pattern of economic organisation in industrialised countries. While the neoclassical and new economics theories emphasise the supply side of migration, the dual labour market theory focuses on the intrinsic demand for labour in the receiving country (Piore, 1979). Therefore, it allows the analysis of the labour market at two levels: the primary (e.g. capital-intensive method of production, i.e. both skilled and unskilled labour are utilised), and secondary (e.g. labour-intensive method of production segment, i.e. predominantly for unskilled migrants) sectors (Doeringer and Piore, 1971; Jennissen, 2004; Piore, 1979). That is, in the developed nations, the primary sector has what is perceived as 'good jobs' whose characteristics include substantial responsibility, job security, high wages, and the likelihood of internal promotion. In contrast, jobs in the secondary sector are perceived to be of low class whose characteristics include casual employment, low wages, and menial tasks (Bulow and Summers, 1985; Doeringer and Piore, 1971; Piore, 1979). As skilled migrants get more status, higher income, and better employment conditions, unskilled employees are left to occupy jobs at the bottom of the labour market. The low wage and poor employment conditions of the secondary employment sectors mean that natives see such jobs as demeaning and they are less likely to take up such positions due to motivational problems, especially the new young and aspiring graduates (Jennissen, 2004). The process can also be complicated by the decline in birth rates and demographic transitions that high-income countries have experienced over decades. Young people in rural areas move away from farming activities to urban cities in search of better educational and employment opportunities, leaving the rural areas underserviced. Similarly, the demographic transition becomes a serious issue with an increased ageing population due to improvement in life expectancy and a declining young population due to the declining birth rates, hence distorting the workforce. With young adults not prepared to accept jobs at the bottom of the job hierarchy (Doeringer and Piore, 1971; Jennissen, 2004), the recruitment of foreign workers (labour demand rather than supply) becomes the main option to fill low-skilled jobs.

**World systems theory:** This theory conceptualises migration from a historical–structural perspective within the developed and expanded structure of the world market, characterised by the search for new natural resources, new low-cost labour and new outlets to meet the demands of world markets (Jennissen, 2004; Massey *et al.*, 1987, 1993; Portes and

Walton, 1981). It permits the examination of international migration through factors operating at a global level from a historical and economic globalisation perspective. According to Wallerstein (1974), a world system is a *"multicultural territorial division of labour in which the production and exchange of basic goods and raw materials is necessary for the everyday life of its inhabitants"*. This division of labour creates two independent regions differentiated by the power hierarchy: the core societies which are wealthy and powerful, dominating and exploiting the periphery societies, which are known to be weak and poor (Jennissen, 2004). Unlike the colonial era when the market penetration was facilitated by colonial regimes' administrators, the expanded world market that followed the decolonisation of the peripheral countries created structures through which these newly independent nations became major sources of primary commodities for their former colonisers (Jennissen, 2004). However, the terms of trade were often unfavourable for these peripheral countries, and in recent years, the imbalanced economic relations brought about by free trade agreements have favoured core nations, resulting in slow and unfavourable economic conditions, hence precipitating mass internal (within periphery country) and international (from periphery to core countries) migration (Ibarra and Carlos, 2015). This pattern is aggravated by neocolonial governments and multinational firms that promote structures that advance the power of elites in peripheral countries (Jennissen, 2004). The resulting differences in economic development and cultural exchanges and linkages between core and peripheral countries influence the pattern of international migration. Therefore, the theory sees migration as a natural development growing out of the dislocations and disruptions of capitalist development and market penetration of low- and middle-income countries. As Massey and colleagues (1993) noted, world systems theory sees *"immigration as a natural consequence of economic globalization and market penetration across national boundaries"* (p. 432).

## *Theories related to migrant settlement in a new environment*

**Acculturation theory:** Regardless of their migration status, cultural differences and different expectations characterise migrants. They experience varying inequalities, ranging from difficulties establishing social networks, finding accommodation or employment, learning the host country's language, and looking after their general health. However, the level of inequality differs according to the degree of cultural transition (Renzaho, 2009). Consequently, the acculturation theory has become a dominant framework used to explain disparities among migrant groups. Early research on acculturation emphasised that the acculturation process happens at a group level with the whole group experiencing structural, cultural, biological, psychological, economic and political changes (for more details, see Flannery *et al.*, 2001). In addition, it was implied that mutual changes occur in both groups: the dominant group (host society) and the acculturating groups (migrants or refugees). However, due to influences from the host society, most changes occur in the acculturating group (Graves, 1967). Nowadays, anthropologists have demonstrated that acculturation occurs at the individual level (Berry, 1990). At this level, acculturation has been termed psychological acculturation, that is, changes in both overt behaviours and covert traits of an individual from a cultural group going through the collective acculturation process (Graves, 1967).

Notwithstanding the structural level at which the acculturation process occurs, two theoretical models have dominated the literature on acculturation: the linear or unidirectional model (UDM), also known as the single-continuum model, and the bi-directional or bi-dimensional model (BDM) also known as the two-culture matrix model (Renzaho, 2009). The UDM assumes that it is not possible to be a fully integrated member of two cultures with two differing sets of cultural values. According to Flannery *et al.* (2001), *"the UDM describes acculturation as the shedding off of an old culture and the taking on of a new culture ... [and] describes only one outcome of acculturation — assimilation"* (p. 1035). In this respect, the UDM considers acculturation as a linear process where an individual moves from being traditional to assimilating. The problem with this assumption is that the model fails to identify those who are bi-cultural. Unfortunately, the UDM has dominated research on acculturation and has become the standard view of acculturation (Park and Miller, 1921). In contrast, the BDM measures two cultural orientations — the home and host cultures (Figures 1(a) and 1(b)), and assumes that the identifications with traditional and host cultures are independent. This model identifies

## Figure (a): Berry's acculturation attitudes

Is it of value to maintain cultural identity and characteristics?

|  | Yes | No |
|---|---|---|
| Is it of value to maintain relationships with other groups? — Yes | Intergation | Assimilation |
| Is it of value to maintain relationships with other groups? — No | Separation | Marginalisation |

(a)

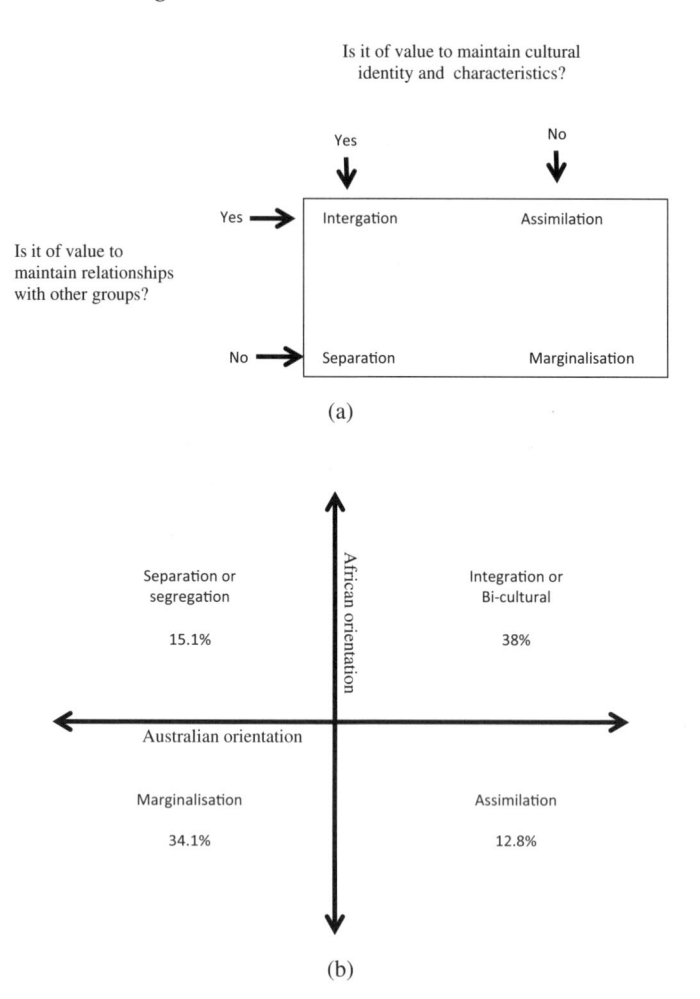

## Figure (b): African vs Australian orientation

- Separation or segregation: 15.1% (African orientation high, Australian orientation low)
- Integration or Bi-cultural: 38% (African orientation high, Australian orientation high)
- Marginalisation: 34.1% (African orientation low, Australian orientation low)
- Assimilation: 12.8% (African orientation low, Australian orientation high)

(b)

**Figures 1:** (a) Berry's acculturation attitudes (Berry, 1997). (b) Conceptualising the results among African migrants in Australia (Renzaho *et al.*, 2008)

migrants on four cultural orientations: (1) traditional, also known as separation (keeps loyalty to traditional culture and does not recognise the host/dominant culture) (Berry and Kim, 1988; MacLachlan, 1997), (2) assimilation, also known as 'cultural shift' (Berry, 1990) or the 'melting pot' theory of acculturation (MacLachlan, 1997) (rejects traditional culture and fully embraces the host/dominant culture), (3) integration, also known as bi-cultural orientation or cultural incorporation (retains cultural identity at the same time moving to join the dominant society) (MacLachlan, 1997), and (4) marginalisation (rejects traditional culture and fails to connect with the host/dominant culture by exclusion or withdrawal (MacLachlan, 1997). Existing and emerging data have led to the formulation of another model of acculturation: the multidimensional model (MDM) of acculturation (Im and Yang, 2006; Keefe and Padilla, 1987). According to Im and Yang (2006), the MDM is not about the general levels of overall acculturation, but it emphasises the acculturation process that closely relates to individual cultural traits with individuals undergoing acculturation selectively acquiring some new traits from the host or dominant culture more quickly than others. That is, the MDM of acculturation offers acculturation typologies based on awareness and ethnic loyalty characterised by migrants' selective adoption of traits and behaviours from the new culture while not giving up certain values from their original culture (Abraído-Lanza *et al.*, 2006; Im and Yang, 2006). Under this model, migrants are perceived to use the adopted or acquired acculturation strategies independent of each other and in a non-consistent manner across areas of daily life, but not mutually exclusively in order to achieve targeted outcomes. This could include, for example, the use of assimilation strategies at work to fit in while at the same time using the separation strategy with choice of friends or food habits to connect with the culture of origin or integration strategy to get by and live in the wide society (Berry *et al.*, 1989; Im and Yang, 2006; Keefe and Padilla, 1987; Lee *et al.*, 2003). Therefore, it is this independent, selective, and stepwise acquisition traits and behaviours or use of each aspect of the culture that distinguishes the MDM from the BDM of acculturation.

**Selective migration theory:** This theory conceptualises migration as a natural selection whereby migrants are inherently healthier mainly due to the pre-migration selection with those migrating having better health profiles than those staying behind. The upheaval of moving to another country implies that those migrating feel (and probably are) fit enough and resilient to cope with the stress of adaptation to a new environment, and other challenges related to the access and utilisation of services associated with migration (Im and Yang, 2006; Renzaho, 2007b). Under this theory, migrants are seen as more willing to take risks and associated changes and hence more prepared to confront successfully challenges of adaptation (Messias and Rubio, 2004). The fact that healthy people leave to relocate to a new country means that the consequences of these patterns are characterized by the sending country losing a significant portion of its healthy young population and the receiving country's population being rejuvenated by an influx of migrants who are younger and more healthy (Im and Yang, 2006).

**Intergenerational discrepancy theory:** It is a theory that conceptualises the clash of values and expectations between migrant parents and their children, resulting in increased family conflicts, parent–child alienation and children maladjustment (Birman, 2006; Hwang, 2006). That is, the acculturative family distancing, the distancing that occurs between immigrant parents and their children due to differing pace of acculturation, leads to breakdown of communication (both verbal and nonverbal), resulting in poor parent–child relations and poor health among children (Hwang, 2006).

**The culture shock stage theory:** First proposed by Oberg (1960), culture shock refers to the personal disorientation experienced by migrants as a result of an unfamiliar way of life in their new country. According to Oberg (1960), culture shock is *"precipitated by the anxiety that results from losing all our familiar signs and symbols of social intercourse"* (p. 142). The culture shock stage theory conceptualises culture shock into four distinct phases: honeymoon (e.g. migrants being fascinated by the new environment and its characteristics such as locals' habits, the food system or pace of life), frustration (e.g. migrants are confronted with the problems that the new environment brings, namely how to navigate it and overcome problems such as language, accommodation, transportation, shopping, or access, and utilise available services leading to frustration, anxiety and anger), adjustment (e.g. as migrants grow accustomed to the new culture and start to understand the new environment's routines they can put in place measures on how to deal with challenges, problem-solving skills for managing expectations, and acceptance of the new culture), and mastery (e.g. cultural adaption and full participation in the new culture). However, the concept of culture shock has not been adequately defined and various authors have provided various models (see for example, Adler, 1975; Taft, 1977; Yue and Le, 2012). Kuo (1976) notes that earlier researchers emphasised role instability and role displacement, severe feelings of personal inefficacy and normlessness as the main determinants of culture shock, while others noted the unstructured and incompletely defined field that migrants found themselves in as the source of their anxiety. Notwithstanding these differing perspectives, there seems to be a consensus that the culture shock stage theory is concerned with the difficulties of adjusting to a new environment when two different cultures come into contact with each other, and migrants in a society with a similar cultural background will tend to adjust more easily. When the two cultures are dissimilar, the shorter the length of stay in the host culture, the greater the shock and associated mental health issues. With time they become acculturated, leading to improvements in their mental health (Kuo, 1976).

**Goal-striving stress:** According to Kuo (1976), the theory of goal-striving stress *"delineates a unique aspect of the immigrant's adjustment problem, that of unfulfilled aspiration"* (p. 298). That is, the theory is concerned with the gap between migrants' aspiration and their actual achievement and associated level of psychological stress. Some researchers have proposed that the psychological stress that characterises culture shock may be balanced by a lower degree of goal-striving stress (Parker *et al.*, 1966, Parker and Kleiner, 1969). With studies showing that people from urban areas have higher levels of goal-striving stress than those from the rural (Parker *et al.*, 1966), Kuo (1976) concluded that

> *"we may generalize that among foreign immigrants from less urbanized and industrialized societies, the first generation will experience lower goal-striving stress than their descendants … the newly arrived immigrants hold a reasonable level of aspiration while they strive hard for achievement. In contrast, their descendants may continue to strive as hard as their parents but suffer a setback: a much higher level of aspiration due to the socialization experience in the new society. The descendants believe that they possess opportunities for success equal to those of the dominant group members but in fact cannot overcome the consequences of segregation and other forms of de facto discrimination"* (p. 298).

Such a conclusion suggests that higher levels of aspiration among migrants may be associated with poor mental health outcomes. Therefore, higher degrees of goal-striving stress could be an indicator of mental illness among migrants.

## Relevance to this book content

All the theories described above are connected with globalisation in three different ways: (1) the diversified international trade and markets which maximise the exchange of capital, goods, and services between countries, (2) the global financial system that facilitates foreign aid (e.g. foreign aid as an anti-migration instrument), international capital flows (e.g. capital flows that induces labour movements or vice versa), remittances (e.g. giving family members in the country of origin a strong purchasing power and improved socio-economic status which are associated with the likelihood of migrating), and international trade (e.g. the liberalisation of the labour market and brain drain/brain gain), and (3) improved and expanded transport and communication infrastructures and technologies which are associated with rapid and diverse flow of information, affordable and rapid communication as well as effective modes of transportation at a reduced cost (making it possible to cover long distances very quickly). However, no single migration theory can address these complex phenomena, and the purpose of this book is not to promote one theory over the other. Despite the differences in scope, their field of application, and methodological approaches, they are complementary and a combination of two or more theories is needed to answer the following migration-related questions: Where do migrants come from and why do they migrate? how do migrants reach their country of destination? to what extent do policies and practices in the destination country facilitate migrants' integrations and/or continuity of contacts in country of origin? or what are the conditions in the country of origin that encourage the return of the diaspora or facilitate remittance flows in order to contribute to the economic growth of the native country?

Therefore, this book examines the effects of the process of migration on the health of migrants from a global perspective. It is divided into three sections: (1) internal and international migration patterns, burden of diseases, and policy response, (2) case studies — asylum seekers, healthy migrant effect, and access and utilisation of health services, and (3) concluding remarks.

Section 1 provides an opportunity to examine the effectiveness of both legally and non-legally binding instruments as well as the 1951 Convention Relating to the Status of Refugees and its related protocols in addressing the needs of forced migrants. It also provides an opportunity to examine the impact of the brain drain in sending and receiving countries, and how remittances can help leverage the consequences associated with the brain drain. The section contains three chapters. Chapter 1 summarises the trends and patterns of internally displaced persons (IDPs) across the globe. It moves on to discuss key health conditions and burden of diseases among IDPs, followed by a thorough examination of the various policy responses and both legally and non-legally binding declarations related to the protection and assistance of IDPs. Chapter 2 explores the demography of refugees across the globe and identifies the key drivers of humanitarian emergencies. It then provides an overview of the burden of disease among refugees and its impacts on health system delivery in low- and middle-income countries. It concludes by examining the current policy responses to refugees' needs globally and their effectiveness. Finally, Chapter 3 focuses on the key features of voluntary and economic migration. It starts by examining the phases of migration, moves on to discuss the brain drain and its consequences, including the role of remittances as a policy option for not only addressing the consequences of the brain drain but also for overcoming poverty. Next, the burden of disease among migrants and the impact of this on health policy and health system are described. The chapter concludes by examining current policy responses to voluntary immigration as well as other policy options that could yield economic gains in sending and receiving countries, including the implications associated with the General Agreement on Trade in Services, and so-called 'medical tourism'.

Section 2 of the book highlights important features of south–north migration. A brief outline of the key health conditions faced by migrants in selected countries, with specific emphasis on asylum seekers, the healthy migrant effect and salmon bias, access and utilisation of health services, the response from governments in handling high inflows, and the role of non-government organisations (NGOs) in the provision of health care. Case studies have been chosen to answer the following research questions: (1) What is the health status of south–north asylum seekers? What are the policy options available to improve their health and wellbeing? (2) What is the health status of south–north migrants? To what extent is the 'healthy migrant effect' true? Does the salmon bias matter? What are the commonalities and differences? and (3) What are the factors associated with accessing and utilising health services among immigrants? Are there regional differences? The section contains 11 case studies, each representing a chapter. Case studies have been chosen to represent a diversity of health issues faced by migrants to exemplify political, social and economic changes associated with immigration occurring in various regions of the world, and to provide the reader with an overall broad understanding of some of the key features particular to that region. They address serious gaps in the literature and represent a diversity of challenges and opportunities rather than aiming at achieving the geographic coverage.

Section 3 is the concluding chapter. It brings the book contents together in terms of conclusions that can be drawn and the way forward. It reiterates that migration is a complex issue which requires a multi-level and comprehensive response. The policy response sections in each chapter have detailed the inadequacies currently prevailing in each region. Although health governance has been supported by organisations such as the World Health Organisation or the World Bank globally, there is currently no formal agreement to support global migration policies. This chapter brings together some of the most effective policies that could help maximise the benefits associated with migration.

## References

Abraído-Lanza, A.F. *et al.* (2006). Toward a theory-driven model of acculturation in public health research. *American Journal of Public Health*, 96(8), 1342–1346.

Adler, P.S. (1975). The transitional experience: An alternative view of culture shock. *Journal of Humanist Psychology*, 15, 13–23.

Arnsperger, C. & Varoufakis, Y. (2006). What is neoclassical economics? The three axioms responsible for its theoretical oeuvre, practical irrelevance and, thus, discursive power. *Panoeconomicus*, 53, 5–18.

Bairoch, P. & Kozul-Wright, R. (1996). Globalization myths: Some historical reflections on integration, industrialization and growth in the world economy. Discussion Paper No. 113, United Nations Conference on Trade and Development, Geneva, SWI.

Bauer, T.K. & Zimmermann, K.F. (1999). Assessment of possible migration pressure and its labour market impact following EU enlargement to Central and Eastern Europe. IZA Research Report No. 3, UK Department of Education and Employment, Bonn, GER.

Bayly, C.A. (2004). *The Birth of the Modern World, 1780–1914: Global Connections and Comparisons*. Blackwell, Oxford, UK.

Ben-Gad, M. (2004). The economic effects of immigration — a dynamic analysis. *Journal of Economic Dynamics and Control*, 28, 1825–1845.

Berry, J.W. & Kim, U. (1988). Acculturation and mental health. In: Dasen, P., Berry, J.W. & Sartorius, N. (eds.), *Health and Cross-cultural Psychology*, Sage, London, UK.

Berry, J.W. et al. (1989). Acculturation attitudes in plural societies. *Applied Psychology: An International Review*, 38(2), 185–206.

Berry, J.W. (1990). Acculturation and adaptation: Health consequences of culture contact among circumpolar peoples. *Arctic Medical Research*, 49, 142–150.

Berry, J.W. (1997). Immigration, acculturation, and adaptation. *Applied Psychology: An International Review*, 46, 5–68.

Birman, D. (2006). Acculturation gap and family adjustment findings with Soviet Jewish refugees in the United States and implications for measurement. *Journal of Cross-Cultural Psychology*, 37(5), 568–589.

Borjas, G.J. (1987). Self-selection and the earnings of immigrants. NBER Working Paper No. 2248, National Bureau of Economic Research, Cambridge, UK.

Borjas, G.J. (1989). Economic theory and international migration. *International Migration Review*, 23(3), 457–485.

Borjas, G.J. (2008). *Issues in the Economics of Immigration*. University of Chicago Press, Chicago, IL.

Bourdieu, P. (1986). The forms of capital. In: Richardson, J.G. (ed.), *Handbook of Theory and Research for the Sociology of Education*, Greenwood Press, New York, NY.

Bulow, J.I. & Summers L.H. (1985). A theory of dual labor markets with application to industrial policy, discrimination and Keynesian unemployment. *Journal of Labor Economics*, 4, 376–414.

Castles, S. (2000). International migration at the begining of the twenty-first century: Global trends and issues. *International Social Science Journal*, 52, 269–281.

Castles, S. (2008). Development and Migration — Migration and Development: What comes first? Migration and Development: Future Directions for Research and

Policy, 28 February – 1 March 2008, Social Science Research Council Conference, New York, NY.

Cohen, R. (2008). *Global Diasporas: An Introduction*. Routledge, New York, NY.

Coleman, J.S. (1988). Social capital in the creation of human capital. *American Journal of Sociology*, S95–S120.

de Haas, H. (2008). *Migration and Development: A Theoretical Perspective*. International Migration Institute, University of Oxford, Oxford, UK.

de Haas, H. & Vezzoli S. (2010). Migration and development lessons from the Mexico–US and Morocco–EU experiences. International Migration Institute, University of Oxford, Oxford, UK.

Deaux, K. (2000). Surveying the landscape of immigration: Social psychological perspectives. *Journal of Community & Applied Social Psychology*, 10, 421–431.

Doeringer, P.B. & Piore M.J. (1971). *Internal Labor Markets and Manpower Analysis*. Heath Lexington Books, Lexington, MA.

Du Toit, A. & Ewert J. (2002). Myths of globalisation: Private regulation and farm worker livelihoods on Western Cape farms. *Transformation: Critical Perspectives on Southern Africa*, 50, 77–104.

Ferguson, M. (1992). The mythology about globalization. *European Journal of Communication*, 7, 69–93.

Flannery, W.P., Reise, S.P. & Yu, J. (2001). An empirical comparison of acculturation models. *Personality and Social Psychology Bulletin*, 27, 1035–1045.

Fouron, G.E. & Schiller N.G. (2001) The generation of identity: Redefining the second generation within a transnational social field. In: Cordero-Guzmán, H.R. et al. (eds.), *Migration, Transnationalization, and Race in a Changing New York*, Temple University Press, Philadelphia, PA.

Geo-JaJa, M.A. & Zajda J. (2015). Globalisation and the future of education in Africa. In: Zajda, J. (ed.), *Second International Handbook on Globalisation, Education and Policy Research*, Springer, Dordrecht.

Graves, T. (1967). Psychological acculturation in a tri-ethnic community. *South Western Journal of Anthropology*, 23, 337–350.

Haque, M.Z. et al. (2015). Corporate social responsibility, economic globalization and developing countries: A case study of the ready made garments industry in Bangladesh. *Sustainability Accounting, Management and Policy Journal*, 6, 166–189.

Hicks, J.R. (1932). *The Theory of Wages*. Macmillan, London, UK.

Holton, R.J. (1997). Four myths about globalisation [defined as a single world society]. *Flinders Journal of History and Politics*, 19, 141–156.

Hwang, W. (2006). Acculturative family distancing: Theory, research and clinical practice. *Psychotherapy: Theory, Research, Practice and Training*, 43, 397–409.

Ibarra, A. & Carlos A. (2015). Mexican mass labor migration in a not-so changing political economy. *Ethnicities*, 15, 211–233.

Im, E.O. & Yang, K. (2006). Theories on immigrant women's health. *Health Care for Women International*, 27(8), 666–681.

International Monetary Fund Staff (2000). Threat of opportunity? 12 April 2000 (Corrected January 2002). Available at: http://www.imf.org/external/np/exr/ib/2000/041200to.htm. Accessed 28 October 2014.

Jennissen, R. (2004). *Macro-economic Determinants of International Migration in Europe*. Dutch University Press, Amsterdam, NED.

Keefe, S. & Padilla, A. M. (1987). *Chicano Ethnicity*. University of New Mexico Press, Albuquerque, NM.

Keeley, B. (2009). *International Migration: The Human Face of Globalisation*. OECD Publications, Paris, FRA.

Kellner, D. (2002). Theorizing globalization. *Sociological Theory*, 20, 285–305.

Kirigia, J.M. *et al.* (2006). The cost of health professionals' brain drain in Kenya. *BMC Health Services Research*, 6, 89–99.

Kobayashi, K. *et al.* (2006). *Structural Change in Transportation and Communications in the Knowledge Society*. Edward Elgar Publishing, Cheltenham, UK.

Kuo, W. (1976). Theories of migration and mental health: An empirical testing on Chinese-Americans. *Social Science & Medicine*, 10(6), 297–306.

Lavoie, M. (1992). *Foundations of Post-Keynesian Economic Analysis*. Edward Elgar Publishing, Aldershot, UK.

Lee, E.S. (1966). A theory of migration. *Demography*, 3, 47–57.

Lee, S.K., Sobal, J.A. & Frongillo, E.A. (2003). Comparison of models of acculturation: The case of Korean Americans. *Journal of Cross-Cultural Psychology*, 34(3), 282–296.

Lewis, W.A. (1954). Economic development with unlimited supplies of labor. *Manchester School of Economic and Social Studies*, 22, 139–191.

Li, P.S. (2008). World migration in the age of globalization: Policy implications and challenges. *New Zealand Population Reviews*, 33/34, 1–22.

Liang, Y. (2014). The causal mechanism of migration behaviors of African immigrants in Guangzhou: From the perspective of cumulative causation theory. *The Journal of Chinese Sociology*, 1, 1–25.

Massey, D. *et al.* (1987). *Return to Aztlan: The Social Process of International Migration from Western Mexico*. University of California Press, Berkeley and Los Angeles, CA.

Massey, D.S. (1990). Social structure, household strategies, and the cumulative causation of migration. *Population Index*, 56, 3–26.

Massey, D.S. *et al.* (1993). Theories of international migration: A review and appraisal. *Population and Development Review*, 19(3), 431–466.

Massey, D.S. et al. (1994). Continuities in transnational migration: An analysis of nineteen Mexican communities. *American Journal of Sociology*, 99, 1492–1533.

MacLachlan, M. (1997). *Culture and Health*. John Wiley & Sons Ltd, Chichester, UK.

McCabe, I.B. et al. (2005). *Diaspora Entrepreneurial Networks Four Centuries of History*. Oxford University Press, New York.

McLuhan, M. (1962). *The Gutenberg Galaxy: The Making of Typographic Man*. University of Toronto Press, Toronto, CAN.

McLuhan, M. (1965). *Understanding Media: The Extensions of Man*. McGraw Hill, New York, NY.

Messias, D.K. & Rubio, M. (2004). Immigration and health. *Annual Review of Nursing Research*, 22, 101–134.

Oberg, K. (1960). Cultural shock: Adjustment to new cultural environments. *Practical Anthropology*, 7, 177–182.

Packer, C. et al. (2009). Globalization and the cross-border flow of health workers. In: Labonté, R., Schrecker, T., Packer, C. & Runnels, V. (eds.), *Globalization and Health: Pathways, Evidence and Policy*. Routledge, New York, NY, pp. 213–234.

Palloni, A. et al. (2001). Social capital and international migration: A test using information on family networks 1. *American Journal of Sociology*, 106, 1262–1298.

Pang, T. et al. (2002). Brain drain and health professionals. *BMJ*, 324(7336), 499–500.

Park, R. & Miller, H. (1921). *Old Word Traits Transplanted*. Arno Press, New York, NY.

Parker, S. et al. (1969). Migration and mental illness. *Social Science & Medicine*, 3(1), 1–9.

Parker, S. & Kleiner R. J. (1966). *Mental Illness in the Urban Negro Community*. Free Press, Glencoe, SCO.

Perraton, J. et al. (1997). The globalisation of economic activity. *New Political Economy*, 2, 257–277.

Piore, M. (2002). Economics and sociology. *Revue économique*, 53, 291–300.

Piore, M.J. (1979). *Birds of Passage: Migrant Labor and Industrial Societies*. Cambridge University Press, Cambridge, UK.

Portes, A. & Walton J. (1981). *Labor, Class, and the International System*. Academic Press, New York, NY.

Ravenstein, E.G. (1885). The laws of migration. *Journal of the Statistical Society of London*, 48, 167–235.

Ravenstein, E.G. (1889). The laws of migration. *Journal of the Royal Statistical Society*, 52, 241–301.

Renzaho, A.M.N. (2007a). Unpacking the brain drain in Sub-Sahara Africa through public health lenses: Implications for development aid. In: A.M.M. Renzaho (ed.), *Measuring Effectiveness in Humanitarian and Development Aid: Conceptual Frameworks, Principles and Practice*, Nova Science Publishers, Hauppauge, New York, NY, pp. 279–299.

Renzaho, A. (2007b). Ischaemic heart disease and Australian immigrants: The influence of birthplace and language skills on treatment and use of health services. *Health Information Management Journal*, 36(2), 26–36.

Renzaho, A. et al. (2008). Maintenance of traditional cultural orientation is associated with lower rates of obesity and sedentary behaviours among African migrant children to developed countries. *International Journal of Obesity*, 32, 594–600.

Renzaho, A.M. (2009). Immigration and social exclusion: Examining health inequalities of immigrants through acculturation lenses. In: Taket, A., Crisp, B.R., Nevill, A., Lamaro, G., Graham, M. & Barter-Godfrey, S. (eds.), *Theorising Social Exclusion*, Routledge, Abingdon, pp. 117–126.

Rochon, L.-P. (1999). The creation and circulation of endogenous money: A circuit dynamique approach. *Journal of Economic Issues*, 33, 1–21.

Schiff, M. (1994). *How Trade, Aid, and Remittances Affect International Migration*. International Economics Department, World Bank, Washington, DC.

Sheffer, G. (2003). *Diaspora Politics: At Home Abroad*. Cambridge University Press, Cambridge, UK.

Sjaadstad, L. (1962). The costs and returns of human migration. *Journal of Political Economy*, 70, 80–93.

Soubbotina, T. (2004). *Beyond Economic Growth. An Introduction to Sustainable Development*. WBI Learning Resources Series, World Bank, Washington, DC.

Stark, O. (2003). Tales of migration without wage differentials: Individual, family, and community contexts. ZEF Discussion Papers on Development Policy, No. 73, Center for Development Research, Bonn, GER.

Taft, R. (1977). Coping with unfamiliar cultures. In: Warren, N. (ed.), *Studies in Cross-cultural Psychology, Volume 1*, Academic Press, London, pp. 121–153.

Taylor, J.E. (1987). Undocumented Mexico — US migration and the returns to households in rural Mexico. *American Journal of Agricultural Economics*, 69, 626–638.

Thompson, H. (1997). Ignorance and ideological hegemony: A critique of neoclassical economics. *Journal of Interdisciplinary Economics*, 8, 291–305.

Todaro, M.P., Smith S. (2006). *Economic Development*. Addison-Wesley, Boston, MA.

Upegui-Hernandez, D. (2014). Transnational migration theory. In: Teo, T. (ed.), *Encyclopedia of Critical Psychology*, Springer, New York, NY, pp. 2004–2015.

Wallerstein, I. (1974). *The Modern World System I: Capitalist Agriculture and the Origins of the European World-Economy in the Sixteenth Century*. Academic Press, New York, NY.

Wood, C.H. (1982). Equilibrium and historical-structural perspectives on migration. *International Migration Review*, 16(2), 298–319.

Yue, Y. & Le, Q. (2012). From "cultural shock" to "ABC framework": Development of intercultural contact theory. *International Journal of Innovative Interdisciplinary Research*, 2, 133–141.

Zelinsky, W. (1971). The hypothesis of the mobility transition. *Geographical Review*, 61(2), 219–249.

Zoomers, A. (2010). Globalisation and the foreignisation of space: Seven processes driving the current global land grab. *The Journal of Peasant Studies*, 37, 429–447.

# Section 1:

# Forced and voluntary migration: patterns of internal and international migration, burden of diseases and policy response

# Chapter 2

# Forced internal displacement: pattern, health impacts and policy response

Professor André M.N. Renzaho

Internal displacement is one form of forced migration. Forced migration refers to a situation where people or the community is displaced or forced to flee or leave their home or usual place of residence as a result of human-made (e.g. civil strife, armed conflict, generalised violence or human rights violations) and natural or environmental (e.g. volcanic eruption, flooding, hurricanes, earthquakes, cyclone, drought, infectious disease such as Ebola, deforestation, and chemical or nuclear disasters) disasters, large-scale development projects (e.g. extraction of mineral resources such as mining or oil extraction, construction of dam, airport or roads, military installations or conservation projects), and slavery and human trafficking (e.g. smuggling people for economic gain) (United Nations Commission on Human Rights, 1993). If the displaced people do not cross international borders they are known as internally displaced persons (IDPs), and if they cross international borders and their application for a legal status under the Refugee Convention is approved, they are considered refugees. However, if their application for a legal status cannot be substantiated or has not yet been determined, they are known as asylum seekers. In this chapter, we only focus on IDPs. Issues related to refugees are addressed in Chapter 3, while

34  *Globalisation, Migration and Health*

issues related to asylum seekers are addressed in Chapter 6. We start by summarising the current pattern of IDPs.

## Pattern of IDPs

Data by the United Nations High Commissioner for Refugees (UNHCR, 2014) show that the number of people forcibly displaced as a result of persecution, conflict, generalised violence, or human rights violations increased from 45.2 million at the end of 2012 to 51.2 million at the end of 2013, representing an increase of six million people forcibly displaced within 12 months. Of these, 33.3 million were IDPs, 16.7 million were refugees (i.e. 11.7 million under UNHCR's mandate and 5 million Palestinian refugees registered by UNRWA), and 1.2 million were asylum seekers. These UNHCR statistics show that the top five countries hosting the largest number of IDPs worldwide were Pakistan (1.6 million), The Islamic Republic of Iran (857,400), Lebanon (856,500), Jordan (641,900), and Turkey (609,900). However, the majority of IDPs (86%) were hosted in developing countries, while 63% of all IDPs came from five countries affected by conflicts, namely Syria, Colombia, Nigeria, the Democratic Republic of Congo (DRC), and Sudan (Albuja *et al.*, 2014). It is interesting to note that there is an inverse relationship between the number of armed conflicts and the number of IDPs. Over the past four decades, the number of IDPs has been steadily increasing, while the number of armed conflicts has significantly declined (Buhaug *et al.*, 2007). For example, the number of armed conflicts and civil wars totalled 450 between 1816 and 2002 (i.e. 199 international wars and colonial conquest and liberation, and 251 civil wars) (Gleditsch, 2004). This number declined significantly between the 1980s and 1990s, dropping to less than 10 armed conflicts and civil wars since 1999 (Gleditsch, 2004). In contrast, data by the Internal Displacement Monitoring Centre (IDMC) suggest that the number of IDPs has increased incrementally from 16.7 million people in 1989 to 33.3 million people in 2013, representing an increase of 99.4% over 25 years (4% per year) and 16% since 2012 (IDMC, 2013).

Sub-Saharan Africa (SSA) remains disproportionally affected by internal displacement with 37.5% out of the 33.3 million IDPs (or 12.5 million people) coming from 21 SSA countries (Table 1). This pattern could be

Table 1: Number of IDPs by region

| Region | No. of IDPs | No. of countries affected |
| --- | --- | --- |
| North Africa and Middle East | 9.1 million | 6 countries |
| Americas | 6.3 million | 4 countries |
| Europe, the Caucasus & Central Asia | 2.2 million | 12 countries |
| South-east Asia | 3.2 million | 7 countries |
| **SSA** | **12.5 million** | **21 countries** |

Source: Albuja et al. (2014).

explained by many factors, predominantly ethnic conflicts, the ongoing political instability and power struggle in the region as well as the improvement in the collection of data related to IDPs (Albuja et al., 2014). However, the number of IDPs reported by the IDMC does not include development-induced displacement such as urban renewal measures, the construction of dams, large infrastructure projects (e.g. construction of roads), or tourism-oriented development of natural parks. While the number of people displaced by development projects is hard to estimate, Terminski (2012) as well as Cernea (2006) have suggested that development projects displace approximately 15 million people each year. Such data suggest that the reported number of IDPs is severely underestimated due to the difficulties associated with monitoring displacement.

## The health burden among IDPs

There is a synergic relationship between poverty and the likelihood of conflict outbreak with four out the five world's poorest countries experiencing major conflicts (Bustreo et al., 2005). The cost of conflicts in the affected countries in terms of economic development and health outcomes is enormous. Current projections suggest that conflict is associated with a 1% to 3% reduction in annual economic output (Chen et al., 2007; Collier, 1999). Both poverty and conflict limit the ability of the state and its health system to provide adequate health care to IDPs and the host communities (Table 2). The inability of the state to meet the health needs of IDPs could also be a consequence of poor public policies. O'Hare and Southall (2007) have shown that the proportion of central expenditures in countries ravaged by conflicts is significantly lower for health and education but higher for defence when compared to countries not affected by conflicts (Figure 1). Although 90% of conflict- and war-related deaths are predominantly civilians (Levy, 2002), they are unequally affected, with the most affected sections of IDPs and host communities including children, particularly under five years, women, especially pregnant and lactating women, chronically sick people, elderly, and people with disability. In addition, while assistance of IDPs has focused on those living in camps for practical as well as political reasons, IDPs outside the camps and their host communities are often not adequately reached, with their assistance occurring on an ad hoc basis, leaving them with unmet needs (Albuja et al., 2014).

## Mortality

Although mortality data among IDPs are scarce, generally mortality rates are higher in countries experiencing conflicts when compared with those without recent conflict. O'Hare and Southall (2007) analysed data from 42 SSA countries (21 countries which have and 21 which have not experienced recent conflict). They found that infant, under-five, mortality rates were significantly more in countries which have experienced recent conflict when compared to those without recent conflict (Table 2). Available mortality data among IDPs across SSA countries are summarised in Table 3. These data suggest that mortality rates among IDPs are two to up to ten times the emergency thresholds for SSA, and several times above the expected rate in non-emergency situations. A population-based survey to quantify associations between human rights violations and health outcomes among IDPs in eastern Burma (Mullany et al., 2007) found that the under-five mortality rate (U5HR) was 218 (95% confidence interval [CI]: 135–301) per 1,000 live births and increased child mortality was associated with force migration (odds ratio (OR) = 2.80; 95% CI: 1.04–7.54). Guerrier and colleagues (2009) undertook a study to examine mortality patterns among IDP and non-displaced population living in a camp, a village or a town in eastern Chad and reported a crude mortality rate of 1.8 (95% CI: 1.2–2.8), 0.3 (95% CI: 0.2–0.4), 0.3 (95% CI: 0.2–0.5) per 10,000 per day, respectively. The respective figures for the under-five mortality were 4.1 (95% CI: 2.1–7.7), 0.5 (95% CI: 0.3–0.9) and 0.7 (95% CI 0.4–1.4) per

Table 2: Comparing the median demographics between countries with and without recent conflict

| Variables | Conflict | Non-conflict | $p$-value |
|---|---|---|---|
| **Key mortality variables** | | | |
| U5MR/live births (2004) | 197/1000 | 137/1000 | 0.009 |
| Adjusted maternal mortality ratio (2000) | 1,000/100,000 | 690/100,000 | 0.005 |
| Reported maternal mortality (1990–2004) | 710/100,000 | 520/100,000 | 0.044 |
| Infant mortality rate/live births (2004) | 115/1000 | 84/1000 | 0.002 |
| Skilled attendant at delivery (1996–2004) | 40% | 61% | <0.001 |
| **Key health determinants** | | | |
| Improved drinking water sources (2002) | 57% | 68% | 0.026 |
| Adequate sanitation facilities (2002) | 30% | 42% | 0.004 |
| One-year-olds vaccinated (DTP3) (2004) | 64% | 80% | 0.018 |
| Primary school enrolment (1996–2004) | 52% | 65% | 0.005 |
| Adult female literacy rate (2000–2004) | 50% | 60% | 0.057 |

*Note*: Significance tested using the independent samples Mann–Whitney $U$ test. Adapted from O'Hare and Southall (2007).

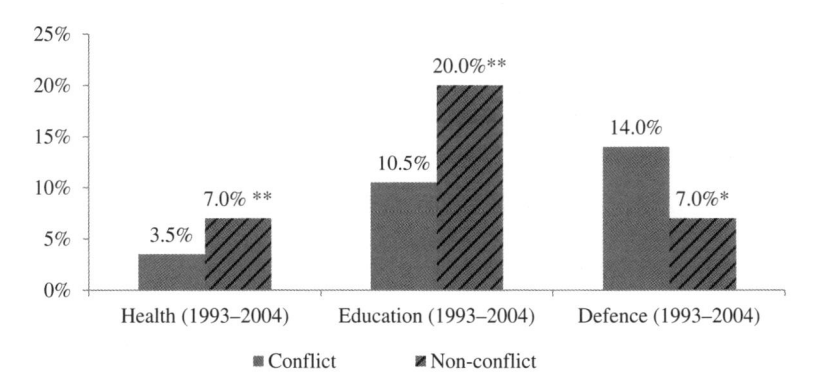

Figure 1: Median spending (% of central government expenditure) on health, education and defence (1994–2004) in SSA countries with and without recent conflict.

*Note*: Significance tested using the independent samples Mann–Whitney $U$ test; * < 0.05, ** < 0.01, and *** < 0.001. Data used to construct the figure were extracted from O'Hare and Southall (2007).

Table 3: CMR and U5MR in selected countries

| Country | CMR (deaths/10,000 population/day) Outside camp | In camp | U5MR (deaths/10,000 population/day) Outside camp | In camp |
|---|---|---|---|---|
| **Emergency threshold for SSA** (*deaths/10,000 population/day*) | 0.9 | | 2.3 | |
| Country | | | | |
| **Sudan, 2004–2005** | | | | |
| West Darfur (Depoortere et al., 2004) | | | | |
| Zalingei | 5.9 | 1.3 | 2.8 | 1.6 |
| Murnei | 9.5 | 1.2 | 2.1 | 1.4 |
| Niertiti | 7.3 | 1.3 | 1.5 | 2.1 |
| El Geneina | NA | 5.6 | NA | 14.1 |
| Darfur (Guha-Sapir and Degomme, 2005) | | | | |
| Darfur Region | 0.7 | NA | 1.0 | NA |
| North Darfur | | | | |
| Abu Shok Camp | NA | 2.2 | NA | 6.8 |
| Kabkabiya | 1.2 | NA | 2.9 | NA |
| Serif Umra | 0.8 | NA | 1.8 | NA |
| Entire province | 1.5 | NA | 2.5 | NA |
| West Darfur | | | | |
| Mukjar, Wade Saleh | 3.6 | NA | 5.2 | NA |
| Habilah | 2.6 | NA | 6.7 | NA |
| Fur Baranga | 0.9 | NA | 1.8 | NA |
| Entire province | 2.9 | NA | 3.1 | NA |
| South Darfur | | | | |
| Kass camp | NA | 3.2 | NA | 5.9 |
| Muhajiria | 1.2–2.3 | | 0.7–1.0 | |
| Kalma | NA | 1.6–3.8 | NA | 2.9–11.7 |

(*Continued*)

Table 3: (*Continued*)

| Country | CMR (deaths/10,000 population/day) Outside camp | CMR (deaths/10,000 population/day) In camp | U5MR (deaths/10,000 population/day) Outside camp | U5MR (deaths/10,000 population/day) In camp |
|---|---|---|---|---|
| Greater Darfur, 2005 (WHO, 2005) | | | | |
| North | 0.9 | 0.8 | 1.8 | 1.5 |
| West | 0.5 | 0.8 | 0.8 | 1.0 |
| South | NA | 0.8 | NA | 2.6 |
| **Uganda, 2005** | | | | |
| Northern Uganda (WHO, 2005) | | | | |
| Acholi region | 1.5 | NA | 3.2 | NA |
| Gulu district | 1.2 | NA | 2.3 | NA |
| Gulu Municipality | 1.3 | NA | 2.5 | NA |
| Kitgum District | 1.9 | NA | 4.0 | NA |
| Pader District | 1.9 | NA | 4.2 | NA |
| **DRC, 2005–2006** | | | | |
| Ituri, (Ahoua et al., 2006) | 4.1 | NA | 6.9 | NA |
| Katanga, (Médecins Sans Frontières, 2006) | 4.3 | NA | 12.7 | NA |
| **Guinea-Bissau, 1998–1999 (Nielsen et al., 2006)** | | | | |
| Pre-war | 0.43 | NA | NA | 1.02 |
| During the war: before peace treaty signed | 1.7–1.8 | NA | NA | 1.8–2.3 |
| After peace treaty signed | 1.0–1.1 | NA | NA | 1.2–1.4 |
| **Chad, 2004 (Guha-Sapir and Degomme, 2005)** | | | | |
| Iridimi, Touloum camp | NA | 1.3–2.6 | NA | 1.6–2.2 |
| Bahai, Cariari | 0.6–1.1 | | 0.4 | |
| Koumoungo | 1.6 | NA | 1.5 | NA |

NA — Not available.

10,000 per day. These findings suggest that mortality was significantly higher among IDPs than non-displaced people. Excess mortality has also been reported among IDPs in Asia (Mullany et al., 2007; Nishikiori et al., 2006) and the Middle East (Guha-Sapir and Panhuis, 2004), however the majority of the surveys have been undertaken in SSA countries.

## *Democratic Republic of Congo (DRC)*

Since 1998, the International Rescue Committee has commissioned a number of retrospective mortality national surveys to assess the impact of war and ethnic conflict in DRC. These surveys also included IDPs. The first survey completed covered the eastern region of the country. Between January 1999 and April 2000, the CMR (deaths/10,000 population per day) among IDPs was found to be 2.1 while U5MR was 4.7 (International Rescue Committee, 2000). The CMR and U5MR among IDPs were found to have decreased over 4 years, estimated respectively at 1.2 and 3.0 in 2002 (Roberts et al., 2003), and 1.0 and 2.0 in 2004 (Coghlan et al., 2006). However, in these studies, the process of identifying IDPs suffered various limitations and displacement was defined based mainly on regions affected by wars and ethnic conflicts (the eastern region). Studies from IDP camps in DRC show a different pattern. Using a systematic sampling approach, Médecins Sans Frontières (2006) carried out a retrospective mortality survey among 1,980 IDPs from three camps of Dubie, Katanga. CMR (deaths/10,000 population/day) was found to be 4.3 while U5MR was estimated at 12.7. Ahoua and colleagues (2006) conducted a retrospective mortality survey in 2005 in Tché camp (population in the camp: 12,000) in Ituri. The survey involved a total of 450 IDP families with a sample size of 2,216 persons. The recall period was divided into two periods to account for the response by international community and humanitarian organisations: period 1 was a pre-response 70-day recall interval (18 December 2004 to 25 February 2005) and represented severe conflicts and violent incidents, and period 2 represented a post-response 30-day recall interval (26 February to 27 March 2005). The study reported an overall CMR (death/10,000 population/day) of 4.1 and an overall U5MR of 6.9. However, when the CMR was examined by the recall period, the rate was lower in period 2. That is, the CMR was 4.7 in period 1 vs. 2.7 in period 2. This pattern was also true for the U5MR: 6.2 in period 1 vs. 8.8 in period 2. Notwithstanding the difference in CMR and U5MR in both periods, they remained significantly higher than the emergency thresholds. The authors suggested that the slight advantage observed in period 2 could be a result of the response by international community and humanitarian organisations that included regrouping displaced civilians near military bases, hence providing them with protection. However, regrouping IDPs near military bases did not significantly reduce the level of insecurity. As the authors speculate, the failure to significantly impact on CMR and U5MR in period 2 following the internal community's response could be related to the spontaneous and unplanned nature of the camps and compromised security conditions, leading to poor public environments characterised by poor living and sanitary conditions and inadequate access to food, basic health services, and clean water.

## *Uganda*

The World Health Organisation (2005) conducted a retrospective mortality survey among IDPs residing in Gulu, Kitgum and Pader districts in collaboration with the Ugandan Ministry of Health and other key partners. The survey involved 3,840 households and data were collected from January to July 2005. The CMR was 1.22 in Gulu District, 1.29 in Gulu Municipality, 1.91 in Kitgum District, and 1.86 in Pader District, giving an overall CMR of 1.54 per 10,000 population per day for the whole Acholi Region. The U5MR was 2.31 in Gulu District, 2.49 in Gulu Municipality, 4.04 in Kitgum District, 4.24 in Pader District, giving an overall U5MR of 3.18 in the whole Acholi Region. The overall CMR and U5MR among IDPs in the Acholi Region were higher than the emergency thresholds.

## *Angola*

Sapir and Gomez (2006) undertook a review of data collected in Angola by means of nutritional and mortality surveys between 1999 and 2005 and included it on the online Complex Emergencies Database (CE-DAT), a database dedicated to gathering data on the human impact of conflict to inform an evidence-based programme to prevent and respond to conflicts.

By 2005, the CE-DAT included more than 1,150 surveys from more than 35 countries experiencing conflict and/or internal displacement. Of these, 88 field surveys were carried out in Angola and were included in this study. The study found that the CMR (death/10,000 population/day) was 2.47 during the conflict and transition period and 1.05 during the post-conflict period. U5MR (death/10,000 population/day) was 5.23 during the conflict and transition period and 2.35 in the post-conflict period. These findings suggest that mortality rates during the conflict were higher than the emergency thresholds, but comparable to the emergency thresholds during the post-conflict period.

## Guinea-Bissau

Nielsen and colleagues (2006) examined mortality patterns among people displaced during the 1998–1999 conflict in Guinea-Bissau. The survey examined mortality rates during three critical periods: pre-war, during the conflict and before signing the peace treaty, and returning home after the cessation of hostilities and signing the peace treaty. The study included 49,731 persons. The CMR and U5MR before the conflict were respectively estimated at 0.43 and 1.02. CMR and U5MR increased significantly during the conflict, rising respectively to 1.78 and 2.07. Although the CMR and U5MR decreased when IDPs returned home after the cessation of the conflict, mortality rates were still higher than the pre-war rate, with the post-conflict CMR and U5MR estimated at 1.05 and 1.31.

## Darfur, Sudan

Grandesso *et al.* (2005) conducted retrospective mortality surveys in 2004 among 137,000 IDPs in south Darfur. The surveys covered three sites with a total sample of 16,082: Kass ($n = 5,776$), Kalma ($n = 5,050$), and Muhajiria ($n = 5,256$). The study found that the CMR (death/10,000 population/day) was 3.2 in Kass, 2.3 in Muhajiria, and 2.0 in Kalma. For children, the U5MR was: 5.9 in Kass, 1.0 in Muhajiria, and 3.5 in Kalma. The reported CMR at all three sites were significantly higher than the 0.9 emergency thresholds for SSA (Checchi and Roberts, 2005). With the exception of Kass, U5MR were also above the 2.3 emergency thresholds for

SSA (Checchi and Roberts, 2005). Using a two-stage cluster sampling standard methodology, the World Health Organisation and the Federal Ministry of Health of Sudan (2005) conducted retrospective mortality surveys in 2004 in IDP settlements in North ($n = 8,843$), West ($n = 7,651$) and South (3,267) Darfur. CMR (deaths/10,000/day) was found to be 1.5 in North, 2.9 in West, and 3.8 in South Darfur. U5MR was 2.5 in North, 3.1 in West, and 11.7 in South Darfur. These findings suggest that the CMR and U5MR in North, West and South Darfur were above the emergency thresholds. Depoortere *et al.* (2004) conducted retrospective mortality surveys in 2004 among 215, 400 IDPs in four sites of West Darfur: Zalingei ($n = 2,386$), Murnei ($n = 4754$), Niertiti ($n = 5188$), and El Geneina ($n = 5191$). CMR and U5MR among IDPs living outside camps were, respectively, 5.9 and 2.8 in Zalingei, 9.5 and 2.1 in Murnei, and 7.3 and 1.5 in Niertiti. However, IDPs living in camps recorded lower CMR and U5MR than those residing outside camps, but at all study sites, the figures remained significantly higher than the emergency thresholds for SSA. The respective CMR and U5MR among IDPs living in camps were 1.3 and 1.6 in Zalingei, 1.2 and 1.4 in Murnei, 1.3 and 2.1 in Niertiti, and 5.6 and 14.1 in El Geneina (Table 3).

## Morbidity

As can be seen from the mortality data summarised above, high mortality among IDPs occur in the early phase of displacement and among IDPs living outside camps mainly due to war or violence-related injury. However, in established camps, the most common causes of deaths are communicable diseases (especially diarrheal diseases and measles), respiratory tract infections, measles, and malaria. Mortality due to these diseases is often exacerbated by high levels of acute malnutrition. Other diseases that contribute to the morbidity of IDPs to a lesser extent include chronic diseases such as tuberculosis, HIV/AIDS and diabetes.

### *War or violence-related injuries*

During conflicts and/or wars, civilians become the most affected, accounting for up to 90% of war-related deaths (Levy, 2002). While during settlement the majority of deaths (80–90%) are predominantly caused by medical causes (Grandesso *et al.*, 2005), in very volatile situations violence and war-related injuries account for a significant share of deaths among IDPs in SSA countries (Depoortere *et al.*, 2004; Grandesso *et al.*, 2005), in Asia (Mullany *et al.*, 2007) and the Middle East (Benini and Moulton, 2004). Available data suggest that depending on the nature and intensity of the war or conflict, war and violence-related injuries account for 67–76% of deaths among adults and 44–91% among children under five-year-old depending on the nature and intensity of the war or conflict and the phase of settlement, in DRC (Ahoua *et al.*, 2006), 3.4–11.7% of all deaths among IDPs in Uganda (World Health Organisation, 2005), 4–11% in Somalia (Toole, 2000), 6.7–72% in Sudan (Depoortere, 2004; Depoortere *et al.*, 2004; Grandesso *et al.*, 2005). In Darfur, Sudan violence accounted for 68–93% of deaths, significantly so among young men (Depoortere *et al.*, 2004; Grandesso *et al.*, 2005). However, in the post-fleeing phase and in stable conditions, the proportion of deaths due to violence is significantly lower, varying from 3.4% to 11.7% (World Health Organisation, 2005). Civilians suffer in different ways depending on their gender and age, and are victims of armed attacks, arbitrary killings and abductions, forced recruitment as well as sexual violence. While physical injuries are frequently used against men during conflicts, for women, sexual torture constitutes a significant weapon of war and women of reproductive age are the main target. Physical injuries include individual (e.g. torture and gunshots, unlawful detention and torture, beating, and mutilation) and collective (e.g. looting or destruction of property) violent events.

However, the prevalence of physical injuries and sexual violence among IDPs has varied by region. It has varied between 17% and 35% (Ahoua *et al.*, 2006; Swiss *et al.*, 1998). Hence war or violence-related injuries are of great concern in the early stage of conflict, and especially among IDPs living outside camps. Sexual violence encompasses rape, assault, trafficking and prostitution or 'survival sex' to pay for food and other essential goods, and harmful traditional practices such as forced and early marriages may be promoted and/or used as an intentional strategy of domination (Watts and Zimmerman, 2002; Wood, 2006). While quantifying the magnitude of sexual violence in conflict zones has proved to be a daunting task, characterised by serious under-reporting (Marsh et al., 2006), data from Liberia suggest that half of IDP women suffer sexual violence (Swiss et al., 1998). Among IDPs in northern Uganda, the prevalence of sexual abuse and torture against women was estimated to be between 14.6% and 20% (Liebling-Kalifani et al., 2013). In the eastern DRC, the lifetime prevalence of sexual abuse and other gender-based violence against women was estimated at 39.7% vs. 23.6% against men (Johnson et al., 2010). However, among those subjected to sexual violence, 74.3% of women and 64.5% of men experienced war or conflict-related sexual violence (Johnson et al., 2010). Among IDPs in western Africa, the prevalence of war-related and non-war-related sexual assault against women was estimated at 17% (i.e. war-related sexual violence was 8% vs. 9% non-war-related sexual violence) in Sierra Leone (Amowitz et al., 2002) and 15% in Liberia (Swiss et al., 1998). Sexual violence occurred in different forms and included violent penetrative sexual acts such as rape, gang rape and defilement, sexual slavery (e.g. forced to cook for a fighters and meet their sexual needs), sexual coercion, and incest. War or conflict-related sexual abuses were mainly committed by combatants against non-combatants whereas non-war-related sexual assaults were committed by family members, friends, or other civilians.

## *Diarrhoea diseases*

While violence continues to account for a significant share of deaths during the early phase period of displacement, diarrhoeal diseases are the primary causes of morbidity and mortality among IDPs. Predisposing factors for diarrheal diseases among IDPs include unsafe water supply, inadequate sanitation and hygiene, often exacerbated by crowded conditions in IDP camps which precipitate the rapid spread of these diseases. Most documented diarrheal diseases among IDPs include dysentery and cholera. The prevalence of diarrheal diseases among IDPs varies between 19.7% and 20.3% (Doocy and Burnham, 2006) and accounts for 18% and 47% of deaths in IDP camps (Grandesso et al., 2005). They disproportionately affect children younger than 5 years and people aged 50 years or older (Kim et al., 2007; Grandesso et al., 2005). It has been estimated that appropriate water, hygiene and sanitation interventions can reduce diarrheal mortality by 65% and incidence by 26% (World Health Organisation, 2003), hence highlighting the importance of providing IDPs with improved water supply and sanitation systems as well as hygiene education and promotion.

## *Measles*

Similar to diarrhoeal diseases, measles is a highly contagious disease and outbreaks have been documented among IDPs (CDC, 2004; Coronado *et al.*, 2006; Kouadio *et al.*, 2010; Salama *et al.*, 2001). The measles attack rate is often used as a measure of frequency of morbidity or speed of spread. The measles attack rate has ranged from 0.4/1000 to 6.9/1000 among IDP populations, which is significantly lower than the attack rate of 9.5/1000 to 31/1000 reported among refugee populations (Kouadio *et al.*, 2010). Although among non-IDPs, measles fatality is stable with a fatality rate between 1% and 5%, the fatality rate among IDPs is extremely high and varies between 9.8% and 30% and is associated with poor vaccination coverage (<60% coverage), poor access to IDPs and overcrowding (Kouadio *et al.*, 2010; Salama *et al.*, 2001; Moodley *et al.*, 2013). Proportional mortality rates due to measles among IPDs have been estimated to vary between 18.7% and 40% of deaths (United Nations Administrative Committee on Coordination Sub-Committe on Nutrition, 2002). However, high mortality due to measles is preventable through measles mass immunisation, complemented by mass vitamin A distribution. For example, mass measles immunisation among IDPs in northern Uganda reduced measles case admissions by 82%, measles mortality by 80% and measles bed-days by 88% (Mupere *et al.*, 2005). These findings are supported by studies quantifying child mortality reductions related to measles vaccination in non-emergency settings (Dabbagh *et al.*, 2009; Goldhaber-Fiebert *et al.*, 2010).

## *Malaria*

Malaria constitutes a leading cause of morbidity among IDPs in endemic regions, with the prevalence of malarial parasitaemia estimated at 11.2% to 37.5% in malaria-endemic regions (Spencer *et al.*, 2004; West Africa

Regional Health Working Group, 2012). A study by Médecins Sans Frontières among IDP camps in Bundibugyo, south-west Uganda (Spencer *et al.*, 2004) reported a prevalence of malarial parasitaemia of 11.2% (95% CI 9.4–13.0), but the prevalence was significantly lower among IDPs who used insecticide-treated bednets than non-users (9.2% vs. 13.8%; relative risk: 0.63, 95% CI: 0.46–0.87). A cross-border community-based integrated malaria control programme among IDPs in eastern Burma/Myanmar reported a baseline prevalence of 8.4% (95% CI: 8.3–8.6) which declined significantly to 1.1% (95% CI: 1.1–1.2) at follow-up after two years of long-lasting insecticide treated net distribution (Richards *et al.*, 2009). Therefore, malaria is a significant cause of morbidity among IDPs with proportional morbidity due to malaria estimated at 43% in Liberia (Johns Hopkins Bloomberg School of Public Health and International Federation of Red Cross and Red Crescent Societies, 2008) and between 6.3% and 20.8% in South Sudan (International Organsation for Migration, 2014; World Health Organisation, 2014). Among IDPs attending outpatient clinics, treatment for malaria constitutes about 45% of all outpatient attendance, and 60% among children below the age of five years (Kolaczinski *et al.*, 2006). In very endemic regions, malaria has accounted for 22.5% to 52.5% of deaths among IDPs (World Health Organisation, 2005; World Health Organisation and Federal Ministry of Health of Sudan, 2005). For children, malaria alone is responsible for 42.9% to 52.5% of child deaths (World Health Organisation, 2005). The distibution of insecticide-treated bednets is an effective way of preventing malaria among IDPs (Richards *et al.*, 2009; Spencer *et al.*, 2004).

## *Acute respiratory infections*

Acute respiratory infections (ARIs) are a significant cause of morbidity and mortality among IDPs, with a high prevalence of approximately 19% (Liebling-Kalifani *et al.*, 2013). The proportional morbidity due to ARIs has been estimated at 68% for upper respiratory tract infections and 19% for lower respiratory tract infections in South Sudan (International Organization for Migration, 2014), 18% in Liberia (Johns Hopkins Bloomberg School of Public Health and International Federation of Red Cross and Red Crescent Societies, 2008) and Chad (West Africa Regional Health Working

Group, 2012), and 21% in Mali (West Africa Regional Health Working Group, 2012). It has been estimated that ARI accounts for 10–19% of deaths among IDPs across SSA, and disproportionately affects children (Bellos *et al.*, 2010; United Nations Administrative Committee on Coordination Sub-Committee on Nutrition, 2002).

## *HIV/AIDS*

Although not leading causes of deaths among IDPs, HIV/AIDS contribute to the burden of diseases. Spiegel and Harroff-Tavel (2006) conducted a literature review of peered and non-peered publications to establish the burden of HIV/AIDS among conflict-affected IDPs covering eight priority countries with large IDP populations. They found that claims related to the increase of HIV/AIDS, high HIV infection rates or lack of adequate HIV interventions among IDPs due to conflict cannot be substantiated due to the paucity of data. They noted that various reports and policy papers, as well as research articles, made strong declarations on the effects of HIV among IDPs without substantiating their claims with data. The few available data the authors identified suggest that the HIV prevalence ranged from 0.3% to 12.4% with a median of 3.2% among countries with an IDP population of 11.1–14.7 million persons. In a follow-up study examining data from seven countries affected by conflict (DRC, Southern Sudan, Rwanda, Uganda, Sierra Leone, Somalia and Burundi) where violence and rape were believed to fuel the HIV epidemic, Spiegel and colleagues (2007) found that the HIV prevalence remained low and fairly stable. Overall, the HIV prevalence among IDP populations has been estimated at 1% (vs. 2.3% in the general population) in Sudan and 7.1% (vs. 4.2% in the general population) in DRC (Spiegel and Harroff-Tavel, 2006) and 10.5% (vs. 11.1% in the general population) in Rwanda (Spiegel *et al.*, 2007). In countries with a high prevalence of HIV/AIDS, AIDS accounts for 6.1% to 19.7% of all deaths among adults (World Health Organisation, 2005).

## *Tuberculosis*

While few data on tuberculosis exist among refugees, the burden on tuberculosis among IDPs is poorly documented and data are scarce. In a recently published systematic review looking at the burden of tuberculosis in crisis-affected populations, Kimbrough and colleagues (2012) identified 51 reports of which 23 focused on refugees living in camps, only five focused on IDPs, 20 on non-displaced populations affected by conflicts and three on populations affected by natural disasters. Only 10 out of the 51 studies reported prevalence data, and none among IDPs. However, the authors found that the tuberculosis case fatality rate among IDPs varied from 4.5% (vs. 3.7% in the host population) in South Sudan to 10.4% in northern Uganda, which is significantly lower than the 20% case fatality rate for developing countries. The risk of dying from tuberculosis increases with levels of acute malnutrition and HIV-tuberculosis co-infection.

## *Acute malnutrition*

It is well documented that among IDPs, acute malnutrition increases the risk of infection and mortality from malaria, diarrhoea, cholera, pneumonia and measles. Table 4 summarises the prevalence of acute malnutrition among IDPs. In most cases (79% of the surveys), the prevalence is well above the "serious" thresholds of 10% used to classify emergencies. While quantifying the proportion of deaths due to undernutrition among IDPs is difficult due to its comorbidity with other diseases, data from DRC indicate that acute malnutrition was a primary or contributing cause in 8.1 to 10.9% of all deaths (Coghlan *et al.*, 2006).

## *Mental health*

When discussing the health of IDPs across SSA, mental health has not featured prominently in the literature and few studies have attempted to describe the mental health of IDPs and the traumatic experiences associated with forced displacement. There is emerging evidence that there are extremely high levels of psychiatric morbidity among the IDP populations. The prevalence of depression among IDPs has been estimated at 31% in south Darfur, Sudan (Kim *et al.*, 2007) and 16.3% in Nigeria (Sheikh *et al.*, 2015). However, higher rates have been reported in the most volatile and war-torn parts of SSA. In a cross-sectional multi-staged, random cluster survey, Roberts and colleagues (2008) obtained data on 1,210 adult IDPs in Gulu and Amuru districts of northern Uganda. Mental health was measured using *Diagnostic and Statistical Manual for Mental Disorders, Fourth*

Table 4: Prevalence of acute malnutrition among IDPs across SSA

| Date | Country | Prevalence | Source |
|---|---|---|---|
| 2004 | *Sudan, South Darfur* | | Grandesso *et al.* (2005) |
| | Kass camp | 14.1% | |
| | Kalma camp | 23.6% | |
| | Muhajiria camp | 10.7% | |
| 2005 | *Sudan* | | Guha-Sapir and Degomme (2005) |
| | North Darfur | 22.5% | |
| | South Darfur | 12.4% | |
| | West Darfur | 8.8% | |
| 2004 | *Sudan, West Darfur* | | Depoortere (2004) |
| | Zalingei camp | 23.4% | |
| | Murnei camp | 20.6% | |
| 2004 | *Sudan, West Darfur* | *25.8%* | Checchi (2004) |
| 2006 | *DRC, Katanga* | *19.2%* | Médecins San Frontières (2006) |
| 2006 | *Angola* | | Sapir and Gomez (2006) |
| | During conflict | 14.9% | |
| | Post conflict | 6.3% | |
| 2008 | *Uganda* | *6.0%* | Olwedo *et al.* (2009) |
| 2009 | *Chad* | *20.6%* | Guerrier *et al.* (2009) |

*Edition* (*DSM-IV*) as well as the *Hopkins Symptoms Check List-25*. They found that 54% of IDPs met symptom criteria for post-traumatic stress disorder (PTSD) while 67% met symptom criteria for depression. Using the same methodology in South Sudan post conflict, Roberts *et al.* (2009) established that of the 1,242 adults interviewed, 36% met symptom criteria for PTSD and 50% met symptom criteria for depression, and IDPs were at increased risk of poor mental health (PTSD: OR 1.81, 95% CI: 1.18–2.76; and depression: OR 2.22, 95% CI: 1.70–2.89) when compared to participants who have never been displaced. These findings were not limited to adults only. In a study of children aged 6–17 years, Morgos *et al.* (2007) obtained data on 331 participants from three IDP camps in Southern

Darfur. The authors found that 75% of the children met the DSM-IV criteria for PTSD, and 38% met symptom criteria for depression. Studies have also attempted to establish the magnitude of suicide with the prevalence of suicidal ideation and suicide attempts over the previous year estimated respectively at 5% and 2% (Kim et al., 2007).

## Policy response

Any policy response to meet the need of IDPs needs to be comprehensive and should examine the displacement continuum: the fleeing phase, the transitional settlement (e.g. post-fleeing settlement and the host communities) and the returning phase (including re-integration). Although IDPs tend to receive varying degrees of assistance during the fleeing and transitional settlement phases, the biggest challenge remains when they return home post-conflict. The main problems in dealing with post-conflict, some of which may have led to their fleeing in the first place, include land disputes, marginalisation and ethnic conflicts, and seizure, occupation and destruction of owned homes, owned lands and farms littered with explosive remnants of war (Albuja et al., 2014). So it is important that response to the needs of IDPs adopts a long-term approach in addition to the short-term relief response. Given that traditionally, by virtue of the fact that IDPs did not cross the border, they have been perceived to be the responsibilities of their government as prescribed by the principles of state sovereignty, any approach to address the needs of IDPs needs to engage the government at all levels to ensure accountability, protection and durable solutions. In the push to meet these requirements, a number of international frameworks and legal principles have been proposed and implemented in SSA.

### *The 1981 African Charter on Human and Peoples' Rights*

Following independence in the late 1950s and early 1960s, most countries in SSA were plagued by internal conflicts, wars and human right abuses. Perhaps the first legal framework to protect the rights of war and conflict-affected populations in SSA countries was the adoption of the 1981 African Charter on Human and Peoples' Rights at the Eighteenth Assembly of Heads of State and Government of the Organization of African Unity in Nairobi, Kenya. It is not the purpose of this chapter to provide a comprehensive historical perspective on the evolution of the legal process that led to the African Charter on Human and Peoples' Rights (for those interested, please see Gittleman, 1981). However, it worth noting that the formulation of the charter can be traced back to 1961 when, under the auspice of the International Commission of Jurists, African jurists (194 African judges, practising lawyers and law teachers, and nine representatives from countries outside of Africa) convened a conference in Lagos, Nigeria. At this conference, the attendees proposed the creation of an African Human Rights Charter under which a court would be established to assist victims of human rights abuses. (Gittleman, 1981; Hazarika, 2010, Umozurike, 1983). The resolution from this conference was the declaration of the 'Law of Lagos'. The creation of such a commission was later discussed in the 1969 Establishment of Regional Commissions on Human Rights with Special Reference to Africa in Cairo, Egypt, which was convened by the United Nations Division of Human Rights in partnership with the Government of the United Arab Republic. After a number of follow-up seminars, colloquia and conferences between 1970 and 1978, the idea had gained momentum and in 1979 a seminar was organised in Monrovia, Sierra Leone, attended by 30 African states. The aim of the seminar was to establish Regional Commissions on Human Rights under the auspices of the United Nations, the result of which was the Monrovia Proposal for the setting up of an African Commission on Human Rights (Gittleman, 1981). The draft was discussed and refined in three different meetings, once in Dakar, Senegal in 1979, and twice in Banjul, Gambia in 1980 and in 1981 (Umozurike, 1983). The final draft was adopted unanimously at the eighteenth assembly of heads of State and government of the then Organisation of African Unity held in Nairobi and signed on 26 June 1981 and entered into force on 21 October 1986. The charter was later complemented by the 1998 Protocol on the African Court on Human and People's Rights and the 2003 Protocol on the Rights of Women, ratified by all 53 African Union member states. The charter and its protocols acknowledge the need to promote human rights and covers both civil and political rights, including the right to development, right to self-determination and generally economic, social and cultural rights.

When the African Charter on Human and People's Rights entered into force on 21 October 1986, the African Commission on Human and People's Rights was established to monitor state parties' compliance with the Charter as well as to promote and protect human rights across SSA countries including accepting and considering complaints of violations of the Charter. However, experts have noted that the African Charter on Human and People's Rights is unrealistic and the least effective when it comes to protecting human rights for many reasons. First of all, the existence of the commission, its role and responsibilities are not well understood by SSAs due to its inability to advertise its activities (Wachira, 2008). How can victims of human rights abuses take their grievances to an organisation they are not aware of or whose operation is not understood? Secondly, the commission is entrusted with documenting human rights abuses as well as investigating complaints and making recommendations. The commission has been unable to implement and enforce its own recommendations as it does not have the authority to interfere with states' internal affairs and some countries such as Nigeria have questioned the commission's mandate to consider cases or make recommendations due to the commission's lack of judicial capacity to make such recommendations (Wachira, 2008; Wachira and Ayinla, 2006). Thirdly, the commission has been seen as lacking independence and influenced by external forces. In its early phase of operation, the commission was made up of nominated rather than elected government officials, which violated the African Charter which prescribes that commission members be elected, hence questioning the credibility of the commission. Being appointed by the same governments that are responsible for human rights abuses, the victims of human rights abuses view these commissions as part of the same repressive governments. Although this issue was overcome when the African Union outlined the nomination process to state parties prohibiting commission members to be members of the government, another challenge arose that jeopardised the commission's independence. As a result of being poorly funded by the African Union, the commission has relied heavily on extra funding from international donors, which in the eyes of state parties made the commission subject to all the influences described by the agenda and activities of international NGOs and their vested interests (Wachira, 2008; Wachira and

Ayinla, 2006). Finally, there have been delays in the commission's dealing with cases due to the volume of cases the commission have had to deal with (Wachira, 2008; Wachira and Ayinla, 2006). All these limitations raise the question of the effectiveness of the African charter in dealing with the immense challenge associated with IDPs.

## The 1998 United Nations Guiding Principles on Internal Displacement

The Guiding Principles form a legal and institutional framework acknowledging the urgent need to assist and protect persons forcibly uprooted from their homes by traumatic events, gross violation of human rights and/or violent conflicts. With a dramatic increase in IDPs in the 1980s and 1990s, the international community found it difficult to meet their needs and to ensure their protection due to the lack of an international treaty dealing with internal displacement or IDP-specific institutional or legal framework to guide a response. Consequently, the UN Commission on Human Rights created a new position in 1992 related to the needs and protection of IDPs, and Francis M Deng was the first appointee as the Representative of the UN Secretary-General on the Human Rights of IDPs (Cohen and Deng, 1998; Deng, 2001). Francis M Deng completed a series of studies documenting international standards relevant to IDPs in 1993 pursuant to Commission on Human Rights Resolution 1992/73 (United Nations Commission on Human Rights, 1993), in 1995 pursuant to Commission on Human Rights Resolution 1995/57 (United Nations Economic and Social Council, 1995) and 1998 pursuant to Commission on Human Rights Resolution 1997/39 (United Nations Economic and Social Council, 1998). In a two-part *Compilation and Analysis of Legal Norms* (Deng, 2001), the studies found that existing institutional and legal frameworks were not adequately equipped to protect IDPs. The identified gaps included the general nature of the existing legal framework with no specific dimensions related to IDPs in terms of identity (personal documentation), compensation (e.g. for lost properties during displacement), protection against forcible return to the place of origin before it is safe, protection against actions by non-state actors controlling IDPs (who unlike state authorities may not be bound by internal laws) and negligence and abandonment of IDPs in states that are non-signatories of the Geneva Refugee Convention and associated additional Protocols (United Nations Commission on Human Rights, 1996).

Therefore, while existing laws provided the basis for protection and assistance of IDPs, they did not directly address very important aspects that characterise IDPs including the fact that they have not crossed the borders (hence not covered by the refugee law), many of them may have been displaced for reasons other than armed conflicts (hence not covered by the humanitarian law) and, most importantly, the human rights law does not directly cover forcible displacement and access to humanitarian assistance (United Nations Commission on Human Rights, 1993). The findings emphasised the evident gaps in the legal protection of IDPs and proposed new and specific standards related to IDPs. The resulting Guiding Principles, although not legally binding, were developed and presented to the commission in 1998. They borrowed significantly from existing human rights, humanitarian and refugee laws and included 30 principles addressing various aspects of IDPs including the rights and guarantees relevant to the assistance and protection of IDPs during displacement, resettlement or re-integration, and return. Principle 3 states that *"(1) National authorities have the primary duty and responsibility to provide the protection and humanitarian assistance to internally displaced persons within their jurisdiction"* and *"(2) internally displaced have the right to request and receive protection and humanitarian assistance from these authorities. They shall not be persecuted or punished for making such a request"* (UN Commission on Human Rights, 1998; p. 2). The emphasis is on equality with respect to rights and freedom under international and domestic laws (23 principles), principles related to humanitarian assistance (four principles) and principles related to return, resettlement and re-integration (three principles) (United Nations Economic and Social Council, 1998).

By virtue of how they were developed and given that they are practically soft laws, the Guiding Principles are prone to being demeaned by states as non-binding, and perceived as not negotiated and adopted by states and not endorsed by a declaration, resolution or recommendation by international organisations (Mutua, 2007). Therefore, the Guiding Principles are vulnerable to political obstruction, not being fully owned and embraced by states as bearers of responsibility and the IDP constituencies may feel that they are not fully engaged and/or neglected by those entrusted by their protection and assistance. Notwithstanding these limitations, the Guiding Principles have gained acclaim from, and have been endorsed by many organisations including the European Union, the UN General Assembly, regional organisations, as well as state governments in Africa and Asia (Mutua, 2007). These principles have been the backbone of legal instruments addressing the needs of IDPs in SSA and have informed the Great Lakes Protocol, the Kampala Convention, the Inter-Agency Standing Committee (IASC) framework on durable solutions for IDPs and the Nations Framework on Ending Displacement in the Aftermath of Conflict.

## The 2006 Great Lakes Protocol

Between 1992 and 2003, the great lakes experienced some of the deadliest interstate conflicts and wars the region has ever experienced. However, intrastate conflicts continue to be prevalent in the region. One of consequences of the interstate and intrastate conflicts that characterise the region has been mass population displacements. In an effort to implement sustainable solutions to end the conflicts and, above all, to meet the challenges associated with IDPs, the International Conference on the Great Lakes Region (ICGLR) was formally initiated in 1996 through a United Nations special envoy who was deployed in the region to consult states and experts in a process to promote peace, security, democracy and development (Internal Displacement Monitoring Centre and International Refugee Rights, 2008). However, the process did not gain momentum until the 2004 Dar es Salaam summit that brought together the eleven member states of the Great Lakes, namely Angola, Burundi, Central African Republic, Republic of the Congo, Democratic Republic of the Congo, Kenya, Rwanda, Sudan, Tanzania, Uganda and Zambia (Internal Displacement Monitoring Centre and International Refugee Rights, 2008). The summit was a success as these eleven members signed the Declaration on Peace, Security, Democracy and Development (known as the Dar es Salaam Declaration). This declaration outlined action and principles that will guide the ICGLR process in the development of the Pact on Security, Stability, and Development in the Great Lakes Region (known as the Great Lakes Pact). The process of developing the Great Lakes Pact was complex, extensive, multitiered and inclusive, and addressed four pillars: (1) peace and security, (2) democracy and good governance, (3) economic development and regional integration, and (4) humanitarian and social issues (Internal Displacement Monitoring Centre and International Refugee Rights, 2008). The process sought input from technical experts, academics and civil society, as well as political endorsement from the Regional Preparatory and Inter-Ministerial Committees (Internal Displacement Monitoring Centre and International Refugee Rights, 2008). The developed pact was adopted at the second summit of heads of states of the ICGLR in Nairobi on 15 December 2006 and ratified by eight member states when it entered into force on 21 June 2008.

The Pact detailed the primary instruments for achieving durable peace in the region and incorporated the Dar es Salaam Declaration, ten protocols, four programmes of action (comprising 33 priority projects), making it a comprehensive and holistic legal framework (Internal Displacement Monitoring Centre and International Refugee Rights, 2008; Kälin, 2007). It is encouraging that the Pact and its instruments outlined measures and mechanisms for protecting the rights of IDPs in the Great Lakes regions. Out of the 10 protocols, two are specifically dedicated to human rights and displacement: (1) the Protocol on the Protection and Assistance to Internally Displaced Persons (the IDP Protocol); and (2) the Protocol on the Property Rights of Returning Populations. The robustness of these two protocols is the recognition that in order to effectively protect IDPs and meet their needs, the assistance needs to be tailored at all phases of displacement (the fleeing phase, settlement in places of displacement, and upon return or resettlement) as well as the recognition that the rights of IDPs cannot be protected if peace, security and development are compromised. The IDP protocol is a hard law and legally binding, it provides a legal framework for implementing the 1998 Guiding Principles and the International Humanitarian Law. In addition, it provides a legal framework for protecting the physical and material needs of IDPs and makes states accountable for preventing and eliminating the root causes of displacement. The advantage of the IDP protocol lies in the fact that while acknowledging states have the primary responsibility of protecting and assisting IDPs, it commits states to enact national legislation to promote coherence and minimise the negative impact of having multiple government ministries and agencies at the national level with different responsibilities in the protection and assistance of IDPs. The Great Lakes Protocol addresses the six most neglected aspects of displacement which existing conventions or treaties have not addressed adequately: the need to effectively deal with development induced displacement (Article 5), the need to support and assist host communities (Article 4), the need to engage IDPs at the national level as key players in the preparation and design of the national legislation that enact the Guiding Principles into national laws (Article 6), the need to maintain an IDP registration database and the provision of identification documents (Article 3), IDPs' freedom of movement as citizens of the affected states (Article 4), and a legal framework that governs the return of IDPs, including protection on return, dispute resolution and the recovery of lost, confiscated or expropriated land and property as well as compensation (Article 5) (International Conference on the Great Lakes Region, 2012).

In order for the Great Lakes Pact and its Protocols to achieve durable solutions for IDPs, there are a number of challenges that need to be overcome beyond its immediate ratification by member states of the ICGLR. These challenges are well articulated by Kälin (2007) into four themes: (1) the tension between accountability and reconciliation, (2) the solution of conflicts between competing property claims, (3) the inclusion of sub-national authorities and traditional communities and the IDPs into efforts to find durable solutions, and (4) the gap between humanitarian assistance and development. The Guiding Principles, especially principle 1 prescribes the needs to assist without prejudice. It states *"these Principles are without prejudice to individual criminal responsibility under international law, in particular relating to genocide, crimes against humanity and war crimes"* and Principle 2 notes *"these Principles shall not be interpreted as restricting, modifying or impairing the provisions of any international human rights or international humanitarian law instrument or rights granted to persons under domestic law"* (International Conference on the Great Lakes Region, 2012). However, human rights treaties prescribe the prosecution and punishment of individuals who commit serious violations of international humanitarian law, yet they are powerless to impose criminal sanctions (Dugard, 1998). Therefore, accountability and reconciliation should not be seen as mutually exclusive (Kälin, 2007) and further efforts are needed to ensure that actioning criminal proceedings does not hamper the implementation of peace agreements, the re-integration of IDPs and the process of solving conflicts between competing property claims. Article 6 of the Great Lakes Protocol outlines the need to engage IDPs at the national level as key players in the preparation and design of the national legislation that enact the Guiding Principles into national laws. This process is more likely to involve other stakeholders such as sub-national authorities and community leaders, hence requiring more clarity about the respective roles and responsibilities as well as relationships (Kälin, 2007).

## *The 2009 Kampala Convention*

With more than one in three IDPs living in Africa, the African Union sought to devise a legally binding framework to govern the protection of IDPs at all phases of displacements. At the Special Summit of Heads of State and Government in 2009, the African Union adopted the Convention for the Protection and Assistance of Internally Displaced Persons in Africa (or the Kampala Convention) on 23 October 2009, which entered into force on 6 December 2012. The Kampala Convention is binding and requests state parties to provide legal protection for the rights and wellbeing of IDPs. It builds on and endorses the International Human Rights Law, International Humanitarian Law and the Refugee Law, as well as the 1998 Guiding Principles and this is well articulated in the preamble which recognises *"the inherent rights of internally displaced persons as provided for and protected in international human rights and humanitarian law and as set out in the 1998 United Nations Guiding Principles on Internal Displacement, which are recognized as an important international framework for the protection of internally displaced persons"* p. 2 (African Union, 2009). The convention also acknowledges the protection expertise of, and role played by, the UNHCR in assisting refugees as well as the International Committee of the Red Cross in assisting people affected by armed conflict and violence. The convention notes the

> *"specific roles of international Organizations and agencies within the framework of the United Nations inter-agency collaborative approach to internally displaced persons, especially the protection expertise of the Office of the United Nations High Commissioner for Refugees and the invitation extended to it by the Executive Council of the African Union in*

*Decision EX/CL.413 (XIII) of July 2008 at Sharm El Sheikh, Egypt, to continue and reinforce its role in the protection of and assistance to internally displaced persons, within the United Nations coordination mechanism; and noting also the mandate of the International Committee of the Red Cross to protect and assist persons affected by armed conflict and other situations of violence, as well as the work of civil society organizations, in conformity with the laws of the country in which they exercise such roles and mandates."*

The Kampala Convention differs from the 1998 Guiding Principles in many aspects. Unlike the 1998 Guiding Principles that are seen as soft laws with no legally binding force, the Kampala Convention contains hard law standards (Ojeda, 2010). As noted by Kälin (2007), the Kampala Convention deals with the successful return of IDPs to their homes or former places of habitual residence under three prescriptions: guaranteeing the safety of returnees, ensuring the return of property to the displaced and the reconstruction of their houses, and maintaining a sustainable environment that promotes economic, social and political returns. The Convention prescribes states parties' obligation to prohibit arbitrary displacement of populations, exclusion and marginalisation (Article 3), protect and assist during displacement (Article 9), sustainable return, local integration or relocation (Article 11), maintain registration and personal documentation (Article 13) and offer compensation (Article 12) (African Union, 2009). In this respect, the Kampala Convention went further than existing international humanitarian laws in three aspects, namely the states' obligation to ensure sustainable return, local integration or relocation of IDPs (a right not explicitly outlined in the international humanitarian laws), proper documentation of IDPs and the provision of identification documents, and reparation through effective remedies and the provision of compensation (elements absent in international humanitarian laws) (Ojeda, 2010). However, the biggest challenge is to ensure the uptake and implementation of the Kampala Convention in order to achieve tangible outcomes. Of the 54 African countries, 39 (72.2%) have signed the Convention since its adoption and only 22 (40.7%) have ratified it. States that have not yet ratified the Kampala Convention include those with the highest burden of IDPs, including Somalia, Sudan, DRC, South Sudan and Burundi. The reluctance of these countries to ratify the Kampala Convention means that its effectiveness to protect IDPs and promote their wellbeing across the continent will remain compromised. There is a need to develop a clear implementation plan and monitoring system couched within states' domestic laws, which need to be promoted and supported by all the international key players.

## *The 2010 Inter-Agency Standing Committee framework on durable solutions for IDPs*

The IASC framework on durable solutions did not seek to replicate the great work achieved in the area of the protection and assistance of IDPs. Instead, the framework seeks to deepen our understanding of the concept of durable solutions for IDPs, to outline guidelines, right-based processes and conditions for achieving a durable solution, and to provide indicators for determining the extent to which durable solutions have been achieved (Inter-Agency Standing Committee, 2010). All proposed strategies in the framework are informed by the 1998 Guiding Principles and the international legal framework including the International Human Rights Law as well as the International Humanitarian Law. The framework considers the rights-based process to be gradual and complex and involving multiple challenges grouped into four pillars: (1) the human rights challenge (e.g. the right to reparation, justice, truth and closure for past injustices), (2) the humanitarian challenge (e.g. addressing the needs of IDPs during the emergency, rehabilitation and re-integration phases), (3) the development challenge (e.g. helping to establish or re-establish local governance structures and the rule of law), and (4) peace-building or reconstruction challenge (e.g. investing in local and national political, economic and social stabilisation). The greatest addition this framework makes to previous declarations and conventions is to highlight the eight criteria that may be used to determine the extent to which a durable solution has been achieved. These criteria are safety and security, adequate standard of living, access to livelihoods, restoration of housing, land and property, access to documentation, family reunification, participation in public affairs, and access to effective remedies and justice. The International Organisation for Migration (IOM) has used the IASC framework to measure progress towards community stabilisation and to determine the point of exit from IOM-partnered assistance programmes as part of the Community Stabilization and Recovery across Africa (International Organization for Migration, 2013).

## The 2011 United Nations framework on ending displacement in the aftermath of conflict

Like the IASC framework, the United Nations framework on ending displacement in the aftermath of conflict is geared towards supporting a more coherent and effective response to the needs of IDPs (United Nations, 2011). It is also significantly informed by the 1998 Guiding Principles, the Kampala Convention and the IASC framework. While the IASC focused on determining indicators for measuring progress, the UN framework focuses on outlining priorities, roles and responsibilities that should govern the delivery of durable solutions for IDPs. In describing the UN engagement with affected states, the framework outlines the principles and laws underpinning its approach focusing on principles related to the (1) state responsibility, (2) the need to adopt rights- and community-based participatory approaches, (3) the need to adhere to the do no harm principles, (4) mainstreaming age, gender, diversity and specific environmental factors into all aspects of protection for IDPs, and (5) the adherence to evidence-based programming (United Nations, 2011). Most importantly, the framework identifies some of the gaps in the current approaches in achieving durable solutions for IDPs. These gaps are related to:

1. Processes
   a. Joint integrated process: mainly the ineffectiveness of the coordination between development, human rights, humanitarian and peace-building actors, and the challenges associated with coordination in the context of emergency–rehabilitation–development continuum.
   b. Planning: the mismatch between the differing needs of IDPs at different phases of displacement (especially in areas of return, settlement or local integration) and UN planning processes as well as recovery and development strategies.
   c. Partnerships, e.g. not giving sufficient support to national capacities to better address the needs of IDPs, and limited partnerships, joint

programming or strategies between UN and non-UN development partners.

d. Funding, e.g. national budgets not allowing sufficient funds to cater for the added needs brought about by displacement and peace-building priorities.

2. Programmes

   a. Social and Economic Recovery: difficulty in capitalising on local resources, hence limiting the stimulation of the local economic recovery, difficulty in involving IDPs in recovery programmes, failure to account for the humanitarian consequences of rapid urban growth due to displacement and limited access to basic services including quality and affordable education and social protection services.
   b. Protection, Security and Rule of Law: poor mechanisms for understanding security risks of returning IDPs, and reporting and monitoring protection concerns, and limited access to justice and legal aid.
   c. Governance: failure to recognise and reinforce national and local governments as the principal duty bearers, capacity-building programmes focusing on national authorities and civil society while neglecting local-level government authorities that closely interact with IDPs, governance interventions for local authorities that neglect the specificities of IDPs' needs, including peace-building, social cohesion and access to basic services and land.
   d. Social Cohesion: neglect of reconciliation and peace-building efforts and psychosocial programmes in recovery programmes for IDPs.

Therefore, the UN Framework on Ending Displacement in the Aftermath of Conflict provides a template for implementing the Kampala Convention and the Great Lakes Protocols. Some of the SSA countries have taken steps to implement the UN framework (Albuja *et al.*, 2014)

## Conclusion

IDPs experience a high burden of diseases and lost opportunities. Those living outside the camp rely heavily on the generosity of local NGOs, hence predisposing them to greater risks of mortality and morbidity than those living in camps. However, there has been significant progress in the development of priorities and strategies related to the protection and assistance of, and durable solutions for, IDPs. Such progress has been characterised by the development, adoption and ratification of soft (Guiding Principles) and hard (the Great Lakes Protocols and the Kampala Convention) laws, complemented by implementation frameworks (IASC and UN frameworks). Notwithstanding this, there are a number of challenges that need to be overcome to maximise the impact of the soft laws and legal instruments. All the soft and hard laws related to the durable solutions for IDPs agree on one thing. That is, the states are responsible for the protection and assistance of IDPs. Yet, not all states have ratified existing legal instruments, and those who have not ratified these hard laws have the highest number of IDPs. In addition, states most hit by internal displacement experience ongoing political instability and may have varying degrees of preparedness and capacity to respond to the needs brought about by internal displacements, hence compromising partnership opportunities. Similarly, all legal instruments acknowledge the need to safeguard state sovereignty. This can mean that any international intervention may need state's clearance, thereby hindering humanitarian assistance. The legal instruments also acknowledged the need to engage all stakeholders at all levels nationally and regionally. At the national levels, the protection and assistance of IDPs may fall under various ministries and government departments (e.g. Ministry of Health, Ministry of Social Development, Ministry of Internal Affairs, Ministry of Foreign Affairs or Ministry of Security and Justice) with different roles and responsibilities making harmonisation of the response and the translation of hard laws into domestic legal instruments difficult. Most of the time it is difficult to monitor progress over time and establishing a database to monitor progress locally and regionally on agreed indicators should be a good start. This is more likely to be an issue given the sensitivity around IDPs as some states tend to not prioritise or underestimate the magnitude of internal displacement. Finally, the protection and assistance of IDPs need to be interpreted through the emergency–rehabilitation–development continuum. Most national and international key players tend to specialise in some but not all aspects of the displacement continuum, which dictates the timing of their involvement. Those who specialise in emergency response tend to intervene in the early phase of displacement and during the settlement in IDP camps or new locations, and those who specialise in rehabilitation and development tend to intervene during the returning phase or re-integration in another location. This makes the coordination and integration of the response at various levels of displacements very difficult.

# References

African Union (2009). African Union Convention for the protection and assistance of internally displaced persons in Africa (Kampala Convention). Available at: http://www.unhcr.org/4ae9bede9.html. Accessed 12 September 2014.

Ahoua, L. *et al.* (2006). High mortality in an internally displaced population in Ituri, Democratic Republic of Congo, 2005: Results of a rapid assessment under difficult conditions. *Global Public Health*, 1, 195–204.

Albuja, S. *et al.* (2014). Global Overview 2014: People Internally Displaced by Conflict and Violence. Internal Displacement Monitoring Centre, Norwegian Refugee Council, Geneva, SWI.

Amowitz, L.L. *et al.* (2002). Prevalence of war-related sexual violence and other human rights abuses among internally displaced persons in Sierra Leone. *Journal of American Medical Association*, 287, 513–521.

Bellos, A. *et al.* (2010). The burden of acute respiratory infections in crisis-affected populations: A systematic review. *Conflict and Health*, 4, 1–12.

Benini, A.A. & Moulton, L.H. (2004). Civilian victims in an asymmetrical conflict: Operation Enduring Freedom, Afghanistan. *Journal of Peace Research*, 41, 403–422.

Buhaug H. *et al.* (2007). *Global Trends in Armed Conflict.* Centre for the Study of Civil War, Peace Research Institute, Oslo, NOR.

Bustreo, F. *et al.* (2005). *Improving Child Health in Post-Conflict Countries: Can the World Bank Contribute?* World Bank, Washington, D.C.

CDC (2004). Emergency measles control activities–Darfur, Sudan. *Morbidity and Mortality Weekly Report*, 53, 897–899.

Cernea, M. (2006). Development-induced and conflict-induced IDPs: Bridging the research divide. *Forced Migration Review*, 261, 25–27.

Checchi, F. (2004). A survey of internally displaced persons in El Geneina, Western Darfur: Final report. Médecins Sans Frontères, Paris, FRA.

Checchi, F. Roberts, L. (2005). Interpreting and using mortality data in humanitarian emergencies: A primer for non-epidemiologists. HPN Network Paper Number 52, 2005. Overseas Development Institute, London, UK.

Chen, S. *et al.* (2007). The aftermath of civil war. Post-Conflict Transitions Working Paper Number 4. World Bank, Washington, DC.

Coghlan, B. *et al.* (2006). Mortality in the Democratic Republic of Congo: A nation-wide survey. *The Lancet*, 367, 44–51.

Cohen, R. & Deng, F. (1998). Masses in Flight: The Global Crisis of Internal Displacement. Brookings Institution Press, Washington, D.C.

Collier, P. (1999). On the economic consequences of civil war. *Oxford Economic Papers*, 51, 168–183.

Coronado, F. *et al.* (2006). Retrospective measles outbreak investigation: Sudan, 2004. *Journal of Tropical Pediatrics*, 52, 329–334.

Dabbagh A. *et al.* (2009). Global measles mortality, 2000–2008. *Morbidity and Mortality Weekly Report*, 58, 1321–1326.

Deng, F. (2001). The global challenge of internal displacement. *Washington University Journal of Law and Policy*, 5, 141–144.

Depoortere, E. (2004). Health assessment in emergencies: Murnei & Zalingei, West Darfur, Sudan. Epicentre, Médecins Sans Frontières, Paris, FRA.

Depoortere, E. *et al.* (2004). Violence and mortality in West Darfur, Sudan (2003–2004): Epidemiological evidence from four surveys. *The Lancet*, 364, 1315–1320.

Doocy, S. & Burnham, G. (2006). Point-of-use water treatment and diarrhoea reduction in the emergency context: An effectiveness trial in Liberia. *Tropical Medicine & International Health*, 11, 1542–1552.

Dugard, J. (1998). Bridging the gap between human rights and humanitarian law: The punishment of offenders. *International Review of the Red Cross*, 38, 445–453.

Gittleman, R. (1981) The African Charter on Human and Peoples' Rights: A legal analysis. *Virginia Journal of International Law*, 22, 667–714.

Gleditsch, K. (2004). A revised list of wars between and within independent states, 1816–2002. *International Interactions*, 30, 231–262.

Goldhaber-Fiebert, J.D. *et al.* (2010). Quantifying child mortality reductions related to measles vaccination. *PloS One* 5, e13842.

Grandesso, F. *et al.* (2005). Mortality and malnutrition among populations living in South Darfur, Sudan: Results of 3 surveys, September 2004. *Journal of American Medical Association*, 293, 1490–1494.

Guerrier, G. *et al.* (2009). Malnutrition and mortality patterns among internally displaced and non-displaced population living in a camp, a village or a town in Eastern Chad. *PloS One* 4, e8077.

Guha-Sapir, D. & Panhuis, W.G. (2004). Conflict-related mortality: An analysis of 37 datasets. *Disasters*, 28, 418–428.

Guha-Sapir, D. & Degomme, O. (2005). Darfur: Counting the deaths. Mortality estimates from multiple survey data. Centre for Research on the Epidemiology of Disasters Report, Brussels, BEL.

Hazarika, R. (2010). The African Charter on Human and Peoples' Rights 198. Available at: http://ssrn.com/abstract=1696363. Accessed 2 April 2014.

Inter-Agency Standing Committee (2010). IASC Framework on durable solutions for internally displaced persons. The Brookings Institution, University of Bern, and Project on Internal Displacement, Washington, DC.

Internal Displacement Monitoring Centre (2013). Conflict and violence-induced displacement. Available at: http://www.internal-displacement.org/global-figures. IDMC, Geneva, SWI. Accessed 11 May 2014.

Internal Displacement Monitoring Centre, International Refugee Rights (2008). The Great Lakes Pact and the rights of displaced people: A guide for civil society. IDMC and IRR, Geneva, SWI.

International Conference on the Great Lakes Region (2012). Protocol on the Protection and Assistance to Internally Displaced Persons. Available at: http://www.brookings.edu/fp/projects/idp/greatlakes_idpprotocol.pdf. Accessed 12 September 2014.

International Organization for Migration (2013). Humanitarian Assistance to Vulnerable Populations Affected by Migration. IOM, Harare, ZIM.

International Organsation for Migration. (2014). IOM South Sudan Situation Report. IOM, Juba.

International Rescue Committee (2000). *Mortality in Eastern DRC: Results from Five Mortality Surveys.* IRC, Bukavu, DRC.

Johns Hopkins Bloomberg School of Public Health, International Federation of Red Cross and Red Crescent Societies (2008). The Johns Hopkins and Red Cross Red Crescent Public Health Guide in Emergencies. International Federation of Red Cross and Red Crescent Societies, Geneva, SWI.

Johnson, K. *et al.* (2010). Association of sexual violence and human rights violations with physical and mental health in territories of the Eastern Democratic Republic of the Congo. *Journal of American Medical Association*, 304, 553–562.

Kälin, W. (2007). The Great Lakes Protocol on Internally Displaced Persons. Responses and Challenges, Statement to Symposium on International Law in Post-Conflict Situations: The Great Lakes Process, London School of Economics, London, UK.

Kim, G. *et al.* (2007). Basic health, women's health, and mental health among internally displaced persons in Nyala Province, South Darfur, Sudan. *American Journal of Public Health*, 97, 353–361.

Kimbrough, W. *et al.* (2012). The burden of tuberculosis in crisis-affected populations: A systematic review. *The Lancet Infectious Diseases*, 12, 950–965.

Kolaczinski, J.H. *et al.* (2006). Adherence of community caretakers of children to pre-packaged antimalarial medicines (HOMAPAK®) among internally displaced people in Gulu district, Uganda. *Malaria Journal*, 5, 1–9.

Kouadio, I.K. *et al.* (2010). Measles outbreaks in displaced populations: A review of transmission, morbidity and mortality associated factors. *BMC International Health and Human Rights*, 10, 1–10.

Levy, B.S. (2002). Health and peace. *Croatian Medical Journal*, 43, 114–116.

Liebling-Kalifani, H. *et al.* (2013). Violence against women in Northern Uganda: The neglected health consequences of war. *Journal of International Women's Studies*, 9, 174–192.

Marsh, M. *et al.* (2006). Addressing sexual violence in humanitarian emergencies. *Global Public Health*, 1, 133–146.

Médecins San Frontières (2006). Food, Nutrition and Mortality Situation of IDPs in Dubie, Katanga, 23–25 March, 2006. MSF, Katanga, DRC.

Moodley, K. *et al.* (2013). Ethical considerations for vaccination programs in acute humanitarian emergencies. *Bulletin of the World Health Organization*, 91, 290–297.

Morgos, D. *et al.* (2007). Psychosocial effects of war experiences among displaced children in southern Darfur. *OMEGA–Journal of Death and Dying*, 56, 229–253.

Mullany, L.C. *et al.* (2007). Population-based survey methods to quantify associations between human rights violations and health outcomes among internally displaced persons in eastern Burma. *Journal of Epidemiology and Community Health*, 61, 908–914.

Mupere, E. *et al.* (2005). Impact of emergency mass immunisations on measles control in displaced populations in Gulu District, Northern Uganda. *East African Medical Journal*, 82, 403–408.

Mutua, M. (2007). Standard setting in human rights: Critique and prognosis. *Human Rights Quarterly*, 29, 547–630.

Nielsen, J. *et al.* (2006). Mortality patterns during a war in Guinea-Bissau 1998–1999: Changes in risk factors? *International Journal of Epidemiology*, 35, 438–446.

Nishikiori, N. *et al.* (2006). Who died as a result of the tsunami? Risk factors of mortality among internally displaced persons in Sri Lanka: A retrospective cohort analysis. *BMC Public Health*, 6, 1–8.

O'Hare, B. & Southall, D. (2007). First do no harm: The impact of recent armed conflict on maternal and child health in Sub-Saharan Africa. *Journal of the Royal Society of Medicine*, 100, 564–570.

Ojeda, S. (2010). The Kampala convention on internally displaced persons: Some international humanitarian law aspects. *Refugee Survey Quarterly*, 29, 58–66.

Olwedo, M.A. *et al.* (2009). Factors associated with malnutrition among children in internally displaced person's camps, northern Uganda. *African Health Sciences*, 8, 244–252.

Richards, A.K. et al. (2009). Cross-border malaria control for internally displaced persons: Observational results from a pilot programme in eastern Burma/Myanmar. *Tropical Medicine & International Health*, 14, 512–521.

Roberts, B. et al. (2008). Factors associated with post-traumatic stress disorder and depression amongst internally displaced persons in northern Uganda. *BMC Psychiatry* 8(38) doi:10.1186/1471-244X-8-38.

Roberts, B. et al. (2009). Post-conflict mental health needs: A cross-sectional survey of trauma, depression and associated factors in Juba, Southern Sudan. *BMC Psychiatry* 9(7) doi:10.1186/1471-244X-9-7.

Roberts, L. et al. (2003). Mortality in the Democratic Republic of Congo: Results from a Nationwide Survey. International Rescue Committee, New York, NY.

Salama, P. et al. (2001). No less vulnerable: The internally displaced in humanitarian emergencies. *The Lancet*, 357, 1430–1431.

Sapir, D.G., Gomez, V.T. (2006). Angola: The humanitarian impact of war. A data review of field surveys in Angola between 1999 and 2005. Centre for Research on the Epidemiology of Disasters, Brussels, BEL.

Sheikh, T.L. et al. (2015). Correlates of depression among internally displaced persons after post-election violence in Kaduna, North Western Nigeria. *Journal of Affective Disorders*, 170, 46–51.

Spencer, S. et al. (2004). Malaria in camps for internally-displaced persons in Uganda: Evaluation of an insecticide-treated bednet distribution programme. *Transactions of the Royal Society of Tropical Medicine and Hygiene*, 98, 719–727.

Spiegel, P. & Harroff-Tavel, H. (2006). *HIV/AIDS and Internally Displaced Persons in 8 Priority Countries*. UNHCR, Geneva, SWI.

Spiegel, P.B. et al. (2007). Prevalence of HIV infection in conflict-affected and displaced people in seven sub-Saharan African countries: A systematic review. *The Lancet*, 369, 2187–2195.

Swiss, S. et al. (1998). Violence against women during the Liberian civil conflict. *Journal of American Medical Association*, 279, 625–629.

Terminski, B. (2012). Environmentally-Induced Displacement: Theoretical Frameworks and Current Challenges. Centre d'Etude de l'Ethnicité et des Migrations, Université de Liège, Liège, BEL.

Toole, M.J. (2000). Displaced persons and war. In: Levy, B.S., Sidel, V.W. (eds.), *War and Public Health*, APHA, Washington, DC, pp. 197–212.

Umozurike U.O. (1983). The African Charter on Human and Peoples' Rights. *American Journal of International Law*, 77, 902–912.

United Nations Commission on Human Rights (1998). Report of the Representative of the Secretary-General, Mr. Francis M. Deng, submitted pursuant to Commission resolution 1997/39. Addendum: Guiding Principles on Internal Displacement,

11 February 1998, E/CN.4/1998/53/Add.2. Available at: http://www.refworld.org/docid/3d4f95e11.html. Accessed 19 September 2014.

United Nations (2011). Ending Displacement in the Aftermath of Conflict: Preliminary framework for supporting a more coherent, predictable and effective response to the durable solutions needs of refugee returnees and internally displaced persons. Available at: http://siteresources.worldbank.org/EXTSOCIALDEVELOPMENT/Resources/244362-1265299949041/6766328-1265299960363/SG-Decision-Memo-Durable-Solutions.pdf. Accessed 4 July 2013.

United Nations Administrative Committee on Coordination Sub-Committee on Nutrition (2002). Refugee Nutrition Information System (RNIS), No. 39 — Report on the Nutrition Situation of Refugees and Displaced Populations. United Nations, Geneva, SWI.

United Nations Commission on Human Rights (1993). Comprehensive study prepared by Mr. Francis M. Deng, Representative of the Secretary-General on the human rights issues related to internally displaced persons, pursuant to Commission on Human Rights resolution 1992/73. Available at: http://daccess-dds-ny.un.org/doc/UNDOC/GEN/G93/105/95/PDF/G9310595.pdf?OpenElement. Accessed 12 August 2014.

United Nations Commission on Human Rights (1996). Report of the Representative of the Secretary-General on internally displaced persons, compilation and analysis of legal norms. UN Doc. E/CN.4/1996/52. Available at: http://www1.umn.edu/humanrts/commission/thematic52/96-52idp.htm. Accessed 20 September 2014.

United Nations Economic and Social Council (1995). Internally displaced persons: Report of the Representative of the Secretary-General, Mr. Francis M. Deng, submitted pursuant to Commission on Human Rights resolution 1995/57. Available at: http://daccess-dds-ny.un.org/doc/UNDOC/GEN/G95/146/89/PDF/G9514689.pdf?OpenElement. Accessed 2 September 2014.

United Nations Economic and Social Council (1998). Questions of human right, mass exoduses, and displaced persons: Report of the Representative of the Secretary-General Mr. Francis Deng, submitted pursuant to Commission on Human Rights resolution 1997/39. Available at: http://daccess-dds-ny.un.org/doc/UNDOC/GEN/G98/104/87/PDF/G9810487.pdf?OpenElement. Accessed 1 September 2014.

UNHCR (2014). War's human cost: UNHCR global trend 2013. United Nations High Comissioner for Human Rights, Geneva, SWI.

Wachira, G.M. (2008). African Court on Human and Peoples' Rights: Ten years on and still no justice. Minority Rights Group International, London, UK.

Wachira, G.M. & Ayinla, A. (2006). Twenty years of elusive enforcement of the recommendations of the African Commission on Human and Peoples' Rights: A possible remedy. *African Human Rights Law Journal* 6, 465–492.

Watts, C. & Zimmerman, C. (2002). Violence against women: Global scope and magnitude. *The Lancet* 359, 1232–1237.
West Africa Regional Health Working Group (2012). Sahel food and health crisis: Emergency health strategy. Available at: http://www.who.int/hac/sahel_health_strategy_21june2012rev.pdf. Accessed 12 September 2014.
Wood, E.J. (2006). Variation in sexual violence during war. *Politics & Society*, 34, 307–342.
World Health Organisation (2003). Looking back, looking ahead: Five decades of challenges and achievements in environemental sanitation and health. WHO, Geneva, SWI.
World Health Organisation (2005). Health and Mortality Survey among Internally Displaced Persons Gulu, Kitgum and Pader Districts, Northern Uganda. Available at: http://www.who.int/hac/crises/uga/who_nuganda_idp_survey_0408.pdf. Accessed 12 June 2013.
World Health Organisation (2014). Early warning and diseases surveillance bulleting (IDP camps and communities). WHO, Juba, SS. Available at: http://www.who.int/hac/crises/ssd/epi/en/. Accessed 12 June 2013.
World Health Organisation and the Federal Ministry of Health of Sudan (2005). Mortality survey among Internally Displaced Persons and other affected populations in Greater Darfur. WHO and FMOH, Darfur, SU.

# Chapter 3

# The social and health dimensions of refugees and complex humanitarian emergencies

Mr Joseph Kamara and Professor André M.N. Renzaho

## Introduction

The concept of "refugee" and its definition has a complex history and dates back to the eighteenth century. The 1793 French Constitution declared that France would take in people fleeing their homelands in search for freedom (Noiriel, 1991). Similarly, the 1905 British Aliens Act emphasised that an immigrant who sought

> "admission to avoid prosecution or punishment on religious or political grounds or for an offence of a political character, or persecution, involving danger of imprisonment or danger to life and limb, on account of religious belief would be protected in Britain" (Collyer, 2005, p. 289).

At the turn of the twentieth century, the League of Nations defined a refugee as a person who was unable to obtain any protection or representation from his or her own country (Glynn, 2011). This definition was included in the 1919 League of Nations Charter, which was drafted by a handful of countries led by the USA under President Thomas Woodrow Wilson. The charter came into effect in early 1920 to reduce human suffering after the First World War (Riga, 1989). However, the process of a universally-accepted definition of what constituted a "refugee" did not gain momentum until the 1940s. The emphasis was mainly on who qualified to be protected by The International Refugee Organisation (IRO). There were disagreements among key member states led by the USA and France who favoured a geographical- and time-based definition limited to European events before 1951 due to a fear of financial commitments necessary to protect a broader range of refugees (Glynn, 2011). Britain, Belgium and Germany preferred a universal definition and were supported by other members such as Israel, China and African countries (Glynn, 2011). As Robinson (1953) notes, in order to eliminate any confusion over what constitutes a refugee and to address the lack of international agreements on how to protect post-Second World War refugees, the United Nations Economic and Social Council requested the Secretary-General of The United Nations to evaluate issues related to the protection of stateless persons and to make recommendations under Resolution 116 (VI) (D) adopted on 2 March 1948. Consequently, the Secretary-General, under Resolution 248 (IX) (B), appointed an Ad Hoc Committee on Statelessness and Related Problems which consisted of representatives from 13 governments. This committee completed its work, the outcome of which was the drafting of a consolidated Convention Relating to the Status of Refugees and a Protocol Relating to the Status of Stateless Person (the Refugee Convention). The draft of the Refugee Convention was adopted at the United Nations Conference of Plenipotentiaries that took place in Geneva from 2 to 25 July 1951, and came into force on 22 April 1954 (Robinson, 1953). The adopted consolidated Refugee Convention defined a refugee as any person who

> *"owing to well-founded fear of being persecuted for reasons of race, religion, nationality, membership of a particular social group or political opinion, is outside the country of his nationality and is unable or, owing to such fear, is unwilling to avail himself of the protection of that country"* (UNHCR, 1951, p.14).

The Refugee Convention became the key legal document that authoritatively outlined the refugee's rights and entitlements as well as the legal obligations of states (UNHCR, 2010). However, the Refugee Convention specified geographic and temporary restrictions, thus limiting protection to European refugees only and those affected prior to 1 January 1951. These restrictions were removed in the 1967 Protocol Relating to the Status of Refugees, which subsequently strengthened the universal protection of refugees.

Refugees flee due to the loss of confidence in their own governments to protect and provide a secure environment that meets their basic needs and rights. To be recognised as a refugee, one needs to cross a border to another country. Those who experience the same problems as refugees but are unable to cross their country's border to seek protection of another country are known as internally displaced persons (IDPs). It is not the purpose of this chapter to define and discuss IDPs (for more information on IDPs, please see Chapter 2). Similarly, a person fleeing their own country to seek protection in another country but whose application for protection as a refugee is pending or denied is an asylum seeker. Issues related to asylum seekers are detailed in Chapters 5 and 6. This chapter focuses on refugees in complex humanitarian emergencies (CHEs). It starts with a historical perspective on CHEs and the description of key health consequences. It then examines the governance and political dimensions of CHEs.

## CHEs: history and patterns

The concept of people fleeing injustice across borders dates back to the seventeenth century when the French protestant minorities fled to neighbouring countries and the USA. This was in response to the Catholic King Louis XIV's revoking of the edict of Nantes issued by an earlier King Henry IV in 1598 to protect the religious minorities (Barnett, 2002). The 1648 Peace Treaty of Westphalia to end a 30-year period of wars in Europe marked the birth of the modern refugee concept in Europe (Croxton, 1999). Since then, refugees have become an integral component of the modern state as many people continue to flee their home countries in search of protection from persecution due to their ideals, beliefs, religious affiliations or race. For example, in the nineteenth century, violent European revolutions caused many people to flee their affected home countries (Barnett, 2002). The 1917–1921 Russian Revolution left over one million Russians stateless across Europe. The 1933–1945 Jewish holocaust sparked another wave of people fleeing persecution from Nazi Germany, also known as the Third Reich. The increased refugee needs overwhelmed the IRO and led to the establishment of a stronger office of the United Nations High Commissioner for Refugees (UNHCR) in 1950 with a three-year mandate to streamline refugee affairs (Maynard, 1982). However, refugees continued to be a hallmark of a troubled world and required the extension of the UNHCR's mandate beyond the initially approved three years. This was vindicated by the new wave of refugees fleeing the defeat of the Hungarian revolution by the Union of Soviet Socialist Republics in 1956 and refugees fleeing conflicts that emerged out of the 1960s era of decolonisation of Africa. More refugee crises unfolded in Asia, Latin America in the 1970s, Africa in the 1980s, the Balkans in the 1990s and early 2000s, and more recent crises in North Africa, the Middle East, South and South East Asia.

These historic events mean that the Refugee Convention has gone through transitions. What began as a convention to protect victims of the Falangists during the Spanish Civil War and the Third Reich, as well as other Europeans displaced by the Second World War, became a rallying point for the protection of refugees across the world. The 1960s brought an end to years of Africa's colonisation which was replaced by weak comprador governments, systems and structures. Many new independent African countries descended into civil wars causing waves of IDPs and refugees who were not protected by the Refugee Convention due to the geographical limitations discussed earlier. This shortcoming led to the creation of NGOs such as Médecins Sans Frontières (MSF) in 1971 in the aftermath of the 1967–1970 humanitarian emergency response to the Biafran War in Nigeria. MSF reinvented the concept of emergency aid and has since led the humanitarian industry in shaping responses and policies on complex emergencies (Redfield, 2005). Consequently, a CHE is a non-partisan response to mitigate a major crisis of a *"multi-causal nature requiring a system-wide response including long-term combination of political solutions, conflict resolution and peacekeeping"* (Duffield, 1994, p. 4). Therefore, the United Nations Office for the Coordination of

Humanitarian Affairs (1999) has defined a CHE as

*"a humanitarian crisis in a country, region, or society where there is total or considerable breakdown of authority resulting from internal or external conflict and which requires an international response that goes beyond the mandate or capacity of any single and/or ongoing UN country program"* (p. 4).

A CHE has six characteristics that differentiate it from natural disasters. These characteristics are "extensive violence and loss of life", "massive displacements of people", "widespread damage to societies and economies", "the need for large-scale, multi-faceted humanitarian assistance", "the hindrance or prevention of humanitarian assistance by political and military constraints", and "significant security risks for humanitarian relief workers in some areas" (United Nations Office for the Coordination of Human Affairs, 1999; p. 4). As such, CHEs are man-made and politically-induced disasters closely related to political mismanagement, weak government institutions and oppressive regimes that collapse when challenged by armed insurrections. Most CHEs are characterised by the disintegration of socioeconomic structures and marginalisation of specific groups, which compromises their rights and results in massive displacements. An example of typology used for CHEs is provided in Table 1.

Perhaps the conflicts that characterised decolonised countries in the 1950s and 1960s could explain the exponential increase in the number of refugees requiring humanitarian responses over the past four decades. For example, between 1970 and 2014, refugees across Africa increased from 153,700 to almost four million (Table 2). The majority of the refugees on the African continent are mainly hosted by the countries of the Central and Eastern African regions. In the 1990s, Sudan, Malawi, Ethiopia, Somalia, DR Congo, Guinea and Burundi were hotspots that hosted more refugees than any other African country. To date, Chad, Ethiopia and Kenya host the highest number of refugees in the region. Similarly, the entire Asian region hosted 2,200 and six million refugees in 1960 and 2014, respectively. However, most of the refugees are currently concentrated in Pakistan, Islamic Republic of Iran and Lebanon (Table 2). With the exception of Lebanon, the same countries have hosted most of Asia's refugees since the

Table 1: A typology of CHEs

| | War | Disease | Hunger | Displacement | Type |
|---|---|---|---|---|---|
| Afghanistan | x | x | x | x | acute |
| Mozambique | x | x | x | x | acute |
| Angola | x | x | x | x | acute |
| Somalia | x | x | x | x | acute |
| Rwanda | x | x | x | x | acute |
| Liberia | x | x | | x | serious |
| Burundi | x | x | | x | serious |
| Sri Lanka | x | x | | x | serious |
| Sierra Leone | x | x | | x | serious |
| Sudan | x | | x | x | serious |
| Ethiopia | | x | x | x | serious |
| Eritrea | | x | x | x | serious |
| Myanmar | | x | x | x | serious |
| Bosnia | x | | | x | violent |
| Croatia | x | | | x | violent |
| Tajikistan | x | | | x | violent |
| Colombia | x | | | x | violent |
| Azerbaijan | x | | | x | violent |
| Armenia | x | | | x | violent |
| Georgia | x | | | x | violent |
| Iraq | x | | | x | violent |
| Niger | | x | x | | poverty |
| Nigeria | | x | x | | poverty |
| Bangladesh | | x | x | | poverty |
| Laos | | x | x | | poverty |
| Central African Repub. | | x | x | | poverty |
| India | x | | x | | mixed |

*Source*: Klugman, 1999.

Table 2: Refugee population by region of asylum between 1960 and 2016

| Region | 1960 | 1970 | 1980 | 1990 | 2000 | 2010 | 2014* |
|---|---|---|---|---|---|---|---|
| Total Africa | 153,700 | 992,085 | 4,123,590 | 5,890,673 | 3,627,130 | 2,408,676 | 3,987,405 |
| Eastern Africa | — | 328,030 | 2,613,930 | 3,284,669 | 1,662,103 | 971,009 | 1,078,814 |
| Middle Africa | 150,000 | 524,650 | 841,110 | 485,559 | 602,800 | 797,406 | 1,174,093 |
| Northern Africa | 3,700 | 67,780 | 546,780 | 1,202,492 | 605,508 | 376,312 | 946,261 |
| Southern Africa | — | 4,565 | 16,770 | 43,467 | 46,567 | 68,898 | 362,355 |
| Western Africa | — | 67,060 | 105,000 | 874,486 | 710,152 | 195,051 | 425,882 |
| Total Latin America and the Caribbean | 548,629 | 624,518 | 675,053 | 1,814,522 | 673,064 | 803,990 | 634,445 |
| Caribbean | — | 1,000 | 6,770 | 5,954 | 1,602 | 1,099 | 33,847 |
| Central America | — | 3,000 | 95,000 | 1,161,394 | 27,656 | 38,361 | 106,885 |
| South America | — | 102,000 | 76,920 | 27,526 | 8,593 | 334,407 | 333,229 |
| North America | 548,629 | 518,518 | 496,363 | 619,648 | 635,213 | 430,123 | 160,484 |
| Total Asia | 2,200 | 152,930 | 2,631,990 | 8,163,888 | 5,383,418 | 5,715,818 | 5,853,790 |
| Central Asia | — | — | — | — | 99,085 | 10,368 | 436,366 |
| Eastern Asia | — | 67,000 | 292,380 | 302,691 | 298,851 | 304,096 | 10,899 |
| Southern Asia | — | 64,560 | 1,766,930 | 7,661,114 | 4,191,287 | 3,484,526 | 1,889,915 |
| South-eastern Asia | — | 20,000 | 437,530 | 159,117 | 294,225 | 181,310 | 292,247 |
| Western Asia | 2,200 | 1,370 | 135,150 | 40,966 | 499,970 | 1,735,518 | 3,224,363 |

(Continued)

Table 2: (Continued)

| Region | 1960 | 1970 | 1980 | 1990 | 2000 | 2010 | 2014[*] |
|---|---|---|---|---|---|---|---|
| **Total Europe** | 700,835 | 569,397 | 485,329 | 1,295,803 | 2,144,635 | 1,441,831 | **1,598,669** |
| Eastern Europe | — | — | 1,000 | 45,123 | 40,628 | 39,111 | 65,307 |
| Northen Europe | 193,000 | 182,000 | 168,000 | 153,295 | 343,468 | 320,779 | 1,155,564 |
| Southern Europe | 31,000 | 74,330 | 56,371 | 29,418 | 517,369 | 159,865 | 152,223 |
| Western Europe | 476,835 | 313,067 | 259,958 | 1,067,967 | 1,243,170 | 922,076 | 225,575 |
| **Total Oceania** | — | 44,000 | 315,000 | 109,680 | 71,032 | 33,814 | **47,982** |
| Australia and New Zealand | — | 44,000 | 314,000 | 102,581 | 65,169 | 24,112 | 35,906 |
| Melenasia | — | — | 1,000 | 7,099 | 5,863 | 9,702 | 11,984 |
| Micronesia | — | — | — | — | — | — | 35 |
| Polynasia | — | — | — | — | — | — | 57 |
| **Uncategorised** | 152,000 | 21,000 | 167,650 | 5,284 | — | — | — |

[*] Estimates by mid-2014 and is subject to change. Note: Data for 1960–2010 cover refugees protected by UNHCR and other people in refugee-like situations. Data for 2014 cover only people recognised as refugees under the 1951 UN Convention, 1967 protocol, the 1969 OAU Convention, people granted a complementary form of protection and those with temporary protection. All data exclude resettled refugees and Palestinian Refugees under UNRWA. Data especially for industrialised regions are based on UNHCR estimates. A dash (—) denotes zero or unavailable.

Source: UNHCR (2015a), Statistical online population database. Geneva: UNHCR. Available at http://www.unhcr.org/pages/4a013eb06.html. Accessed on 3 April 2015.

1980s. Africa and Asia produce and host more than half of the total global refugees. Some of the hosting countries in these regions are overwhelmed by the refugee burden. For example, Lebanon, a small country of 10,452 km² with a population of 4.467 million hosts 178 refugees per 1,000 citizens (Holmes, 2014). Data by the United Nations (2014) suggest that by April 2014, Lebanon had over one million refugees, making it one of the countries with the highest per capita concentration of refugees. Similarly, Chad, one of the poorest countries in the world, hosts 34 refugees per 1,000 persons which is proportionally a significant burden on the barely functional social services. In 2013, Afghanistan, Syrian Arab Republic and Somalia produced approximately 6 million refugees and half of these were children. It is interesting to note that in forced mass displacements such as the Syrian refugees in Lebanon, the recipient country may have limited capacity to address the rapid influx, hence making CHEs a significant political, security and public health burden (Brennan and Nandy, 2001). As Brennan and Nandy (2001) note, natural disasters, which often relate to major adverse events resulting from natural processes of the environment such as drought, volcanic eruption, avalanches, earthquakes, wildfires, flooding, tsunami or health threats such as the flu pandemic or Ebola outbreak, can aggravate CHEs and vice versa. However, overall CHEs account for more mortality than all natural and technological disasters.

## Refugees' health and burden of disease

Globally, refugees' health remains a key challenge in humanitarian responses. At the onset of CHEs, the most significant burden of disease is mainly infectious and communicable diseases. However, chronic non-communicable diseases (NCDs) continue to affect refuges in CHEs, especially in the Middle East, even though they attract limited or no attention. Overall, there have been improvements in the quality and delivery of humanitarian assistance over time. This has significantly contributed to the reduction of mortality among refugees in CHEs. With the exception of the 31.9 crude mortality rate (CMR) reported among Cambodian refugees in Thailand in 1979 (CDC 1992) and the 1994 Rwandese refugee crisis in DR Congo, where CMR was estimated between 20 and 35 per 1000 per day (Goma Epidemiology Group, 1995), there has been a remarkable reduction in refugee mortality across

## 82　Globalisation, Migration and Health

**Table 3:** Estimated daily crude mortality rates (deaths per 10,000/day) in selected refugee populations 1979–2014

| Reference | Period | Country of origin | Country of refugee | Name of refugee camp | CMR | U5MR | CMR (b) thresholds: emergency (baseline) | U5MR (b) thresholds: emergency (baseline) |
|---|---|---|---|---|---|---|---|---|
| Toole and Waldman (1990) | August 1980 | Ethiopia | Somalia | Gedo & Woqooyi Galbeed | 10.1 (a) | NR | 0.8 (0.41) | 2.1 (1.07) |
| CDC (1993) | October 1979 | Cambodia | Thailand | Khao-I-Dang | 10.6 (a) | NR | 0.4 (0.19) | 0.3 (0.15) |
| CDC (1993) | August 1992 | Mozambique | Zimbabwe | Chambuta | 3-50 | NR | 0.8 (0.41) | 2.1 (1.07) |
| CDC (1993) | Jan–September, 1992 | Mozambique | Malawi | Lisungwe | 1.0–3.6 | 5.0 | 0.8 (0.41) | 2.1 (1.07) |
| Goma Epidemiology Group (1995) | July–August, 1994 | Rwanda | Zaire | Katale | 41.3 | NR | 0.8 (0.41) | 2.1 (1.07) |
|  |  |  |  | Kibumba | 28.1 | NR | 0.8 (0.41) | 2.1 (1.07) |
|  |  |  |  | Mugunga | 29.4 | NR | 0.8 (0.41) | 2.1 (1.07) |
|  |  |  |  | All camps | 32.9 | NR | 0.8 (0.41) | 2.1 (1.07) |
| Friedman and Spiegel (2000) | February 2000 | East Timor | Indonesia | 14 unnamed sentinel sites | 0.2 | NR | 0.4 (0.19) | 0.3 (0.15) |
| CDC (2001) | January–May, 2001 | Liberia/Sierra Leon | Guinea | Parrots Beak | 0.3–0.9 | 0.9 | 0.8 (0.41) | 2.1 (1.07) |
| Tomczyk et al. (2004) | June 2004 | Sudan | Chad | Iridimi/ Touloum/ Kounoungo | 1.56 | 1.46 | 0.8 (0.41) | 2.1 (1.07) |

*(Continued)*

Table 3: (Continued)

| Reference | Period | Country of origin | Country of refugee | Name of refugee camp | CMR | U5MR | CMR (b) thresholds: emergency (baseline) | U5MR (b) thresholds: emergency (baseline) |
|---|---|---|---|---|---|---|---|---|
| UNHCR (2008a) | October 2006 | Sudan | Ethiopia | Dimma | 0.04 (a) | 0.00 (a) | 0.8 (0.41) | 2.1 (1.07) |
| UNHCR (2008a) | October 2007 | Eritrea/Somalia/Ethiopia | Djibouti | Ali Adde | 0.06 (a) | 0.11 (a) | 0.8 (0.41) | 2.1 (1.07) |
| UNHCR (2008a) | June 2007 | Sudan and DRC | Uganda | Adjumani | 0.05 (a) | 0.16 (a) | 0.8 (0.41) | 2.1 (1.07) |
| Spiegel et al. (2011) | July–August, 2011 | Somalia | Kenya | Dabab | 0.44 | 1.53 | 0.8 (0.41) | 2.1 (1.07) |
| UNHCR (2013a) | October 2012/September 2013 | Syria | Iraq | Domiz | <0.16 (a) | <0.16 (a) | 0.3 (0.16) | 0.5 (0.27) |
|  | October 2012/July 2013 |  | Jordan | Za'atri | 0.07 | 0.04 | 0.3 (0.16) | 0.5 (0.27) |
| UNHCR (2013b) | March 2013 | Somalia | Ethiopia | Hilaweyn camp | 0.32 | 1.08 | 0.8 (0.41) | 2.1 (1.07) |
| Andresen et al. (2014) | June–July, 2014 | Sudan |  | Kule | 1.63 | 5.64 | 0.8 (0.41) | 2.1 (1.07) |

(a) Converted from /1000/month to /10,000/day for ease of interpretation; (b) Sphere emergency (baseline) thresholds; NR = Not reported; CMR = Crude Mortality Rate; U5MR = under-five mortality rate.

regions (Table 3). In subsequent paragraphs, we discuss the most common communicable diseases that affect refugees.

## Communicable diseases

**Diarrhoeal diseases:** While violence associated with conflict causes most morbidity and mortality in the early phases of CHEs, diarrhoeal diseases are among the primary causes of mortality and morbidity among refugees. Although diarrheal diseases are preventable through the provision of safe water and its storage, good sanitation, and hygiene education, they still account for more than 40% of deaths in the acute phase of an emergency (Connolly et al., 2004). Of those dying from diarrheal diseases, over 80% occur in children aged younger than two years old. There have been some cases where mortality attributable to diarrhoeal diseases is higher than 40%, namely the 1994 Rwandese refugee crisis in Goma, Zaire. In this emergency, 85% of all deaths in the first month were due to diarrheal diseases especially cholera and shigella dysentery (Goma Epidemiology Group 1995). Earlier studies suggest diarrhoeal diseases accounted for 28% to 85% of deaths in refugee camps in Somalia in 1980, Ethiopia in 1982 and Malawi in 1988 (Porter et al., 1990).

**Acute respiration infections (ARIs):** ARIs account for a high proportions of morbidity and mortality in refugee camps. The prevalence of ARIs among refugees has been reported to vary from 27.7% among adults to 34.4% among one-year-old children or younger (Bellos et al., 2010). Diaz and Achi (1989) reported that 63% of morbidity in Nicaraguan refugees in Costa Rica in 1998 was due to ARIs. Of all primary health care consultations, ARIs account for the biggest share of the burden of communicable diseases, making up 62.9%, 41.2% and 30.3% of the communicable disease burden among Syrians in refugee camps in Iraq, Jordan and Lebanon, respectively (UNHCR, 2013a). The proportion of deaths attributable to ARI among refugees varies between 25% and 36% among children younger than five years and 9% and 26% across the whole refugee population, making ARIs second only to diarrhoeal diseases (Bellos et al., 2010). In Kakuma refugee camp in Kenya, ARIs were identified as the leading cause of mortality and morbidity among Sudanese refugees, accounting for 30–40% of deaths among children younger than five years (World Health Organisation, 2008).

**Measles:** Several studies have examined the impact of measles on children in CHEs. This highly infectious viral disease is easily transmitted through contact with bodily fluids and air droplets. Measles is often rampant in refugee populations because of concentrated exposure in high population density (Aaby *et al.*, 1984; Toole *et al.*, 1989). Well known documented risk factors include inadequate or poor measles vaccination status, vaccination campaigns, and surveillance; living conditions such as overcrowding and high density camps; frequent movement of refugees in the neighbouring community and in other camps; malnutrition and famine including vitamin A deficiency; and insecurity and inaccessibility to target zone (Aaby *et al.*, 1984; Kouadio *et al.*, 2010; Toole *et al.*, 1989). Measles severity is measured by its attack rate which is defined as the number of cases per population at risk in a specific area at a given time (Kouadio *et al.*, 2010). For example, Porter and colleagues (1990) found that, between November 1988 and January 1989, measles outbreaks occurred in 11 Mozambican refugee camps in Malawi. They reported measles attack rates as high as 10–26% among children aged 6–9 months and 3–21% among children aged less than six months. Kouadio and colleagues (2010) found other measles outbreaks with a high attack rate, including Vietnamese refugees in Hong Kong (attack rate of 25.5%) and Cambodian refugees in Thailand (attack rate of 17.4%).

They also reported lower attack rate (<5%) among Ethiopians in refugee camps in Sudan (attack rate of 3.1%). Measles case fatality rates have varied with a rate as high as 15–21% reported among less than five-year-old Mozambican children in refugee camps in Malawi (Porter *et al.*, 1990). Other high-case fatality rates have been documented among Ethiopian refugees in Wad Kowli in Sudan in 1985 (32.4%) (Shears *et al.*, 1987). Prior to the 1990s when measles immunisation in refugee camps was inadequate, measles accounted for 42–53% of deaths (Toole and Waldman, 1988). However, some studies suggest that there has been a reduction in measles mortality among the refugee population due to improved surveillance, quick mass immunisation and vitamin A supplementation in early stages of emergencies (Paquet and Hanquet, 1998). For example, the measles case fatality rate averaged 13.1% (median = 10%) prior to 2000 compared to an average of 6.3% (median = 1.3%) after 2000 (Kouadio *et al.*, 2010).

**Malaria:** Malaria is common in endemic tropical and sub-tropical regions, and is life-threatening in CHEs. In 2013, there were 584,000 deaths due to malaria, of which 90% occurred in Sub Saharan Africa (SSA) (World Health Organisation, 2014a). These data suggest that malaria is a major cause of morbidity and mortality in SSA including refugee populations. Malaria outbreaks and transmission are facilitated by conducive environmental factors such as warm temperatures, plenty of stagnant water and bushes in areas where refugee camps are often located. Approximately two-thirds (63%) of CHEs occur in malaria-endemic areas, and in areas of high transmission, malaria accounted for up to 40–50% of all deaths in CHEs (World Health Organisation, 2005). There is no doubt that progress has been made in reducing the burden of malaria among refugees in CHEs due to the declining transmission rates as a result of effective support and promotion of malaria control policies and programmes in the early phase of emergencies (UNHCR, 2008b). Available evidence suggests that between 2006 and 2009 the annual incidence of malaria in children younger than five years of age decreased more than one-third in refugee sites in Kenya, Tanzania and Uganda, reflecting the pattern of the host countries (O'Meara *et al.*, 2010). This is consistent with a reduction in malaria incidence rates of 25% globally, and 31% in the WHO Africa region observed between 2000 and 2012 as a result of the scale-up of intervention strategies (World Health Organisation, 2014a). Notwithstanding this decline, malaria remains a significant burden in the post-emergency refugee sites with an overall incidence in refugee sites in Tanzania of 399 cases per 1,000 refugees and 728 cases per 1,000 in children younger than five years (Anderson *et al.*, 2011). In a retrospective mortality survey of 51 post-emergency camps in Azerbaijan, Ethiopia, Myanmar, Nepal, Tanzania, Thailand and Uganda covering the 1998–2000 period, Spiegel *et al.* (2002) reported an overall malaria incidence of 576 cases per 1,000 persons and 936 cases per 1,000 children. Among Congolese refugees in Lugufu camp in Tanzania, malaria accounted for 33.3% of all deaths (Talley *et al.*, 2001). The progress made to reduce the burden of malaria in CHEs needs to be consolidated both within and outside post-emergency sites. The focus needs to be on managing movement of malaria across regions and international borders, which if not controlled poses a major obstacle to achieving malaria elimination (Richards *et al.*, 2009). Because of its adaptive capacity, malaria is likely to remain as one of the major causes of refugee morbidity and mortality in the tropics especially those in poor camp conditions.

**HIV/AIDS:** HIV/AIDS is a chronic disease with a negative toll on vulnerable populations in CHEs where conditions make it thrive. However, available evidence suggests that it is not among the leading causes of refugee mortality and morbidity. Despite the common belief that CHE conditions create more vulnerability in accelerating the HIV/AIDS epidemic, there is insufficient evidence to support mass HIV/AIDS interventions among refugees in CHEs (Spiegel, 2004). A systematic review of HIV among refugee populations in Africa by Spiegel and colleagues (2007) found that there is lower HIV prevalence among refugees compared to neighbouring non-refugee populations. They found, for example, that the prevalence for HIV in the Dadaab refugee camp in Kenya was only 0.6% in 2003 compared with 26% in 2002 in the neighbouring sentinel site in Garisa. Similarly, the HIV prevalence in 2004 was 1.0% in the Palorinya Sudanese refugee settlement in Uganda, compared with 5.9% in the neighbouring non-refugee populations. Similar trends were observed by the same study in refugee camps in Zambia, Tanzania and Rwanda. In Mae La refugee camp on the Thai–Myanmar border, the HIV prevalence between 1995 and 2003 was estimated at 0.2–0.4% among refugees compared with a prevalence of 1.8–2.4% observed among neighbouring non-refugee populations (Plewes *et al.*, 2008). Nonetheless, the impact of the disease on refugee health cannot be underestimated because HIV spreads fastest in conditions of poverty and social instability, lack of protection and weak bargaining power in transactional sex, conditions that typify refugees in CHEs (Hankins *et al.*, 2002). The HIV risk in CHEs can be aggravated by the breakdown of social structures, sexual violence, alcohol and drug abuse (Spiegel, 2004). While combating HIV in CHEs requires integrated interventions, such an approach remains too difficult to implement especially during the acute period of the emergency. For example, mandatory HIV testing in refugee circumstances is a difficult initiative to implement. Besides, mandatory blood testing for transfusion contravenes the refugees' basic rights and hence is a contraindicated policy.

**Tuberculosis:** Studies on the impact of tuberculosis among refugees in CHEs are scarce but generally it is not a leading cause of mortality post-1990s and traditionally became only a critical issue after measles and diarrheal diseases were under control (CDC, 1992). A study in two refugee camps in Asia found that the disease incidence varied from 2.2% to 5.8% in refugee camps in Thailand and the Philippines (Sutter and Haefliger, 1990). A 2012 systematic review of the disease in crisis-affected populations identified 51 studies. Of these, only 23 focused on camp-based refugees. The other studies were based on populations in similar conditions as refugees (Kimbrough et al., 2012). The study reported that the case fatality rate among refugees varied from 2% among Somali refugees in Kenya to 11% among Burundian and Rwandese refugees in Tanzania, which is significantly lower than the 20% case fatality rate for developing countries. Prior to the 1990s, tuberculosis was a serious issue among refugees, accounting for 26% of all deaths among refugees in Somalia 1985, 38–50% of all deaths among refugees in Eastern Sudan, and during this time tuberculosis ranked the third leading cause of death overall and the leading cause of mortality among adults (CDC, 1992). However, improvements in humanitarian aid delivery have led to the establishment of effective tuberculosis prevention and control programmes (Coninx, 2007). These interventions are often not rolled out during the acute phases of the emergencies due to competing lifesaving interventions and the multifaceted and complex nature of tuberculosis programmes. It is difficult to follow the standard treatment requirements such as the directly observed treatment as it lasts six months while a patient is under supervision of a health worker (Coninx, 2007). In these CHE contexts, ensuring patient compliance with the treatment, the required personnel to supervise treatment, the uncertain duration of stay, frequent changes of camp locations and poor camp organisation may hinder tuberculosis treatment programmes (CDC, 1992).

## Non-communicable diseases

Globally, the impact of NCDs has surpassed that of communicable diseases, maternal and perinatal, nutrition-related mortality combined (World Health Organisation, 2011). According to the latest data by the World Health Organisation from 194 countries, only 15% of NCDs mortality occur in high-income countries, and a staggering 85% occur in low- and middle-income countries (World Health Organisation, 2014b), which also have high incidences of CHEs.

Despite being a significant burden of disease in CHEs, especially in the Middle East, NCDs remain a neglected health care need among refugees. A study by MSF Switzerland among refugees in Lebanon and Iraq concluded that while high mortality rate during acute phases of emergencies have traditionally been fuelled by the exacerbation of endemic infectious diseases and acute malnutrition, in the Middle East, excess morbidity and mortality are closely rated to the exacerbation of existing chronic diseases such as cardio-vascular diseases, hypertension and diabetes (Abu Sa'Da and Serafini, 2013). While treatment continuation becomes essential, the study found that for Syrian refugees in Lebanon, 52% could not afford treatment for chronic diseases and a further 30% had no choice but to suspend treatment because of the exorbitant prices of drugs. Some of the challenges of addressing NCDs in refugee settings are complex and multifaceted. They include inadequate linkage between the refugee registration process and access to services, camp-based vs. non-camp-based refugees, lack of funding for the treatment of NCDs and the continuity of care and poorly equipped health care infrastructure of host countries (Abu Sa'Da and Serafini, 2013; Elliott, 2015). In the case of Syrian refugees in Lebanon, for example, 41% were not registered due to lack of information on how and where to register, the fact that the registration centres were too far away, delays at the registration centres and fear of being sent back to Syria as a result of not having proper legal documents. With 65% of Syrian refugees in Lebanon living outside camps, they are scattered over 1,000 municipalities, most of which are impoverished urban areas. In contrast, in Iraq, refugees live predominantly in camps as well as in cities (Abu Sa'Da and Serafini, 2013). These factors affect negatively the continuity of care for those with NCDs such as diabetes as non-registered refugees need to fund their own treatment, and for those registered they may have difficulty accessing available services due to distance (if they live outside camps) or lack of information.

**Diabetes and cardio-vascular diseases:** Diabetes causes a significant health burden for both refugees and non-refugee populations albeit not being prioritised in humanitarian interventions (Zimmet, 2003). Various studies assert that diabetes and its complications can be exacerbated by lack of basic care and treatment in CHEs, hence negatively impacting on refugees' wellbeing and quickly progressing to mortality (Coffey *et al.*, 2002; Rubin and Peyrot, 1999). The UNHCR (2013a) has reported that the proportion of all primary health care consultations accounted for by NCDs is 7.4% among Syrian refugees in Iraq, 21.8% among Syrian refugees in Jordan and 8.3% among Syrian refugees in Lebanon. Recent data by Médecins Sans Frontières (2014) suggest that nearly 90% of Syrian refugees in Lebanon attending their health services arrive with prior diagnoses of chronic disease, mainly hypertension and diabetes. In a systematic review of NCDs among urban refugees in developing countries, Amara and Aljunid (2014) found that other than the UNHCR ordinary reports, there are limited studies on the prevalence of NCDs among refugees. The overall prevalence of NCDs among urban refugees ranged from 9% to 50% among refugees in the Middle East and 1% to 30% among refugees in Asia and Africa with the most prevalent NCDs being musculoskeletal disease and pain problems, cardio-vascular diseases, diabetes and chronic respiratory disease. However, cancer and renal disease were reported less frequently. More specifically, screening prior to resettlement in a third country estimated a prevalence of hypertension of 33% among Iraqi refugees and 18.7% among Palestinian refugees (Amara and Aljunid, 2014). In Asia, prevalence of hypertension among Cambodian refugees in Thailand was reported to be 16.5% (Culhane-Pera *et al.*, 2009) while among urban refugees in SSA it was estimated at 1% in Kenya, 3% in Togo and 28% in Congo (Amara and Aljunid, 2014). Similarly, Amara and Aljunid (2014) reported that the prevalence of cardiovascular diseases varied from 7% among Burmese urban refugees in Malaysia to 10% among Afghanistan urban refugees in Iran. The prevalence of diabetes was significantly higher among refugees from the Middle Eastern Region, ranging from 7.6% to 9.8% among Palestinian and Iraqi refugees. In SSA, it was estimated at 8% among refugees from DR Congo, Rwanda and Angola living in urban Congo compared to 1% to 2% among other refugees in African urban centres. In Asia, the prevalence of diabetes ranged between 6% and 8% among urban refugees while that of the metabolic syndrome, a clustering of abdominal obesity, hypertension, elevated fasting plasma glucose and dyslipidaemia, was estimated at 15.3% in women and 20.8% in men among North Korean refugees in Seoul (Amara and Aljunid, 2014). However, these prevalence rates should be taken with caution because of the heterogeneity of the studies' designs, variation in sample sizes and the use of different instrumentations' diagnostic criteria.

**Malnutrition:** Food shortages remain very frequent in CHEs, and together with an impaired health environment, can lead to two types of nutrition problems: macronutrient and micronutrient deficiencies. The macronutrient deficiencies are universally described under the "protein-energy malnutrition" umbrella and include acute malnutrition or wasting chronic malnutrition or stunting and underweight, defined respectively as weight-for-height (WFH), height-for-age (HFA) and weight-for-age (WFA) indices below minus two standard deviations of the median reference population. While stunting and underweight are also very prevalent among refugees, only wasting is used to classify the degree of severity of CHEs (Table 4a) and for decision-making purposes (Table 4b). When anthropometrically defined, a child is classified as acutely malnourished when their WFH index is <-2 $z$-score and/or has bilateral oedema. The prevalence of acute malnutrition in CHEs has consistently been between the serious and critical categories. An alarming prevalence of acute malnutrition was reported among refugee children in eastern and central Africa over the past three decades. For example, monitoring data by the United Nations System Standing Committee on Nutrition in the late 1990s and early 2000s indicate that the prevalence of global acute malnutrition among refugees varied between 12.8% and 16.9% in Eritrea, 7.5% and 12% in Ethiopia, 16.8% and 34.4% in Kenya, 15.9% and 21% in Somalia, and 12.1% and 21.5% in Sudan. The Goma Epidemiological Group (1995) reported a prevalence of global acute malnutrition of 23.1% in Katale camp, 20.1% in Kibumba

Table 4: (a) WHO classification of severity of malnutrition in a community

| Severity of malnutrition | Prevalence of wasting (% weight-for-height below median — 2SD) | Mean weight-for-height $z$-score |
| --- | --- | --- |
| Acceptable | <5%> | > –0.40 |
| Poor | 5–9% | –0.40 to –0.69 |
| Serious | 10–14 | –0.70 to –0.99 |
| Critical | >15% | < –1.00 |

Table 4: (b) Decision-making and programming

| GAM ($z$-score) | Other contributing factors | Classification | Intervention |
| --- | --- | --- | --- |
| <3% | • CMR < 0.5/10,000/d<br>• Food: >2,100 kcal/p/d<br>• Water: >15 litres/p/d<br>• Adequate livelihood assets | Generally food secure | Targeted assistance of food insecure; investment in food and economic production systems |
| >3% but <10% | • CMR: <0.5/10,000/d<br>• U5MR: <1/10,000/d<br>• Food: borderline (2,100/p/d)<br>• Water: borderline (15L/p/d) | Chronically food insecure | "Safety nets" to high-risk groups; advocacy; close monitoring; increase resilience of livelihood systems |
| 10–15% | • CMR: 0.5–1/10,000/d<br>• U5MR : 1–2/10,000/d<br>• Food: ≤2,100kcal/d<br>• Water: 7.5–15L/p/d | Acute food and livelihood crisis | GFD+ targeted SFP + TFP; advocacy, address underlying structural causes |
| >15% | • CMR: 1–2/10,000/d<br>• U5MR: >2/10,000/d<br>• Food: <2,1000kcal/p/d<br>• Water: <7.5L/p/d | Humanitarian emergency | GFD + blanket SFP +TFP; advocacy, address underlying structural causes |
| >30% | • CMR: >2/10,000/p/d<br>• Disease outbreaks(pandemic)<br>• Food: <2,100 kcal/p/d<br>• Water: <4 L/p/d | Humanitarian catastrophe | GFD + blanket SFP +TFP; comprehensive assistance with basic needs: sanitation, water, health, soaps etc. |

*Source*: Adapted from Food and Agriculture Organisation (2006). CMR = crude mortality rate; U5MR = under-five mortality rate; p/d = per person per day; L/p/d = litres per person per day; kcal/p/d = kilocalories per person per day; GFD = general food distribution; SFP = supplementary feeding program; TFP = therapeutic feeding program.

camp and 17.7% in Mugunga camp among Rwandan refugee children in Zaire (now the Democratic Republic of Congo). Although the prevalence of global acute malnutrition was lower in western Africa (3.4–7.8%), central Africa (3.7–15.7%) and southern Africa (6.9–15.5%) than eastern Africa, it was still higher than what is acceptable (United Nations System Standing Committee on Nutrition, 2004). Precarious nutrition situations have also been reported among refugee children in Asia (Young and Jaspars, 2006). Among recent Syrian refugees in Jordan, the prevalence of global acute malnutrition has been estimated at 5.1% among refugees living outside camps and 5.8% among those in refugee camps (UNHCR, 2013a). Among Syrian refugees in Lebanon, the prevalence of global acute malnutrition was slightly higher, varying from 4.1% to 8.9% (United Nations Children's Fund, 2014). High-case fatality of 19–30% was reported among children treated for severe acute malnutrition prior to the 1990s (Schofield and Ashworth, 1996), but it has since plummeted due to better protocols and evidence-based guidelines and products (Salama *et al.*, 2004).

**Micronutrient deficiencies:** In terms of micronutrient deficiencies, the most prevalent among refugees are Vitamin A deficiency (xerophtalmia), iron deficiency and anaemia, scurvy (Vitamin C deficiency), beriberi (Thiamin deficiency), iodine deficiency and pellagra (Niacin deficiency) (Prinzo and De Benoist, 2002). Some of the best known approaches to address micronutrient deficiencies in CHEs include mass vitamin A distribution to all children younger than 5 years (and older children when required) every 4 to 5 months, and a short-term supplementation strategy for other micronutrients as required, compulsory fortification of food aid commodities, mainly oil, salt, blended foods and cereal flour, effective identification, treatment, and prevention of malaria and diarrhoeal disease, deworming, and small-scale home gardening programmes.

Prior to the 1990s, vitamin A deficiency was common among refugees in Asia and Africa and was associated with various morbidities such as measles, diarrhoeal diseases and preventable blindness (Semba, 1998). The prevalence of vitamin A deficiency among refugees varied between 20.5% and 61.7% (Seal *et al.*, 2005). However, improved standards of care and guidelines around mass measles immunisation and vitamin A distribution in CHEs have improved the vitamin A status of refugees. Mass measles immunisation is critical because of the well-known synergistic relationship between measles and vitamin A deficiency (Toole *et al.*, 1989; Tomczyk *et al.*, 2004; Dabbagh *et al.*, 2009). Evidence suggests that adequate vitamin A intake among young children up to 6 years old through vitamin A supplementation and food fortification increases children's likelihood of surviving an infection, and reduces the risk of death from measles by 50%, from diarrhoea by about 40% and overall mortality by 23–30% (Beaton *et al.*, 1993; Glasziou and Mackerras, 1993; Fawzi *et al.*, 1993).

Anaemia is among the major causes of poor health in refugees and affects nearly half of the children in complex emergencies (Kemmer *et al.*, 2003; Ramakrishnan and Semba, 2008). Iron deficiency and anaemia attributed to inadequate intake of iron found in foods such as beef, chicken and seafood that are not often available to refugees varies by region. In Asia, the prevalence of iron deficiency and anaemia among refugees was estimated at 84% (iron deficiency) and 72% (anaemia) among Burmese refugees (Kemmer *et al.*, 2003). In the Middle Eastern region, refugee studies have documented an anaemia prevalence of 67% (Hassan *et al.*, 1997) and in SSA, the prevalence among refugee populations was reported to vary between 15% and 75% for iron deficiency and 12.8 and 90% for anaemia (Seal *et al.*, 2005; Toole, 1992; Woodruff *et al.*, 2006). Vitamin C is another important micronutrient that refugees often lack albeit being commonly available in citrus fruits. Its deficiency leads to scurvy which is rare but can be debilitating among refugee populations who are mainly dependent on food aid rations, a diet that does not include fruit and vegetables. Scurvy outbreaks have been documented in various CHEs in recent times among refugee populations in SSA (CDC, 1989; Magan *et al.*, 1983; Toole, 1992), Bhutanese refugees in Nepal (Save the Children, 1997) and people in refugee-like conditions in Afghanistan (Cheung *et al.*, 2003). The prevalence of scurvy has been estimated between 13.6% and 44% among refugees in Sudan and Somalia (Desenclos *et al.*, 1989; Magan *et al.*, 1983) and 6.3% among refugee-like population in Afghanistan (Cheung *et al.*, 2003).

Beriberi is common in south-east Asia, especially among refugee populations that primarily subsist on rice (polished) and is a result of thiamine deficiency (Hansch, 1999). Thiamine deficiency poses a significant health burden and can cause fatalities if left untreated for prolonged periods. Prior to 2000, the prevalence of thiamine deficiency varied from 8% among Cambodian refugees (Berry-Koch *et al.*, 1990) to 57.7% among Burmese refugee women (McGready *et al.*, 2001). A study by Luxemburger *et al.* (2003) found that thiamine deficiency accounted for 40% of infant mortality among refugees in Thailand between 1987 and 1990. Since then, the disease prevalence has been on the decline due to improved surveillance and fortified food rations for refugees.

Finally, pellagra is caused by niacin and/or tryptophan deficiency and is mainly localised in refugee populations on maize-based rations with an inadequate supply of protein, especially in east and southern Africa (Hansch, 1999). Often characterised by "the three Ds" for diarrhea, dermatitis, and dementia (and a possible 4th D for death), pellagra remains a disease difficult to diagnose in the absence of the skin lesion. Pellagra outbreaks have been documented in various emergency situations and its prevalence was reported to be 6.3% during a major outbreak among refugees in Malawi (Malfait *et al.*, 1993). Other outbreaks have been reported among refugees in Angola (Table 5). Since then, humanitarian agencies have learnt to prevent further outbreaks of the disease through food fortification and supplementation (Hansch, 1999).

**Mental health:** Even though poor mental health remains one of the significant burdens of diseases in CHEs, it does not feature among the top emergency response priorities (Box 1) due to many factors: the controversies and disagreement over the public health value of the post-traumatic stress disorder (PSTD) a disease and concept as well as the appropriateness of non-integrated vertical trauma-focused services (Van Ommeren *et al.*, 2005). Nevertheless, in 2005, Porter and Haslam published a meta-analysis to examine the degree of compromised mental health among refugees. They found that despite the large heterogeneity in retained studies, refugees scored 0.41 standard deviations lower on mental health indices than their non-refugee counterparts. However, the effect size had overlapping confidence intervals suggesting that refugees had only moderately poorer mental health outcomes. The study also found that post-displacement conditions moderated mental health outcomes, and poor mental health outcome among forced migrants was associated with living in institutional accommodation, restricted economic opportunity, internal displacement

Table 5: Early outbreaks of micronutrient deficiencies in refugee populations

| year | Location | Prevalence/incidence |
|---|---|---|
| Pellagra (WHO 2000) | | |
| 1988 | • Zimbabwe | 1.5% |
| 1989 | • Malawi (11 camps) | 0.5% |
| 1990 | • Malawi (11 camps) | 6.3% |
| 1990 | • Malawi (all camps) | 2.0% |
| 1991 | • Malawi (Nsanje district) | 0.2% |
| 1994 | • Nepal (Bhutanese refugees) | 0.5/10 000/day (incidence) |
| 1994 | • Nepal (Bhutanese refugees) | 0.005/10 000/day (incidence) |
| 1995 | • Mozambique | 1.4% |
| 1999 | • Angola | 2.6/1000/week |
| Vitamin A deficiency (Xerophthalmia) (CDC, 1992) | | |
| 1986–1987 | • Somalia | 7% |
| 1985 | • Niger | 2.1% |
| 1982 | • Thailand (Kampuchean refugees) | 4.3% |
| 1984 | • Mauritania | 2.7% |
| Scurvy (CDC, 1992) | | |
| 1984 | • Sudan | 22% |
| 1985 | • Somalia | 6.9–44.0% |
| 1989 | • Ethiopia | 1.0–2.0% |
| Iron Deficiency (Anaemia) (CDC, 1992) | | |
| 1990 | • Syria, Jordan, West Bank & Gaza | 54.5–73.9% (children) |
| 1990 | • Syria, Jordan, West Bank & Gaza | 12.5–62.5% (women) |
| 1990+ | • Ethiopia | 10.0–13.0% |
| Thiamine deficiency/Beriberi (WHO, 1999) | | |
| 1995 | • Thailand (Karen refugee women) | 57.7% in postpartum women |
| 1980 | • Thailand (Cambodian refugees) | 8% in adults only |
| 1981 | • Thailand (Cambodian refugees) | 5% |
| 1992 | • Thailand (Karen refugees) | 6% of breast-feeding women/cases of infantile beriberi |
| 1995 | • Nepal (Bhutanese refugees) | 0.85–1.83/10,000/day |

> **Box 1: Top priorities to address in emergencies**
>
> 1. Rapid assessment of the health status of the population
> 2. Mass vaccination against measles
> 3. Water and sanitation
> 4. Food and nutrition
> 5. Shelter and site planning, and non-food items
> 6. Health care: curative care based on the use of standardized therapeutic protocols using essentials drugs
> 7. Control and prevention of communicable diseases and potential epidemics
> 8. Public health surveillance and alert
> 9. Assessment of human resources and training, and supervision of community health workers
> 10. Coordination of different operational partners
>
> *Source*: Bigot *et al.* (1997).

and repatriation to the country they previously fled. However, the homogeneity analysis indicated a significant variability among studies with heterogeneity rather than sampling error explaining 96% of the variance in effect size points.

The review of evidence of the pre-2004 burden of mental health in complex emergencies by Mollica *et al.* (2004) found that mental health disorders are a significant burden among both adults and children. In adults, the prevalence of PSTD among refugees in Thailand varied from 4.6% among Burmese refugees to 37.2% in Cambodian refugees, and was estimated at 17.1% among Albanian refugees in Kosovo and 26% among Bosnian refugees in Croatia. The prevalence of depression was estimated at 41.8% and 67.9% among Burmese and Cambodian refugees in Thailand, respectively, and 39% among Bosnian refugees in Croatia. Similar patterns were reported among children. The prevalence of PTSD varied between 24% and 50% while that of depression varied between 11% and 68%. A number of studies have reported a high prevalence of mental health disorders among refugees in south America (Sabin *et al.*, 2003; Cardozo *et al.*, 2004), in the Middle East (United Nations Relief Works Agency 2009) and Africa (Reeler and Immerman 1994; Onyut *et al.*, 2009; Neuner *et al.*,

2004; Tang and Fox, 2001; Fox and Tang, 2000). The proportion of all primary health care consultations accounted for by mental health disorders was 0.5%, 1.3% and 1.4% among Syrian refugees in Iraq, Jordan and Lebanon respectively (UNHCR, 2013a). Given the stigma associated with mental disorders in low- and middle-income countries, this pattern of service use may reflect an underutilisation of primary health care. However, it is difficult to compare results summarised across studies as they use different scales and criteria, exacerbated by the lack of accurate population estimates and culturally validated screening instruments (Mollica et al., 2004). The various instruments used to measure mental health in complex emergencies include the Harvard Trauma Questionnaire, the Hopkins Symptom Checklist-25, Diagnostic and Statistical Manual of Mental Disorders criteria, the Posttraumatic Diagnostic Scale, the Composite International Diagnostic Interview, the Impact of Event Scale and many others.

While there are emergency thresholds for communicable diseases and malnutrition, and cut-off points for establishing the effectiveness of interventions in complex emergencies as specified in the Sphere guidelines, there are no standardised thresholds for mental health disorders. However, emerging evidence suggests that early intervention could be effective in addressing mental health issues in CHEs. Wietse et al. (2008) evaluated the efficacy of school-based mental health intervention for children affected by political violence in Indonesia using a cluster randomised trial. The intervention included 15 sessions delivered over 5 weeks of a manualised school-based group intervention such as trauma-processing activities, cooperative play and creative expressive elements. They found that after adjusting for clustering of participants within schools, the intervention improved PTSD symptoms and retained hope in the treatment, but did not improve traumatic idioms (stress-related physical symptoms), depressive symptoms, anxiety and functioning impairment when compared to the control group. Similarly, Layne et al. (2001) used a school-based psychotherapeutic intervention for war-traumatised Bosnian adolescents which included a four-module, 20-session trauma and grief-focused group psychotherapy. The authors found that the intervention not only reduced levels of PSTD but also reduced depression and grief symptoms. Reduced stress was associated with psychosocial adaptation. These findings are consistent with those reported by Gordon *et al.* (2004) but not supported by other studies. For example, Thabet *et al.* (2005) found that a short-term, seven-session group crisis intervention for children (drawing, free play, storytelling and expression of feelings) experiencing ongoing conflict in the Gaza Strip and presenting with PTSD symptoms had no significant impact on children's PTSD or depressive symptoms. Lack of intervention effect has also been reported by Dybdahl (2001) in a study of mother/child during the Bosnian war and Paardekooper (2002) among Sudanese refugee children. These contradictory results could be explained by many factors including differences in intervention scope and implementations (e.g. involving vs. not involving parents during interventions), small sample sizes, variations in measurements in the intervention outcomes (e.g. use of different scales) and variation in study designs (quasi-experimental vs. randomised controlled trials). Notwithstanding these limitations, emerging literature advocates for standardisation of mental health care interventions in CHEs (Van Ommeren *et al.*, 2005; Thabet *et al.*, 2005; Dybdahl 2001; Paardekooper 2002).

## Refugee governance and regional mechanisms in CHEs

The refugee governance in CHEs is complex and involves various stakeholders such as the UNHCR, the host government, other UN agencies and partner Non governmental organisations (NGOs) to provide humanitarian assistance and to mitigate human suffering. The governance of refugees varies by regions. In this section we summarise some of the most relevant mechanisms. In SSA, the refugee governance is mandated by the 1951 Refugee Convention and its 1967 Protocol and the 1969 African Refugee Convention by the African Union (AU). These are enshrined in local legislations and translated into operational policies. In other regions such as south-east Asia, refugee governance is also guided by national legislations and other regional mechanisms summarised below. However, many countries in Asia and the Pacific according to the WHO's regions are not a party to the Refugee Convention. Only 11 out of the 38 countries in the WHO's Asia and the Pacific region (28.9%) have ratified the 1951 Refugee Convention and its 1967 protocols. These countries are Australia, New Zealand, Timor-Leste, Papua New Guinea, Fiji, Samoa, Solomon

Islands, China, Japan, the Philippines and Korea (UNHCR, 2015b). In the Middle Eastern region, refugee governance is more complex. In theory, it is guided by the 1951 Refugee Convention and its 1967 Protocol but in practice the refugee governance is informal and varies between contexts, countries and localities. For example, Hanafi (2010) suggests that Palestinian refugee camps across the Middle East are governed by smaller but powerful non-state actors with allegiance to political and religious groups which undermine formal agencies such as United Nations Relief Works and Agency (UNRWA). In the Americas, refugee governance during the 1980s was predominantly based on state interests. Most of the countries affected by CHEs did not have formal mechanisms and had not ratified the 1951 Refugee Convention and its 1967 protocols (Hartigan, 1992).

## *Africa*

Africa is one of the most politically volatile regions at the forefront of human rights violations resulting in producing and hosting a continuum of large waves of refugees (Table 2). To address this shortfall, the region has created various mechanisms to address human rights issues. Since the 1960s, when most African states gained independence from the European colonial powers, the region has had a unique refugee context in that it generated and hosted large numbers of refugees including freedom fighters. The creation of new African states and the large numbers of people displaced by the various conflicts that emerged out of the collapse of colonialism necessitated an indigenous African refugee solution. In 1969, the Organisation of the African Unity (OAU) member states ratified the African Refugee Convention which became a centrepiece of refugee protection in Africa (Okoth-Obbo, 2001). The African Refugee Convention promoted the sharing of the refugee burden among member states, equipped member states with commensurate skills in refugee protection and monitored the enactment of national laws consistent with the principles of refugee protection. In 2001, the OAU transitioned into the AU which continues to influence and lead the humanitarian thinking, policies and action related to refugee protection in the region. Some of the African Refugee Convention's achievements include the establishment of various regional coordination mechanisms such as the Protocol Relating to the Establishment of Peace and

Security Council of the AU. This protocol came into effect in December 2003 to address conflicts that transformed millions of people into refugee life (African Union, 2002). This protocol also addresses capacity-building of member states and sub-regional organisations in coordination, management and resolution of conflicts and crises in tandem with management of other humanitarian and emergency affairs (United Nations, 2010; Inter-Agency Standing Committee, 2014).

In April 1999, the AU Ministerial conference held in Mauritius established the Mauritius Grand Bay Declaration and Plan of Action (Keetharuth, 2009). The Ministerial conference was held at the backdrop of escalating human rights violations including crimes against humanity and genocide that had earlier transpired in Rwanda. The Grand Bay declaration committed member states to emphasise the respect for human rights, establish social justice, uphold good governance and the rule of law. In addition, the Grand Bay declaration emphasised the independence of the judiciary and the eradication of crimes against humanity and genocide as core tenets for Africa's security and stability (African Commission on Human and Peoples' Rights, 1999). Later, in 2004, the African Commission on Human and Peoples' Rights held its 35th session which was dedicated to the protection of the rights of all displaced people including asylum seekers, refugees and IDPs. During the session, member states created the Special Rapporteur on Refugees, Asylum Seekers, Migrants and IDPs as a mechanism to research and identify, investigate and make recommendations for member states on how to improve the protection of all categories of displaced (African Commission on Human and Peoples' Rights, 2004; Sahli-Fadel, 2012). However, the creation and operationalisation of this new mechanism has not improved the protection of refugees or mitigated the emergence of new refugee situations as ongoing conflicts among member states of Burundi, Chad, Central Africa, Mali, Sudan, South Sudan and Somalia continue to uproot millions of refugees from their homelands (Mukirya Nyanduga, 2006). Despite the quest to promote and uphold human rights, Africa continues to trail other regions in refugee protection. Scholars such as Okoth-Obbo (2001) and Rutinwa (1996) noted that some member states like DR Congo, Kenya, Rwanda, Tanzania and Uganda, among others have openly undermined refugee protection mechanisms through forced repatriations, refoulement of large numbers of refugees at gun point or closing borders to refugees fleeing violence. These practices are inconsistent with the principles of refugee protection.

## *Middle East*

The Middle Eastern region has experienced a significant refugee burden for the past six decades and remains a politically volatile region producing and hosting vast numbers of refugees. Responding to the 1948 mass displacement of Palestinians, the UN General Assembly under resolution 302 (IV) of 8 December 1949 established the United Nations Relief and Works Agency (UNRWA) as a temporary mechanism to provide humanitarian assistance and protection to Palestinians refugees (Bartholomeusz, 2009). Since its creation, UNRWA's mandate has been renewed and broadened to include non-Palestinians displaced by conflict and in need of humanitarian assistance in the region (Bartholomeusz, 2009). However, UNRWA's mandate does not include refugees' resettlement due to political restrictions instituted during UNRWA's formation and by countries hosting Palestinian refugees as they see the refugee burden as a security and political risk (Adelman, 1982). The UNRWA reports directly to the UN Secretary-General but relies on the host governments' permission to operate within their borders. Nonetheless, the UNRWA remains the leading formal agency providing social services such as refugees' welfare and health care, education and protection in the region.

There are other complex and intricate non-state actors providing an alternative governance of the humanitarian assistance for Palestinian refugees. These non-state actors include political and religious factions and popular committees known locally as lijan sha'biyya. The lijan sha'biyya are very influential but undertake their activities with little or no coordination with the mainstream agencies (Hanafi, 2010; Hanafi and Long, 2010). Each non-state actor is independent and controls a specific camps or group of camps with private militias which undermine the role and responsibilities of formal agencies and host governments (Sayigh, 1995; Hanafi and Hassan, 2009). The absence of a unified and authoritative structure makes standardisation of humanitarian assistance across camps difficult while constraining refugees in poor living conditions. Prior to the emergence of the non-state actors, the regional governments exercised control (parallel to the UNRWA) of Palestinian refugees by placing armed forces in the camps (Peteet, 1987; Sayigh, 1995). The militarisation of the humanitarian assistance caused resentment among refugees, the consequence of which was the formation of refugees' own coordination committees in the camps. These refugee committees were later infiltrated by various political factions such as Fatah loyalists and dissidents aligned to different power brokers in the region such as the Shi'ites, Hezbollah, Maronites and the Arab Socialist Baathists to control the camps for political reasons.

## *South-east Asia*

The south-eastern Asia region is a refugee-prone area with large numbers of refugees concentrated in the Meakong countries. A number of countries such as Indonesia, Malaysia, Myanmar, Thailand and Vietnam, in the WHO geographical region of south-east Asia have generated or hosted most refugees since 1960 but are not signatories to the 1951 Refugee Convention and its 1967 Protocol. Out of the 11 countries in south-east Asia, only Cambodia, China, the Philippines and Timor-Leste are signatories to the 1951 Refugee Convention. However, the region's member states have put in place several mechanisms to address the refugee burden. Such mechanisms include the International Covenant on Economic, Social and Cultural Rights, the Comprehensive Plan of Action (CPA), the Bali Process on People Smuggling, Trafficking in Persons and Related Transnational Crime, and the Emergency Transit Agreement between the UNHCR and the government of the Philippines. Although all the mechanisms are not refugee-specific, they have provisions for refugees.

The CPA began in 1989 and ended in 1997. It was a refugee mechanism that replaced an earlier commitment made by 65 countries at a UN conference on Indochinese refugees in Geneva in July 1979 to respond to the burgeoning refugee crisis in south-east Asia. The crisis mainly involved boat loads of refugees fleeing from repressive regimes in Cambodia, Laos and Vietnam. In a study of the 1970s to 1980s refugee crisis in south-east Asia, Robinson (2004) noted that the Indochinese conference committed itself to resettle refugees from the first countries of asylum, halt the refoulement of boatloads of refugees and speed up refugee processing to decongest the overcrowded camps in the region. Inadvertently, the third-country resettlement policy led to a further influx of boat loads of refugees in the region which outweighed the Indochinese conference commitments by 1998. Ten years after the Indochinese conference, the CPA was adopted by 70 countries in a follow-up conference held in Geneva to address the protracted Indochinese refugee situation in the region (Francis and Maguire, 2013). The CPA was funded by the international donor community and implemented by the UNHCR. It hinged on promoting cooperation between affected countries which included refugees' countries of origin (mainly Cambodia, Vietnam and Laos), countries of asylum or transit (predominantly Malaysia, Hong Kong, Thailand and Indonesia) and final countries of settlement (mainly in North America, Europe and Australia). The success of this cooperation was premised on the desire to reduce illegal departures and clamp down on people smugglers, to provide first asylum to all arrivals and establish their status until a durable solution is found, to apply international standards in determining the refugee status for all asylum seekers, to resettle all those meeting requirements for a refugees status in third countries and to repatriate those found to be ineligible for a refugee status (Robinson, 2004). This cooperation promoted international cooperation on resettlements and ended the turning away of refugees on boats and pushing them back to sea by the affected countries. It further prevented loss of refugee lives at sea and led to significant reductions in the number of asylum seekers. However, it also introduced the controversial regional screening and forced repatriation of those deemed ineligible.

Since the end of the CPA, new migration trends such as people smuggling which affect refugees emerged in Asia. In 2002, the UNHCR supported by Australia advanced a new regional mechanism known as the Bali Process on People Smuggling, Trafficking in Persons and Related Transnational Crime which is still ongoing (Francis and Maguire, 2013; Piper, 2005). The Bali Process was founded by a coalition of 45 Asian and Oceania countries together with UNHCR and the International Organisation for Migration (The Bali Process Regional Support Office, 2015). The main objectives of the Bali Process have been to address the causes of migration, combat people trafficking and smuggling, assist victims of human trafficking; and promote the principles of the 1951 Refugee Convention. Since inception, it has attracted more membership from Europe, South Africa and international agencies such as the United Nations Office of Drug and Crime, European Commission and the International Committee of the Red Cross among others. Recently, Rohingya refugees fleeing Myanmar have been stuck at sea because Indonesia, Malaysia and Thailand were refusing to welcome and process them. Instead the boats are being pushed back to the sea. These events suggest that the Bali Process is not effective in addressing people smuggling and illegal movement of people in the region (Human Rights Watch, 2015).

Other important regional mechanisms in the refugee affairs include the 2009 Emergency Transit Agreement (ongoing) between the International Organisation for Migration (IOM), UNHCR and the government of the Philippines. The agreement established mechanisms for processing refugees at risk of refoulement and those awaiting processing and resettlement to third countries (International Organisation for Migration, 2009). Specific areas covered under the agreement have included transporting refugees to and from the Philippines, refugees' health care, and preparation for life in third countries. The agreement is unique in that it provides for the evacuation of refugees at high risk of refoulement to the Philippines for protection (International Organisation for Migration, 2009).

## *The Americas*

The Americas have emerged from serious conflicts and oppressive regimes through the 1980s and 1990s which displaced large numbers of refugees especially in Guatemala, Argentina, Chile and Uruguay. The region has implemented various mechanisms addressing broad issues such as human rights which also cover refugees. The main mechanisms include the Inter-American Commission on Human Rights, the American Convention on Human Rights and the Centre for Justice and International Law (CEJIL). These play different but critical roles complementing each other in the protection of refugees.

The Inter-American Commission on Human Rights was the first regional mechanism to protect human rights and was created in 1959 during the Fifth Meeting of Consultation of Ministers of Foreign Affairs of the Organization of American States (OAS) in Santiago and became operational in 1960 (Scheman, 1965). The Commission was established to promote and monitor human rights among member states, and handle petitions on human rights violations and recommend measures for improving human rights. Additionally, the Commission was tasked to report on its performance, document member states' human rights records and advise member states on matters of human rights. The Commission, which is still functional, operates within the framework of each member state's constitution and laws which in some instances contradict the Commissions' own constitution as validated in Haiti where the repressive regime used laws to violate citizens' rights (Goldman, 2009). Although the Commission was later on augmented by the Inter-American Human Rights Court in 1978 to investigate and prosecute human rights abuses (Buergenthal, 1982), it lacks the authority to police and enforce appropriate action for non-compliant member states. It relies on the moral sanction of naming and shaming human rights violators through its reports that it made public (Fox, 1988). The Commission performs a dual mandate as a charter body of the OAS and as a Convention agency whose activities and involvement are confined within the member states of the American Convention on Human Rights.

The American Convention on Human Rights (the Pact of San José) is an ongoing regional human rights mechanism that was adopted in 1969 after a long period of negotiations and refinement by member states (Fox, 1973). The Pact obliges member states to respect the rights and freedom of their citizens without discrimination and where necessary adopt appropriate legislation to guarantee the citizens' rights and freedoms (The Organisation of American States, 1969). The strength of the Pact lies in the assurance of guaranteeing socio-cultural as well as political and civil rights, and articulating how these rights should be protected (Goldman, 2009). The Pact also unites the efforts of American states to pursue the ideals of democracy and to promote social justice for all (Fox, 1973). The Pact is monitored by the Inter-American Commission on Human Rights and the Inter-American Court of Human Rights to ensure compliance by the member states. However, some of the criticisms of the Pact include the duplication of roles of the Inter-American Commission on Human Rights, especially the latter's jurisdictional court. Goldman (2009) observed that the Pact is one of the most ambitious regional mechanisms to guarantee maximum citizens' rights especially in member states where constitutions and domestic laws have not pronounced themselves on the subject matter.

The Center for Justice and International Law (CEJIL) is a private organisation advocating for the protection of human rights in the region. CEJIL was created in 1991 in Caracas by a group of individuals motivated by the desire to equip human rights advocates with the capacity to navigate the complex regional mechanisms to seek justice for those whose rights and freedom guaranteed by the Inter-American System were violated (Centre for Justice and International Law, 2014). CEJIL provides pro-bono services to victims of human rights abuses who would otherwise be denied the opportunity to seek justice in their own countries (Centre for Justice and International Law, 2014). CEJIL's objectives include responding to state-orchestrated human rights violations, promoting equality before the law, strengthening the region's democratisation process and promoting access to the Inter-American mechanisms (Centre for Justice and International Law, 2015). Since the end of the civil wars that plagued the Americas in the 1980s and 1990s, CEJIL has led various initiatives towards negotiating mutual settlements that have underpinned the improvement of member states' human rights records (Baluarte, 2006). Additionally, CEJIL plays a critical role in monitoring the performance of the Inter-American organisations and the implementation of the recommendations of the Inter-American Commission and its jurisdictional court to ensure justice for human rights victims. Some of the CEJIL's acclaims include the championing of the pioneer Brazilian law on violence against women (Centre for Justice and International Law, 2014) and compelling Peru to withdraw amnesty from individuals who violated human rights on a large scale during the armed conflict that raged between 1980 and 2000 (Sikkink and Walling, 2007).

## Social and health policy response

One of the best known frameworks to guide the humanitarian response to refugees' needs is the SPHERE project. It specified minimum standards in humanitarian assistance based on evidence, experience and best practice. However, policy discussions on refugee health are often considered with limited understanding of the local context of health service provision. There have been some successful country policies that have improved refugee access to health service information, health care and cultural competency. We explore some randomly selected examples of country refugee policies to reflect diversity in social response and geographic representation:

**Pakistan** has a national policy operationalised in July 2013 specifically to address the social and health needs of Afghan refugees, who make up the majority of refugees in its borders. The policy focuses on safety and dignity, voluntary repatriation and support to host communities (Khan, 2014). Prior to this policy, Pakistan's federal laws were silent on refugees and relied on the Foreigners Order of October 1951. The Foreigners Order was enshrined into Pakistani domestic laws and gave power to immigration and custom officers at Pakistan's borders to grant or deny entry into Pakistan. The Foreigners Order stipulated that foreigners not in possession of a passport or valid visa to Pakistan, or those who have not been exempted from passport and visa requirements can be denied entry. This mainly affected refugees who often fled their domiciles to enter Pakistan without any relevant travel documents. The Foreigners Order did not articulate the basis to grant or deny entry of asylum seekers and refugees and their protection. The Foreigners Order restricted refugee movements beyond gazetted areas and areas of residence (National Legislative Bodies/ National Authorities, 1951). In July 2013, the government operationalised a new national policy specifically for Afghan refugees in anticipation of the withdrawal of NATO forces from Afghanistan in 2014. NATO's withdrawal was expected to trigger a further influx of refugees into Pakistan due to perceived increases in insecurity. In spite of the Foreigners Order and the new policy on Afghanistan refugees, Pakistan still lacks a comprehensive policy covering all aspects of refugees under its care.

**Islamic Republic of Iran** promotes a holistic approach to enhance prospects of permanent solutions especially for protracted refugee situations (UNHCR, 2015c). Article 155 of the Iranian Constitution recognised political refugees provided they are not traitors or criminals under the Iranian law. In 1963, Iran instituted a legal framework on refugees that was supplemented by the ratification of the Refugee Convention in 1976. In the same year, Iran commissioned a special Bureau of Aliens and the Foreign Immigrant Affairs to oversee refugee matters such as the provision of health care, education and resettlement (Alborzi, 2006).

**Kenya** enacted a Refugee Act in 2006 to enable the implementation of the 1951 Refugee Convention and its 1967 Protocol, together with the 1969 African Refugee Convention. The Act classified refugees into two groups, namely, the statutory refugees and prima facie refugees. Statutory refugees are those defined in paragraph 1A(1) of the 1951 Refugee Convention and refers to the categories of refugee before, during and shortly after The Second World War (Maynard, 1982). Prima facie refugees are recognised based on the obvious conditions that caused their influx (Rutinwa, 2002). In other words, it is the country's mechanism to manage admission, protection and provision of humanitarian assistance to large groups of refugees that come under its care. The Refugee Act laid out the conditions for the exclusion and withdrawal of refugee status which included those who have committed crimes either outside or within Kenya, have dual nationality and are able to seek refuge in their second country of origin or people from places where the factors that led to them seeking refuge no longer exist. The Refugee Act established a Department for Refugee Affairs (DRA) to coordinate and manage refugee-related matters including refugee health care and protection. The DRA is responsible for policy development, coordinating international assistance, receiving and processing applications for refugee status, registration, issuing identity cards and travel documents, and management of refugee camps (Government of Kenya, 2006).

**Ethiopia** is a signatory to the 1951 Refugee Convention and its 1967 Protocol. It is also a signatory to the 1969 African Refugee Convention. Article 55(1) of the Ethiopian Constitution provides the same level of refugee recognition and protection as the 1951 Refugee Convention (Government of Ethiopia, 2004). However, provisions for refugees' integration in the community are limited as the law maintains reservations on matters pertaining to refugees' employment. Nonetheless, the law allows refugees to live outside camps and engage in informal livelihood opportunities. It also provides for refugees' health care and education.

**Turkey** is one of the original signatories to the 1951 Refugee Convention but still maintains a selective preference of only refugees from Europe (Burch, 2013). Refugees from other regions are not entitled to protection in Turkey. However, its geographical location between Asia and Europe as well as its good living conditions make it an attractive destination for refugees and a transit point to Europe. Under Turkey's refugee law, non-European refugees must apply only for "temporary asylum" to remain in Turkey while their claims are evaluated (Burch, 2013). As they wait for processing, refugees are required to live only in gazetted areas and to seek police permission to travel outside of the gazetted area. While non-European applicants found to be genuine refugees are referred to UNHCR for resettlement, European applicants found to be genuine refugees are provided the same level of health care as that are accorded to Turkish natives at no cost. Unregistered refugees and those living outside the gazetted areas are not permitted to access free health care and other essential services (World Health Organisation, 2014c). Nonetheless, the preference of European over non-European is discriminatory and leaves non-European refugees without protection while they wait for the processing of their application and resettlement. This waiting period is often characterised by harsh conditions which push many of them to attempt to enter Europe illegally, and those who are caught trying to escape are subject to refoulement (Levitan, 2009).

**Lebanon** does not have refugee legislation and commensurate institutions to address refugees' needs and is not a signatory to the 1951 Refugee Convention and its 1967 Protocol (Crisp *et al.*, 2009). This could be attributed to a precedent set by the 1948 mass arrival of Palestinian refugees who remained indefinitely. Ratifying the 1951 Refugee Convention or its 1967 Protocol would compel Lebanon to accept and protect more refugees from the country's politically turbulent neighbours. Refusing to ratify the 1951 Refugee Convention and institutionalise local mechanisms to protect refugees did not stop the influx of new refugees especially from Iraq and Syria. Instead, it has created a vacuum that is bridged by non-state actors, local communities as well as the private sector which provide refugee services such as health care. Similarly, the government has realised that ignoring the existence of refugees within its borders was counterproductive and has since decided to provide refugees with free access to public primary health care. However, the country's health care system is often overstretched and inefficient. The secondary health care system is privatised and too costly for refugees (Crisp *et al.*, 2009).

## Conclusion

Refugees are a product of failed political systems and require political solutions. Refugees continue to be a significant strain on the host countries' social protection as host governments struggle to respond to the needs of their own constituencies while at the same time fulfilling their international obligations to refugees. As the mass movement of refugees continues, those that host them in large numbers will get overwhelmed while the refugee push factors remain unaddressed across regions. While there has been significant improvements in refugee protection as reflected in the reduced mortalities and morbidities, there is still need to research into how to improve wellbeing especially in protracted refugee conditions given that some of the refugees will never experience a durable solution in their lifetime. For example, Palestinian refugees have lived in camps across the Middle East since 1948 and Bhutanese refugees have lived in camps in eastern Nepal since the early 1990s. Therefore, the integration of humanitarian and political solutions should be paramount to any humanitarian response in CHEs because apolitical humanitarianism has only focused on reducing the suffering of refugees while failing to address causes of refugee conditions.

## References

Aaby, P. *et al.* (1984). Overcrowding and intensive exposure as determinants of measles mortality. *American Journal of Epidemiology*, 120(1), 49–63.

Abu Sa'Da, C. & Serafini, M. (2013). Syria crisis—humanitarian and medical challenges of assisting new refugees in Lebanon and Iraq. *Forced Migration Review*, 44, 70–73.

Adelman, H. (1982). Politics and refugees: The United Nations Relief and Works agency for Palestine refugees in the near east. *Refuge: Canada's Journal on Refugees*, 1(8), 1–4.

African Commission on Human and Peoples' Rights (1999). *Grand Bay (Mauritius) declaration and plan of action, 1999*. ACHPR, Banjul, GAM. Available at: http://www.achpr.org/instruments/grandbay/. Accessed 29 May 2015.

African Commission on Human and Peoples' Rights (2004). *Special rapporteur on refugees, asylum seekers, migrants and internally displaced persons*. ACHPR, Banjul, GAM. Available at: http://www.achpr.org/mechanisms/refugees-and-internally-displaced-persons/. Accessed 25 May 2015.

African Union (2002). Protocol relating to the establishment of the peace and security council of the African Union, 9 July 2002. Available at: http://www.refworld.org/docid/3f4b1d374.html. Accessed 28 May 2015.

Alborzi, M.R. (2006). *Evaluating the Effectiveness of International Refugee Law: The Protection of Iraqi Refugees*. Martinus Nijhoff Publishers, Leiden, NED.

Amara, A. & Aljunid, S. (2014). Noncommunicable diseases among urban refugees and asylum-seekers in developing countries: A neglected health care need. *Globalization and Health*, 10, 1–14.

Anderson, J. et al. (2011). The burden of malaria in post-emergency refugee sites: A retrospective study. *Conflict and Health*, 5(1), 1752–1505.

Andresen, E. et al. (2014). Malnutrition and elevated mortality among refugees from South Sudan — Ethiopia, June–July 2014. Centres for Diseases Control, Atlanta, GA. Available at: http://www.cdc.gov/mmwr/preview/mmwrhtml/mm6332a5.htm. Accessed 5 April 2015.

Baluarte, D.C. (2006). Inter-American justice comes to the Dominican Republic: An island shakes as human rights and sovereignty clash. *Human Rights Brief*, 13(2), 7.

Barnett, L. (2002). Global governance and the evolution of the international refugee regime. *International Journal of Refugee Law*, 14(2–3), 238–262.

Bartholomeusz, L. (2009). The mandate of UNRWA at sixty. *Refugee Survey Quarterly*, 28(2–3), 452–474.

Beaton G.H. et al. (1993). Effectiveness of vitamin A supplementation in the control of young child morbidity and mortality in developing countries. United Nations Administrative Committee on Coordination, Sub-committee on Nutrition State-of-the-Art Series: Nutrition Policy. Discussion Paper No. 13.

Bellos, A. et al. (2010). The burden of acute respiratory infections in crisis-affected populations: A systematic review. *Conflict and Health*, 4, 1–12.

Berry-Koch, A. et al. (1990). Alleviation of nutritional deficiency diseases in refugees. *Food & Nutrition Bulletin*, 12(2), 106–112.

Bigot, A. et al. (1997). *Refugee Health: An Approach to Emergency Situations*. MacMillan Education Ltd, London, UK.

Brennan, R.J. & Nandy, R. (2001). Complex humanitarian emergencies: A major global health challenge. *Emergency Medicine*, 13(2), 147–156.

Buergenthal, T. (1982). The Inter-American court of human rights. *American Journal of International Law*, 76(2), 231–245.

Burch, J. (2013). Turkey has new law on asylum, but sets limits for non-Europeans. Reuters, Ankara, TUR. Available at: http://www.reuters.com/article/2013/04/12/us-turkey-refugees-idUSBRE93B0XO20130412. Accessed 6 March 2005.

Cardozo, B.L., et al. (2004). Karenni refugees living in Thai-Burmese border camps: Traumatic experiences, mental health outcomes, and social functioning. *Social Science & Medicine*, 58(12), 2637–2644.

Centre for Justice and International Law (2014). The selection process of the Inter-American commission and court on human rights: Reflections on necessary reforms. CEJIL, Buenos Aires, ARG. Available at: https://cejil.org/sites/default/files/Position%20Paper%20No.%2010_3.pdf. Accessed 10 May 2015.

Centre for Justice and International Law (2015). Mission, vision and principal objectives. Washington, D.C. Available at: https://cejil.org/en/cejil/about-cejil. Accessed 10 May 2015.

CDC (1989). Nutritional status of Somali refugees in Eastern Ethiopia, September 1988–May 1989. *Morbidity and Mortality Weekly Report*, 38, 455–456.

CDC (1992). Famine-affected, refugee, and displaced populations: Recommendations for public health issues. *Morbidity and Mortality Weekly Report*, 41, No. RR-13. US Epidemiology Program Office. Public Health Service; US Department of Health and Human Services.

CDC (1993). Mortality among newly arrived Mozambican refugees–Zimbabwe and Malawi, 1992. *Morbidity and Mortality Weekly Report*, 42(24), 468. US Epidemiology Program Office. Public Health Service; US Department of Health and Human Services.

CDC (2001). Surveillance of mortality during a refugee crisis–Guinea, January–May 2001. *Morbidity and Mortality Weekly Report*, 50(46), 1029. US Epidemiology Program Office.

Cheung, E. et al. (2003). An epidemic of scurvy in Afghanistan: Assessment and response. *Food & Nutrition Bulletin*, 24(3), 247–255.

Coffey, J.T. et al. (2002). Valuing health-related quality of life in diabetes. *Diabetes Care*, 25(12), 2238–2243.

Collyer, M. (2005). Secret agents: Anarchists, Islamists and responses to politically active refugees in London. *Ethnic and Racial Studies*, 28(2), 278–303.

Coninx, R. (2007). Tuberculosis in complex emergencies. *Bulletin of the World Health Organization*, 85(8), 637–640.

Connolly, M.I.A. et al. (2004). Communicable diseases in complex emergencies: Impact and challenges. *The Lancet*, 364(9449), 1974–1983.

Crisp, J., et al. (2009). Surviving in the city: A review of UNHCR's operation for Iraqi refugees in urban areas of Jordan, Lebanon and Syria. UNHRC, Geneva, SWI.

Croxton, D. (1999). The peace of Westphalia of 1648 and the origins of sovereignty. *The International History Review*, 21(3), 569–591.

Culhane-Pera, K.A. et al. (2009). Cardiovascular disease risks in Hmong refugees from Wat Tham Krabok, Thailand. *Journal of Immigrant and Minority Health*, 11(5), 372–379.

Dabbagh, A., et al. (2009). Global measles mortality, 2000–2008. *Morbidity and Mortality Weekly Report*, 58(47), 1321–1326.

Desenclos, J.-C., et al. (1989). Epidemiological patterns of scurvy among Ethiopian refugees. *Bulletin of the World Health Organization*, 67(3), 309.

Diaz, T. & Achi, R. (1989). Infectious diseases in a Nicaraguan refugee camp in Costa Rica. *Tropical Doctor*, 19(1), 14–17.

Duffield, M. (1994). *Complex emergencies and the crisis of developmentalism.* Institute of Development Studies, University of Sussex, Brighton, UK.

Dybdahl, R. (2001). Children and mothers in war: An outcome study of a psychosocial intervention program. *Child Development*, 72(4), 1214–1230.

Elliott, J. (2015) Survival management: Syrian refugees living with diabetes face extraordinary challenges. Médecins Sans Frontières, Canada. Available at: http://www.msf.ca/en/article/survival-management-syrian-refugees-living-with-diabetes-face-extraordinary-challenges. Accessed 3 June 2015.

Fawzi, W.W. et al. (1993). Vitamin A supplementation and child mortality: A meta-analysis. *Journal of the American Medical Association*, 269, 898–903.

Food and Agricultural Organisation (2006). Integrated food security and humanitarian phase classification (IPC) framework. FAO's Agriculture and Development Economics Division (ESA), Rome, ITA. Available at: ftp://ftp.fao.org/es/ESA/policybriefs/pb_03.pdf. Accessed 5 May 2015.

Fox, D. T. (1973). Convention on human rights and prospects for United States ratification. *Human Rights*, 3(2), 243–281.

Fox, D. T. (1988). Inter-American commission on human rights finds United States in violation. *American Journal of International Law*, 82(3), 601–603.

Fox, S.H. & Tang, S.S. (2000). The Sierra Leonean refugee experience: Traumatic events and psychiatric sequelae. *The Journal of Nervous and Mental Disease*, 188(8), 490–495.

Francis, A. & Maguire, R. (2013). Shifting Powers: Protection of refugees and displaced persons in the Asia pacific region. In: Francis, A. & Maguire, R. (eds.), *Protection of Refugees and Displaced Persons in the Asia Pacific Region*, Ashgate Publishing, Farnham, UK. pp. 1–11.

Friedman, C. & Spiegel, P. (2000). West Timor mission report, January 24–March 2, 2000. United Nations High Commissioner for Refugees and Centers for Disease Control, Kupang, WTI.

Glasziou, P.P., Mackerras, D.E. (1993). Vitamin A supplementation in infectious diseases: A meta-analysis. *British Medical Journal*, 306, 366–370.

Glynn, I. (2011). The genesis and development of article 1 of the 1951 refugee convention. *Journal of Refugee Studies*, 25(1), 134–148.

Goldman, R.K. (2009). History and action: The Inter-American human rights system and the role of the Inter-American commission on human rights. *Human Rights Quarterly*, 31(4), 856–887.

Goma Epidemiology Group (1995). Public health impact of Rwandan refugee crisis: What happened in Goma, Zaire, in July, 1994? *Lancet,* 345(8946), 339–344.

Gordon, J.S., *et al.* (2004). Treatment of posttraumatic stress disorder in post war Kosovo high school students using mind-body skills groups: A pilot study. *Journal of Traumatic Stress,* 17(2), 143–147.

Government of Ethiopia (2004). Proclamation No. 409/2004 of 2004, Refugee Proclamation. Federal Negarit Gazeta, Addis Ababa, ETH.

Government of Kenya (2006). *The refugee act.* Gazette Supplement, Nairobi, KEN.

Hanafi, S. (2010). Governing Palestinian Refugee Camps in the Arab East. Issam Fares Institute for Public Policy and International Affairs, AUB, Beirut, LEB.

Hanafi, S. & Hassan, I.S. (2009). Constructing and governing Nahr el-Bared camp. An 'ideal' model of exclusion. *Majallat al-Dirasat al-Falastiniyya (Journal of Palestine Studies). Beirut: Institute of Palestine Studies,* 78, 39–52.

Hanafi, S. & Long, T. (2010). Governance, governmentalities, and the state of exception in the Palestinian refugee camps of Lebanon. *Journal of Refugee Studies,* 23(2), 134–159.

Hankins, C.A., *et al.* (2002). Transmission and prevention of HIV and sexually transmitted infections in war settings: Implications for current and future armed conflicts. *Aids,* 16(17), 2245–2252.

Hansch, S. (1999). Enhancing the nutritional quality of relief diets overview of knowledge and experience: Background paper prepared for the Workshop by the Congressional Hunger Center, April 1999. Congressional Hunger Center, Washington DC. Available at: http://pdf.usaid.gov/pdf_docs/pnacj175.pdf. Accessed 6 May 2015.

Hartigan, K. (1992). Matching humanitarian norms with cold, hard interests: The making of refugee policies in Mexico and Honduras, 1980–1989. *International Organization,* 46(03), 709–730.

Hassan, K., *et al.* (1997). Factors associated with anaemia in refugee children. *The Journal of Nutrition,* 127(11), 2194–2198.

Holmes, D. (2014). Chronic disease care crisis for Lebanon's Syrian refugees. *Lancet Diabetes Endocrinal,* 3(2), 102.

Human Rights Watch (2015). Southeast Asia: accounts from Rohingya boat people. HRW, New York, NY. Available at: http://www.hrw.org/news/2015/05/27/southeast-asia-accounts-rohingya-boat-people. Accessed 1 June 2015.

Inter-Agency Standing Committee (2014). Inter-agency standing committee: Concise terms of reference and action procedures. IASC, Geneva, SWI. Available at: http://www.humanitarianinfo.org/iasc/pageloader.aspx?page=about-default. Accessed 8 May 2015.

International Organisation for Migration (2009). Philippine government, IOM, UNHCR Sign refugee transit agreement. IOM, Manila. Available at: https://www.iom.int/news/philippine-government-iom-unhcr-sign-refugee-transit-agreement. Accessed 9 May 2015.

Kemmer, T.M., et al. (2003). Iron deficiency is unacceptably high in refugee children from Burma. *The Journal of Nutrition*, 133(12), 4143–4149.

Keetharuth, S.B. (2009). Major African legal instruments. In: Bösl, A. and Diescho, J. eds. *Human Rights in Africa: Legal Perspectives on their Protection and Promotion*. Macmillan Education Namibia, Windhoek, NAM.

Khan, A.M. (2014). Pakistan's national refugee policy. *Refugee Migration Review*, 46 (May 2014), 22.

Kimbrough, W., et al. (2012). The burden of tuberculosis in crisis-affected populations: A systematic review. *The Lancet Infectious Diseases*, 12(12), 950–965.

Klugman, J. (1999). Social and economic policies to prevent complex humanitarian emergencies: Lessons from experience. United Nations University & World Institute for Development Economics Research, Helsinki, FIN.

Kouadio, I.K. et al. (2010). Measles outbreaks in displaced populations: A review of transmission, morbidity and mortality associated factors. *BMC International Health and Human Rights*, 10(1), 5.

Layne, C.M. et al. (2001). Trauma/grief-focused group psychotherapy: School-based post war intervention with traumatized Bosnian adolescents. *Group Dynamics: Theory, Research, and Practice*, 5(4), 277.

Levitan, R. (2009). Refugee protection in Turkey. *Forced Migration Review*, 32, 56–57.

Luxemburger, C. et al. (2003). Beri-beri: The major cause of infant mortality in Karen refugees. *Transactions of the Royal Society of Tropical Medicine and Hygiene*, 97(2), 251–255.

Magan, A. M. et al. (1983). An outbreak of scurvy in Somali refugee camps. *Disasters*, 7(2), 94–96.

Malfait, P. et al. (1993). An outbreak of pellagra related to changes in dietary niacin among Mozambican refugees in Malawi. *International Journal of Epidemiology*, 22(3), 504–511.

Maynard, P.D. (1982). The legal competence of the United Nations High Commissioner for Refugees. *International and Comparative Law Quarterly*, 31(3), 415–425.

McGready, R. et al. (2001). Postpartum thiamine deficiency in a Karen displaced population. *The American Journal of Clinical Nutrition*, 74(6), 808–813.

Médecins Sans Frontières (2014). Treating chronic diseases among Syrian refugees. Available at: http://www.doctorswithoutborders.org/news-stories/field-news/treating-chronic-diseases-among-syrian-refugees. Accessed 26 May 2015.

Mollica, R.F. et al. (2004). Mental health in complex emergencies. *The Lancet*, 364(9450), 2058–2067.

Mukirya Nyanduga, B.T. (2006). Special rapporteur on refugees, asylum seekers, migrants and internally displaced persons. African Commission on Human and Peoples' Rights. Banjul, GAM.

National Legislative Bodies/National Authorities, 1951. Foreigners order, 1951. National Assembly of Pakistan. Available at: http://www.refworld.org/docid/3ae6b4f717.html. Accessed 5 March 2015.

Neuner, F. et al. (2004). A comparison of narrative exposure therapy, supportive counseling, and psychoeducation for treating posttraumatic stress disorder in an African refugee settlement. *Journal of Consulting and Clinical Psychology*, 72(4), 579.

Noiriel, G. (1991). *La Tyrannie du National. Le Droit d'Asile en Europe 1793–1993*. Calmann-Lévy, Paris, FRA.

Okoth-Obbo, G. (2001). Thirty years on: A legal review of the 1969 OAU refugee convention governing the specific aspects of refugee problems in Africa. *Refugee Survey Quarterly*, 20(1), 79.

O'Meara, W.P. (2010). Changes in the burden of malaria in sub-Saharan Africa. *Lancet Infectious Diseases*, 10, 545–555.

Onyut, L.P. et al. (2009). Trauma, poverty and mental health among Somali and Rwandese refugees living in an African refugee settlement — an epidemiological study. *Conflict and Health*, 3(6), 90–107.

Paardekooper, B.P. (2002). *Children of the Forgotten War: A Comparison of Two Intervention Programs for Promotion of Well-being of Sudanese Refugee Children*. Vrije Universiteit Academic Proefschrift, Amsterdam, NED.

Paquet, C. & Hanquet, G. (1998). Control of infectious diseases in refugee and displaced populations in developing countries. *Bulletin de l'Institut Pasteur*, 96(1), 3–14.

Peteet, J. (1987). Socio-political integration and conflict resolution in the Palestinian camps in Lebanon. *Journal of Palestine Studies*, 16(2), 29–44.

Piper, N. (2005). A problem by a different name? A review of research on trafficking in South-East Asia and Oceania. *International Migration*, 43(1–2), 203–233.

Plewes, K. et al. (2008). Low seroprevalence of HIV and syphilis in pregnant women in refugee camps on the Thai–Burma border. *International Journal of STD & AIDS*, 19(12), 833–837.

Porter, J.D. et al. (1990). Measles outbreaks in the Mozambican refugee camps in Malawi: The continued need for an effective vaccine. *International Journal of Epidemiology*, 19(4), 1072–1077.

Porter, M. & Haslam, N. (2005). Predisplacement and postdisplacement factors associated with mental health of refugees and internally displaced persons: A meta-analysis. *Journal of American Medical Association*, 294(5), 602–612.

Prinzo, Z.W. and De Benoist, B. (2002). Meeting the challenges of micronutrient deficiencies in emergency-affected populations. *Proceedings of the Nutrition Society*, 61(02), 251–257.

Ramakrishnan, U. & Semba, R.D. (2008). Iron deficiency and anaemia. In: Semba, R. & Bloem, M. (eds.), *Nutrition and Health in Developing Countries, 2nd edn.* Humana Press, Totowa, NJ.

Redfield, P. (2005). Doctors, borders, and life in crisis. *Cultural Anthropology*, 20(3), 328–361.

Reeler, A.P. & Immerman, R. (1994). A preliminary investigation into psychological disorders among Mozambican refugees: Prevalence and clinical features. *The Central African Journal of Medicine*, 40(11), 309–315.

Richards, A.K. et al. (2009). Cross-border malaria control for internally displaced persons: Observational results from a pilot programme in eastern Burma/Myanmar. *Tropical Medicine & International Health*, 14(5), 512–521.

Riga, J.F. (1989). Defenses for sanctuary movement: A humanitarian plea falling upon deaf ears. *Boston College International and Comparative Law Review*, 12(1), 225–263.

Robinson, N. (1953). *Convention Relating to the Status of Refugees: Its History, Contents and Interpretation*. Institute of Jewish Affairs, New York, NY.

Robinson, W.C. (2004). The comprehensive plan of action for Indochinese refugees, 1989–1997: Sharing the burden and passing the buck. *Journal of Refugee Studies*, 17(3), 319–333.

Rubin, R.R. & Peyrot, M. (1999). Quality of life and diabetes. *Diabetes/Metabolism Research and Reviews*, 15(3), 205–218.

Rutinwa, B. (1996). The Tanzanian government's response to the Rwandan emergency. *Journal of Refugee Studies*, 9(3), 291.

Rutinwa, B. (2002). Prima facie status and refugee protection. UNHCR, Geneva, SWI.

Sabin, M. et al. (2003). Factors associated with poor mental health among Guatemalan refugees living in Mexico 20 years after civil conflict. *Journal of the American Medical Association*, 290(5), 635–642.

Sahli-Fadel, M. (2012). Report of the mechanism of the Special Rapporteur on rights of refugees, asylum seekers and internally displaced and migrants in Africa since its creation. African Commission on Human & Peoples' Rights, Yamoussoukro, CIV.

Salama, P. et al. (2004). Lessons learned from complex emergencies over past decade. *The Lancet*, 364(9447), 1801–1813.

Save the Children UK (1997). *Household Food Assessment of Shudunabari and Bedlangi Refugee Camps, Jhapa District, South-East Nepal.* Save the Children UK, London.

Sayigh, R. (1995). Palestinians in Lebanon: Harsh present, uncertain future. *Journal of Palestine Studies,* 25(1), 37–53.

Scheman, L.R. (1965). The Inter-American commission on human rights. *The American Journal of International Law,* 59(2), 335–344.

Schofield, C. & Ashworth, A. (1996). Why have mortality rates for severe malnutrition remained so high? *Bulletin of the World Health Organization,* 74(2), 223.

Seal, A.J. et al. (2005). Iron and vitamin A deficiency in long-term African refugees. *The Journal of Nutrition,* 135(4), 808–813.

Semba, R.D. (1998). The role of vitamin A and related retinoids in immune function. *Nutrition Reviews,* 56(1), S38–S48.

Shears, P. et al. (1987). Epidemiological assessment of the health and nutrition of Ethiopian refugees in emergency camps in Sudan, 1985. *British Medical Journal,* 295(6593), 314–318.

Sikkink, K. & Walling, C.B. (2007). The impact of human rights trials in Latin America. *Journal of Peace Research,* 44(4), 427–445.

Spiegel, P., et al. (2002). Health programmes and policies associated with decreased mortality in displaced people in postemergency phase camps: A retrospective study. *The Lancet,* 360(9349), 1927–1934.

Spiegel, P.B. (2004). HIV/AIDS among conflict affected and displaced populations: Dispelling myths and taking action. *Disasters,* 28(3), 322–339.

Spiegel, P.B. et al. (2007). Prevalence of HIV infection in conflict-affected and displaced people in seven sub-Saharan African countries: A systematic review. *The Lancet,* 369(9580), 2187–2195.

Spiegel, P.B. et al. (2011). Notes from the field: Mortality among refugees fleeing Somalia — Dadaab Refugee Camps, Kenya, July – August 2011. Centres of Disease Control, Atlanta, GA. Available at: http://www.cdc.gov/mmwr/preview/mmwrhtml/mm6033a4.htm. Accessed 5 April 2015.

Spiegel, P. et al. (2012). Health programmes and policies associated with decreased mortality in displaced people in post emergency phase camps: A retrospective study. *Lancet,* 360, 1927–1934.

Sutter, R.W. & Haefliger, E. (1990). Tuberculosis morbidity and infection in Vietnamese in Southeast Asian refugee camps 1, 2. *American Review of Respiratory Diseases,* 141, 1483–1486.

Talley, L. et al. (2001). An investigation of increasing mortality among Congolese refugees in Lugufu camp, Tanzania, May–June 1999. *Journal of Refugee Studies,* 14(4), 412–427.

Tang, S.S. & Fox, S.H. (2001). Traumatic experiences and the mental health of Senegalese refugees. *The Journal of Nervous and Mental Disease*, 189(8), 507–512.

Thabet, A.A. *et al.* (2005). Group crisis intervention for children during ongoing war conflict. *European Child & Adolescent Psychiatry*, 14(5), 262–269.

The Bali Process Regional Support Office (2015). The Bali process on people smuggling, trafficking in persons and related crime. RSO, Bankok, THA. Available at: http://www.baliprocess.net/files/RSO/RSO%20Information%20Sheet%20-%20 Bali%20Process%20Conclusions.pdf. Accessed 1 June 2015.

The Organisation of American States (1969). American convention on human rights "Pact of San Jose, Costa Rica" (B-32). San Jose, CRA. Available at: http://www.mindbank.info/item/1254. Accessed 10 May 2015.

Tomczyk, B., *et al.* (2004). Emergency nutrition and mortality surveys conducted among Sudanese refugees and Chadian villagers in North East Chad, June 2004. Centre for Disease Control, Atlanta, GA.

Toole, M.J. & Waldman, R.J. (1988). An analysis of mortality trends among refugee populations in Somalia, Sudan, and Thailand. *Bulletin of the World Health Organization*, 66(2), 237–247.

Toole, M. J. *et al.* (1989). Measles prevention and control in emergency settings. *Bulletin of the World Health Organization*, 67(4), 381–388.

Toole, M.J. & Waldman, R.J. (1990). Prevention of excess mortality in refugee and displaced populations in developing countries. *Journal of American Medical Association*, 263, 3296–3302.

Toole, M. (1992). Micronutrient deficiencies in refugees. *The Lancet*, 339(8803), 1214–1216.

Toole, M.J. *et al.* (1989). Measles prevention and control in emergency settings. *Bulletin of the World Health Organization*, 67(4), 381.

United Nations (2010). Peace and security cluster: Report to the 11th session of the regional coordination mechanism (RCM-Africa). NEPAD, Addis Ababa, ETH. Available at: http://www.nepad.org/system/files/PeaceandSecurity.pdf. Accessed 20 May 2015.

United Nations (2014). Report of the United Nations High Commissioner for refugees covering the period 1 July 2013–June 2014. United Nations, New York, NY.

United Nations Children's Fund (2014). Joint Nutrition Assessment Syrian Refugees in Lebanon. UNHCR, UNICEF and WFP, Amman, JDN. Available at: https://data.unhcr.org/syrianrefugees/download.php?id=4600. Accessed 20 May 2015.

UNHCR (2008a). 2008 Annual report: East and horn of Africa. United Nations High Commissioner for Refugees, Geneva, SWI.

UNHCR (2008b). UNHCR's strategic plan for malaria control 2008–2012. United Nations High Commissioner for Refugees, Geneva, SWI.

UNHCR (2010). The convention and protocols relating to the status of refugees. United Nations High Commissioner for Refugees, Geneva, SWI. Available at: http://www.unhcr.org/protect/PROTECTION/3b66c2aa10.pdf. Accessed 21 July 2015.

UNHCR (2013a). Inter-agency regional response for Syrian refuges in Jordan host communities and Za'Atri refugee camps. United Nations High Commissioner for Refugees, Amman, JDN. Available at: https://data.unhcr.org/syrianrefugees/download.php?id=2744. Accessed 20 May 2015.

UNHCR (2013b). Joint nutrition and health surveys Dollo Addo refugee camps. United Nations High Commissioner for Refugees, ARRA, WFP, UNICEF, SC-I, ACF, IMC, GOAL, Addis Ababa, ETH.

UNHCR (2014). War's human cost: UNHCR global trends 2013. United Nations High Commissioner for Refugees, Geneva, SWI.

UNHCR (2015a). Statistical online population database. United Nations High Commissioner for Refugees, Geneva, SWI. Available at: http://www.unhcr.org/pages/4a013eb06.html. Accessed 3 April 2015.

UNHCR (2015b). State parties to the 1951 convention relating to the status of refugees and the 1967 protocol. United Nations High Commissioner for Refugees Available at: http://www.unhcr.org/3b73b0d63.html. Accessed 4 May 2015.

UNHCR (2015c). 2015 UNHCR country operations profile — Islamic Republic of Iran. United Nations High Commissioner for Refugees, Geneva, SWI. Available at: http://www.unhcr.org/pages/49e486f96.html. Accessed 5 March 2015.

UNRWA (2009). The Gaza labour market in 2008: A briefing paper. December 2009. United Nations Relief Works Agency. Available at: http://www.unrwa.org/userfiles/201001196450.pdf. Accessed 29 April 2015.

United Nations Office for the Coordination of Humanitarian Affairs (1999). *Orientation Handbook on Complex Emergencies*. United Nations, New York, NY.

United Nations System Standing Committee on Nutrition (2004). Nutrition information in crisis situations: Report No. 2 — summary. Available at: http://apps.who.int/disasters/repo/13489.pdf. Accessed 4 May 2015.

Van Ommeren. et al. (2005). Mental and social health during and after acute emergencies: Emerging consensus? *Bulletin of the World Health Organization*, 83(1), 71–75.

Wietse, A.T. et al. (2008). School-based mental health intervention for children affected by political violence in Indonesia: A cluster randomized trial. *Journal of the American Medical Association*, 300(6), 655–662.

Woodruff, B.A. et al. (2006). Anaemia, iron status and vitamin A deficiency among adolescent refugees in Kenya and Nepal. *Public Health Nutrition*, 9(01), 26–34.

World Health Organization (1999). Thiamine deficiency and its prevention and control in major emergencies. Report No: WHO/NHD/99.13. Department of Nutrition for Health and Development, WHO, Geneva, SWI.

World Health Organization (2000). Pellagra and its prevention and control in major emergencies. WHO, Geneva, SWI.

World Health Organisation. (2005). *Malaria Control in Complex Emergencies: An Inter-agency Field Handbook*. WHO, Geneva, SWI.

World Health Organisation (2008). East and horn Africa 2008 annual report. WHO, Geneva, SWI. Available at: http://www.unhcr.org/4b506cca9.html. Accessed 4 April 2015.

World Health Organisation. (2011). Global status report on non communicable diseases 2010. WHO, Geneva, SWI.

World Health Organisation. (2014a). World malaria report 2014. WHO, Geneva, SWI.

World Health Organisation. (2014b). Noncommunicable diseases country profiles 2014. WHO, Geneva, SWI.

World Health Organisation. (2014c). WHO donor snapshot–Turkey: January–June 2014. WHO, Geneva, SWI.

Young, H. & Jaspars, S. (2006). The meaning and measurement of acute malnutrition in emergencies: A primer for decision-makers. Overseas Development Institute (ODI). Humanitarian practice network (HPN).

Zimmet, P. (2003). The burden of type 2 diabetes: Are we doing enough? *Diabetes & Metabolism*, 29(4), 6S9–6S18.

# Chapter 4

# Health, social and economic impact of voluntary migration

Professor André M.N. Renzaho

This chapter will focus on voluntary migration. As opposed to forced migrations (Chapters 2 and 3, and case studies in Section 2), voluntary migration examines a form of migration in which individuals migrate based on their free will due to various reasons as extensively examined in the migration theories summarised in Chapter 1. Voluntary migration is not a new phenomenon and dates back to the pre-modern period. Throughout history it has occurred in various forms and has included migration from low- and middle-income countries (LMICs) to developed nations (south–north migration), from developed nations to LMICs (north–south migration), between LMICs (south–south migration) and between developed nations (north–north migration). The purpose of this chapter is not to cover these various and dynamic forms of voluntary migration. The chapter is intended to examine the socioeconomic and health impacts of voluntary migration. We start with a brief historical perspective on voluntary migration, followed by an examination of the international migration patterns. We then move on to examine the health burdens of international migration as well as its socioeconomic impact, focusing mainly on the brain drain/gain and remittances. We conclude by examining the policy responses and directions.

## Patterns of international migration

The most comprehensive and recent data on international migration are summarised in the "World Migration in Figures" which is a joint contribution by the United Nations' Department of Economic and Social Affairs (UN-DESA) and the Organisation for Economic Co-operation and Development (OECD) to the United Nations' high-level dialogue on migration and development that took place in New York on 3–4 October 2013 (UN-DESA & OECD, 2013). The report suggests that there were around 232 million international migrants worldwide (or about 3.2% of the world population) in 2013 with the global north experiencing an increase of 65% (or around 53 million) compared to only 34% in the global south (or around 24 million) since 1990. The proportion of international migrants to the total population increased from less than 9% in 2000 to 11% in 2013 in the developed countries, but has remained stable in developing countries (estimated at 2%) as a result of significant natural population growth and higher return levels (UN-DESA & OECD, 2013). LMICs were a destination for 96 million (41.4%) international migrants, suggesting that south–south migration was significant (Table 1). For example, of the 232 million international migrants, SSA was a destination for 17 million migrants or 7.4% of the total migrant stock. Of those emigrating within SSA, only 3.6% came from outside the continent with 96.4% representing intra-African migration. However, there has been an increase in African migrants relocating to developed countries, growing more than any other community (UN-DESA & OECD, 2013). Establishing the real figure of African migrants within and outside SSA is a daunting task due to lack of migration registries and databases in countries of origin.

## The health burden of voluntary migrants

Managing and controlling migration flows is part of measures to maintain national sovereignty and border protection (Glendenning et al., 2003). The border protection's outcome is to protect the population from public health risks, hence the need for pre-migration compulsory health screening as a pre-requisite for entry into a country. The aim of pre-migration health checks is twofold: to reduce public health and safety risks as much

Table 1: Data on international migrants worldwide

| Major region of destination | 1990 | 2000 | 2010 | 2013 |
|---|---|---|---|---|
| **Migrant stock** | | | | |
| WORLD | 154,161,984 | 174,515,733 | 220,729,300 | 231,522,215 |
| HICs | 82,306,645 | 103,388,690 | 129,737,280 | 135,583,436 |
| LMICs | 71,855,339 | 71,127,043 | 90,992,020 | 95,938,779 |
| SSA | 14,625,619 | 14,520,681 | 15,812,664 | 17,228,396 |
| LMICs as % of world stock | 46.6% | 40.8% | 41.2% | 41.4% |
| SSA as % of world stock | 9.5% | 8.3% | 7.2% | 7.4% |
| **Migrant stock as a % of the population** | | | | |
| WORLD | 2.9% | 2.8% | 3.2% | 3.2% |
| HICs | 7.2% | 8.7% | 10.5% | 10.8% |
| LMICs | 1.7% | 1.4% | 1.6% | 1.6% |
| SSA | 2.9% | 2.2% | 1.8% | 1.8% |
| **Refugee stock** | | | | |
| WORLD | 18,618,158 | 15,631,959 | 15,384,945 | 15,659,622 |
| HICs | 2,011,751 | 3,116,076 | 2,044,208 | 1,992,078 |
| LMICs | 16,606,407 | 12,515,883 | 13,340,737 | 13,667,544 |
| SSA | 5,329,768 | 3,451,220 | 2,237,845 | 2,719,846 |
| **Refugee as a % of migrant stock** | | | | |
| WORLD | 12.1% | 9.0% | 7.0% | 6.8% |
| HICs | 2.4% | 3.0% | 1.6% | 1.5% |
| LMICs | 23.1% | 17.6% | 14.7% | 14.2% |
| SSA | 36.4% | 23.8% | 14.2% | 15.8% |

*Source*: Author's own computations. Data extracted from United Nations database on International Migrant Stock, 2013 revision (UN-DESA, 2013).

as possible to the host population, and to control and minimise health expenditure associated with migration-related burden of diseases. While many developed nations continue to state that their pre-migration checks are in line with global non-discriminatory immigration policies, some countries have restrictions on entry, based on health status (Ofori-Asenso, 2013). For example, as many as 59 countries, territories and areas have specific restrictions on entry, residence and stay, based on HIV status (United Nations Programme on HIV/AIDS, 2009). The pre-migration health checks also include tuberculosis and hepatitis, and applicants have to meet the health requirement for entry into Australia, Canada, USA and other high-income countries before they are granted an entry visa (Aldridge et al., 2014; Ofori-Asenso, 2013). The pre-migration screening means that migrants who are granted entry visas could have a lower prevalence of communicable diseases than those remaining behind. That is not the case. Many studies from different industrialised countries show the re-emergence of diseases such as tuberculosis (TB) and an increase in the incidence of hepatitis and HIV/AIDS, and migrants represent an increasing proportion of new cases. However, the health of voluntary migrants is not just about infectious diseases and falls into four categories: communicable diseases, non-communicable diseases, occupational diseases and reproductive health.

## Communicable diseases

Mortality from infectious diseases is more than 25% higher among migrants than the host population in OECD countries (Bos et al., 2004). Infectious diseases most prevalent among migrant populations include Helicobacter pylori, gastric schistosomiasis, chronic hepatitis viral infections, HIV/AIDS and TB (Gibney et al., 2009; Tiong et al., 2006). However, studies on infectious diseases among migrants have mainly been based on the retrospective audit of medical records of patients attending a tertiary referral centre, and hence representing a highly selected population seeking treatment, which could lead to the overestimation of these conditions.

**Tuberculosis:** TB has been reported to be a serious issue which is significantly higher among south–south migrants, especially those working in mines, compared to the host population (Karim et al., 2009; Rees et al., 2010). It is also an emerging problem among south–north migrants. Recently, Walter et al. (2014) published data on persistent latent TB reactivation risk in US migrants. The TB screening occurred between 2001 and 2009, and involved a total of 333,768 adult migrants, of whom 123,114 intended to settle in California. In the California-bound migrants, 17,160

(14%) had abnormal pre-immigration radiograph results. The study found a rate of latent TB infection reactivation of 31.6% per 100,000 person-years among migrants with normal pre-migration examination and radiography results during the first 9 years in the USA, a rate which did not change with the length of stay in the country. Of the 123,114 migrants intending to settle in California, 793 had TB, and within 1 year of pre-migration examination, more than three-quarters (85%) of TB cases were imported, 6% were latent TB infection reactivation and 9% were inactive TB. However, after one year of entry (i.e. years 2–9) in the USA, 76% of TB cases were latent TB infection reactivation and 24% were inactive TB. Interestingly, the study also found that among migrants without active TB at baseline, the reported number of TB did not decline over nine years, suggesting that the increased risk of TB in the long run is mainly from sustained high risk of latent TB infection reactivation. The post-migration increase in cases of TB among foreign persons is consistent with other studies in OECD countries (Wörmann and Krämer, 2011). Data by the European Centre for Disease Prevention and Control (2010) and Wörmann and Krämer (2011) suggest that the incidence of TB was 52.2 per 100,000 populations in the WHO European region and 16.7 per 100,000 populations within the European Union in 2008 with higher incidence rates reported in countries such as Romania (115.1), Lithuania (66.8), Latvia (47.1), Bulgaria (41.2) and Estonia (33.1). Overall, the proportion of all TB cases accounted for by migrant populations in the European Economic Area averaged 22.4%. However, this figure was higher for many European countries, ranging from 20% to 40% for the Czech Republic, Greece, Ireland, Slovenia and Spain; 30% to 40% for Belgium, France, Germany and Italy, 60–70% for Denmark, Iceland, the Netherlands and the United Kingdom, and more than 70% for Cyprus, Malta, Norway and Sweden.

**HIV/AIDS:** In the case of south–north migration, Schulden *et al.* (2014) undertook a study on HIV among migrant populations in five US states. The study involved rapid HIV testing between 2005 and 2007, and a total of 5,247 persons were tested. The prevalence of HIV-positive cases was 0.1%, suggesting very low HIV infection rates. These low rates occurred despite participants reporting a relatively high frequency of self-reported HIV/STD risk behaviours, characterised by having two or more sex partners (45%), having sex while intoxicated (30%) and transactional sex (29%). This pattern of high HIV/STD risk behaviours and low HIV infection rate (<1%) is consistent with other studies (European Centre for Disease Prevention and Control/WHO Regional Office for Europe, 2010; Madeddu et al., 2007; Wörmann and Krämer, 2011). However, a higher prevalence has been reported among migrants in Spain. In a study of 8,861 subjects of whom 2,810 (31.7%) were migrants, Castilla and colleagues (2002) reported an overall HIV prevalence of 1.8%, but the prevalence was significantly higher among migrants from SSA (men: 9.1%, women: 7.5%, all: 8.4%) and migrant men from Latin America (men: 11.3%, women: 0.3%) than Spanish-born nationals (men: 2.3%, women: 1.0%, all: 1.8%). Because of the rigorous pre-migration medical checks, most of the prevalence of HIV among migrants is low on arrival, but the post-migration incidence is higher than that of the host populations (Pezzoli et al., 2009). For example, the proportion of new HIV infections among migrants in Italy increased from 2.4% in 1997–2000 to 17.6% in 2001–2004 (Madeddu et al., 2007). The number of new HIV cases tends to be significantly higher among migrants from SSA than migrants from other regions, with 8.3% and 16.2% of all reported new HIV cases in 2009 in the WHO European Region and European Union respectively originating from SSA (European Centre for Disease Prevention and Control/WHO Regional Office for Europe, 2010). Nevertheless, as Wörmann and Krämer (2011) argue, the extent to which migration has impacted on the overall burden of HIV/AIDS in host countries is not entirely clear.

**Hepatitis:** Liu et al. (2014) studied chronic Hepatitis B virus (HBV) infection among foreign-born persons from six population-based surveillance sites in the USA between 2001 and 2010. They found that chronic HBV was 9.2 times more prevalent among foreign-born persons than the US-born population. Data from US national surveys indicate that the prevalence of HBV among migrants is 5.6 times higher than that found among the US-born population (Wasley et al., 2010). Overall, the prevalence of hepatitis B core antigen (anti-HBc), which is a measure of acute HBV infection, 12.2% among foreign-born participants which is significantly higher than the 3.5% reported among their US-born counterparts. Among Somali migrants to Minnesota, the prevalence of HBV infection is 10 times that found in the baseline population (Shire *et al.*, 2012). Meta-analyses of European data and systematic reviews indicate that 53–77% of chronic HBV infections are found among migrants born outside the European Union and the prevalence is significantly higher among migrants from Asia and SSA (Marschall *et al.*, 2008; Rossi *et al.*, 2012).

The prevalence of hepatitis C virus (HCV) infection is also a serious problem among migrant populations, estimated at 9.9% and 6.6% among African migrant males and females in the USA, respectively (Shire *et al.*, 2012). In Europe, the prevalence of HCV infection varies between 0.4% and 5.2% in the general population and up to 23.4% in migrant populations (Hahné *et al.*, 2013). These results suggest that the prevalence of HCV infection in migrant populations is more than two times higher than that in the general population. Migration-related inequalities have also been reported for hepatitis A and hepatitis E virus infections with their prevalence significantly higher among migrants than the host population (Wörmann and Krämer, 2011).

## *Non-communicable diseases*

Non-communicable chronic diseases are diverse and can be classified into two groups: (1) life-threatening diseases including cardiovascular and cerebrovascular diseases and associated major modifiable risk factors such as hypertension, smoking, obesity and diabetes; cancer, diseases of the thyroid, Crohn's disease and mental health disorders; and (2) non-life threatening diseases including chronic respiratory diseases such as asthma, back pain, allergies, ulcers and diseases of the joints such as arthritis, and nutrition deficiencies such as vitamin deficiencies. This chapter does not intend to review all these diseases due to limited data in the literature. We focus on the most important diseases for which data are available.

**Cardiovascular diseases:** Most of the life-threatening chronic diseases have four common features that determine their relevance among migrants: ethnicity and genetic predisposition (i.e. a pre-migration risk), food habits (e.g. pre-migration dietary habits and post-migration dietary acculturation), lifestyle such as physical activity and sedentary behaviours, and stress (i.e. migration-related acculturative stress). For example, whether living in their country of birth or not, South Asian migrants in the USA, Canada and Europe have coronary artery disease risks and coronary artery disease mortality rates that are two to three times higher than that of their Caucasian counterparts, irrespective of gender, religion, social class or dietary practices (Boon et al., 2015; Dodani, 2008; Tan et al., 2014). A study looking at the risk of hospitalisation for ischaemic heart disease among Asian-Americans in Northern California reported age-adjusted hospitalisation rates for South Asian men that were two to four times higher than that of their White counterparts. The study found that among men aged 45–59 years, rates per 1,000 person-years were 5.6 for Whites, 2.9 for Chinese and 21.9 for South Asians; and 16.0 for Whites, 8.3 for Chinese and 34.7 for South Asians among men aged 60 years or older (Klatsky et al., 1994). Studies from Canada have consistently reported that South Asian migrants have higher rates of cardiovascular diseases compared to other migrants or the host population, with a prevalence of 11% comparing unfavourably with 5% and 2% reported among Caucasian and Chinese migrants, respectively (Anand et al., 2000). South Asian migrants have premature heart diseases causing them to die at a younger age compared to the host population. Whether living in their country of birth or as migrants in other countries, South Asians have 40–60% higher mortality rates from coronary heart disease than native populations in OECD countries (Boon et al., 2015; Forouhi et al., 2006; McKeigue et al., 1991, 1993; Turin et al., 2013).

Although many studies have hypothesised that the metabolic syndrome (central obesity, insulin resistance, type-2 diabetes and dyslipidaemia), which is increasingly common among South Asians, may explain the increased risk for coronary artery diseases in this sub-populations, by itself, this syndrome is not sufficient to adequately explain the observed excess coronary artery disease risk (Boon et al., 2015; Dodani, 2008). Emerging evidence to explain the disadvantageous metabolic phenotype among South Asians points the finger at non-classical risk factors which are higher among South Asian migrants than Caucasians (Boon et al., 2015; Dodani, 2008). These include a lower amount of brown adipose tissue which results in lower energy expenditure, lower lipid oxidation and glucose uptake as well as a high prevalence of inflammatory risk factors including visceral adipose tissue inflammation, endothelial dysfunction and high-density lipoprotein dysfunction (Boon et al., 2015; Dodani, 2008). Apart from South Asian migrants, the trend of cardiovascular diseases has varied considerably among migrants from other regions. In the Netherlands for example, compared to the native Dutch population, all-cause cardiovascular mortality was 49% and 17% lower among Moroccan and Antillean/Aruban male migrants, respectively, and 13% higher among Surinamese male migrants. Among female migrants, the mortality was 14% higher among Surinamese migrants, and although not statically significant 13% and 15% lower among Turkish and Moroccan migrants, respectively (Bos et al., 2004). Similar ethnic differences in cardiovascular disease mortality have been reported in Spain, with lower mortality reported among migrants from northern Africa and southern America, and higher mortality among migrants from Asia, the Caribbean and SSA (Regidor et al., 2009).

**Hypertension and stroke:** Hypertension remains a serious issue among migrant populations and varies by ethnicity. The prevalence of hypertension among South Asian migrants has been estimated at 37% among 35–60-year-olds in the UK which is significantly higher than the corresponding figure of 22% reported among their Caucasian counterparts (Chambers et al., 2001). Among South Asian migrants to the USA, the prevalence of hypertension has been estimated at 35.6% (Misra et al., 2010). Given that hypertension is a significant risk factor for stroke, it contributes to the high risk for stroke among many migrant groups. In the UK, rate ratios for stroke mortality remain higher for migrants (Harding et al., 2008). In the Netherlands, compared with Dutch-born people, the incidence of stroke is lower among Moroccan migrants but higher in Surinamese migrants and similar for Turkish migrants (Agyemang et al., 2014). In Sweden, no difference in the incidence of stroke was found between Swedish-born and migrant women (4.7% vs. 4.5%) (Nayak et al., 2014).

**Cancers:** In general, migrants have a lower incidence and prevalence of major cancers than the host population in OECD countries, but this health advantage varies according to the type of cancers and migrants' country of birth. For example, in the USA, Japanese migrants in Hawaii were found to have lower rates of stomach, oesophageal, pancreatic, liver and cervical cancers, but higher rates for all other cancers, compared to the Caucasians in Hawaii (Maskarinec and Noh, 2004). In Australia, compared to the Australian-born population, migrants have a lower prevalence of colon, prostate, lung and breast cancers, but a higher prevalence of bladder and nasopharyngeal cancers (Anikeeva et al., 2010). While some studies have found migrants to have elevated risks for stomach and liver cancers (Stirbu et al., 2006) and cancers of the respiratory system, lymphoid, hematopoietic and related tissue (Hemminki et al., 2002; Spallek et al., 2009), overall migrants in most OECD countries have consistently been found to have lower incidence rates for skin cancer (Spallek et al., 2009; Supramaniam et al., 2008; Visser and Van Leeuwen, 2007), cancer of the genital organs including testicular, gynaecological, ovarian and cervical cancers (Azerkan et al., 2008; Spallek et al., 2009; Visser and Van Leeuwen, 2007), cancer of the digestive system and the urinary tract (Spallek et al., 2009; Wild et al., 2006), and breast cancer (Hemminki et al., 2002; Spallek et al., 2009; Stirbu et al., 2006; Visser and Van Leeuwen, 2007) than the host population. In Sweden, Azerkan et al. (2008) found that compared to the native Swedish, the relative risk of cervical cancer was higher among migrants from high-income countries such as those from Denmark and Norway, and lower among migrants from LMICs such as those from eastern Africa, south-central Asia, and south-western Asia. However, the incidence and prevalence of cancers among migrants need to be interpreted with caution because they are under-represented in research and the majority of studies are based on cancer registries. Available evidence suggests that the rate of cancer screening is 30–60% lower among migrants than the host population (Weber et al., 2009).

In terms of mortality, most available evidence suggests that all-cancer mortality rates are 20% to 60% lower among migrants than the host population in OECD countries (Kunst et al., 2011; Stirbu et al., 2006; Visser and Van Leeuwen, 2007), but cancer mortality patterns vary by type of cancers and country of birth. For example, in the Netherlands, all-cancer mortality is 37% and 53% lower among Turkish, 53% and 61% lower among Moroccan, 38% and 42% lower among Surinamese, and 17% and 34% lower among Antillean/Aruban male and female migrants, respectively, when compared to native Dutch (Bos et al., 2004). In

England, all cancer mortality rates have been reported to be higher among people born in Scotland and Ireland, but lower among migrants from LMICs such as those from Bangladesh, India, Pakistan or China, West Africa and the West Indies (Wild *et al.*, 2006). In Australia, compared to the Australian-born population, migrants have higher mortality rates of stomach, lung and bladder cancers, but lower mortality for colorectal cancer and melanoma, with the greatest advantage found among migrants from southern Europe, south-eastern Europe, Chinese Asia and southern Asia (Anikeeva *et al.*, 2012). In France, North African migrant populations have been found to have an overall higher mortality from cancer of the nasopharynx, gall bladder and bladder but lower mortality from melanoma, cancer of the oral cavity, pharynx, oesophagus, stomach, colon, rectum, lung, larynx, kidney, nervous system, breast, ovary and cervix uteri (Bouchardy *et al.*, 1996).

**Type-2 diabetes:** The burden of type-2 diabetes (T2DM) is significantly higher among migrant populations than the host population in OECD countries with a prevalence that is two times higher and diabetes-related mortality three to four times higher than that of native populations (Deboosere, 2005; Kunst *et al.*, 2011). While the prevalence of T2DM among migrant populations varies by ethnicity, migrants from south Asia and SSA remain among the most affected, with a prevalence of T2DM of 15–30%, which compares unfavourably with a prevalence of less than 10% in most OECD countries (Chambers *et al.*, 2001; Ruwanpathirana *et al.*, 2014; Saleh *et al.*, 2002). South Asian migrants have a three- to four-fold increased risk of developing T2DM, which develops 10 years earlier than in Europeans (Chowdhury *et al.*, 2003; Mather and Keen, 1985). Misra *et al.* (2010) found that among South Asian migrants to the USA the prevalence of the metabolic syndrome was 38.2% as per the International Diabetes Federation criteria and that of T2DM was 17.4%. The prevalence of T2DM observed among south Asian migrants in the USA was significantly higher than that reported among non-Hispanic whites (7.8%), non-Hispanic blacks (13%), Hispanic Latinos (10.2%) and Native Americans/Alaskan natives (15.1%). Similarly, the prevalence of impaired fasting glucose was more than twice that reported for Mexican Americans, African-Americans and Whites. Among migrants to Canada, the risk of T2DM increased at a younger age (35–49 years) and was three- to four-fold higher among south Asian, Latin American, the Caribbean and African migrants than that found among migrants from western Europe and North America (Creatore *et al.*, 2010). Other studies have reported a prevalence of T2DM among migrants in the USA from 14% to 26%, which is significantly higher than the 7% reported among white Caucasians (Kanaya *et al.*, 2008). Migrants also have higher levels of poor diabetes management and diabetes-related complications including diabetic nephropathy and retinopathy (Mukhopadhyay *et al.*, 2006; Shaw *et al.*, 2002).

**Other non-communicable diseases:** Other non-communicable diseases and associated risk factors worth mentioning include mental health disorders, disease of the respiratory system and nutrition deficiencies. Most studies on mental health among migrants have predominantly focused on forced migrants such as refugees and asylum seekers, and not economic migrants. Nevertheless, available data suggest that suicide deaths are 20–50% lower among migrants in the Netherlands than native Dutch (Bos *et al.*, 2004). These findings are supported by data from Canada which indicate that the suicide rates among migrants are about half of those found in their Canadian-born counterparts (Malenfant, 2004). In contrast, excess suicide deaths have been reported among Indian migrants in the UK (Raleigh *et al.*, 1990). A recent systematic review examining suicide among migrants in Europe concluded that migrants from countries known to have high suicide risks such as northern and eastern European countries experience higher suicide rates than people without a migration background (Spallek *et al.*, 2015). Homicide deaths are two to three times higher among migrants in the Netherlands than the native Dutch (Bos *et al.*, 2004) and excess homicide deaths have been linked with migration-related inequalities in the USA (Krueger *et al.*, 2004; Sorenson and Shen, 1996). Other studies have reported that there is no relationship between levels of homicide and migration or migration-related processes when all other influences are controlled for (Lee *et al.*, 2001).

In terms of disease of the respiratory system, mortality has been reported to be 20–46% lower among migrants when compared to the native population in OECD countries (Bos *et al.*, 2004). Epidemiological data in Australia have reported a prevalence of up to 60% for asthma and allergic diseases, a prevalence which is higher than the national average (Leung, 1996). Due to the majority of migrants developing asthma and allergy for the first time after arriving in Australia, the author stipulates that the post-migration environment plays an important role in the pathogenesis of these conditions. These findings mirror those reported in the Netherlands (Kunst et al., 2011) but are not supported by data from Italy (Ventura et al., 2004). While the post-migration environment's role in the pathogenesis of allergic diseases was also evident in Italy, prevalence of these conditions among Albanian migrants was found to be significantly lower than that of the native Italians and Albanians back home in the country of origin (Ventura et al., 2004). Findings from the European Community Respiratory Health Survey suggest that when compared to non-migrant populations, migrants have a higher prevalence of asthma, but a similar prevalence of bronchial responsiveness, atopy and use of health services (Tobias et al., 2001). Studies on chronic obstructive pulmonary diseases (COPD) are scarce, but the few available data indicate that apart from the high prevalence of smoking among migrants, there are no differences in the prevalence and mortality patterns related to COPD between migrants and the host population in OECD countries (Kunst et al., 2011).

Nutritional deficiencies continue to account for a significant burden of disease among migrants and the most documented deficiencies include vitamin D deficiency-related diseases, iron deficiency anaemia and over-nutrition (Wandel, 1993). The prevalence of vitamin D deficiency (25OHD <50 nmol/L) among migrants varies between 23% and 92% depending on skin colour (Eggemoen et al., 2013; Renzaho et al., 2011; Tiong et al., 2006) and that of iron varies between 9% and 22% (Wandel, 1993; Morrone et al., 2012). Migrants have been found to gain weight rapidly following migration to OECD countries, recording a prevalence equal to or higher than the host population within a short span of arrival (Gele and Mbalilaki, 2013; Hervey et al., 2009; Kaplan et al., 2004; Renzaho et al., 2008, 2011).

## *Occupational diseases*

Due to difficulties and challenges associated with the recognition of overseas qualifications in OECD countries, many migrants found themselves in low-paid semi-skilled and unskilled jobs. Although most migrants have jobs, their skills are often undervalued (Arcury et al., 2012; Friberg et al., 2014). While employment rates are lower among highly educated migrants, they are comparable between low-educated migrants and natives in OECD countries. That is, migrants tend to be overqualified for their job hence more likely to be classified in the 'low skilled and low social status jobs' that are unattractive to the host population (Johnston et al., 2015; Mahmud et al., 2014; Reyneri and Fullin, 2011). Consequently, migrants are overrepresented in the manufacturing industry and dangerous jobs. However, they are neither provided with nor use job-appropriate safety mechanisms, and where such safety mechanisms exist migrants may be poorly trained in procedures which can be exacerbated by linguistic and cultural factors and adverse employment arrangements (Arcury et al., 2012; Bollini and Siem, 1995; Ronda Pérez et al., 2012; Solé et al., 2013). Nevertheless, studies in occupational diseases among migrants have produced conflicting results. In Spain for example, Solé et al. (2013) found that despite migrants' working conditions being objectively worse, they exhibited a lower probability of work-related disability than the native Spanish. Similarly, in the USA, migrants have been found to experience an agricultural injury risk of 9.3 per 100 full-time equivalent employees, which is comparable to that of non-migrant agricultural workers in other US settings (Brison and Pickett, 1992; Browning et al., 1998; McCurdy et al., 2003; Pratt et al., 1992; Zhou and Roseman, 1994). In a study examining the role of migrant factors in work-related fatalities in Australia, Corvalan et al. (1994) found that the overall fatality incidence per 100,000 person-years was 7.1 among migrants, which was similar to the fatality incidence of 6.6 reported for Australian-born persons. Interestingly though, compared with Australian-born persons, the fatality incidence increased significantly among migrants in rural and mining occupations. The mortality ratios standardised separately for occupation and age were significantly elevated among migrants from non-English speaking backgrounds who had been in Australia for less than 5 years, converging to the Australian rate with increased duration of residence. Notwithstanding the above findings, the majority of studies in OECD countries have consistently found that occupational injury rates are significantly higher among migrants than native populations (Agudelo-Suárez *et al.*, 2011).

In Norway, the incidence of injuries and exposure to physical, chemical, mechanical and psychosocial strains has been reported to be significantly higher among migrant workers than native Norwegians (Langeland, 2009). Bollini and Siem (1995) have reported higher rates of occupational accidents and disability among migrants than native workers in OECD countries. The authors note that although the types of reported accidents varied considerably, overall occupational accident rates are approximately two times higher for migrant workers than their native counterparts. Many hypotheses have been postulated to explain the higher rates of occupational injury among migrant workers. These include difficulties in employment, working conditions characterised by a high incidence of temporary work and work rotation required to juggle multiple jobs and tasks; longer working hours; harsh working conditions and physical and psychological risks; mismatches between occupation specifications and status and migrants' skills, attributes and qualifications (e.g. the pre-migration and post-migration occupation being different); and problems with workplace integration (Agudelo-Suárez *et al.*, 2011).

## *Reproductive health*

Reproduction health, especially pregnancy-related morbidity and mortality, have been widely documented among migrants. Compared to native populations, migrants have a lower rate of obstetrical interventions (David *et al.*, 2006; Schutte *et al.*, 2010) and a higher incidence of pregnancy and labour complications such as anaemia, pre-eclampsia, antepartum hospitalisations, miscarriages, induced abortions and excessive bleeding (David *et al.*, 2006; Fedeli *et al.*, 2010; van Roosmalen *et al.*, 2002), congenital malformations (David *et al.*, 2006), poor ante and post-natal care such as no prenatal care or late entry into antenatal care, postpartum sterilisation after vaginal delivery, and hospital discharge after birth without birth control (Choté *et al.*, 2011; Janevic *et al.*, 2011; Thurman *et al.*, 2009; Thurman and Janecek, 2010), postpartum depression (Eastwood *et al.*, 2011; Stewart *et al.*, 2008); perinatal death (Essén *et al.*, 2002; Roosmalen *et al.*, 2002) and maternal death (Philibert *et al.*, 2008; Ravelli *et al.*, 2010). However, some studies have suggested that in some countries migrants do not differ from native populations in terms of access to health care services during pregnancy. Such findings suggest that any differences in reproductive health outcomes are closely linked to the quality and content of antenatal care (Reeske *et al.*, 2011; Schutte *et al.*, 2010). For example, Philibert *et al.* (2008) found that compared to native French women, postpartum maternal death rates were two times higher among migrant women, and the risk of dying from hypertensive disorder and infections was four times higher for migrant women. Interestingly, the study found that migrant women who died received quality of care that was less optimal than native French women. These findings of poor quality of care for migrant women mirror those reported in the Netherlands (Schutte *et al.*, 2010; van Roosmalen *et al.*, 2002).

## Social and economic impact of voluntary migration

### The brain drain

The brain drain has become a dilemma for policymakers due to the complexity of the phenomenon. It has become an issue of intense discussion in the human rights literature and has been linked to structural and economic factors. However, the costs and benefits of the brain drain have been controversial and continues to divide opinion. Earlier researchers linked ongoing poverty and lack of economic growth in low-income countries to the brain drain (Bhagwati and Hamada, 1974). Nevertheless, more recently, researchers have pointed out that migration of skilled migrants from low- to high-income countries could benefit both sending countries through remittances and skill transfers and receiving countries through labour markets, paying tax for the public purse and economic growth (Commander *et al.*, 2004; Stark, 2004; OECD, 2014). The latest data by the United Nations Department of Economic and Social Affairs in collaboration with the OECD suggest that the number of highly educated migrants to OECD countries reached 27.3 million people in 2011, an increase of 70% over 10 years (UN-DESA & OECD, 2013). Although the proportion of all migrants settling in OECD countries who are highly educated has averaged 30%, the brain drain is highest among countries and small island states in Africa, Latin America and the Caribbean (Table 2).

**South–north brain drain:** The increase in the ageing population in most developed countries means that south–north migration will continue to dominate the literature in the next 30 years or so. For example, the proportion of the population aged 60 years or over in developed countries has increased from 12% in 1950 to 23% in 2013 and projected to reach 32% in 2050. In contrast, in most low- and middle-income countries, the proportion of older persons increased slowly, from 6% in 1950 to 9% in 2013 and is projected to reach 19% in 2050 (United Nations, 2013). The increase in the ageing population in developed countries is accompanied by a decrease in the working-age population with the population of 10–64 years estimated to decrease by almost a quarter (23%) from 741 million in 2005 to 571 million in 2050. During this same period, the 20-to-64-year-old population will more than triple in Africa (from 408 million to 1.12 billion or to 1.4 billion without migration), and increase by 40% (from 2.21 billion to 3.08 billion or to 3.12 billion without migration) in Asia and 45% (from 303 million to 404 million or to 467 million without migration) in Latin America (Szilard, 2009). These demographic trends suggest that the demand for human capital in most developed countries will increase significantly over the next 30 years. In absolute terms, south–south migration outweighs south–north migration. However, when figures are adjusted for population sizes of each region, the south–north brain drain accounts for the biggest share of the shortage of highly skilled professionals in LMICs (Table 2).

Emigration rates suggest that countries hit by poverty and who need human capital the most are among the main losers (Tables 2 and 6; Fig. 1). For example, the African continent has already lost one-third of its human capital, and the continent has been losing approximately 20,000 highly qualified professionals (doctors, university lecturers, engineers and other professionals) every year since 1990 (Brain Drain in Africa: Facts and Figures, 2014). It has been estimated that 36 (63%) out of the 57 poorest countries experiencing a critical shortage of doctors, nurses and midwives worldwide are located in the African continent (O'Brien and Gostin, 2011). In his recent book *Trade in Health: Economics, Ethics and Public Policy*, Professor David Reisman has summarised the extent of the brain drain in Africa. He notes that while South Africa lost only 14% of its highly skilled doctors between 1925 and 1975, the number increased significantly

Table 2: Emigrant population 15+ years in the OECD in 2010/11 and emigration rates of highly educated in thousands

| | Total population | | | |
|---|---|---|---|---|
| Country and region of origin | Emigrant population (in thousands) | Highly educated emigrants | Emigration rate | Emigration rate of the highly educated |
| **AFRICA** | 10,490 | 2,856 | 2.4 | 10.8 |
| Morocco | 2,630 | 392 | 9.9 | 14.6 |
| Algeria | 1,504 | 306 | 5.5 | 9.2 |
| South Africa | 540 | 281 | 1.6 | 11.6 |
| Tunisia | 507 | 94 | 5.8 | 8.9 |
| Egypt | 395 | 193 | 0.7 | 3.2 |
| Ghana | 337 | 103 | 2.2 | 14.3 |
| Kenya | 255 | 108 | 1.1 | 12.8 |
| Senegal | 248 | 48 | 3.1 | 14.0 |
| Zimbabwe | 193 | 89 | 2.3 | 43.6 |
| Democratic Republic of Congo | 190 | 60 | 0.5 | 6.5 |
| Cameroon | 159 | 66 | 1.5 | 14.7 |
| Côte d'Ivoire | 140 | 39 | 1.2 | 5.2 |
| Mauritius | 132 | 42 | 11.7 | 41.0 |
| Sudan | 97 | 31 | 0.4 | 3.0 |
| Uganda | 95 | 45 | 0.6 | 7.6 |
| **ASIA** | 26,329 | 10,436 | 0.9 | 3.3 |
| China | 3,862 | 1,655 | 0.4 | 1.8 |
| India | 3,441 | 2,080 | 0.4 | 3.2 |
| Philippines | 2,854 | 1,417 | 4.5 | 7.4 |
| Turkey | 2,550 | 251 | 4.3 | 3.7 |
| Vietnam | 1,879 | 524 | 2.8 | 10.3 |
| Republic of Korea | 1,453 | 637 | 3.4 | 3.5 |
| Pakistan | 1,088 | 378 | 1.0 | 5.5 |
| Kazakhstan | 935 | 134 | 7.4 | 6.0 |

(*Continued*)

Health, Social and Economic Impact of Voluntary Migration 141

Table 2: (*Continued*)

| Country and region of origin | Emigrant population (in thousands) | Highly educated emigrants | Emigration rate | Emigration rate of the highly educated |
|---|---|---|---|---|
| Iran, Islamic Rep. of | 845 | 424 | 1.5 | 4.0 |
| Japan | 660 | 371 | 0.6 | 0.9 |
| Iraq | 555 | 151 | 2.7 | 6.1 |
| Sri Lanka | 553 | 168 | 3.2 | 5.7 |
| Bangladesh | 528 | 179 | 0.5 | 3.2 |
| Thailand | 515 | 153 | 1.0 | 2.6 |
| Afghanistan | 347 | 71 | 1.8 | 4.8 |
| **EUROPE** | 32,759 | 9,270 | 5.0 | 5.3 |
| UK and Northern Ireland | 3,505 | 1,384 | 6.5 | 10.8 |
| Poland | 3,195 | 884 | 8.9 | 15.5 |
| Germany | 3,162 | 1,168 | 4.2 | 8.4 |
| Romania | 2,643 | 483 | 12.7 | 18.4 |
| Italy | 2,309 | 401 | 4.4 | 7.9 |
| Russian Federation | 1,953 | 660 | 1.6 | 1.0 |
| Portugal | 1,492 | 147 | 14.2 | 12.9 |
| France | 1,291 | 573 | 2.5 | 5.3 |
| Ukraine | 1,136 | 433 | 2.9 | 2.8 |
| Albania | 977 | 82 | 28.7 | 26.7 |
| Spain | 738 | 212 | 1.9 | 2.3 |
| Netherlands | 728 | 284 | 5.0 | 8.3 |
| Ireland | 679 | 227 | 16.1 | 17.4 |
| Greece | 655 | 143 | 6.4 | 5.8 |
| Serbia | 562 | 61 | 6.1 | 6.1 |
| **Northern America** | 2,406 | 1,164 | 0.9 | 0.8 |
| United States of America | 1,224 | 590 | 0.5 | 0.5 |
| Canada | 1,163 | 566 | 3.9 | 5.4 |

(*Continued*)

Table 2: (Continued)

| Country and region of origin | Emigrant population (in thousands) | Highly educated emigrants | Emigration rate | Emigration rate of the highly educated |
|---|---|---|---|---|
| **Oceania** | 1,314 | 422 | 4.4 | 4.8 |
| New Zealand | 538 | 164 | 13.9 | 8.8 |
| Australia | 317 | 157 | 1.8 | 2.6 |
| Fiji | 159 | 46 | 20.5 | 31.3 |
| Tonga | 46 | 6 | 40.9 | 44.1 |
| Papua New Guinea | 29 | 11 | 0.7 | 17.9 |
| **Latin America & The Caribbean** | 25,837 | 4,399 | 5.7 | 7.4 |
| Mexico | 11,249 | 867 | 12.1 | 6.0 |
| El Salvador | 1,228 | 125 | 19.5 | 19.6 |
| Colombia | 1,217 | 365 | 3.4 | 10.5 |
| Cuba | 1,205 | 345 | 11.4 | 20.2 |
| Ecuador | 1,140 | 160 | 10.3 | 8.3 |
| Brazil | 998 | 267 | 0.7 | 2.4 |
| Dominican Republic | 996 | 168 | 12.6 | 11.9 |
| Jamaica | 920 | 272 | 32.3 | 46.3 |
| Peru | 833 | 252 | 3.8 | 5.3 |
| Guatemala | 807 | 79 | 8.9 | 17.2 |
| Haiti | 665 | 157 | 10.2 | 73.9 |
| Argentina | 583 | 223 | 1.9 | 5.6 |
| Honduras | 523 | 62 | 9.3 | 13.8 |
| Venezuela (Bolivarian Republic of) | 419 | 200 | 2.0 | 4.0 |
| Guyana | 354 | 109 | 39.4 | 92.7 |

Extracted from UN-DESA & OECD (2013).

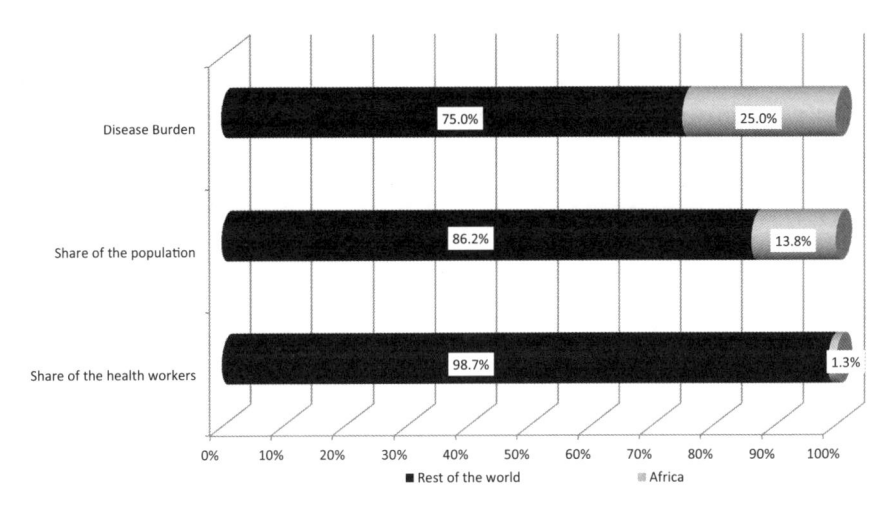

Health, Social and Economic Impact of Voluntary Migration 143

[Figure: horizontal bar chart showing Disease Burden: Rest of world 75.0%, Africa 25.0%; Share of the population: Rest of world 86.2%, Africa 13.8%; Share of the health workers: Rest of world 98.7%, Africa 1.3%]

**Figure 1: Burden of disease, share of population and share of health workers, Africa and rest of world.**
*Source*: Packer *et al.* (2009).

post-1960s with 44–47% of South African-trained doctors between 1960s and the 1990s residing outside the country. Similarly, more than half (61%) of doctors trained in Ghana between 1986 and 1995, 56% of Kenyan-trained doctors and 43% of Liberian doctors practice abroad. Approximately one in three (30%) and one in four (25%) doctors trained in Ghana and Uganda respectively work in Canada and the USA. Overall, the proportion of doctors trained and registered in SSA practicing outside the continent has been estimated between 6% and 10% in the USA and 6% in the UK, averaging 23% in OECD countries which equates to more than 12% of doctor shortfall in the African continent (Reisman, 2014). The nursing sector has also been severely affected with more than 11% of nurses practicing in the USA being foreign-born, 80% of whom are from LMICs (Adkoli, 2006).

Tankwanchi *et al.* (2013) found that in terms of the number of physicians per 100,000 people, there has been a negative growth in Africa, but a positive growth in most OECD countries since the 1970s. Over four decades (i.e. between the 1970s and mid-2010s), the physician-to-patient ratio decreased significantly in SSA, decreasing by 17.0% in Senegal and 87.1% in Liberia. Ironically, during the same period, most

OECD countries recorded a two- to six-fold increase in physician coverage (Table 3). A total of 17,376 physicians practising in the USA were born or trained in Africa, of whom 62.3% were either born or trained in 28 countries from SSA and 37.7% were born in North Africa (Table 4). Of the 10,819 physicians from SSA, 7,370 (68%) were trained in SSA medical schools, 2,126 (20%) were US-trained and 1,323 (12%) were trained outside both SSA and the USA. Over a 10-year period (2001–2011), emigration trends of SSA-trained doctors increased for all countries except South Africa, which experienced a decrease of 8%. During this period, the number of doctors from Nigeria (+1,113) and Ghana (+243) increased by more than 50%, while those from Ethiopia (+274) and Sudan (+244) more than doubled (Tankwanchi et al., 2013). Similarly, Clemens and Pettersson (2008) conducted a study to estimate the number of SSA-born doctors and professional nurses working abroad circa 2000. The data suggest that the percentage of doctors and nurses born in SSA appearing in a census of nine receiving OECD countries averaged 28% and 11%, respectively. However, 16 out of 48 African countries (33.3%) lost more than 50% of their trained doctors to foreign countries. In order of magnitude, these countries were Mozambique (75.4%), Guinea Bissau (70.9%), Angola (70.5%), Equatorial Guinea (63.3%), Liberia (63.3), Sao Tome & Principe (60.6%), Malawi (59.4%), Zambia (56.9%), Ghana (55.9%), Gambia (53.5%), Republic of Congo (52.7%), Tanzania (51.8%), Senegal (51.4%), Zimbabwe (51.1%), Cape Verde (51.1%) and Kenya (50.8%). As a share of doctors emigrating abroad, the top five destinations for emigrating doctors were Britain (13,350 or 36.4%), USA (8,558 or 23.3%), France (4,199 or 11.5%), Portugal (3,847 or 10.5%) and Canada (2,800 or 7.6%). When all professions are taken into account, the problem is more acute with approximately 40% of doctors, teachers, engineers, technicians and managers departing from the continent's shores (Owolabi and Rafiu, 2010).

Other regions of the world have also been affected by the brain drain. Data from Bangladesh indicate that about 6.57 million citizens left the country to work abroad between 1976 and 2008. Of these, 50% were unskilled, including household workers, agricultural workers, hotel and cleaning staff, 31% were skilled, such as production workers and computer operators, 16% were semi-skilled, such as tailors and masons, and 4% were

Health, Social and Economic Impact of Voluntary Migration  145

Table 3: Changes in physician-to-population ratios (density) and medical schools in selected African and non-African countries ranked by change in physician density (5)

| Country | Circa 1970 Population (in thousands) | No. of physicians | Physicians/ 100,000 people | No. of medical schools | Circa 2010 Population (in thousands) | No. of physicians | Physicians/ 100,000 people | No. of medical schools | Change over time Physician density (absolute) | Physician density (%) | No. of medical schools |
|---|---|---|---|---|---|---|---|---|---|---|---|
| Liberia | 1,397 | 132 | 9.4 | 1 | 4,190 | 51 | 1.2 | 1 | −8.2 | −87.2 | 0 |
| Tanzania | 14,354 | 576 | 4.0 | 1 | 47,783 | 300 | 0.6 | 5 | −3.4 | −85.0 | 4 |
| Zimbabwe | 5,515 | 1,035 | 18.8 | 1 | 13,724 | 827 | 6.0 | 1 | −12.8 | −68.1 | 0 |
| Mozambique | 9,304 | 510 | 5.5 | 1 | 25,203 | 548 | 2.2 | 4 | −3.3 | −60.0 | 3 |
| Sierra Leone | 2,789 | 149 | 5.3 | 0 | 5,979 | 136 | 2.3 | 1 | −3.0 | −56.6 | 1 |
| Zambia | 4,248 | 527 | 12.4 | 1 | 14,075 | 836 | 5.9 | 1 | −6.5 | −52.4 | 0 |
| Somalia | 3,667 | 193 | 5.3 | 1 | 10,195 | 300 | 2.9 | 2 | −2.4 | −45.3 | 1 |
| Djibouti | 180 | 52 | 28.9 | 0 | 906 | 185 | 20.4 | 1 | −8.5 | −29.4 | 1 |
| Congo | 1,272 | 163 | 12.8 | 1 | 4,337 | 401 | 9.2 | 1 | −3.6 | −28.1 | 0 |
| Niger | 4,841 | 109 | 2.3 | 1 | 17,157 | 288 | 1.7 | 1 | −0.6 | −26.1 | 0 |
| Ghana | 8,789 | 856 | 9.7 | 2 | 25,366 | 2,033 | 8.0 | 4 | −1.7 | −17.5 | 2 |
| Senegal | 4,318 | 281 | 6.5 | 1 | 13,726 | 741 | 5.4 | 4 | −1.1 | −16.9 | 3 |
| Guinea Bissau | 620 | 55 | 8.9 | 0 | 1,664 | 124 | 7.5 | 1 | −1.4 | −15.7 | 1 |
| Lesotho | 1,067 | 50 | 4.7 | 0 | 2,052 | 89 | 4.3 | 0 | −0.4 | −8.5 | 0 |
| Togo | 1,964 | 95 | 4.8 | 1 | 6,643 | 349 | 5.3 | 1 | 0.5 | 10.4 | 0 |
| Swaziland | 455 | 54 | 11.9 | 0 | 1,231 | 173 | 14.1 | 0 | 2.2 | 18.5 | 0 |

(Continued)

## Table 3: (Continued)

| Country | Population (in thousands) | Circa 1970 No. of physicians | Physicians/ 100,000 people | No. of medical schools | Population (in thousands) | Circa 2010 No. of physicians | Physicians/ 100,000 people | No. of medical schools | Physician density (absolute) | Change over time Physician density (%) | No. of medical schools |
|---|---|---|---|---|---|---|---|---|---|---|---|
| South Africa | 22,740 | 12,060 | 53.0 | 7 | 52,386 | 38,236 | 73.0 | 8 | 20.0 | 37.7 | 1 |
| Ethiopia | 29,469 | 374 | 1.3 | 2 | 91,729 | 2,152 | 2.3 | 12 | 1.0 | 76.9 | 10 |
| Angola | 5,606 | 383 | 6.8 | 1 | 20,821 | 2,946 | 14.1 | 7 | 7.3 | 107.4 | 6 |
| Rwanda | 3,769 | 77 | 2.0 | 1 | 11,458 | 568 | 5.0 | 1 | 3.0 | 150.0 | 0 |
| Gambia | 485 | 19 | 3.9 | 1 | 1,791 | 175 | 9.8 | 1 | 5.9 | 151.3 | 0 |
| Niger | 59,607 | 2,343 | 3.9 | 12 | 169,000 | 55,376 | 32.8 | 25 | 28.9 | 741.0 | 13 |
| SSA | 287,856 | 25,504 | 8.9 | 53 | 913,302 | 150,305 | 16.5 | 109 | 7.6 | 85.4 | 56 |
| Canada | 22,479 | 37,277 | 165.8 | 16 | 34,838 | 69,699 | 200.1 | 17 | 34.3 | 20.7 | 1 |
| Brazil | 58,854 | 59,573 | 101.2 | 77 | 199,000 | 341,849 | 171.8 | 90 | 70.6 | 69.8 | 13 |
| USA | 211,909 | 338,111 | 159.6 | 126 | 318,000 | 909,749 | 286.1 | 147 | 126.5 | 79.3 | 21 |
| UK | 55,968 | 75,141 | 134.3 | 26 | 62,783 | 172,553 | 274.8 | 33 | 140.5 | 104.6 | 7 |
| Belgium | 9,757 | 16,476 | 168.9 | 7 | 11,090 | 39,690 | 357.9 | 11 | 189.0 | 111.9 | 4 |
| Australia | 12,959 | 17,972 | 138.7 | 8 | 23,050 | 81,639 | 354.2 | 21 | 215.5 | 155.4 | 13 |
| South Korea | 32,905 | 16,377 | 49.8 | 19 | 49,003 | 98,293 | 200.6 | 52 | 150.8 | 302.8 | 33 |
| Cuba | 8,074 | 7,000 | 86.7 | 7 | 11,271 | 76,506 | 678.8 | 14 | 592.1 | 682.9 | 7 |

*Source*: Extracted from Tankwanchi et al. (2013).

Table 4: African-origin physicians appearing in the US physician workforce in 2011

| Location of medial school of training | Africa | Americas | Asia Pacific | Europe | Sub-total |
|---|---|---|---|---|---|
| SSA | 7,370 | — | — | — | 7,370 |
| USA | — | 2,126 | — | — | 2,126 |
| India | — | — | 420 | — | 420 |
| Caribbean | — | 254 | — | — | 254 |
| Euro zone | — | — | — | 168 | 168 |
| UK | — | — | — | 154 | 154 |
| Middle East | — | — | 79 | — | 79 |
| Other | 28 | 70 | 23 | 127 | 248 |
| Sub-total sub-Saharan | 7,398 | 2,450 | 522 | 449 | 10,819 |
| North Africa | 6557 | — | — | — | 6,557 |
| Total | 13,955 | 2,450 | 522 | 449 | 17,376 |

*Source*: Extracted from Tankwanchi *et al.* (2013).

professionals, such as doctors, engineers, teachers and nurses (Naim and Iftikhar, 2008). Similarly, the number of Pakistanis who were skilled professionals and living outside the country was estimated at 7 million in 2008, of whom more than 4 million have a legal status in the host country while the rest are non-registered migrants including graduating students overstaying their visa (Naim and Iftikhar, 2008). The evidence suggests that of all doctors trained in Asia and practicing in OECD countries in 2006, 12.8% were Malaysian, 10.2% were Singaporean, 9.7% were Filipino and 3.3% were Thai (Reisman, 2014). Half of the approximately 5,000 Pakistani doctors graduating each year and more than two-thirds of Jamaican-trained nurses leave their respective countries to work abroad. Of all the nurses practicing in the USA, 14% are Filipino, two-thirds are Bangladeshi and 25% are Sri Lankan (Reisman, 2014). Adkoli (2006)'s data on the brain drain in south-east Asia are compelling. By 2006, the number of Indian doctors in the USA had exceeded 50,000, which was the largest group of physicians after native-born American doctors translating favourably into a doctor–patient ratio of one. India has also been one of the leading exporters of doctors to the UK; for example in 2006, around 30% of doctors in the UK National Health Service were found to be Indians with the majority being specialists including anaesthetists, radiologists and psychiatrists. Of the 302 Sri Lankan postgraduate medical trainees qualifying between 1993 and 1996, 13% left the country, a proportion that increased to 28% (146/524) between 1997 and 2000. In Bangladesh, 65% of newly graduated doctors attempt to get jobs abroad, while an average of 200 doctors from the government sector leave the country every year. Asian doctors working in OECD countries represent approximately 9% of doctor shortfall in south-east Asia (Reisman, 2014).

**South–south brain drain:** However, there seems to be a misconception that the south–south migration is characterised by the movement of unskilled refugees. That is not the case. For example, contrary to popular myths that the majority of migrants relocate to developed countries, south–south migration accounts for the greatest share of African migration (Fig. 2). The intra-African emigration rate for SSA is estimated at 65%, which represents the largest south–south migration (Shimeles, 2010). Significant intra-African migration has been recorded across all regions in SSA, however, it clusters around neighbouring countries. For example, Tanzania and Kenya receive a high number of migrants from east

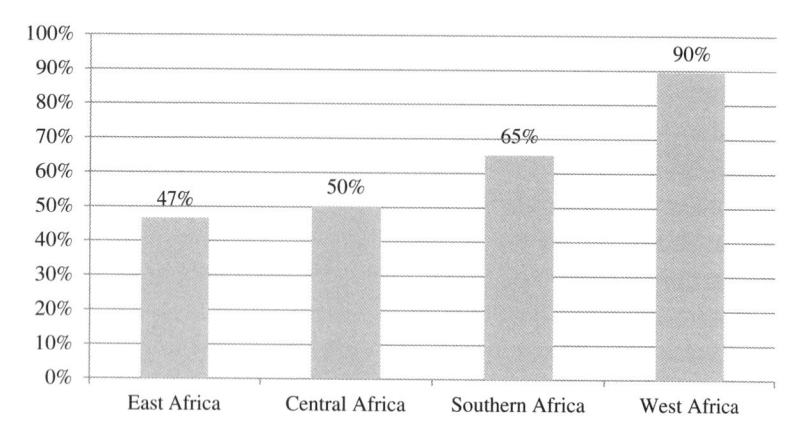

**Figure 2:** Percentage of migration taking place within SSA (intra-continental migration).
*Source*: Figure constructed using data extracted from Shimeles (2010).

and central Africa while Sudan is the preferred destination for migrants from Chad, Eritrea and Ethiopia, Nigeria is a hub for migrants from Ghana, Niger and Benin, and South Africa is the preferred destination for migrants from Botswana, Lesotho, Swaziland and Mozambique, as well as migrants from east and central Africa (Shimeles, 2010). As can be seen from Figure 1A, in western Africa region, Southern Africa, Central Africa and East Africa, 90%, 65%, 50% and 47% of intra-African migration took place within the same sub-regions respectively.

Similarly, in 2005, 50% of migrants residing in the Caribbean region originated from other Caribbean countries, the main sending country being Haiti with 71.5% of its 122,000 emigrant stock residing in the Dominican Republic (IOM & ACP Observatory on Migration, 2010). Approximately 33% of Guyanese intra-Caribbean migrants reside in Trinidad and a further 45% reside in Antigua, Barbuda and Barbados. The intra-Caribbean migration is characterised by population flows towards island-states of the English-speaking Caribbean with a high human development index, predominantly highly skilled and semi-skilled migrants including university graduates, artists, musicians, media workers, sportspersons, teachers, nurses, artisans and household domestic workers with a Caribbean vocational qualification (IOM & ACP Observatory on Migration, 2010). However, the Caribbean region has a number of policies that facilitate the intra-regional free movement of skilled migrants and support the management of labour migration such as the 1989 Caribbean Free Movement Protocol, the Caribbean Single Market Economy and the Caribbean Vocation Qualification framework which is a regional system harmonising skills evaluation of Caribbean workers based on agreed occupational standards (IOM & ACP Observatory on Migration, 2010). These policies serve the majority of the Caribbean countries with 12 out of the 16 African, Caribbean and Pacific Group of States being full members of both the Caribbean Community and the Caribbean Single Market Economy, and allow a "Hassle-Free travel" within the region without a passport (IOM & ACP Observatory on Migration, 2010).

South–south migration of skilled and semiskilled people is also extremely prevalent in Asia and the Middle East (Fiddian-Qasmiyeh, 2015). Over decades, Chinese and Indians have migrated to Africa and the Middle East while more recently Africans are increasingly moving to China, Latin

America, the Middle East and the Caribbean. For example, it has been estimated that the Gulf States employ more than 20,000 doctors, the majority of whom are from the Indian subcontinent (Adkoli, 2006). More than three-quarters (80%) of Bangladeshi doctors leaving the country to work abroad are in the Middle East while the number of Bangladeshi nurses working in the Middle East is far greater than those practicing at home (Siddiqui and Parvin, 2012). Of the 4 million Pakistanis working outside the country in 2008, 47.6% resided in the Middle East, and 2.8% worked in Asia and Africa and the rest in Europe, the USA, Australia and New Zealand (Naim and Iftikhar, 2008).

However, intra-regional migration of highly skilled people has had some devastating effects in SSA. For example, as South Africa loses its doctors to OECD countries, it aggressively recruits doctors across SSA to fill the shortage (Table 5). In addition, Shinn (2008) notes that even countries like the Democratic Republic of Congo which is burdened by wars and ethnic conflicts and is in desperate need of medical staff, managed to offer its doctors to Zimbabwe, while Tanzania and South Africa sent their nurses and doctors to Swaziland. Both Zimbabwe and Swaziland are among the countries in SSA who are losing a significant share of their health workers to OECD countries and to HIV/AIDS (Shinn, 2008). Our re-analysis of Clemens and Pettersson (2008) found that in 2000, the 1,434 foreign doctors working in South Africa represented 1.1% of all doctors born in SSA, 3.9% of SSA-born doctors working abroad and 5.2% of the South African medical workforce (Table 5). In absolute number of doctors born in SSA emigrating abroad, the top 10 countries supplying the majority of foreign doctors to South Africa are Zimbabwe, Namibia, Zambia, Nigeria, Uganda, the Democratic Republic of Congo, Republic of Congo, Ghana, Kenya and Mozambique. Regarding the training country's contribution towards the national supply of doctors, some countries are more affected than others with more than one in four doctors trained in Namibia (34.3%) and Lesotho (28.7%), and more than one in five doctors trained in Swaziland (23.7%) and Zimbabwe (20.5%) emigrating to South Africa (Table 5). The nursing profession followed a similar pattern but not as pronounced as the pattern observed among doctors.

Table 5: African doctors' emigration abroad and to South Africa in 2000

| Country | National stock | Domestic | Abroad | % Abroad | Number | as a % of stock in country of origin | as a % of those practicing abroad |
|---|---|---|---|---|---|---|---|
| Angola | 2,983 | 881 | 2,102 | 70.5 | 31 | 1.0 | 1.5 |
| Benin | 629 | 405 | 224 | 35.6 | 0 | 0.0 | 0.0 |
| Botswana | 598 | 530 | 68 | 11.4 | 26 | 4.3 | 38.2 |
| Burkina Faso | 392 | 314 | 78 | 19.9 | 0 | 0.0 | 0.0 |
| Burundi | 366 | 230 | 136 | 37.2 | 9 | 2.5 | 6.6 |
| Cameroon | 1,852 | 1,007 | 845 | 45.6 | 3 | 0.2 | 0.4 |
| Cape Verde | 413 | 202 | 211 | 51.1 | 0 | 0.0 | 0.0 |
| Cent. Afr. Rep. | 207 | 120 | 87 | 42.0 | 0 | 0.0 | 0.0 |
| Chad | 318 | 248 | 70 | 22.0 | 0 | 0.0 | 0.0 |
| Comoros | 74 | 50 | 24 | 32.4 | 3 | 4.1 | 12.5 |
| Congo, DR | 6,199 | 5,647 | 552 | 8.9 | 98 | 1.6 | 17.8 |
| Congo Rep | 1,417 | 670 | 747 | 52.7 | 135 | 9.5 | 18.1 |
| Cote d' Ivoire | 2,047 | 1,763 | 284 | 13.9 | 3 | 0.1 | 1.1 |
| Djibouti | 112 | 86 | 26 | 23.2 | 0 | 0.0 | 0.0 |
| Equatorial Guinea | 128 | 47 | 81 | 63.3 | 0 | 0.0 | 0.0 |
| Eritrea | 271 | 173 | 98 | 36.2 | 0 | 0.0 | 0.0 |
| Ethiopia | 1,863 | 1,310 | 553 | 29.7 | 9 | 0.5 | 1.6 |
| Gabon | 433 | 368 | 65 | 15.0 | 0 | 0.0 | 0.0 |
| Gambia | 86 | 40 | 46 | 53.5 | 0 | 0.0 | 0.0 |
| Ghana | 2,933 | 1,294 | 1,639 | 55.9 | 82 | 2.8 | 5.0 |
| Guinea | 1,013 | 898 | 115 | 11.4 | 0 | 0.0 | 0.0 |
| Guinea Bissau | 354 | 103 | 251 | 70.9 | 0 | 0.0 | 0.0 |
| Kenya | 7,830 | 3,855 | 3,975 | 50.8 | 81 | 1.0 | 2.0 |
| Lesotho | 171 | 114 | 57 | 33.3 | 49 | 28.7 | 86.0 |
| Liberia | 199 | 73 | 126 | 63.3 | 0 | 0.0 | 0.0 |

(Continued)

**Table 5:** (*Continued*)

|  | Number of doctors ||||Supply to south Africa |||
| --- | --- | --- | --- | --- | --- | --- | --- |
| Country | National stock | Domestic | Abroad | % Abroad | Number | as a % of stock in country of origin | as a % of those practicing abroad |
| Madagascar | 2,348 | 1,428 | 920 | 39.2 | 0 | 0.0 | 0.0 |
| Malawi | 493 | 200 | 293 | 59.4 | 48 | 9.7 | 16.4 |
| Mali | 686 | 529 | 157 | 22.9 | 0 | 0.0 | 0.0 |
| Mauritania | 376 | 333 | 43 | 11.4 | 0 | 0.0 | 0.0 |
| Mauritius | 1,782 | 960 | 822 | 46.1 | 19 | 1.1 | 2.3 |
| Mozambique | 1,769 | 435 | 1,334 | 75.4 | 61 | 3.4 | 4.6 |
| Namibia | 848 | 466 | 382 | 45.0 | 291 | 34.3 | 76.2 |
| Niger | 423 | 386 | 37 | 8.7 | 0 | 0.0 | 0.0 |
| Nigeria | 35,741 | 30,885 | 4,856 | 13.6 | 180 | 0.5 | 3.7 |
| Rwanda | 273 | 155 | 118 | 43.2 | 10 | 3.7 | 8.5 |
| Sao Tome & P. | 160 | 63 | 97 | 60.6 | 0 | 0.0 | 0.0 |
| Senegal | 1,318 | 640 | 678 | 51.4 | 3 | 0.2 | 0.4 |
| Seychelles | 170 | 120 | 50 | 29.4 | 4 | 2.4 | 8.0 |
| Sierra Leone | 587 | 338 | 249 | 42.4 | 4 | 0.7 | 1.6 |
| Somalia | 461 | 310 | 151 | 32.8 | 0 | 0.0 | 0.0 |
| South Africa | 34,914 | 27,551 | 7,363 | 21.1 | 834 | 2.4 | 11.3 |
| Sudan | 5,731 | 4,973 | 758 | 13.2 | 10 | 0.2 | 1.3 |
| Swaziland | 186 | 133 | 53 | 28.5 | 44 | 23.7 | 83.0 |
| Tanzania | 2,620 | 1,264 | 1,356 | 51.8 | 40 | 1.5 | 2.9 |
| Togo | 445 | 265 | 180 | 40.4 | 0 | 0.0 | 0.0 |
| Uganda | 4,266 | 2,429 | 1,837 | 43.1 | 179 | 4.2 | 9.7 |
| Zambia | 1,553 | 670 | 883 | 56.9 | 203 | 13.1 | 23.0 |
| Zimbabwe | 3,132 | 1,530 | 1,602 | 51.1 | 643 | 20.5 | 40.1 |
| SSA | 133,058 | 96,405 | 36,653 | 27.50 | 1434 | 1.1 | 3.9 |

Further analysis undertaken for ease of interpretation. Data extracted from Clemens and Pettersson (2008).

**Internal brain drain:** Apart from the transnational brain drain (health personnel moving from one country to another), possibly a more severe issue in many low-income countries is the internal brain drain, which occurs in two forms: local health staff being poached by international NGOs and staff moving from rural and regional service areas to urban centres with technologically advanced facilities. While a strong presence of NGOs in most low-income countries has resulted in increased access to services, it has also translated into scarcity of staff for the public sector. By hiring specialised staff from the public system on very high salaries, international NGOs have deprived governments from workforces much needed to effectively run the public system. Even if the international NGOs do not poach staff from the public sector, the increasing number of NGOs and their financial power mean that there are plenty of opportunities for consultancies, which offer better remuneration than the government, and result in taking highly qualified personnel away from their usual poorly-paid work. Perhaps one of the most comprehensive studies to shed light on the challenges posed by the internal brain drain is the study by Mullan *et al.* (2011) which undertook an inventory of medical schools in SSA and identified a total of 168 schools. Of the 146 medical schools invited to participate in the study, 105 responded, giving a response rate of 72%. The authors found that at five years post-graduation, 22% of doctors migrate outside Africa, a further 6% migrate to other African countries and 72% were still practicing in the country of training. Of those remaining in the country of training, more than half (53%) practiced in urban areas (21% in urban public general practice, 13% in urban private general practice and 19% in urban specialist practice), only 17% remained or relocated to rural areas (5% rural private general practice, 9% rural public general practice and 3% rural specialist practice), 2% left the practice of medicine all together, and a small proportion (<1%) were in other sectors. These data illustrate an unequal distribution of doctors across the rural/urban (17% vs. 53%) and public/private (21% vs. 32% in urban areas; 9% vs. 8% in rural areas) divides. The authors noted that in some countries medical graduates declined to work in rural areas due to lack of clinical support while others were prepared to forgo employment due to low salaries and poor working conditions (Mullan *et al.*, 2011).

## Consequences and impact of the brain drain

Samet (2013) has summarised the effect of the brain drain into three assumptions: an induced effect, a direct effect and a feedback effect. The induced effect encompasses the brain drain-related stimulus to domestic education. Under this assumption, the emigration rate of highly skilled people is positively associated with a higher schooling rate in the sending country. That is, the perceived improvement in the quality of life of highly educated emigrants acts as a motivation for those staying behind to take education seriously and to change their course structures through additional classes and smart course choices to maximise their likelihood of emigrating once they complete their studies. Therefore, further education is used as a passport for emigration. However, there are always uncertainties about the likelihood of obtaining a visa post-graduation, meaning that although the increasing emigration of highly skilled people leads to an increasing number of people engaged in higher education in the source country, not all those graduating may end up emigrating. Such a scenario turns the demand for higher education by aspiring emigrants into a significant brain gain for the source country. There needs to be an optimal level of both development and the brain drain that would yield some benefits in the educational attainment rates in the sending country because low levels of development generate strong incentives for the highly educated to emigrate, but such levels should not be so low such that there are constraints related to personal liquidity, which in turn make it impossible for individuals to invest in education. Current estimates suggest that a small but positive skilled emigration rate of 5–10% can yield development-related benefits with human capital accumulation maximised when the level of the brain drain is around 10% (Beine *et al.*, 2008; Docquier, 2014). The brain drain becomes harmful for development in most LMICs when the emigration rate of highly skilled people is above 20%. Unfortunately, most countries affected by the brain drain in LMICs are above that threshold (Docquier, 2014).

The direct effect assumption includes the decline in the economic growth due to the depreciation of the human capital. With a one-year increase in the average education of the workforce of a nation associated with an increase of 5–15% of the production per worker, any brain drain that is not associated with a stimulus in education in the source country leads to serious economic losses (Samet, 2013). Therefore, under the direct effect assumption, the brain drain is associated with a depreciated human capital stock, the consequence of which includes reduced competitiveness and productivity, and poor economic growth of a nation. The diminished skilled manpower and the loss of entrepreneurs and specialists in the sending country lead to increased dependence on foreign technical assistance, slowed transfer and institutionalisation of knowledge thereby hindering development, and the financial loss associated with training (Brain Drain in Africa: Facts and Figures, 2014). For example, estimates by the United Nations Commission for Trade and Development suggest that each professional leaving Africa costs the continent US$ 184,000 (Marchal and Kegels, 2003) while the African's share of world scientific outputs has declined from 0.5% to 0.3% over the past 15 years (Brain Drain in Africa: Facts and Figures, 2014). Ironically, there are over 300,000 highly qualified Africans in the diaspora, 10% of whom (30,000) have PhDs (Anyangwe and Mtonga, 2007), yet the continent is home to only 1.3% of the global health workforce (Packer *et al.* 2009). Consequently, the continent spends approximately $4 billion to meet the salary of 100,000 western expatriates performing generic technical assistance tasks, a figure which equates to 35% of the official development aid to the continent. In some African countries, up to 90% of private firms are managed by expatriates (Brain Drain in Africa: Facts and Figures, 2014). Similarly, the current density of physicians and nurses per 10,000 populations was lowest in the African region, and highest in OECD countries (Table 6). These figures are well below the Millennium Development Goals standard of 25/10,000 health workers per population. The shortage of doctors, nurses and midwives in SSA presents a serious problem to its health system with an overall shortfall ranging from 800,000 to 1.5 million health workers (Scheffler *et al.*, 2009). The overall consequence of this imbalance is a significant decline in the availability and quality of health care with fewer doctor visits, diminished time with patients and increased cost of health care. The extremely low ratio of health workers per population makes it very difficult for many SSA countries to meet the health needs of their constituencies and to compete internationally. It has been estimated that SSA will need to increase the output of health professionals by 140% in order to provide adequate health care and meet the health needs of its constituencies (Anyangwe and Mtonga, 2007).

Table 6: Latest WHO estimates for the size of the international health workforce

| WHO Region | Doctors Number | Doctors Density | Nurses Number | Nurses Density | Total density (doctors + nurses) |
|---|---|---|---|---|---|
| African Region | 118,621 | 2.2 | 467,487 | 9.0 | 11.2 |
| Region of the Americas | 1,555,428 | 20.0 | 4,749,397 | 72.5 | 92.5 |
| South-east Asia Region | 901,006 | 5.6 | 1,736,755 | 10.9 | 16.4 |
| European Region | 2,942,286 | 33.2 | 5,766,646 | 65.0 | 98.2 |
| Eastern Mediterranean Region | 626,923 | 10.9 | 856,744 | 15.6 | 26.5 |
| Western Pacific Region | 2,507,843 | 14.8 | 3,112,221 | 18.4 | 33.3 |

**Countries with the lowest health worker density worldwide vs. seven EU countries with the highest**

| | | | |
|---|---|---|---|
| Norway | 42 | 319 | 361 |
| Finland | 29 | 240 | 269 |
| Denmark | 34 | 161 | 195 |
| Ireland | 32 | 157 | 189 |
| Sweden | 38 | 119 | 157 |
| Germany | 36 | 111 | 147 |
| United Kingdom | 27 | 101 | 128 |
| Mozambique | <0 | 3 | 3 |
| Mali | <0 | 3 | 3 |
| Malawi | <0 | 3 | 3 |
| Liberia | <0 | 3 | 3 |
| Bhutan | <0 | 3 | 3 |
| Tanzania | <0 | 2 | 2 |
| Sierra Leone | <0 | 2 | 2 |
| Ethiopia | <0 | 2 | 2 |
| Somalia | <0 | 1 | 1 |
| Niger | <0 | 1 | 1 |
| Guinea | 1 | <0 | 1 |

Density/10,000 people.
*Source*: Jensen (2013).

The financial loss associated with the brain drain is staggering. For example, for SSA to eliminate its shortage of health workers, the continent may require an additional annual wage bill of approximately $2.6 billion (Scheffler et al., 2009). While accounting for only 13.8% of the world's population but bearing a staggering 25% of the world's total burden of disease, SSA contributes only 1.3% to the world's health workforce and only 1% to the economic resources (Figure 1). As an illustration, over the years most countries in SSA have been unable to fill the vacancies for doctors and nurses created by those emigrating abroad. Vacancy rates for public facility health professionals increased from 36% in 1998 to 72% in 2003 for Malawi, and averaged 43% for Ghana and 48% for Lesotho (Liese et al., 2003). As recently as 2012, South Africa had more than 829,000 unfilled vacancies for skilled people in the private sector alone (Höppli, 2014). While the economic impact of unfilled vacancies has not been estimated in most LMICs, the annual loss of unfilled vacancies in potential GDP in OECD countries is approximately $160 billion for the US economy, $36 billion for the German economy, $29 billion for the UK economy and $6 billion for the Australian economy (Indeed, 2014). Similarly, the economic growth of some eastern European countries was negatively affected in the 1990s (Lowel and Findlay, 2001). By 2004, the annual tax revenue loss to India due to the brain drain was well above $700 million (Desai et al., 2004) while recent data suggest migration of Indian skilled labour to US alone translates into an annual loss of approximately US$2.0 billion to the Indian economy (Naim and Iftikhar, 2008). Mills and colleagues (Mills et al., 2011) estimated the lost investment of domestically educated doctors migrating from SSA to four OECD countries. Data were obtained from nine SSA countries with at least one medical school and a HIV prevalence of 5% or greater or with more than 1 million people with HIV/AIDS: Ethiopia, Kenya, Malawi, Nigeria, South Africa, Tanzania, Uganda, Zambia and Zimbabwe. They also obtained data on the number of doctors practicing in destination countries. The authors estimated that the government subsidised cost of a doctor's education ranged from $21,000 in Uganda to $58,700 in South Africa, translating into an overall loss of about US$2.2 billion in returns from the investment made in training physicians who are working abroad. The loss of investment ranged from $2.16 million for Malawi to $1.41 billion for South Africa. Based on the ratio of lost investment over gross domestic product, the authors found that Zimbabwe and South Africa experience the biggest losses. The data suggest that SSA's loss is OECD countries' gain with the United Kingdom and USA saving $2.7 billion and $846 million in training costs respectively by recruiting doctors trained in SSA. These findings are similar to those previously reported by Kirigia and colleagues (Kirigia et al., 2006). The authors estimated that from primary school to university, the total cost of educating a single medical doctor and one nurse in Kenya was respectively US$65,997 and US$43,180, but for every doctor and nurse who emigrates, Kenya loses respectively about US$517,931 and US$338,868 worth of returns from the investment.

The feedback effect relates to the brain gain through various diaspora options such as technology transfer, remittances, links with the international trade and the foreign direct investment, the diaspora networks, and/or the return option through the physical return of professional and skilled migrants to their country of origin (Samet, 2013). The idea that there is a net gain of professional mobility from LMICs to OECD countries through financial support to the families "back home" has gained momentum. LMICs have been receiving a significant share of their foreign exchange from remittances, which constitute a stable and predictable source of revenue. Data summarised in Table 7 provide a trend in remittances per region of the world. In 2013, remittances to LMICs equalled $404 billion, an increase of 24.7% compared to 2010. Impoverished regions of the world are also experiencing increases in remittances. SSA accounted for 7.9% of remittances to LMICs and remittances to SSA are projected to increase from $32 billion in 2013 to $41 billion in 2016, representing an annual growth of 9.4%. The largest recipients of remittances in SSA are Nigeria ($20.6 billion), Senegal ($1.4 billion), Kenya ($1.2 billion), Sudan ($1.1 billion) and South Africa ($1.1 billion). These five countries accounted for 85% of remittances to SSA, and Nigeria alone received 66.4% of the total remittances to SSA (Table 8). In most LMICs, remittances make up a sizeable share of the country's economy. In SSA remittances account for 3.9% of the GDP with higher contributions of remittances to the GDP recorded for Lesotho (28.6%), Togo (12.2%), Senegal (11%), Gambia (10%) and Cape Verde (9.9%). The reported remittances and their contribution to the GDP in SSA may have been

Table 7: Migrants' remittances per region

| Remittance | 2010* | 2011* | 2012* | 2013* | 2014** | 2015** | 2016** |
|---|---|---|---|---|---|---|---|
| **In $ billion** | | | | | | | |
| World | 464 | 508 | 529 | 542 | 581 | 628 | 681 |
| SSA | 29 | 31 | 31 | 32 | 35 | 38 | 41 |
| All LMICs | 324 | 373 | 392 | 404 | 436 | 473 | 516 |
| HICs | 140 | 135 | 137 | 137 | 145 | 155 | 165 |
| **Annual growth** | | | | | | | |
| World | 8.7% | 9.5% | 4.1% | 2.5% | 7.3% | 8.1% | 8.4% |
| SSA | 7.0% | 6.9% | 0.1% | 3.2% | 8.7% | 9.1% | 9.4% |
| All LMICs | 10.3% | 15.1% | 3.1% | 3.3% | 7.8% | 8.6% | 8.9% |
| HICs | 4.5% | −3.6% | 1.5% | 0.1% | 5.7% | 6.5% | 6.8% |

*Author's own computations. Data extracted from the World Bank database on bilateral migration and remittances (World Bank, 2014). **Projection by Ratha et al. (2014).

underestimated as a significant proportion is sent through informal channels (e.g. hand delivery) and hence unaccounted for (Ratha et al., 2011).

The positive impact of remittances in receiving countries has been documented and includes improved sanitary conditions, healthier lifestyles and adequate health care resulting from the accumulation of human capital and assets (Dhillon and Mehra, 2014). According to recent surveys (Ratha et al., 2011), money received through remittances is predominantly spent on education, health care, buying land, building houses, starting businesses or improving farms. In countries such as Senegal, the majority of money that families receive through remittances is predominantly spent on human capital, mainly food, education and health care. In contrast, in Kenya and Nigeria, such money is spent on physical capital as part of investment plans, mainly homebuilding, land purchases and farm improvements. The authors argue that remittances directly affect the economic growth of most receiving countries through increased consumption and investment, and in turn increased spending on health, education and nutrition improves and sustains the long-term wellbeing and productivity families and communities (Ratha et al., 2011). Other studies have found

Table 8: Remittances to SSA by country

| Remittance in millions | 2010 | 2011 | 2012 |
| --- | --- | --- | --- |
| SSA | 29,078.38 | 31,342.00 | 30,986.78 |
| Nigeria | 19,817.84 | 20,618.85 | 20,568.29 |
| Senegal | 1,477.68 | 1,477.68 | 1,366.85 |
| Kenya | 685.76 | 934.15 | 1,227.62 |
| Sudan | 1,100.12 | 1,419.61 | 1,126.13 |
| South Africa | 1,119.27 | 1,212.01 | 1,114.61 |
| Uganda | 768 | 948.64 | 976.6 |
| Lesotho | 610.13 | 649.33 | 601.87 |
| Ethiopia | 345.15 | 513.24 | 524.2 |
| Mali | 472.74 | 472.74 | 444.45 |
| Liberia | 31.44 | 359.99 | 372.39 |
| Côte d'Ivoire | 373.48 | 373.48 | 325.09 |
| Togo | 336.6 | 336.6 | 320.71 |
| Benin | 184.6 | 184.6 | 179.18 |
| Cape Verde | 132.54 | 177.85 | 176.8 |
| Rwanda | 103.15 | 103.15 | 156.2 |
| Ghana | 135.85 | 151.6 | 151.5 |
| Burkina Faso | 139.6 | 110.59 | 130.35 |
| Niger | 134.29 | 101.72 | 122.36 |
| Cameroon | 114.86 | 114.86 | 109.22 |
| Mozambique | 131.86 | 156.83 | 99.12 |
| The Gambia | 115.7 | 90.67 | 89.25 |
| Sierra Leone | 57.52 | 77.32 | 79.01 |
| Tanzania | 55.03 | 75.77 | 75.34 |
| Guinea | 60.39 | 78.31 | 74.77 |
| Botswana | 62.64 | 62.64 | 54.85 |
| Swaziland | 54.69 | 54.69 | 46.89 |
| Zambia | 43.7 | 46.3 | 45.55 |
| Guinea-Bissau | 45.89 | 45.89 | 42.18 |

(*Continued*)

Table 8: (*Continued*)

| Remittance in millions | 2010 | 2011 | 2012 |
|---|---|---|---|
| Burundi | 34.5 | 45.46 | 42.15 |
| Djibouti | 32.64 | 32.36 | 31.52 |
| Seychelles | 17.38 | 25.51 | 25.9 |
| Namibia | 15.86 | 16.05 | 16.51 |
| Malawi | 16.74 | 17.41 | 16.01 |
| São Tomé and Principe | 6.36 | 6.88 | 6.5 |
| Angola | 17.97 | 0.2 | 0.19 |

Author's own computations. Data extracted from the World Bank database on bilateral migration and remittances (World Bank, 2014).

that medical migrants send medications, medical supplies and diagnostic equipment to support the health system (Tankwanchi *et al.*, 2013), making the diaspora a significant source of capital, trade, investment, knowledge and technology transfers (Canuto and Rafha, 2011). Higher remittance flows are associated with lower poverty levels (Acosta *et al.*, 2007; Bouoiyour and Miftah, 2015; Ratha *et al.*, 2011), higher child's educational attainment (Acosta *et al.*, 2007; Dhillon and Mehra, 2014) and increased child survival and overall reduced infant mortality (Hildebrandt *et al.*, 2005; Kanaiaupuni and Donato, 1999; Ssengonzi *et al.*, 2002). However, the impact of remittances on child's education varies by gender, across rural and urban areas, and parental educational level with remittances bridging gender gaps in primary school education and achieving larger impacts among parents with lower levels of schooling (Acosta *et al.*, 2007; Roy *et al.*, 2015). In a study assessing migrants' willingness to remit to education, De Arcangelis *et al.* (2015) found that soft commitment (e.g. simply labelling remittances as being used for education) raises remittances by more than 15% and adding a hard option (e.g. having funds directly paid to a school and the student's educational performance monitored) added only a further 2.2% remittance commitment. These findings suggest remittance commitments to education can be increased through soft policies that allow migrants to exert some control over their use rather than hard forms of commitments.

## Some policy options

The six "Rs" are a set of policies that have been identified to facilitate the return of migrants to their source country (Lowell, 2002): return (migration), restriction (migration), recruitment (migration), reparation (monetary), resourcing (diaspora options) and retention (opportunities). The first three Rs relate to migration policies that directly affect the movement of people (Table 9). The fourth R for reparation is particularly concerned with monetary compensation to source countries who lose their highly educated and skilled people to other countries. The fifth R for resourcing is more about harnessing the skills and resources of diasporas to foster development in source countries. The sixth R for retention encompasses policies to improve socioeconomic conditions and opportunities domestically wherein highly skilled people do not feel the need to leave the country (Lowell, 2002).

However, Samet (2013) conceptualises relevant policies to address the consequences of the brain drain into two major rubrics: the return option and the diaspora option. The return option could encompass direct investment and technology transfer (e.g. temporary or permanent return of migrants and technology transfer through direct investment and human capital transfer) and policies encouraging the circular migration. Policies encouraging the circular migration could adopt the reverse brain drain model through (a) offer of material and non-material incentives; (b) the establishment of a lead coordinating body to facilitate the integration of returnees and research institutes that track highly qualified nationals abroad and encourage them to return or to join professional associations to facilitate skill transfers, and (c) setting up and maintaining networks and databases that employers can use to identify and recruit highly educated nationals abroad. Such policies could also adopt a direct business model whereby such nationals abroad are attracted back home using financial capital, dual nationality and flexible residential rights (Samet, 2013). The diaspora option could encompass the recovery of economic losses in sending countries by recovering taxes and other forms of remittances in receiving countries and depositing the money in a national fund in the sending country to support the development of human resources. Such policies could also harness and maximise the economic benefits from migrants' remittances for consumption and productive purposes through financial

Table 9: Policy responses to high-skilled emigration: The Six "Rs"

**Return of migrants to their source country**

The return of emigrants is one sure way to cultivate human capital for source countries, especially when there is value added from working abroad. Permanent return tends to be the focus of most such policies (kindred temporary return programmes are under diaspora options below).

**Restriction of international mobility**

Many developing countries have restrictive emigration policies that make it difficult for their nationals to take jobs abroad. Most countries restricted the immigration of foreign nationals to protect their domestic workers from competition.

**Recruitment of international migrants**

If there are domestic shortages of skilled workers, for any reason, why not court foreign workers? For example, the information technology revolution sparked a worldwide competition for workers: new policies worldwide ease numerical and "protective" regulations on admissions.

**Reparation for loss of human capital (tax)**

A favourite but never implemented economic prescription in the 1970s, the idea is that developed countries either compensate source countries, or that emigrants directly submit taxes to deal with externalities created by the immediate loss of human capital.

**Resourcing expatriates (diaspora options)**

Skilled emigrants abroad can be a significant resource, especially if ongoing contact between academic and private sector institutions is fostered. Government and private sector initiatives seek to increase communications, knowledge transfer, remittances and investment.

**Retention**

**(through educational sector policies)**

Creating a highly educated workforce begins with strengthening domestic educational institutions. A viable system that encourages graduates to stay with the system that retains people and ensures that the source country keeps its original investment in education.

**(through economic development)**

Giving people a reason to stay (or return) is without doubt the most effective policy for reducing emigration and the surest long-term means of boosting average human capital as well as economic growth.

Source: Lowell (2002).

investments (savings) and the development of the assets such as firms, and technology transfer. Sending countries could use diaspora networks and links to facilitate international trade and direct foreign investment in development projects and technology transfer (Samet, 2013). Below we examine some policy examples and how they could be implemented.

**Return of migrants to their source country: brain drain circulation or reverse brain drain:** Perhaps the best way to conceptualise policies related to the return of migrants to their source country is through the so-called brain drain circulation or reverse brain drain. The brain circulation simply refers to the inter-countries' movement of professionals such as the return of the diaspora to their country of origin after training and work experience in industrialised nations as well as the return of international students who have graduated abroad. It could also involve movement of highly skilled people between countries other than their country of origin. Many researchers have noted that the basic tenet of the reverse brain drain is that professionals who migrated to, and students studying in, industrialised nations constitute potential human resources for the socioeconomic development of their home countries (Chacko, 2007; Ismail *et al.*, 2014; Mutume, 2003; Song, 1997). In this case, the brain drain should be viewed as a potential brain gain which can be facilitated and achieved through various policies including policies supporting and promoting the return of students studying abroad and effective engagement with the diaspora to return as expatriates and entrepreneurs, to act as bridges for foreign investment and trade, to remit savings, and to facilitate technology, skills and knowledge transfer (Ismail *et al.*, 2014; Kapur, 2001; Mutume, 2003). Professionals who migrated to industrialised countries and international students may also be drawn back home due to the improvement in the political and socioeconomic environment in countries of origin or failure to socially and culturally integrate into the destination country's way of life (Han *et al.*, 2015).

For example, while China continues to be one of the countries supplying most of the world's highly skilled migrants, it also receives a large backflow of overseas talents, especially from other LMICs (Han *et al.*, 2015; Xue, 2012). Similarly, Han *et al.* (2015) have noted that in the early 1990s, there were approximately 900,000 researchers, scientists, engineers and technopreneurs in the USA, many of whom were predominantly from India, Taiwan, China, Russia and other OECD countries. The majority of those skilled migrants from Taiwan, India and China were in their reverse mode to return to their homeland at the turn of the millennium. The percentage of Chinese graduating abroad and returning home increased from 25% in 2006 to 28% in 2008 and 32.6% in 2010 (Han et al., 2015). Since the beginning of the global financial crisis in 2008, 359,000 highly-skilled South Africans practicing abroad have returned home (Höppli, 2014). The Chinese government launched its "Thousand Talent Program" in 2008 in an attempt to attract 2,000 Chinese IT experts and scholars practicing abroad. By April 2012, 2,263 professionals had returned to China, filling strategic positions in 29 provinces and regions (Harvey and Groutsis, 2015; Zhang, 2012). Recent data have suggested that the Indian diaspora has contributed positively and significantly to the growth of the Indian economy by investing in government bonds and through start-up organisations and filling highly skilled labour market shortages in high-technology clusters (Harvey and Groutsis, 2015; Khadria, 2002). Between 2000 and 2004, about 25,000 IT professionals returned to India (Gupte and Jadhav, 2014). For professional Indians returning home, reasons were multiple, but centred around a feeling of dissatisfaction in the destination country and availability of opportunities in the country of origin (Gupte and Jadhav, 2014): career prospects, better job opportunities, flexibility in types of research, ease in availability of funds and job security in India (45%), family-related factors such as aging, parents, family ties and raising children (36%), not fitting in culturally in country of destination (32%) and migration-related issues such as spouse not being able to find a job (27%). Some countries such as India have developed policies geared towards encouraging returns of citizenships including the introduction of dual citizenship, tax breaks, attractive salary packages and rights to ownership of agricultural land for foreign passport holders (Han et al., 2015). Although there is inconclusive evidence on the best practices in the reverse brain drain (Ismail et al., 2014), a number of countries have developed incentive-based policies to both retain the brightest students and attract the return of the diaspora (Table 10) and there has been some best practice policies related to the reverse brain drain (Table 11).

Table 10: Programmes for the return of qualified diaspora: selected policy examples

| Country | Programme name | Programme description |
|---|---|---|
| SSA | IOM African return programme | Include the Return of Qualified African Nationals (RQAN) and Migration for Development in Africa (MIDA). RQAN and MIDA aim to develop a country's economy by seeking persons who are highly trained and qualified to either return or find positions in each country that benefits from the person's training. They provide durable solutions to governments in need by using the country's diaspora as the primary instrument. They complement key partners' broader development strategies by providing support to the social and economic advancement of developing countries to foster their national human resource development and to counter the negative effects of the brain drain by encouraging brain circulation instead. |
| Sub-Saharan Africa | Homecoming Revolution | Started in 2003, the goal of Homecoming Revolution is to bring highly-skilled Africans back to their homelands. |
| Ireland | Irish Christmas recruitment | The Irish Ministers of Enterprise, Trade and Development are recruiting expatriates to return to build the software industry, targeting those returning home for Christmas. |
| Malaysia | Malaysian return incentives | Malaysia hopes to provide incentives for return by giving out tax exemptions, permanent resident status for spouses and children, and relaxed immigration policies. |
| Malaysia | Malaysian internet job postings | Created on an exploratory basis with hopes to expand, Malaysia's JobsDB.com lists domestic high-skill jobs to inform expatriates about positions available back home. |
| Mexico | Mexican studen loan forgiveness | The Mexican government programme Becas CONACYT grants loans to students who study abroad: if they return, much of the loan is forgiven and if they go on to work at a Mexican university, the loan is forgiven. |
| Canada | Canadian tax incentives | Now discontinued, Canada for a short time gave federal income tax holidays for up to three years to its emigrants who returned for employment. |

(Continued)

Table 10: (*Continued*)

| Country | Programme name | Programme description |
|---|---|---|
| Argentina | R@ICES | A programme under the Ministry of Science, Technology and Productive Innovation of Argentina. The goals of the programme are to strengthen the link between Argentine researchers in the country and abroad, bring Argentines abroad back to Argentina to develop research and implement retention policies that promote the return of Argentines. |
| Bavaria | Return to Bavaria | Sponsored by the Bavarian Ministry of Economic Affairs and Media, Energy and Technology, the programme was initiated in 2012 to motivate Bavarian and German professionals to return home. |
| Brazil | Science Without Borders "Young Talent Programme" (i.e. Jovens Talentos) | A joint effort from Brazil's Ministry of Education and the Ministry of Science and Technology, the programme aims to (1) place 100,000 Brazilian students and researchers in top universities worldwide by 2014, and (2) to attract talented young researchers from outside the country, especially Brazilians, to Brazil. |
| Chile | Start-up Chile | Programme started by the Chilean government in 2010 to attract early stage entrepreneurs to build their startup companies in Chile. |
| China | 1000 Talents Programme | Launched by the Central Organization Department of the Chinese Communist Party in 2008, the programme aims to recruit 1,000 outside Chinese talents to return to China. |
| Europe | Horizon 2020 | Commencing in 2014, Horizon 2020 is an initiative aimed at securing Europe's global competitiveness. There are many different programmes (e.g. European Research Council Starting Grants, European Research Council Advanced Grants, Marie Sklodowska-Curie Actions Programme, etc.) that facilitate the return of young European scientists back to Europe. |

(*Continued*)

**168** *Globalisation, Migration and Health*

Table 10: (*Continued*)

| Country | Programme name | Programme description |
|---|---|---|
| Germany | German Academic International Network (GAIN) | Created by the Deutscher Akademischer Austausch Dienst (i.e. German Academic Exchange Service) in cooperation with the German Research Foundation and the Alexander von Humboldt Foundation, the programme provides support, networking opportunities, workshops and job postings for German scholars and scientists working in North America. GAIN promotes the dissemination of information across the Atlantic and prepares German scientists to return to Germany. |
| Israel | Gvahim | Initiated in 2006, this non-governmental organisation promotes Israel's "Brain Bain" efforts by offering highly-skilled Olim (migrants) with opportunities and networking in Israel. |
| Italy | Dulbecco Telethon Institute | Founded in 1999, the Institute provides funding to early-stage researchers who work on human genetic diseases. |
| Moldova | Gsorm Gala Studenilor | Moldovan students abroad participated in the competition "Academic Excellence Moldova". The programme encourages Moldovan students abroad to return to Moldova. |
| Portugal | Cienca 2007 | An international call for 1,000 post-doctoral research positions, for both Portuguese and foreign nationals, at Portuguese scientific institutions. The programme was launched and closed in 2007. |
| Russia | Mega Grant (i.e. Resolution No. 220) | Launched in 2010 by the government of the Russian Federation, the programme provides grants of up to $5 million USD to conduct research in Russia. The programme hopes to bring Russian scientists residing abroad as well as foreign scientists to Russian institutions. |
| South Korea | Brain Return 500 | Established by the Institute for Basic Science, the goal of the programme is to attract 500 talented young scholars and scientists back to South Korea by 2017. |
| Spain | Spanish Ramón y Cajal Programme | Funded by the Spanish Ministry of Economy and Competitiveness, the programme provides financial support to PhD researchers for a period of 5 years. |

(*Continued*)

Table 10: (*Continued*)

| Country | Programme name | Programme description |
|---------|----------------|----------------------|
| Sweden | Study in Sweden Swedish Institute | The Institute is a public agency that provides grants to researchers around the world in order to establish cooperating and lasting relations with other countries. A variety of programmes and grants are available depending on the applicant's nationality. |
| Thailand | Reverse Brain Drain (RBD) | The RBD initiative by Thailand's National Science and Technology Development Agency began in 1990. Initially, the primary goal of the initiative was to promote the permanent return of overseas Thai professionals. In 1997, the RBD's main objective shifted to the promotion of temporary returns of science and technology professionals. As of 2007, RBD promotes the brain circulation of Thai professionals overseas. |
| Turkey | 2232 Repatriation Research Scholarship Programme | Enacted by the Scientific and Technological Research Council of Turkey, the programme encourages the return of successful Turkish researchers from abroad to continue their work in their home country. |

*Sources*: Han *et al.* (2015) and Lowell (2002).

**Restriction of international mobility:** Restriction of international mobility of skilled labour can be applied in both sending and receiving countries, but the effectiveness of such policy has been questioned. For example, before the expansion of the European Union, countries such as Germany and Austria had strict transitional measures, but migrants found other innovative modes of entry into the country. However, those who entered the country were less likely to be skilled migrants (as restrictive transitional measures discouraged migrants who had competitive alternatives), hence these countries attracted older and lower-skilled migrants than the older European Union member states that had opened their borders earlier to the newer European Union states (Kahanec and Zimmermann, 2011). Similarly, Australia has a number of restrictive transition measures to regulate the mobility of skilled labour. The Skilled Graduate Visa (485) gives overseas students gaining an Australian qualification with at least

**Table 11: Best practices of reverse brain drain and suggested strategies for other countries to adopt**

| | Example | Some elements some other countries can adopt |
|---|---|---|
| 1 | Collecting a database of diaspora overseas, including students, academics and professionals. China has demonstrated great success in this initiative. | Comprehensive databases about the diaspora abroad, capturing professionals according to fields of expertise, job positions, institutions to which they are affiliated, age, work experience and other demographic characteristics such as gender and family status. These databases should be updated periodically. |
| 2 | Funded best scientific research projects and research institutions. | Governments should fund the best scientific research through collaboration research centres in which returning researchers and professionals may be deployed and provide mentorship for local staff and trainees. Not only does the country receive returnees, it also gains in terms of transfer of technology from foreign researchers. |
| 3 | Reverse brain drain projects that enhanced human talent inflow. Some lessons can be learnt from China, e.g. the Spring Light Project (1996), the Hundred Top Talent Programme (1998) and Green Channel (2007). | Governments should continuously develop many more reverse brain drain projects that enhance human talent inflows to the country. Existing programmes should be further nurtured and injected with innovations to make them attractive and sustainable. |
| 4 | Human capital development. Lessons can be learnt from South Korea, e.g. by employing heavy and aggressive investments in education and training, and the borrowing of foreign capital, the country created a smooth road to success. China blended Human Resource Development policy in their 10th Economic Plan (2001–2005) by focusing on education, training, and research and development. | Countries should blend human resource development policy plans by emphasising education, training, and research and development right from the primary school up to tertiary level. More government agencies should be given the tasks to attract, retain and develop global talents. Human resource development should be treated as a key strategy for regional development by integrating social and economic development through which these resources can be implemented. |

Source: Han et al. (2015).

two years' study in Australia, an 18-month temporary visa to work in Australia during which time they can apply for a provisional or permanent General Skilled Migration Visa subject to passing the Department of Immigration and Border Protection's points test. A similar scheme is the Skilled Recognised Graduate visa (476) for graduates with a degree from recognised overseas educational institutions who have skills in demand in Australia. It provides holders up to 18 months of skilled work experience in their occupations. There is also the Working Holiday Programme that promotes cultural exchange through reciprocal agreements allowing young people (18–30 years) to live and work in Australia on a temporary basis and for Australian young people to work temporarily in partner countries. Similar schemes exist in the USA (Massey and Liang, 1989) and other OECD countries and Asia (Mesnard, 2004), making temporary migration a universal phenomenon. In most cases, temporary migrant workers are often on contracts and expected to return once their contract expires.

These kinds of arrangements create temporal constraints and differential inclusion in the labour market characterised by the lack of access to any government-sponsored social welfare (e.g. subsidised health care and education or unemployment benefits) and differentiated tax statuses (Robertson, 2014). Holders of temporary working visas may end up in low-paying and flexible jobs that are not commensurate with their qualifications such as taxi driving, late-night retail or hospitality jobs, and sex work, (Lantz, 2005; Neilson, 2009; Robertson, 2014), hence making them vulnerable to exploitation, discriminatory practices and abuses. According to Massey and Liang (1989), temporary migrants, once in the system, are more likely to make repeated trips with or without legal documents; and eventually end up settling permanently in the host country. They conclude that in the long run, there is no such thing as a temporary worker programme. All these factors combine to affect the effectiveness of policies geared towards restricting international mobility of labour to address the brain drain. The evidence suggests that temporary migrant workers' optimal investment into country-specific human capital is lower when compared to permanent migrant workers due to many factors: Temporary migrant workers' earnings tend to be lower than national averages, temporary migrant workers are positively selected only under certain labour market conditions, and the length of the working contract in the host country has an effect on their investment into human capital and purchasing power (Dustmann, 1993). While restrictive policies through the issuing of temporary visas can benefit both sending (e.g. remittances, enhanced human capital of returning migrants) and receiving countries (e.g. filling in labour shortages) (Lowell, 2002), taken together, it is possible that restricting labour mobility can be counterproductive in many ways (Massey and Liang, 1989). Temporary migrant workers' repeated trips between sending and receiving countries may involve trips with and without legal documents, and these workers introduce their children and extended families to the migratory careers (Massey and Liang, 1989), thereby increasing the likelihood of illegal migration. In their recent work, Massey and Pren (2012) indicate that in 1942, the US government instigated the Bracero programme to facilitate the free movement of temporary workers from Mexico to work in the farming industries in California and Texas. By 1959, 437,643 Mexicans had entered the USA on a temporary work visa and an additional 23,061 entered the USA legally under different type of visas, but there were 20,131 who entered the country illegally. The programme ended in 1964, but other border control and restrictive policies were introduced. Despite these initiatives, by 1979 the number of undocumented migrants increased dramatically to reach 427,033 while the number of legal migrants only rose to about 52,479 and the number of temporary migrants shrunk significantly and numbered only 1,725 people from more than 437,643 in 1959 (Massey and Pren, 2012). Other negative effects associated with restrictive measures and stricter immigration policies have been documented in Spain (López-Sala, 2013) and Germany (Constant *et al.*, 2013).

**Compensation and reform:** Over the past three decades, many experts have called on receiving countries to impose taxes on migrant workers' salaries and deposit the revenue into a national fund into the sending countries. Implementing and evaluating the effectiveness of this strategy is too difficult mainly due to the under-development of the financial services in sending countries, where more than three-quarters (85%) of the population are excluded from the formal financial system and do not have a bank account as well (Ondiege, 2010). Therefore, the disbursement of these funds at the grassroots' level for meaningful development projects

> **Box 1: Recommendations to promote and improve medical education and population health**
>
> 1. Launch campaigns to develop the capacity of medical school faculties, including recruitment, training and retention.
> 2. Increase investment in medical education infrastructure.
> 3. Build structures to promote interministerial collaboration for medical education.
> 4. Fund research and research training at medical schools.
> 5. Promote community-oriented education based on principles of primary health care.
> 6. Establish national and regional postgraduate medical education programmes to promote training, excellence and retention.
> 7. Establish national or regional bodies that are responsible for accreditation and quality assurance of medical education.
> 8. Increase donor investment in medical education aligned with national health needs.
> 9. Recognise and review the growing role of private institutions in medical education.
> 10. Revitalise the African Medical Schools Association.
>
> *Source*: Mullan *et al.* (2011).

could be compromised by leaving the money in a corrupt system which could be a disincentive for migrant workers. In addition, this policy option could lead to unintended consequences as some of the migrants are temporary, and those who are permanent may one day decide to return, so a taxation system that is solely based on their increased income may reduce their motivation to upskill themselves (improvement in skill and knowledge), hence negatively affecting knowledge and skill transfer and direct investments.

However, it is possible to compensate sending countries through programme exchange, work placement and the strengthening of institutions (Box 1). For example, the USA has been spearheading innovative initiatives in SSA. The most well known and documented initiatives are the Medical Education Partnership Initiative (MEPI) and the Nursing Education Partnership Initiative (NEPI). The MEPI aims to provide up to

$130-million as a 5-year award to 13 African medical schools by the US government and bring together 30 regional partners including health and education ministries as well as 20 US collaborators (Glass *et al.*, 2014; Goosby and von Zinkernagel, 2014; Omaswa, 2014). NEPI is now operational in six countries: the Democratic Republic of Congo, Zambia, Lesotho, Malawi, Ethiopia and South Africa. These two initiatives have been established to support the US President's Emergency Plan for AIDS Relief's goal of increasing the number of health workers by 140,000. Their primary objective is to address the critical shortage of health workers in SSA through the strengthening of medical, nursing and midwifery education systems, expanding clinical and research capacity, and supporting innovative retention strategies for health workers in beneficiary countries. By expanding the pool of health professionals, target countries would be in a position to meet the full range of health needs of their constituencies. Importantly, initial evidence suggests that these initiatives have established robust networks that facilitate information exchange between education institutions and training facilities within and across SSA countries. Hence, they augment a platform for research opportunities, the improved quality of clinical practice and excellence in patient care, elements that can act as an incentive to retain professionals (Glass *et al.*, 2014; Goosby and von Zinkernagel, 2014; Omaswa, 2014).

However, the added technical expertise may not be sufficient to retain the health workforce if they are not complemented by other measures. Such measures could include a legislation binding doctors and nurses to compulsory service for a period of time before they can emigrate. The length of the time must be adjusted such that it is commensurate with the cost of the degree. For example, Australia provides scholarships to students under the Australia Awards Scholarships. The scholarships are available for undergraduate and postgraduate degrees as well as vocational education and training courses, and aim to contribute to the long-term development needs of the beneficiary countries including the brain drain. On completion of their degrees, it is compulsory that scholarship holders return to their country of citizenship for two years to contribute to the development of their country. The Australian government effort to address the brain drain through capacity building is ratified in a memorandum of understanding between Australia and the African Union (Commonwealth of

Australia, 2012). Available data suggest that Australia has offered more than 4,000 scholarships to Africa since 1960, and 69% (2,750) were offered between 2011 and 2013 (Udah, 2014). The compulsory service postgraduation needs to be supported by competitive financial rewards, which may require reforming the employment and labour market to address issues related to wages and employment benefits. This is not an easy task in SSA due to socioeconomic (e.g. unemployment and poverty) and political (e.g. wars, conflicts or political instability) factors as well as a heavy presence of international NGOs that tend to distort the labour market. Therefore the reform of the labour market in SSA should occur in tandem with the reform of the NGO sector. There is an urgent need to reform the NGO and private sectors in the most affected countries across SSA, and such reform should consider regulating the NGOs' recruitment process and remuneration and align them with ethically acceptable standards and in line with national policies. Most countries could benefit from establishing a clearing house that should regulate the NGO sector in terms of NGO recruitment, and coordination of NGO and government efforts in order to maximise synergy and integration while minimising duplication of effort (efficiency in the use of the scarce resources).

**Return of and retaining talents:** One of the proposed policies to address the brain drain is to encourage and support the return of the highly skilled to their country of origin. For example, Tankwanchi et al. (2013) estimated that if half the number of Ghanaian doctors practicing in the USA were to return to Ghana, the Ghanaian physician workforce would increase by >30%. Countries like Liberia would benefit the most as the return of Liberian doctors practicing in the USA would more than double the Liberian physician workforce. However, putting in place strategies/incentive-based systems to encourage migrants to go back to help re-build their shattered countries is not an easy task. It is encouraging to note that the International Organisation for Migration has put in place programmes encouraging health professionals to assist their country of origin (IOM) with the most notable schemes being the Return of Qualified African Nationals and the Migration for Development in Africa (Ghosh, 2000). Under this plan, the IOM pays the returnees' air fare including any excess baggage and provides a relocation allowance plus a local salary supplement of up to $800 dollars per month for 6–12 months (International Development Research Centre, 2004; Ngunjiri, 2003). However, this scheme has been less successful because those professionals returning home are struck by the reality of poverty and poor infrastructure on arrival, which prompts them to pack their bags and move to South Africa for better economic returns (International Development Research Centre, 2004). In addition, incentives to return home through the provision of free air fare, loans for housing and temporary salary supplements are not enough to attract significant numbers of returnees, and those more likely to embrace incentivised return tend to be recent retirees (Shinn, 2008).

However, there have been more successful models that have yielded positive outcomes. For example, as part of the Africa Action Plan, the World Bank (2013) launched the Africa Diaspora Initiative in 2007, renaming it to the Africa Diaspora Programme in 2010. The aim of the programme is to enable the human and financial capital contributions of the African diaspora to the economic development of their countries of origin. The programme has four pillars: (1) partnering with the African Union to enhance its global diaspora policies, programmes and projects, (2) engaging with partner countries to enable policy and institutional environments conducive to engaging their diaspora in economic and social development activities, (3) working with partner donors to improve the flow of remittances including transfer costs and methods of leveraging and securing remittances for development, and (4) engaging with Diaspora Professional Networks to increase knowledge-sharing and transfer (brain gain) between the diaspora and their home countries (World Bank, 2013). Since its establishment, the programme has developed a Database of Professional Skills in the African Diaspora and received €720,000 from European donors (Belgium, the Netherlands, Germany and France) in support of the Development Marketplace for African Diaspora in Europe (D-MADE), €1,696,350 from the European Commission in support of the establishment of the African Institute for Remittances in the African Union Commission, and US$960,000 equivalent from Italy to support the Ethiopia Diaspora Health and Education Professionals project. The Diaspora Health and Education Professionals project is operating in Ethiopia focusing on strengthening and building the capacity of the health system to improve the delivery of education and health services in

Ethiopia. The strengthening and capacity-building centres on engaging, deploying and utilising the Ethiopian diaspora professionals in the area of neurology, tele-medicine and social work. In contrast, the D-MADE provides small grants to individual diaspora organisations engaged in 16 development projects in 10 beneficiary home countries. The award of small grants and technical assistance to entrepreneurial African diaspora has led to a number of innovative projects ranging from the production of high-end textiles in Mali, a semi-artisanal cashew nuts processing plant in Cote d'Ivoire, cheap, clean and mobile public toilets in the Democratic Republic of Congo and Benin, to storage facilities for the preservation of marine resources in Sierra Leone. The D-MADE represents a more robust model for engaging the African diaspora and is being replicated in other regions of the world. Following the D-MADE's success, the Development Marketplace for African Diaspora Action (DMADA) has been established to promote youth and employments (World Bank, 2013).

**Remittance markets and diaspora savings for development:** Remittances have a significant role to play in the economic development of sending countries, and more so than foreign aid (official development assistance). Baldé (2011) carried out a study to investigate the macroeconomic impact of remittances on savings and investment. The author found that both remittances and foreign aid promote savings and investment, but the effect was greater for remittances. That is, for every 10% increase in remittances, there is an increase in savings by 7% and investment by 6.5%. In contrast, for every 10% increase in foreign aid, there is an increase in savings by only 1.6% and investment by only 1%. These findings suggest that the effect of remittances in stimulating the economy is six to seven times higher than that of foreign aid. For example, while foreign aid accounts for approximately 17% of the GDP in SSA (Baldé, 2011), the 3.9% that remittances contribute to the GDP across SSA represents a more effective and sustainable model for boosting savings and investment in the continent than foreign aid. Notwithstanding the benefits of remittances, there are significant barriers that may negatively impact the economic impact of remittances. Recently, remittances have been identified as a potential avenue for channelling money to terrorist organisations and the emerging evidence suggests a statistically significant short- and long-run relationship between remittances and terrorism (Mascarenhas and Sandler, 2014; Ullah *et al.*, 2015). This has led to anti-money laundering and the war against financial terror where banks in the USA and the UK have closed the accounts of the money transfer operators in countries such as Somalia (Ratha *et al.*, 2014).

In addition, sending money to SSA is more expensive than other regions, and the region has not benefitted from the remittance price reduction interventions. The World Bank successfully lobbied and secured the commitment of the G8 and G20 Heads of State to reduce the global average costs of transferring remittances from 10% to 5% in five years through enhanced information, transparency, competition and cooperation with partners (Cirasino, 2014). The evaluation of remittance price reduction interventions show that remittance costs in most remittance corridors average between 5% and 10% (Cirasino, 2014) compared to a staggering 22% for SSA (Ratha *et al.*, 2014). The high remittance cost observed in Africa is due to the fact that most transactions are done as cash transfer through money transfer companies instead of potentially cheaper account-to-account and cash-to-account transfer options (Ratha *et al.*, 2014). Therefore, high remittance costs are limiting SSA's competitiveness in the remittance market. To overcome these costs, a taxation-based method could be an option. However, taxing methods need to be planned along the lines of reciprocal tax agreements so that half the tax on income is being remitted in the country where they earn it, and the other half in their home country. Given the level of corruption in many of the receiving SSA countries, it may also be necessary to suggest that any such tax revenue goes into special funds that are rigorously audited so that the money is indeed used for development projects. However, this would require proper governance structures and functioning banking systems as well as transparent and healthy policies free of corruption and nepotism.

The annual growth of the diaspora savings is about 7.1% with the overall pool of saving increasing from $307.5 billion in 2009 to $511 billion in 2012 (Table 12). However, savings of the diaspora from impoverished regions of the world have been significant. For example, savings by the diaspora from SSA in countries of residence were significant and represented 3.2% of the regional GDP. Their savings increased from $30.4 billion in

Table 12: Estimates of diaspora savings in 2009 and 2012 across regions

|  | 2009* | | | 2012** | Change*** | |
|---|---|---|---|---|---|---|
|  | Diaspora stock (millions) | Diaspora savings estimate ($ billions) | Diaspora savings as % of regional GDP | Diaspora savings estimate ($ billions) | Over 4 years (%) | Per year (%) |
| SSA | 21.80 | 30.4 | 3.2% | 37.0 | 21.7 | 5.4 |
| Middle East and North Africa | 18.00 | 41.2 | 3.9% | 47.0 | 14.1 | 3.5 |
| South Asia | 26.70 | 53.2 | 3.3% | 72.0 | 35.3 | 8.8 |
| Europe and Central Asia | 43.00 | 72.9 | 2.8% | 93.0 | 27.6 | 6.9 |
| East Asia and the Pacific | 21.70 | 83.9 | 1.3% | 116.0 | 38.3 | 9.6 |
| Latin America and the Caribbean | 30.20 | 116.0 | 2.9% | 146.0 | 25.9 | 6.5 |
| **Total LMICs** | 161.50 | 397.5 | 2.4% | 511.0 | 28.6 | 7.1 |

*Data from Ratha and Mohapatra (2011). **Data from Ratha et al. (2014). ***Author's own computations based on the data in the table.

2009 to $37 billion in 2012, representing an increase of 21% over four years or an annual growth of 5.4%. Such large pool of funds represents an opportunity for development in many ways. The diaspora can use the savings to invest heavily in the country of origin through small- and large-scale businesses as well as investing in land and real estates. The other option is through the diaspora bonds. This is an area that remains untapped, given some of the recent successes documented in the Middle East, Israel and India. For example, in 1951, Israel launched its diaspora bond through the Development Corporation for Israel. The bonds were diversified including fixed, floating rate bonds and notes with 1- to 20-year maturity periods. Through this diaspora bond system, it is estimated that Israel has raised bonds worth more than $32 billion for development- and infrastructure-related initiatives including the transport, energy, water and telecommunication sectors (Gumede et al., 2012). Similarly, India raised an estimated $11.3 billion between 1991 and 2000 through diaspora bonds, which were fixed rate bonds with a five-year maturity. And more recently, Middle-Eastern countries have launched Islamic bonds for people of the Islamic faith as opposed to a country-specific diaspora (Gumede et al., 2012). While diaspora bonds represent a great opportunity for impoverished regions such as SSA, there are a number of challenges that make the implementation of the scheme very difficult. The continent is a collection of many nations with no shared identity, has a high level of political instability, poor governance and governments' mismanagement, and a lack of democracy, making the African diaspora bonds less appealing. Gumede et al. (2012) remarked that there are three-fold challenges to be overcome to make the diaspora bond a success in SSA: (1) how to instill confidence in potential diaspora investors and persuade them to invest in Africa, (2) how to make investment in Africa easy and hassle-free, and (3) how to make long-term profitability of investment in Africa. Any framework geared towards maximising the impact of the diaspora bonds in SSA would not be complete without developed countries' commitment to political stability and conflict prevention, and investing in the promotion of social capital. The environment would need to be safe enough for the diaspora to have confidence in the investment system.

## *The 2010 Global Voluntary Code of Practice on the International Recruitment of Health Personnel*

In the 2000s, a number of key international government and non-government organisations had called for the development of a code of practice to minimise the negative impact of the brain drain. By 2003, Commonwealth countries had adopted and signed a Code of Conduct to guide the recruitment of health professionals from developing countries. The Commonwealth Code focuses on obligation-free sets of agreements related to ethical principles to address the issue of the brain drain (Commonwealth Secretariat, 2003). The UK embarked on a number of reforms geared towards setting up standards for bilateral agreements and ethical recruitment. The outcomes of these reforms included the restrictions on the recruitment of health workers from more than 150 developing countries and the announcement of a US$187 million health package to Malawi which included a $103 million Emergency Human Resource programme, whose aim was to attract and retain health workers, expand training and send volunteers to Malawi (Nullis-Kapp, 2005). Another outcome of these reforms was a memorandum of understanding between the UK and South Africa in 2002, which restricted the number of health workers migrating to the UK from South Africa (Nullis-Kapp, 2005). In 2006, the NGO Physicians for Human Rights set forth some guidelines for rich countries in search of additional health care labour (Physicians for Human Rights, 2006). At the 2004 World Health Assembly, the idea of compensating countries losing their health workers was mooted and the WHA57.19 resolution was adopted by 192 countries (World Health Assembly, 2004). This resolution urged member states (1) to develop strategies to mitigate the adverse effects of the migration of health personnel and minimise its negative impact on health systems, (2) to frame and implement policies and strategies that could enhance the effective retention of health personnel including, but not limited to, strengthening of human resources for health planning and management, and review of salaries and implementation of incentive schemes, (3) to use government-to-government agreements to set up health personnel exchange programmes as a mechanism for managing their migration, and (4) to establish mechanisms for the receiving countries to support the strengthening of health systems, in particular human resources development, in the countries of origin (World Health Assembly, 2004). The code of conduct was also intended to cover the internal brain drain by requiring international NGOs not to poach specialised staff from the public sector and to focus instead on improving the health system in countries of operation (Bristol, 2008).

All the above initiatives were occurring on an ad hoc basis. It was not until 2008 that the first Global Forum on Human Resources for Health took place in Kampala, Uganda from 2 to 7 March 2008, which led to the adoption of the Kampala Declaration. The declaration called for the development of an ethical code of practice to guide the recruitment of international health workers. Subsequently, the G8 made successive communiqués in 2008 and 2009 requesting that the WHO accelerate the development and adoption of a code of practice to halt the negative consequences of the brain drain. Building on the Kampala Declaration, in 2010 the World Health Assembly unanimously adopted the first WHO Global Code of Practice on the International Recruitment of Health

Personnel as a core component of bilateral, national, regional and global responses (World Health Organisation, 2010). This code of practice represents an international soft law and non-binding instrument and contains 10 articles: Article 1 outlines the objectives of the code of practice, Article 2 defines the nature and scope of the code, stressing that it is voluntary and not legally binding, Article 3 provides the Guiding Principles, Article 4 clarifies responsibilities, rights and recruitment practices, Article 5 stresses the need to invest in the health workforce development and health systems sustainability, Article 6 notes the importance of data gathering and research, and recognises the importance of formulating effective policies and plans based on a sound evidence base, Article 7 highlights the importance of information exchange and the establishment and maintenance of an updated database of laws and regulations related to health personnel recruitment and migration, Article 8 emphasises the need to publicise the code and incorporate it into applicable laws and policies, Article 9 notes the need for monitoring and institutional arrangements, and Article 10 emphasises partnerships, technical collaboration and financial support.

## The NGO Code of Conduct for Health Systems Strengthening Initiative

While the 2010 Global Voluntary Code of Practice on the International Recruitment of Health Personnel seeks to address the south–north brain drain, it does not address the internal brain drain. It is widely recognised that international NGOs contribute significantly to the internal brain drain in most LMICs. As Farmer (2008) sums it up,

> "The NGOs that fight for the right to health care by serving the African poor directly frequently do so at the expense of the public sector. Their efforts too often create a local brain drain by luring nurses, doctors, and other professionals from the public hospitals ... to "NGOland," where salaries are better and the tools of our trade more plentiful. The chronic dearth of resources that undermines staff retention in the public sector is due not only to corruption... but also to the structural adjustment programs imposed by the international financial institutions". (p. 10)

Finances raised from voluntary and private sources together with donor aid to LMICs, which has continually and disproportionately been channeled through international NGOs rather than through ministries of health, have led to the proliferation of international NGOs. The end results of the rapid proliferation of NGOs in LMICs include duplication, and to some extent fragmentation, of services, the increased management burdens for local authorities to monitor multiple projects being implemented by NGOs, and the high demand for local staff the consequence of which is the NGOs' aggressive recruitments of employees in the public sector by offering higher salaries, hence leading to the internal brain drain (Pfeiffer et al., 2008). In recognising that the global expansion of international NGOs and their actions undermine the strengthening of public primary health care systems in countries of operation, a number of civil society and non-governmental organisations launched and signed the NGO code of conduct on 29 May 2008 in Washington, DC. The original drafters of the Code were primarily health-focused NGOs such as ActionAid, Health GAP, Partners in Health, Oxfam UK, Equinet, African Medical and Research Foundation, Physicians for Human Rights, Health Alliance International and others (Global Health Alliance, 2008). The NGO code of conduct is a framework for good practice whose purpose is (1) to discourage international NGOs from poaching health workers from the already struggling public-health systems in most LMICs, and (2) to implement policies that strengthen health systems in country of operation through the pursuit of practices that bolster the public sector (Health Alliance International, 2015). The Code targets six important areas: (1) hiring policies, (2) compensation schemes, (3) training and support, (4) minimising the management burden on government due to multiple NGO projects in their countries, (5) helping governments connect communities to the formal health systems, and (6) providing better support to government systems through policy advocacy (Health Alliance International, 2015). Although a soft law and non-binding instrument, the code has six articles (Box 2). Data by the Health Alliance International (2015) suggest that there were an initial group of 22 signatories at the launch of the Code in 2008, but the number has grown exponentially to 63 signatories as of 13 April 2015.

**Trade agreement for brain gain-a win–win:** The role of international trade agreements to address the brain drain is well documented (Shaffer

> **Box 2: The NGO Code of Conduct for Health Systems Strengthening**
>
> **Preamble**
>
> The purpose of this Code of Conduct for Health Systems Strengthening is to offer guidance on how international non-governmental organizations (NGOs) can work in host countries in a way that respects and supports the primacy of the government's responsibility for organizing health system delivery.
>
> Articles:
>
> 1. Article I: NGOs will engage in hiring practices that ensure long-term health system sustainability.
> 2. Article II: NGOs will enact employee compensation practices that strengthen the public sector.
> 3. Article III: NGOs pledge to create and maintain human resources training and support systems that are good for the countries where they work.
> 4. Article IV: NGOs will minimize the NGO management burden for Ministries of Health.
> 5. Article V: NGOs will support Ministries of Health as they engage with communities.
> 6. Article VI: NGOs will advocate for policies which promote and support the public sector.
>
> *Source*: Health Alliance International (2015).

*et al.*, 2005; Packer *et al.*, 2009). Some of the most recent and known regional trade agreements include the 2006 Japan–Philippines bilateral agreement allowing for up to 500 Filipino nurses or caregivers to temporary enter Japan each year for work, professional education or language training, the EU's inclusive model of mutual recognition of qualifications whereby registered nurses can freely work in any EU member state subject to recognition of qualification and proficiency in the host country's language; the North American Free Trade Agreement which enables temporary employment of Canadian, Mexican and American citizens in each other's countries through mutual recognition of professional competency, the Association of Southeast Asian Nations Trade Area which is geared towards creating a single market to facilitate free flows of skilled labour, capital, and other goods and services, and the Southern Common Market

Agreement which is a regional free-trade agreement ratified by 10 South American countries to facilitate trade in health services (Packer *et al.*, 2009). However, there are three trade agreements that underpin the World Trade Organization (WTO): the General Agreement on Tariffs and Trade (GATT), the Agreement on Trade-Related Aspects of Intellectual Property Rights (TRIPS), and the General Agreement on Trade in Services (GATS). The GATS is the agreement most relevant to the brain drain and came into force in 1995. GATS allow members to liberalise trade in service and commit particular services under four modes of service delivery.

**Mode 1** relates cross-border supply of health services through virtual medicine, telemedicine or e-health. In this mode of service trade, users of health services have the opportunity to consult with health professionals in different countries. Similarly, health professionals have the opportunities to consult with patients in different countries. It is about the remote provision of health services from one country to another, and is not limited to the doctor–patient interaction. It also includes interactions between the provider and diagnostic procedures or surgery, and the interaction between the government providing the service and citizens in the recipient country such as internet-based training, and the capacity-building of doctors or public information sites. While this mode of service trade has the potential to harness and maximise the impact of the diaspora's expertise in reaching out to under-served areas, evidence from pilot studies suggests that there are some challenges that need to be overcome (Brauchli *et al.*, 2005; Geissbuhler *et al.*, 2003, 2007). These challenges include the limited relevance of telemedicine when there are major differences in the availability of resources as well as the sociocultural context between the collaborating parties, induced digital divide due to major differences in technological advancements and the need to develop local medical content management skills (Brauchli *et al.*, 2005; Geissbuhler *et al.*, 2003, 2007).

**Mode 2** of service trade relates to the consumption of health services abroad, where health service users go to another country for treatment (either seeking treatment or becoming sick while abroad). Known as health tourism, it is a form of service trade that has flourished over the past two decades. By 2009, it was estimated that there were more than four million international patients per year, which equated to a worldwide market of about $20–40 billion with a project growth of roughly 133% per year (Smith *et al.*, 2009). Contrary to popular belief that health tourism is predominantly characterised by the south–north migration, the majority of patients seeking health care abroad are predominantly from north to south and from south to south. SSA medical tourists tend to be from the middle class as well as politicians and their extended families whose destinations vary with a significant number seeking treatment in Europe and the USA and an increasing number seeking treatment in Asia (e.g. India), the Middle East (e.g. Dubai) and in other African countries such as South Africa (Connell, 2006; Crush and Chikanda, 2014; Kachipande, 2013). Available estimates suggest yearly medical visas granted to Nigerians approximate 40,000 in the UK and 35,000 in India, while those granted to Kenyans equate 50,000 in India annually (Kachipande, 2013). Most scholars argue that medical tourists are attractive in destination countries because they pay higher out-of-pocket rates than local patients as well as spend money on entertainment, dining and lodging for themselves and their family entourage (Kachipande, 2013) and represent good value for business. For example, with Nigeria generating about 5,000 medical tourists per month, this translates into $20 billion on health costs outside Nigeria and a loss to Nigeria's economy of US$500 million per year (Connell, 2006; Kachipande, 2013). The south–south medical tourism to South Africa is characterised by three distinctive drivers: (1) middle class and elites from SSA seeking high-quality private care, (2) patients who are unable to obtain specialised care in their own country, and (3) patients from neighbouring countries with public health care systems near collapse or in a state of crisis (Crush and Chikanda, 2014). South Africa receives approximately 2,477,000 medical tourists per year, of whom 2,196,000 (88.7%) come from the African continents (Kachipande, 2013). In contrast, the north–south medical tourism to South Africa is more driven by the affordability of health care and the added opportunity for a Safari post-treatment. The cost of surgery in South Africa equates to one-third of the surgery cost in the UK (US$5,428 vs. US$13,953 for a facelift; US$310 vs. US$70 for a Botox) and the low cost is complemented by a "Surgery and Safari tour" package, making it very attractive for patients from OECD countries (Kachipande, 2013). This is an area where the medical diaspora can play a significant role. They are often highly trained, possess the knowledge on cultural factors, and may have a burning desire to contribute towards and reconnect with their homeland. Visiting their country of origin is also an opportunity to visit some of the most touristic sites. Harnessing the medical diaspora could save millions of dollars for the countries sending medical tourists abroad while strengthening their own health system through knowledge and skill transfer.

**Mode 3** of the service trade relates to foreign investments characterised by foreign ownership of health services in a given country as a result of such a country opening up to foreign investments mainly in the area of health operations, health management and health insurance. This mode of service trade has remained smaller than other sectors as most health facilities tend to be publicly owned, compounded by the existence of regulatory barriers (Smith, 2004; Smith *et al.*, 2009). A number of scholars have extensively discussed the issues associated with this mode of service trade, and if adopted in SSA it could lead to more health inequalities and non-affordability of health care as a result of the nation's inability to restrict or limit foreign investments in its health care systems. They note that foreign control of health care provision and the liberalisation (service trade under mode (2) as well as the increased privatisation of health would lead to the diversion of much needed resources to curative and high-end procedures, domestic brain drain and advantageous patient selection (Janjaroen and Supakankunti, 2000; Pollock and Price, 2000; Shaffer *et al.*, 2005; Smith *et al.*, 2009).

**Mode 4** of service trade relates to the movement of health professionals rather than companies. Strictly, under the trade agreement, the movement is temporary and not permanent, and can involve the movement of doctors, nurses and pharmacists as well as supporting manpower such as paramedics and medical technicians. There are some ambiguities around what constitutes temporary as this mode of service trade "temporary" is not defined and most importantly statistics on the migration of health professionals do not tend to distinguish temporary from permanent. Like in Modes 1–3, there is no formal process to facilitate the public debate in GATS' decisions concerning committing services. Therefore, countries' requests for commitments of services under Mode 4 are confidential (Shaffer et al., 2005). Other factors constraining Mode 4 of service trade relate to the procedural requirements for recognising overseas qualifications and professional licensing, which may create a serious imbalance and disadvantage many SSA countries. This could explain why most south–north and south–south emigration of health professionals are done through the private sector rather than through states' trade agreements, making states unable to fill the void left by emigrating health professionals and with no mechanisms to seek compensations for lost investments.

## Conclusion

Eliminating the brain drain in the long run is going to be impossible and should not be a policy priority. Instead, there is a need to embrace it and celebrate the many benefits associated with it, and put in place policies geared towards turning the brain drain into the brain gain. As discussed in this chapter and elsewhere in the book, most OECD countries are characterised by a dramatic decline in birth rates and an increasingly ageing population. Such demographic changes mean that there will be a significant decline of the working age population and increase in the dependency ratio over the next 50 years, with serious fiscal, social and macroeconomic implications. If proper policies are not put in place, some of the implications and consequences of a declining working age population and increased ageing include labour shortages, less government income but increased government expenditures to service public pensions and aged care, and overall reductions in production. Policies to mitigate the effects of an aging population and the old age dependency ratio will certainly include prioritising professional and skilled migrants together with other options such as increasing the retirement age and the age at which pension is entitled. Both sending and receiving countries should not necessarily view the brain drain as a negative issue, but seize the opportunity to explore better ways to reshape the brain drain into brain gain through the repatriation of skills and knowledge, better engagement of the diaspora and benefits from remittances. Similarly, the internal brain drain is also a significant issue in most LMICs. Strategies to address the brain drain need to consider the complexities inherent in working within an environment where the NGO presence is greater than ever. To achieve brain gain, major structural changes will need to occur predominantly in sending countries, in terms of how to better capture patterns of emigration through adequate registrations or direct recruitment of professionals and skilled people by international public and private firms, to make the socio-political and economic environment appealing to the diaspora in terms of investments and incentivised strategies to attract their return, and improve the financial service systems to facilitate better management of remittances.

In addition, strategies addressing push factors could be put in place to retain talents including policies geared towards promoting conflict prevention, and work safety and security. There is also an opportunity to explore the benefits that medical tourism may offer. While it may be easy to dismiss medical tourism as a key player in promoting development in impoverished countries, it brings with it many advantages. If sending countries modernise their health care system, then medical tourism could grow exponentially and could constitute a significant source of revenue and employment. Not only would the modernised health care system provide local communities access to health care, it would also provide health workers with a better equipped health care, hence addressing one of the factors that push health professionals to emigrate. The lure and advantage of building the medical tourism industry is that, unlike developed countries that have very complicated processes of obtaining visas, there are lesser visa restrictions in developing countries. While GATS permits states to liberalise their care systems, their viability in sending countries remains questionable. They would, in fact, introduce more inequalities if they are part of the state commitment because when the state is faced with unforeseen challenges it would not be able to withdraw as once commitments have been agreed they are not reversible. GATS would lead to the privatisation of public services and reduce the government's sovereign authority to regulate the employment sector. Releasing such power to multinational corporations, who are interested in the bottom line, may prove to be disastrous for most sending countries.

# References

Acosta, P.A. *et al.* (2007). The impact of remittances on poverty and human capital: Evidence from Latin American household surveys. World Bank Policy Research Working Paper WPS4247. World Bank, New York, NY.

Adkoli, B. (2006). Migration of health workers: Perspectives from Bangladesh, India, Nepal, Pakistan and Sri Lanka. *Regional Health Forum*, 10, 49–58.

Agudelo-Suárez, A. *et al.* (2011). Occupational health. In: Rechel, B., Mladovsky, P., Devillé, W., Rijks, B., Petrova-Benedict, R., McKee, M. (eds.), *Migration and health in the European Union*. Open University Press, McGraw-Hill House, Maidenhead, UK, pp. 155–168.

Agyemang, C. *et al.* (2014). Socioeconomic inequalities in stroke incidence among migrant groups analysis of nationwide data. *Stroke*, 45, 2397–2403.

Aldridge, R.W. *et al.* (2014). Pre-entry screening programmes for tuberculosis in migrants to low-incidence countries: A systematic review and meta-analysis. *Lancet Infectious Diseases*, 14, 1240–1249.

Anand, S.S. *et al.* (2000). Differences in risk factors, atherosclerosis, and cardiovascular disease between ethnic groups in Canada: The Study of Health Assessment and Risk in Ethnic groups (SHARE). *Lancet*, 356, 279–284.

Anikeeva, O. *et al.* (2010). The health status of migrants in Australia: A review. *Asia-Pacific Journal of Public Health*, 22, 159–193.

Anikeeva, O. *et al.* (2012). Trends in cancer mortality rates among migrants in Australia: 1981–2007. *Cancer Epidemiology*, 36, e74–e82.

Anyangwe, S.C. & Mtonga, C. (2007). Inequities in the global health workforce: The greatest impediment to health in SSA. *International Journal of Environmental Research and Public Health*, 4, 93–100.

Arcury, T.A. *et al.* (2012). Personal protective equipment and work safety climate among Latino poultry processing workers in Western North Carolina, USA. *International Journal of Occupational and Environmental Health*, 18, 320–328.

Azerkan, F. *et al.* (2008). Risk of cervical cancer among migrants by age at immigration and follow-up time in Sweden, from 1968 to 2004. *International Journal of Cancer*, 123, 2664–2670.

Baldé, Y. (2011). The impact of remittances and foreign aid on savings/investment in SSA. *African Development Review*, 23, 247–262.

Beine, M. *et al.* (2008). Brain drain and human capital formation in developing countries: Winners and losers. *The Economic Journal*, 118(528), 631–652.

Bhagwati, J. & Hamada, K. (1974). The brain drain, international integration of markets for professionals and unemployment: A theoretical analysis. *Journal of Development Economics*, 1, 19–42.

Bollini, P. & Siem, H. (1995). No real progress towards equity: Health of migrants and ethnic minorities on the eve of the year 2000. *Social Science & Medicine,* 41, 819–828.

Boon, M.R. et al. (2015). High prevalence of cardiovascular disease in South Asians: Central role for brown adipose tissue? *Critical Reviews in Clinical Laboratory Sciences.* Early online view. DOI: 10.3109/10408363.2014.1003634, 1–8.

Bos, V. et al. (2004). Ethnic inequalities in age- and cause-specific mortality in The Netherlands. *International Journal of Epidemiology,* 33, 1112–1119.

Bouchardy, C. et al. (1996). Cancer mortality among north African migrants in France. *International Journal of Epidemiology,* 25, 5–13.

Bouoiyour, J. & Miftah, A. (2015). The impact of migrant workers' remittances on the living standards of families in Morocco: A propensity score matching approach. *Migration Letters,* 12, 13–27.

Brain Drain in Africa: Facts and Figures (2014). Available at: http://www.aracorporation.org/files/factsandfigures.pdf. Accessed 2 February 2015.

Brauchli, K. et al. (2005). iPath-a telemedicine platform to support health providers in low resource settings. *Studies in Health Technology and Informatics,* 114, 11–17.

Brison, R.J. & Pickett, C.W.L. (1992). Non-fatal farm injuries on 117 Eastern Ontario beef and dairy farms: A one-year study. *American Journal of Industrial Medicine,* 21, 623–636.

Bristol, N. (2008). NGO code of conduct hopes to stem internal brain drain. *The Lancet,* 371, 2162.

Browning, S.R., et al. (1998). Agricultural injuries among older Kentucky farmers: The farm family health and hazard surveillance study. *American Journal of Industrial Medicine,* 33, 341–353.

Canuto, O. & Rafha, D. (2011). Migration and Remittances. Factbook 2011. World Bank, Washington, DC.

Castilla, J. et al. (2002). HIV infection among people of foreign origin voluntarily tested in Spain. A comparison with national subjects. *Sexually Transmitted Infections,* 78, 250–254.

Chacko, E. (2007). From brain drain to brain gain: Reverse migration to Bangalore and Hyderabad, India's globalizing high tech cities. *GeoJournal,* 68, 131–140.

Chambers, J.C. et al. (2001). C-reactive protein, insulin resistance, central obesity, and coronary heart disease risk in Indian Asians from the United Kingdom compared with European whites. *Circulation,* 104, 145–150.

Choté, A. et al. (2011). Explaining ethnic differences in late antenatal care entry by predisposing, enabling and need factors in The Netherlands. The Generation R Study. *Maternal and Child Health Journal,* 15, 689–699.

Chowdhury, T.A. *et al.* (2003). Preventing diabetes in south Asians: Too little action and too late. *British Medical Journal*, 327, 1059–1060.
Cirasino, M. (2014). Remittance Cost Reduction Intervention, Monitoring and Impacts. The 12th Coordination Meeting on International Migration. 21 February 2014. World Bank, New York, NY.
Clemens, M.A. & Pettersson, G. (2008). New data on African health professionals abroad. *Human Resources for Health*, 6, 1–11.
Commander, S. *et al.* (2004). The brain drain: Curse or boon? A survey of the literature. In: Baldwin, R., Winters, L.A. (eds.), *Challenges to Globalization: Analyzing the Economics.* University of Chicago Press, Chicago, IL, pp. 235–278.
Commonwealth of Australia. (2012). Australia and Africa: Partners into the Future. Commonwealth of Australia, Canberra, AUS.
Commonwealth Secretariat. (2003). Commonwealth code of practice for the international recruitment of health workers. Commonwealth Secretariat, London, UK.
Connell, J. (2006). Medical tourism: Sea, sun, sand and… surgery. *Tourism Management*, 27, 1093–1100.
Constant, A.F. *et al.* (2013). The economics of circular migration. In: Constant, A.F. & Zimmermann, K.F. (eds.), *International Handbook on the Economics of Migration.* Edward Elgar, Cheltenham, UK, pp. 55–74.
Corvalan, C.F. *et al.* (1994). Role of migrant factors in work-related fatalities in Australia. *Scandinavian Journal of Work, Environment & Health* 20(5), 364–370.
Creatore, M.I. *et al.* (2010). Age-and sex-related prevalence of diabetes mellitus among migrants to Ontario, Canada. *Canadian Medical Association Journal*, 182, 781–789.
Crush, J. & Chikanda, A. (2014). South–south medical tourism and the quest for health in Southern Africa. *Social Science & Medicine*, 124, 313–320.
David, M. *et al.* (2006). Perinatal outcome in Berlin (Germany) among migrants from Turkey. *Archives of Gynecology and Obstetrics*, 274, 271–278.
De Arcangelis, G. *et al.* (2015). Directing remittances to education with soft and hard commitments: Evidence from a lab-in-the-field experiment and new product take-up among Filipino migrants in Rome. *Journal of Economic Behavior & Organization*, 111, 197–208.
Deboosere, P. (2005). Adult migrant mortality advantage in Belgium: Evidence using census and register data. *Population*, 60, 655–698.
Desai, M.A. *et al.* (2004). Sharing the spoils: Taxing international human capital flows. *International Tax and Public Finance*, 11, 663–693.
Dhillon, T.S. & Mehra, A. (2014). Organised or unorganised collective remittances for the development of rural Punjab: A comparative study of two Doaba villages. *Asian Journal of Multidisciplinary Studies*, 2, 34–44.

Docquier, F. (2014). The brain drain from developing countries. *IZA World of Labor*, 31, 1–10.

Dodani, S. (2008). Excess coronary artery disease risk in South Asian migrants: Can dysfunctional high-density lipoprotein explain increased risk? *Journal of Vascular Health and Risk Management*, 4, 953–961.

Dustmann, C. (1993). Earnings adjustment of temporary migrants. *Journal of Population Economics*, 6, 153–168.

Eastwood, J.G. *et al.* (2011). Postnatal depression and socio-demographic risk: Factors associated with Edinburgh Depression Scale scores in a metropolitan area of New South Wales, Australia. *Australian and New Zealand Journal of Psychiatry*, 45, 1040–1046.

Eggemoen, Å.R. *et al.* (2013). Vitamin D status in recently arrived migrants from Africa and Asia: A cross-sectional study from Norway of children, adolescents and adults. *BMJ Open*, 3, e003293.

Essén, B. *et al.* (2002). Are some perinatal deaths in migrant groups linked to suboptimal perinatal care services? *BJOG: An International Journal of Obstetrics & Gynaecology*, 109, 677–682.

European Centre for Disease Prevention and Control (2010). Tuberculosis Surveillance in Europe 2008. WHO Regional Office for Europe, ECDC, Stockholm, SWE.

European Centre for Disease Prevention and Control/WHO Regional Office for Europe (2010). HIV/AIDS Surveillance in Europe 2009. European Centre for Disease Prevention and Control, WHO Regional Office for Europe, ECDC, Stockholm, SWE.

Farmer, P. (2008). Challenging orthodoxies: The road ahead for health and human rights. *Health and Human Rights*, 10(1), 5–19.

Fedeli, U. *et al.* (2010). Obstetric hospitalizations among Italian women, regular and irregular migrants in North-Eastern Italy. *Acta Obstetricia et Gynecologica Scandinavica*, 89, 1432–1437.

Fiddian-Qasmiyeh, E. (2015). *South–South Educational Migration, Humanitarianism and Development: Views from Cuba, North Africa and the Middle East.* Routledge, New York, NY.

Forouhi, N. *et al.* (2006). Do known risk factors explain the higher coronary heart disease mortality in South Asian compared with European men? Prospective follow-up of the Southall and Brent studies, UK. *Diabetologia*, 49, 2580–2588.

Friberg, J.H. *et al.* (2014). Nordic labour market institutions and new migrant workers: Polish migrants in Oslo, Copenhagen and Reykjavik. *European Journal of Industrial Relations*, 20, 37–53.

Geissbuhler, A. *et al.* (2007). The RAFT network: 5 years of distance continuing medical education and tele-consultations over the internet in French-speaking Africa. *International Journal of Medical Informatics*, 76, 351–356.

Geissbuhler, A. et al. (2003). Telemedicine in Western Africa: Lessons learned from a pilot project in Mali, perspectives and recommendations, AMIA Annual Symposium Proceedings. American Medical Informatics Association, p. 249.

Gele, A.A. & Mbalilaki, A.J. (2013). Overweight and obesity among African migrants in Oslo. *BMC Research Notes*, 6, 119.

Ghosh, B. (2000). Return migration: Journey of hope or despair? *International Organization for Migration*, Geneva, SWI, pp. 181–226.

Gibney, K.B. et al. (2009). The profile of health problems in African migrants attending an infectious disease unit in Melbourne, Australia. *The American Journal of Tropical Medicine and Hygiene*, 80, 805–811.

Glass, R.I. et al. (2014). The importance of research in the MEPI program: Perspectives from the National Institutes of Health. *Academic Medicine*, 89, S9–S10.

Glendenning, P. et al. (2003). *No liability–tragic results from Australia's deportations.* Edmund Rice Centre for Justice & Community Education and the Australian Catholic University, Homebush West, AUS.

Global Health Alliance (2008). Launch of NGO Code of Conduct to support public health systems. Available at: http://www.who.int/workforcealliance/news/code-of-conduct/en/. Accessed 28 July 2015.

Goosby, E.P. & von Zinkernagel, D. (2014). The Medical and Nursing Education Partnership Initiatives. *Academic Medicine*, 89, S5–S7.

Gumede, W. et al. (2012). An African Diaspora Bond for infrastructure development: Lessons learnt from India, Israel and Islamic bonds. Policy brief No. 6. Development Bank of Southern Africa, Midrand, SA.

Gupte, M. & Jadhav, K. (2014). The concept of reverse brain drain and its relevance to India *International Monthly Refereed Journal of Research in Management & Technology*, 3, 83–87.

Hahné, S.J. et al. (2013). Infection with hepatitis B and C virus in Europe: A systematic review of prevalence and cost-effectiveness of screening. *BMC Infectious Diseases*, 13, 181.

Han, X. et al. (2015). Will they stay or will they go? international graduate students and their decisions to stay or leave the us upon graduation. *PLoS One*, 10, e0118183.

Harding, S. et al. (2008). Trends for coronary heart disease and stroke mortality among migrants in England and Wales, 1979–2003: Slow declines notable for some groups. *Heart*, 94, 463–470.

Harvey, W.S. & Groutsis, D. (2015). Reputation and talent mobility in the Asia Pacific. *Asia Pacific Journal of Human Resources*, 53, 22–40.

Health Alliance International (2015). The NGO code of conduct for health systems strengthening. Available at: http://ngocodeofconduct.org. Accessed 28 July 2015.

Hemminki, K. et al. (2002). Cancer risks in first-generation migrants to Sweden. *International Journal of Cancer*, 99, 218–228.

Hervey, K. et al. (2009). Overweight among refugee children after arrival in the United States. *Journal of Health Care for the Poor and Underserved*, 20, 246–256.

Hildebrandt, N. et al. (2005). The effects of migration on child health in Mexico. *Economia*, 6(1), 257–289.

Höppli, T. (2014). Is the Brain Drain really reversing? New evidence. Policy Research on International Services and Manufacturing Working Paper 1. PRISM, University of Cape Town, Cape Town, SA.

Indeed, 2014. The economic costs of unfulfilled jobs in the U.S. Available at: https://fortunedotcom.files.wordpress.com/2014/11/report-empty-desk-final-.pdf. Accessed 10 March 2015.

International Development Research Centre (2004). *Stakeholder Roundtable Engaging the African Diaspora in Africa's Capacity Building Efforts*. IDRC, Ottawa, CAN.

IOM & ACP Observatory on Migration (2010). Overview on South–South Migration and Development in the Caribbean: Trends and research needs. ACPOBS/2010/PUB14. Available at: http://www.acpmigration-obs.org/sites/default/files/Regional%20Overview%20Caribbean.pdf. Accessed 10 March 2015.

IOM & ACP Observatory on Migration (2011). Overview on South–South Migration and Development in East Africa: Trends and Research Needs. Available at: http://www.acpmigration-obs.org/sites/default/files/Regional%20Overview%20East%20Africa.pdf. Accessed 10 March 2015.

Ismail, M. et al. (2014). Evidence of reverse brain drain in selected asian countries: Human resource management lessons for Malaysia. *Organizations and Markets in Emerging Economies*, 5, 31–48.

Janevic, T. et al. (2011). Maternal education and adverse birth outcomes among migrant women to the United States from Eastern Europe: A test of the healthy migrant hypothesis. *Social Science & Medicine*, 73, 429–435.

Janjaroen, W. & Supakankunti, S. (2000). International trade in health services in the millenium: A case of Thailand. Centre for Health Economics, Bankok, THA.

Jensen, N. (2013). *The Health Worker Crisis: An Analysis of the Issues and Main International Responses*. Health Poverty Action, London.

Johnston, R., Khattab, N., & Manley, D. (2015). East versus West? Over-qualification and Earnings among the UK's European Migrants. *Journal of Ethnic and Migration Studies*, 41(2), 196-218.

Kachipande, S. (2013). *Medical Tourism in Africa: Sun, Sea, Scalpel and Safari*. Consultancy Africa Intelligence, Johannesburg, SA.

Kahanec, M. & Zimmermann, K.F. (2011). *High-skilled Immigration Policy in Europe*. DIW Berlin, German Institute for Economic Research, Berlin, GER.

Kanaiaupuni, S.M. & Donato, K.M. (1999). Migradollars and mortality: The effects of migration on infant survival in Mexico. *Demography*, 36, 339–353.

Kanaya, A.M. et al. (2008). South Asians and diabetes: Higher risk with traditional beliefs. Paper presented at the 68th Scientific Sessions of the Amedican Diabetes Association; June 6–10, San Francisco, CA.

Kaplan, M.S. et al. (2004). The association between length of residence and obesity among Hispanic migrants. *American Journal of Preventive Medicine*, 27, 323–326.

Kapur, D. (2001). Diasporas and technology transfer. *Journal of Human Development*, 2, 265–286.

Karim, S.S.A. et al. (2009). HIV infection and tuberculosis in South Africa: An urgent need to escalate the public health response. *The Lancet*, 374, 921–933.

Khadria, B. (2002). Skilled labour migration from developing countries: Study on India. *International Migration Papers*, 49. International Labour Office, Geneva, SWI.

Kirigia, J.M. et al. (2006). The cost of health professionals' brain drain in Kenya. *BMC Health Services Research*, 6, 89–99.

Klatsky, A.L. et al. (1994). The risk of hospitalization for Ischemic Heart Disease among Asian Americans in Northern California. *American Journal of Public Health*, 84, 1672–1675.

Krueger, P. et al. (2004). Neighbourhoods and homicide mortality: An analysis of race/ethnic differences. *Journal of Epidemiology and Community Health*, 58, 223–230.

Kunst, A. et al. (2011). Non-communicable diseases, in: Rechel, B., Mladovsky, P., Devillé, W., Rijks, B., Petrova-Benedict, R. & McKee, M. (eds.), *Migration and Health in the European Union*. Open University Press, McGraw-Hill House, Maidenhead.

Langeland, B.T. (2009). Work-related accidents and risks among migrant workers. National Institute of Occupational Health, Norwegian Ministry of Labour and Social Affairs, Oslo, NOR.

Lantz, S. (2005). Students working in the Melbourne sex industry: Education, human capital and the changing patterns of the youth labour market. *Journal of Youth Studies*, 8, 385–401.

Lee, M.T. et al. (2001). Does immigration increase homicide? *The Sociological Quarterly*, 42, 559–580.

Leung, R. (1996). Asthma and migration. *Respirology*, 1, 123–126.

Liese, B., et al. (2003). The human resource crisis in health services in SSA. The World Bank, Washington, DC.

Liu, S.J. et al. (2014). Characterization of chronic Hepatitis B cases among foreign-born persons in six population-based surveillance sites, United States 2001–2010. *Journal of Migrant and Minority Health*, 17(1), 7–12.

López-Sala, A. (2013). Managing uncertainty: Immigration policies in Spain during economic recession (2008–2011). *Migraciones Internacionales*, 7, 21–69.

Lowel, L.B. & Findlay, A.M. (2001). Migration of Highly Skilled Persons from Developing Countries: Impact and Policy Responses: Synthesis Report. *International Migration Papers*, 44. International Labour Office, Geneva, SWI.

Lowell, B.L. (2002). Policy responses to the international mobility of skilled labour. *International Migration Papers*, 45. International Labour Office, Geneva, SWI.

Madeddu, G. et al. (2007). The changing face of the HIV epidemic in Northern Sardinia: Increased diagnoses among pregnant women. *Infection*, 35, 19–21.

Mahmud, S., et al. (2014). Mismatches in skills and attributes of migrants and problems with workplace integration: A study of IT and engineering professionals in Australia. *Human Resource Management Journal*, 24, 339–354.

Malenfant, É.C. (2004). Suicide in Canada's migrant population. *Health Reports* 15, 9–17.

Marchal, B. & Kegels, G. (2003). Health workforce imbalances in times of globalization: Brain drain or professional mobility? *The International Journal of Health Planning and Management*, 18, S89–S101.

Marschall, T. et al. (2008). High impact of migration on the prevalence of chronic hepatitis B in the Netherlands. *European Journal of Gastroenterology & Hepatology*, 20, 1214–1225.

Mascarenhas, R. & Sandler, T. (2014). Remittances and terrorism: A global analysis. *Defence and Peace Economics*, 25, 331–347.

Maskarinec, G. & Noh, J.J. (2004). The effect of migration on cancer incidence among Japanese in Hawaii. *Ethnicity & Disease*, 14, 431–439.

Massey, D.S. & Liang, Z. (1989). The long-term consequences of a temporary worker program: The US Bracero experience. *Population Research and Policy Review*, 8, 199–226.

Massey, D.S. & Pren, K.A. (2012). Unintended consequences of US immigration policy: Explaining the post-1965 surge from Latin America. *Population and Development Review*, 38, 1–29.

Mather, H.M. & Keen, H. (1985). The Southall Diabetes Survey: Prevalence of known diabetes in Asians and Europeans. *British Medical Journal*, 291, 1081–1084.

McCurdy, S.A. et al. (2003). Agricultural injury in California migrant Hispanic farm workers. *American Journal of Industrial Medicine*, 44, 225–235.

McKeigue. et al. (1993). Association of early-onset coronary heart disease in South Asian men with glucose intolerance and hyperinsulinemia. *Circulation*, 87, 152–161.

McKeigue, P. et al. (1991). Relation of central obesity and insulin resistance with high diabetes prevalence and cardiovascular risk in South Asians. *The Lancet*, 337, 382–386.

Mesnard, A. (2004). Temporary migration and capital market imperfections. *Oxford Economic Papers*, 56, 242–262.

Mills, E.J. et al. (2011). The financial cost of doctors emigrating from SSA: Human capital analysis. *British Medical Journal*, 343: d7031 doi: 10.1136/bmj.d7031.

Misra, R. et al. (2010). Prevalence of diabetes, metabolic syndrome, and cardiovascular risk factors in US Asian Indians: Results from a national study. *Journal of Diabetes and its Complications*, 24, 145–153.

Mukhopadhyay, B. et al. (2006). A comparison of glycaemic and metabolic control over time among South Asian and European patients with Type 2 diabetes: Results from follow-up in a routine diabetes clinic. *Diabetic Medicine*, 23, 94–98.

Morrone, A. et al. (2012). Iron deficiency anaemia prevalence in a population of immigrated women in Italy. *The European Journal of Public Health*, 22(2), 256–262.

Mullan, F. et al. (2011). Medical schools in SSA. *The Lancet*, 377, 1113–1121.

Mutume, G. (2003). Reversing Africa's brain drain. *Africa Recovery*, 17, 1–9.

Naim, S. & Iftikhar, Z. (2008). Migration of highly skilled and its impact on the economic and technological development of Pakistan and Bangladesh. *South Asia Network of Economic Research Institutes*, 10, 2–23.

Nayak, R.K. et al. (2014). Incidence of stroke among Swedish-born and migrant women–the role of socio-economic status, smoking, and physical activity. *World Journal of Cardiovascular Diseases*, 4, 556–566.

Neilson, B. (2009). The world seen from a taxi: Students-migrants-workers in the global multiplication of labour. *Subjectivity*, 29, 425–444.

Ngunjiri, P. (2003). Africa to Lost Professionals: 'Come Home'. Pacific News Service, Nairobi, KEN.

Nullis-Kapp, C. (2005). Efforts under way to stem 'brain drain' of doctors and nurses. *Bulletin of the World Health Organization*, 83, 84–85.

O'Brien, P. & Gostin, L. (2011). *Health Worker Shortages and Global Justice*. Milbank Memorial Fund, New York, NY.

OECD (2014) Is migration good for the economy? Available at: http://www.oecd.org/migration/mig/OECD%20Migration%20Policy%20Debates%20Numero%202.pdf. Accessed 8 March 2015.

Ofori-Asenso, R. (2013). HIV-Related Travel Restrictions: A Focus On US And Canada. The Internet Journal of World Health and Societal Politics 8. Available at: https://ispub.com/IJWH/8/1/14678. Accessed 24 February 2015.

Omaswa, F.G. (2014). The contribution of the Medical Education Partnership Initiative to Africa's renewal. *Academic Medicine*, 89, S16–S18.

Ondiege, P. (2010). Mobile banking in Africa: Taking the bank to the people. *Africa Economic Brief*, 1, 1–15.

Owolabi, R. & Rafiu, L. (2010). Chemical engineering education in Nigeria: Challenges and prospects. *International Journal of Chemical Engineering and Applications*, 1, 138–141.

Packer, C. et al. (2009). Globalization and the cross-border flow of health workers. In: Labonté, R., Schrecker, T., Packer, C. & Runnels, V. (eds.). *Globalization and health: Pathways, evidence and policy.* Routledge, New York, NY, pp. 213–234.

Pezzoli, M.C. et al. (2009). HIV infection among illegal migrants, Italy, 2004–2007. *Emerging Infectious Diseases,* 15, 1802–1804.

Pfeiffer, J. et al. (2008). Strengthening health systems in poor countries: A code of conduct for nongovernmental organizations. *American Journal of Public Health,* 98(12), 2134–2140.

Philibert, M. et al. (2008). Can excess maternal mortality among women of foreign nationality be explained by suboptimal obstetric care? *BJOG: An International Journal of Obstetrics & Gynaecology,* 115, 1411–1418.

Physicians for Human Rights (2006). *An Action Plan to Prevent Brain Drain: Building Equitable Health Systems in Africa.* Physicians for Human Rights, Boston, MA.

Pollock, A.M. & Price, D. (2000). Rewriting the regulations: How the World Trade Organisation could accelerate privatisation in health-care systems. *The Lancet,* 356, 1995–2000.

Pratt, D.S. et al. (1992). The dangers of dairy farming: The injury experience of 600 workers followed for two years. *American Journal of Industrial Medicine,* 21, 637–650.

Raleigh, V.S. et al. (1990). Suicides among migrants from the Indian subcontinent. *The British Journal of Psychiatry,* 156, 46–50.

Ratha, D. & Mohapatra, S. (2011). Preliminary Estimates of Diaspora Savings. *Migration and Development Brief,* 14. The World Bank, Washington, DC.

Ratha, D. et al. (2011). Leveraging migration for Africa: Remittances, skills, and investments. The World Bank, Washington, DC.

Ratha, D., et al. (2014). Migration and Remittances: Recent Developments and Outlook. *Migration and Development Brief,* 22. The World Bank, Washington, DC.

Ravelli, A.C. et al. (2010). Ethnic differences in stillbirth and early neonatal mortality in The Netherlands. *Journal of Epidemiology and Community Health,* 65, 696–701.

Rees, D. et al. (2010). Oscillating migration and the epidemics of silicosis, tuberculosis, and HIV infection in South African gold miners. *American Journal of Industrial Medicine,* 53, 398–404.

Reeske, A. et al. (2011). Stillbirth differences according to regions of origin: An analysis of the German perinatal database, 2004–2007. *BMC Pregnancy and Childbirth,* 11, 63. doi:10.1186/1471-2393-1111-1163.

Regidor, E., et al. (2009). Mortality from cardiovascular diseases in migrants residing in Madrid. *Medicina Clinica,* 132, 621–624.

Reisman, D. (2014). *Trade in Health: Economics, Ethics and Public Policy.* Edward Elgar Publishing, Cheltenham, UK.

Renzaho, A. et al. (2008). Maintenance of traditional cultural orientation is associated with lower rates of obesity and sedentary behaviours among African migrant children to Australia. *International Journal of Obesity*, 32, 594–600.

Renzaho, A. et al. (2011). Prevalence of vitamin D insufficiency and risk factors for type 2 diabetes and cardiovascular disease among African migrant and refugee adults in Melbourne. *Asia Pacific Journal of Clinical Nutrition*, 20, 397–403.

Reyneri, E. & Fullin, G. (2011). Labour market penalties of new migrants in new and old receiving West European countries. *International Migration*, 49, 31–57.

Robertson, S. (2014). Time and temporary migration: The case of temporary graduate workers and working holiday makers in Australia. *Journal of Ethnic and Migration Studies*, 40, 1915–1933.

Ronda Pérez, E. et al. (2012). Differences in working conditions and employment arrangements among migrant and non-migrant workers in Europe. *Ethnicity & Health*, 17, 563–577.

Roosmalen, J. et al. (2002). Substandard care in migrant versus indigenous maternal deaths in The Netherlands. *BJOG: An International Journal of Obstetrics & Gynaecology*, 109, 212–213.

Rossi, C. et al. (2012). Seroprevalence of chronic hepatitis B virus infection and prior immunity in migrants and refugees: A systematic review and meta-analysis. *PLoS One*, 7, e44611.

Roy, A.K. et al. (2015). Impact of rural–urban labour migration on education of children: A case study of left behind and accompanied migrant children in India. *Space and Culture, India*, 2, 17–34.

Ruwanpathirana, T. et al. (2014). Assessment of vitamin D and its association with cardiovascular disease risk factors in an adult migrant population: An audit of patient records at a Community Health Centre in Kensington Melbourne Australia. *BMC Cardiovascular Disorders*, 14, 1–8.

Saleh, A. et al. (2002). The effect of migration on dietary intake, type 2 diabetes and obesity: The Ghanaian Health and Nutrition Analysis in Sydney, Australia (GHANAISA). *Ecology of Food and Nutrition*, 41, 255–270.

Samet, K. (2013). Circular migration between the North and the South: Effects on the source Southern economies. *Procedia-Social and Behavioral Sciences*, 93, 2234–2250.

Scheffler, R.M. et al. (2009). Estimates of health care professional shortages in SSA by 2015. *Health Affairs*, 28, w849–w862.

Schulden, J. et al. (2014). HIV testing histories and risk factors among migrants and recent migrants who received rapid HIV testing from three community-based organizations. *Journal of Migrant and Minority Health*, 16, 798–810.

Schutte, J. et al. (2010). Rise in maternal mortality in the Netherlands. *BJOG: An International Journal of Obstetrics & Gynaecology*, 117, 399–406.

Shaffer, E.R. et al. (2005). Ethics in public health research: Global trade and public health. *American Journal of Public Health*, 95, 23–34.

Shaw, P.C. et al. (2002). Increased end-stage diabetic nephropathy in Indo-Asian migrants living in the Netherlands. *Diabetologia*, 45, 337–341.

Shimeles, A. (2010). Migration Patterns, Trends and Policy Issues in Africa. Working Paper Series No. 119. African Development Bank Group, Tunis, TUN.

Shinn, D.H. (2008). African migration and the brain drain, Institute for African Studies and Slovenia Global Action, 20 June 2008, Ljubljana, SVN.

Shire, A.M. et al. (2012). Viral hepatitis among Somali migrants in Minnesota: Association of hepatitis C with hepatocellular carcinoma. *Mayo Clinic Proceedings*, 87(1), 17–24.

Siddiqui, T. & Parvin, N. (2012). Circulation of Highly Skilled Professionals and its Impact on Development of Bangladesh. Background paper for the Least Developed Countries Report 2012: Harnessing Remittances and Diaspora Knowledge to Build Productive Capacities. Background Paper No. 2. United Nations Conference on Trade and Development, Geneva, SWI.

Smith, R.D. (2004). Foreign direct investment and trade in health services: A review of the literature. *Social Science & Medicine*, 59, 2313–2323.

Smith, R.D. et al. (2009). Trade in health-related services. *The Lancet*, 373, 593–601.

Solé, M., Diaz-Serrano, L., Rodríguez, M. (2013). Disparities in work, risk and health between migrants and native-born Spaniards. *Social Science & Medicine*, 76, 179–187.

Song, H. (1997). From brain drain to reverse brain drain: Three decades of Korean experience. *Science Technology & Society*, 2, 317–345.

Sorenson, S.B. & Shen, H. (1996). Homicide risk among migrants in California, 1970 through 1992. *American Journal of Public Health*, 86, 97–100.

Spallek, J. et al. (2009). Cancer incidence rate ratios of Turkish migrants in Hamburg, Germany: A registry based study. *Cancer Epidemiology*, 33, 413–418.

Spallek, J., Reeske, A., Norredam, M., Nielsen, S. S., Lehnhardt, J., & Razum, O. (2015). Suicide among immigrants in Europe — a systematic literature review. *The European Journal of Public Health*, 25(1), 63–71.

Ssengonzi, R. et al. (2002). The effect of female migration on infant and child survival in Uganda. *Population Research and Policy Review*, 21, 403–431.

Stark, O. (2004). Rethinking the brain drain. *World Development*, 32, 15–22.

Stewart, D.E., et al. (2008). Postpartum depression symptoms in newcomers. *Canadian Journal of Psychiatry*, 53, 121–124.

Stirbu, I. et al. (2006). Cancer mortality rates among first and second generation migrants in the Netherlands: Convergence toward the rates of the native Dutch population. *International Journal of Cancer*, 119, 2665–2672.

Supramaniam, R. et al. (2008). Future cancer trends to be influenced by past and future migration. *Australian and New Zealand Journal of Public Health*, 32, 90–92.

Szilard, A. (2009). New migration challenges for hungary since the EU and the Schengen area accession. Centre International de Formation Européenne Institut Européen, Nice, FRA.

Tan, S.-T. et al. (2014). Coronary heart disease in Indian Asians. *Global Cardiology Science & Practice*, 2014, 13.

Tankwanchi, A.B.S. et al. (2013). Physician emigration from SSA to the United States: Analysis of the 2011 AMA physician masterfile. *PLoS Medicine*, 10, e1001513.

Thurman, A.R. et al. (2009). Unfulfilled postpartum sterilization requests. *The Journal of Reproductive Medicine*, 54, 467–472.

Thurman, A.R. & Janecek, T. (2010). One-year follow-up of women with unfulfilled postpartum sterilization requests. *Obstetrics & Gynecology*, 116, 1071–1077.

Tiong, A. et al. (2006). Health issues in newly arrived African refugees attending general practice clinics in Melbourne. *Medical Journal of Australia*, 185, 602–606.

Tobias, A. et al. (2001). Symptoms of asthma, bronchial responsiveness and atopy in migrants and emigrants in Europe. *European Respiratory Journal*, 18, 459–465.

Turin, T.C. et al. (2013). Burden of cardio-and cerebro-vascular diseases and the conventional risk factors in South Asian population. *Global Heart*, 8, 121–130.

Udah, H. (2014). The African Diaspora in Australia and African Renaissance: Harnessing Diaspora Resources and Encouraging Diaspora Investments and Linkages with Africa., African Renaissance and Australia, 26–28 November 2013. African Studies Association of Australasia and the Pacific, Perth, AUS.

Ullah, I. et al. (2015). Terrorism and worker's remittances in Pakistan. *Journal of Business Studies Quarterly*, 6, 178–189.

United Nations (2013). World Population Ageing 2013. ST/ESA/SER.A/348. UN Department of Economic and Social Affairs, Population Division, New York, NY.

UN-DESA (2013) Trends in International Migrants Stock: The 2013 Revision (United Nations database, POP/DB/MIG/Stock/Rev.2013, Table 1), http://esa.un.org/unmigration/TIMSA2013/Data/UN_MigrantStock_2013.xls Accessed 27 July 2015.

UN-DESA & OECD (2013). World Migration in Figures. Available at: http://www.oecd.org/els/mig/World-Migration-in-Figures.pdf. Accessed 1 September 2014.

United Nations Programme on HIV/AIDS (2009). Mapping of restrictions on the entry, stay and residence of people living with HIV. UNAIDS/09.20E/JC1727E. UNAIDS, Geneva, SWI.

van Roosmalen, J. et al. (2002). Substandard care in migrant versus indigenous maternal deaths in The Netherlands. *BJOG: An International Journal of Obstetrics & Gynaecology*, 109, 212–213.

Ventura, M. *et al.* (2004). Allergy, asthma and markers of infections among Albanian migrants to Southern Italy. *Allergy,* 59, 632–636.
Visser, O. & Van Leeuwen, F. (2007). Cancer risk in first generation migrants in North-Holland/Flevoland, The Netherlands, 1995–2004. *European Journal of Cancer,* 43, 901–908.
Walter, N.D. *et al.* (2014). Persistent latent tuberculosis reactivation risk in United States migrants. *American Journal of Respiratory and Critical Care Medicine,* 189, 88–95.
Wandel, M. (1993). Nutrition-related diseases and dietary change among Third World migrants in northern Europe. *Nutrition and Health,* 9, 117–133.
Wasley, A. *et al.* (2010). The prevalence of Hepatitis B virus infection in the United States in the era of vaccination. *Journal of Infectious Diseases,* 202, 192–201.
Weber, M.F. *et al.* (2009). Cancer screening among migrants in an Australian cohort; cross-sectional analyses from the 45 and Up Study. *BMC Public Health,* 9, 144. doi:110.1186/1471-2458-1189-1144.
Wild, S. *et al.* (2006). Mortality from all cancers and lung, colorectal, breast and prostate cancer by country of birth in England and Wales, 2001–2003. *British Journal of Cancer,* 94, 1079–1085.
World Bank (2013). The African Diapsora Programme: Mobilising the African diaspora for development. World Bank, Washington, DC.
World Bank (2014). World Bank database on bilateral migration and remittances. Available at: http://go.worldbank.org/JITC7NYTT0. Accessed 12 March 2015.
World Health Assembly (2004). Resolution WHA57.19. Fifty-seventh World Health Assembly. Eighth plenary meeting, 22 May 2004. WHO, Geneva, SWI.
World Health Organisation (2010). WHO Global Code of Practice on the International Recruitment of Health Personnel. WHO, Geneva, SWI.
Wörmann, T. & Krämer, A. (2011). Communicable diseases. In: Rechel, B., Mladovsky, P., Devillé, W., Rijks, B., Petrova-Benedict, R. & McKee, M. (eds.), *Migration and health in the European Union.* Open University Press, McGraw-Hill House, Maidenhead.
Xue, P. (2012). Why does overseas Chinese talent intend to return? A Case Study on The Determinants of Return-Intentions of Chinese Talent in Japan. Working Paper Series, 8. The International Centre for the Study East Asian Development. Kitakyushu Fukuoka, JPN.
Zhang, Y. (2012). Thousand talent program brings more pros. *China Daily.* Available at: http://www.chinadaily.com.cn/bizchina/2012-04/28/content_15168335.htm. Accessed 10 March 2015.
Zhou, C. & Roseman, J.M. (1994). Agricultural injuries among a population-based sample of farm operators in Alabama. *American Journal of Industrial Medicine,* 25, 385–402.

# Section 2:
# Case Studies — Asylum Seekers, Healthy Migrant Effect, and Access and Utilisation of Health Services

# Chapter 5

# Invisible and suffering: prolonged and systematic detention of asylum seekers living in substandard conditions in Greece

Dr Sheila Cyril and Professor André M.N. Renzaho

## Introduction

Detention of irregular migrants and asylum seekers is becoming an increasingly common practice in many countries. Irregular migrants include those arriving in the country with a legal visa either to visit or to work and overstaying their visa without any residence status. In contrast, asylum seekers are people fleeing dangerous war-torn regions with human right abuses and seeking international protection in another country but whose claim for refugee status has not yet been determined. The so-called "undocumented" or "illegal" arrivals are asylum seekers arriving either by boat, land, or plane without a valid visa. Both irregular migrants and undocumented arrivals are subject to immigration detention. The use of the terms "irregular migrants" and "undocumented arrivals" has attracted criticism and has been labelled as insulting. We recognise that asylum-seeking is neither a criminal act nor should it be criminalised. However, we use these terms in this chapter for ease of narration, and do not place any value judgement on them. We use the term "third-country national" to refer to individuals in transit and applying for a visa to stay in a country other than their country of origin or to go to a destination country that is not their country of origin. In the European Union (EU) context, "third-country nationals" refer to individuals who are neither from the EU member state in which they apply for a visa nor from any other EU member states.

The concept of mandatory detention has become a global phenomenon and most countries employ detention as a way of regulating irregular migration. Data from the Global Detention Project (2015) indicate that low- and middle-income countries, some with poor human rights track record, have also adopted mandatory detention policies. However, compared to other regions, the number of countries with mandatory detention centres is significantly higher in Europe. The increasing number of detention centres worldwide led the United Nations High Commissioner for Refugees (UNHCR) to develop guidelines for detention in 2012, which are summarised in Box 1 (UNHCR, 2012a). It is worth noting that several international NGOs and multilateral agencies have condemned the practice of detention as violation of human rights within the migration framework (Amnesty International, 2014; Human Rights Watch, 2008; UNHCR, 2012a). Nevertheless, a plethora of definitions exist for the term "detention" or "immigration detention" with some positioning it as legitimate and others positioning it as a breach of international standards. For example, the European Commission considers immigration detention as "a *non-punitive administrative measure applied by the state to restrict the movement of an individual through confinement in order for an immigration procedure to be implemented*" (European Commission, 2014). Consequently, the EU has put in place procedural safeguards and legal frameworks stipulating that "*immigration detention is justified only for a set of specific grounds applied in specific situations, such as preventing unauthorised entry into the territory of a Member State, preventing absconding in return procedures and under certain conditions within the asylum procedure*" (European Commission, 2014, p. 4). In contrast, the UNHCR considers immigration detention as nothing more than "*a deprivation of liberty or confinement in a closed place which an asylum-seeker is not permitted to leave at will, including, though not limited to, prisons or purpose-built detention, closed*

> **Box 1: UNHCR detention guidelines**
>
> **Guideline 1**  The right to seek asylum must be respected.
> **Guideline 2**  The rights to liberty and security of person and to freedom of movement apply to asylum seekers.
> **Guideline 3**  Detention must be in accordance with and authorised by law.
> **Guideline 4**  Detention must not be arbitrary, and any decision to detain must be based on an assessment of the individual's particular circumstances, according to the following:
>
> > **Guideline 4.1**  Detention is an exceptional measure and can only be justified for a legitimate purpose.
> > **Guideline 4.2**  Detention can only be resorted to when it is determined to be necessary, reasonable in all the circumstances and proportionate to a legitimate purpose.
> > **Guideline 4.3**  Alternatives to detention need to be considered.
>
> **Guideline 5**  Detention must not be discriminatory.
> **Guideline 6**  Indefinite detention is arbitrary and maximum limits on detention should be established in law.
> **Guideline 7**  Decisions to detain or to extend detention must be subject to minimum procedural safeguards.
> **Guideline 8**  Conditions of detention must be humane and dignified.
> **Guideline 9**  The special circumstances and needs of particular asylum seekers must be taken into account.
> **Guideline 10**  Detention should be subject to independent monitoring and inspection.
>
> *Source*: UNHCR (2012a).

*reception or holding centres or facilities."* (UNHCR, 2012a, p. 9). Such a definition implies that immigration detention may be illegal in some cases, especially if detention policies, conditions and operational approaches contravene international standards. For example, in its assessment of Australian immigration detention centres in the Republic of Nauru in 2013, the UNHCR concluded that these detentions did not comply with international standards on arbitrary and mandatory detention, and do not provide a fair and expeditious processing system for refugee claims as well as safe and humane conditions to asylum seekers in detentions under international law (UHNCR, 2014a).

Discussions around the legality or illegality of immigration detention are beyond the purpose of this chapter (recommended further reading — Macgrady, 1997; Schriro, 2009). Instead, this chapter discusses the impact of detention on the health of migrants seeking asylum in Europe, using Greece, which is a member of the EU, as a case study. The chapter begins by describing the trends and characteristics of undocumented migration flows into Greece followed by a discussion on the use of detention as a migration management tool. It then proceeds to explore the challenges faced by inmates in detention centres, including key health issues and access to health care, followed by an overview of the policy response to irregular migration and highlighting important gaps in the asylum system in Greece. The chapter then discusses the role of NGOs in identifying and addressing the risks and challenges in detention centres and concludes by giving an overview of the key policy recommendations for improving the health and wellbeing of detained asylum seekers in Greece.

## Trends and patterns in the flow of irregular migrants into Greece

In the recent past, Greece has become the main gateway into Europe for irregular migrants and asylum seekers coming from Asia and Africa. The flow mainly includes people fleeing war, violence and conflict in their home countries. Greece has close proximity to regions that have been experiencing serious conflict which results in the country receiving more than its fair share of the EU's asylum seekers, a phenomenon which has been growing steadily over the years. For instance, in 2010, 90% of all arrests for illegal entry into the EU took place in Greece, compared to 75% in 2009 and 50% in 2008 (Charalambos, 2012). Since 2012, the majority of "illegal arrivals" originated from Syria, followed by Somalis, Afghans and Eritreans. In 2014 alone, approximately 43,500 irregular migrants and illegal arrivals reached Greece by sea, equating to an increase of 280% when compared to 2013 (UNHCR, 2014b).

The Greek–Turkish border has been one of the main points of irregular border crossings into Europe. To control these flows, border control was tightened from 2010 onwards in compliance with the Schengen Agreement. The Schengen Agreement was originally signed on 14 June 1985 between the governments of Belgium, Luxembourg, The Netherlands, The Federal Republic of Germany and France followed by the establishment of the Schengen Convention in 1990 which led to the abolition of internal border controls to enable passport-free movement between 26 European countries in the Schengen Area (EUR-LEX Access to European Union Law, 2009). The Schengen Area includes Greece. The creation of an internally borderless Europe was characterised by common rules applying to people crossing external borders in the Schengen area and cross-border surveillance by police authorities. However, increasing irregular migrant flows at its various borders including Italy, France and Greece led to calls requesting the reinstatement of border control procedures. It is worth noting that under the Schengen Borders Code, each member state in the Schengen area is responsible for tightening its external border security and controls, covering land and sea borders as well as international airports. Member states' border security and control strategies are complemented by FRONTEX's technical expertise in coordination of deployment. FRONTEX is the European Agency for the Management of Operational Cooperation at the External Borders of the EU member states, which was established in 2004 for purposes of border control against irregular migration and human trafficking (FRONTEX, 2015). In 2010, FRONTEX supported the Poseidon Land and Poseidon Sea Joint Operations with personnel, equipment, technical and operational expertise to equip the border control authorities, namely the police and the Hellenic Coast Guard (UNHCR, 2014b). Later in 2012, the Greek authorities launched Operation Aspida (Shield) by deploying 1,800 additional police officers from Greece to block crossings at the Greek–Turkish land border in the Evros region (Council of Europe, 2013). Findings from the UNHCR (2014b) suggest that the border control policy proved effective in reducing the number of land arrests in Greece which dropped from 30,433 in 2012 to a mere 1,122 in 2013 (Figure 1). Nevertheless, the decline in irregular arrivals by land as a result of the border control

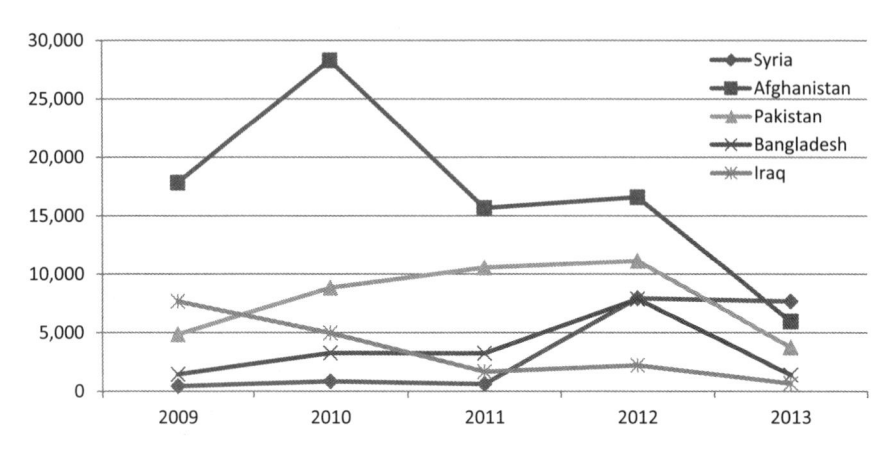

Figure 1: Five-year trends in arrests among leading Asian nationalities for illegal entry/residence in Greece (2009–2013).
Source: Figure constructed using data from Hellenic Police (2015).

intervention was accompanied by a dramatic increase in irregular boat arrivals with the number of sea arrests increasing from 3,651 in 2012 to 11,447 in 2013. A five-year trend analysis of illegal entry and/or residence in Greece for asylum seekers from Asian countries between 2009 and 2013 suggests an increase in arrests in 2010 followed by a sharp decline in 2013.

Additionally, as can be seen from Figure 2, there was a sharp drop in asylum applications in 2010. This drop could have been a result of the 2010 strict border protection measures, the restrictive asylum policy, inhumane reception conditions and poor infrastructure which hindered migrants' applications for asylum (Charalambos, 2012). Data in Figures 1 and 2 show that the number of asylum applications was not proportionate to the number of arrests. For example, while Afghanistan recorded the highest number of arrests between 2009 and 2013, this pattern was not reflected in their applications for asylum. In its 2014 report, the UNHCR (2014b) stated that the top nationalities applying for asylum did not match the top nationalities of illegal arrivals, hence confirming that many arrivals choose not to apply for asylum. Such findings are supported by data in Figure 3.

*Invisible and Suffering* 213

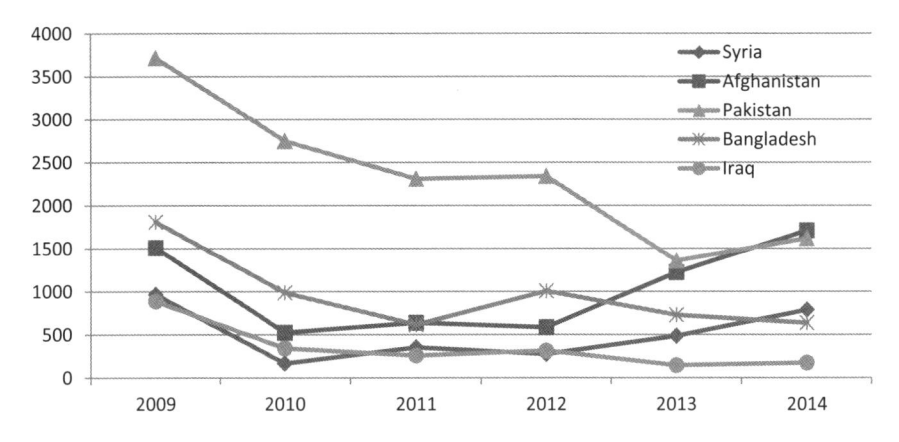

**Figure 2:** Six-year trends in asylum applications in Greece from the corresponding Asian countries (2009–2014).
*Source*: Figure constructed based on data from UNHCR Asylum Trends (UNHCR, 2010, 2011, 2012b, 2014c).

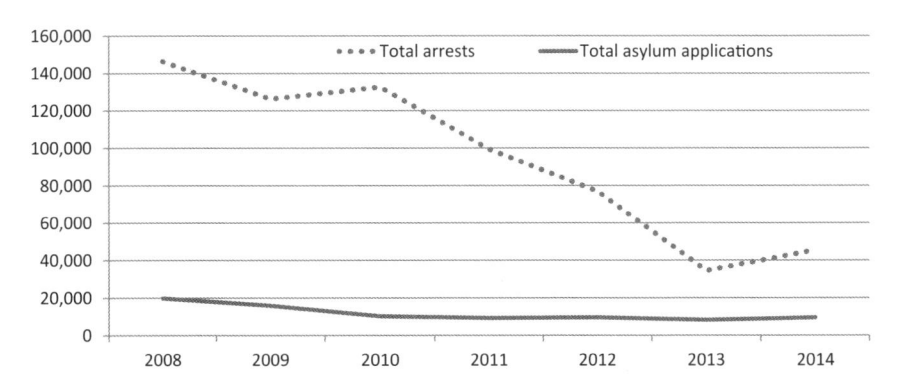

**Figure 3:** Trends in total number of arrests and total number of asylum applications in Greece (2008–2014).
*Source*: Figure constructed based on data from UNHCR Asylum Trends. (UNHCR, 2010, 2012b, 2014c; Hellenic Police, 2015).

# Detention practice in Greece as a migration management tool

The systematic detention of irregular migrants and asylum seekers is increasingly being used, worldwide and by EU member states including

Greece, as a core migration management tool to restrict the influx of migrants and to pressurise detained migrants into joining voluntary return programmes. However, the effectiveness of detention as a deterrent for irregular or otherwise "illegal" migration has not been established. As Edwards (2011) noted *"there is no empirical evidence that the prospect of being detained deters irregular migration, or discourages persons from seeking asylum"* (p. 1). According to the UNHCR (2012a), detention is applicable where it pursues a legitimate purpose and has been determined to be both necessary and proportionate in each individual case. From 2010 onwards, Greece adopted a new policy governed by the Presidential Decree 114/2010 on the asylum procedure, which uses detention as a sole means of managing its irregular migrant inflows (Council of Europe, 2013). Under this policy, irregular migrants including asylum seekers without legal documentation are routinely and systematically placed in detention.

Detention in Greece is regulated by two laws, namely, Law 3386/2005 which applies to those detained upon entry at the external border, and Law 3907/2011, which implements the EU Returns Directive, for those detained while already residing in Greece (OHCHR, 2013; para 42). Following its adoption of Law 4075/2012, Greece was heavily criticised as this law extended the grounds for detention, mainly on health-related grounds. Law 4075/2012 amended both Presidential Decree 114/2010 and Law 3386/2005, providing for irregular migrants and asylum seekers to also be detained if they represent a "danger to public health", when they "suffer from an infectious disease", "belong to groups vulnerable to infectious diseases" or are living in "conditions that do not meet minimum standards of hygiene" (OHCHR, 2013; para 44).

The detention period has been an issue of growing concern and controversy with the length of detention having been extended three times within the past few years. Initially in 2009, the maximum period of detention was increased from 3 to 6 months. In 2011, following the transposition of the Returns Directive, the period was increased to 18 months. Finally, on 24 February 2014, the Greek Legal Council published the Advisory Opinion no. 44/2014, which specified that Greek authorities were legally permitted to detain irregular migrants beyond 18 months, which exceeded the maximum time limit set by the Greek law. (Triandafyllidou, 2014; Majcher and Flynn 2014) Incidentally, this policy has a two-fold aim: first, to ensure that all irregular migrants are sent back to their home countries, and second, to use this system of detention as a warning to those who are seeking asylum in Greece and not yet under the international protection status (Triandafyllidou, 2014).

## *Operation Xenios Zeus*

Operation Xenios Zeus is an initiative led by police authorities to track illegal immigration in Athens by conducting verification checks on migrants' legal status. Launched in August 2012, the aim of this operation is three-fold: (1) to seal the Greece–Turkey border in order to deter entry by illegal immigrants, (2) to identify illegal (undocumented) migrants in urban areas in order to facilitate their return to home countries, and (3) to improve the quality of life for Athens' residents and visitors by restoring Athens as a city of law (Headquarters of the Hellenic Police, 2012; Human Rights Watch, 2013a). Since the commencement of Operation Xenios Zeus, thousands of foreigners have been taken to police stations for verification of their documents. In February 2013 alone, there were 4,811 arrests for illegal entry, and within two months this number rose to 5,194, following which the Athens police refused to release any further statistics on the arrests for illegal entry into Greece (Human Rights Watch, 2013a). Those arrested under Operation Xenios Zeus, as is the case for any other irregular migrants, are subject to administrative detention (UNHCR, 2014b). Administrative detention is defined as *"the arrest and detention of individuals by State authorities outside the criminal law context, for reasons of security, preventive detention, as well as to restrain irregular migrants"* (UN, 2010, para 77).

While police officials considered Operation Xenios Zeus to be a huge success in reducing illegal immigration in Greece, one of the operation tenets is ethnic profiling. Ethnic profiling refers to police operations geared towards identifying irregular and illegal migrants based on people's skin colour and ethnicity (Amnesty International, 2014). Human Rights Watch (2013a, p. 25), based on Article 14 of the European Convention on Human Rights, has stated that *"no difference in treatment which is based exclusively or to a decisive extent on a person's ethnic origin is capable of being objectively justified in a contemporary democratic society"*.

Therefore, Operation Xenios Zeus and the practice of ethnic profiling are incongruent with, and in violation of, human rights and have been publicly condemned by several humanitarian organisations (Human Rights Watch, 2013a; Amnesty International, 2014).

## Detention centres and their conditions

In Greece, the immigration detention facilities can be classified into three types, namely, pre-removal detention centres, detention centres and identification centres (AIDA, 2015). All illegal arrivals are routinely issued a detention order and held in detention until a decision on their asylum application is made by the immigration authorities. Illegal maritime arrivals are held in custody by the Hellenic coast guards, while illegals arriving on land are held in police stations until the prosecution process is commenced (UNHCR, 2014b). The Greek laws permit three specific grounds for pre-removal detention of third-country nationals, namely, (1) risk of absconding, (2) avoidance of or hindrance to the return or the removal process, and (3) posing a threat to public order or national security (Majcher and Flynn, 2014). Pre-removal detention involves detaining irregular migrants prior to the "removal process", which involves the authorities either granting a visa and releasing them into the community, or repatriating them to their country of departure. As of October 2013, there were six pre-removal detention centres with a total detention capacity of 5,000, including Fylakio (inmate capacity of 2,034), Amygdaleza (1,665), Corinth (1,022), Xanthi (440), Komotini (427) and Paranesti Dramas (320) (Majcher and Flynn, 2014). Apart from these centres, unused warehouses are commonly used as detention centres. In contrast, identification centres are regular police stations with holding cells, which are not equipped to hold detainees for longer than 24 hours but are often used to detain irregular migrants for several weeks or months. All detention facilities are managed solely by police staff and considered "secure", where inmates are physically prevented from leaving.

Detention centres have been found to have substandard living conditions. Although the capacity of detention centres in Greece have been increased to hold more than 5,000 detainees in total, most centres have detainees in excess of their capacity, thus forcing them to live in crowded and inhuman conditions. Several substandard conditions have consistently been recorded including overcrowded cells without proper ventilation or sunlight, poor sanitation and low hygiene. For instance, in the case of confinement and shelter, the Sphere guidelines (*The Sphere Handbook*, 2011) recommend 3.5 m$^2$ of sleeping space per person which is in congruence with the UNHCR Handbook's recommendation of 3.5 m$^2$ of sleeping space per person in a warm climate and 4.5–5.5 m$^2$ sleeping space per person in a cold climate (UNHCR, 2000). Table 1 shows the current conditions prevailing in the detention facilities in Greece, mapped out in accordance with the Sphere guidelines. Most of the detention facilities, with the exception of the pre-removal facilities which were recently refurbished following repeated recommendations by the European Committee for the Prevention of Torture and inhuman or degrading treatment or punishment (CPT), have not met the minimum standard Sphere guidelines (Council of Europe, 2014). The supply of hygiene items is uniformly poor, which has led to rodent infestations in many of these facilities. However, these findings are not just limited to detention facilities in Greece, but are seen across Europe. For example, Bieber *et al.* (2013) reported that pre-removal detention centres in central and eastern Europe have less than the specified space limit, which leads to overcrowding (Table 2).

Data in Table 1 suggest that detention conditions in Greece violate the human rights of detention inmates. As one of the MSF humanitarian workers summed it up,

"*What we witness every day inside the detention facilities is not easy to describe. In Feres, with a capacity of 35, last night we distributed sleeping bags to 115 detained migrants. One woman with a serious gynaecological problem mentioned there was no space to sleep and she had no other option but to sleep in the toilet. In the detention centre of Fylakio, several cells were flooded with sewage from broken toilets*" (Kotsioni et al., 2013, p. 12).

In identification centres, men, women and children are thrown together in the same cells under filthy, unhygienic, cage-like conditions with no access to physical exercise, poor diet and inadequate health care provision. Inmates are treated like prisoners and only allowed in the yard

Table 1: Living conditions in detention facilites in Greece

| Facility | Space # | Toilet^ & bathing | Hygiene items* | Beds/ blanket | Light | Ventilation | Safe drinking water | Outdoor exercise |
|---|---|---|---|---|---|---|---|---|
| **Police stations** | | | | | | | | |
| Aghios Panteleimonas | × | × | × | × | × | — | — | × |
| Drapetsona | × | × | × | × | × | × | × | × |
| Exarchia | × | × | × | × | × | — | × | × |
| Tychero | ✓ | ✓ | × | — | — | — | ✓ | × |
| Kypseli | × | × | × | × | × | × | × | × |
| Soufli | ✓ | ✓ | × | — | ✓ | — | — | ✓ |
| Perama | × | × | × | × | × | × | × | × |
| Feres | ✓ | × | × | ✓ | × | × | ✓ | × |
| **Coast guard detention facility** | | | | | | | | |
| Igoumenitsa | × | × | × | × | × | × | × | × |
| **Pre-removal detention centres** | | | | | | | | |
| Amygdaleza | ✓ | ✓ | × | ✓ | ✓ | ✓ | ✓ | ✓ 2 hours/day |
| Komotini centre | ✓ | × | × | ✓ | ✓ | ✓ | × | ✓ 2 hours/day |
| Paranesti centre | × | × | × | ✓ | ✓ | ✓ | ✓ | ✓ 1.5 hours/day |
| Xanthi centre | × | ✓ | × | ✓ | ✓ | ✓ | ✓ | ✓ 1 hour/day |
| **Holding facilities** | | | | | | | | |
| Athens airport | × | × | × | × | × | × | ✓ | × |
| Filakio | × | × | × | × | × | × | × | × |
| Petrou Ralli | × | × | × | × | × | × | × | × |
| **Transfer centres** | | | | | | | | |
| Metagogon | × | × | × | × | × | × | × | × |
| Thessaloniki | × | × | × | × | × | × | × | × |
| **Holding facility for unaccompanied minors** | | | | | | | | |
| Amygdaleza Special facility | ✓ | × | × | ✓ | × | × | ✓ | ✓ |

# <3.5 m$^2$ per person; *soaps, laundry detergents, menstrual hygiene materials; ^ maximum of 20 people per toilet; "–" = not mentioned; × — not provided or present; ✓ — provided or present.
*Source*: Council of Europe (2014).

Table 2: Trend in occupancy rate (%) in pre-removal detention facilities across Europe

| Country | 2000 | 2009 | 2010 | 2011 |
|---|---|---|---|---|
| Albania | NA | 141 | 143 | 143 |
| Bulgaria | 90 | 110 | 130 | 130 |
| Czech Republic | NA | 94 | 98.5 | 104.7 |
| Greece | 220 | 248 | 279 | 366 |
| Hungary | 165 | 135 | 142 | 145 |
| Lithuania | NA | 88 | 76 | 86 |
| Montenegro | NA | 236 | 269 | 91 |
| Poland | NA | 104 | 102 | 98.5 |
| Russia | 103 | 80 | 78.6 | 88 |
| Ukraine | NA | 103 | 106 | 99.5 |

NA — Not available.
Source: Bieber et al. (2013) and Council of Europe (2014).

for a maximum of one hour in the morning and one hour in the afternoon (MSF, 2014). Further, detainees are also exposed to extreme temperatures when housed in warehouses which lack insulation, heating and cooling systems, and generally deemed unfit for human habitation.

The absence of a regulatory framework for the operation of immigration detention facilities and lack of sufficient human resources, have been implicated in the cause of deplorable detention conditions. This situation is prevalent in several European countries, for instance in Turkey, Albania, Poland, Lithuania and Romania, and it has been observed that detention conditions are equivalent to those faced by convicted prisoners. Whereas in Bulgaria, Hungary, Czech Republic, Montenegro and Moldova, it was reported that detention conditions were worse than prisons (Bieber et al. 2013). Over the past several years, detention centres have been struggling to cope with meeting the requirements of the inmates, which far exceed their material and staff capacities. Hence, the Greek Action Plan on Asylum and Migration Management proposed to launch three new detention facilities within the first six months of 2014 in Lesvos, Macedonia and Euboea in order to increase the capacity of detention centres. However, these facilities have not yet been established (AIDA, 2015). The widening gap between the demand and availability of accommodation facilities drives asylum seekers to desperation, and those who manage to escape detention centres often end up being homeless, including sleeping in the streets, parks and abandoned buildings. The UNHCR (2014b) has recorded the majority of homelessness among single men and persons with mental illness, probably due to the fact that women and children are often given preference in reception accommodations. Finally, detention centres do not provide information on asylum applications, interpreter or legal services to the inmates. The lack of interpreters negatively impacts the communication between detainees and detention centre staff, often creating tensions and serious constraints on the work performance of the detention staff (MSF, 2010).

## Health of migrants in detention centres

By virtue of their pre-migration conditions and their long and dangerous journey, migrants in detention centres are at increased risk of ill-health. Many of them have been victims of violence, armed attack, bombing, rape and other forms of violence. Their vulnerability is further exacerbated by uncertainty about the future, poor living conditions and the restrictions of detention. Below we examine some of the health conditions of migrants in detention centres.

### *Physical health conditions*

The increasing importance of migration in the national infectious disease epidemiology in the receiving country is well documented (Gushulak and Macpherson, 2004). The majority of migrants in detention centres in Greece come from countries where infectious diseases represent major causes of death and morbidity, and these migrants display strong manifestations of the risks of infectious disease acquisition from the country of origin. Factors such as incomplete vaccination, poor diagnosis and treatment of disease in native countries, also play an important role in the prevalence of infectious disease among irregular migrants. ECDC (2010) and MSF (2014) have identified active cases of tuberculosis, HIV and Hepatitis B in Greek detention centres. However, due to lack of proper surveillance, there is no accurate data on the prevalence of these diseases among detained migrants. There is no standard protocol regarding the medical screening of asylum seekers upon arrival in Greece and surprisingly all other EU countries have implemented this screening process (Norredam et al., 2005). Factors related to the ineffective screening process of asylum seekers in Greece are closely associated with the limited medical personnel in detention centres, the high mobility of asylum seekers and the lack of interpretation services.

Apart from health screening and pre-migration health risks, substandard detention conditions could be responsible for the majority of health problems suffered by detention inmates (ECDC, 2011; Kotsioni et al., 2013). The most debilitating conditions are overcrowding, lack of hygiene and poor sanitation. Most of the third-country nationals suffer from the so-called "refugee disease" consisting of cumulative health problems such as gastrointestinal, respiratory and dermatological problems, and symptoms of depression directly related to living conditions (Médecins du Monde Greece, 2015). According to MSF (2014) medical data, the most frequently diagnosed conditions in detention centres are upper respiratory tract infections (24.7%), gastrointestinal disorders (14.7%), musculoskeletal problems (13.7%), skin diseases (8.5%) and dental problems (7.9%). Kotsioni et al. (2013) found that respiratory problems, which account for the majority of the disease burden, occur due to frequent exposure to cold, closeness with infected inmates and lack of treatment for infections. Many inmates complain of difficulty in breathing and worsening of pre-existing conditions such as asthma, due to poor ventilation and lack of fresh air (Jesuit Refugee Service, 2011). MSF (2013) consultations have revealed that skin diseases such as scabies, bacterial and fungal infections are a result of overcrowding and poor hygiene. The lack of physical exercise, poor diet and high levels of stress lead to gastrointestinal problems including gastritis, constipation and haemorrhoids. Further, prolonged confinement, where detainees spend up to 17 months inside the cell with no access to the outdoors increases the risk of musculoskeletal problems due to limited space and lack of movement (Kotsioni et al., 2013; MSF, 2014). Overcrowding by itself increases the risk of viral infections such as measles and the lack of isolation facilities for people with contagious diseases increases the risk of infectious disease transmission between detainees.

222   *Globalisation, Migration and Health*

Substandard detention conditions aggravate chronic diseases such as diabetes, cardiovascular conditions, arthritis and epilepsy. Those suffering from chronic diseases are not promptly identified and referred to the hospital for appropriate treatment. This causes disruption in their medical treatment with them not receiving the necessary medication which leads to complications such as heart attack, stroke and diabetic coma. Further, inmates with conditions such as diabetes or renal failure do not receive an appropriate diet (MSF, 2010). Due to the lack of medical staff in detention centres, police officers function as sole decision-makers on the type of patients requiring emergency care, the urgency of the medical problem and requirement of referrals. Since police officers do not undergo medical training and lack the expertise required for the identification of an urgent medical problem, detainees are at significant risk for their health. However, MSF

| Condition | Number |
| --- | --- |
| Non-bloody diarrhea | 150 |
| Bloody diarrhea | 3 |
| Gastrointestinal disorder | 45 |
| Urinary tract infection | 25 |
| Upper respiratory tract infection | 339 |
| Lower respiratory tract infection | 125 |
| Sexually transmitted disease | 2 |
| Intentional violence | 4 |
| Unintentional violence/trauma | 73 |
| Skin disease | 94 |
| Epilepsy | 4 |
| Musculoskeletal problems | 197 |
| Gynecological problems | 21 |
| Hypertension | 1 |
| Conjunctivitis | 31 |
| Psychological complaint | 97 |
| Psychiatric disorder | 28 |
| Dental problems | 94 |
| Frostbite | 16 |
| Cardiovascular disease | 7 |
| Headache | 73 |
| Others | 176 |

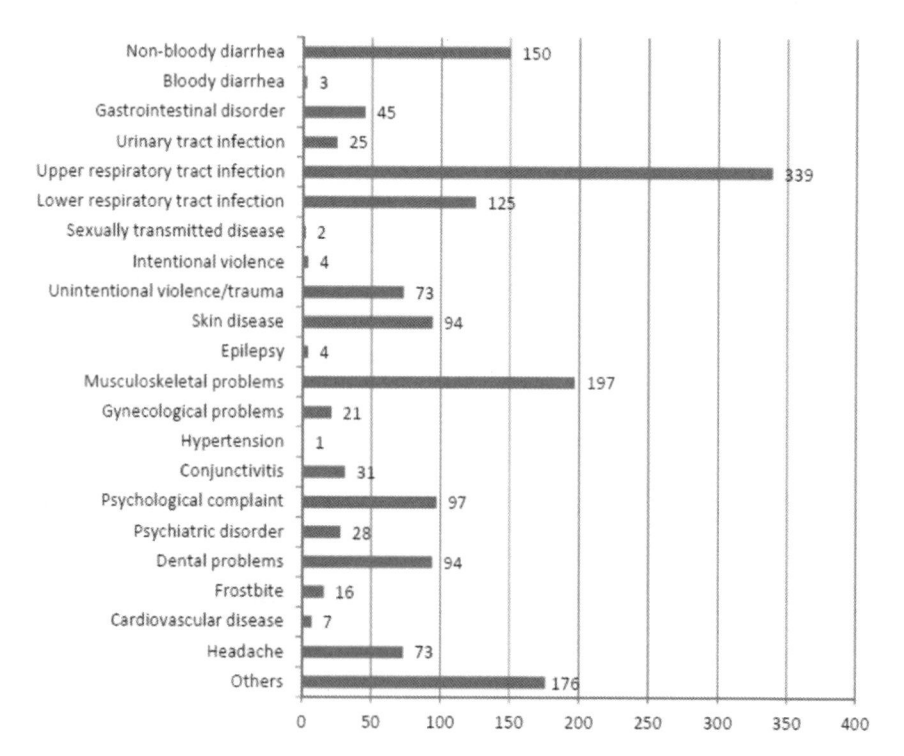

**Figure 4:** Diagnosed medical conditions (in numbers) among detainees as reported by MSF in Soufli and Tychero detention centres (1 December 2010–2 March 2011).
*Source*: Figure constructed using data extracted from MSF (2011).

(2010) noted that in the few centres that are equipped with medical personnel, the staff failed to conduct routine cell visits which force the inmates to seek their attention by gathering at the doors of the cells. This often results in the weakest or sickest people not being noticed, and being denied medical attention. The detention centres do not have any system requiring regular monitoring from public health authorities to assess the health of the inmates and quality of health care in the centres. Only the larger detention centres through the implementation of EU-funded projects by the Hellenic Centre for Disease Control and Prevention (HCDCP) had medical services available for short periods of time (MSF, 2014). Nonetheless, due to the lack of sustainable funding, these medical services are no longer affordable. The failure of the government to bear the health expenditure of detainees has resulted in the violation of their basic health rights.

## *Mental health conditions*

The traumatic events experienced by asylum seekers prior to, and during, their dangerous journey to Greece leads to psychological illness, depression, anxiety, aggression, and other physical and emotional consequences. Detention has been known to aggravate these conditions, and in some cases, while asylum seekers do not present with mental symptoms at the time of detention, they often show signs of illness post-detention. The risk of "re-traumatisation" among traumatised inmates is high since many detention centres have a prison-like atmosphere (Jesuit Refugee Service, 2011). Difficult living conditions, the abusive behaviour of guards, lack of physical activities, constant noise, dependence on other people's decisions, and social isolation caused by limited opportunities to communicate with the outside world and their families, contribute to detainees' poor mental health (MSF, 2010, 2013). During the detention process, asylum seekers are often separated from their families, resulting in high levels of stress especially for parents whose children are separated from them. High stress levels in turn lead to insomnia or sleeplessness, loss of appetite and mental tension. Insomnia also lowers energy levels and affects cognitive capacities, which result in emotional imbalances (Koopowitz and Abhary, 2004). Recently, MSF (2010, 2014) has documented several stress-related psychosomatic problems, such as sleeplessness, stomach-ache, headache, general body pain and poor appetite among inmates confined in Greek detention centres. Other risk factors for mental illness among detainees include the length and uncertainty of the period of detention, and the constant threat of forced repatriation. For example, following the police announcement on increases in the length of detention from three to six months in 2009, the mental health of inmates deteriorated, with 39% suffering from anxiety including constant worry and fear, 31% showing symptoms of depression, 9.5% experiencing post-traumatic stress disorder, and 3% attempting self-harm or suicide (MSF, 2010). These observations are consistent with the evidence on the higher prevalence of mental illness found among detainees (Cohen, 2008) and refugees who had endured torture (Steel et al., 2009) than the general population. Other factors increasing the risk of mental illness include language difficulties, limited knowledge of their rights, being treated like criminals, exclusion and discrimination. Overall, the burden of disease among detainees in Greece remains gravely under-researched due to the lack of reliable, routinely collected data on the health status of asylum seekers (Kotsioni and Hatziprokopiou, 2009).

## *Violence, abuse and racism*

Asylum seekers frequently suffer violence and abuse at the hands of immigration authorities during various phases of their detention in Greece. First, illegal arrivals experience physical violence at the hands of coast guards and police upon their arrest on arrival. Second, they face physical, verbal and emotional abuse by detention centre staff during their stay in detention centres, which cause physical injuries, disabilities, psychological trauma and stress. Finally upon release from detention centres, they are exposed to attacks arising from racism, discrimination, xenophobia and racist violence which altogether undermine the safety, dignity, health and wellbeing of asylum seekers. Racism was found to cause psychological distress, high blood pressure and reduced appetite among victims (Jesuit Refugee Service, 2011). The UNHCR (2014b) has also documented the increased risk of racist attacks among homeless asylum seekers. The physical and psychological trauma experienced by asylum seekers are aggravated by the non-existence of public health structures specialised in identifying or assisting violence victims in their rehabilitation process

(AIDA, 2015). Of all the victims of racist attacks seeking help for their injuries, 90% do not report the attacks to Greek authorities for fear of being arrested, detained and deported (Triandafyllidou, 2014).

Several international human rights bodies have criticised Greece concerning the excessive use of force by law enforcement officials and ill-treatment of undocumented migrants and asylum seekers (Amnesty International, 2014; Human Rights Watch, 2008). In 2007, the CPT reported numerous allegations of ill-treatment by irregular migrants in the custody of state agents and stated that those who are deprived of their liberty by law enforcement officials face an increased risk of ill-treatment (Council of Europe, 2008). In response to these crimes, the UN Refugee Agency and the National Commission for Human Rights established the Racist Violence Recording Network in 2011 to monitor and record racist attacks against irregular migrants (UNHCR, 2013). Consequently, in 2014, the Greek government passed a new anti-racist legislation through Law 4285/2014 (AIDA, 2015). Following these legislative changes, all caseworkers from the Asylum Service in Greece are scheduled to receive training based on principles of the International Human Rights Law (AIDA, 2015).

## Detention of children

Detention of children is extremely serious due to its devastating impact on their physical, emotional and psychological development. According to the UNHCR (2012a), children should not be detained at all. Instead those identified as unaccompanied minors should be transferred to reception facilities for children. Unaccompanied minors, as defined in article 1 of the Convention, are children who have been separated from their father and mother and other close relatives, and are not being cared for by an adult who by either law or custom is responsible for doing so (UN Committee on the Rights of the Child, 2005, para 7). However, upon arrival in Greece, children are routinely taken into detention as there are neither official age-assessment procedures nor training for the police officers at entry points to accurately assess the age of children. This leads to children being misreported as adults. For example, between 2013 and 2014 more than 100 children were wrongly registered as adults (MSF, 2014). During the process of detention, minors are particularly vulnerable to violence and physical abuse including being beaten, kicked or slapped by police officers and coast guards (Human Rights Watch, 2013b). Due to the absence of proper screening, it is possible that many minors who are victims of trafficking are not identified as such, which results in them being denied referral to specialised services. Human Rights Watch (2008) has noted that unaccompanied minors are also subject to an increased risk of sexual exploitation, child prostitution or commercial sex, and child pornography. Several children are detained alongside adults for lengthy periods of time despite being recorded as minors, which increases their risk of being abused.

Children arriving illegally in Greece experience a double whammy of being unaccompanied and trafficked, yet the asylum system is not equipped well enough to address their needs in terms of accommodation, material resources and asylum applications. For example, in 2012, a total of 1,519 unaccompanied minors had been recorded from Syria alone (EMN, 2014) which led to a severe shortage of accommodation in the reception facilities for children. Additionally, there is an average 25-day waiting period before minors are placed in reception facilities during which time they either become homeless or seek employment to pay for their accommodation. Children often end up being illegally employed in exploitative work, performing heavy and hazardous tasks which lead to a combination of health and safety risks. These risks include lifting heavy loads, falling from heights, exposure to cold temperatures over long hours as well as substandard and unhygienic accommodation. All of these risks fall under the category of worst form of child labour, as defined by Article 3 of the Worst Forms of Child Labor Convention (International Labour Organisation, 1999).

Regarding the asylum process for unaccompanied minors, the police are responsible for the entire process of detention and asylum, while the Ministry of Health and Social Solidarity is responsible for providing accommodation and access to medical services, and the juvenile prosecutors act as temporary guardians for all unaccompanied minors, regardless of whether or not they apply for asylum (Human Rights Watch, 2008). However, the process suffers from two fundamental flaws: children released from detention are not referred to proper care; and on release from detention they are accompanied by adults without prior assessment of a family link (UNHCR, 2014b). In both these circumstances, the protocol for dealing with unaccompanied minors in terms of registration and care is violated. In 2007, the Greek National Commission for Human Rights (2007) called on the government to refrain from detaining children; to systematically register, identify and represent children, to adopt a formal age assessment procedure, and to provide adequate accommodation. Despite these recommendations, the Greek law does not actively prohibit the administrative detention of children arriving without valid documents.

## Detention of vulnerable persons

In the majority of EU member states including Greece, there is no definition of vulnerable persons or the existence of formal identification processes to accurately identify persons with special needs (ECRE, 2013). According to MSF (2014), "vulnerable migrants" include patients with serious chronic or infectious conditions with disruptions in their treatment, women in advanced pregnancy and nursing mothers, victims of human trafficking, those with physical disabilities requiring assistance with their mobility, people with mental health disorders, unaccompanied minors, and certified victims of torture. The lack of a consistent health screening process of detainees upon arrival at immigration detention facilities has resulted in sick people and other vulnerable people being detained without taking into account their physical and mental health condition and needs. Once in detention, authorities have no way of discerning the level of specialised care required by vulnerable asylum seekers, or the availability of such care. For instance, those with disabilities such as missing limbs, as a result of being victims of bomb or mine explosions are detained in the same cells as others, without access to facilities for people with disabilites (MSF, 2010). Pregnant women are denied safe, hygienic facilities with adequate medical care which predisposes them to unfavourable health outcomes. Evidence shows that undocumented migrants, especially those who have been politically persecuted in their home country, show a higher risk of unfavourable perinatal health outcomes such as stillbirth, neonatal and perinatal mortality than women living in the host countries (Rechel et al., 2011). These findings clearly indicate the failure of detention centre authorities to accurately identify vulnerable asylum seekers and provide appropriate facilities for them, which can lead to deleterious health outcomes. Detention centres lack a proper system for the speedy release of vulnerable detainees on medical grounds or referrals to secondary care. Even for those who are eligible for referrals to secondary care in hospitals, the process is often delayed by significant transport difficulties. In January 2013, the Greek government announced that vulnerable persons should not be detained and should instead be accommodated in two open reception centres. However, those centres are yet to be built (AIDA, 2015).

## Immigration policy response to irregular migration

In Greece, there are two procedures within the asylum system: the Old Asylum System for processing applications lodged prior to 7 June 2013 which was handled entirely by the police, and the New Asylum System for processing applications lodged after 2013, which is under the authority of the Asylum Service. Law 3907/2011 has been responsible for reforming the asylum system in four key areas, namely, (1) setting new standards for the first reception of irregular migrants, (2) establishing the distinction between irregular migrants and asylum seekers, (3) processing asylum applications and reducing the waiting period of these applications, and (4) removing the asylum committees from the authority of the Greek police (Triandafyllidou, 2014). In 2011, Law 3907/2011 introduced the Asylum Service, an Appeals Committee and a First Reception Service (FRS) (Greece, 2011). The Asylum Service is an administrative body comprising a Central Office in Athens and Regional Asylum Offices including mobile units. The Appeals Committee, on the other hand, is responsible for examining appeals against first instance asylum decisions issued by the police (Old System) and Asylum Service (New System). The FRS has a Central Service and Regional Services which include multiple centres and the mobile units. It organises the needs assessment, screening, appropriate routing and assistance for illegal arrivals. Law 3907/2011 allows two types of permits for asylum seekers and irregular migrants: (1) the so-called "tolerated asylum seekers", representing people who have no formal permission to stay in Greece but are unable to return to their country of origin, and (2) a new permit for "exceptional reasons" given to irregular migrants who have been living in Greece for a minimum period of 12 years with a mandatory 10 years' continuous stay before their application for this permit. This law also provides for the before assisted voluntary return for irregular migrants and re-integration in their country of origin (Triandafyllidou, 2014).

Although many asylum seekers do not plan to continue living in Greece, they are unable to leave, as a result of EU policies such as the Dublin II Regulation. This regulation stipulates that only one EU member state is responsible for examining an asylum application, the objective being to prevent one asylum seeker from submitting several applications to various EU member states (Europa, 2011). The Dublin II Regulation is based on the Council Regulation (EC) No. 343/2003 Act for determining which member state is responsible for examining an asylum application lodged in any one of the member states by a third-country national (EUR-LEX Access to European Union Law, 2003). Under certain circumstances, the regulation permits the transfer of asylum seekers from one EU state to another. However, the EU member states including Greece do not accurately follow the Dublin Regulation. For example, when a family member applies for asylum, the Dublin criteria are applied in a restrictive manner without acknowledging the presence of other family members, which often leads to the separation of families (ECRE, 2013). There is also no consistency between the EU member states in the implementation of the process for managing unaccompanied children in terms of age assessment, assignment of a guardian and tracing family members in other EU states. Asylum seekers subject to the Dublin Regulation are not always guaranteed a fair and efficient examination of their asylum claim, and are also granted fewer rights in terms of access to reception conditions both before and after a Dublin transfer.

One of the major obstacles in accessing the asylum procedure in Greece has been the practice of informal forced returns ("push-backs") of third-country nationals at its sea and land borders, by which Greece could be violating the principle of non-refoulement, which is the cornerstone of international refugee protection (AIDA, 2015). This process results in incriminating those who are in the very need of international protection. An important deficit in the Greek asylum system has been the non-respect of asylum seekers' rights, as shown by poor information provision to asylum seekers and lack of granting complete and effective access to the asylum-seeking procedure. Overall, several gaps in the policies handling irregular migration have been highlighted including (a) lack of information to irregular migrants at border areas or when apprehended, (b) difficulty in accessing relevant services for filing asylum applications, (c) asylum application decisions based on country of origin, (d) lack of substantial asylum interviews, (e) mishandling of the application process by police personnel who have not received any asylum training, and (f) lack of political will for improvement (Triandafyllidou, 2014). These gaps have violated the European human rights standards as articulated by the European Court of Human Rights (Council of Europe, 2011). Evidence also shows that asylum seekers fleeing persecution, conflict and torture have a limited knowledge of migration policies, and due to language and literacy barriers are unable to navigate the asylum application process (ECRE, 2013; UNHCR, 2014b). Despite various reforms, the Greek asylum system has not demonstrated competency in dealing with the asylum applications. The process of assessing asylum claims is often significantly delayed due to inadequate resources and improper guidelines. The FRS is unable to cope with the demands of migration inflows, resulting in the majority of the irregular migrants being denied its service and accommodated in inhuman detention facilities. In 2014 alone, the FRS registered 6,228 individuals accounting for only 20% of total new arrivals in that year (UNHCR, 2014b). Although Law 3907/2011 specifies a total staff of 235 persons for the Asylum Service, currently only 176 persons have been appointed. Due to huge inadequacies in the reception facilities and the inability of the Greek asylum system in coping with the claims overload, several EU member states have stopped sending asylum seekers to Greece. There is no doubt that the poor handling of asylum seekers has had an impact on the Greek economy. Studies have shown that the Greek irregular migration policy with its expensive lengthy detention has led to resource depletion, as demonstrated by repeated appeals from Greece to other EU member states for financial support in the past three years (Bloomfield, *et al.*, 2015: Angeli and Triandafyllidou, 2014).

## *Alternatives to detention*

Alternatives to detention (ATD) refer to *"any legislation, policy or practice that allows asylum-seekers to reside in the community subject to a number of conditions or restrictions on their freedom of movement*" (UNHCR, 2012a, p. 10). The legal framework underpinning alternative detention principles is based on the European Convention on Human Rights, the 1951 Refugee Convention, the International Covenant on Civil and Political Rights and the EU law (Bloomfield *et al.*, 2015). For the past few years, the UNHCR has been advocating for ATD that are more humanitarian and less expensive in nature. Although a range of strategies exist for consideration as ATD, currently there is no EU law regulating a specific approach and member states are free to choose their own alternatives. Some examples of alternatives commonly used in Europe are summarised in Box 2.

---

**Box 2: Alternatives to detention: a European perspective**

**Monitoring requirements** where an asylum seeker is released from detention on the condition that she/he reports regularly (weekly or monthly) to a monitoring authority. The various monitoring mechanisms include registration with authorities, nominated address and reporting requirements.

**Deposit of identity or travel documentation** such as passports by the asylum seekers, in which case they need to be issued a substitute documentation that authorises their stay in the country.

**Directed residence** is where asylum seekers are permitted to live in a specific residence, the location details of which have been notified to the authorities; further, they need to seek approval from the authorities and notify the change of address in case of relocation.

**Provision of guarantor/surety** by the asylum seeker, who would take responsibility for ensuring the attendance of the asylum seeker at hearings, meetings and official appointments, the failure of which would result in the guarantor being fined.

**Release on bail/bond** — Release from detention is granted if the asylum seeker can pay a specified bail or bond sum, sometimes in conjunction with a guarantor/surety.

**Open centres** are group accommodation facilities allowing the free movement of irregular migrants, where people can leave the premises at will within specified times, usually coupled with monitoring requirements/reporting.

---

(*Continued*)

> **Box 2:** (*Continued*)
>
> **Case management** can be considered as a benchmark of a good ATD system as it involves an integrated approach starting from the commencement of the asylum process until its resolution which may be either refugee recognition or return. A case manager is assigned to each asylum seeker living independently in the community for conducting screening, holistic assessment, case planning, intervention, ongoing review, follow-up, resolution and case closure.
>
> **Community supervision** involves release of the asylum seeker into the community with supervision from the local service providers to support arrangements with regard to local accommodation, schools, employment and the direct provision of goods.
>
> **Electronic tagging** is one of the most coercive forms of ATD used more frequently among criminals rather than illegal immigrants. However in the UK, it is used for tracking asylum seekers and irregular migrants by placing an electronic bracelet around their ankle which is linked to a receiver in their homes. This process enables authorities to monitor the movements of the individual.
>
> **Home curfew** is another severe form of ATD amounting to significant deprivation of liberty where the asylum seeker is confined to a specific residence with enforcement of curfew at specified times and is often used along with electronic tagging.
>
> *Source:* Bloomfield *et al.* (2015), Jesuit Refugee Service (2013), UNHCR (2012a), and Edwards (2011).

In Greece, open centres and reporting requirements are ATD commonly used by the government, while community supervision is often the method preferred and supported by the NGOs. Reporting requirements involve the individual either physically presenting themselves at the police station or immigration office to sign a register, or phoning a particular number at a specified time, and recording a statement which is verified using voice recognition technology. The frequency of reporting depends on the stage of the individual asylum claim and compliance with the requirements. For example, if the date of return is fast approaching, the frequency of reporting increases in order to monitor the individual more closely. On the other hand, once the authorities are satisfied with the character of the asylum seeker due to his/her compliance with the initial reporting requirements, the frequency lessens. Sometimes, immigration authorities also use distribution of food vouchers and basic supplies as a "de facto" reporting mechanism to keep a check on irregular migrants (Sampson *et al.*, 2011).

Responses to the use of alternatives have varied across countries: case management has been overwhelmingly successful in Sweden and has become part of its immigration system, whereas in the UK, case management has no place and ATD such as electronic monitoring, reporting and bail seem to be popular. The bail or bond systems can discriminate against those asylum seekers who have no funds, hence using an NGO as a guarantor in this situation may be a valuable option. In EU member states such as Lithuania, the UK, Belgium, Slovenia, Austria and Sweden, designated open centres, designated residence and reporting to authorities are the most commonly used alternatives (Bloomfield *et al.*, 2015). From the EU governments' perspective, reporting is one of the cheapest alternatives as asylum seekers are staying in their own accommodation, but dealing with non-reporting can be a challenge. Apart from the ATD mentioned above, "return houses" are options made available in the UK and Belgium for asylum seeker families with children, the aim being to house them for a temporary period before organising their return to home countries.

ATD can include any strategy where asylum seekers are accommodated in the community with minimal restriction on their movement. While both governments and NGOs are involved in their implementation, there are some similarities and differences in the key challenges they encounter. Governments are concerned with the risk of absconding, while NGOs are challenged with a mismatch between the suitability of strategies and the characteristics of the asylum seekers. To avoid these dilemmas in choosing between alternatives, Amaral (2013) identified certain key features of well-functioning alternatives. They include information provision and legal assistance, as well as proper accommodation, food, clothing, public transport and access to medical care, as it is envisaged that once basic necessities are taken care of, asylum seekers will be empowered to take the necessary steps towards their claim applications.

The aim of ATD is to not only remove asylum seekers from detention but also keep them engaged in the immigration procedures while they are living in the community. Shifting the focus from mere location tracking

> **Box 3: The five-step IDC CAP model**
>
> Step 1: Presume detention is not necessary.
> Step 2: Screen and assess each case individually.
> Step 3: Assess the community context.
> Step 4: Apply conditions to release if necessary.
> Step 5: Detain only as the last resort in exceptional cases (Sampson, et al., 2011).

of asylum seekers to providing them with the necessary infrastructure, support and skills to enable the resolution of their migration case can be a sustainable and humanitarian approach. This approach has been outlined in the International Detention Coalition's 5-Step Community Assessment and Placement (CAP) Model, which allows governments to assess the suitability of an individual to a specific alternative programme (Box 3). Based on these and several other recommendations, on 17 February 2015, the Greek government announced that alternatives to detention will be implemented as a proactive measure to end the punitive approach of detention (AIDA, 2015).

## Guidelines for detention

It is clear that authorities in Greece are not following the guidelines set out by the UNHCR (Box 1). For instance, Guideline 8 specifies the segregation of men and women in detention facilities, prompt medical treatment including psychological counselling, provision of basic necessities to detainees and opportunities for physical exercise. However, none of these requirements have been accurately adopted in the management of detention facilities. Further, the UN Working Group on Arbitrary Detention recognises that although administrative detention does not contravene international human rights, criminalisation of irregular migration leading to detention should be abolished (UN, 2010). In order to prioritise the human rights of detention inmates, a global strategy for 2014–2019 was launched by the UNHCR (2014d) to urge governments to end the detention of refugees. The Global strategy has three goals, namely, (1) to end the detention of children, (2) to ensure that alternatives to detention are implemented, and (3) to ensure that conditions of detention (where detention is necessary and unavoidable) meet international standards by, inter alia, securing access to places of immigration detention for UNHCR and/or its partners for regular monitoring.

## Migration health policy

The Greek health care system is based on the National Health Service (NHS), primarily on obligatory social insurance and to a lesser degree on private insurance (Kotsioni and Hatziprokopiou, 2009). The Ministry of Health & Welfare released a circular in July 2000, which stated that non-EU nationals are entitled to the same health care benefits as EU nationals, provided they possess a stay/work permit, which is linked to the possession of social insurance (Council of Europe, 2000). However, according to Presidential Decree 668, refugees and asylum seekers without work permits or social insurance are also entitled to free primary and secondary care as long as they possess legal documentation of stay. Hence, asylum seekers who are legally recognised as refugees have equal access to the health care system as Greek citizens. However, the majority of asylum seekers whose application is in process and are awaiting their claim decision are not covered by any interim health schemes. This poses a great danger to their health as those requiring medical assistance often postpone their treatment in order to avoid out-of-pocket expenses for health care utilisation and medication. Additionally, a new Migration Code established in April 2014 prohibits Greek authorities, public services, and social security organisations from offering services to foreigners who are unable to prove that they have entered and are residing in the country legally (Triandafyllidou, 2014). The exception to this rule is provision of emergency care and health care to minors under the age of 18. Hence, unregistered asylum seekers including minors are permitted to access the health care system only in emergency situations such as treatment of pregnancy-related complications and delivery, HIV/AIDS and other infectious diseases treatment, provided they have been released from detention. Nevertheless, the health care delivery to registered migrants is compromised by the absence of culturally sensitive services in the NHS, such as the lack of access to interpreters, cultural mediators and health care professionals trained in culturally competent health care approaches (Kotsioni and Hatziprokopiou, 2009).

## Role of NGOs in detention centres in Greece

NGOs and charities often play an invaluable role in meeting the needs of migrants in detention centres. Issues addressed by NGOs are complex and include reporting racist crimes, protection of victims of crime and advocacy against human right violations by law enforcement officials (Amnesty International, 2014), detention of vulnerable persons and unaccompanied minors (Red Cross EU Office, 2013), raising awareness on the implications of child labour on the wellbeing of children (PRAKSIS, 2015), and health problems directly related to living conditions (MSF, 2014). There are approximately 90 NGOs contributing towards the welfare of migrants and refugees in Europe and Greece. In Greece alone, a total of 15 reception centres with a maximum capacity of 1,006 places are managed by various NGOs across the country (Red Cross EU Office, 2013). Despite this assistance from the NGOs, the failure of Greek authorities to take adequate measures to end the substandard inhumane conditions prevailing in detention centres has led to an active intervention by the International Detention Coalition (IDC). The IDC is a global network comprising more than 300 civil society organisations and individuals from more than 70 countries, that advocate for, research and provide direct services to refugees, asylum seekers and migrants affected by immigration detention (International Detention Coalition, 2015). In 2012, the IDC along with the Greek Council for Refugees (GCR) organised the first EU Workshop on Immigration Detention in Greece with participation from NGOs in 15 EU countries who discussed the Global Campaign to End Immigration Detention of Children and a reduction in the maximum timeframe for immigration detention (International Detention Coalition, 2015).

Apart from the IDC, the European Council on Refugees and Exiles (ECRE) is an important pan-European alliance of 87 NGOs, whose role is to protect the rights of refugees, asylum seekers and displaced persons in accordance with the international human rights law (European Council on

Refugees and Exiles, 2013). The three NGOs who are ECRE members from Greece include the Greek Council for Refugees (GCR), Aitima and Klimaka. The GCR was founded in 1989 to provide food, shelter, clothing, legal assistance, psychosocial support and vocational counselling to asylum seekers and refugees, and is also an implementing partner of the UNHCR (European Council on Refugees and Exiles, 2013). Another important initiative aimed at effectively handling the influx of asylum seekers and strengthening the cooperation between NGOs and other authorities is the SOAM programme (Supporting Organizations that Assist Migrant asylum seeking population in Greece) which was established by the International Organization for Migration during 2011–2012 with funding from the European Economic Area Grants (IOM, 2013). The SOAM programme aims to improve the overall situation of asylum seekers in Greece by providing long-term support to asylum seekers and NGOs who assist asylum seekers and supporting the Greek government's efforts to manage migration processes in unaccompanied minors, single-parent families and vulnerable women (IOM, 2013).

### *Médecins Sans Frontières/doctors without borders*

Médecins Sans Frontières (MSF) is an international, independent, medical humanitarian organisation that delivers emergency aid to people affected by armed conflict, epidemics, natural and man made disasters, and exclusion from health care. The main objective of MSF is to improve the health of detained migrants through the amelioration of poor living conditions, the delivery of medical assistance and facilitation of medical follow-up through the national health care system. From 1996 to 2004, MSF has provided assistance to irregular migrants and refugees in Greece through polyclinics. From 2008 onwards, MSF (2013) has been working in detention facilities at the Greek–Turkish borders including the Evros and Lesvos Islands. In detention facilities, MSF contribute in two ways: (1) medical — provision of primary health care, and (2) logistical — involving (a) distribution of non-food items including sleeping bags, personal hygiene kits, gloves, socks and hats, and (b) technical support such as the maintenance and plumbing of heating systems and toilets, disinfection and provision of cleaning material, and minor construction work in detention centres (MSF, 2011).

In 2011, MSF (2013) noted that 63% of their total consultations involved treatment of communicable diseases following which they urgently advocated for an improvement in the detention centres' living conditions. However, despite their persistent calls to improve conditions in detention facilities, no concrete actions were taken by the Greek government to address the problems. In 2013 alone, MSF teams provided 5,441 medical consultations, organised 365 referrals to secondary health facilities, 100 referrals for dental care and provided specialised scabies treatment for 1,500 patients in the detention facilities (MSF, 2014). Apart from providing medical assistance for physical illnesses, MSF also provides social, interpretive and psychological assistance at the detention centres. Over the past decade, through its daily work in the detention centres in Greece, MSF (2010) has witnessed the negative impact of detention on the mental health of migrants and asylum seekers, and observed that following their arrest in detention centres, they do not receive information about their legal status, the detention system or the right to apply for asylum. MSF has also noted that the administration of detention centres has been challenged by lack of planning and organisation, and deficiencies in human and material resources. For example, between August 2009 and April 2010, MSF psychologists consulted 305 patients in three detention centres with majority of the patients originating from an Asian background. Of all the patients receiving psychological services in that year, 89% were males, 46% were young adults (younger than 26 years) and 12% were minors (<18 years) (MSF, 2010). Gaps in psychological services addressed by MSF include: trust building and screening sessions, individual and group counselling sessions including play therapy sessions involving group-based sports, music, craft and recreational activities, referrals of patients to psychiatric services, provision of translated information services (medical care, legal support, food and non-food items distributions) which migrants can access after being released from detention, and conducting sensitisation sessions with detention centres' staff to raise awareness regarding inmates' psychosocial needs (MSF, 2010). MSF teams also enabled separated families to communicate with each other in the detention centres by obtaining permission from police authorities for children to visit their parents who were held in different and separate detention facilities.

## Greek Forum of Refugees

GFR oversees a network involving the Afghan, South Sudanese and Somali communities in Greece (International Detention Coalition, 2015) and collaborates with organisations such as IDC, ECR, Racist Violence Recording Network, Campaign of Access to Asylum and Platform for International Cooperation on Undocumented Migrants. These organisations work with refugee communities concerning their rights in Greece, in Europe and internationally (Greek Forum of Refugees, 2012). GFR raises awareness of the public on human rights violations and provides information to refugees and asylum seekers on their rights, and conducts systematic dialogue with the organisations of civil society and Greek authorities to advocate for a functional and fair asylum system. It is actively involved in updating the profile of refugees in Greece, in terms of documenting the reasons they fled their homeland, problems experienced during their journey, as well as their needs and challenges in the host country. There are several NGOs which target racist crime attacks in Greece and fight for the rights of refugees, asylum seekers and migrants. ANTIGONE (2013) is an NGO which runs a programme called Experience Crime, which aims to improve responses to racist, hate and related crimes through innovative and experiential learning methods by equipping police officers and legal practitioners with the knowledge and skills on racist crime, hate and homophobic crime. This programme also promotes an anti-racist ethos in law enforcement bodies through a network of champions selected among the trainees. Aitima is another Greek NGO founded in 2008 which undertakes awareness-raising activities and participates in the Racist Violence Recording Network (European Council on Refugees and Exiles, 2013).

## Amnesty International

Established in 1961, with over 7 million members and supporters around the world, Amnesty International (AI) has been enraged by the numerous acts of human rights violations committed by law enforcement officials in Greece over the past decade. Between 2012 and 2014, AI conducted research among refugee/asylum seeker victims of ill-treatment while in detention, during sweep operations, when intercepted crossing the border or as sole victims of hate crime. It found that police authorities arrested the irregular migrant victims instead of the perpetrators, and discouraged the victims from filing complaints against the perpetrators (Amnesty International, 2014). Additionally, AI has documented gaps in the investigations which include failure of the police and judicial authorities to conduct prompt, effective and impartial investigations, and the prosecution and punishment of the law enforcement officials involved in human rights abuses in Greece. Although AI has called upon the Greek authorities to make changes including amendments to the current definition of torture, ratification of the Optional Protocol to the Convention against Torture and other Cruel, Inhuman or Degrading Treatment or Punishment (OPCAT), and the establishment of an independent police complaint mechanism, the Greek government has failed to action these recommendations (Amnesty International, 2014).

## *Hellenic Red Cross*

Hellenic Red Cross (HRC) is a member of the Red Cross EU Office and since 1915, has facilitated family reunification procedures (Red Cross EU Office, 2013). Since 2003, HRC has been operating two reception centres in Greece, one in Lavrio accommodating up to 200 asylum seekers, and the other centre in Volos for about 100 unaccompanied minors. The centres prioritise the most vulnerable groups (large families, single-headed households, chronically ill), and offer short-term accommodation, psychosocial support, counselling on access to the labour market and intercultural activities. In Volos, HRC provides to minors much needed social and legal support services including legal support proceedings before the Juvenile Court, Greek and English language courses, computer courses as well as integration (Red Cross EU Office, 2013). HRC is also a member of the Social Inclusion and Vocational Integration of Asylum Seekers and Victims of Human Trafficking (SAVIAV) which promotes the social, economic and human rights of trafficked people. With funding from the European Refugee Fund, HRC enabled the development of a framework for ongoing improvement in the education of asylum seeker minors (Red Cross EU Office, 2013).

## Association for the Social Support of Youth

Association for the Social Support of Youth (ARSIS) is an NGO established in 1992, which provides social support services for youth and advocates for their rights during rescue operations at sea and at reception facilities (ARSIS, 2015). ARSIS operates three shelters for unaccompanied minors in Metoikos, Oraiokastro and Makrinitsa, which provide accommodation, basic necessities such as food, Greek language lessons and health care, educational, social and recreational events, psychosocial support, information and support on how to become independent and self-sufficient, and legal assistance with the process of seeking asylum. For example, the "Loghos kai Ifasma" programme trains female prisoners in fabric elaboration techniques, conducts sales of their artworks at exhibitions and organises deposits of the financial proceeds into asylum seekers' bank accounts. In 2011, ARSIS initiated a painting workshop programme at the Avlona's Special Juvenile Detention Centre. Since its inception, more than 15 ex-detainees have managed to successfully secure a job and a permanent place of residence in Greece due to the support and skills gained in these programmes. Additionally, ARSIS (2015) runs a service named "Sym-Parastasi" to enable asylum seekers and migrants to grasp the complexities of the Greek legal system. This is achieved through the provision of free legal support including mediation, information on the available free legal assistance programmes and referrals to institutions for supplementary assistance.

## Programmes of Development, Social Support and Medical Cooperation

Programmes of Development, Social Support and Medical Cooperation (PRAKSIS) is an NGO whose main goal is to deliver humanitarian and medical interventions to vulnerable social groups including asylum seekers, refugees, unaccompanied minors and victims of trafficking. Through the "ASK FIRST" mobile units and polyclinics, PRAKSIS provides medical care, health education and health promotion on HIV and Hepatitis. One of its programmes assisting asylum seekers, the "Unaccompanied Children on the Move" programme is run through the operation of the Drop-In

Centre in Patras. Patras is the second largest port in Greece and the main point of entry and exit for irregular migrants. Due to its strategic location, the Drop-in Centre is able to identify gaps in relation to children's protection and provide services for the reception, consultation and appropriate referral for unaccompanied children who need international protection (PRAKSIS, 2015). PRAKSIS is also actively involved in collaborative efforts with Médecins du Monde (Doctors of the World), Positive Voice and Centre for Life, the Thessaloniki Solidarity Centre, the Red Cross and IOM. The main outcomes of these partnerships include prompt examination for HIV and Hepatitis C, socio-psychological support and legal counselling, information on the prevention of HIV and Hepatitis C, voluntary repatriation of unaccompanied minors, medical assistance including free visits to doctors and psychiatrists and the provision of free medicines, and housing assistance and accommodation for people in need of international protection (PRAKSIS, 2015).

### *Médecins du Monde-Greece*

Médecins du Monde-Greece (Doctors of the World) was founded in 1990 and is a medical humanitarian NGO. It is a member of the Médecins Du Monde International which consists of 15 national delegations and their long-term goal is to make health care a basic human right. Médecins du Monde is one of the largest medical NGOs assisting asylum seekers in Greece and in 2014 it contributed more than 600 medical volunteers towards Médecins du Monde's initiatives in Greece (Médecins du Monde-Greece, 2015). The various services operating within Médecins du Monde-Greece include (a) medical services by volunteer doctors and nurses such as mobile medical units providing medical and pharmaceutical coverage to people living in remote areas who face difficulties in accessing health care services, (b) psychological support to vulnerable social groups, as well as specialised services to children and adolescents with developmental disabilities and learning difficulties, (c) nutritional services providing monthly family packages (pasta, lentils, rice, olive oil and milk) to families unable to afford basic foods, and (d) social services providing individualised coverage of needs and social support (Médecins du Monde Greece, 2015). One of Médecins du Monde's interventions most used by asylum seekers is the open polyclinics which provide primary health care, paediatric and specialist

Table 3: Snapshot of the NGO initiatives addressing the health and wellbeing of migrants, refugees and asylum seekers in Greece

| NGO | Initiative | Funding | Outcomes |
| --- | --- | --- | --- |
| ARSIS | You are not alone! Action for protection of unaccompanied minors | Norwegian Directorate of Immigration, funds of EEA grants | Develop an operational framework for the shelters for unaccompanied minors who are asylum seekers in Greece |
| ARSIS | Shelter "House of ARSIS" | Solidarity Now | Provision of food, shelter, clothing, medicines; inclusion in the educational and social environment, for abused, trafficked-victim children (5–18 years) |
| PRAKSIS | Polyclinics in Athens and Thessaloniki | European Refugee Fund (ERF), Stavros Niarchos Foundation, John S. Latsis Public Benefit Foundation, PFIZER | Provision of free medical services, paediatric clinic, vaccination, referrals, medication and social services to vulnerable groups |
| PRAKSIS | Let's Play Together | European Fund — Integration of Third Country Nationals, Ministry of Internal Affairs | Using sport to promote equality for all, conducting sports competitions and activities for immigrant children |
| PRAKSIS | ERF-Mobile Support | ERF | Fully equipped mobile medical unit to deliver medical, psychosocial support and interpreter services in northern Greece |
| PRAKSIS | TOPEKO | European Social Fund (ESF), Ministry of Social Security, Public Expenditure (EU) National funds, Public Investment | Local Actions for Social Integration of Vulnerable Groups; identifying, selecting, preparing and promoting the re-employment of unemployed people |
| PRAKSIS | Business Coaching Centre | JPM Chase Foundation, Athens American Embassy AMKE Vapori | Training and coaching for vulnerable unemployed to develop their entrepreneurial skills for small business |

(*Continued*)

## Table 3: (Continued)

| NGO | Initiative | Funding | Outcomes |
|---|---|---|---|
| PRAKSIS | ERF — Housing | ERF | Providing temporary shelter (currently 23 apartments) in Attica, central Macedonia and prefecture of Lesvos, Greece |
| Hellenic Red Cross | Multifunctional Centre for Social Support, and integration of refugees | ERF and the Ministry of Health and Social Solidarity | Assistance to asylum seekers/refugees to find employment, provision of social counselling through a hotline service to enable their integration into Greek society |
| Hellenic Red Cross | Mobile Intervention Unit in the city of Patras | Hellenic Red Cross | Improve the living conditions of asylum seekers; accelerate the process of asylum requests in Patras; provide information on the rights of migrants; provide legal aid and interpretation services; and raise awareness of the local authorities with regards to issues in the asylum system |
| Doctors of the World/Médecins du Monde — (MdM-Greece) | First Reception Mobile Units in high migration flow areas | European Commission and the External Borders Fund | Fully-equipped mobile unit which provides primary health care services, psychosocial support, medication, personal hygiene items, clothing and footwear for migrants in Moria of Lesvos island |
| MdM-Greece/ Greek Council for Refugees | "ENOUGH!" (APKETA!) | Open Society Foundations | Provides medical, psychosocial and legal support to victims of racist violence. Conduct information sessions using multimedia in schools to raise awareness on racist crimes |
| Ecumenical Refugee Programme | Asylum Reform Project (CCME) | UNHCR, ERF, European Commission | Provides legal assistance and legal representation to refugees and asylum seekers |

(*Continued*)

Table 3: (Continued)

| NGO | Initiative | Funding | Outcomes |
|---|---|---|---|
| PRAKSIS/ARSIS | Mobile School | Bodossaki Foundation | Removal of children from the streets, providing psychosocial support to them, and facilitating their integration into the school environment |
| PRAKSIS/Klimaka, Municipality of Athens, MDM, Equal Society | Social structures tackling poverty in Athens Municipality | ESF | Provision of primary health care, basic supplies, disposable hygiene kits, laundry services, referrals to social service agencies and hospitals, access to internet and phone, organising play areas for children |
| PRAKSIS/IOM | Addressing the needs of Unaccompanied Minors (UAMS) in Greece | European Union, Sweden, the Netherlands and Denmark | Conduct street-work to identify unaccompanied minors, provide information on programme of voluntary repatriation and re-integration of minors who wish to return to their families in their respective countries of origin |
| PRAKSIS/Hellenic Red Cross | STEGI Plus/ accommodation centre for minor asylum seekers in Patras & Athens | Current/ European Economic Area (Iceland, Liechtenstein and Norway), IOM | Accommodation centres, psychosocial/medical support, mediation services, legal counselling, tutoring in Greek, study support, interpretation, intercultural and recreational activities, job counselling for integration in the labour market |

*Source:* ARSIS (2015); PRAKSIS (2015); Red Cross EU Office (2013); Médecins du Monde Greece (2015); and CCME (2012).

services, vaccination, preventive care, health education and pharmaceutical coverage to people without social insurance or those challenged by administrative and language barriers to accessing the national health care system.

## Conclusion and policy recommendations

In conclusion, migrants flee war, poverty and violence to seek asylum in developed countries. For undocumented migrants who are Europe-bound, Greece is the main point of entry. Upon arrival in Greece, undocumented arrivals are arrested and routinely placed in systematic and prolonged detention. Substandard living conditions, the abusive behaviour of detention staff and lack of access to medical care lead to deleterious health effects. Deleterious health effects associated with detention are aggravated by the lack of adequate assessment on arrival, ethnic profiling by Greek authorities, sweep operations and detention of children, which in some cases separate them from their parents. The Greek government, in collaboration with the UNHCR, has developed policies aligning its activities in detention centres with the international human rights guidelines. These include the new asylum policy in 2013 which improved services on processing asylum applications and issuing permits to asylum seekers, the adoption of UNHCR guidelines on detention, the implementation of alternatives to detention, and the systematic, independent monitoring of detention centres. However, there has been poor coordination and integration of these policies and guidelines, and compliance remains a serious challenge. NGOs have played a powerful role in improving the conditions in detention facilities, and enabling the health and social wellbeing of asylum seekers on arrival, and during and after detention. Consequently, the following policies would augment current efforts to address the issues faced by asylum seekers and undocumented migrants in Greece:

1. **Reception and detention facilities**: In order to improve the living conditions in detention facilities in Greece and elsewhere in Europe, there is an urgent need for the mobilisation of developed nations to ratify the UNHCR guidelines on applicable criteria and standards relating to the detention of asylum seekers, and embed core international human rights treaties into their domestic laws. The most important

core human right treaties to protect asylum seekers are International Convention on the Elimination of All Forms of Racial Discrimination, International Covenant on Civil and Political Rights, International Covenant on Economic, Social and Cultural Rights, Convention on the Elimination of All Forms of Discrimination against Women, Convention against Torture and Other Cruel, Inhuman or Degrading Treatment or Punishment, Convention on the Rights of the Child, International Convention on the Protection of the Rights of All Migrant Workers and Members of Their Families, and Convention on the Rights of Persons with Disabilities. It is worth noting that while Greece is a signatory to most human rights treaties, it is not a party to the Convention against Torture and the Convention for the Rights of Migrant Workers.

2. **Dublin II Regulation**: While the Dublin II Regulation leaves the responsibility for processing applications from people seeking international protection under the Geneva Convention to each EU member state, the system has experienced significant flaws. In the case of Greece, as can be seen from this chapter, such flaws have included the failure to provide a fair and efficient system for processing asylum seekers' applications, subjecting asylum seekers to abuses with little protection, and asylum seekers' lack of access to adequate legal and welfare services. The implementation and effectiveness of the Dublin II regulation need to be evaluated and practical steps put in place to streamline national practices on the detention of asylum seekers.

3. **Systematic monitoring of detention centres**: Practices and service delivery in detention centres need to be monitored to identify any human rights violations at both the individual and systemic levels. The monitoring should also help improve the social and health environments of detention facilities through the provision of basic necessities such as food, clothing and personal hygiene items; strengthening surveillance systems and practice guidelines to prevent and control communicable disease outbreaks, and provide timely secondary referral for specialist medical conditions.

4. **Post-detention**: There is an urgent need for the Greek government to address the health and welfare of asylum seekers post-detention through the provision of suitable accommodation and basic necessities, ensure

the continuity of adequate medical and mental health care, and provide an environment that promotes a healthy lifestyle.
5. **Human resources**: The Greek government should pay specific attention to staffing in detention centre facilities. There is an urgent need to ensure adequate staffing and training of personnel at detention facilities. The priority should be on training staff in human rights principles and culturally competent practices, and the coordination of activities between different levels of government ministries and local government areas.
6. **End of immigration detention**: In the real world, immigration detention should not be a first option to deal with undocumented migrants as it is in violation of international human rights treaties. There is an urgent need to abandon the practice of indefinite detention of undocumented migrants and asylum seekers, and the detention of children. The focus should be on timely information on the right to apply for asylum, processes of dealing with applications from people seeking international protection, and asylum seekers' rights and entitlements. The Greek government should put in place practical policies that do not detain children except in exceptional circumstances as a measure of last resort, and make the speedy processing of asylum seekers' applications, family tracing and reunification, and alternatives to detention, the cornerstone of its asylum seeker strategies.

## References

AIDA (2015). Asylum Information Database. Country Report: Greece. Third Update — April 2015. Available at: http://www.asylumineurope.org/reports/country/greece. Accessed 16 May 2015.

Amaral, P. (2013). Detention, alternatives to detention, and deportation: Immigration detention: looking at the alternatives. *Forced Migration Review*, 44, 40–42.

Amnesty International (2014). A Law unto themselves: A culture of abuse and impunity in the Greek Police. Available at: https://www.amnesty.org/en/documents/eur25/005/2014/en/. Accessed 6 May 2015.

Angeli, D. & Triandafyllidou, A. (2014). Is the indiscriminate detention of irregular migrants a cost-effective policy tool? A case-study of the Amygdaleza Pre-Removal Center. MIDAS research project, policy brief, ELIAMEP, Athens, GRE. Available at: http://www.eliamep.gr/wp-content/uploads/2014/05/Policy-brief_the-case-study-of-Amygdaleza-1.pdf. Accessed 12 May 2015.

ANTIGONE (2013). Information and Documentation Centre on Racism, Ecology, Peace and NonViolence: ExperienceCrime. Available at: http://www.antigone.gr/en/projects/project/20/description/. Accessed 9 May 2015.

ARSIS (2015). Home. Available at: http://arsis.gr/en/home/. Accessed 9 May 2015.

Bieber, I., Buzatu, C., Moldova, Z. & Novoszádek, N., 2013. Promoting the Reform of Pre-trial Detention in CEE-FSU Countries — Introducing Good Practices. Available at: http://helsinki.hu/wp-content/uploads/Pre-trial_detention_in_CEE-FSU_countries.pdf. Accessed 4 June 2015.

Bloomfield, A. *et al.* (ed.), (2015). Alternatives to Immigration and Asylum Detention in the EU. Available at: http://www.justiceandpeace.nl/public/Publication/22/download/MadeReal-report-%20Alternatives%20to%20detention%20in%20the%20EU.pdf. Accessed 24 May 2015.

CCME (2012). Ecumenical Refugee Program — Church of Greece Available at: http://www.ccme.be/members-info/greece/. Accessed 12 May 2015.

Charalambos, K. (2012). Greece: Illegal Immigration in the Midst of Crisis. Migration Information Source. Available at: http://www.migrationpolicy.org/article/greece-illegal-immigration-midst-crisis. Accessed 19 May 2015.

Cohen, J. (2008). Safe in our hands? A study of suicide and self-harm in asylum seekers. *Journal of Forensic and Legal Medicine*, 15, 235–244.

Council of Europe (2000). Official Gazette of the Council of Europe: Committee of Ministers part-volume. Council of Europe Publishing, Strasbourg, FRA.

Council of Europe (2008). Report to the Government of Greece on the visit to Greece carried out by the European Committee for the Prevention of Torture and Inhuman or Degrading Treatment or Punishment (CPT) CPT/Inf (2008) 3. Available at: http://www.cpt.coe.int/documents/grc/2008-03-inf-eng.pdf. Accessed 28 May 2015.

Council of Europe (2011). M.S.S. v. Belgium and Greece, Application no. 30696/09, Council of Europe: European Court of Human Rights, 21 January 2011. Available at: http://www.refworld.org/docid/4d39bc7f2.html. Accessed 4 May 2015.

Council of Europe (2013) Migration and asylum: mounting tensions in the Eastern Mediterranean. Committee on Migration, Refugees and Displaced Persons. Available at: http://assembly.coe.int/ASP/Doc/XrefViewPDF.asp?FileID=19349&Language=en. Accessed 20 April 2015.

Council of Europe (2014). Report to the Government of Greece on the visit to Greece carried out by the European Committee for the Prevention of Torture and Inhuman or Degrading Treatment or Punishment (CPT) CPT/Inf (2014) 26. Available at: http://www.cpt.coe.int/documents/grc/2014-26-inf-eng.pdf. Accessed 4 June 2015.

ECDC (2010). Tuberculosis Surveillance in Europe 2008. European Centre for Disease Prevention and Control, Stockholm, SWE.

ECDC (2011). Mission Report: Increased influx of migrants at the Greek–Turkish border. Available at: http://ecdc.europa.eu/en/publications/Publications/1105_ MIR_Joint_WHO_Greece.pdf. Accessed 1 May 2015.

ECRE (2013). Dublin II Regulation: Lives on Hold. Available at: http://www.ecre.org/component/content/article/56-ecre-actions/317-dublin-ii-regulation-lives-on-hold.html. Accessed 3 May 2015.

Edwards, A. (2011). Back to Basics: The Right to Liberty and Security of Person and "Alternatives to Detention" of Refugees, Asylum-Seekers, Stateless Persons and Other Migrants, UNHCR Legal and Protection Policy Research Series, PPLA/2011/01.Rev.1, April 2011. Available at: http://www.unhcr.org/refworld/docid/4dc935fd2.html. Accessed 19 April 2015.

EMN (2014). Policies, practices and data on unaccompanied minors in 2014. European Migration Network. Available at: http://ec.europa.eu/dgs/home-affairs/what-we-do/networks/european_migration_network/reports/docs/emn-studies/unaccompanied-minors/greece_national_report_uams_en.pdf. Accessed 4 June 2015.

EUR-LEX Access to European Union Law (2003). Official Journal of the European Union: COUNCIL REGULATION (EC) No. 343/2003. L 50/1. Available at: http://eur-lex.europa.eu/legal-content/EN/TXT/PDF/?uri=CELEX:32003R0343&from=EN. Accessed 23 May 2015.

EUR-LEX Access to European Union Law (2009). The Schengen area and cooperation. Available at: http://eur-lex.europa.eu/legal-content/EN/TXT/?uri=URISERV:l33020. Accessed 8 June 2015.

Europa (2011). Summaries of EU Legislation: Dublin II Regulation. Available at: http://europa.eu/legislation_summaries/justice_freedom_security/free_movement_of_persons_asylum_immigration/l33153_en.htm. Accessed 2 June 2015.

European Commission (2014). The use of detention and alternatives to detention in the context of immigration policies. Synthesis Report for the EMN Focussed Study 2014. Available at: http://ec.europa.eu/dgs/home-affairs/what-we do/networks/european_migration_network/reports/docs/emn studies/emn_study_detention_alternatives_to_detention_synthesis_report_en.pdf. Accessed 02 June 2015.

European Council on Refugees and Exiles (2013). Available at: http://www.ecre.org/. Accessed 10 May 2015.

FRONTEX (2015). Origin. Available at: http://frontex.europa.eu/about-frontex/origin/. Accessed 18 May 2015.

Global Detention Project (2015). Available at: http://www.globaldetentionproject.org. Accessed 3 June 2015.

Greece (2011). Law No. 3907 of 2011 on the establishment of an Asylum Service and a First Reception Service, transposition into Greek legislation of Directive 2008/115/EC "on common standards and procedures in Member States for returning illegally staying third country nationals" and other provisions. [Greece], 26 January 2011. Available at: http://www.refworld.org/docid/4da6ee7e2.html. Accessed 4 June 2015.

Greek Forum of Refugees (2012). Actions. Available at: http://www.refugees.gr/en/activities/actions. Accessed 9 May 2015.

Greek National Commission for Human Rights (2007). Observations regarding the issue of Unaccompanied Minors, February 15, 2007. Available at: http://www.nchr.gr/images/English_Site/Ektheseis/eng2007.pdf. Accessed 10 April 2015.

Gushulak, B.D. & Macpherson, D.W (2004). Globalization of infectious diseases: the impact of migration. *Clinical Infectious Diseases*, 38, 1742–1748.

Headquarters of the Hellenic Police (2012). "Police Operation 'XENIOS ZEUS' in Athens and Evros to tackle illegal immigration. Statements by the Spokesperson of the Hellenic Police," Press Release, August 4, 2012. Available at: http://www.astynomia.gr/index.php?option=ozo_content&lang='..'&perform=view&id=18424&Itemid=950&lang=. Accessed 13 April 2013.

Hellenic Police (2015). Statistical Data: Statistics on Illegal Immigration. Available at: http://www.astynomia.gr/index.php?option=ozo_content&perform=view&id=24727&Itemid=73&lang=EN. Accessed 18 May 2015.

Human Rights Watch (2008). Left to Survive: Systematic Failure to Protect Unaccompanied Migrant Children in Greece. Available at: http://www.hrw.org/reports/2008/12/22/left-survive. Accessed 28 April 2015.

Human Rights Watch (2013a). Unwelcome Guests: Greek Police Abuses of Migrants in Athens June 2013. Available at: http://www.hrw.org/sites/default/files/reports/greece0613_ForUpload.pdf. Accessed 20 May 2015.

Human Rights Watch (2013b). Turned Away: Summary Returns of Unaccompanied Migrant Children and Adult Asylum Seekers from Italy to Greece. Available at: http://www.hrw.org/sites/default/files/reports/italy0113ForUpload_0.pdf. Accessed 4 June 2015.

International Detention Coalition (2015). Available at: http://idcoalition.org/. Accessed 6 May 2015.

International Labour Organisation (1999). C182 — Worst Forms of Child Labour Convention, 1999 (No. 182) art. 3. Available at: http://www.ilo.org/dyn/normlex/en/f?p=NORMLEXPUB:12100:0::NO::P12100_INSTRUMENT_ID:312327. Accessed 15 April 2015.

IOM (2013). International Organisation for Migration: Overview of SOAM Program. Available at: http://eeagrants-iomathens-soam.gr/?lang=en. Accessed 11 May 2015.

Jesuit Refugee Service (2011). Europe: Becoming Vulnerable in Detention, June 2011. Available at: http://www.refworld.org/docid/4ec269f62.html. Accessed 28 April 2015.

Jesuit Refugee Service (2013). Detention in Europe. Available at: http://www.detention-in-europe.org/index.php?option=com_content&view=article&id=309&Itemid=262. Accessed 5 June 2015.

Koopowitz, A. & Abhary (2004). Psychiatric aspects of detention: illustrative case studies. *Australian and New Zealand Journal of Psychiatry*, 38, 495–500.

Kotsioni, I. & Hatziprokopiou, P. (2009). MIGHEALTHNET: State of the Art Report on the Greekcase. Available at: http://www.academia.edu/7865591/MIGHEALTHNET_State_of_the_Art_Report_on_Greek_Case. Accessed 21 April 2015.

Kotsioni, I. *et al.* (2013). Detention, alternatives to detention, and deportation: Health at risk in immigration detention facilities. Available at: http://www.fmreview.org/en/detention.pdf. *Forced Migration Review*, 44, 12–14.

Macgrady B., (1997). Resort to international human rights law in challenging conditions in US immigration detention centers. *Brooklyn Journal of International Law*, 23, 271.

Majcher, I., A., Flynn, M. (2014). Immigration Detention in Greece. Available at: http://www.globaldetentionproject.org/countries/europe/greece/introduction.html. Accessed 20 April 2015. Global Detention Project, Geneva, SWI.

Médecins du Monde Greece (2015). Annual Activity Report 2014: Doctors of the World Greek delegation. Available at: http://mdmgreece.gr/en/activity-report-2014-doctors-of-the-world-greece/. Accessed 10 May 2015.

MSF (2010). Migrants in detention: lives on hold. Available at: http://www.doctorswithoutborders.org/news-stories/special-report/greece-lives-hold. Accessed 25 April 2015.

MSF (2011). Médecins Sans Frontières (MSF) Emergency Intervention in Migrants' Detention Facilities in Evros. Available at: http://www.msf.org/sites/msf.org/files/old-cms/fms/article-documents/Greece_Evros_Report.pdf. Accessed 14 May 2015.

MSF (2013). Medical assistance to migrants and refugees in Greece: Findings from MSF's intervention in detention facilities for migrants. Available at: http://www.msf.org.uk/sites/uk/files/greece_refugees_2013.pdf. Médecins Sans Frontières. Accessed 14 May 2015.

MSF (2014). Invisible Suffering: Prolonged and systematic detention of migrants and asylum seekers in substandard conditions in Greece. Available at: http://www.doctorswithoutborders.org/sites/usa/files/attachments/invisible_suffering.pdf. Accessed 20 May 2015.

Norredam, M., Mygind, A. & Krasnik, A., (2005). Access to healthcare for asylum seekers in the European Union — a comparative study of country policies. DOI: http://dx.doi.org/10.1093/eurpub/cki191. *The European Journal of Public Health*, 16(3), 285–289.

OHCHR (2013). Report of the Special Rapporteur on the human rights of migrants, Mission to Greece, April 2013. Office of the High Comissioner for Human Rights. Available at: http://ap.ohchr.org/documents/dpage_e.aspx?si=A/HRC/23/46/Add.4. Accessed 12 April 2015.

PRAKSIS (2015). Current intervention. Available at: http://www.praksis.gr/en/our-programs/current-interventions. Accessed 9 May 2015.

Rechel, B. *et al.* (eds.) (2011). *Migration and health in the European Union.* Open University Press, New York, NY.

Red Cross EU Office (2013). Mapping of the migration activities of European National Red Cross Societies 2012–2013 Update Greece. Available at: http://redcross.eu/en/upload/documents/pdf/2013/Migration/GREECE_mapping_FINAL_01.2013.pdf. Accessed 9 May 2015.

Sampson, R., Mitchell, G. & Bowring, L., 2011. *There are Alternatives: a Handbook for Preventing Unnecessary Immigration Detention.* The International Detention Coalition, Malbourne, AUS. Available at: http://www.ohchr.org/Documents/Issues/Migration/Events/IDC.pdf. Accessed 2 June 2015.

Schriro, D.B. (2009). Immigration detention overview and recommendations. US Department of Homeland Security, Immigration and Customs Enforcement, Washington, DC.

Steel, Z. *et al.* (2009). Association of torture and other potentially traumatic events with mental health outcomes among populations exposed to mass conflict and displacement: a systematic review and meta-analysis. *Journal of American Medical Association*, 302, 537–549.

The Sphere Handbook (2011). Humanitarian Charter and Minimum Standards in Humanitarian Response. Available at: https://www.ifrc.org/PageFiles/95530/The-Sphere-Project-Handbook-20111.pdf. Accessed 2 June 2015.

Triandafyllidou, A. (2014). Migration in Greece: Recent Developments in 2014. OECD Network of International Migration Experts, Paris, FRA.

UN (2010). Working Group on Arbitrary Detention, Report A/HRC/13/30 58 p. 17 10 January 2010. Available at: http://www1.umn.edu/humanrts/wgad/2010report.pdf. Accessed 15 April 2015.

UN Committee on the Rights of the Child (2005). Treatment of unaccompanied and separated children outside their country of origin. General Comment No. 6,

UN Doc. CRC/GC/2005/6 (2005), paras. 7–8. Available at: http://www.refworld.org/docid/42dd174b4.html. Accessed 23 May 2015.

UNHCR (2000). Handbook for emergencies. United Nations High Comissioner for Refugees. Available at: www.aidworkers.net/resources/unhcr-handbook.html. Accessed 3 June 2015.

UNHCR (2010). Asylum levels and trends in industrialized countries, 2009. United Nations High Comissioner for Refugees. Available at: http://www.unhcr.org/4ba7341a9.html. Accessed 19 May 2015.

UNHCR (2011). Asylum levels and trends in industrialized countries, 2010. United Nations High Comissioner for Refugees. Available at: http://www.unhcr.org/4d8c5b109.html. Accessed 19 May 2015.

UNHCR (2012a). Detention guidelines: Guidelines on the applicable criteria and standards relating to the detention of asylum-seekers and alternatives to Detention. United Nations High Comissioner for Refugees. Available at: http://www.unhcr.org/refworld/docid/503489533b8.html. Accessed 24 April 2015. United Nations High Commissioner for Refugees, Geneva, SWI.

UNHCR (2012b). Asylum trends 2012. United Nations High Comissioner for Refugees. Available at: http://www.unhcr.org/5149b81e9.html. Accessed 19 May 2015.

UNHCR (2012c). A Framework for the Protection of Children, June 2012. United Nations High Comissioner for Refugees. Available at: http://www.refworld.org/docid/4fe875682.html. Aaccessed 28 April 2015.

UNHCR (2013). 1 against racism: Members of the Racist Violence Recording Network. United Nations High Comissioner for Refugees. Available at: http://www.unhcr.gr/1againstracism/en/members-of-the-racist-violence-recording-network/. Accessed 8 May 2015.

UNHCR (2014a). UNHCR monitoring visit to the Republic of Nauru, October 2013. United Nations High Comissioner for Refugees. Available at: http://unhcr.org.au/unhcr/images/2013-11-26%20Report%20of%20UNHCR%20Visit%20to%20Nauru%20of%207-9%20October%202013.pdf. Accessed 8 June 2015.

UNHCR (2014b). Observations on the Current Situation of Asylum in Greece, December 2014. United Nations High Comissioner for Refugees. Available at: http://reliefweb.int/report/greece/unhcr-observations-current-situation-asylum-greece-december-2014. Accessed 20 April 2015.

UNHCR (2014c). Asylum Trends, 2014. United Nations High Comissioner for Refugees. Available at: http://www.unhcr.org/551128679.html. Accessed 19 May 2015.

UNHCR (2014d). Beyond detention: A global strategy to end the detention of asylum seekers and refugees, 2014. United Nations High Comissioner for Refugees. Available at: http:// www.unhcr.org/53aa929f6.pdf. Accessed 10 April 2015.

# Chapter 6

# The health status, service needs and barriers to accessing care for detention and community-based asylum seekers in Australia

Ms Emily Hadgkiss and Professor André M.N. Renzaho

According to the UNHCR, of 51.2 million individuals forcibly displaced worldwide at the end of 2013, 1.2 million were asylum seekers (UNHCR, 2014a). Between 2009 and 2013, the USA, Germany, France, Sweden and the United Kingdom received the largest number of new asylum seekers, over one-third (38%) of all requests submitted in industrialised countries (UNHCR, 2014b). In 2013, Australia was ranked seventh of the countries receiving asylum seekers, accounting for about 4% of the share of total applications (UNHCR, 2014b). This chapter will focus on asylum seekers in Australia and not internally displaced people (covered in Chapter 2) or refugees (covered in Chapter 3). For the purpose of this chapter, an asylum seeker is defined as a person outside of their country of origin and is seeking international protection as a refugee but whose refugee status has not yet been determined. It gives a brief historical and migration governance overview followed by more in-depth analysis of the physical and mental health status of asylum seekers with some comparison of immigration detention and community-based arrangements. It concludes by summarising some of the social and health policy responses of government and non-government bodies.

## Australian legal framework governing asylum seeking

Australia is one of 147 countries who are signatories to the 1951 United Nations Convention Relating to the Status of Refugees and its 1967 Protocol ("the Refugee Convention") (UNHCR, 2010) and one of 26 countries regularly participating in the UNHCR resettlement programme. A protection visa may be granted to a person who is found to have protection obligations by Australia and meets the definition of a refugee or the "complementary protection" criteria under the Migration Act 1958 (Commonwealth of Australia, 2015). In addition to the Refugee Convention, there are other international human rights conventions to which Australia is a party. These include the International Covenant on Civil and Political Rights, the International Covenant on Economic, Social and Cultural Rights, the Convention against Torture and Other Cruel, Inhuman or Degrading Treatment or Punishment, the Convention on the Rights of the Child, and the International Convention on the Elimination of all Forms of Racial Discrimination (Australian Human Rights Commission, 2012b). The discussion of these conventions is beyond the purpose of this chapter. Below, we focus on the points most relevant to asylum seekers.

Under the Refugee Convention (UNHCR, 2010), persons may be owed protection if they are outside their country and are unable or unwilling to return due to a well-founded fear that they will be persecuted because of their race, religion, nationality, political opinion or membership of a particular social group. People who have left their country of residence or nationality due to war, famine, environmental collapse or to seek economic opportunities, but do not fear persecution, are not owed protection under the Refugee Convention. Nor is Australia obliged to protect those who already have effective protection in another country. In contrast, under the Migration Amendment (Complementary Protection) Act 2011, Australia also assesses asylum seekers' claims for protection under 'complementary protection' criteria which state that people are owed protection by Australia if they have substantial grounds for fearing they will suffer significant harm if returned to their home country (Commonwealth of Australia, 2015). The criteria for complementary protection takes into consideration Australia's broader international obligations under the International Covenant on Civil and Political Rights and the Convention against Torture and Other Cruel, Inhuman or Degrading Treatment or Punishment. It considers if a person will be subject to arbitrary deprivation of his or her life, the death penalty, torture, cruel or inhuman treatment or punishment, or degrading treatment or punishment (Commonwealth of Australia, 2015). However, in accordance with the Refugee Convention, penalties should not be imposed on people seeking asylum. It is not illegal to enter Australia as an asylum seeker even if a person arrives into Australian territory without authorisation or travel documents (Commonwealth of Australia, 1958). According to the UNHCR, this includes not only refugees coming straight from their country of origin but also refugees coming from any other country where their protection, safety and security cannot be assured (UNHCR, 1999).

Collectively, these international human rights conventions have important implications for the protection and treatment of asylum seekers in Australia. Some of these rights are legally binding and absolute while others are subject to reasonable limitations for the purpose of protecting national security, public order or promoting the general welfare of a democratic society. Some of the rights that Australia is obliged to uphold, and yet may be questioned with regard to the treatment of asylum seekers include the right to not subject anyone to cruel, inhuman or degrading treatment, the right to liberty of movement and freedom to choose one's residence, the right to a fair and public hearing by a competent, independent and impartial tribunal, the right to non-discrimination based on race, colour, sex, language, religion, political or other opinion, national or social origin, property, birth or other status, the right to work, the right to social security, the right to protection and assistance for the family, the right to an adequate standard of living, and the right to health.

While there was an intake of approximately 14,000 refugees and humanitarian entrants in the 2013–2014 Australian Refugee and Humanitarian Programme (Commonwealth of Australia, 2014a), of relevance to this chapter are only asylum seekers that arrive in Australia by boat or plane and then apply for a protection visa under the "onshore" component of the Refugee and Humanitarian Programme. Asylum seekers arriving with or without a substantive visa (such as a student, tourist or business visa) and claim asylum on arrival are referred to by the Australian Government as "Illegal Maritime Arrivals" (IMAs) if arriving by boat, or "Unauthorised Air Arrivals" (UAA) if arriving by plane. In 2013–2014 programme year, there were 10,624 protection visa applications through the "onshore" programme. Of those, 2,752 people were granted a protection visa through the onshore programme, fewer than 20% were people who had arrived by boat (Commonwealth of Australia, 2014a). This is the lowest allocation of visas to this group in several years, which reflects Australia's increasingly restrictive policies towards IMAs.

## History of asylum seekers in Australia and current political context

Over the past few decades, a global increase in the number of people seeking asylum and the number of "unauthorised" arrivals across national borders has been a concern for many governments and a focus of political and social debate. Historically, most asylum seekers arrived by plane, but the issue that has consumed the Australian media and the attention of the public over the last four decades has largely been that of "boat arrivals". The first wave of people seeking asylum who arrived by boat was in the 1970s following the Vietnam War (Phillips and Spinks, 2013). In the 1990s, Australia saw a second wave of asylum seekers arriving by boat, mostly from Cambodia, Vietnam and southern China, and a third wave predominantly from the Middle East from 1999 (Phillips and Spinks, 2013). In most recent years, the majority of asylum seekers have been from southern and central Asia, north Africa and the Middle East or north-east Asia (Commonwealth of Australia, 2013). A multitude of factors result in asylum seekers choosing to take a perilous boat journey to Australia, usually with the aid of people smugglers in Indonesia. There have been over one thousand deaths among asylum seekers trying to reach the Australian mainland by boat, including at least 15 children between 2008 and 2013 (Australian Human Rights Commission, 2014). Subsequently over the past two decades, there have been many rapid changes to the policies and legislation that govern Australia's approach to the processing and treatment of people seeking asylum in Australia.

## Immigration detention in Australia

Increasingly, industrialised countries such as Australia have resorted to "policies of deterrence" in an effort to reduce the number of people seeking asylum in those countries. Mandatory immigration detention policy has existed in Australia since 1992 and still maintains bipartisan support. This means that any "unlawful non-citizens" (people without a valid visa) must be detained, including people arriving by boat or air without valid documentation and people who have overstayed their visa or had their visa cancelled. They may only be released from immigration detention if they are granted a visa, moved into an alternative "Community Detention" arrangement, or are deported from Australia — the first two conditions being at the discretion of the Minister for Immigration and Border Protection (who under the Migration Act, does not have a *duty* to exercise this power). Under Australian law, there is no prescribed limit to the length of time that an adult or child can be detained.

The Australian government maintains that mandatory detention is deemed necessary to enable health and security checks to be undertaken, to prevent asylum seekers from absconding, and to act as a deterrent for other asylum seekers. This stance has been maintained despite a number of independent inquiries resulting in domestic and international criticism, and significant lobbying from community groups concerned about the rights and welfare of asylum seekers in detention settings. The UN Committee against Torture has noted with concern that practices in immigration detention appear cruel and inhumane including punitive practices, solitary confinement of detainees, mistreatment by officers and a dehumanising environment (United Nations General Assembly, 2008). Other concerns raised have been around the remoteness and poor conditions of detention centres, absence of time limits on detention, the lack of meaningful activities for detainees to engage in, and the subsequent effects of detention on mental health and community adjustment (discussed later in this chapter) (Joint Select Committee on Australia's Immigration Detention Network, 2012).

In July 2008, the New Directions in Detention Policy was released, based on seven key government immigration detention values. This outlined that immigration detention should be for the shortest period possible and if a person is compliant with immigration processes and is not deemed a risk to the community, then the presumption was that they will remain in the community while their immigration status is resolved (Commonwealth of Australia, 2009). The policy was not enshrined in legislation, however, and subsequent policy directions (outlined below) have again resulted in increasing numbers of asylum seekers being detained for lengthy periods of time. In terms of children in detention centres, the 2005 provision in the Migration Act outlined that a child should only be detained as a "measure of last report". In response to this, since 2010, many families have been transferred to "community detention" arrangements as an alternative to a closed detention facility while they await a decision on their refugee claims. Yet in recent years, the number of children and families in closed detention facilities has steadily risen again with the highest number recorded at just under 2,000 children in July 2013. The average period of time in detention is also increasing with many of these children having been detained for a year or more (Australian Human Rights Commission, 2014). The United Nations Committee on the Rights of the Child has expressed deep concern about Australia's mandatory detention policy and its failure to conform with the Convention on the Rights of the Child (United Nations Committee on the Rights of the Child, 2012). Recent political pressures have resulted in the release of many families and unaccompanied minors from detention centres, but there remain significant numbers that are ineligible for transfer either because of the mode and timing of their arrival, or because a parent has been assessed as a potential security risk and cannot be released. These families are likely to remain in detention for extended periods of time.

### *Third country processing and offshore detention*

In September 2001 the Australian Government adopted the "Pacific Solution", a suite of legislative changes that included the transfer of asylum seekers to third country processing centres. This was dismantled in 2008 and remaining asylum seekers were resettled in Australia, but was again re-introduced in 2012 following the release of a report from an appointed Expert Panel on Asylum Seekers (Houston *et al.*, 2012). Agreements were made with the governments of the Republic of Nauru and Papua New Guinea, and detainee transfers to Nauru and Manus Island commenced in the following months. The Australian government also made an earlier attempt in 2011 to make a bilateral agreement with the government of

Malaysia to "exchange" 4,000 people in Malaysia who had been assessed as refugees with 800 asylum seekers who had arrived in Australia by boat. However, this was ruled invalid by the High Court of Australia on the grounds that Malaysia is not a signatory to the Refugee Convention and the agreement would contravene human rights protections. In June 2013, even tougher measures were put in place that stipulated that all asylum seekers arriving by boat would be subject to offshore processing and resettlement, and that no one found to be a refugee would be resettled in Australia.

## Alternative to detention: community-residing asylum seekers

**Bridging visas:** Asylum seekers arriving by plane usually enter Australia with a valid visa, such as a student or tourist visa before seeking protection. They are generally not subject to immigration detention and instead are granted a "bridging visa". Bridging visas allow asylum seekers to live lawfully in the community while they wait for a decision on their visa application. Since November 2011, the Australian government has also permitted some unauthorised boat arrivals to be released from immigration detention to live freely in the community with a bridging visa. This means that although immigration detention is still mandatory for this group, in some cases time spent in detention is limited to conducting health, security and character checks before they are released (Commonwealth of Australia, 2012b). These can be granted at the discretion of the Minister for Immigration and Border Protection. At the end of the 2013–2014 programme year, there were more than 28,000 asylum seekers living in the Australian community awaiting a decision on their protection claims (Commonwealth of Australia, 2014a). Most bridging visas granted to asylum seekers arriving by plane (with a valid visa) allow them to work. Many asylum seekers arriving by boat are not granted work rights, or lose their right to work along the long visa resolution pathway. Policy around bridging visas and permission to work is complex, changes frequently and is dependent on a number of operational and discretionary factors including an individual's mode and timing of arrival in Australia. Asylum seekers living in the community without work rights are particularly vulnerable — without being able to earn an income and with very limited government support, individuals are at high risk of poverty and homelessness (Asylum Seeker Resource Centre, 2010). There are a number of welfare schemes and support services offered to asylum seekers by the Australian government, but eligibility criteria exclude many individuals, or the financial support is insufficient or only short-lived. Legal assistance is no longer available to any asylum seekers arriving by boat since recent policy changes were made. Restrictive policies result in increased pressure on charitable organisations and community groups to provide welfare, legal and social support to this vulnerable population.

**Community detention:** Families, unaccompanied minors and vulnerable adults may be transferred into a supportive "community detention" programme, regardless of their mode of arrival. People living in community detention arrangements have no lawful status in Australia, they do not hold a visa or have any rights or entitlements. While in community detention, asylum seekers are required to live at the allocated address and regularly report to the immigration department or another service provider (Commonwealth of Australia, 2012a). A case worker is assigned to each family or individual, but the level of support provided is considered inadequate, except for unaccompanied minors who receive 24-hour support. Asylum seekers in community detention are provided with a basic living allowance, which is a proportion of what an Australian living on basic welfare would receive. In addition, housing, furniture, medical and schooling expenses are mostly covered (Australian Red Cross, 2012). A local general practitioner and pharmacist are assigned to support their needs and they have the right to access the same health services as an Australian citizen. Community detention is considered a much better environment for mental and physical wellbeing than other detention arrangements. It allows individuals to begin to settle into the community while they await a decision on their visa. The number of asylum seekers living in community detention fluctuates, but there are usually several thousand in this situation at any given time.

## Deterrence policies 2012–2014

Although the number of unauthorised asylum seekers has fluctuated over the previous decade, there has been a rise since 2008, resulting in many tragic deaths at sea which has placed significant pressure on the Australian government to combat people smuggling and address the apparent border security deficiencies. This has resulted in the introduction of a number of complex deterrence policies that apply to asylum seekers travelling by boat (and sometimes those arriving by plane but without clearing immigration). Such policies are justified by the government as seeking to deter asylum seekers considering a boat journey to Australia, but the reality is that it only serves to punish those who have already safely arrived.

**"No advantage" principle:** In 2012, the Expert Panel on Asylum Seekers (Houston *et al.*, 2012) outlined a suite of short- and long-term deterrence strategies. One of these that the Australian government elected to introduce was the "No advantage" principle, which suspended processing of asylum seekers arriving by boat so that they were not granted any benefit over asylum seekers waiting for resettlement offshore via the regular humanitarian pathway. One consequence of these changes means that asylum seekers, including children, have had to wait for increasingly longer periods of time (in detention or the community) before their protection claims are assessed.

**Regional resettlement arrangement:** The regional resettlement arrangement policy was announced in July 2013. It stipulated that asylum seekers arriving by boat from this point onwards would never be resettled in Australia and instead would be offered third country resettlement (or voluntary repatriation). Over this period, other restrictions have been placed on IMAs, such as denial of work rights, ineligibility for family reunion pathways and reduced income support.

**Temporary protection visas:** TPVs were re-introduced under legislative changes in December 2014 and apply to any "unauthorised" asylum seekers (i.e. those arriving by boat or by plane without clearing immigration) (Commonwealth of Australia, 2014b). TPVs do not offer a pathway to permanent protection in Australia but rather provide temporary settlement for three years with work rights and access to Medicare. After three years, asylum seekers will be required to reapply and have their refugee claims re-assessed. Under the same legislative amendments, the government introduced Safe Haven Enterprise Visas, valid for up to

5 years, which require asylum seekers to live and work in certain regional areas in Australia. TPVs were previously used in Australia (from around 1999–2008) and studies found they had detrimental effects on the well-being of asylum seekers as they were left in a state of limbo unsure of what their future held without the rights and protections offered to permanent visa holders (Momartin *et al.*, 2006; Steel *et al.*, 2011).

**Refugee criteria and the fast track process:** Recent amendments have also introduced a "fast track" protection claim process, which denies "unauthorised" asylum seekers access to a review tribunal should they receive an initial negative outcome. This means that they can only appeal a negative decision through the courts to determine if the law has been properly applied, but cannot have the merits of their case re-heard. The Australian government has also removed references to the Refugee Convention in key legislation, allowing the government greater flexibility in determining the criteria for assessing a refugee. As this amendment was only recently introduced, it is not yet clear what the potential ramifications will be, or what proportion of asylum seekers this may affect.

**Border control:** As well as the transfer of all unauthorised asylum seekers to offshore detention centres, the "Operation Sovereign Borders" policy, introduced in September 2013, included a military-led operation used to intercept unauthorised boats entering Australian waters and forcibly turn them back to prevent asylum seekers from reaching Australia. It is part of a Regional Deterrence Framework aimed at preventing people smuggling, and the actions taken to date have been largely obscured from public knowledge. One legal case — with regard to the return of asylum seekers from Sri Lanka — was challenged in the High Court of Australia as to Australia's non-refoulement obligations under international law.

## Understanding the health needs of asylum seekers

There are important differences between settled refugees and asylum seekers, and such factors can have a significant impact on their physical and mental health outcomes. In countries such as Australia with formal policies and legislation, refugees who have received a positive assessment of their protection claims are granted access to health services and certain benefits including access to work and study opportunities, social and welfare rights and support to help them transition to their new life circumstances. Asylum seekers on the other hand remain in a state of legal limbo, faced with the constant threat of deportation, and in many cases denied work rights, and limited access to health, social, welfare and even legal services. Asylum seekers also face additional challenges related to the refugee determination process including discrimination due to societal misconceptions around their mode of arrival (Grove and Zwi, 2006; McKay, 2012).

In the Australian context, there are very few studies published on the health needs of asylum seekers. Firstly, it is difficult to access reliable data on the numbers of asylum seekers residing in the community, and the proportion of those that have access to work rights or welfare support. Asylum seekers are not "counted" in census data, electoral rolls or other official registries, and the Australian government appear reluctant to provide such figures (Correa-Velez and Gifford, 2007). The government has also been reluctant to allow researchers access to detention centres. This is a point of conflict with public health researchers, who need the data to inform service provision and to advocate for the health needs of asylum seekers. Researchers also highlight a number of practical and ethical reasons why undertaking research studies with this population group can be particularly challenging, including fear of deportation, the cultural appropriateness of consultation around sensitive issues, risks of re-traumatisation or exacerbation of feelings of anxiety and sadness (Silove et al., 2002).

Notwithstanding the limited research, the physical and mental health of asylum seekers arriving in Australia is likely to have been adversely affected by experiences in their country of origin, refugee camps, transit countries or the journeys between these destinations. The very nature of this journey is related to the persecution they face in their home country. Some asylum seekers have suffered the loss or abuse of family members and friends, imprisonment for political reasons, torture or sexual abuse. Such trauma can have a devastating impact on the psychological and physical wellbeing of an individual and his or her family. Having experienced torture has been identified as the strongest risk factor for post-traumatic stress disorder (Steel et al., 2009). Asylum seekers often travel to Australia from transit countries such as Indonesia in poorly constructed vessels. The conditions during these journeys can be hazardous and highly stressful. Pre-migration factors are likely to contribute to the types of physical and mental health conditions experienced by asylum seekers, and health professionals need to be appropriately trained to assess, detect and manage these patients.

## *Physical health of asylum seekers*

Asylum seekers may have complex medical profiles, including both infectious and chronic diseases similar to recently arrived refugees in the community (Hadgkiss and Renzaho, 2014). However, unlike refugees, individuals arriving in Australia by boat will not have undergone any pre-arrival medical screening and are likely to have no documented medical history. They may also be experiencing physical health conditions that are related to the nature of their journey to Australia by boat including sunburn, injuries or dehydration (Shaw and Leggat, 2006; Cheng and Kumarasinghe, 2014). Existing Australian policies require people arriving in Australian territory by boat without valid documentation to undertake standardised health screening upon arrival at a detention centre, the primary aim of which is to ensure that any diseases of public health significance are detected and treated immediately (Commonwealth of Australia, 2007). Asylum seekers may be at increased risk of infectious as well as chronic diseases and their risk factors. Risk factors and chronic conditions may lie undetected, or they may have been inadequately managed as a result of forced migration (Lightfoot, 2005; Bowers and Cheng, 2010). In addition, nutritional deficiencies may also exist as a result of intestinal parasites or inadequate nutritional intake. Left untreated, this can lead to vitamin and iron deficiency or delayed growth and developmental delays in children (Bowers and Cheng, 2010; Smith, 2000). Dental diseases are common among asylum seekers who may have poor nutritional status, poor dental hygiene or had limited access to dental care and treatment (Smith, 2000; Cheng and Kumarasinghe, 2014). One study found that close to 70% of asylum seekers had dental problems requiring consultation (Blackwell *et al.*, 2002). However asylum seekers' physical health may vary depending on many different pre-migration factors and whether they are in detention centres or community-based settings.

**Physical health of community-based asylum seekers:** A systematic review of international literature on the physical health of asylum seekers living in the community found that asylum seekers' perceived general health status is poorer than comparative refugee samples, immigrants or a general, non-immigrant population with at least one chronic physical symptom or complaint being self-reported by 49–77% of asylum seekers (Hadgkiss and Renzaho, 2014). Although asylum seekers' health is commonly associated with conditions that are infectious or nutritional in nature, the review found that the health profiles of asylum seekers can be considerably more complex. The most common conditions reported in studies included dental, headache or migraine, musculoskeletal, neck, back or shoulder pain, dermatological, respiratory, and gastrointestinal problems (Hadgkiss and Renzaho, 2014). In fact, infectious and parasitic diseases accounted for only 6.3% of individual diagnoses in a large study, whereas musculoskeletal and respiratory were the most frequently diagnosed conditions (Bischoff *et al.*, 2009). Sexual and reproductive issues were also reported in some studies; compared to the general population, asylum seekers were 4.5 times more likely than the general population to experience severe acute maternal morbidity, and more likely to have experienced sexual assault and had higher rates of unwanted pregnancy and induced abortions (Hadgkiss and Renzaho, 2014).

**Physical health of asylum seekers in detention centres:** A study reporting the results of 7,000 documented screenings of recently arrived asylum seekers in immigration detention centres found that rates of infectious disease were higher than the general Australian population for tuberculosis, malaria, hepatitis and some infectious skin conditions (King and Vodicka, 2001). New health complaints may also be related to the living conditions of the detention setting itself. For example, skin diseases such as eczema, fungal infections and infected sores may result from stress or unhygienic living conditions, while injuries incurred may be accidental or related to self-harming (Shaw and Leggat, 2006). An Australian study of the medical records of people in detention centres (Green and Eagar, 2010) showed that on average, detainees presented with 1.2 health complaints per week (new or existing), the most common of which were dental problems, respiratory conditions and lacerations (including self-harm). Asylum seekers who had arrived by boat, rather than by air, were more likely to present with new complaints. Conditions more commonly reported among detainees were musculoskeletal conditions, respiratory, ear and skin infections and injuries (Green and Eagar, 2010). A study from an acute hospital in the Northern Territory of Australia reported that over two-thirds of people at a nearby detention centre required transfer to the emergency department in a 12-month period. Most emergency department presentations were for chronic or non-specific conditions, including musculoskeletal, gastrointestinal, respiratory and neurological conditions (Deans *et al.*, 2013). A recent report demonstrated that maternal health care, including pregnancy monitoring, is also important in immigration detention settings (Australian Human Rights Commission, 2014). At offshore detention centres, due to the geography and climate, it is possible that asylum seekers may be at risk of malaria, dengue fever and other mosquito-borne diseases. The safety of asylum seekers may also be compromised in detention settings. On Manus Island in Papua New Guinea, riots within a detention centre led to the violent death of an asylum seeker at the hand of a detention employee, while there have been allegations of rape and assault on male detainees (Asylum Seeker Resource Centre, 2013).

## *Mental health of asylum seekers*

There are many pre-migration factors that may affect the mental health of asylum seekers, in particular previous experiences of trauma and torture. Mental health-related problems are among the most common reasons for seeking care among asylum seekers (Correa-Velez *et al.*, 2008). The most common psychiatric conditions are post-traumatic stress disorder, major depressive disorder, minor depression, dysthymia (mild chronic depression), generalised anxiety disorder, and panic disorder, with many individuals suffering from multiple conditions (Silove *et al.*, 2002). Additionally, the immigration process itself is a major cause of mental distress, and asylum seekers are left in a state of limbo, unsure about their future with the possibility of deportation, and worrying for the wellbeing of family and friends left behind in the country they fled. Further, asylum seekers are required to relive their horrific past as they tell their story for the purpose of assessment against refugee and complementary protection criteria.

Currently, many asylum seekers are experiencing lengthy delays in a decision on their protection claims due to harsh policies aimed at deterring people from travelling by boat to seek asylum.

**Mental health of community-based asylum seekers:** If permitted to live in the Australian community, a number of other challenges and issues create additional distress for asylum seekers as they try to navigate unfamiliar legal, employment, housing and health systems, and unfamiliar social and cultural customs. Language barriers can hinder attempts to learn more about their new community environment, compounding social isolation. In Australia, some asylum seekers may be able to access orientation and language services to support their settlement while they await a decision on their application, but this tends to be ad hoc and poorly resourced (Hadgkiss *et al.*, 2012). Restrictive policy in Australia at present creates an environment of significant stress and vulnerability for most community-residing asylum seekers (Steel *et al.*, 2011). Financial insecurity is a major problem with many asylum seekers being denied work rights and available financial support being inadequate to pay for rental accommodation, food and other basic needs (Asylum Seeker Resource Centre, 2010). Being denied work rights impacts mental wellbeing as it leads to boredom, social isolation and a sense of worthlessness. Other factors that negatively affect community-based asylum seekers' mental health are discrimination and stigmatisation (Royal Australian and New Zealand College of Psychiatrists, 2012).

**Mental health of asylum seekers in detention:** There is overwhelming evidence and wide consensus that immigration detention has an adverse effect on mental health. The risks to mental health are compounded when individuals are detained in offshore and remote centres, where the delivery of high quality services is often compromised. Among asylum seekers in detention centres who attend an emergency department, psychiatric problems (24.3%) including self-harm (17.9%) account for a significant share of primary diagnoses (Deans *et al.*, 2013). Overall, Australian and international literature consistently demonstrates high rates of major depression and anxiety disorders, post-traumatic stress disorder, self-harming and suicidal ideation among detainees (Robjant *et al.*, 2009; Silove *et al.*, 2007).

Data provided by the medical contractor in Australian detention centres estimated that around 30% of adults have a mental health problem and the severity and rates of these problems increase with the length of time in detention (Australian Human Rights Commission, 2014). The landmark study conducted by Steel *et al.* revealed the rate of psychiatric illness among detainees was substantially higher than that found in refugee populations who have not been in detention (Steel *et al.*, 2004). For adults there was a three-fold increase in psychiatric disorders, and for children a 10-fold increase since being detained. One study found that rates of new mental health diagnoses were 3.6 times higher in people who had been detained for over 24 months compared to those who were released within 3 months (Green and Eagar, 2010). Detainees also have a higher dependence on medication and greater need for case-worker support (Steel *et al.*, 2004), and once in the community are more likely to seek health care, particularly for mental health issues, than those who had never been detained (Mitchell and Kirsner, 2004). A systematic review of the international literature on the mental health impact of immigration detention also concluded that worse outcomes are associated with longer periods of time in detention (Robjant *et al.*, 2009). The detention environment in Australia is likely to have an adverse psychological impact on individuals for a number of reasons. These include the deprivation of liberty, social isolation and the harsh, punitive and dehumanising environment characteristic of detention centres (Coffey *et al.*, 2010). Individuals may be exposed to disturbing events such as riots, hunger strikes and lip sewing, forced confinement, and mental health disturbance among fellow detainees including self-harming (Coffey *et al.*, 2010; Rees, 2003; Sultan and O'Sullivan, 2001). In addition, asylum seekers have complained of boredom, aimlessness and apathy, difficulties accessing interpreters and barriers to accessing health care as other factors which contribute to poor mental health outcomes in detention (Sultan and O'Sullivan, 2001). A previous investigation by the Australian Human Rights Commission (2012a) found that the detrimental effects of detention continue to be pervasive even once an individual was released into the community to await the outcome of their protection claims. Previously detained refugees studied in Australia were found to suffer an ongoing sense of insecurity and injustice from their detention experience, and continued to suffer from depression, concentration and memory disturbances, and persistent anxiety (Coffey *et al.*, 2010).

## Families and children in immigration detention

A comprehensive report investigating the detention of children was released in early 2015 by the AHRC (Australian Human Rights Commission, 2014). It draws attention to issues of significant concern and validates the findings of previous Australian studies conducted with families in detention centres. Around the time that the report was released by the AHRC, there were several hundred children including unaccompanied minors in detention centres on the Australian mainland, Christmas Island and Nauru. The Australian government appeared to be making a concerted effort to release families and unaccompanied minors into the community, but many of them had been detained for many months. Over a 14-month period from January 2013–March 2014, there were 128 babies born to women in detention centres in Australia, 19 miscarriages suffered and one infant died (Australian Human Rights Commission, 2014). At least four requests for a pregnancy termination were made by detainees on Nauru; the parents revealed that they feared for their health and safety during pregnancy and could not perceive how a baby could be raised in the conditions present (Australian Human Rights Commission, 2014).The report found that difficult living conditions in detention centres impacts on parents' ability to bond with, nurture and care for their children. Normal family functioning is affected by the inadequate accommodation with poor hygiene and sanitation, cramped spaces and a lack of privacy in some detention centres, as well as restrictions on their movements and lack of access to recreation facilities. Detention denies children the environmental and social conditions that they require to optimise their development and learning, and places them at risk of harm. For example, children on Christmas Island for a period of around one year were not able to attend school. Limited and even unsafe physical environments make it difficult for infants to crawl and explore their surroundings while cramped living conditions and overcrowding result in the increased spread of infections. Asthma is also common and the symptoms may be exacerbated by infections and dust (Australian Human Rights Commission, 2014).

The AHRC investigation also found that not only are children in detention not meeting their expected developmental milestones, they are exposed to incidents of violence and the behaviours of traumatised adults who may be depressed, anxious, self-harming or displaying signs of psychosis. Children experience inadequate care including a lack of regular health monitoring and specialist paediatric services in some detention settings. More than three-quarters (85%) of children and parents surveyed indicated that their emotional and mental health had been affected since being in detention (Australian Human Rights Commission, 2014). Most reported feelings of worry, anxiety, and difficulties with eating and sleeping. The mental health assessments of more than 200 children in detention on the Australian mainland and Christmas Island revealed that 34% of children had mental health disorders that would normally require acute psychiatric treatment. Over a 15-month period, 128 children engaged in self-harm (Australian Human Rights Commission, 2014). While the mental and emotional health of children appears to improve once they are released into the community, the long-term impacts of prolonged detention on children remain largely unknown. When surveyed in community detention, over three-quarters of parents and children continued to feel that their mental health had been negatively affected by their experience of detention (Australian Human Rights Commission, 2014).

The high prevalence of mental health problems reflects the findings of landmark studies conducted in Australia in the past. Researchers conducting interviews with asylum seeker families in prolonged detention found that nearly all children and adults reported extreme distress associated with fear of being sent home and disturbing events experienced in the detention centre (Steel *et al.*, 2004). Psychological assessment of the families revealed that all adults interviewed suffered from major depressive disorder and most (86%) met the criteria for PTSD. Nearly all adults (93%) had experienced suicidal ideation and one-third had tried self-harming. Psychiatric conditions in children were equally alarming with all individuals receiving a diagnosis of at least one psychiatric condition and 80% being diagnosed with multiple disorders. Similar findings were reported in other studies (Sultan and O'Sullivan, 2001; Mares *et al.*, 2002) that also noted behavioural disorders, language and developmental delays among the children. This is likely to impact children's neurological development and functioning as well as increase their risk of mental illness in later life (Procter, 2005).

## *Access to health services for asylum seekers*

**Immigration detention:** The Australian government does not directly provide the detention and health services but rather contracts this out to service providers. Policy stipulates that detention facilities should provide health care to detainees at a level that is commensurate with that received by Australians in the public health system. The contracted organisation providing health care in detention facilities is required to meet accreditation standards that have been set by the Royal Australian College of General Practitioners and in detention centres on the mainland, torture and trauma counselling services are offered by a reputable specialist service that operates throughout Australia. Immigration and detention health advisory groups previously existed to provide expertise and oversight to improve the delivery of health care in the detention setting. These bodies were made up of independent, multidisciplinary health professionals and over the course of their operation, succeeded in making a number of important health policy and practice reforms. However, the most recent group was disbanded in December 2013, and a single individual remains serving as an independent health advisor.

Upon arrival at a detention centre, detainees undergo a health assessment including screening for communicable diseases, which is required to be conducted within 48 hours. The Royal Australian College of Physicians state that to do this comprehensively according to best practice is just not possible in this time frame and they have previously questioned the adequacy of the assessments and the clinical experience of health professionals performing this role, particularly with children in detention centres (Australian Human Rights Commission, 2014). Asylum seekers should also be offered regular consultations for the purpose of assessing both physical and mental health status, or as requested by the detainee. But despite appropriate policies and guidelines, ongoing concerns have been raised about the extent to which the health care occurs in a timely and high quality manner. A 2013 Auditor-General report found that 40% of surveyed immigration detainees stated that their basic health care needs had not been met (Australian National Audit Office, 2013). There have been several high profile cases of asylum seekers who have died while in immigration detention. For example, on Nauru, it has been reported that the standards of the local hospital are inadequate, lacking some essential medical and surgical equipment, and serious limitations should someone require a blood transfusion (Australian Human Rights Commission, 2014). Transfers to acute health services from offshore detention centres for medical investigations or treatment are often delayed with a recent avoidable death resulting from a skin infection that led to fatal septicaemia. Detention health advisory groups in Australia in the past have been particularly critical of the inadequate provision of health services in the detention facilities, in particular mental health services (Detention Health Advisory Group, 2011). They were concerned that policies relating to psychological support and survivors of torture and trauma were not being adhered to. It appears that mental health screening has been unsatisfactory and that detainees at risk of self-harm and suicide are either not consistently identified, or not managed appropriately (Joint Select Committee on Australia's Immigration Detention Network, 2012). The remoteness of detention facilities is one factor that makes it challenging to facilitate specialist psychiatric services. Given that the detention environment exacerbates mental health conditions, one would expect that under professional guidance, detainees be removed and placed in a more supportive environment in the community, yet this often fails to occur. The return of individuals to the detention environment following in-patient treatment for serious psychological conditions raises serious concerns (Joint Select Committee on Australia's Immigration Detention Network, 2012).

**Community-residing asylum seekers:** The majority of asylum seekers living in the community on bridging visas are granted access to Medicare — Australia's publicly funded universal health system. There are some people, however, who are not eligible for Medicare including individuals whose refugee claims have been rejected and are pursuing alternative pathways or awaiting deportation. It is very difficult to estimate the proportion of asylum seekers in Australia that are in this situation. The health care needs of asylum seekers in the community (including a minority that cannot access Medicare) are met through a variety of federal and state government policies with enormous support from charitable organisations and pro-bono services. While some state health departments have policies that mandate fee-waivers for community-residing asylum seekers, the extent of free services is highly varied between states and there is often confusion or misinformation that creates delays or deficiencies in the delivery of care (Hadgkiss et al., 2012; Corbett et al., 2014). In the Australian context, usually, fee-waivers or subsidies for some out-of-pocket health services and medicines are provided to people who are identified as having a limited capacity to pay, such as pensioners or those on welfare support. Asylum seekers are not, however, eligible for a health care card that would recognise their low income. By comparison, asylum seekers in community detention can also access public health services but their care is coordinated by a contracted health service provider who arranges access to physical and mental health care via a network of pre-approved community-based providers, including specialists. They are not expected to pay out-of-pocket expenses for health care.

## Barriers to accessing health care in the community

International and Australian literature (Hadgkiss and Renzaho, 2014) and consultations with Australian service providers (Hadgkiss *et al.*, 2012) point to a number of factors that may affect asylum seekers' access to health care. These factors can broadly be categorised into political barriers, systemic barriers and sociocultural barriers. The implications of these barriers can be devastating: delayed or inadequate care can result in detrimental short- and long-term health outcomes including preventable hospitalisations.

**Political barriers:** Policy related to the provision of health care to asylum seekers is directly linked with immigration policy which frequently changes, creating fragmentation of service delivery and confusion for asylum seekers navigating the health system (Correa-Velez *et al.*, 2005). This fragmentation extends to differences between Australia's State and Federal policies. Under-funded services and restrictions on the eligibility of services and benefits to asylum seekers compromise their health. The main political barriers relate to eligibility and costs. In Australia, like in many other high-income host countries, community residing asylum seekers are eligible for free health care funded by the government or national insurance schemes. However, in some circumstances, eligibility is affected by the stage of the visa process and, subsequently, asylum seekers face difficulties seeking out free clinics or other pro-bono services. With limited or no income, asylum seekers may face significant difficulties paying for out-of-pocket health care expenses. This may include consultation fees for some specialist services, high costs of medicines, pathology and other diagnostics, dental procedures, medical equipment or aids, or even the cost of transportation to medical appointments (Spike *et al.*, 2011; Rees, 2003; Hadgkiss *et al.*, 2012). Service providers report difficulties negotiating fee-waivers for asylum seekers who cannot afford to pay (Hadgkiss *et al.*, 2012). Charitable organisations may try to assist in covering these costs, but their resources are always over-stretched. A survey of asylum seekers in Melbourne, Australia, found that around one-quarter had been refused medical treatment at some point due to being unable to pay, their visa status or lack of Medicare eligibility (Mitchell and Kirsner, 2004). For chronic or complex conditions, the ongoing costs of treatment including medication or medical items like blood glucose monitoring can serve as a significant financial burden and may result in poor adherence or the cessation of treatment. Prescription medication is a common outcome of primary care consultation for asylum seekers (Correa-Velez *et al.*, 2008) and can be a huge cost burden. Australia subsidises many medications through the Pharmaceutical Benefits Scheme, which asylum seekers can access if they are eligible for Medicare, but many remain unable to afford the gaps, particularly if a number of medications are prescribed concurrently.

**Systemic barriers:** The major problem in Australia is that specialty clinics targeting and addressing the needs of asylum seekers are few and far between, and those that do exist are therefore over-stretched and under-resourced, particularly in mental health (Phillips *et al.*, 2011; Hadgkiss *et al.*, 2012). This means that there may be long delays, waiting lists, or restrictive eligibility or triage criteria (Mitchell and Kirsner, 2004; Hadgkiss *et al.*, 2012). Refugee and asylum seeker health profiles are constantly changing — as global issues change over time, so do the countries of origin that asylum seekers flee from. Subsequently, the cultural and health needs of individuals are different. Many health professionals in Australia may be unfamiliar with the kinds of medical conditions that are more prevalent among asylum seekers and refugees (Phillips *et al.*, 2011; Johnson *et al.*, 2008), which can result in inadequate assessment and treatment. This is further compounded by difficulties encountered when trying to accurately record the full medical history of asylum seekers, many of whom have been transient and living in refugee camps. The systemic barriers that asylum seekers experience occur in various forms. First, in terms of general health service access, primary care services with a larger number of refugee and asylum seeker patients may find complex assessments time consuming and therefore overwhelming for the practice (Bowers and Cheng, 2010). Beyond specialist services for refugees, it can be difficult to engage general practitioners in private practice to help meet the needs of asylum seekers in Australia (Hadgkiss *et al.*, 2012). There are several factors at play, including the complexity of their general health, mental health, and social or welfare needs that subsequently require the allocation of longer time periods for consultation. Asylum seekers are usually not able to pay gap fees, and for those without Medicare, the service must be provided pro-bono. There is also the added challenge of language barriers, which is discussed later. Increasingly, Refugee Health Nurses are being trained to provide specialist care and they are integral to filling some of the primary care gaps, but they too have limited time and resources, and are restricted by their scope of practice. Like many Australian residents outside of metropolitan areas, asylum seekers also face difficulties accessing health and community services in regional and rural areas due to an absence of bulk billing services, lack of on-site interpreters and female physicians, and lack of local specialist services (Correa-Velez *et al.*, 2005).

In Australian states where there is a public hospital fee-waiver for asylum seekers, the emergency department of a public hospital may be utilised if there are significant barriers to seeking care in the community. The policy of fee waivers, however, is not always clear or familiar to emergency department staff and so asylum seekers presenting to such services may face barriers (Hadgkiss *et al.*, 2012). Furthermore, it is inappropriate for non-urgent health issues to be dealt with by acute services and so it is likely an asylum seeker would need to wait many hours before seeing a doctor.

Second, in terms of specialist health services, such as dental care, mental health care or chronic disease management programmes, access is problematic for asylum seekers (Hadgkiss *et al.*, 2012). The same reasons are commonly cited: long waiting times, difficulties accessing interpreters and ineligibility for asylum seekers without Medicare. For example, there is currently no routine, mandatory screening of asylum seekers in the community for mental health issues. Therefore, psychological morbidity may remain undetected among many asylum seekers. For a range of reasons including cultural factors and poor health literacy, asylum seekers may be unlikely to recognise mental health problems and, subsequently, very few self-refer for mental health services (Hadgkiss *et al.*, 2012). Similarly, except for highly acute mental health needs, there are limited referral pathways to access schemes that cover the costs of consultation by a mental health professional. The barriers are even greater for asylum seekers who may have unique and complex mental health needs, require culturally-appropriate services and access to an interpreter. In each state in Australia, there are specialist torture and trauma services, which collectively form the Forum of Australian Services for Survivors of Torture and Trauma. These services are reputable leaders in the field, offering high quality care for asylum seekers and refugees. However, high demand and insufficient funding requires these services to triage clients, and asylum seekers with mental health needs not directly related to torture or trauma may not be eligible for their services. Beyond the specialist torture and trauma services, there exist a few dedicated but small pro-bono mental health services, often run through asylum seeker support agencies. However, despite the high quality and dedication of these services, sudden and unexpected growth in the number of asylum seekers living in the community has placed additional demands that just cannot be met. Asylum seeker support agencies rely on donations, small grants and volunteer staff, which makes it difficult to make long-term planning decisions or provide continuity of service provision. The alternative for asylum seekers is to try and access mainstream community mental health services. These services are not always trained to manage the unique needs of asylum seekers and the complex interaction of social factors that affect mental health, and are therefore unlikely to provide culturally-appropriate care. Private psychologists and psychiatrists are difficult to engage because few have appropriate cultural competence expertise or free access to translator services. Crisis support for asylum seekers with very acute needs is limited. Community crisis response teams, emergency services and inpatient psychiatric units have very high thresholds of response and do not currently understand the complexity of asylum seeker mental health needs. It appears, however, that expertise is growing in some areas of Australia where there are larger populations of asylum seekers residing and more opportunities for professional and service development are available (Hadgkiss *et al.*, 2012).

Finally, asylum seekers may find the health system too complex to navigate. The health system in an industrialised country like Australia is likely to be structured very differently to the health system in an asylum seeker's country of origin. Even where asylum seekers are eligible for Medicare, this does not always translate to service utilisation unless the individual is living in an area where the health and welfare needs of refugees and asylum seekers are being addressed through targeted, well-resourced programmes (Hadgkiss et al., 2012). As one would expect, a lack of culturally appropriate, translated information on eligibility and availability of health services can hinder access (Spike et al., 2011). It can be difficult for asylum seekers trying to navigate the health system and differentiate between public and private services (Correa-Velez et al., 2005). Asylum seekers may be worried about being charged for services and so may be reluctant to seek help, resulting in the neglect or inadequate treatment of underlying health problems with potentially devastating consequences. International studies have found that poor understanding of the concept of primary health care and referral pathways sometimes leads to the inappropriate utilisation of emergency services for non-urgent needs (O'Donnell et al., 2008), and that physically accessing the service can be affected by lack of transportation or difficulties locating a service (Asgary and Segar, 2011; Bhatia and Wallace, 2007). In Australia, the cost of public transportation to get to a service can be high for someone who has little or no income, and can be difficult to navigate (Correa-Velez et al., 2005). Social and community supports are integral for providing information and resources to facilitate service access (Hadgkiss and Renzaho, 2014). Specialist roles, such as dedicated support nurses or bilingual health care workers are highly beneficial for ensuring that asylum seekers feel supported. It can be difficult to engage asylum seekers that are not finding their way into available health services. While asylum seekers that are released from detention facilities are likely to be given some formal orientation to enable primary care registration and initial case worker support, asylum seekers arriving by plane receive no formal orientation and may subsequently be a more "hidden" population group in Australia.

**Sociocultural factors:** Asylum seekers in Australia are often living in unstable environments with little or no income, insecure housing and many have minimal social supports (Asylum Seeker Resource Centre, 2009; 2010). Such factors are known to contribute to stress and poor health, but also mean that proactively addressing health issues may not be a first priority. Asylum seekers are an ethnically, culturally and linguistically diverse population group. They are likely to have different beliefs, behaviours and perceptions of prevention, treatment and expectations of health services. Health care providers with poor cultural understanding may unintentionally deter or even exclude certain ethnic groups from seeking assistance. Poor health literacy due to difficulties accessing and understanding health-related information will affect asylum seekers' ability to make informed decisions. Some health professionals find it challenging to explain disease processes and treatment needs, and it may be difficult for asylum seekers to adhere to treatment recommendations as a result. Available evidence suggests that continuity of care is an important factor for improving trust and confidence among asylum seekers (Bhatia and Wallace, 2007; O'Donnell et al., 2007). Asylum seekers can be a mobile group, as they are vulnerable to homelessness due to insecure income and dependence on the government or charitable organisations to provide accommodation in the community (Asylum Seeker Resource Centre, 2009). This increased mobility can make it difficult to provide continuity of care. Asylum seekers may be reluctant to attend health services where they feel they face discrimination from staff. A number of studies have found that asylum seekers have experienced or observed hostility or disrespect, or suspected they were receiving insufficient or poorer quality care as a result of their immigration status or race (Asgary and Segar, 2011; Bhatia and Wallace, 2007; O'Donnell et al., 2007). By contrast, health professionals that listen and show empathy and kindness improve rapport with the patient and therefore facilitate greater trust in the care being provided.

It is well known that poor two-way communication between a health care professional and client can result in ineffective, unnecessary, time-consuming and even dangerous intervention. In Australia access to interpreter and translator services is different between various health and community services — some have unlimited access to funded services, while others must allocate a significant proportion of their operational budgets to cover interpreter and translator services. Different again are some services that employ bilingual health workers to bridge the gap for common languages. Even where interpreter and translator services are available, there may be other factors that create communication barriers. Some health professionals are unaware of interpreter services available to them, or reluctant to work with interpreters, even when they are readily available at no additional cost (Victorian Foundation for Survivors of Torture, 2012; Atkin, 2008). This may be related to a lack of training or familiarity with working with interpreter services, or overestimation of an individual's grasp of the host country language. Another issue is the use of family members or friends as informal interpreters (Asgary and Segar, 2011; Bhatia and Wallace, 2007). The appropriateness of this practice will depend on the sensitivity of the health information being conveyed and other cultural factors, but in general, this should be discouraged and professional interpreters employed to reduce the risk of miscommunication (Atkin, 2008).

Additionally, asylum seekers may be fearful of contact with medical services for a number of reasons. They may be reluctant to engage with agencies and authorities, particularly those associated with government services. This may relate to concerns over the degree of confidentiality and security of their medical history. Or it may be linked to the perception that immigration and health systems are interconnected, and that their health information, lack of documentation or inability to pay would affect the asylum process, or increase their risk of deportation or detention (Asgary and Segar, 2011; Murray and Skull, 2005). This is particularly the case for asylum seekers with mental health problems, who may be concerned that a mental health diagnosis will influence immigration-related decisions (Procter, 2006). For some cultural groups, mental health problems are stigmatised and there is a poor understanding of treatment options (Procter, 2006). This can make it challenging to engage asylum seekers in early intervention and appropriate treatment. Issues of mistrust may also arise with interpreters during physical or mental health consultations — there may be concerns about the accuracy and quality of translation and whether confidentiality of health information will be upheld (Bernardes *et al.*, 2010; Bhatia and Wallace, 2007; O'Donnell *et al.*, 2007). Furthermore, some asylum seekers may have experienced torture prior to fleeing, and they may associate these experiences with medical procedures.

## Social and health policy response

To address some of the health gaps for asylum seekers in the community, some Australian State Departments of Health have developed policies to provide better support and services for refugees and asylum seekers. This includes memoranda of understanding with acute public health services to provide fee-waivers for asylum seekers without Medicare. A more comprehensive and proactive approach has been adopted by Victoria through the Victorian refugee and asylum seeker health action plan 2014–2018 (State Government Victoria, 2014), which describes a funded model of refugee and asylum seeker health care built around five priority areas for action: accessibility, expertise in refugee health, service coordination, cultural responsiveness, and health, literacy and communication.

While action at the state level is crucial to fill social and health service gaps, the main factors affecting the health and welfare of asylum seekers are dependent on Federal government policy and legislative reform. Over the years, many independent bodies, community agencies and charities have called on the Australian government to create a more just system for the processing of asylum seekers and bring about a more humane approach to the treatment of asylum seekers while they await immigration decisions. In the past five years alone, there have been a number of inquiries pertaining to asylum seekers that have yielded strong responses from the community including

- National Inquiry into Children in Immigration Detention (2014);
- Parliamentary Joint Committee on Human Rights' inquiry into the regional processing of asylum seekers (2013);
- Expert Panel on Asylum Seekers (2012);
- Senate Standing Committees on Legal and Constitutional Affairs Inquiry into Australia's agreement with Malaysia in relation to asylum seekers (2011);
- Inquiry of the Joint Select Committee on Australia's Immigration Detention Network (2011).

The Australian Council of Social Service released a statement in 2011 urging both major political parties to "de-politicise policies about the treatment of asylum seekers by immediately abandoning the policy of offshore processing and focusing on policies that uphold Australia's human rights obligations domestically and internationally" (Australian Council of Social Service, 2011). The statement was signed by more than 260 organisations in Australia. The Law Council of Australia maintains a policy position that Australia is obliged under international law to ensure that laws and policies concerning asylum seekers adhere to the Refugee Convention principles, and other relevant international conventions to which Australia is a signatory (Law Council of Australia, 2014). Central to the policy position is a sentiment echoed by many community groups that all people seeking Australia's protection should be treated with fairness, humanity and dignity. The Refugee Council of Australia has also been a strong advocate for the rights of asylum seekers, and recently published a report with 49 clearly articulated recommendations (Refugee Council of Australia, 2014), urging the government to

- Abandon the Regional Resettlement Arrangement with Papua New Guinea (PNG) in light of the inability of PNG to provide sustainable protection and support to refugees on a permanent basis.
- Ensure that all asylum seekers are eligible to apply for legal assistance regardless of their mode of arrival.
- Abandon the re-introduction of Temporary Protection Visas.
- Use immigration detention only as a matter of last resort and give priority to finding community-based alternatives for all asylum seekers currently in closed immigration detention.
- End the arbitrary and indefinite detention of asylum seekers and expedite the processing of asylum claims.
- Ensure that appropriate services, living conditions, health care and activities are provided to all people who remain in closed detention.
- Release all children including unaccompanied minors from closed detention as a matter of urgency.
- Consolidate existing support programmes into a holistic, consistent and client-driven service delivery framework that allows equal access to services and support regardless of status or mode of arrival — and support with orientation, English language tuition, education and employment.
- Grant work rights to all asylum seekers, offer employment support services and maximise opportunities for asylum seekers to be self-supporting while their status is resolved.
- Provide meaningful educational opportunities for asylum seekers.
- Ensure that policies and processes enable families to remain together.

## Conclusion

Australia's annual intake of asylum seekers is very minimal, ranking seventh of the countries receiving asylum seekers and accounting only for about 4% of the share of total applications. There is no doubt that some aspects of Australia's asylum seeker policies are in violation of international human rights laws and conventions. There is an opportunity for Australia to take international leadership in providing evidence-based community practices to effectively deal with the various needs of asylum seekers. Yet, despite numerous calls to action, both major political parties continue to take a tough stance on the policies affecting asylum seekers. This only exacerbates the trauma suffered by people seeking protection from persecution, resulting in poorer physical and mental health outcomes.

## Acknowledgements

This chapter builds on some content from the Asylum Seeker Health and Wellbeing Scoping Study (2012), commissioned by St Vincent's Health Australia. Emily Hadgkiss would like to acknowledge the contributions of co-authors Dr Carolyn Lethborg, Dr Ahmad Al-Mousa and Dr Claudia Marck.

## References

Asgary, R. & Segar, N. (2011). Barriers to health care access among refugee asylum seekers. *Journal of Health Care for the Poor and Underserved*, 22, 506–522.

Asylum Seeker Resource Centre (2009). Locked out: Position paper on homelessness of asylum seekers living in the community. ASRC, Melbourne, AUS.

Asylum Seeker Resource Centre (2010). Destitute and uncertain: The reality of seeking asylum in Australia. ASRC, Melbourne, AUS.

Asylum Seeker Resource Centre (2013). Offshore processing and resettlement mythbuster. ASRC, Melbourne, AUS. Available at: http://www.asrc.org.au/wp-content/uploads/2013/07/Offshore-Processing-Resettlement-Mythbuster_November-2013-1.pdf. Accessed 15 March 2015.

Atkin, N (2008). Getting the message across — professional interpreters in general practice. *Aust Fam Physician*, 37, 174–176.

Australian Council of Social Service (2011). Asylum seekers and refugees: ACOSS writes to MP's calling for onshore processing. Available at: http://acoss.org.au/policy/law_justice/community_sector_statement_on_asylum_seeker_malaysia_deal_high_court_ruling/. Accessed 3 March 2015.

Australian Human Rights Commission (2012a). Community arrangements for asylum seekers, refugees and stateless persons: Observations from visits conducted by the Australian Human Rights Commission from December 2011 to May 2012 Sydney, Australia.

Australian Human Rights Commission (2012b). Human rights at your fingertips (2012). Sydney, AUS. Available at: https://www.humanrights.gov.au/human-rights-your-fingertips-2012. Accessed 15 March 2015.

Australian Human Rights Commission (2014). The forgotten children: National inquiry into children in immigration detention 2014. AHRC, Sydney, AUS.

Australian National Audit Office (2013). ANAO Audit Report No. 21 2012–2013: Individual Management Services Provided to People in Immigration Detention. Canberra, AUS.

Australian Red Cross (2012). Fact Sheet: Community Detention. Australian Red Cross, Melbourne, AUS.

Bernardes, D. et al. (2010). Asylum seekers' perspectives on their mental health and views on health and social services: Contributions for service provision using a mixed-methods approach. *International Journal of Migration, Health & Social Care*, 6, 3–19.

Bhatia, R. & Wallace, P. (2007). Experiences of refugees and asylum seekers in general practice: A qualitative study. *BMC Family Practice*, 8, 48.

Bischoff, A. et al. (2009). Health and ill health of asylum seekers in Switzerland: An epidemiological study. *European Journal of Public Health*, 19, 59–64.

Blackwell, D. et al. (2002). An interim report of health needs assessment of asylum seekers in Sunderland and North Tyneside. *Public Health*, 116, 221–226.

Bowers, J.E. & Cheng, I. (2010). Meeting the primary healthcare needs of refugees and asylum seekers *Research RoundUp*. Available at: http://www.phcris.org.au/phplib/filedownload.php?file=/elib/lib/downloaded_files/publications/pdfs/phcris_pub_8342.pdf. Accessed 10 April 2015.

Cheng, H.M. & Kumarasinghe, S.P. (2014). Dermatological problems of asylum seekers arriving on boats: A case report from Australia and a brief review. *Australasion Journal of Dermatology*, 55, 270–274.

Coffey, G.J. et al. (2010). The meaning and mental health consequences of long-term immigration detention for people seeking asylum. *Social Science & Medicine*, 70, 2070–2079.

Commonwealth of Australia (1958). Migration House of Representatives, Parliament of Australia, Canberra, AUS.

Commonwealth of Australia (2007). Detention health framework: A policy framework for healthcare for people in immigration detention. Department of Immigration and Citizenship. Canberra, AUS.

Commonwealth of Australia (2009). Annual Report 2008–2009. Department of Immigration and Citizenship, Canberra, AUS.

Commonwealth of Australia (2012a). Fact Sheet 83a: Community detention. Department of Immigration and Citizenship, Canberra, AUS.

Commonwealth of Australia (2012b). Irregular maritime arrivals on Bridging Visa E. Department of Immigration and Citizenship, Canberra, AUS.

Commonwealth of Australia (2013). Asylum trends: Annual publication 2012–13. Department of Immigration and Border Protection, Canberra, AUS.

Commonwealth of Australia (2014a). Annual report 2013–14. Department of Immigration and Border Protection, Canberra, AUS.

Commonwealth of Australia (2014b). Migration and Maritime Powers Legislation Amendment (Resolving the Asylum Legacy Caseload) Bill 2014. House of Representatives, Parliament of Australia, Canberra, AUS.

Commonwealth of Australia (2015). Complementary Protection — Act Amendments. Department of Immigration and Border Protection. Canberra, AUS. Available at: http://www.immi.gov.au/legislation/amendments/2012/120324/lc24032012-05.htm. Accessed 22 March 2015.

Corbett, E.J., Maycock, A., & Isaacs, D. (2014). Australia's treatment of refugee and asylum seeker children: The views of Australian paediatricians. *Medical Journal of Australia*, 201 393–398.

Correa-Velez, I. & Gifford, S.M. (2007). When the right to be counted doesn't count: The politics and challenges of researching the health of asylum seekers. *Critical Public Health*, 17, 259–267.

Correa-Velez, I. et al. (2005). Australian health policy on access to medical care for refugees and asylum seekers. *Australia and New Zealand Health Policy*, 2, 23.

Correa-Velez, I. et al. (2008). Community-based asylum seekers' use of primary health care services in Melbourne. *Medical Journal of Australia*, 188, 344–348.

Deans, A.K. et al. (2013). Use of Royal Darwin Hospital emergency department by immigration detainees in 2011. *Medical Journal of Australia*, 199, 776–778.

Detention Health Advisory Group (2011). Submission to the Joint Select Committee on Immigration Detention. Canberra, AUS.

Green, J.P. & Eagar, K. (2010). The health of people in Australian immigration detention centres. *Medical Journal of Australia*, 192, 65–70.

Grove, N.J. & Zwi, A.B. (2006). Our health and theirs: Forced migration, othering, and public health. *Social Science and Medicine*, 62, 1931–1942.

Hadgkiss, E.J. et al. (2012). Asylum seeker health and wellbeing scoping study. St Vincent's Health Australia; Sydney AUS.

Hadgkiss, E.J. & Renzaho, A.M. (2014). The physical health status, service utilisation and barriers to accessing care for asylum seekers residing in the community: A systematic review of the literature. *Australian Health Review*, 38, 142–159.

Houston, M.A. et al. (2012). Report of the expert panel of asylum seekers.

Johnson, D.R. et al. (2008). I don't think general practice should be the front line: Experiences of general practitioners working with refugees in South Australia. *Australia and New Zealand Health Policy*, 5, 20.

Joint Select Committee on Australia's Immigration Detention Network (2012). Joint Select Committee on Australia's Immigration Detention Network: Final report. Canberra, AUS.

King, K. & Vodicka, P. (2001). Screening for conditions of public health importance in people arriving in Australia by boat without authority. *Medical Journal of Australia*, 175, 600–602.

Law Council of Australia. (2014). Asylum seeker policy, Canberra, AUS.

Lightfoot, T. (2005). Asylum Seeker Healthcare in Victoria: A Briefing Paper Prepared by the Refugee and Asylum Seeker Health Network (RASHN), Victoria.

Mares, S., et al. (2002). Seeking refuge, losing hope: Parents and children in immigration detention. *Australasian Psychiatry*, 10, 91–96.

Mckay, F. (2012). 'It would be ok if they came through the proper channels': Community perceptions and attitudes toward asylum seekers in Australia. *Journal of Refugee Studies*, 25 113–133.

Mitchell, G. & Kirsner, S. (2004). Asylum seekers living in the Australian community: A casework and reception approach, Asylum Seeker Project, Hotham Mission, Melbourne. *Refuge: Canada's Journal on Refugees*, 22(1), 119–128.

Momartin, S. et al. (2006). A comparison of the mental health of refugees with temporary versus permanent protection visas. *Medical Journal of Australia*, 185, 357–361.

Murray, S.B. & Skull, S.A. (2005). Hurdles to health: Immigrant and refugee health care in Australia. *Australian Health Review*, 29, 25–29.

O'Donnell, C.A. et al. (2007). "They think we're OK and we know we're not". A qualitative study of asylum seekers' access, knowledge and views to health care in the UK. *BMC Health Services Research*, 7, 75.

O'Donnell, C.A. et al. (2008). Asylum seekers' expectations of and trust in general practice: A qualitative study. *British Journal of General Practice*, 58, 870–876.

Phillips, C.B. et al. (2011). The Refugee Health Network of Australia: Towards national collaboration on health care for refugees. *Medical Journal of Australia*, 195, 185–186.

Phillips, J. & Spinks, H. (2013). Boat arrivals in Australia since 1976. Department of Parliamentary Services, Canberra, AUS.

Procter, N.G. (2005). 'They first killed his heart (then) he took his own life'. Part 1: A review of the context and literature on mental health issues for refugees and asylum seekers. *International Journal of Nursing Practice*, 11, 286–291.

Procter, N.G. (2006). 'They first killed his heart (then) he took his own life'. Part 2: Practice implications. *Interntional Journal of Nurse Practiners*, 12, 42–48.

Rees, S. (2003). Refuge or retrauma? The impact of asylum seeker status on the wellbeing of East Timorese women asylum seekers residing in the Australian community. *Australasian Psychiatry*, 11, S96–S101.

Refugee Council of Australia (2014). Australia's Refugee and Humanitarian Programme 2014–15: Community views on current challenges and future directions. Sydney, AUS.

Robjant, K. et al. (2009). Mental health implications of detaining asylum seekers: Systematic review. *British Journal of Psychiatry*, 194, 306–312.

Royal Australian and New Zealand College of Psychiatrists (2012). Position statement 46 – the provision of mental health services to asylum seekers. Available at: https://www.ranzcp.org/Files/Resources/College_Statements/Position_Statements/ps46-pdf.aspx. Accessed 12 March 2015.

Shaw, M.T.M. & Leggat, P.A. (2006). Medical screening and the health of illegal immigrants in Australia. *Travel Medicine & Infectious Disease*, 4, 255–258.

Silove, D. et al. (2007). No refuge from terror: The impact of detention on the mental health of trauma-affected refugees seeking asylum in Australia. *Transcultural Psychiatry*, 44, 359–393.

Silove, D. et al. (2002). Towards a researcher-advocacy model for asylum seekers: A pilot study amongst East Timorese living in Australia. *Transcultural Psychiatry*, 39, 452–468.

Smith, M. (2000). Desperately seeking asylum: The plight of asylum seekers in Australia. *New Doctor*, 74, 21–23.

Spike, E.A. et al. (2011). Access to primary health care services by community-based asylum seekers. *Medical Journal of Australia*, 195, 188–191.

State Government Victoria (2014). Victorian refugee and asylum seeker health action plan 2014–18. Department of Health, Melbourne, AUS.

Steel, Z. et al. (2009). Association of torture and other potentially traumatic events with mental health outcomes among populations exposed to mass conflict and displacement: A systematic review and meta-analysis. *Journal of American Medical Association*, 302, 537–549.

Steel, Z. et al. (2004). Psychiatric status of asylum seeker families held for a protracted period in a remote detention centre in Australia. *Australian & New Zealand Journal of Public Health*, 28, 527–536.

Steel, Z. et al. (2011). Two year psychosocial and mental health outcomes for refugees subjected to restrictive or supportive immigration policies. *Social Science and Medicine*, 72, 1149–1156.

Sultan, A. & O'Sullivan, K. (2001). Psychological disturbances in asylum seekers held in long term detention: A participant-observer account. *Medical Journal of Australia*, 175, 593–596.

United Nations Committee on the Rights of the Child (2012). Concluding observations on the fourth periodic report of Australia under the Convention on the Rights of the Child.

United Nations General Assembly (2008). Report of the Committee Against Torture: Fortieth Session.

UNHCR (1999). UNHCR revised guidelines on applicable criteria and standards relating to the detention of asylum seekers. February report, Geneva, SWI.

UNHCR (2010). Convention and protocol relating to the status of refugees, Geneva, SWI.

UNHCR (2014a). UNHCR Global Trends 2013: War's Human Cost, Geneva, SWI.

UNHCR (2014b). Asylum trends 2013: Levels and trends in industrialised countries. Geneva, SWI.

Victorian Foundation for Survivors of Torture (2012). Exploring barriers and facilitators to the use of qualified interpreters in health. Melbourne, AUS.

# Chapter 7

# Women, children and men trapped in unsafe corridors

Dr Kevin Pottie, Dr Chuck Hui, and Mr Fabien Schneider

## Introduction

During the 2015 World Health Assembly, Dr Margaret Chan, the Director General of the World Health Organization, called for sustainable and resilient health systems for all nations. World Health Assembly delegates cited the recent Ebola crisis, the 2015 earthquake in Nepal and the repeated drownings of irregular migrants in the Mediterranean as imperatives to develop resilient health systems for all nations within our interconnected world. To accompany these health systems, there was a call for universal access (Ravenscroft and Marcos, 2012) with more primary health care and the integration of public health care practitioners. Health systems of the future must also be able to look after irregular migrants, i.e. women, children and men who may be trapped between countries but who may not be fundamentally different from other persons who flee when abandoned by their state. In recent years, however, irregular migrants have become frequently and aggressively politically branded as "undesirables".

## Irregular migrants

Irregular migration is, by definition, not well documented. Mass migrant burial sites, however, have surfaced in Mexico and more recently in Malaysia (2015). Between 2000 and 2014, there have been 40,000 deaths in migrant corridors and in border zones. Deaths have resulted from Syrians, Somalis, Sudanese and Eritreans attempting entry into Europe (IOM, 2014). Six thousand central Americans have died at the Mexican–US border. Other deadly migrant corridors include the Red Sea, Eritrea to Yemen (see Table 1) and the crossings in south-east Asia where more than 20,000 irregular migrants from Afghanistan, Sri Lanka, Burma and Bangladesh have risked the three-month ocean crossing in recent years. Stricter border control measures do not reduce the numbers of irregular migrants but rather result in migrants undertaking greater risks.

Unsafe migrant corridors refer to undocumented and precarious movements of women, men and children who are forced to seek unauthorised transit, stay on route or entry to the global north, which includes 49 countries with a human development index of above 0.8 (although not all these countries are located in the north) (UNDP, 2014). These persons include irregular migrants and asylum seekers. They enter the global north clandestinely via land, sea routes, air and frequently have to seek assistance of criminal networks of smugglers. Migrant smuggling is a growing global criminal activity that preys on poverty, and social and political instability. While young men have historically been the face of irregular migration, recently smuggling boats in the Mediterranean have carried up to 50% women and children, and older adults (See Box 1).

Table 1: Regional estimates of migrant border-related deaths (IOM, 2014)

| Region | Number of deaths | Period | Source |
| --- | --- | --- | --- |
| Sahara | 1,790 | 1996–2013 | Fortress Europe |
| US–Mexican border | 6,029 | 1998–2013 | US Border Patrol |
| European external borders | 22,394 | 2000–2014 | IOM based on The Migrant Files |
| Australian waters | 1,495 | 2000–2014 | Australian Border Deaths Database |
| Horn of Africa | 3,014 | 2006–2014 | UNHCR, IOM |
| Bay of Bengal | 1500–2000 | 2012–2014 | UNHCR; Arakan Project |
| Caribbean | 188 | 2012–2014 | UNHCR; IOM for 2014 |

> **Box 1: Migration trends for year 2013 (IOM, 2014)**
>
> — There are an estimated 50 million irregular migrants in the world, many of whom have paid to illegally cross borders; 3 million people illegally enter the USA each year, mostly smuggled across the border.
> — Women account for 48% of the global migration. Migrants in the north are on average older than migrants in the south (42 years as median age in the north, 33 in the south), and most international migrants are of working age.
> — 11.4 million women and girls are victims of forced labour, 9.5 million men and boys.
> — Of the total recorded fatalities, 66% have occurred in the Mediterranean, 11% of deaths globally occurred in the Bay of Bengal, 6% in the Horn of Africa and 6% along the US–Mexico border. More than 85% of deaths occurred along sea routes.
> — The number of forcibly displaced people has grown and the reality of global displacement is increasingly complex. Refugees were estimated at 16.7 million, people internally displaced by conflict and violence were estimated at 33.3 million.
> — More than 86% of world's refugees were being hosted by developing countries. Pakistan and the Islamic Republic of Iran are the main host countries in absolute terms (1.6 million and more than 850,000 refugees respectively), followed by Lebanon (more than 856,000), Jordan (more than 640,000) and Turkey (almost 610,000).

As of 2014, 38 million people have been forced from their homes by armed conflict and violence, and have been living within the borders of their own country (internally displaced peoples). This was a 15% increase from the previous year and included 11 million people who were newly displaced, the most seen in 10 years. The number of forced crossings of the Mediterranean reached its peak, 207,000, in 2014.

The UNHCR estimates that 866,000 asylum applications were recorded in 2014, representing a 45% increase or 269,400 more claims compared to the year before (UNHCR, 2014a). Since the beginning of the conflict, over 500,000 asylum applications from Syrians have been received in Europe. More than 40% of the applications are for Germany and Sweden (UNHCR, 2015). Two hundred and thirty two million people are international migrants, or 3.2% of the world population (UNFPA 2015). Seven hundred and forty million people live as internal migrants (Bell, 2009). The five-year Syrian crisis is, in this regard, a poignant example of forced migration. Seven million, six hundred thousand are displaced within the country (Internal Displacement Monitoring Centre, 2015). In 2015, the total number of refugees registered in third countries was more than 4 million, 98% of which are in Turkey, Lebanon, Jordan, Egypt and Iraq and more than 26,000 in north African countries (UNHCR, 2015).

Data on the detention of migrants or the capacity to detain is difficult to obtain as many countries do not publish this information. The best estimates are country-specific data that the International Detention Project provides: http://www.globaldetentionproject.org/countries.html. The European Migration Network study estimated that 93,000 migrants were detained in 2013. Amnesty International (2013) estimates that for the purposes of migration control, approximately 600,000 men, women and children are detained in Europe annually.

Politically branded as "undesirables", irregular migrants and asylum seekers face repeated discrimination. Negative attitudes in the host country may also arise from lack of acknowledgement of migrant contributions to destination countries. Irregular migrants and asylum seekers are also at risk of being blamed for rising unemployment and for being a drain on the economy. In reality, migrants are viewed and welcomed differently, depending on the receiving countries. Some African countries like Uganda and Kenya for example have hosted refugees for many years, in camps and within their communities. Uganda, despite its status as a developing country, has been recognised for its hospitality and asylum policies (Biffl and Altenburg, 2012).

## Field reports

Fleeing migrating persons fight to overcome political and economic constraints, and socioeconomic, language, ethnic and gender discrimination and bureaucratic barriers (Viruell-Fuentes *et al.*, 2012). There are critical periods during migration when pregnant women, young children and persons with mental health problems face emergent health care needs. Yet access to health care is extremely limited for irregular migrants and fleeing asylum seekers. Migration stress and illnesses accumulate over time. Displaced persons often reach a point where they are no longer able to continue. But often it is impossible to return due to risk of imprisonment or the shame of facing family who invested in them to go abroad to earn money. From the MSF field perspective (Pottie *et al.*, 2015), current migration control policies grind down displaced persons with repeated low-intensity attacks.

In so-called transit countries, MSF provides basic health care and support to irregular migrants who often suffer from having travelled under extremely hard conditions. This has serious effects on their health and well-being. Most people treated by MSF have either experienced violence themselves during their journey or witnessed violence first-hand (Medecins Sans Frontieres, 2011). Many faced abuse and ill-treatment. Accordingly, some of the most frequent diagnoses by MSF teams among migrants after their journey have included traumas and traumatic lesions as a result of abuse and violence (Medecins Sans Frontieres, 2013). In Yemen, for instance, between 2007 and 2008, MSF treated many migrants who had bruises, body pains and lacerations after their journeys across the Gulf of Aden. Fourteen per cent of diagnoses in Yemen were for violent trauma, often resulting from patients being beaten by smugglers with sticks, pipes, rifle butts and knives (Medecins Sans Frontieres, 2011). Other frequent health problems detected by MSF included dehydration, due to the lack of access to drinking water during the journey, hypothermia, due to being exposed to the cold outside or on a boat, and musculoskeletal complaints caused by the inability to move in cramped boats or trucks, and being forced to remain in the same position over a long period of time.

## Response to uncontrolled migratory flows

In response to the escalating forced and uncontrolled migratory flows of asylum seekers, displaced persons and irregular migrants, and related anti-migrant sentiment, states have focused on protection of their respective sovereign borders. These policies have made it more and more difficult to cross borders, even for persons fleeing war and violence, and increases the health and social risks for displaced persons. Restrictive policies include the closing of borders, reinforcement of border control, rejection of asylum seekers and obstacles to asylum processes, and other policies include lack of access to basic health care and social services.

One example is the European irregular migrant and asylum seeker crisis. The annual flow, and death rate, is dependent on several push and pull migratory factors. The migrants attempting this dangerous crossing are a mixed group that may include women, children and elderly who may be irregular migrants, displaced persons or asylum seekers from the Middle East and Africa, Syria, Eritrea, Somalia and other countries. In Europe, migrant policies have become restrictive and certain states such as Greece, Italy and Malta have received the largest number of irregular migrants. The EU president in Belgium has called for renewed discussions on country quotas and other measures to support safety and proportionate sharing of irregular migrants to Europe (Le Monde, 2015).

## Detention centres and alternatives

Migration has been a part of human history from the earliest times. More recently, the large numbers of irregular migrants and asylum seekers have stressed migration systems of many countries and continents. The increase in migration occurs in association with the context of broader free trade agreements and regional governing bodies that have taken the migration decisions out of the hands of local politicians. However, the issue has been further politicised by pointing to irregular migrants as global security concerns. In recent years, there has been an increase in the use of detention in the context of immigration policies (Committee on Migration, Refugees, and Displaced Persons, 2014). Detention and its processes may threaten the health and a number of human rights of migrant women, children and men. In an attempt to reduce these harms, centres in Europe are to follow principles of necessity, proportionality, brevity, non-arbitrariness, lawfulness, access to legal aid and judicial review. European Union (EU) asylum and migration detention is now only officially justified in specific situations, such as preventing unauthorised entry into the territory of an EU state.

On 9 March 2015, the UN Special Rapporteur on Torture, Juan E. Méndez, reported that the immigration detention of children is not only a violation of child rights (International Convention on the Rights of the Child, article 37b) and often violates the principle of family unity but also rises to the level of "cruel, inhuman or degrading treatment" in violation of the international prohibition on torture (United Nations, 2015). The report recommended better care for children and more alternatives for detention, concluding that children deprived of their liberty are at a heightened risk of torture and ill-treatment due to their unique vulnerability and needs.

## Most common grounds for detention

National legal frameworks do show variations across EU states with regard to the categories of third-country nationals that can be placed in detention and the corresponding grounds for detention. Table 2 outlines reasons cited for detention.

The EU states that comprehensive and robust assessment procedures for placing third-country nationals in detention are essential for ensuring non-arbitrariness, necessity and proportionality. Challenges to assessment, however, arise around criteria for assessment, legal frameworks and lack of review of detention practices. While differences exist across EU states in the types of detention facilities and the basic material conditions provided to detainees, some common patterns are also discernible, notably related to the provision of basic services such as medical care, legal aid, language support and the right to have contact with the outside world.

The vulnerabilities of migrants extend from their situation pre-departure and continue through their journey and do not end in the detention centre. Lack of access to health care, exploitation and violence pervades the journey. Migrants, especially irregular, lack access to preventative health services due to fear of being reported, lack of information about their rights, lack of legal entitlements, the cost of services, discriminatory attitudes among health professionals and other barriers related to language, culture and gender. The United Nations Special Rapporteur on the Human Rights of

Table 2: The most common grounds for detention in Europe

| | |
|---|---|
| 1. | Risk of absconding. |
| 2. | Establishing identity of the third-country national. |
| 3. | Threat to national security and public order. |
| 4. | Non-compliance with the alternatives to detention. |
| 5. | Presenting destroyed or forged documents. |
| 6. | Reasonable grounds to believe that the person will commit an offence. |

Migrants, François Crépeau, has stated that "[r]esearch shows that immigration detention has widespread and seriously damaging effects on the mental (and sometimes physical) health of detainees" as reported at the UN General Assembly in 2012.

Health services are equally heterogenous and of poor quality. This is compounded by the fact that there is lack of training for migrant-related health issues and the conflict of interest inherent in the dual loyalty of many health care professionals employed by the detention facilities.

## Alternative to detention

The International Detention Coalition has compiled the benefits of alternatives to administrative detention: maintains high rates of compliance, costs less than detention, reduces wrongful detention and litigation, reduces overcrowding, protects and fulfils human rights, improves client health and welfare, and increases voluntary return and departure (Sampson et al., 2011). This needs to be balanced by the potential benefit of a decreased rate of absconding. There has been a lack of evidence in the outcomes of detention and the efficacy of various strategies of detention due to the heterogeneity of practices, changing trends over time, lack of follow-up and lack of appropriate comparators among others. However, most importantly, the evidence that detention plays a role in the deterrence of migrants is not compelling. (International Detention Coalition, 2015). The fundamental driving principle should be the human rights and health of the migrants who have been placed in an administrative system.

Alternatives to detention have been advocated by international organisations (UNHCR, 2012), NGOs (Sampson et al., 2011), and regional governments (Council of Europe, 2014). The Community Assessment and Placement model developed by the International Detention Coalition outlines five key steps to prevent unnecessary detention with the primary assumption that detention is not necessary. Individualised assessment of the migrant followed by community assessment and application of conditions in the community if required are the other core elements to the approach. Community conditions may include registration and/or deposit/surrender of documents, bond/bail/sureties, reporting conditions, community release and supervision, designated residence, electronic monitoring or home curfew.

The UNHCR has published similar guidelines for alternatives to detention and the alternatives to detention for children and families (UNHCR, 2014b).

## UNHCR guidelines

The UNHCR and other humanitarian partners continue to work to provide safety, services and, above all, to save lives of asylum seekers and refugees during humanitarian crises. In 2012, the UNHCR published internationally unique detention guidelines and have updated them in 2014 with the Beyond Detention strategy 2014–2019 (UNHCR, 2014b). These guidelines aim to set standards for detention and include special protection for asylum seekers (see Table 3).

## The role of the health sector in migration

Unmet medical and humanitarian needs of vulnerable individuals drive the MSF operational and advocacy response, irrespective of status, label or stigma. When the categorisation of certain population groups (i.e. irregular migrants) is used to justify their exclusion from basic health care or dignified treatment, MSF will work to expose this injustice.

Migration has implications for health and health systems in both the countries of origin and host countries. At times, migrants arrive sick, suffering from petrol burns, dehydration, scabies and lice, or even gunshot wounds (Medecins Sans Frontieres, 2013). Many have suffered sexual violence as well as psychological and emotional trauma as in the case of torture camps in Yemen. Therefore, as soon as they arrive in the host country or are rescued, they require urgent medical attention in order to avoid further mortality and morbidity (Medecins Sans Frontieres, 2011). It is possible

Table 3: United Nations High Commission for Refugees detention goals

Goal 1: End the detention of children.
Goal 2: Ensure that alternatives to detention are available in law and implemented in practice.
Goal 3: Ensure that conditions of detention, where detention is necessary and unavoidable, meet international standards.

Table 4: Lessons learned from field health care (Pottie *et al.*, 2015)

- Mobile clinics reach migrants who are too afraid or unable to come to stationary medical clinics.
- Cultural mediators improve triage for emotional, physical and emergency medical needs of migrants.
- Collaboration with local migrant-friendly NGOs improves reach and access to hidden migrant populations.
- Field programmes that address mental health and social needs along with medical conditions play an important role in supporting migrants' dignity.
- Programmes focused on the most vulnerable migrant populations and tailored field programmes to the local sociocultural context are viewed as most successful.
- Migrant health care projects need more research and eventually international best practices.
- Ongoing education of health care providers to migrant health issues is crucial.

that the rise in the number of arriving migrants could pressurise the health systems in the receiving countries, but all human beings have the right to health as enshrined in the International Covenant on Economic, Social and Cultural Rights (1966).

Key areas to focus on include provision of quality health care for migrants, regardless of refugee status. Evidence-based migrant health guidelines now exist to guide programmes and care (Pottie *et al.*, 2011), and Health Impact Assessment is emerging as a promising tool to include migrants in system development (Povall *et al.*, 2013). Advocacy should be through a health equity, human rights and humanitarian framework. Migrant populations also need to be recognised in the post-2015 health agenda if migrants are to be included in WHO-led resilient health system initiatives for all nations. Finally, promising practices are emerging from the field missions of organisations such as MSF (see Table 4) and these early approaches need to be developed as organisations launch projects for mobile and irregular migrant populations.

## Conclusions

The first priority for irregular and asylum-seeking migrants must be saving lives and this endeavour should be linked to ensuring access to life-saving health care and ensuring human rights. Bit by bit, countries are working towards pan-national migration policies, but outreach medical relief programmes and other measures to support the health of irregular migrants and asylum seekers continue to be needed.

Migration is a priority for many nation states and for economic development. It may even be an effective way of reducing global poverty and also may be a powerful tool in achieving health equity. It has been suggested that sustainable efforts to build stable governments, thriving economies and resilient health systems across all states is the most promising way to address unsafe and sometimes deadly migration. In the meantime, the global north and United Nations agencies should continue to uphold their moral duty to humanity and health for all. Restricting access to health and social services, and the use of intimidating political propaganda will not help produce durable solutions. Ultimately, between the global north and the developing countries, we need win–win partnerships with pan-national policies and mutual benefits for all sides.

## Acknowledgements

We would like to thank Jorge Pedro Martin, Stephen Cornish, Linn Maria Biorklund, Ivan Gayton and Frank Doerner for contributions to the Médecins Sans Frontiers/Doctors Without Borders Working Group on migrant health. We would also like to acknowledge Andre Renzaho for his helpful comments on earlier versions of this paper.

## References

Amnesty International (2013). The State of the World's Human Rights. Amnesty International Report 2013. Available at: https://www.amnesty.org/en/documents/pol10/001/2013/hu/. Accessed July 2015.

Bell, M. & Muhidin, S. (2009). Cross-national comparisons of internal migration. Available at: http://hdr.undp.org/sites/default/files/hdrp_2009_30.pdf. Accessed 27 October 2015.

Biffl, G. & Altenburg, F. (Hg). (2012) Migration and Health in Nowhereland — Access of Undocumented Migrants to Work and Health Care in Europe, omninum, Bad Vöslau, AUT.

Council of Europe (2014). Report to the Government of Greece on the visit to Greece carried out by the European Committee for the Prevention of Torture and Inhuman or Degrading Treatment or Punishment (CPT) CPT/Inf (2014) 26. Available at: http://www.cpt.coe.int/documents/grc/2014-26-inf-eng.pdf. Accessed 4 June 2015.

Committee on Migration, Refugees, and Displaced Persons (2014). The alternatives to immigration detention of children, Parliamentary Report, Doc. 13597, 15 September 2014, Council of Europe. Available at: http://www.refworld.org/pdfid/547c7c834.pdf. Accessed June 2015.

European Migration Network (2014). The use of detention and alternatives to detention in the context of immigration policies: Synthesis Report for the EMN Focussed Study 2014. Available at: http://ec.europa.eu/dgs/home-affairs/what-we-do/networks/european_migration_network/reports/docs/emn-studies/emn_study_detention_alternatives_to_detention_synthesis_report_en.pdf. Accessed June 2015.

Internal Displacement Monitoring Centre (2015). Global Overview 2015. People internally displaced by conflict and violence. Available at: http://www.internal-displacement.org/assets/library/Media/201505-Global-Overview-2015/20150506-global-overview-2015-en.pdf. Accessed June 2015.

International Detention Coalition (2015). Briefing Paper: Does Detention Deter? Available at: http://idcoalition.org/detentiondatabase/does-detention-deter/. Accessed June 2015.

IOM. (2014). Global Migration Trends: An overview. Available at: http://missingmigrants.iom.int/sites/default/files/documents/Global_Migration_Trends_PDF_FinalVH_with%20References.pdf. Accessed 31 May 2015.

Le Monde (2015). Quels pays accueilleraient le plus de migrants, après la proposition de la Commission. Available at: http://www.lemonde.fr/les-decodeurs/article/2015/05/28/quels-pays-accueilleraient-le-plus-de-migrants-apres-la-proposition-de-la-commission_4642760_4355770.html. Accessed 31 May 2015.

Medecins Sans Frontieres (2011). Medecins Sans Frontieres, Annual reports 2011, reports on Libya. Available at: http://www.msf.org.uk/reports-0. Accessed 28 April 2015.

Medecins Sans Frontieres (2013). Violence, Vulnerability and Migration: Trapped at the Gates of Europe. A report on the situation of sub-Saharan migrants in an irregular situation in Morocco. Available at: http://www.msf.org.uk/reports-0. Accessed 9 March 2015.

Pottie, K. *et al.* (2011). Overview: Evidence-based clinical guidelines for immigrants and refugees. *CMAJ*, 183(12), E824–E925.

Pottie, K. *et al.* (2015). Access to healthcare for the most vulnerable migrants: A humanitarian crisis. *Conflict and Health*, 9, 16, doi:10.1186/s13031-015-0043-Published: 7 May 2015.

Povall, S.L. *et al.* (2013). Health equity impact assessment. *Health Promotion International*. Oxford Journals, doi: 10.1093/heapro/dat012. Available at: http://heapro.oxfordjournals.org/content/early/2013/02/28/heapro.dat012.full.pdf+html. Accessed June 2015.

Ravenscroft, J. & Marcos, L. (2012). Civil society organisations and universal health care. *Lancet* 380, 888.

Sampson, R. *et al.* (2011). There are alternatives: A handbook for preventing unnecessary immigration detention. The International Detention Coalition Malbourne, AUS. Available at: http://www.ohchr.org/Documents/Issues/Migration/Events/IDC.pdf. Accessed June 2015.

United Nations (2015). 28th session of the Human Rights Council: Report A/HRC/28/68 Torture and ill-treatment of children deprived of their liberty. Available at: http://www.ohchr.org/EN/HRBodies/HRC/RegularSessions/Session28/Pages/ListReports.aspx. Accessed June 2015.

UNDP (2014). HDI Indicators By Country 2014. https://data.undp.org/dataset/HDI-Indicators-By-Country-2014/5tuc-d2a9. Accessed 31 July 2015.

UNFPA. (2015). Migration Overview. Available at: http://www.unfpa.org/migration. Accessed October 27, 2015.

UNHCR (2012). Detention Guidelines on the applicable criteria and standards relating to the detention of asylum-seekers and alternatives to detention. Available at: http://www.unhcr.org/505b10ee9.html. Accessed June 2015.

UNHCR (2014a). Asylum trends 2014. Available at: http://www.unhcr.org/551128679. Accessed 30 May 2015.

UNHCR (2014b). Beyond Detention, A Global Strategy to support governments to end the detention of asylum-seekers and refugees 2014–2019. Available at: http://www.unhcr.org/53aa929f6.html. Accessed June 2015.

UNHCR (2015). Syria Regional Refugee Response. Available at: http://data.unhcr.org/syrianrefugees/regional.php. Accessed 2015 Oct 27.

Viruell-Fuentes, E.A. *et al.* (2012) More than culture: Structural racism, intersectionality theory, and immigrant health. *Soc Sci Med.*, 75(12), 2099–2106. doi: 10.1016/j.socscimed.2011.12.037.

# Chapter 8

# Migration and health effects in the Netherlands

Dr Paul Herfs and Dr Olta Gishti

## Introduction

In this chapter, the authors describe the history of migration in the Netherlands. The starting point is the description of migration since the sixteenth century, the so-called Golden Century. After describing migration globally, the authors describe the migration flows from the 1960s in depth. The focus lies on the major ethnic minority groups in the Netherlands: the Turks, the Moroccans, the Surinamese and the Antilleans. The refugees will also be discussed. Furthermore, the authors describe the health problems facing migrants in the Netherlands. In the final paragraph, measures to push back the extraordinary health problems of migrants are discussed.

## Migration into the Netherlands since 1588

Migration movements into the Netherlands are not new. Already in the sixteenth century, many foreigners tried to settle in the Republic of the Seven United Netherlands. The Republic started in 1588 and ended in 1795 when the French occupied the Republic. After ending the Spanish oppression in 1588, the Dutch leaders could not find a "good" king (Bekkers, 1999).

So they decided to create a Republic, which was a rare phenomenon in Europe at that time. Although the Republic was just a small country with 2–2.5 million citizens and not very different from the Netherlands as we know it today, it was a major player in the world. The reason for its important role lay in the country's success in world trade. The Dutch East and the Dutch West India Company were extremely powerful. In the Golden Age (seventeenth century), the Dutch fleet was bigger than the fleets of England and France. Through this trade, the standard of living in the Republic was the highest in this part of western Europe (Bekkers, 1999; Verkuil *et al.*, 2008). Trade, art (e.g. Frans Hals and Rembrandt van Rijn) and science flourished. This wealth created a tolerant attitude towards dissidents. Migrants were both needed and therefore welcomed. Migrants from Spain and France, who were persecuted for their religious beliefs in their home countries, fled to the Republic of the Seven United Netherlands. Jews from countries in eastern Europe tried to escape from extreme poverty and migrated to the Netherlands. Despite the tolerant attitude in the Republic, there was certainly oppression against religious groups that were deviating from the mainstream Protestant beliefs. For instance, Jews were not allowed to become members of the guilds and Catholics could not celebrate Mass.

The reasons for migrants to leave their countries were the same. They left to survive, to find work and earn money, or to start a relationship elsewhere. Migration should be considered as a normal historical phenomenon with short- and long-term consequences.

Migration is defined by Obdeijn and Schrover as geographical mobility of people in which they cross boundaries in order to live elsewhere for a longer period of time (Obdeijn and Schrover, 2008). In the beginning of the Republic, persons who crossed city boundaries or regional boundaries were seen as foreigners or migrants. Later on that point of view changed, as migrants were those people who crossed boundaries of one country or more.

In the period between 1600 and 1800, several groups of refugees settled in the Republic. They came from the southern part of the Netherlands (Protestants), from France (Huguenots), from Spain and Portugal (Sephardic Jews) and from eastern Europe (Ashkenazic Jews). Besides the refugees, a great number of economic migrants from Germany settled in the Republic. It is estimated that between 1600 and 1800, 350,000 Germans and 155,000 refugees lived in the Netherlands (Obdeijn and Schrover, 2008). At that time, the Republic had about 2 million citizens. So, during this period of prosperity in the Republic, one-quarter of all inhabitants had foreign roots.

In the nineteenth century, the Republic came to an end. It changed into the Kingdom of Holland during the French occupation. Louis, the brother of Napoleon, became the Dutch king. After Napoleon lost the Battle of Leipzig in 1813, King William I became the first Dutch king. In 1830, Belgium was separated from the Kingdom of the Netherlands. Although mass migration took place — 60 million Europeans left the continent — only 300,000 Dutch people left the Netherlands (Obdeijn and Schrover, 2008). Still the Netherlands was quite attractive for economic migrants (from Germany and Belgium) and for refugees (Lucassen and Lucassen, 2012). The attractiveness of the Netherlands is accounted for by three factors according to Lucassen *et al.* (Lucassen and Lucassen, 2012):

- The fact that salaries were much higher than in surrounding countries.
- The relative prosperity (there were very poor citizens too).
- The relative tolerance (although Jews and Catholics were discriminated against).

Health problems as a consequence of migration in the nineteenth century have been described by Curtin (1989). The majority of Europeans who migrated to the tropics died because they lacked immunity to tropical diseases. Also, migrants from Germany who stayed temporarily in the Netherlands were confronted with diseases. They suffered from endemic malaria and were even excluded in Germany from their health insurance (Lucassen, 1984).

Between 1865 and 1900, the number of immigration flows (entering the Netherlands) and emigration flows (leaving the Netherlands) did not differ strongly. About 555,000 persons migrated to the Netherlands and about 440,000 left the Netherlands (Obdeijn and Schrover, 2008). Even at the end of the nineteenth century, the Netherlands was wealthier than the surrounding countries, so the country retained its attractiveness. It was however no longer a refuge for persecuted people. Until World War I, it was quite easy for foreigners to cross the Dutch borders. World War I marked an end to the freedom of movement of persons in many countries. During World War I, the Netherlands stayed neutral. As many as 1 million Belgian citizens fled the war in their country and found a safe haven in the Netherlands. About 100,000 Belgians stayed until 1918, the end of World War I, in the Netherlands. Between the two world wars, German Jews and left-wing citizens fled to the Netherlands from the Nazi regime. Immigration flows before and during World War II from other countries (e.g. Italy, China) were modest.

## Migration in the Netherlands after World War II

After World War II, it appeared that in certain industrial sectors there were shortages of unskilled workers. These shortages were revealed in the coal mines in the province of Limburg, in the docking yards in Rotterdam and Amsterdam, and in the textile industry in the province of Overijssel. Among the Dutch there was hardly unemployment, so for employers it was hard to attract personnel. The call for the recruitment of temporary and unskilled workers from abroad became louder and louder in the 1950s. But there was not only a shortage of unskilled workers. In hospitals, there were shortages of nurses (Lucassen and Lucassen, 2012). Nurses from Surinam, Indonesia and the Philippines were recruited. The emphasis of recruitment efforts concentrated on unskilled workers. At first employers tried to recruit Italians and Spaniards. However, the efforts to find sufficient amounts of Mediterranean workers were inadequate. So they went to Morocco and Turkey in order to attract unskilled workers. Table 1 shows the change in the efforts of recruitment officers (Wentholt, 1967).

When these migrants — mostly single men — from Mediterranean origin came to the Netherlands, the common opinion was that after some time they would return to their home countries. Even the migrants themselves shared that opinion. Sahin, the daughter of a Turkish migrant and nowadays working at the Education Inspectorate, described her personal

Table 1: Numbers of recruited workers since 1960

|      | Italians | Spaniards | Turks  | Moroccans | Other | Total   |
|------|----------|-----------|--------|-----------|-------|---------|
| 1960 | 2,740    | 151       | 22     | 3         | 375   | 3,291   |
| 1970 | 18,000   | 16,946    | 20,615 | 19,445    | 8,239 | 83,255  |
| 1977 | 20,000   | 17,475    | 42,300 | 29,125    | 9,925 | 118,825 |

migration history (Sahin, 2003). She and her family joined her father in the Netherlands at the age of seven. She observed that since 1960 "… both parties, migrants and the Dutch government, were convinced of the fact that the residency of the migrants was only temporary. This perspective lasted for at least 35 years." Employers and politicians disagreed about the necessity of regulations. Employers wanted the government to be as less demanding towards migrants as possible. Because of this pressure, many migrants received residence permits and once they had obtained residence permits they tried to reunify with their families. Once these migrated workers obtained residency, their wives and children came to the Netherlands as well. As mentioned before, the common opinion until 1979 was that "guest workers" (literal translation of the Dutch word "gastarbeiders") eventually would return to their home countries (Netherlands Scientific Council for Government Policy, 1990). The Netherlands Scientific Council for Government Policy concluded that "it is safe to assume that immigration will continue for the present and that the share of the non-indigenous communities in the total population will continue to grow, whereas the Council advised in 1979 that the presence of *immigrants* should in principle be regarded as permanent." (Netherlands Scientific Council for Government Policy, 1990, p. 20). For a long period of time, the Dutch government failed to develop a policy towards these migrants. There was no felt necessity because of their temporary stay in the Netherlands. As a consequence of this non-policy, there were no language requirements towards migrants. On the shop floor, it was fully accepted that migrants could not communicate in the Dutch language. Courses in Dutch as a second language were not present overall (Extra, 1996). And when these migrants started to reunify with their families, the language they spoke at home was not the Dutch language, except for the Surinamese, as most of them speak Dutch at home.

The housing of migrants was also problematic. According to Engbertsen, "most migrants lived in segregated districts of the big cities. The sociological characteristic of these groups is that they live in a very isolated position" (Engbertsen, 2006). The international economic crisis that took place in 1980–1985 had great impact on the Dutch migrant communities. Many of them came to the Netherlands as unskilled workers, so when the crisis came to a head the unskilled workers were the first ones to lose their jobs. The major conditions for positive participation of the migrants in

Dutch society in the 1990s were no longer met — the first generation of migrants hardly mastered the Dutch language, they lived in isolated districts where only a few Dutch citizens lived and because of the economic crisis they lost their jobs to a massive extent. The consequences of these developments were that migrant groups and the Dutch majority lived in one country but without having real contacts. In Table 2, the numbers of Dutch nationals and of migrants in the Netherlands in 1992 are presented (Roijen et al., 1994).

In 2012, the Central Bureau for Statistics presented the following statistics on the Dutch population in 2011 (Centraal Bureau voor de Statistiek, 2012). Table 3 shows the numbers of the major minority groups in the Netherlands in 2011. A distinction is made between the first and second generations.

Table 2: The numbers of Dutch nationals and of minority groups in the Netherlands in 1992

| | |
|---|---|
| Dutch | 12,764,767 |
| Italians | 32,818 |
| Spaniards | 29,046 |
| (former) Yugoslavians | 27,117 |
| Turks | 240,810 |
| Moroccans | 195,536 |
| Surinamese | 262,839 |
| Antillean/Aruban | 90,650 |

Table 3: Minority groups in the Netherlands in 2011

| | First generation | Second generation | Total |
|---|---|---|---|
| Dutch | 197,000 | 192,000 | 16,656,000 |
| Turks | 197,000 | 192,000 | 389,000 |
| Moroccans | 168,000 | 188,000 | 356,000 |
| Surinamese | 184,000 | 160,000 | 343,000 |
| Antillean/Aruban | 82,000 | 59,000 | 141,000 |

# The major minority groups in the Netherlands

## *The Surinamese minority group*

The Surinamese minority group had different motives to migrate to the Netherlands than the Turks and the Moroccans. Suriname was a former colony of the Netherlands. When in 1975 the Republic of Suriname was proclaimed, many Surinamese, mostly Hindu and Javanese, migrated to the Netherlands. They feared that the Creole party, the majority in Suriname, would create chaos in the government of their home country. That fear was fostered by the domination of the Surinamese army by the Creole population. In December 1982, 15 prominent young Surinamese men, who had criticised the military dictatorship then ruling Suriname, were executed by the military who were under the command of Desi Bouterse. He became the President of the Republic of Suriname in 2010. The relationship between Suriname and the Netherlands deteriorated since the seizure of power by the military. It led to the migration of many Hindu, Javanese and Chinese Surinamese to the Netherlands as long as they had Dutch nationality. In addition, part of the Creole population left Suriname and came to the Netherlands as long as they had the possibilities. Most Surinamese are living in the big cities of the Netherlands. The majority of the Creoles (71,420) are living in Amsterdam (Bijlmermeer), while the Hindustani majority (43,685) lives in The Hague (Obdeijn and Schrover, 2008). The Central Bureau for Statistics declared that in 2007, 327,000 Surinamese were living in the Netherlands, while 494,000 people were living in the Republic of Suriname (Centraal Bureau voor de Statistiek, 2007).

## *The Antillean and Aruban minority group*

In the sixteenth century, the Antillean islands became colonised. Slaves were transported from Africa to work on the plantations. The Dutch managed these plantations. The Antillean islands served also as a transitional station for the slave trade. After the abolition of slavery in 1863, the ties between the Netherlands and the Antillean islands were not cut. Since 1954, the Antillean islands have been an autonomous area within the Kingdom of the Netherlands. As a consequence, Antillean and Aruban citizens hold Dutch nationality. Migration from the Antillean islands and Aruba existed for a long period of time. Mostly, young men from these islands came to the Netherlands to study at Dutch universities (Verkuil *et al.*, 2008). In the

1960s, workers and nurses were recruited. The economic crisis in the 1980s lead to unemployment on the Antillean islands and Aruba, and subsequently to the growth of migration flows from these islands to the Netherlands. In 2004, it was estimated that nearly 23% of the Antillean and Aruban population (84,400) lived in the European part of the Netherlands. In total, 275,800 inhabitants lived on the Antillean and Aruban islands (Centraal Bureau voor de Statistiek, Jaargang 53, 2005). Nowadays there is a continuous flow of young students, both male and female, from the Antillean islands and Aruba to the Netherlands in order to obtain a degree at one of the universities (Herfs, 1994). All Antilleans and Arubans who study in higher education are eligible for Dutch study grants.

## *The Turkish minority group*

Since 1965, the migration flows from Turkey grew. The Dutch economy was booming and there was a great need for unskilled workers. In 1964, the Dutch government reached a recruitment agreement with the Turkish government. Most Turks worked first in other countries (Belgium and Germany) before they decided to settle in the Netherlands. Two-thirds of the Turkish migrants came originally from rural regions in central and eastern parts of Turkey. In the beginning, the guest workers obtained contracts for one or two years. But, as they proved to be good workers, the contracts were made up for an indefinite period. Employers put pressure on politicians and government to face Turkish workers with as few restrictions as possible. Nevertheless, the common opinion was that one day the Turkish workers would leave the Netherlands. But once the (male) Turks got the possibility of reunifying with their families, who stayed behind in Turkey, it became clear that their stay in the Netherlands changed from temporary to permanent. The economic crisis that started in the 1980s had severe consequences for the first generation of Turkish migrants. Many Turks lost their jobs and stayed unemployed for the rest of their life. Their start in the Dutch society was a false one. Although they had permanent residency, they did not master the Dutch language and they lived in isolated parts of the bigger cities.

## *The Moroccan minority group*

The Moroccan minority migration history has roughly the same characteristics as the Turkish migration one. In 1969, the Dutch government reached a recruitment agreement with the Moroccan government. Since 1970, great numbers of Moroccan unskilled workers were recruited. Most of them came from the Rif area in the north of Morocco.

In the beginning, the guest workers received contracts for one or two years. But once they proved to be good workers, the contracts were made for an indefinite period. Dutch employers put pressure on the government and politicians to face Moroccan workers with as few restrictions as possible. Nevertheless, the common opinion was that one day the Moroccan workers would leave the Netherlands. But once the (male) Moroccans got the possibility of reunifying with their families, who stayed behind in Morocco, it became clear that their stay in the Netherlands changed from temporary to permanent.

The economic crisis that started in the 1980s had severe consequences for the first generation of Moroccan migrants. Many lost their jobs and stayed unemployed for the rest of their life. Their start in the Dutch society was a false one. Although they had permanent residency, they did not master the Dutch language and they lived in isolated parts of the bigger cities.

### *Refugees*

The four major groups in 2010 with a refugee status living in the Netherlands are the Iraqis, the Afghans, the Iranians and the Somalians (Dourleijn, 2011a; Dourleijn, 2011b). Since 1980, refugees from Iraq, Afghanistan and Iran fled from persecution. The majority of the first refugees from these countries were highly educated. Since 1990, the number of Somalian refugees grew. In contrast with the other refugee groups, the Somalian refugees were not highly educated. The number of refugees accounts for 8% of the non-western migrants in the Netherlands (Table 4). In 2010 in total 1,858,294 non-western migrants are living in the Netherlands.

## Migrants' health issues

As previously described, large ethnic differences in socioeconomic status and wealth were observed in the Netherlands since 1855. All these differences have continuously influenced health status among ethnic minorities' groups. Also nowadays ethnic differences in health status have been reported worldwide and especially large differences were observed in European countries

Table 4: Number of the major refugee groups in the Netherlands

| 2010 | Number of refugees or children of refugees |
|---|---|
| Iraqi | 52,102 |
| Afghan | 38,664 |
| Iranian | 31,653 |
| Somalians | 27,011 |

(Anand *et al.*, 2000; Berry *et al.*, 2012; Bhopal *et al.*, 2013; Walker *et al.*, 2012; Winkleby *et al.*, 1999). Because of a continuous migration, a large variety in ethnic groups is present in western Europe. The largest ethnic minority groups in western European countries are from north African, south American, Turkish and Asian backgrounds (Crul and Vermeulen, 2003). Although these migrant groups form a considerable part of current European populations, they are often poorly represented in studies (Ranganathan and Bhopal, 2006). As previously described, based on colonial and working immigration history, the largest ethnic minority groups in the Netherlands are Dutch Antilleans, Moroccans, Surinamese-Creoles, Surinamese-Hindustani and Turkish (Nicolaas, 2010; Statistics Netherlands, 2003).

## *Ethnic differences in health status among childhood populations*

Given that health problems in early life, when left untreated, are likely to persist or become worse later in life, it is of great importance to explore how migration influences health in childhood, and if these influences persist in adult life.

**Childhood mortality:** In the Netherlands, ethnic differences in health status among children are being observed. These differences might originate from foetal life onwards. Table 5 gives the ethnic differences in infant mortality and it shows that Moroccan, Turkish, Antillean and Surinamese populations have an increased risk of infant mortality compared to the Dutch population (Troe *et al.*, 2006). The most important determinants in explaining these differences in foetal growth and birthweight were maternal

Table 5: Number of live births, early neonatal mortality (ENM), late neonatal mortality (LNM), post neonatal mortality (PNM), number of deaths and infant mortality rates (IMR) per ethnic group

|  | Live births | ENM | LNM | PNM | Deaths | IMR (95% CI) |
|---|---|---|---|---|---|---|
| Dutch | 935,858 | 2,715 | 718 | 1,089 | 4,522 | 4.8 (4.7, 4.9) |
| Turkish | 41,348 | 105 | 44 | 106 | 255 | 6.2 (5.5, 7.0) |
| Moroccan | 39,210 | 135 | 34 | 94 | 263 | 6.7 (5.9, 7.5) |
| Surinamese | 27,313 | 117 | 27 | 32 | 176 | 6.4 (5.5, 7.4) |
| Antillean | 10,654 | 44 | 15 | 18 | 77 | 7.2 (5.6, 8.8) |
| Total | 1,178,848 | 3,455 | 931 | 1,493 | 5,879 | 5.0 (4.9, 5.0) |

and paternal height, educational level of the mother, maternal age and marital status (Drooger *et al.*, 2005; Troe *et al.*, 2006).

In general, the non-Dutch populations in the Netherlands have a lower socioeconomic position and are less educated than the native Dutch population (Statistics Netherlands, 2004). Women from ethnic minorities give birth usually at a younger age and are more often single mothers, compared to Dutch mothers. A higher prevalence of teenage pregnancies are observed among Surinamese mothers (Schulpen *et al.*, 2001). Single motherhood and teenage pregnancy are previously shown to be associated with these adverse pregnancy outcomes, such as low birthweight and preterm birth and infant mortality (Fraser *et al.*, 1995; Raatikainen *et al.*, 2005). Second, there are also several etiological factors that can mediate the associations between maternal socioeconomic status and birthweight, gestational age and infant mortality. These factors include smoking habits, bacterial vaginosis, low gestational weight gain, short stature and psychosocial stressors that present among mothers from ethnic minority groups (Kramer *et al.*, 2000, 2001). Third, previous studies have found that a higher percentage of pregnant women in the Turkish and Moroccan populations had a consanguineous partner (Teeuw *et al.*, 2014; Ten Kate *et al.*, 2014). Consanguinity has been shown to be a risk factor for congenital anomalies (Bromiker *et al.*, 2004; Zlotogora, 2002). Moreover, consanguinity is associated with perinatal and infant mortality (Grant and Bittles, 1997; Hussain *et al.*, 2001; Tuncbilek and Koc, 1994). In the literature, relative risks of infant mortality associated with parent's consanguinity are described ranging from 1.3 to 2.1 for first cousin relationships and from 1.2 to 2.4 for second cousin relationships (Grant and Bittles, 1997; Stoltenberg *et al.*, 1998; Khoury *et al.*, 1987). Altogether, this relatively high frequency of consanguinity in the Turkish and Moroccan population potentially contributes to the increased risk of infant death from congenital anomalies and to the excess infant mortality observed in the Turkish and Moroccan ethnicities.

**Cardiovascular risk factors:** The adverse health status seems to persist also among children at older ages. Higher prevalence rates of overweight and obesity have been shown among Turkish, Moroccan and Surinamese school-age children compared to Dutch children (de Wilde *et al.*, 2009). Another study among 7,801 children at the age of five years reported that not Surinamese, but children from other ethnic minority groups in the Netherlands have higher risk of being overweight than Dutch children (Veldhuis *et al.*, 2013). Moreover, a registry-based study among 50,961 children aged 3–16 years living in The Hague, the Netherlands, observed higher prevalences of obesity among Turkish, Moroccan and Surinamese children as compared to Dutch children (de Wilde *et al.*, 2009). The obesity rates obtained from this registry-based study are given in Table 6.

A prospective cohort study among 5,244 children at the age of six years showed that compared to Dutch, Moroccan, Surinamese-Hindustani and Turkish had not only higher risk of obesity but also an adverse body fat distribution (Table 7) (Gishti *et al.*, 2014). Body fat distribution is shown to be more strongly related to cardiovascular disease in later life (Gishti *et al.*, 2015).

Differences in other cardiovascular risk factors have also been previously reported. A Dutch study among 2,509 children aged 5–6 years found that Turkish children have a higher blood pressure compared to Moroccan and Dutch children. These differences were partly explained by differences in body mass index and waist circumference (de Hoog *et al.*, 2012). Other studies among children suggested that Turkish children had higher total- and low-density lipoprotein-cholesterol levels than Dutch children (de Hoog *et al.*, 2011; van Vliet *et al.*, 2009). Consistently, previous studies among children in the Netherlands have shown that Turkish children have higher risk for developing metabolic syndrome as compared to Dutch children (Dannemann *et al.*, 2011; van Vliet *et al.*, 2009). An overview for

Table 6: Obesity rates (%) per ethnic group

|  | 1999 | 2007 | 1999–2007 | OR (95% CI, unadjusted) | OR (95% CI, adjusted) |
|---|---|---|---|---|---|
|  | % (n) | % (n) | % (n) |  |  |
| **Dutch** |  |  |  |  |  |
| Boys | 2.2 (2,712) | 2.3 (2,904) | 2.4 (25,588) | 1.010 (0.979, 1.041) | 0.997 (0.965, 1.029) |
| Girls | 3.7 (2,637) | 3.3 (2,889) | 3.4 (24,805) | 0.973 (0.947, 0.999)* | 0.978 (0.951, 1.005) |
| **Turkish** |  |  |  |  |  |
| Boys | 7.9 (647) | 13.1 (1,008) | 10.0 (7,350) | 1.075 (1.043, 1.107)*** | 1.188 (1.063, 1.329)** |
| Girls | 8.0 (613) | 10.7 (881) | 8.8 (6,821) | 1.042 (1.008, 1.076)* | 1.041 (1.007, 1.077)* |
| **Moroccan** |  |  |  |  |  |
| Boys | 5.6 (535) | 7.2 (720) | 6.1 (5,452) | 1.019 (0.976, 1.064) | 1.011 (0.968, 1.056) |
| Girls | 7.2 (528) | 6.6 (760) | 7.0 (5,545) | 0.973 (0.936, 1.012) | 0.970 (0.933, 1.010) |
| **Surinamese** |  |  |  |  |  |
| Boys | 5.1 (550) | 5.4 (592) | 5.3 (4,976) | 0.994 (0.948, 1.042) | 0.962 (0.916, 1.010) |
| Girls | 4.4 (527) | 4.5 (554) | 3.8 (4,697) | 0.995 (0.940, 1.053) | 0.975 (0.919, 1.034) |

Sex and age group in 1999 and 2007 and for the whole period 1999–2007. Unadjusted and adjusted odds ratio (OR) and 95% confidence interval (CI) for 1999–2007 with year of examination as independent variable adjusted for socioeconomic status (age group) or socioeconomic status and age (totals per sex per ethnic group). *$p < 0.05$; **$p < 0.01$; ***$p < 0.001$.

differences in blood pressure, lipid levels and insulin levels among ethnic groups in the Netherlands are given in Table 8. These data were obtained from Generation R study, a multiethnic cohort study in Rotterdam, the Netherlands (Jaddoe et al., 2012).

All the above studies have suggested that ethnic differences in health status are mostly explained from differences in lifestyle, socioeconomic status and environmental inequalities between ethnic groups. Moreover, the previous studies described how low birthweight and preterm birth

Table 7: Ethnic differences in body fat distribution

| | Body mass index, (kg/m$^2$) | Body fat percentage (%) | Android/ gynoid fat mass ratio | Pre-peritoneal area (cm$^2$) | Overweight (%) | Obesity (%) |
|---|---|---|---|---|---|---|
| Dutch $n = 3,584$ | 15.7 (13.7, 19.7) | 24.0 (4.9) | 0.2 (0.1) | 0.4 (0.2, 1.0) | 10.0 | 2.1 |
| Turkish $n = 501$ | 16.6 (13.9, 23.7)* | 28.2 (6.5)* | 0.3 (0.1)* | 0.5 (0.2, 1.7)* | 23.8* | 12.0* |
| Moroccan $n = 378$ | 16.5 (14.1, 22.3)* | 27.0 (6.0)* | 0.3 (0.1)* | 0.5 (0.2, 1.6)* | 20.6* | 7.7* |
| Surinamese $n = 194$ | 16.1 (13.4, 23.8)* | 23.7 (6.7) | 0.2 (0.1) | 0.4 (0.1, 1.5) | 13.4* | 7.7* |
| Antillean $n = 196$ | 16.5 (14.0, 24.1)* | 25.5 (6.6) | 0.3 (0.1)* | 0.4 (0.2, 2.5) | 18.4* | 13.8* |

Values are means (standard deviation), percentages or median (95% range). p-value was estimated by using One-Way ANOVA test and Chi-square tests, and Dutch ethnicity was used as reference groups. *$p < 0.05$ body fat percentage and android/gynoid fat mass ratio, which reflects the waist to hip ratio, were measured from DXA scanning. Pre-peritoneal fat, which reflects visceral adipose tissue, was measured by abdominal ultrasound.

among ethnic populations is shown to be associated with the development of obesity and cardiovascular disease in later life (Gluckman et al., 2008). Lower socioeconomic status is also shown to be associated with unhealthy diet, lower physical activity and, subsequently, higher risk of disease in these populations. Therefore, reducing the socioeconomic and environmental inequalities between ethnic populations could result in a decrease in ethnic differences in health status.

## *Ethnic differences in health status among adulthood populations*

All the above-mentioned ethnic differences in childhood look likely to persist also among adults.

**Adverse cardiovascular outcomes:** Dutch nationwide register-based cohort study ($n = 7,423,174$) was conducted between 1998 and 2010 and studied the ethnic disparities in ischaemic stroke, intracerebral haemorrhage and subarachnoid haemorrhage incidence (Agyemang et al., 2014).

Table 8: Ethnic differences in blood pressure, lipid levels and insulin

| | SBP (mmHg) | DBP (mmHg) | Total cholesterol (mmol/L) | HDL-cholesterol (mmol/L) | LDL-cholesterol (mmol/L) | TG (mmol/L) | Insulin (U/L) | MSC (%) |
|---|---|---|---|---|---|---|---|---|
| Dutch $n = 3,584$ | 102.2 (8.0) | 60.3 (6.6) | 4.2 (0.6) | 1.3 (0.3) | 2.3 (0.6) | 1.0 (0.4, 2.4) | 118.1 (17.1, 386.4) | 9.0 |
| Turkish $n = 501$ | 105.1 (9.0)* | 62.4 (7.2)* | 4.3 (0.7)* | 1.3 (0.3) | 2.5 (0.6)* | 1.0 (0.4, 2.6)* | 100.0 (13.3, 392.4)* | 20.6* |
| Moroccan $n = 378$ | 103.4 (8.3)* | 60.3 (6.8) | 4.1 (0.6) | 1.3 (0.3) | 2.3 (0.6) | 0.9 (0.4, 2.3) | 110.7 (14.3, 423.8) | 10.3 |
| Surinamese $n = 194$ | 104.0 (7.7)* | 61.3 (6.4)* | 4.4 (0.8)* | 1.4 (0.3)* | 2.5 (0.7)* | 0.8 (0.4, 1.8)* | 114.6 (14.8, 457.7) | 9.6 |
| Antillean $n = 196$ | 103.7 (8.7)* | 61.7 (7.2)* | 4.2 (0.6) | 1.4 (0.3)* | 2.3 (0.5) | 0.8 (0.3, 2.1)* | 103.0 (24.1, 489.4)* | 14.4* |

SBP, systolic blood pressure; DBP, diastolic blood pressure; HDL-cholesterol, high density lipoproteine cholesterol; LDL-cholesterol, low density lipoproteine cholesterol; TG, triglycerides; MSC, clustering of cardiovascular outcomes; Values are means (standard deviation), percentages or median (95% range). $p$-value was estimated by using One-Way ANOVA test and Chi-square tests, and Dutch ethnicity was used as reference groups. *$p < 0.05$.

Higher rates of ischaemic stroke, intracerebral haemorrhage and subarachnoid haemorrhage were observed among Surinamese and Antillean adults as compared to Dutch adults, whereas lower incidence rates were observed among Moroccans (data shown in Table 9). The ethnic differences reflect the variations in the underlying risk factors. As previously described, higher cardiovascular risk factors are present among Turkish, Surinamese and Antillean as compared to Dutch, starting from childhood onwards. The lower incidence of all the various stroke subtypes found among Moroccan people is in line with previous studies that showed a low prevalence of hypertension in Moroccan people as compared with ethnic Dutch people. This previous study observed that the prevalence of hypertension was 26.1% and 19.6% in Moroccan men and women as compared with 48.8% and 35% in ethnic Dutch men and women, respectively (Agyemang et al., 2006). The rate of smoking has also been shown to be low among Moroccan and Turkish people in the Netherlands (Ujcic-Voortman et al., 2011). The Mediterranean diet, which has cardio-protective effects, may also contribute to their favourable cardiovascular disease outcomes. Thus, all these factors might also explain, at least in part, the relatively low stroke incidence observed among Turkish women in this study.

Few studies have looked at differences in cardiovascular health between first- and second-generations minorities and the Dutch population. Studying whether these changes converge towards the Dutch population might be important in understanding whether migrants in the Netherlands can adopt healthy lifestyle factors in the country. A nationwide register-based cohort study observed that changes in myocardial infarction incidence over migrant generations were unbeneficial for most of the ethnic groups (van Oeffelen et al., 2013). This could be explained by the loss of beneficial health behaviours from the country of origin, the adoption of unhealthy behaviours in the host country and by the weakening of the healthy migrant effect over generations (Landrine and Klonoff, 2004). Only minorities from the former Dutch colonies (Suriname, Indonesia, Netherlands Antilles) showed beneficial intergenerational changes. These minority groups are more closely related to native Dutch because of colonial heritage. Therefore, second-generation minorities may have an advantage in adopting healthy lifestyle factors in the Netherlands while retaining healthy lifestyle factors of their parents.

Table 9: Age-standardized* absolute incidence rates of stroke subtypes per 100,000 person-years at risk by sex

|  | Total n events | Total Incidence rate (95% CI) | Men n events | Men Incidence rate (95% CI) | Women n events | Women Incidence rate (95% CI) |
|---|---|---|---|---|---|---|
| **Combined stroke types** | | | | | | |
| Ethnic Dutch | 298,177 | 300 (299–301) | 139,794 | 332 (330–334) | 158,383 | 274 (273–275) |
| Turkish | 1,404 | 193 (170–216) | 868 | 249 (187–311) | 536 | 154 (129–179) |
| Moroccan | 251 | 89 (60–118) | 173 | 75 (61–90) | 78 | 84 (40–127) |
| Surinamese | 3,280 | 370 (354–387) | 1,573 | 418 (386–449) | 1,707 | 338 (319–358) |
| Antillean | 541 | 314 (270–358) | 259 | 386 (289–483) | 282 | 279 (230–328) |
| **IS** | | | | | | |
| Ethnic Dutch | 119,950 | 187 (186–188) | 58,786 | 215 (213–216) | 61,164 | 166 (164–167) |
| Turkish | 666 | 140 (117–164) | 421 | 204 (131–277) | 245 | 110 (88–132) |
| Moroccan | 94 | 35 (26–44) | 63 | 41 (29–53) | 31 | 23 (13–33) |
| Surinamese | 1,623 | 280 (263–298) | 813 | 326 (294–358) | 810 | 249 (228–270) |
| Antillean | 233 | 220 (176–264) | 115 | 253 (165–342) | 118 | 202 (152–252) |
| **ICH** | | | | | | |
| Ethnic Dutch | 27,658 | 26 (26–26) | 13,575 | 30 (30–31) | 14,083 | 23 (23–23) |
| Turkish | 186 | 23 (15–30) | 122 | 28 (18–38) | 64 | 15 (7–23) |
| Moroccan | 31 | 7 (4–11) | 24 | 8 (4–11) | <10[†] | 7 (0–16) |
| Surinamese | 418 | 42 (37–47) | 220 | 59 (48–69) | 198 | 33 (27–38) |
| Antillean | 58 | 21 (13–30) | 36 | 40 (18–62) | 22 | 12 (4–20) |
| **SAH** | | | | | | |
| Ethnic Dutch | 8,752 | 8 (7–8) | 3,144 | 6 (6–6) | 5,608 | 9 (9–9) |
| Turkish | 60 | 5 (4–6) | 35 | 5 (3–6) | 33 | 5 (3–7) |
| Moroccan | 15 | 2 (1–3) | <10 | 2 (0–3) | <10[†] | 2 (0–4) |
| Surinamese | 150 | 11 (9–13) | 45 | 7 (4–9) | 105 | 13 (10–16) |
| Antillean | 32 | 6 (4–8) | <10 | 4 (1–6) | 23 | 8 (5–12) |

CI, confidence interval; ICH, intracerebral haemorrhage; IS, ischaemic stroke; SAH, subarachnoid haemorrhage.

*Standardised to the age distribution of the Dutch population in 1998.

[†] Actual number of cases not given in line with the Dutch data protection guideline as the cases were < 10.

**Mental health differences:** Ethnic inequalities in depressive symptoms, schizophrenia and sleeping disorders, especially among Turkish and Moroccan ethnic adults, compared to Dutch adults were observed (van Dijk et al., 2013; Anujuo et al., 2014). Prevalence rates for high risk of depression differed across the ethnic groups, from 5.7% (Dutch), 13.1% (Surinamese), 19.5% (Moroccan) to as high as 27.3% (Turkish). Differences in cultural background and socioeconomic status might explain the higher rates among ethnic groups (van Dijk et al., 2013). Additionally, immigrants were observed to use less physical therapy and home care compared to Dutch people. Language competence among the elderly and the additional lower socioeconomic status and education have high explanatory power for all types of health services utilisation (Denktas et al., 2009). Thus, all the above factors might explain the observed differences in mental health status among ethnic groups in the Netherlands.

## Potential interventions to reduce ethnic differences in health status

As it is not possible to alter the migrant status, policies and interventions that aim to reduce these inequalities should tackle the underlying mechanisms that lead to the health disadvantage. One of the first steps in addressing this issue is to broaden the definition of the term "migrant". Currently, the Statistics Netherlands classification of ethnicity is still the most widely used for identifying migrant groups in the Netherlands. However, this approach does not distinguish between first- and second-generation migrants, does not take into account the heterogeneity within ethnic groups and does not differentiate between ethnic subgroups (Statistics Netherlands, 2003). One way to also include next generations in scientific studies is to combine the Statistics Netherlands definition with self-classification of ethnicity.

A second step is to reach high-risk groups of populations and the next generation migrants with policies and interventions. Taking into account that lower education levels, lower income and adverse lifestyle are present among ethnic minorities as compared to the Dutch population, interventions to reduce these inequalities are of great importance. One way to do this may be through online communities or migrant organisations. A good example of an online community in the Netherlands is "Marokko.nl" which is widely accessed by all generations of Moroccan migrants (Verheggen et al.,

2007). In general, socioeconomic factors explain an important part of the vulnerability of migrant children and their parents, but these factors are not easily amendable. Therefore, alongside the policies and interventions that tackle unemployment and other socioeconomic factors, attention should also be directed to enhancing family resilience to stress. One strategy may be to screen mothers for mental health problems during pregnancy which will ensure timely support. Additionally, social workers or other health care workers could provide support to "high risk" families. Religious entities such as churches or mosques, as well as community centres may be good places to begin such initiatives. Inequalities can also be tackled at the neighbourhood level. The mental health of migrant children and their parents was shown to be worst off in ethnically homogeneous neighbourhoods. Lack of social connectedness and increased discrimination in these neighbourhoods were hypothesised to be the underlying mechanisms. Policymakers and urban planners may want to consider diversifying neighbourhoods and/or scale-up the policies and interventions that increase social connectedness and reduce discrimination and prejudiced attitudes at the neighbourhood level.

The high rates of teenage pregnancies and single mothers among Surinamese-Creoles, and Antilleans require special attention. Priority should be given to making interventions that aim to raise the education and awareness to teenage girls (e.g. via awareness-raising campaigns in schools and communities), increasing parental knowledge of teenage pregnancy problems and facilitating help-seeking through friends or mothers. School resources such as peer discussion groups or parent–teacher meetings may be helpful in this regard. Matching the available services to the needs of adolescent girls from diverse ethnic backgrounds and training professionals in working with the age group may also change the negative attitudes towards professional mental health care. Consanguinity is also suggested to be an important determinant on the ethnic differences in health outcomes in the Netherlands. To overcome the health burden imposed by consanguinity, increased public education and awareness on the effects of consanguinity on genetic diseases is needed. Premarital and preconception testing, and prenatal diagnosis and termination of pregnancy (within the allowed limits in religions) should also be part of strategies to reduce the prevalence of congenital anomalies and birth defects.

Finally, the lower utilisation of health systems between ethnic minorities is another challenge the policymakers have to overcome. The lower education and economic status among ethnic groups are important factors that influence the lower utilisation of health systems and subsequently lead to inadequate treatment of different diseases. Interventions that increase patient education about disease and nurse assistance during treatment have been shown to have a beneficial effect on reducing blood pressure among African-Surinamese and Ghanaian patients in the Netherlands, when compared with the usual care (Beune *et al.*, 2014). Moreover, language inability can also be an important factor that impedes people from minority ethnicities from using the health system. Thus, providing health care practices in different languages might help to reduce these differences.

## Conclusions

Large ethnic differences in health status are observed in the Netherlands. These differences persist over time and seem to originate from early life. The observed health differences are partly explained by socioeconomic and lifestyle-related factors among different ethnic groups. Consistent interventions on reducing health differences among ethnic minority groups have been performed in the country. Although there has been a small reduction in these differences, other preventive strategies are needed. Taking into account that ethnic differences in health status are present since early life, future interventions focused on reductions of ethnic disparities are needed to begin from early childhood onwards.

## References

Agyemang, C. *et al.* (2006). Prevalence and management of hypertension among Turkish, Moroccan and native Dutch ethnic groups in Amsterdam, the Netherlands: The Amsterdam Health Monitor Survey. *Journal of Hypertension*, 24, 2169–2176.

Agyemang, C. *et al.* (2014). Ethnic disparities in ischemic stroke, intracerebral hemorrhage, and subarachnoid hemorrhage incidence in the Netherlands. *Stroke*, 45, 3236–3242.

Anand, S.S. *et al.* (2000). Differences in risk factors, atherosclerosis, and cardiovascular disease between ethnic groups in Canada: The Study of Health Assessment and Risk in Ethnic groups (SHARE). *Lancet*, 356, 279–284.

Anujuo, K. et al. (2014). Ethnic differences in self-reported sleep duration in the Netherlands—the HELIUS study. *Sleep Medicine*, 15, 1115–1121.

Bekkers, S. (1999). Winkler Prins *Millennium*, 1000–2000, 320.

Berry, J.D. et al. (2012). Lifetime risks of cardiovascular disease. *New England Journal of Medicine*, 366, 321–329.

Beune, E.J. et al. (2014). Culturally adapted hypertension education (CAHE) to improve blood pressure control and treatment adherence in patients of African origin with uncontrolled hypertension: Cluster-randomized trial. *PLoS One*, 9, e90103.

Bhopal, R.S. et al. (2013). Changes in cardiovascular risk factors in relation to increasing ethnic inequalities in cardiovascular mortality: Comparison of cross-sectional data in the Health Surveys for England 1999 and 2004. *BMJ Open*, 3, e003485.

Bromiker, R. et al. (2004). Association of parental consanguinity with congenital malformations among Arab newborns in Jerusalem. *Clinical Genetics*, 66, 63–66.

Centraal Bureau Voor de Statistiek (2012). Statistisch jaarboek. Tuijtel: *Hardinxveld-Giessendam*, 239.

Centraal Bureau Voor de Statistiek. Jaargang 53 (2005). Bevolkingstrends, 4e kwartaal 2005. *CBS Voorburg*, 79.

Centraal Bureau Voor de Statistiek. Jaargang 55 (2007). Bevolkingstrends, 1e kwartaal 2007. *CBS Voorburg*, 90.

Crul, M & Vermeulen, H. (2003). The second generation in Europe. *Integrational Migration Review*, 37, 965–986.

Curtin, P. (1989). *Death by Migration: Europe's Encounter with the Tropical World in the Nineteenth Century*. Cambridge University Press, Cambridge, UK.

Dannemann, A. (2011). Ethnicity and comorbidities in an overweight and obese multiethnic childhood cohort in Berlin. *Acta Paediatrica*, 100, 578–584.

De Hoog, M.L. et al. (2011). Overweight at age two years in a multi-ethnic cohort (ABCD study): The role of prenatal factors, birth outcomes and postnatal factors. *BMC Public Health*, 11, 611.

De Hoog, M.L. et al. (2012). Ethnic differences in cardiometabolic risk profile at age 5–6 years: The ABCD study. *PLoS One*, 7, e43667.

De Wilde, J.A. et al. (2009). Trends in overweight and obesity prevalence in Dutch, Turkish, Moroccan and Surinamese South Asian children in the Netherlands. *Archives of Disease in Childhood*, 94, 795–800.

Denktas, S. et al. (2009). Ethnic background and differences in health care use: A national cross-sectional study of native Dutch and immigrant elderly in the Netherlands. *International Journal for Equity in Health*, 8, 35.

Dourleijn, E.D. (2011a). Migratie en demografisch profiel. In: Vluchtelingengroepen in Nederland. *Sociaal en Cultureel Planbureau*. Den Haag, 240, NED.

Dourleijn, E.D. (2011b). Vluchtelingengroepen in Nederland; over de integratie van Afghaanse, Iraakse, Iraanse en Somalische migranten. *Sociaal en Cultureel Planbureau*. Den Haag, 240.

Drooger, J.C. (2005). Ethnic differences in prenatal growth and the association with maternal and fetal characteristics. *Ultrasound in Obstetrics and Gyneocology*, 26, 115–122.

Engbertsen, G. (2006). Verhef de onderklasse. In: *De Volkskrant* 11 Februari 2006.

Extra, G. (1996). *De multiculturele samenleving in ontwikkeling: Feiten, beeldvorming en beleid*. Tilburg University Press, 61, NED.

Fraser, A.M. et al. (1995). Association of young maternal age with adverse reproductive outcomes. *New England Journal of Medicine*, 332, 1113–1117.

Gishti, O. et al. (2014). Ethnic disparities in general and abdominal adiposity at school age: A multiethnic population-based cohort study in the Netherlands. *Annals of Nutrition and Metabolism*, 64, 208–217.

Gishti, O. et al. (2015). Body mass index, total and abdominal fat distribution and cardiovascular risk factors in school-age children. *Pediatric Research*, 77, 710–718.

Gluckman, P.D. et al. (2008). Effect of in utero and early-life conditions on adult health and disease. *New England Journal of Medicine*, 359, 61–73.

Grant, J.C. & Bittles, A.H. (1997). The comparative role of consanguinity in infant and childhood mortality in Pakistan. *Annals of Human Genetics*, 61, 143–149.

Herfs, P.G.P. (1994). *Verslag van een studiereis naar Aruba, Bonaire en Curaçao*. Afdeling Studentenzaken., 16, Universiteit Utrecht, NED.

Hussain, R. et al. (2001). Consanguinity and early mortality in the Muslim populations of India and Pakistan. *American Journal of Human Biology*, 13, 777–787.

Jaddoe, V.W. et al. (2012). The Generation R Study: Design and cohort update 2012. *European Journal of Epidemiology*, 27, 739–756.

Khoury, M.J. et al. (1987). An epidemiologic approach to the evaluation of the effect of inbreeding on prereproductive mortality. *American Journal of Epidemiology*, 125, 251–262.

Kramer, M.S. (2000). Socio-economic disparities in pregnancy outcome: Why do the poor fare so poorly? *Paediatric and Perinatal Epidemiology*, 14, 194–210.

Kramer, M.S. et al. (2001). Socio-economic disparities in preterm birth: Causal pathways and mechanisms. *Paediatric and Perinatal Epidemiology*, 15(2), 104–123.

Landrine, H. & Klonoff, E.A. (2004). Culture change and ethnic-minority health behavior: An operant theory of acculturation. *Journal of behavioural Medicine*, 27, 527–555.

Lucassen, J. (1984). *Naar de kusten van de Noordzee; trekarbeid in Europees perspectief 1600–1900*. Thesis Universiteit Utrecht. Gouda, 407, NED.

Lucassen, L. & Lucassen, J. (2012). Winnaars en verliezers; een nuchtere balans van vijfhonderd jaar immigratie. Uitgeverij Bert Bakker, 204, Amsterdam, NED.

Netherlands Scientific Council for Government Policy (1990). Immigrant policy. *Den Haag*, 10, NED.

Nicolaas, H.W.E. & Ooijevaar, J. (2010). Demografie van (niet-westerse) allochtonen in Nederland. *Centraal Bureau voor de Statistiek (CBS)-Bevolkingstrends*, 22–34.

Obdeijn, H. & Schrover, M. (2008). Komen en gaan. *Uitgeverij Bert Bakker*, 412, Amsterdam, NED.

Raatikainen, K. *et al.* (2005). Marriage still protects pregnancy. *BJOG*, 112, 1411–1416.

Ranganathan, M & Bhopal, R. (2006). Exclusion and inclusion of nonwhite ethnic minority groups in 72 North American and European cardiovascular cohort studies. *PLoS Med*, 3, e44.

Roijen, J. (1994). *Minderheden in Nederland: Statistisch vademecum 1993/1994*. SDU/CBS. Rotterdam, 173, NED.

Sahin, S. (2003). *Lessen en aanbevelingen voor het migratiebeleid. In: Christen Democratische Verkenningen*. Den Haag, 164, NED.

Schulpen, T.W. *et al.* (2001). Influences of ethnicity on perinatal and child mortality in the Netherlands. *Archives of Disease in Childhood*, 84, 222–226.

Statistics Netherlands (2003). Migrants in the Netherlands 2003. Voorburg/Heerlen, 10, NED.

Statistics Netherlands (2004). Allochtonen in Nederland 2004. Voorburg/Heerlen, 10, NED.

Stoltenberg, C. *et al.* (1998). Influence of consanguinity and maternal education on risk of stillbirth and infant death in Norway, 1967–1993. *American Journal of Epidemiology*, 148, 452–459.

Teeuw, M.E. *et al.* (2014). Consanguineous marriage and reproductive risk: Attitudes and understanding of ethnic groups practising consanguinity in Western society. *European Journal of Human Genetics*, 22, 452–457.

Ten Kate, L.P. *et al.* (2014). Consanguinity and endogamy in the Netherlands: Demographic and medical genetic aspects. *Human Hereditary*, 77, 161–166.

Troe, E.J. *et al.* (2006). Ethnic differences in total and cause-specific infant mortality in The Netherlands. *Paediatric and Perinatal Epidemiology*, 20, 140–147.

Tuncbilek, E. & Koc, I. (1994). Consanguineous marriage in Turkey and its impact on fertility and mortality. *Annals of Human Genetics*, 58, 321–329.

Ujcic-Voortman, J.K. *et al.* (2011). Ethnic differences in systemic inflammation: An investigation of C-reactive protein levels among Moroccan, Turkish and Dutch groups in the Netherlands. *Atherosclerosis*, 218, 511–516.

Van Dijk, T.K. et al. (2013). Multidimensional health locus of control and depressive symptoms in the multi-ethnic population of the Netherlands. *Social Psychiatry and Psychiatric Epidemiology*, 48, 1931–1939.

Van oeffelen, A.A. et al. (2013). Incidence of acute myocardial infarction in first and second generation minority groups: Does the second generation converge towards the majority population? *International Journal of Cardiology*, 168, 5422–5429.

Van Vliet, M. (2009). Ethnic differences in cardiometabolic risk profile in an overweight/obese paediatric cohort in the Netherlands: A cross-sectional study. *Cardiovascular Diabetology*, 8, 1–9.

Veldhuis, L. (2013). Ethnic background and overweight among 5-year-old children: The "Be Active, Eat Right" Study. *ISRN Pediatrics*, 2013: 861246, doi: 10.1155/2013/861246.

Verheggen, P. (2007). Beraken van Nieuwe Nederlanders: Bereik van cultuurgebonden media. *Motivaction*, Amsterdam, NED.

Verkuil, D. (2008). Dynamiek en stagnatie; de Republiek in de Gouden Eeuw. Noordhoff Uitgevers, 110, Groningen, NED.

Walker, S.E. et al. (2012). Racial/ethnic discrepancies in the metabolic syndrome begin in childhood and persist after adjustment for environmental factors. *Nutrition, Metabolism and Cardiovascular Diseases*, 22, 141–148.

Wentholt, R. (1967). *Buitenlandse arbeiders in Nederland; een veelzijdige benadering van een complex vraagstuk.* Van Mantgem & De Does, Leiden, NED.

Winkleby, M.A. (1999). Ethnic variation in cardiovascular disease risk factors among children and young adults: Findings from the Third National Health and Nutrition Examination Survey, 1988–1994. *Journal of American Medical Association*, 281, 1006–1013.

Zlotogora, J. (2002). What is the birth defect risk associated with consanguineous marriages? *American Journal of Medical Genetics*, 109, 70–71.

# Chapter 9

# Health equity: evidence-based guidelines, e-learning and physician advocacy for migrant populations in Canada

Dr Kevin Pottie and Dr Doug Gruner

## Introduction

Worldwide, there are more than 234 million international migrants whose movement across borders has significant health impacts in many countries (IOM, 2013). Persons living without political status suffer isolation, discrimination and deterioration in health and economic productivity. For example, migrants without a health card or basic social support suffer increased mental and physical health problems (Kirmayer *et al.*, 2011). Visible minority status deserves special attention as it is associated with higher levels of discrimination such as bullying of children in schools, more risk of physical and sexual violence, and reduced access to jobs and health services (Pottie *et al.*, 2014).

Immigration has been and remains an important force shaping Canadian cultural and linguistic identity. Health characteristics associated with the movement of large numbers of people have current and future implications for migrants, health practitioners and health systems (Gushulak *et al.*, 2011).

Until recently, there has been a lack of evidence-based information to support policy, health systems, education and primary care practitioners. Health needs may be unique and access to care aggravated by neglect and disadvantage. Migrant health needs may differ significantly from those of Canadian-born people due to differential prior exposure to certain diseases, lack of access to preventive health care, environmental exposures in source countries that may have limited resources or different health care systems. Language, cultural factors and lack of familiarity with the new health care system can impair access and delivery of primary health care after arrival (Pottie *et al.*, 2015). This may be compounded by health care providers' lack of skills and awareness of the specific health care needs of this population (Mota *et al.*, 2015).

## Health equity

Evidence-based science is the foundation for health equity (O'Neill *et al.*, 2014). Health equity aims to address unfair and unjust health inequality outcomes using a variety of responses. Whitehead (1992) has also noted that inequity has a moral and ethical dimension. Health equity responses aim to increase political will, build provider capacity to ensure equitable service provision, strengthen capacity of state policy-making capacity and service delivery, and use non-state mechanisms for policy coordination, harnessing NGOs as non-state providers (Bornemisza *et al.*, 2010).

Canada is playing a lead role in health equity alongside the United Kingdom. New health equity methods support equity-focused system reviews (Welch *et al.*, 2012) and evidence-based guidelines (Welch *et al.*, in press). At the university level, evidence-based approaches support training to prepare physicians, nurses and frontline staff, and health equity impact assessment is being used to prevent unintended harms and consequences related to programmes and policies (Miramontes *et al.*, 2013).

Health equity responses come from various sectors and include planned and coordinated action. They require civil society and political will, data to make credible equity interpretations, inclusion of disadvantaged migrant communities and Open Access training modules. This article uses three case studies, examples from the Public Health Agency of Canada's Migrant Health Guidelines, University of Ottawa's Refugee and Global Heath e-Learning, and Canadian physician advocacy that mobilised organisations and practitioners to save social services and bring back health care for refugees and asylum seekers in Canada.

## Case 1: Canadian immigrant health guidelines

### *Migration health until 2010*

Over the past decade, researchers and practitioners had begun to recognise the need for guidance to address the unique health needs of migrant populations. Newly arriving migrants often faced poorer health outcomes related to previous living conditions, refugee camp stressor, limited official language proficiency, gender and socioeconomic status (Ng *et al.*, 2011). Beach *et al.* (2006) led a review on ethnic and visible minorities that documented health inequities and showed promising health care interventions that could address them. In Australia, guidelines for community engagement and cultural competency emerged from the public health sector (Australian Government, 2005) as did the Australasian infectious disease screening guidelines for refugees from Africa (Murray *et al.*, 2009). Around the same time, the USA published *Immigrant Health* (Walker *et al.*, 2007) a textbook covering a range of health conditions.

But until very recently, migrant health has been a field led by action and driven by passion and experience — in disadvantaged populations such action may bring benefits but also harms (Leaning *et al.*, 2011). Evidence in the form of effectiveness and harms, especially with a primary health care focus, has begun to play an increasing role in community care guidelines. One example of the new role for evidence is the Public Health Agency of Canada who funded the development of the Evidence Based Guidelines for Newly Arriving Immigrants and Refugees (Pottie *et al.*, 2011). These guidelines were driven by primary care practitioners from across Canada who selected priority preventable and treatable health conditions in which guidelines were needed (Swinkels *et al.*, 2011).

### *Evidence-based migrant health guidelines*

The Canadian guidelines are the most comprehensive evidence-based migrant health guidelines, taking on mental health conditions, women's health conditions as well as infectious diseases (Pottie *et al.*, 2011). The team reviewed the world's published evidence to synthesise benefits and harms of screening, and other interventions for migrants. The guidelines showed that preventive care must be informed by the person's region or country of origin and migration history. Refugees with low income and limited proficiency in English or French have increased risk of a decline in health and should be considered in the assessment and delivery of preventive care. An Open Access App was created to provide clinicians with an instant set of recommendations based on age, gender, region of origin and migration status (CCIRH, 2015), And storyteller versions for each recommendation were created and made available at Cochrane Podcasts: Immigrant Health (Cochrane Community, 2015).

## *Recommendations*

The following snapshots provide a brief look at how the evidence-based recommendations address health equity.

**Vaccinations:** A large proportion of migrant women, children and men are more susceptible to vaccine-preventable diseases than the general population: measles, mumps, rubella, diphtheria, pertussis and tetanus. The Canadian recommendations resolve the confusion among practitioners concerning unclear vaccine records and steer practitioners away from costly and time-consuming serology testing and focus on the benefits of simply updating routine vaccinations.

**Intestinal parasites:** Several novel recommendations arose from seeking evidence for clear benefits and harms. For example, in the case of possible asymptomatic intestinal parasite infections, the guidelines recommend serology (blood) testing for certain parasites that can cause the most harm long term and foregoing traditional stool testing for ova and parasites in asymptomatic patients, marking a shift in practice. These recommendations reduce transportation and unnecessary out-of-pocket costs and focus attention on parasites with highest morbidity, strongyloides and schistosomiasis.

**Varicella:** Among immigrants and refugees from tropical countries, up to 50% of adolescents are susceptible to varicella and are at increased risk of severe varicella. Pregnant migrant women and their babies are at highest risk for complications of varicella infection. The recommendation highlights varicella vaccination for susceptible migrants.

**Tuberculosis:** The recommendations highlight the number needed to treat and the number needed to harm in screening for latent tuberculosis for various migrant groups. Mantoux testing is recommended for high-risk migrant groups as soon as possible after arrival in Canada. It must also be linked to the offer of INH treatment for latent tuberculosis infection in those with a positive result and monitoring for hepatotoxicity harms for patients of all ages.

**Hepatitis C:** About 3% of migrants are infected with the chronic Hepatitis C virus (up to 18% in certain migrant populations) most of whom will be asymptomatic, but the majority of whom will be eligible for treatment. Treatment response rate is better in those who have not yet developed chronic liver disease (cirrhosis) The Canadian guidelines recommendation for routine screening for Hepatitis C has led the screening field with its focus on right to health.

**Post-traumatic stress disorder:** Forty per cent of Canadian migrants come from countries involved in war or with significant social unrest and have been exposed to traumatic events before migration. Some clinics in the USA, UK and Australia have implemented routine trauma screening. But the Canadian recommendations highlight the lack of evidence for benefits from routine screening and the potential for harms and do not recommend routine screening.

**Dental disease:** While many physicians may avoid examination of teeth, our guidelines highlight the two-fold increase in obtaining appropriate dental care when a physician actively examines and refers a patient with dental pathology to a dental specialist. This emphasises the health equity role for physicians in diagnosing and seeking management for treatable diseases.

**Contraception:** Unmet contraceptive needs can lead to unwanted pregnancies, which is associated with negative outcomes such as abortion, failure to adopt healthy pregnancy recommendations and limitation of women's ability to achieve educational, employment and economic goals. The recommendations highlight the importance of giving women choice and considering regional contraceptive preferences (IUD use in Eastern Europe and Middle East and Asia) and the need for early screening for unmet contraceptive needs and education regarding emergency contraception.

## Case 2: Refugee health e-learning for medical students

Historically, medical students have been sent to work in community settings and international settings without training. Programmes have not included realistic training objectives for the student, or realistic expectations for the receiving organisation. Until recently, there has been a focus on experience, and much less on ethics or engagement or on health equity and the prevention of harms for disadvantaged populations.

### *Community service learning*

Community service learning programmes have stood as an exception. Originally devised in the USA in relation to overseas volunteers, they have grown into many areas of universities. In medicine, these programmes have grown alongside overseas elective programmes. At the University of Ottawa, a "pre-departure" training approach has been instituted into a community service learning programme in which junior medical students work in a community shelter with newly arriving refugees.

The Refugees and Global Health e-Learning Program (Pottie *et al.*, 2013) includes seven online modules with learning objectives, and case scenarios to guide the learner through training that lays the groundwork for the unique knowledge, skills and competencies needed for refugee and global health. The 60–80 minute e-Learning Program gives students the chance to learn more about refugees and health systems and to recognise pitfalls and challenges that often come with refugee health issues. Modules and podcasts introduce and examine case studies on neonatal tetanus, suicide, domestic violence, malaria and post-traumatic stress disorder. Refugee and global health experts challenge the learner and provide practical reflections by linking users to evidence-based migrant health guidelines and other readily available resources. The goal of this e-Learning Program is to introduce the learner to the basic concepts of refugee and global health, and prepare them for in-depth discussions on challenges and opportunities of developing health systems in resource-limited settings.

As with the community service learning students, the modules are systematically used for training at a National Summer Institute for Student Leaders in Refugee Health. All participants from across Canada must complete the e-Learning Program. For example, participants who complete a quiz with a score of >75% will receive a Refugee Health Training Certificate and qualify for additional workshop training and refugee patient engagement in the shelter.

## *Research and evaluation*

In an effort to evaluate the effectiveness and usability of these e-learning modules, a mixed method study comparing e-learning to traditional peer-reviewed global health articles was conducted. This evaluation used quantitative quiz and survey and qualitative inquiry consisting of four post-intervention semi-structured focus groups. Outcomes included pre/post quiz and self-assessment measures based on validated tools from a Global Health CanMEDS Competency Model. The results were analysed using statistical software and focus group transcripts were coded using quantitative software and grounded theory.

More than 150 pre-clerkship medical students from three Canadian medical schools participated in the evaluation. Overall, comparing the pre- to post-results, both groups showed a small increase in the mean quiz scores and self-assessed competencies ($p < 0.5$). No statistically significant difference was found between the two approaches. Focus groups highlighted the usefulness of the e-learning to integrate global health concepts as a repository of resources. They also identified personal interest, online learning preferences, convenience and integration into the curriculum as incentives to complete the e-learning. Early integration barriers included content overload and technical difficulties with the beta version, details that were easily revised after the study (Gruner *et al.*, in press).

Students appreciated the pre-refugee shelter training. Both the e-Learning Program and the peer-reviewed articles were effective in the acquisition of global and refugee health concepts. Many students, however, preferred e-learning given its interactive, multi-media approach, access to links and reference materials, and its capacity to engage and re-engage over long periods of time.

This case illustrates the importance of integrating evidence-based medicine into the medical student curriculum, the importance of pre-community entry training when working with refugee or other disadvantaged populations, and the importance of evaluating training tools using both quantitative and qualitative methods to ensure high-quality education and, thus, high-quality health equity initiatives.

## Case 3: Physician advocacy

Canada had for many years an international reputation for ensuring refugees have reasonable access to health care. This case study will focus on recent cuts to government funding for refugee health care, and the response from health care practitioners and others concerned with the consequences for refugees and Canadian society overall.

### *Skills set for advocacy*

Physicians in today's global context need to have knowledge, skills and attitudes that will prepare them for, and enable them to provide, high-quality care to a diverse population. Having medical knowledge is clearly not enough, a good physician needs to be an excellent communicator, they need to be able to work well and collaborate with others, they need to be organised managers but at the very centre they need to be empathetic and passionate as advocates for their patients. Advocacy is manifested in many forms, from making a few extra calls or writing letters to help patients find affordable housing, to confronting the injustice of a poorly devised government policy that puts patient's health at risk. The recent cuts to the Interim Federal Health Programme (IFHP) are an example of physician advocacy on a large scale.

## *Programme for asylum seekers*

Canada has for many years maintained a number of positive policies towards refugees such as access to employment, social assistance, education and, until recently, access to health care through IFHP. Since 1957, the IFHP had provided temporary coverage of medical costs for refugees (Canada Gazette, 2012). The IFHP applied to all resettled refugees and asylum seekers, and covered doctor's visits, diagnostic tests and medications. This health care coverage was similar to that of low-income Canadians.

On 30 June 2012, the Canadian government significantly reduced the scope of the IFHP (Governement of Canada, Citizenship and Immigration Canada, 2012). Coverage of basic medication was eliminated, except for conditions threatening public health or safety, for almost all IFHP beneficiaries. Medical services were no longer covered for asylum seekers from certain designated countries except for conditions posing a risk to public health or safety. Without health care coverage, significant conditions (diabetes, heart conditions and mental health) went untreated (Barnes, 2012). A secondary effect of this government policy has been outright refusal of care or demands for fees by doctors and clinics which may be linked to a number of factors. These include confusion about which services are covered, difficulties checking the person's status, concerns that services may not be reimbursed by the IFHP and time-consuming billing procedures. Faced with uncertainty and additional effort, many clinicians prefer to refuse people with IFHP coverage or to demand fees.

Health care practitioners across Canada have expressed outrage at the IFHP cuts (Canadian Medical Association, 2012), which put the lives of refugees at risk, cost taxpayers more money and threaten public health. The advocacy began with a flurry of e-mails from physicians who serve refugees expressing concern over the ill-conceived policy. What followed was unprecedented as doctors and other health workers across the country participated in sit-ins at cabinet ministers' offices, interrupted ministers during public announcements and organised protests, all to bring attention to the plight of refugees.

## Canadian Doctors for Refugee Care

This ad hoc group would eventually form Canadian Doctors for Refugee Care (CDRC, 2012). On 18 June 2012, CDRC organised the National Day of Action which took place in 13 major cities across the country, shining the media spotlight on the injustice of this very egregious policy that was soon to be implemented. The advocacy was highly effective as the government did backtrack and reversed the cuts for one class of refugee, the government-assisted refugee (GAR). The advocacy did not stop with this victory and CDRC began collaboration with the legal community by taking the federal government to court (Eggertson, 2013).

The legal challenge which began on 25 February 2013 raises two main arguments: first, the denial of IFH coverage to asylum seekers is unconstitutional in that it violates the Canadian Charter of Rights and Freedoms (1982) (Government of Canada, 2015), and second, it is in breach of Canada's international obligations under the Convention Relating to the Status of Refugees (1951) (UNHCR, 1951) and the Convention on the Rights of the Child (1989) (UN General Assembly, 1989).

The Federal Court decision in the matter of *Canadian Doctors for Refugee Care v. Canada (Attorney general)* 2014 FC 651 (Federal Court of Canada, 2014) was released on 4 July 2014. The cuts to the IFHP were deemed unconstitutional in that they were found to violate Sections 12 and 15 of the Charter. The health cuts were thus deemed to be invalid and the federal government was given four months to reinstate the previous IFHP. Surprisingly, the federal government did not fully comply (Government of Canada, 2014) with the decision. In doing so, the federal government is not respecting the Federal Court's order and is in breach of the rule of law and so the advocacy efforts continue with CDRC preparing for its fourth National Day of Action in June 2015.

## Next steps

Canadians can choose to facilitate refugee integration, welcome them as they strive to create a new home in a safe environment for themselves and their children, and as a community grow with them and learn from them. Canadians can also choose to exacerbate the existing barriers, make it more difficult to build communities and create divisions between Canadians born in Canada and our newcomers. The cuts to the IFHP are an example of the latter path. Canadians face a fundamental choice as to whether they want to build a society based on inclusion or exclusion.

## Conclusion

Health equity for disadvantaged migrants requires a diverse range of planned and coordinated actions. It demands assessment and policies to improve social determinants of health, and this is supported worldwide with the Health Equity Impact Assessment movement and led by Australia, New Zealand, the UK and Canada. Evidence-based clinical guidelines to improve quality and consistency of health care services is an emerging movement in many countries including Australia, New Zealand, the USA and the UK, and most recently the European Union.

Health equity responses require evaluated training programmes for students who will be working with disadvantaged persons. Community service learning and social accountability movements at medical schools are supporting these types of initiatives. Finally, equity may require the courage of physician advocacy for migrant populations that face discrimination and withdrawal of basic health care services, a situation which has recently been reversed in Canada and more recently in Spain, thanks in a large part to strong physician advocacy programmes.

Refugees and asylum seekers remain under the jurisdiction of the UNHCR. The Five Country Initiative includes Australia, New Zealand, Canada, the USA and the UK. This group works together to set health screening, presumptive treatment and health education policy. It plays a key role in coordinated mass resettlement of refugees from Burma, Bhutan and other long-term camps. Europe has struggled to define and implement its policies across 31 European Union countries. There continues to be a lack of consensus between southern and northern European countries on the management of irregular migrants and asylum seekers, and this has not solved the precarious migration scenario that continues across the Mediterranean. Europe's inability to find consensus notwithstanding, there does appear to be more coordination and communication between the global north and UN agencies such as the International Organization for Migration (IOM) and UNHCR. In recent years there was a shift towards restrictive policies and when this is done across many countries it will increasingly require a multinational health equity response.

## *Take home message*

- Health equity responses must be grounded in evidence-based science.
- Equity responses must come from all sectors and should take diverse forms.
- Training our next generation of professionals to effectively respond to disadvantage should be a health professional education priority.

## Acknowledgements

We would like to acknowledge Andre Renzaho for his helpful comments on earlier versions of this paper and Sheila Cyril for her expert technical assistance.

## References

Australian Government National Health and Medical Research Council AG (2005). Cultural competency in health: A guide for policy, partnerships and participation. The Council, Canberra, AUS.

Barnes, S. (2012). The Real Cost of Cutting Refugee Health Benefits: A Health Equality Impact Assessment. The Wellesley Institute, Toronto, CAN. Available at: http://www.toronto.ca/legdocs/mmis/2012/hl/comm/communicationfile-30470.pdf. Accessed 20 May 2015.

Beach, M.C. *et al.* (2006). Improving health care quality for racial/ethnic minorities: A systematic review of the best evidence regarding provider and organization interventions. *BMC Public Health*, 6, 104.

Bornemisza, O. *et al.* (2010). Promoting health equity in conflict-affected fragile states. *Social Science and Medicine*, 70, 80–88.

Canada Gazette (2012). Order Respecting the Interim Federal Health Program (2012). P.C. 2012-433, April 5, 2012 — SI/2012-26. Canada Gazette, Part II, Vol.146, No. 9. Available at: http://www.gazette.gc.ca/rp-pr/p2/2012/2012-04-25/html/si-tr26-eng.html. Accessed 20 May 2015.

Canadian Medical Association, Royal College of Physicians and Surgeons of Canada, College of Family Physicians of Canada, Canadian Nurses Association, Canadian Association of Social Workers, Canadian Association of Optometrists, Canadian Dental Association, Canadian Federation of Medical Students, and Canadian Pharmacists Association, 5 December (2012). Letter to the Minister of Citizenship and Immigration, Jason Kenney. Available at: http://www.caswacts.ca/sites/default/files/open_letters/Letter%20-. Accessed 20 May 2015.

CCIRH (2015). Canadian Collaboration for Immigrant and Refugee Health: Migrant Health Knowledge Exchange Network, 2015. Available at: www.ccirhken.ca. Accessed 1 June 2015.

CDRC (2012). Canadian Doctors for Refugee Care (2012). Available at: http://www.doctorsforrefugeecare.ca/. Accessed 20 May 2015.

Cochrane Community (beta) (2015). Available at: http://community.cochrane.org/podcasts/issue/Immigrant%20Health/577. Accessed 1 June 2015.

Eggertson, L. (2013). Doctors promise protests along with court challenge to refugee health cuts. *Canadian Medical Association Journal*, 185(7), E 275–76.

Federal Court of Canada (2014). Canadian Doctors for Refugee Care, The Canadian Association of Refugee Lawyers, *Daniel Garcia Rodrigues, Hanif Ayubi, and Justice for Children and Youth vs. Attorney General of Canada and Minister of Citizenship and Immigration.* Available at: http://cas-ncr-nter03.cas-satj.gc.ca/rss/T-356-13%20Cdn%Doctors%20v%20AGC%20Judgment%20and%20reasons.pdf. Accessed 20 May 2015.

Government of Canada, Citizenship and Immigration Canada (2012). Reform of the Interim Federal Health Program ensures fairness, protects public health and safety. Available at: http://www.cic.gc.ca/english/department/media/releases/2012/2012-04-25.asp. Accessed 20 May 2015.

Government of Canada, Citizenship and Immigration Canada (2014). Interim Federal Health Program Policy. Available at: http://www.cic.gc.ca/english/department/laws-policy/ifhp.asp. Accessed 12 May 2015.

Government of Canada: Justice Laws website (2015).Canadian Charter of Rights and Freedoms (Constitution Act, 1982). 1982, c. 11 (U.K.), Schedule B. Available at: http://laws-lois.justice.gc.ca/eng/Const/page-15.html. Accessed 20 May 2015.

Gruner, D. *et al.* Introducing global health competencies into undergraduate medical school curriculum using an e-learning program: A mixed method pilot study. *BMC Medical Education*, (in press).

Gushulak, B.D. *et al.* (2011). Migration and health in Canada: Health in the global village. *CMAJ*, 183(12), E952–E958.

IOM (2013). World Migration Report 2013. (IOM). ISBN 978-92-9068-668-2. ISSN 1561-5502. Geneva, SWI.

Kirmayer, L.J. *et al.* (2011). Common mental health problems in immigrants and refugees: General approach in primary care. *CMAJ*, 183(12), E959–E967.

Leaning, J. *et al.* (2011). Public health equity in refugee situations. *Conflict and Health*, 5, 6.

Miramontes, L. *et al.* (2013). The top four challenges to considering migrant populations in health impact assessment: A call for migrant equity reporting guidelines. *WHO Bulletin*, Geneva, SWI.

Mota, L. *et al.* (2015). Rejecting and accepting international migrant patients into primary care practices — a mixed method study. *Journal of Migration, Health and Social Care*, 11(2), 108–129.

Murray, R. *et al.* (2009). Diagnosis, management and prevention of infections in recently arrived refugees. Australasian Society for Infectious Diseases, Sydney, AUS. Available at: www.asid.net.au/downloads/RefugeeGuidelines.pdf. Accessed 30 March 2015.

Ng, E. *et al.* (2011). Limited official language proficiency and decline in health status: A dynamic view from the longitudinal survey of immigrants to Canada. *Health Reports*, 22(4), 15–23.

O'Neill, J. *et al.* (2014). Applying an equity lens to interventions: Using PROGRESS to ensure consideration of socially stratifying factors to illuminate inequities in health. *Journal of Clinical Epidemiology*, 67(1), 56–64.

Pottie, K. *et al.* (2011). Overview: Evidence-based clinical guidelines for immigrants and refugees. *CMAJ*, 183(12), E824–E925.

Pottie, K. *et al.* (2013). Refugees and Global Health: A Global Health E-Learning Program, Canadian Collaboration for Immigrant and Refugee Health (CCIRH) and the University of Ottawa, Canada. Available at: www.ccirhken.ca. Accessed 21 May 2015.

Pottie, K. *et al.* (2014). Improving delivery of primary care for vulnerable migrants: Delphi consensus to prioritize innovative practice strategies. *Family Physician*, 60, e32–40.

Pottie, K. *et al.* (2015). Do immigrant adolescents face higher rates of bullying and other violence, peer aggression and suicide than do non-immigrant adolescents? A systematic review. *Journal of Immigrant and Minority Health*. DOI: 10.1007/s10903-014-0108-6.

Swinkels, H. *et al.* (2011). Development of guidelines for recently arrived immigrants and refugees to Canada: Delphi consensus on selecting preventable and treatable conditions. *CMAJ*, 183(12), E928–E932.

UN General Assembly Convention on the Rights of the Child. (1989). 1577 UNTS 3. Available at: http://www.refworld.org/docid/3ae6b38f0.html. Accessed 21 May 2015.

UNHCR, (1951). Convention Relating to the Status of Refugees (1951). 189 UNTS 137. Available at: http://www.unhcr.org/protect/PROTECTION/3b66c2aa10.pdf. Accessed 21 May 2015.

Walker, P.F., Barnett, E.D., Stauffer, W.M. (eds). (2007). *Immigrant Medicine*. Saunders Elsevier, Philadelphia, PA.

Welch, V. *et al.* (2012). PRISMA-Equity 2012 Extension: Reporting Guidelines for Systematic Reviews with a Focus on Health Equity. *PLoS Med*, 9(10), e1001333. doi:10.1371/journal.pmed.1001333.

Welch, V., *et al.* (in press). GRADE Equity: Introduction: Why health equity and GRADE guidelines? *Journal of Clinical Epidemiology.*

Whitehead, M. (1992). The concepts and principles of equity and health. *International Journal of Health Services*, 22(3), 429–45.

# Chapter 10

# Hispanic immigration and the epidemiological paradox

Professor Mary Lou de Leon Siantz

This chapter focuses on describing a population health phenomenon that is unique to the health of Hispanic immigrants in the USA: the epidemiological paradox. "Hispanic" is a term established by the United States Congress in 1976 and refers to a population that reflects diversity through history, nationality, social class, legal status and generation, encompassing both descendants of early Spanish settlers and immigrants from central and Swouth America, and the Caribbean. It is a term used interchangeably with "Latino" in the USA. The most numerous of Hispanics/Latinos are Mexicans who also reflect the largest numbers of Hispanic immigrants to the USA (Rumbaut, 2006). Internationally, the USA is the primary destination for immigrants from Mexico. Approximately 96% of foreign-born Mexicans migrate into the USA (Connor, 2012). Those who are recent newcomers to the USA are also younger, poorer, and less educated than non-Hispanic whites. Surprisingly, despite their poverty and limited education, these Hispanic/Latino immigrants, primarily from Mexico, paradoxically experience better outcomes in certain areas of health than the average US population (Marger, 2011).

This phenomenon has been termed the "epidemiological paradox," as well as the "immigrant health paradox." It refers to consistent research findings that have documented positive health outcomes in two areas, birth and adult mortality, primarily among immigrants of Mexican origin (Markides and Eschbach, 2005; Rumbaut et al., 2006). This paradox was first described by Kyriakos Markides who discovered that the health status of Hispanics in the south-west USA was more like the health status of other Whites than that of African-Americans, despite the fact that the socioeconomic status of Hispanics was closer to African-Americans than that of non-Hispanic whites (Markides and Coreil, 1986).

In the 1990s, growing evidence began to establish a mortality advantage among Mexican Americans as well as among other Hispanic populations. This observation transformed the "epidemiological paradox" to the "Hispanic paradox" (Markides et al., 1997; Palloni and Morenoff, 2001). Others concluded that the paradox was evident in two particular age groups: infants and older adults (Franzini et al., 2001).

Hayes-Bautista (2004) further documented a healthy profile for the 7.7 million California Latinos living in California, from 1985 to 1990, with Mexicans the largest Latino population of California primarily living in Los Angeles. He found that they had the smallest rates of low birthweight infants and infant mortality, equal to non-Hispanic whites and Asians. However, in the same study, California Latinos not only had lower adjusted death rates resulting from disease, strokes and cancers but also higher death rates than non-Hispanic whites, blacks or Asians, due to motor vehicle accidents, and cirrhosis. California Latinos also had a higher rate of diabetes than non-Hispanic whites or Asians.

While much research on the paradox continues to focus on mortality, more recent studies have expanded perspectives. Studies have investigated the impact of the epidemiological paradox across the lifespan in other areas in addition to the established areas of infant outcomes, disease and mortality rates. Researchers have explored additional factors that might help understand the paradox. To date, three possible theories have been used to explain the Hispanic epidemiological paradox. These include (1) the healthy migrant effect, (2) reverse migration or the salmon effect, and (3) the Latino lifestyle (Thomson et al., 2013).

What follows is an overview of these theories. They include (1) emerging topics concerning the impact of the epidemiological paradox across the lifespan for Hispanic/Latinos, especially Mexican immigrants; (2) theories that have helped to conceptualise the epidemiological paradox, (3) limitations of what is known about the paradox, and (4) research that is still needed to fully comprehend the importance of this phenomenon for Latino immigrant population health, especially for foreign-born Mexicans who migrate from Mexico to the USA. About 96% of all Mexicans who leave Mexico immigrate to the USA, the top destination for Mexican immigrants, their top destination internationally (Connor, 2012).

## Epidemiological paradox: a lifespan perspective

While high birth rates and low death rates among Hispanic/Latinos account for most of their increased population growth rate (Fry and Center, 2008; Passel et al., 2011), immigration plays an important role with about 35.5% of all Hispanics in the USA foreign born in 2012, despite a decline since 2000 (Passel et al., 2013). Research has found that foreign-born Hispanic immigrants in the USA experience lower mortality rates in adulthood than do non-Hispanic whites despite their low socioeconomic status. The aged have, to date, been a small proportion of the US Hispanic population. However, the projected Hispanic elderly population is expected to more than double by 2050. It has, therefore, become increasingly urgent to examine the impact of the Hispanic paradox on current and future generations across the lifespan (Thomson et al., 2013). Growing awareness of this paradox, rooted as it is in the strengths and resources of immigrant families and communities, has helped to infuse a positive and more optimistic tone into negative and pessimistic discussions concerning Hispanic immigration.

### *Infant*

Surprisingly, the US Hispanic population has rates of infant mortality and low birthweight comparable to non-Hispanic US whites in the presence of limited education, and low socioeconomic status. While immigrant status is associated with a reduced risk of about 20% for low birthweight among Mexicans, it is not the same across other Latino subgroups which include Puerto Ricans, Cubans, and central and south Americans (Acevedo-Garcia et al., 2007)

Explanations have included the selective migration of immigrant women, social support (Franzini et al., 2001) and accessibility of family networks (Bender and Castro, 2000), as well as Hispanic cultural values and beliefs about health promotion (McGlade et al., 2004). Others have found that Hispanics who live in a community with a higher proportion of Hispanics are likelier to have better pregnancy outcomes and lower rates of smoking during pregnancy (Shaw and Pickett, 2013). For example, US-born mothers of Hispanic origin, similar to Mexican origin mothers, have been found to have infants with lower rates of low birthweight when they live in immigrant neighbourhoods (Osypuk et al., 2010). In general, infants of foreign-born Hispanic immigrant women have been found to have better health outcomes on a variety of indexes that include birthweight, infant mortality, adult obesity, cardiovascular functioning, longevity and mortality when compared with US native-born or later generation immigrants (Cunningham et al., 2008).

## *Childhood*

The immigrant paradox may hold better for some age ranges than others (Crosnoe and Turley, 2011). The children of immigrants have often been viewed as challenges to the American health and education systems because of the various disadvantages they experience. These include limited English proficiency, low socioeconomic status, and entering a new and at times unwelcoming society (Crosnoe and Fuligni, 2012). However, first- and second-generation immigrant children often display less risky behaviour and better health than do their more acculturated native-born peers.

On the other hand, during early childhood, a period that is associated with access to health care and exposure to disease, the health profiles of immigrant children of foreign-born Mexican parents are not as positive compared to their peers with US-born parents (Case et al., 2008). Some have found that these children are likelier to experience more common illnesses of childhood especially ear infections and respiratory diseases. In addition, foreign-born parents are more likely to rate their children's health lower than their US-born counterparts.

When considering if an immigrant educational paradox exists, others have found that immigrant children of Mexican-born parents may do poorer in standardised educational test scores, suggesting an early preschool disadvantage especially in communication and cognitive abilities (Fuller *et al.*, 2015). However, expanding the lens beyond test scores, many of these patterns seem to shift back towards an immigrant paradox. For example, children of Mexican-born immigrant parents have often been highly rated by their teachers on work habits, engagement and general behaviour (Crosnoe, 2006). These Mexican immigrant children of foreign-born parents have been found to overcome their disadvantages and demonstrate more growth in learning across elementary school grades than children of native-born parents. Thus, during the elementary school period, evidence of immigrant risk has been found to decline which more consistently points to an immigrant paradox (Crosnoe *et al.*, 2014). This phenomenon has been well studied by social scientists (Crosnoe *et al.*, 2014).

On the other hand, highly acculturated immigrant youth have been found to have less academic excellence and/or more risky behaviours than do their less acculturated peers (Coll and Marks, 2012). In general, school readiness and early achievement based on the skills that young children possess as they begin their education and how they build on these skills during their first years at school are of concern for immigrant families, especially among US children of Mexican and other Latin American-born parents (Han, 2008). More evidence has been found to support the existence of the paradox during high school than during the elementary school period. Additional research is needed to better understand if this epidemiological paradox continues beyond birth and the impact of its dynamics on the academic success of US immigrant children of Mexican foreign-born parents in particular over time. Among immigrant groups that include Asian as well as Latin American populations, support for this paradox has occurred by controlling for family socioeconomic and English proficiency with bilingualism and family ties associated with immigrant advantage (Crosnoe and Turley, 2011).

## *Adolescence*

Foreign-born, immigrant adolescents have been found to be just as adjusted, if not better than their native adolescent peers (Suárez-Orozco and Qin, 2006). They have a lower prevalence of mental disorders (Alegria et al., 2008), substance abuse (Allen et al., 2008) and better academic achievement (Suárez-Orozco and Qin, 2006) despite the challenges they face as recent immigrants to a new host country. Researchers have referred to this counterintuitive phenomenon as an immigrant paradox for adolescents (Hayes-Bautista, 2004; Guarini et al., 2011). It has helped them interpret their findings (Lara, 2014), and has been used, for example, to understand the high incidence of sexually risky behavioir among Latino adolescents (Rumbaut, 1997; Guarini et al., 2011) and its impact on the individual, family and community as well as society (Control, 2007).

Classic assimilation models have predicted that time in the USA results in increased English language proficiency, and greater access to resources and social capital (Alba et al., 2000; Alba and Nee, 1997; Waters and Jiménez, 2005) with assimilated adolescents likelier to have better health-related behaviours based on assumptions about European immigrant populations. However, this has not been the case with Latino immigrant populations (Portes and Rumbaut, 2001).

Some researchers have found that foreign-born Latino immigrant adolescents have significantly lower levels of sexually risky behaviours than later generations (Hussey et al., 2007). They are also in less danger of the negative outcomes related to sexual risk, than their second- and third-generation peers who were either born in the USA of foreign-born immigrant parents, or whose parents were also born in the USA. Other researchers have found that third-generation adolescents, those of parents born in the USA, were at highest risk for sexually risky behaviours (Guarini et al., 2011). No differences among boys were discovered when their immigration status, generation, birthplace or that of their parents were considered in the data analysis of this study. Their study was unique through its use of the Hispanic immigrant paradox to conceptually guide their study of sexually risky behaviour among immigrant Latino adolescents in the USA and investigate variance by immigrant generation and gender longitudinally.

## *Adults*

The positive effect of the Hispanic epidemiological paradox has also been observed among adults through studies which found that among older

Hispanic/Latino immigrants, mortality surprisingly broadened with age despite socioeconomical disadvantage counterintuitive to research that has consistently supported a significant relationship between low socioeconomic status and poor health outcomes. Studies comparing the mortality experience of Hispanic immigrant adults with non-Hispanic white adults found that Hispanics had similar or lower mortality rates once their ages were adjusted (Elo and Preston, 1997; Ruiz *et al.*, 2013; Sorlie *et al.*, 1993). This established that the age-adjusted mortality rates for Hispanic men and women who were 45 years or older ranged from 18% to 28% lower in comparison to non-Hispanic whites. Similar conclusions were made between Hispanics and whites who were 25–44 years of age (Elo and Preston, 1997) and it was also found that Hispanic mortality advantage increased when they controlled for socioeconomic status. Thus, despite the inverse relationship between socioeconomic status and mortality, the Hispanic paradox continued with US foreign-born Hispanic immigrant adults.

In general, the data that supports the Hispanic epidemiological paradox appears to be stronger for some Hispanic subgroups. For example, one study examined mortality differences between non-Hispanic whites and Hispanics of Mexican, Puerto Rican, Cuban, central American or south American origin and other Hispanic subgroups using National Health Interview Survey-Multiple Cause of Death data (Hummer *et al.*, 2000). In this study, investigators established a large mortality advantage among Hispanics of Mexican, central American or south American and of other Hispanic origin in the data analysis controlling for age, sex and socioeconomic status. This advantage was not found among Puerto Ricans or Cubans. They also reported lower mortality rates among foreign-born immigrant Hispanics compared to US-born Hispanics. Still others have found that Hispanic immigrants of Mexican, Puerto Rican, Cuban and other Hispanic origin had lower mortality than non-Hispanic whites when they controlled for age, sex and socioeconomic status (Abraido-Lanza *et al.*, 1999). Surprisingly, the mortality advantage found in this study included both foreign-born Mexican and other Hispanic-origin born as well as those born in the USA.

Others (Palloni and Arias, 2004) have also established the mortality differences between Hispanic and non-Hispanic white adults longitudinally, using the National Health Interview Survey Multiple Cause of Death data for adults 35 years of age and older. When they controlled for demographic and socioeconomic characteristics, these researchers found that only foreign-born men and women of Mexican and other Hispanic origin were advantaged when compared to non-Hispanic whites. There were no significant mortality differences between non-Hispanic whites and foreign-born or US-born Puerto Ricans, or foreign-born or US-born Cubans. While some Hispanic subgroups may experience mortality advantage over non-Hispanic whites, the findings remain inconsistent with more research needed to determine causality. Nevertheless, Hispanics in general experience worse general health than non-Hispanic whites with an increasing morbidity and mortality burden among US-born Latinos compared to foreign-born Latinos (Vega et al., 2009).

Obesity has become a major risk factor for Hispanic adults (Ogden et al., 2014) contributing to risk for diabetes, hypertension and cardiovascular disease. The incidence of diabetes is twice the frequency among Hispanics of Mexican origin than it is among non-Hispanic whites. If current trends continue, the ageing Hispanic population will be burdened with higher rates of cardiovascular disease, stroke, kidney disease, blindness and other complications of obesity, diabetes and hypertension. These risk factors are thus likely to increase the incidence of disability and mortality among Hispanics (Escarce et al., 2006; Ogden et al., 2014).

In summary, research has provided general support for the existence of the Hispanic epidemiological paradox, with examples across the lifespan. However, controversy continues to question the validity of the paradox (Teruya and Bazargan-Hejazi, 2013). The documented positive outcomes of Hispanic/Latino immigrants go against what is known about the negative impact of low socioeconomic status on the general health and wellbeing of individuals in the USA (Acevedo-Garcia et al., 2007, 2012; Ruiz et al., 2013). Several competing theories have evolved to explain these positive health outcomes and guide future research as the next section will review.

## Understanding the Hispanic epidemiological paradox: alternative explanations

Three major theories have emerged to help understand the root causes of the epidemiological Hispanic paradox. These include (1) the healthy migrant effect, (2) reverse migration or the salmon effect, and (3) the Latino lifestyle (Thomson et al., 2013).

## The healthy migrant effect

Self-selection of the healthiest for migration may contribute to a resilient immigrant profile that is not randomly drawn from their population of origin (Palloni and Arias, 2004; Vega et al., 2009). Hispanic immigrants may have some health advantage with the better mental and physical health status they already possess in their native populations and bring with them into their host country at entry (Abraido-Lanza et al., 1999). In this model, only the healthiest Hispanics migrate to the USA. They are assumed to be healthier than those who do not migrate from their country of origin (Abraido-Lanza et al., 1999; Fry and Center, 2008). They may also be healthier than the population in the host country.

As discussed earlier, some have found that, for example, Mexicans who migrate to the USA experience lower mortality rates in their host countries than the overall mortality rates of their home countries (Palloni and Arias, 2004).

Others have reported that US-born Hispanics were at higher risk for elevated blood pressure, blood glucose and cholesterol after controlling for income and education, while Hispanic immigrants were comparable to non-Hispanic white Americans in their health risks (Crimmins et al., 2005). It may be that those who migrate and experience the challenges of an actual migration are hardier than those who do not. The migration experience itself may lead them to better health outcomes than those Hispanics born in the USA with comparable socioeconomic status (Palloni and Arias, 2004).

The "Healthy Migrant Effect" theory may be of interest because more than one-third of Hispanics in the USA are foreign born. Migrants are, therefore, an important part of the Hispanic population. However, the vigorous health of new immigrants to the USA associated with the protective effect of self-selection has been found to decrease with time following immigration and the consequences of living in the USA as unhealthy behaviours are adopted. A second migratory theory has also been postulated to affect the mortality rates of ageing Hispanic immigrants. As discussed earlier, compared to non-Hispanic whites, Hispanics have higher poverty rates, less education and less health insurance, but a lower all-cause mortality rate. A second migration theory associated with an explanation of the Hispanic epidemiological paradox is the "salmon bias" (Ullmann *et al.*, 2011).

## *Reverse migration: the salmon effect*

This theory has been used to explain the Hispanic immigrant mortality advantage by hypothesising a selective return migration with some evidence to support this theory (Riosmena *et al.*, 2013). According to the "salmon effect," Hispanic immigrants are thought to leave their host countries to return to their country of origin because of ageing, retirement or development of serious illness. They are, therefore, not counted in US mortality rates. Not being counted provides them with a false mortality advantage due to their absent mortality data. By using social security data, Turra and Elo (2008) found some but not enough evidence to explain an immigrant mortality advantage. However, it was only found among foreign-born Mexicans, not among other foreign-born Hispanics (Palloni and Arias, 2004).

This theory not only supports a mortality advantage but also inflates life expectancy estimates. More research is needed to examine the rate of return migration among Hispanic immigrants to their country of origin. Other studies have actually found the emigration rate lower than some might think (Abraido-Lanza *et al.*, 1999; Thomson *et al.*, 2013). An alternative explanation for the Hispanic immigrant mortality advantage is the Latino lifestyle that reflects the social and cultural factors characteristic of the Latinos.

## *Latino lifestyle*

According to this theory, sociocultural factors are thought to provide a protective effect that buffers the risks of low socioeconomic status for Hispanic immigrants (Granillo *et al.*, 2012). This framework is based on the assumption that Latino culture influences mortality outcomes through its effect on individual health and lifestyle behaviours, family networks and social structures (Palloni and Arias, 2004; Thomson *et al.*, 2013). It is thought that the culture of the home country shapes the behavioural risk profile of immigrants through cultural practices. Culture also shapes the nature of the social environment by socialising an individual before migration through norms and beliefs about family relationships and obligations. Cultural values and beliefs also influence decisions about whether to live alone or with extended families, the need for social supports and self-efficacy (Vega et al., 2009, Gruskin, 2004), and results in health-related behaviours that protect Hispanic immigrants from adverse outcomes associated with low socioeconomic status in the USA (Rumbaut et al., 2006; Morales et al., 2002). Some researchers have inconclusively found that health status and mortality are associated with active participation in supportive networks. These networks provide both instrumental and social support, and enhance a sense of control over ones' life (Viruell-Fuentes and Schulz, 2009; Mulvaney-Day et al., 2007). Immigrants who establish social networks and a sense of mastery may be more resilient to the physiological stress that results from migration and the need to establish a new identity in their host country (Palloni and Arias, 2004). Without these protective factors (social supports, self-efficacy), immigrants may be more likely to succumb to the stresses they experience during migration, transition and integration into their host country. They may not have the benefit of new social networks, and experience increased exposure to health risk factors. Furthermore, their mortality advantage may diminish as they assimilate and as they abandon their cultural protective advantage. Surprisingly, this is not the case for positive infant outcomes. Some positive infant outcomes continue even as protective cultural values and beliefs are ignored by the second generation. These are the children of foreign-born immigrants (Escarce et al., 2006).

More research is needed to support this hypothesis and the negative effect of acculturation on Hispanic immigrant risk factors, resilience and the protective factors of the Latino lifestyle over time across the lifespan of Latino immigrants in the USA. The study of the Hispanic immigrant paradox in general is in need of continued research, especially when the gaps and limitations of earlier studies are underscored.

## *Limitations of research*

In general, limitations suggest that the underreporting of Hispanic origin on US death certificates, the prime data-collection tool for mortality statistics may be problematic with 7% of Hispanics not recorded as Hispanic on death certificates (Rosenberg et al., 1999). Thus US vital statistics may underestimate the overall mortality rates for Hispanics. These rates are drawn from two data sources. Mortality rates build on a denominator that integrates census data based on individuals self-identifying their own race and ethnicity. The numerator, on the other hand, depends on death certificates with proxy identification of the race and ethnicity of the deceased. Hispanics may be underidentified on death certificates, resulting in the underreporting of their deaths (Rosenberg et al., 1999). Together, these data challenge may lead to the Hispanic paradoxical advantage (Escarce et al., 2006). An overestimate of ages among the elderly in this population may also exist, producing a more positive mortality pattern. Finally, there may be a mismatch of records with matching procedures that link death records to a population that varies across individuals and groups (Vega et al., 2009; Palloni and Arias, 2004).

To date, a definitive explanation of the Hispanic epidemiological paradox continues to be in need of future research.

## Implications for research: migration and the epidemiological paradox

First-generation Hispanic immigrants, those born in their home countries, have a better health profile than US-born Latinos. With the rapid growth of the second generation (children of foreign-born immigrant parents), the health profile of the total US Latino population is at risk and may worsen over time. What is currently known about the negative consequences of acculturation should support the need to identify specific sociocultural protective factors associated with resilience among foreign-born immigrants to continue their health advantage through the second generation and beyond.

The assumptions about the selection of the healthiest for migration has not been well explained since both genes and behaviours consistent with good health might be passed on to the next generations. However, research is needed on risk, protective factors and resilience to better understand the health advantage that Hispanic immigrants bring to their host country. Binational research is needed to determine how health and immigrant policies may protect and sustain this health advantage for future generations of Hispanic immigrants over time. Additional models to understand the impact of migration on health of immigrants have emerged. They show promise for understanding how latent genetic predisposition may increase risk for expression of disease when people are transplanted from one social and physical environment to another as it occurs during migration (Cooper, 2003). The key mechanism that Cooper describes in his model is the latent dispositions of specific gene mutations that may be dormant in the home country but may be expressed in a new host country through gene environment interplay. The role of biological/genetic factors will provide new insights into understanding the Hispanic epidemiological paradox and the role that genetics has in determining the health advantage that foreign-born Hispanic immigrants bring to their adopted host country.

# References

Abraido-Lanza, A.F. et al. (1999). The Latino mortality paradox: A test of the "salmon bias" and healthy migrant hypotheses. *American Journal of Public Health*, 89 1543–1548.

Acevedo-Garcia, D. et al. (2007). Low birthweight among US Hispanic/Latino subgroups: The effect of maternal foreign-born status and education. *Social Science & Medicine*, 65, 2503–2516.

Acevedo-Garcia, D. et al. (2012). Integrating social epidemiology into immigrant health research: A cross-national framework. *Social Science & Medicine*, 75, 2060–2068.

Alba, R. & Nee, V. (1997). Rethinking assimilation theory for a new era of immigration. *International Migration Review*, 31(4), 826–874.

Alba, R.D. et al. (2000). The changing neighborhood contexts of the immigrant metropolis. *Social Forces*, 79, 587–621.

Alegria, M. et al. (2008). Prevalence of mental illness in immigrant and non-immigrant US Latino groups. *The American journal of Psychiatry*, 165, 359–369.

Allen, M.L. et al. (2008). The relationship between Spanish language use and substance use behaviors among Latino youth: A social network approach. *Journal of Adolescent Health*, 43, 372–379.

Bender, D.E. & Castro, D. (2000). Explaining the birth weight paradox: Latina immigrants' perceptions of resilience and risk. *Journal of Immigrant Health*, 2, 155–173.

Case, A. et al. (2008). The income gradient in children's health: A comment on Currie, Shields and Wheatley Price. *Journal of Health Economics*, 27, 801–807.

Coll, C.G.E. & Marks, A.K.E. (2012). The immigrant paradox in children and adolescents: Is becoming American a developmental risk? American Psychological Association, Worcester, MA.

Connor, P. (2012) Faith on the Move: The Religious Affiliation of International Migrants. Pew Forum on Religion and Public Life, Washington, DC. Available at: http://features. pewforum. org/religious-migration/Faithonthemove. pdf, 2012. 21 April 2015.

Control, C.F.D. (2007). Eliminating racial & ethnic health disparities. Available at: http://www. cdc. gov/omh/AboutUs/disparities. htm. Accessed 10 March 2015.

Cooper, R.S. (2003). Gene-environment interactions and the etiology of common complex disease. *Annals of Internal Medicine*, 139, 437–440.

Crimmins, E.M. et al. (2005). Using anthropometric indicators for Mexicans in the United States and Mexico to understand the selection of migrants and the "Hispanic paradox". *Biodemography and Social Biology*, 52, 164–177.

Crosnoe, R. (2006). *Mexican Roots, American Schools: Helping Mexican Immigrant Children Succeed.* Stanford University Press, Stanford, CA.

Crosnoe, R. & Fuligni, A.J. (2012). Children from immigrant families: Introduction to the special section. *Child Development*, 83, 1471–1476.

Crosnoe, R. et al. (2014). Family background, school-age trajectories of activity participation, and academic achievement at the start of high school. *Applied Developmental Science*, 21, 1–14.

Crosnoe, R. & Turley, R.N.L. (2011). K-12 educational outcomes of immigrant youth. The Future of Children, 21(1), 129–152.

Cunningham, S.A. et al. (2008). Health of foreign-born people in the United States: A review. *Health & Place*, 14, 623–635.

Elo, I.T. & Samuel, H.P. (1997). Racial and ethnic differences in mortality at older ages. In: B, Soldo & L. Martin (eds.), *Racial and ethnic differences in the health of older Americans*, (pp. 10–42), National Academies Press, Washington, DC.

Escarce, J. et al. (2006). National Research Council. Hispanics and the future of America. Panel on Hispanics in the United States, Committee on Population, Division of Behavioral and Social Sciences and Education. The National Academies Press, Washington, DC.

Franzini, L. et al. (2001). Understanding the Hispanic paradox. *Ethnicity & Disease*, 11, 496–518.

Fry, R.A. & Center, P.H. (2008). *Latino Settlement in the New Century.* Pew Hispanic Center, Washington, DC.

Fuller, B. et al. (2015). Differing cognitive trajectories of Mexican American toddlers: The role of class, nativity, and maternal practices. *Hispanic Journal of Behavioral Sciences*. doi:0739986315571113.

Granillo, C.M. et al. (2012). Ethnic immigration status differences on child indicators of health for European Americans and Latinos. *California Journal of Health Promotion*, 10, SI II: Health Disparities on Latino Health, 15–24.

Gruskin, S. (2004). What are health and human rights? *The Lancet*, 363, 329.

Guarini, T.E. et al. (2011). The immigrant paradox in sexual risk behavior among Latino adolescents: Impact of immigrant generation and gender. *Applied Developmental Science*, 15, 201–209.

Han, W.-J. (2008). The academic trajectories of children of immigrants and their school environments. *Developmental Psychology*, 44, 1572.

Hayes-Bautista, D. (2004). *La nueva California: Latinos in the Golden State*. University of California Press, Oakland, CA.

Hummer, R.A. et al. (2000). Adult mortality differentials among Hispanic subgroups and non-Hispanic whites. *Social Science Quarterly*, 81, 459–476.

Hussey, J.M. et al. (2007). Sexual behavior and drug use among Asian and Latino adolescents: Association with immigrant status. *Journal of Immigrant and Minority Health*, 9, 85–94.

Lara, L. (2014). Psychological well-being of immigrants in Spain: The immigrant paradox. *Procedia-Social and Behavioral Sciences*, 132, 544–548.

Marger, M.N. (2011). *Race and Ethnic Relations: American and global Perspectives*. Cengage Learning, Boston, MA.

Markides, K.S. & Coreil, J. (1986). The health of Hispanics in the southwestern United States: An epidemiologic paradox. *Public Health Reports*, 101, 253.

Markides, K.S. & Eschbach, K. (2005). Aging, migration, and mortality: Current status of research on the Hispanic paradox. *The Journals of Gerontology Series B: Psychological Sciences and Social Sciences*, 60, S68–S75.

Markides, K.S. et al. (1997). Health status of Hispanic elderly. In: Soldo, B. Soldo & Maratin, L. (Eds.), *Racial and Ethnic Differences in the Health of Older Americans*, pp. 285–300, National Academies Press, Washington DC.

Mcglade, M.S. et al. (2004). The Latina paradox: An opportunity for restructuring prenatal care delivery. *American Journal of Public Health*, 94, 2062–2065.

Morales, L.S. et al. (2002). Socioeconomic, cultural, and behavioral factors affecting Hispanic health outcomes. *Journal of Health Care for the Poor and Underserved*, 13, 477.

Mulvaney-Day, N.E. et al. (2007). Social cohesion, social support, and health among Latinos in the United States. *Social Science & Medicine*, 64, 477–495.

Ogden, C.L. et al. (2014). Prevalence of childhood and adult obesity in the United States, 2011–2012. *Journal of American Medical Association*, 311, 806–814.

Osypuk, T.L. et al. (2010). Another Mexican birthweight paradox? The role of residential enclaves and neighborhood poverty in the birthweight of Mexican-origin infants. *Social Science & Medicine*, 70, 550–560.

Palloni, A. & Arias, E. (2004). Paradox lost: Explaining the Hispanic adult mortality advantage. *Demography*, 41, 385–415.

Palloni, A. & Morenoff, J.D. (2001). Interpreting the paradoxical in the Hispanic paradox. *Annals of the New York Academy of Sciences*, 954, 140–174.

Passel, J.S. et al. (2011). Hispanics account for more than half of nation's growth in past decade. Pew Hispanic Center, Washington, DC. Available at: http://pewhispanic.org/files/reports/140.pdf. Accessed 20 March 2015.

Passel, J.S. et al. (2013). Population decline of unauthorized immigrants stalls, may have reversed. Pew Hispanic Center, Washington, DC. Available at: http://www.pewhispanic. org/files/2013/09/Unauthorized-Sept-2013-FINAL.pdf. Accessed 20 March 2015.

Portes, A. & Rumbaut, R.G. 2001. *Legacies: The Story of the Immigrant Second Generation*, University of California Press, Oakland, CA.

Riosmena, F. et al. (2013). Migration selection, protection, and acculturation in health: A binational perspective on older adults. *Demography*, 50, 1039–1064.

Rosenberg, H.M. et al. (1999). Quality of death rates by race and Hispanic origin: A summary of current research, 1999. *Vital and health statistics. Series 2, Data evaluation and methods research*, 1–13.

Ruiz, J.M. et al. (2013). Hispanic mortality paradox: A systematic review and meta-analysis of the longitudinal literature. *American Journal of Public Health*, 103, e52–e60.

Rumbaut, R.G. (2006). The making of a people. In Tienda, M. & Mitchell, F. (Eds.), *Hispanics and the Future of America*, pp. 16–65, National Academies Press, Washington DC.

Rumbaut, R.G. et al. (2006). The health status and health behaviors of Hispanics. In: Tienda, M. & Mitchell, F. (eds.) *Hispanics and the Future of America*, pp. 16–65, National Academies Press, Washington, DC.

Rumbaut, R.G. (1997). Assimilation and its discontents: Between rhetoric and reality. *International Migration Review*, 31(4) 923–960.

Shaw, R.J. & Pickett, K.E. (2013). The health benefits of Hispanic communities for non-Hispanic mothers and infants: Another Hispanic paradox. *American Journal of Public Health*, 103, 1052–1057.

Sorlie, P.D. et al. (1993). Mortality by Hispanic status in the United States. *Journal of American Medical Association*, 270, 2464–2468.

Suárez-Orozco, C. & Qin, D.B. (2006). Gendered perspectives in psychology: Immigrant origin youth. *International Migration Review*, 40, 165–198.

Teruya, S.A. & Bazargan-Hejazi, S. (2013). The immigrant and hispanic paradoxes a systematic review of their predictions and effects. *Hispanic Journal of Behavioral Sciences*, 35, 486–509.

Thomson, E.F. *et al.* (2013). The hispanic paradox and older adults' disabilities: Is there a healthy migrant effect? *International Journal of Environmental Research and Public Health*, 10, 1786–1814.

Turra, C.M. & Elo, I.T. (2008). The impact of salmon bias on the Hispanic mortality advantage: New evidence from social security data. *Population Research and Policy Review*, 27, 515–530.

Ullmann, S.H. *et al.* (2011). Healthier before they migrate, less healthy when they return? The health of returned migrants in Mexico. *Social Science & Medicine*, 73, 421–428.

Vega, W.A. *et al.* (2009). Health disparities in the Latino population. *Epidemiologic Reviews*, 31, 99–112.

Viruell-Fuentes, E.A. & Schulz, A.J. (2009). Toward a dynamic conceptualization of social ties and context: Implications for understanding immigrant and Latino health. *American Journal of Public Health*, 99, 2167.

Waters, M.C. & Jiménez, T.R. (2005). Assessing immigrant assimilation: New empirical and theoretical challenges. *Annual Review of Sociology*, 31, 105–125.

# Chapter 11

# Migration and the healthy migrant effect in Australia: current knowledge, gaps and opportunity for future research

Professor André M.N. Renzaho

## Introduction

Over the past 200 years, migration has transformed Australia as a nation, its history and socioeconomic and cultural fabrics. Entry to Australia is regulated by immigration policies and entry visa and can be broadly categorised into four groups: skill stream categories (e.g. point-based skilled migration, permanent employer-sponsored programme, business innovation and investment programme, and distinguished talent), family stream categories (e.g. family reunion, such as partner, child, parent and other family members); special eligibility stream (e.g. former residents with sustained ties with Australia and people subject to resolution of status), and humanitarian programme categories (e.g. refugees and other people with special humanitarian needs) (Australian Bureau of Statistics, 2009). These migration streams suggest that immigrants to Australia come from different environments. Therefore, their physical and mental health is affected by many factors, including the pre-migration environment in country of origin, the timing or wave of migration, the migration stream category and the degree of integration in Australia. This chapter starts with the description of the various aspects of immigration to Australia. It then moves on to examine the health burden among migrant populations and to discuss the validity of the healthy migrant effect. It concludes by outlining research priorities to reduce migration-related inequalities.

## Overview of migration in Australia

While Australia is known to have been created by immigrants, the original inhabitants of this country are Australian Aboriginal people (Jupp, 1990). The year 1788 marked the first arrival of the British, whose aim was to establish a penal colony (Clark, 1969). The adoption of the 'white Australia' policy meant that Australian Aboriginal people were largely excluded from the Australian society (Figure 1). The policy existed prior to the Federation in 1901 and was in place as early as 1830 due to fear that the introduction of non-white migrants would destabilise the country, and enforced until 1973 with related policies surviving as late as 1982 (Jupp, 1990, 2002; O'Neill *et al.*, 2004; Windschuttle, 2004). Although there were some rare cases of non-white migrants entering Australia including the Chinese people during the 1850s gold rushes, Kanakas (a term then used for a worker from various Pacific Islands to work in British colonies such as in Queensland, Australia), and Melanesians many of whom were kidnapped from Pacific Islands as a source of labour to work in plantations (Graves, 1993; O'Neil and Handley, 1994), the 'White Australia' policy was enforced by leaders of all political parties (Burgmann, 1984). By the time the Commonwealth of Australia was declared in 1901, the British were the largest migrant group followed by Germans and in third place were Chinese (Jupp, 2002).

Within the first year of the Federal Parliament, a number of legislations marking out the racial boundaries of the new nation were passed including the Pacific Island Labourers Act which was passed by the House of Representatives and by the Senate on 17 December 1901 and enabled the deportation of most of the Pacific Islanders working in Australia as soon as possible after 1906 (Australian House of Representatives, 1901). Only 700 of the approximately 10,000 Pacific Islanders who were living in Queensland and northern New South Wales when the Bill became law were exempt from

## Migration and the Healthy Migrant Effect in Australia

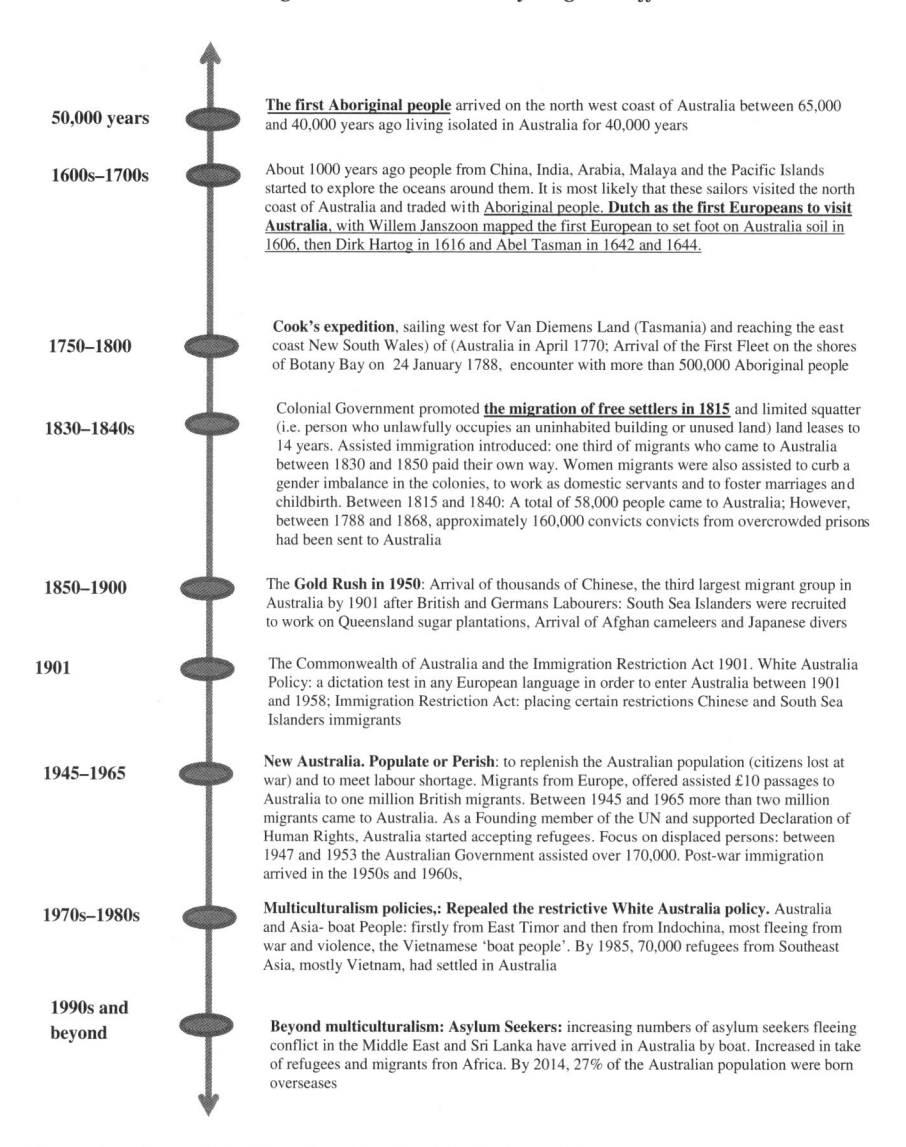

| | |
|---|---|
| 50,000 years | **The first Aboriginal people** arrived on the north west coast of Australia between 65,000 and 40,000 years ago living isolated in Australia for 40,000 years |
| 1600s–1700s | About 1000 years ago people from China, India, Arabia, Malaya and the Pacific Islands started to explore the oceans around them. It is most likely that these sailors visited the north coast of Australia and traded with Aboriginal people. **Dutch as the first Europeans to visit Australia**, with Willem Janszoon mapped the first European to set foot on Australia soil in 1606, then Dirk Hartog in 1616 and Abel Tasman in 1642 and 1644. |
| 1750–1800 | **Cook's expedition**, sailing west for Van Diemens Land (Tasmania) and reaching the east coast New South Wales) of (Australia in April 1770; Arrival of the First Fleet on the shores of Botany Bay on 24 January 1788, encounter with more than 500,000 Aboriginal people |
| 1830–1840s | Colonial Government promoted **the migration of free settlers in 1815** and limited squatter (i.e. person who unlawfully occupies an uninhabited building or unused land) land leases to 14 years. Assisted immigration introduced: one third of migrants who came to Australia between 1830 and 1850 paid their own way. Women migrants were also assisted to curb a gender imbalance in the colonies, to work as domestic servants and to foster marriages and childbirth. Between 1815 and 1840: A total of 58,000 people came to Australia; However, between 1788 and 1868, approximately 160,000 convicts convicts from overcrowded prisons had been sent to Australia |
| 1850–1900 | The **Gold Rush in 1950**: Arrival of thousands of Chinese, the third largest migrant group in Australia by 1901 after British and Germans Labourers: South Sea Islanders were recruited to work on Queensland sugar plantations, Arrival of Afghan cameleers and Japanese divers |
| 1901 | The Commonwealth of Australia and the Immigration Restriction Act 1901. White Australia Policy: a dictation test in any European language in order to enter Australia between 1901 and 1958; Immigration Restriction Act: placing certain restrictions Chinese and South Sea Islanders immigrants |
| 1945–1965 | **New Australia. Populate or Perish**: to replenish the Australian population (citizens lost at war) and to meet labour shortage. Migrants from Europe, offered assisted £10 passages to Australia to one million British migrants. Between 1945 and 1965 more than two million migrants came to Australia. As a Founding member of the UN and supported Declaration of Human Rights, Australia started accepting refugees. Focus on displaced persons: between 1947 and 1953 the Australian Government assisted over 170,000. Post-war immigration arrived in the 1950s and 1960s, |
| 1970s–1980s | **Multiculturalism policies,: Repealed the restrictive White Australia policy.** Australia and Asia- boat People: firstly from East Timor and then from Indochina, most fleeing from war and violence, the Vietnamese 'boat people'. By 1985, 70,000 refugees from Southeast Asia, mostly Vietnam, had settled in Australia |
| 1990s and beyond | **Beyond multiculturalism: Asylum Seekers**: increasing numbers of asylum seekers fleeing conflict in the Middle East and Sri Lanka have arrived in Australia by boat. Increased in take of refugees and migrants fron Africa. By 2014, 27% of the Australian population were born overseases |

**Figure 1: A simplified immigration timeline in Australia.**
*Source*: Data used to construct the figure were extracted from the NSW Migration Heritage Centre's website on the Australian Immigration history timeline at http://www.migrationheritage.nsw.gov.au/exhibition/objectsthroughtime-history/1965-1990/. Accessed 31 July 2015.

deportation. Exempt from deportation were those brought to Australia before 1 September 1879, those working as ships' crews, and those granted Certificates of Exemption under the 1901 Immigration Restriction Act (Australian House of Representatives, 1901). At the closure of the Pacific Island Branch of the Queensland Immigration Department on 31 July 1908, almost all the Pacific Islanders working in plantations were returned home when their work was completed, with only 1,654 allowed to remain in Australia (Moore, 1999). Following Australia's vulnerability during the Second World War in the Pacific, the then immigration minister, Arthur Calwell, controversially expelled all Japanese from the country in 1945 and gradually sought to deport all non-white refugees, mainly Malays, Indonesians and Filipinos who had settled in Australia during the Second World War (Henderson, 1988; Jupp, 1990). Minister Calwell maintained that for every non-British immigrant there will be 10 Britons (Jupp, 1990). It was not until 1949 that Minister Holt, Calwell's successor, decided to allow the only remaining 800 non-white refugees as well as Japanese 'war brides' to settle in Australia (Department of Immigration and Multicultural and Indigenous Affairs, 2002). The 'White Australia' policy was geared towards keeping Australia white and Anglo-Saxon, and this was reflected in the redrafting of section 117 of the constitution removing references to equality before the Australian law and equal application of the law while validating the racist colonial legislation (O'Neill et al., 2004). When introducing the bill, Alfred Deakin, the first Attorney General of the first federal government in 1901, declared:

> *"The ultimate result is a national determination to make no truce with coloured immigration, to have no traffic with the unclean thing, and to put it down in all its shapes without much regard to cost. Those Chinese, Japanese, or coolies who have come here under the law, or in spite of it, are not to be permitted to increase." (O'Neill et al., 2004; p. 698)*

The Australian migration went through waves, with the 1788–1825 first wave characterised by convicts from England transported to Australia (Clark, 1969; Jupp, 1990). The 1825–1850 period constituted the second wave of migration, driven by the 'new Britannia' policy, a period during which the British government's goal was to increase the number of Britons in Australia to create an Australia in Britain's image. This was achieved through an incentivised scheme including meeting relocation expenses to British citizens willing to migrate to Australia. This policy was very successful, resulting in the relocation of 1,068,311 Britons to Australia between 1830 and 1940 (Petrilli and Ponzio, 2009). The third wave of migration in Australia occurred from 1910 to the 1930s with the arrival of predominantly British immigrants and a significant number of Jews, European Christians and anti-Nazis (Jupp, 1990; Windschuttle, 2004). By becoming one of the founding members of the United Nations in 1945, joining the International Refugee Organisation in 1947 and supporting the Declaration of Human Rights (Henderson, 1988), Australia signalled its intention to expand its migration policy beyond the United Kingdom, targeting countries that would provide migrants perceived to assimilate easily. Therefore, the 1947–1972 period was the fourth migration wave which saw a shift away from the British focus and the arrival of predominantly non-British Europeans settlers, followed by the official dismantling of the "White Australia" policy in 1973 by the Whitlam Labour government (Jupp, 1990, 2002). This period saw a significant arrival of migrants from the Baltic States, eastern European and Mediterranean countries, as well as Asian business people and Indian professionals willing to assimilate (Jupp, 1990). It is estimated that around a quarter of a million Italians arrived in Australia in the first 15 years following World War II (MacDonald and MacDonald, 1970). Similarly, while only 12,500 Greeks lived in Australia prior to 1947, the 1947–1983 period saw the arrival of 250,000 Greek migrants in Australia (Giorgas, 2008). There was a significant number of migrants from Poland, the Netherlands, former Yugoslavia and the former USSR, Germany, Malta, Turkey, Lebanon and South Africa (Young, 1991). The end of the "White Australia" policy marked the beginning of the last wave of migration starting in 1974 and beyond, predominantly of refugees fleeing conflicts and political persecution in Asia, Africa and the Middle-East (Commonwealth of Australia, 2002; Jupp, 2002). The change in Australian migration history saw the mass arrival of Vietnamese refugees in 1975 after the Vietnam War, the arrival of 45,000 Cambodian refugees in 1981, a significant number of Chinese refugees in 1989 after the Tiananmen Square demonstration (Jupp, 2002), and migrants from Middle-East and Sub-Saharan Africa (SSA) throughout the 1990s and beyond (Australian Bureau of Statistics, 2015).

The proportion of Australians born overseas has grown from 2.6% in 1933 (Krupinski, 1984) to 27% in 2014 (Australian Bureau of Statistics, 2015).

## Health of migrants in Australia

As shown above, Australian migration has gone through different phases, and each phase represents a unique opportunity to better understand differences in the health of migrants to Australia. However, for the purpose of this chapter, we examine studies on the health of migrants to Australia over two periods: pre-1990 and post-1990.

### Prior to the 1990s

Studies into the health of migrants in Australia were scarce. Last (1960), Saint (1963) and Krupinski (1984) were among some of the earlier researchers attempting to comprehensively describe the health of migrants in Australia. Their findings suggested that the health of Australian migrants varied according to their wave of arrival and region of origin, and could be grouped into four categories: infectious diseases, degenerative chronic diseases, occupational diseases and mental disorders. In terms of physical health, infectious diseases were more prevalent among non-British migrants and constituted the main cause of hospital admission. In contrast, degenerative arterial and chronic respiratory diseases were more prevalent among Australian-born and British migrants (Saint, 1963). Therefore, the Australian government introduced tough pre-migration health screening to prevent entrance to Australia of any prospective migrant with a tuberculosis infection or a chronic disease (Proust, 1974). Despite these measures, the "imported diseases" theory persisted, which was postulated to explain the difference in morbidity patterns between migrants and the Australian-born population. Imported or exotic diseases most documented among migrants included malaria, stomatocytosis, thalassemia, sickle cell disease, leishmaniasis, tropical pulmonary eosinophiha, neurocystlcerocosis and tuberculosis (Krupinski, 1984). For example, between 1959 and 1961, the incidence of tuberculosis was estimated at 130/100,000 population among migrants and 27/100,000 population among Australian-born (Saint, 1963). These results suggest that the incidence of tuberculosis among migrants was more than four times higher than that of their Australian-born counterparts. Similarly, between 1965 and 1969, the pulmonary tuberculosis notification rate among adolescents and young adults was two times higher among migrants than Australians of similar age (Krupinski, 1984).

Degenerative chronic diseases were also a serious problem among migrants. For example, type-2 diabetes was found to be more prevalent in specific groups of migrants than the Australian-born population (Dunt and Parker, 1973). Staszewski (1972) noted that the mortality rate from cancer was several times higher for stomach cancer and lower for cancer of the intestinal track among Polish migrants than that of their Australian-born counterparts. These findings are similar to those reported by McMichael and Bonett (1981). The authors examined cancer incidence in British, Irish and southern-European migrants in South Australia between 1977 and 1978. They found a high risk of stomach cancer in all migrant groups but a low risk of colon cancer in southern-European migrants. In contrast, Stenhouse and McCall (1970) found that, compared to the Australian-born population, mortality rates from arteriosclerotic and degenerative diseases were comparable for Scottish migrants, but significantly lower for migrants born in England, Wales and Italy. Regardless of the country of origin, mortality rates from arteriosclerotic and degenerative diseases were lower among migrants to Australia compared to those remaining back in the country of origin; and for those migrants born in England, Wales and Italy, mortality rates remained significantly lower than that of Australian-born populations regardless of the length of stay in Australia for all age groups. With increasing length of residence in Australia, however, these mortality rates started to approximate those observed among Australian-born people (Table 1). The lower age-standardised mortality rates observed among migrant populations in Australia when compared to the corresponding rates in their own country of origin could be related to either the migration self-selection or the pre-migration medical screening or both. In contrast, the increased risk of stomach cancer among migrants was associated with culturally-determined differences in lifestyle such as changes in dietary and drinking habits, as well as length of residence in Australia (Stenhouse and McCall, 1970; McMichael and Bonett, 1981).

Studies on migrants' occupational diseases were scarce prior to the 1990s. The few available studies reported several cases of asbestosis among

Table 1: Australian death rates per 100,000 at-risk population by age, sex, country of birth and period of residence in Australia for arteriosclerotic and degenerative diseases (ICD 420–422)

| Place of birth and/or residence | Males 40–49 | 50–59 | 60–69 | 70–79 | Females 40–49 | 50–59 | 60–69 | 70–79 |
|---|---|---|---|---|---|---|---|---|
| **Australia** | 169 | 592 | 1,471 | 3,089 | 39 | 167 | 600 | 1718 |
| England and Wales | | | | | | | | |
| Rate in country of origin | 122 | 425 | 1101 | 2,576 | 19 | 91 | 418 | 1510 |
| After migration in Australia | | | | | | | | |
| Residence for 0–6 years | 77γ | 302# | 782γ | 1,593γ | 12 | 38* | 266# | 827γ |
| Residence for 7–19 years | 130 | 405 | 1,030 | 2576 | 11 | 77 | 425 | 1,285 |
| Residence for 20+ years | 134 | 516γ | 1,214γ | 2,678* | 36# | 135γ | 540# | 1,513 |
| Scotland | | | | | | | | |
| Rate in country of origin | 182 | 587 | 1,442 | 3,065 | 39 | 160 | 606 | 1,929 |
| After migration in Australia | | | | | | | | |
| Residence for 0–6 years | 162 | 275# | 1,308 | 2,275 | 61 | 107 | 424 | 1,397 |
| Residence for 7–19 years | 171 | 511 | 1,578 | 2,119 | 45 | 175 | 670 | 1,487 |
| Residence for 20+ years | 180 | 690* | 1,398 | 3,088 | 31 | 186 | 519* | 1,771 |
| Italy | | | | | | | | |
| Rate in country of origin | 70 | 228 | 655 | 1,732 | 20 | 77 | 342 | 1,425 |
| After migration in Australia | | | | | | | | |
| Residence for 0–6 years | 16# | 123* | 260# | 838* | 17 | 41 | 236 | 1,100 |
| Residence for 7–19 years | 51* | 170* | 376* | 1,513 | 8 | 68 | 252 | 1,066 |
| Residence for 20+ years | 130* | 344γ | 758* | 1,933 | 9 | 139* | 542γ | 1,348 |

*Source:* Stenhouse and McCall (1970). γ $p < 0.001$; # $p < 0.01$; * $p < 0.05$.

migrants following an exposure over a relatively short period (Saint, 1963). Data on compensation litigation noted a marked over-representation of non-British migrants in workers' compensation claims and litigation (Parker, 1970; Krupinski, 1984). A study by Parker (1970) found that although non-British European migrants accounted for 6% of the population at the time of his study, they were responsible for 22% of accident litigations. In contrast, British migrants constituted 10% of the population but accounted for only 6% of accident litigations. In terms of mental health, a high incidence of suicide was reported among migrants with a very high incidence reported among migrants from Austria, Czechoslovakia, Hungary, Sweden, a moderate incidence and similar to that of Australian-born migrants from Germany, New Zealand, Poland and the United Kingdom, and a very low incidence among migrants from Greece, Ireland, Italy, Malta and the Netherlands (Whitlock, 1971; Burvill *et al.*, 1973). The incidence of psychiatric disorders, especially schizophrenia and depressive illness, was highest among refugees from eastern Europe, followed by southern-European migrants (Krupinski, 1984).

## *Health of immigrants to Australia post-1990s*

The health of immigrants to Australia post the 1990s somehow mirrors that pattern observed prior to 1990. However, the magnitude of the burden has changed and this could be a result of the rigorous pre-migration health screening policy. As was the case for the pre-1990 period, comprehensive national surveys of the health of immigrants are lacking in Australia, and available evidence comes from audits of health services and/or retrospective case series for infectious diseases, and small studies looking at the burden of chronic diseases. In their review of infectious diseases screening of 2,111 refugee and humanitarian entrants in Western Australia between 2003 and 2004, Martin and Mak (2006) reported that 25% of all participants had a positive Mantoux test for tuberculosis result while 5% were carriers of Hepatitis B, and a further 5% had positive test results for syphilis. The authors reported that 6.4% of SSAs, 6.5% of south-east Asians and 6.8% of north Africans in Australia were Hepatitis B carriers. The authors concluded that "*disease prevalence varied greatly between refugees from different countries and was particularly high in those arriving from sub-Saharan Africa, the region of most Australia's refugee and humanitarian entrants*" (p. 607). This conclusion was flawed, politically motivated, and not supported by their findings. We re-analysed data from this study based on the findings summarised in Table 2 of the published article, comparing the prevalence of selected infectious diseases among refugees from SSA with that of refugees from other regions (Figure 2). Our findings suggest that the various rates of infectious diseases reported among refugees and humanitarian entrants from SSA were comparable to that reported among their north African counterparts for the Mantoux test (>=15 mm

Table 2: Age-standardised mortality rates from arteriosclerotic and degenerative heart disease by country of birth and length of residence in Australia per 100,000 of population, 1979

| Place of birth and/or residence | Males | Females |
|---|---|---|
| Australian-born | 856.3 | 428 |
| Italians in Italy | 404.9 | 300.9 |
| Italian migrants in Australia | 367.5 | 246.4 |
|    Residence for 0–6 years | 181.5 | 220.9 |
|    Residence for 7–19 years | 301.4 | 224.2 |
|    Residence for 20 or more years | 504.7 | 345.3 |

Source: Krupinski (1984).

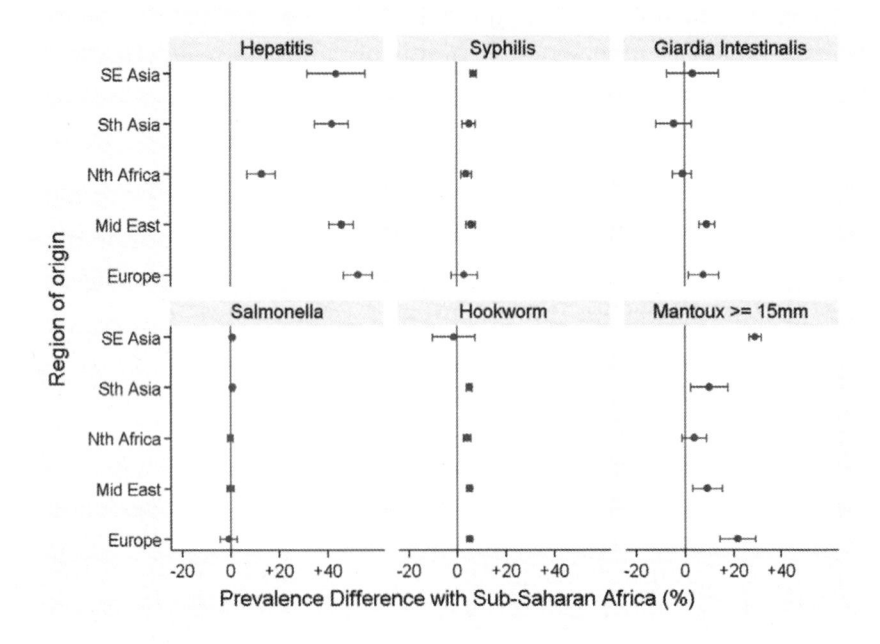

Figure 2: Difference estimate in the prevalence of infectious diseases between refugees and humanitarian entrants from SSA and those from other geographic locations.
Source: Re-analysis of data extracted from Martin and Mak (2006).

induration), refugees from South Asia, south-east Asia and North Africa for Giardia Intestinalis, and refugees from south-east Asia for hookworms. In fact, the prevalence of syphilis and Salmonella among SSA refugees and humanitarian entrants was respectively somewhere between 2.4% and 4.3% lower and 8.4% and 2.7% higher than those of a European background (Figure 2).

Our findings from the re-analysis of Martin and Mak (2006)'s data are to some extent supported by those reported by O'Sullivan and colleagues (2004) who estimated that only 1% of SSA, 5.4% of south-east Asian and 4.9% of north-east Asian migrants in Australia were Hepatitis B carriers. However, in a similar clinical audit at the Darwin Refugee Health Service, Johnston and colleagues (2012) reported that the prevalence of Hepatitis B carrier status and tuberculosis was 22% and 18%, respectively. Other studies reported a prevalence of Hepatitis B status varying from 8% to 16% (Tiong et al., 2006). The authors estimated that approximately 50% of the chronic Hepatitis B burden in Australia is among migrants, predominantly from south-east Asia (33.3%) and north-east Asia (16.2%). Other diseases documented among refugees and humanitarian entrants in Australia include malaria (between 1% and 10%), schistosomiasis (between 7% and 17%), hookworms (5%) and strongyloidiasis (2%) (Martin and Mak, 2006; Tiong et al., 2006). Findings from these studies need to be interpreted with caution due to differences in testing methods, use of difference cut-off points, variation in and skewed sample sizes, clustering of the diseases within families and the selective nature of the sampling strategies (i.e. targeting health services used by certain migrant groups and not others).

Migrants in general have a lower age-adjusted incidence for cancer and other chronic diseases than Australian-born, with a generally lower prevalence of colon, prostate, lung and breast cancers, lower age-adjusted cardiovascular disease mortality and hospitalisation rates, but a higher prevalence of bladder cancer, nasopharyngeal cancer and cardiovascular risk factors such as obesity, high blood pressure and diabetes when compared to Australian-born (Saleh et al., 2002; Anikeeva et al., 2010; Renzaho et al., 2011). In terms of mental health, migrants from countries with high suicide rates have been found to have higher age-adjusted rates of suicide than their Australian counterparts — this pattern is true for women from Oceania and Europe whereas those from Asia and the Middle East have been found to have lower rates than Australian-born. However, overall male migrants displayed a lower rate of suicide than Australian-born males (Anikeeva *et al.*, 2010). The most documented psychiatric disorders among migrants in Australia include higher rates of schizophrenia among Polish, Greek and former Yugoslavian migrants, higher rates of organic psychosis among Italian and Dutch migrants, and overall poorer mental health among Iranian, Sudanese, Vietnamese and Filipino refugees when compared with their Australian counterparts (Anikeeva *et al.*, 2010).

Despite migrants displaying a high prevalence of cardiovascular disease (CVD) risk factors, notably obesity, type-2 diabetes and hypertension, their overall mortality due to chronic and degenerative diseases is lower than their Australian counterparts (Tables 2 and 3). Although adherence to dietary habits such as the Mediterranean diet was put forward to explain the

Table 3: Cardiovascular disease age-standardised mortality ratios among Australians, 1987–1989

| Country of birth | Men | Women |
|---|---|---|
| **ESB countries** | | |
| United Kingdom and Ireland | 92* | 91* |
| South Africa | 89 | 85 |
| Canada | 96 | 66 |
| United States | 96 | 109 |
| New Zealand | 109 | 105 |
| Australia | 103* | 104* |
| **NESB countries** | | |
| Greece | 62* | 55* |
| Italy | 67* | 55* |
| Yugoslavia | 87* | 79* |
| Malta | 103 | 124* |
| Germany | 95 | 90 |
| Netherlands | 91 | 84* |
| Poland | 124* | 117* |
| Lebanon | 80* | 118 |

(*Continued*)

Table 3: (*Continued*)

| Country of birth | Men | Women |
| --- | --- | --- |
| Egypt | 90 | 122 |
| Vietnam | 30* | 35* |
| Malaysia | 71* | 59* |
| Philippines | 81 | 56* |
| China | 62* | 61* |
| Other Oceania (a) | 137* | 165* |
| Central and southern America | 54* | 69* |

*Ratio statistically significant from 100; $p < 0.05$.
*Source*: Adapted from Young (1986).

migrants' health advantage (Kouris-Blazos *et al.*, 1999), it has been hypothesised that risk factors known to be associated with CVDs such as systolic and diastolic blood pressure, total plasma cholesterol, high-density lipoprotein cholesterol, triglyceride, low-density lipoprotein, body mass index, smoking status, alcohol consumption, leisure-time physical activity and high-density lipoprotein cholesterol to triglyceride ratio are not sufficient to explain the lower than expected standardised mortality ratios among migrants in Australia (Dunt, 1982; Renzaho, 2007). Instead the "healthy-migrant effect" has been postulated as one of the possible explanations (Dunt, 1982). How real is the healthy migrant effect? How much of the effects can be explained by the salmon bias? These are the questions we tackle below.

## The healthy migrant effect: challenges

The healthy migrant effect is a well-documented phenomenon whereby migrants from low- and middle-income countries to industrialised countries such as Australia, Canada, the United Kingdom or the USA are often found to be healthier than people in their country of origin and the host population. However, this health advantage diminishes with length of residence, approximating and, among some migrant groups, overtaking the health profile of the host population. This deterioration of health among migrants over time is often linked to migrants' poor living and working conditions, and leads to substantial burden of disability later in life, a concept described in the literature as the "exhausted migrant effect" (Domnich *et al.*, 2012). Four possible explanations have been provided: (1) the rigorous pre-migration health screening means that only healthy migrants are more likely to be granted permanent migration visa, (2) migrant self-selection in country of origin means that migrants relocating to industrialised countries are physically and mentally healthier, wealthier and have healthier behaviours than those remaining behind, (3) the healthy workers effect means that migrant workers are selected for their good health and ability to work in their destination countries and potential migrant workers who are ill and chronically disabled are less likely to be granted a work visa, and (4) the time travellers theory also known as the "cultural buffering" effect whereby relative to the host country, migrants perceived to come from a "past" stage of the health transition characterised by lifestyles that are healthier than those in the host people (exposed to fewer or lower doses of risk factors for CVDs (Dunt, 1982; Rust, 1990; McDonald and Kennedy, 2004; Razum, 2006; Domnich *et al.*, 2012).

There have been a series of evidence to support the healthy migrant effect (Tables 2 and 3). Razum *et al.* (1998) undertook a study to test whether minority Turkish migrants with lower socioeconomic status in Germany experience a higher mortality than their German counterparts. The study covered the 1980–1994 time period and included all-cause mortality rates among people aged 25–65 years. The authors used the death registry data and used the mid-year population estimates to compute mortality rates. They found that over the study period, the overall all-cause death rates among Turkish migrants were 35–70% lower than that of their German counterparts of the same age group and sex. Interesting that the mortality advantage observed among Turkish migrants did not decline with time of residence to approximate to the mortality rate observed among German-born. Turkish migrants' all-cause mortality rate remained consistently lower than that of the German population and Turkish in country of origin. In a follow-up study, Razum and colleagues (2000) documented the mortality experience of Turkish migrants aged between 15 and 64 years using the German Socio-Economic Panel between 1984 and 1997. The dataset contained 23,769 individuals. They found that crude mortality rates (CMR) per 1,000 person-years were significantly lower among Turkish migrants

(CMR: 2.19; 95% CI: 1.72–2.78) than that of their German counterparts (CMR: 8.54; 95% CI: 8.08–9.04). These findings remained consistent after adjusting for gender, age and year of arrival in Germany (adjusted relative risk: 0.63; 95% CI: 0.49–0.82) and there was no secular increase in their mortality. It is interesting to note that the study also found a cohort effect Turkish migrants who arrived in the 1991–1997 period. They recorded lower mortality rates than those who arrived in the 1984–1990 period (adjusted relative risk: 0.77; 95% CI: 0.69–0.86).

McDonald and Kennedy (2004) undertook a comprehensive analysis of pooled cross-sectional data from the National Population Health Survey and the Canadian Community Health Survey to test and confirm the "healthy immigrant effect" hypothesis. They confirmed the existence of the healthy migrant effect among newly arrived migrants in that they were less likely to be diagnosed with a chronic condition than their Canadian-born counterparts. However, the health advantage persisted and the gap in health between migrants and Canadian-born narrowed significantly over time and the incidence of chronic conditions was comparable after approximately 20 years, which is consistent with the literature (Kliewer, 1992). This study was among the few to also report a cohort effect, the effect of the age at arrival and region of origin. The year of arrival was an important determinant of health status among men but not in women. Men arriving in Canada prior to the 1960s had better health than either more recent migrants or the Canadian-born population. The authors note that younger immigrants had significantly better health on arrival than older people and speculate that this could be a result of the negative selection hypothesis where older migrants may be less healthy because they migrate to Canada to take advantage of an advanced health care system. Finally, migrants from a non-English speaking background such as mainly continental Europe and Asia had a significantly lower incidence of chronic diseases than Canadian-born and migrants from an English-speaking background. In fact, there was no difference in incidence of chronic diseases between Canadian-born and migrants from English-speaking countries such as the UK, Ireland, USA, Australia and New Zealand. The effect of region of origin has also been reported in Australia, with migrants in Australia found with better health than Australian-born counterparts but this health advantage declines with length of residence in Australia, plateauing at 20 years (Biddle *et al.*, 2007). Nevertheless, the health advantage among migrants in Australia was more evident for migrants from non-English-speaking countries than those from English-speaking countries, and the latter were found to have a similar health profile as the Australian-born population (Biddle *et al.*, 2007). Data from cohort studies have confirmed the healthy migrant effect. Swerdlow (1991) analysed mortality and cancer incidence data in a cohort of 3,327 Vietnamese refugees who migrated to Britain after the end of the Vietnam war. The author found that there was overall lower mortality rates among Vietnamese refugees when compared to the national mortality rates for England and Wales. He estimated the all-cause standardised mortality ratio at 64 (95% CI: 52–77) for males and 56 (95% CI: 44–71) for females. In other words, compared to the host population, mortality rates among Vietnamese refugees were 36% lower in men and 44% lower in women.

However, the concept of the "healthy migrant effect" needs to be scrutinised for many reasons. It is possible that the magnitude of migrants' health is either underplayed or glossed over due to methodological flaws. It is also possible that culture-related barriers and behaviours that affect the health of migrants are poorly understood by researchers, service providers and policymakers. In the section that follows, we summarise the most pertinent challenges that may help shed light on the relevance of the healthy migrant effect and explore some of the policy implications.

## *Challenge 1: voluntary vs. forced migration*

It is important to make a distinction between voluntary and forced migration. The voluntary migration scheme includes economic/skilled migration or family reunion, while forced migration encompasses refugees and humanitarian entrants such as women at risk or asylum seekers. The healthy migrant effect is more likely to be true for voluntary migrants and less so for refugees and humanitarian entrants for many reasons. Refugees enter industrialised countries either directly from refugee camps or from transition countries. Regardless of their community of origin, refugee populations are well known to have poorer health indicators than the pre-migration communities from which they came (Toole and Waldman, 1997). Forced migrants are often exposed to various levels of traumas such as natural disasters and human-made disasters including wars, ethnic conflicts, political persecutions, living in a refugee camp or human trafficking (Grove and Zwi, 2006), which is in addition to poorer heath care systems in many developing countries from which they originate. Similarly, refugees' pre-migration health will depend on how long they have lived in a refugee camp. Apart from tuberculosis, refugees cannot be denied entry to Australia on medical grounds, pre-departure medical assessment is limited in scope and the post-arrival health care is not formally managed by government agencies as Australian States and Territories do not have routine post-arrival health checks (Davidson *et al.*, 2004). On arrival, most refugees may have limited access to education and hence have poor health literacy, and lack the knowledge to navigate the complex system in their new environment which can be compounded by their poor oral and written English. Therefore, they tend to have poor health and health outcomes than the host population, although some researchers argue that on arrival refugees immediately benefit from better access to medical care for infectious diseases and emergencies, hence providing a mortality advantage (Abraido-Lanza *et al.*, 1999). Despite these important confounding factors, studies examining the healthy migrant effect do not examine the data by migration status. Similarly, studies that have attempted to incorporate the health profile of populations in migrants' country of origin as a comparator, such as the study by Razum and colleagues (1998), relied on crude mortality data rather than age-standardised mortality rates, making comparisons very difficult. Further studies testing the healthy migrant effect would need to examine migrants' health data by migration status and account for their improved access to medical care in host countries which could benefit refugees, especially for infectious diseases and emergencies. It is thus possible that while the healthy migrant effect could be true for voluntary migration, this would not be the case for forced migration (refugees, asylum seekers, internally displaced people or smuggled or trafficked people), and any improved access to health services might in itself increase their mortality advantage.

## *Challenge 2: methodological fallacies and the salmon bias*

There has been a gross underestimation of health issues among migrants due to methodological flaws. Consider for example the issue of alcohol and drug use among migrant populations in Australia. Few studies have found that levels of alcohol and illicit drug use are low among migrant populations when compared to the general Australian population. That is, migrants, especially those from a non-English background are more likely to abstain from both alcohol and illicit drugs than those migrants from an English-speaking background (Department of Human Services, 2000; Australian Institute of Health and Welfare, 2008). However, the issue of alcohol and illicit drug use is a culturally sensitive one, thus self-reported measures may be inhibited because of negative cultural and religious attitudes associated with these behaviours, while obtaining valid or objective measures may be difficult (Department of Human Services, 2000). Similarly, migrants' participation rates in formal research are often low and non-users may be more inclined to participate in surveys than users (United Nations Office on Drugs and Crime, 2004). There is the salmon bias hypothesis, which has been postulated to dispute the merit of the healthy migrant effect. The salmon bias stipulates that many migrants may prefer to return home when they become critically ill to convalesce and possibly to die (Pablos-Méndez, 1994; Weitoft et al., 1999). If these statistics are not included in mortality data examining the healthy migrant effect, migrant mortality rates become distorted. However, it is difficult to assess departing migrants' health or whether they die due to the complexity and methodological complications of tracing migrant health after they return home (Pablos-Méndez, 1994; Turra and Elo, 2008).

## *Challenge 3: under-representation in research*

Migrants remain under-represented in community-based interventions and research. Researchers have often wrongly blamed these communities for this under-representation, arguing that they either fail to understand the importance of the research process or are unable to participate because of language barriers (Sheikh, 2006). However, a landmark systematic review (Wendler et al., 2006) found that socioeconomically disadvantaged communities as well as migrant populations in developed countries are on the whole no less likely, and possibly even more likely, to participate in research when approached than mainstream communities. The authors noted that the main barrier to the participation of socioeconomically disadvantaged communities lies in their reduced likelihood of being invited to participate. Indeed, in major randomised controlled trials (RCTs) (Greaves et al.,

2008; McMurran *et al.*, 2011; O'Neil *et al.*, 2011) and systematic reviews/meta-analyses (Moher *et al.*, 1996), one of the inclusion criteria is proficiency in spoken English, hence excluding migrant populations who do not speak English, yet who are more likely to experience the highest burden of diseases. The reasons for excluding participants from non-English speaking backgrounds or study published in a language other than English are diverse, including the prohibitive costs associated with interpreting and translation during recruitment or data collection. However, adopting such an approach introduces substantial biases, makes the RCTs and the review process flawed, and exaggerates the results or evidence because authors are more likely to publish RCTs in an English-language journal when the results are statistically significant (Moher *et al.*, 1996; Egger *et al.*, 1997; Pham *et al.*, 2005). Similarly, a considerable number of refugees migrating under the Refugee and Humanitarian Entrants scheme lived in refugee camps prior to migration and had little exposure to research prior to migration, apart from surveys to determine their eligibility for humanitarian assistance such as food rations, accommodation/shelter and welfare services. In this sense, any participation in research implies immediate financial return. That is, participation in research is only for instrumental use, which may breach ethical guidelines. This can exacerbate the low participation rate observed among migrant populations. Hence, migrants who can communicate and interact with their new system are more likely to be included in the studies and would benefit from accessing available health services. In contrast, those who are intimidated by the health system due to cultural and linguistic factors are less likely to interact with the health system and could be under-represented in the major health datasets.

## Challenge 4: poor data mapping, integration and coordination

In Australia, a lot of data is being collected by government institutions, and many of the surveys include data on migration status and health. Cases in point include the Longitudinal Survey of Australian Children, the Household, Income, and Labour Dynamics in Australia, the Victorian Child Health and Wellbeing study, Visa Medical Examination & Pre-departure Medical Screening, the Longitudinal Survey of Immigrants to Australia, the Continuous Survey of Australian Migrants, the Survey of New Arrivals, the Survey of Income and Housing; and the Longitudinal Study of Humanitarian Migrants just to name a few. There are similarities in these surveys, but they are often conducted by different organisations for different purposes related to understanding determinants of health, immigration, social security or census. There are no clear data linkages and integration approaches in place, and the extent to which these data can be pooled to examine the healthy migrant effect to inform policies geared towards addressing social and health inequalities is limited.

## Challenge 5: tough immigration law vs. public health gain

Australia has always experienced skill shortages over the years, mainly in construction, mining, hospitality, nursing and farm work. Such skill shortages are often addressed by ensuring the skilled migration stream accounts for the majority of migration programmes (e.g. the number of visas for permanent residence, excluding New Zealand citizens and visas issued under the Humanitarian Program). Ironically, the Australian government has also strong border protection policies, whose aim is two-fold: (1) policies as deterrents to undocumented migrants deemed by the government as unlawful (i.e. those arriving in Australia without a visa or whose visa has expired), and (2) policies geared towards the deportation of unlawful migrants who are not eligible for a refugee status (Glendenning *et al.*, 2003). Migration-related health data to better inform health policies, such as capturing those returning home for health reasons or making the pre-migration health screening comprehensive for public health gains are lacking. The extent to which the merit of the salmon bias or the healthy migrant effect can be tested is limited. It is difficult to address the mismatch between immigration laws and migration health policies.

## Challenge 6: differing cultural values

While the collectivism–individualism continuum has been used to characterise and evaluate management styles and strategies (Healy *et al.*, 2004) and to understand how it influences health-seeking behaviours (Cauce *et al.*, 2002), the influence of individualistic and collectivist values on research methods remains neglected in public health and health promotion programmes. Collectivist communities are strongly characterised by group memberships in which hierarchy, respect for opinion formers and family relations are extremely important, and decisions are based on group consensus and the group regulates what its members do and intend to do while emphasising conformity and compliance to social or group norms (Triandis, 1995, 2000). That is, individuals work for the group and not for own personal gain and they are subordinate to the collective. The emphasis is on inter-dependence. In contrast, individualistic communities are characterised by the emphasis on self-reliance, self-determination, liberty, and, above all, personal independence. The goal is to fulfil individual needs and personal goals and personal excellence and status are extremely important (Triandis, 1995, 2000). The main threads of individualism include taking responsibility for own actions, protection of individual rights by law and the opposition of societal authority over the will of the individual (Schwartz, 1990). In collectivist cultures, such as the case of migrants in Australia who are mostly from non-English backgrounds, everyone is expected get along with each other, and people's actions or competence are evaluated on the basis of their networks and who they know (Diaz-Guerrero, 1979; Triandis, 2000).

These value orientations have relevance when discussing the healthy migrant effect. It is well established that the traditional collectivistic social orientation and the philosophy of harmony that characterise collectivist communities are associated with the valuing of the health and wellbeing of the whole community and family more than the health of individuals (Chesla and Chun, 2005; Deng et al., 2013). This means enforcing behaviours and lifestyle that promote the wellbeing of the community and the family. One example is the effect of the Mediterranean diet in countries bordering the Mediterranean Sea such as Greece, Italy, France and Spain. In this sense, the maintenance of a healthy traditional Mediterranean diet is an expression of cultural values, and their history, and communal lifestyle and identity (Trichopoulou and Lagiou, 1997). Various studies have showed that longer survival among migrants who consume the Mediterranean diet is associated with the adherence to the principles of the traditional Mediterranean diet (Kouris-Blazos et al., 1999; Trichopoulou and Vasilopoulou, 2000; Sofi et al., 2008). Kouris-Blazos and colleagues (1999) reported that for every unit increase in a Mediterranean diet score there was a 17% reduction in overall mortality among Anglo-Celts as among Greek-Australians. These findings are similar to those reported in the literature and meta-analyses (Mitrou *et al.*, 2007; Sofi *et al.*, 2008). However, studies in the healthy migrant effect rarely adjust for dietary habits nor do they consider the influence of culture on health.

## Conclusion

There is a gap in the availability of high-quality information and research in the field of migration health. To better understand the healthy migrant effect, future research needs to examine data by migration status and incorporate mortality data in the populations of origin. Public health interventions need to develop and test models that best conceptualise migrants' health issues and advocate for integrated migration management policies for health. Efficient information systems must be developed which include the collection of data to build indicators to assess migrants' health and needs. Understanding and conceptualising how different cultural processes interact with the social environment and how this subsequently influences the health of migrants beyond the healthy migrant effect would be a better starting point to inform health policies in Australia. Public health programmes need to incorporate social outcomes such as social connectedness and cultural participation, and to focus on bridging the individualism–collectivism gaps to promote the maintenance or the adoption of a healthy, successful life among migrants.

## References

Abraido-Lanza, A. *et al.* (1999). The Latino mortality paradox: A test of the 'salmon-bias' and 'healthy migrant hypotheses'. *American Journal of Public Health*, 89, 1543–1548.

Anikeeva, O. *et al.* (2010). Review paper: The health status of migrants in Australia: a review. *Asia Pacific Journal of Public Health*, 22(2), 159–193.

Australian Bureau of Statistics (2009). Perspectives on Migrants. Cat. No. 3416.0. ABS, Canberra, AUS.

Australian Bureau of Statistics (2015). Migration, Australia, 2011–12 and 2012–13. Cat. No. 3412.0. ABS, Canberra, AUS.

Australian House of Representatives (1901). Pacific Island Labourers Act 1901 (Cth): An Act to provide for the Regulation, Restriction, and Prohibition of the Introduction of Labourers from the Pacific Islands and for other purposes (No. 16 of 1901). Avalable at: http://foundingdocs.gov.au/item-did-15.html. Accessed 31 July 2015.

Australian Institute of Health and Welfare (2008). 2007 National Drug Strategy Household Survey: Detailed findings, Cat. no. PHE 107. AIHW, Canberra, AUS.

Biddle, N. et al. (2007). Health assimilation patterns amongst Australian immigrants. *Economic Record*, 83(260), 16–30.

Burgmann, V. (1984). Racism, socialism, and the Labour Movement, 1887–1917. *Labour History*, 47, 39–54.

Burvill, P. et al. (1973). Deaths from suicide, motor vehicle accidents and all forms of violent death among migrants in Australia, 1962–66. *Acta Psychiatrica Scandinavica*, 49(1), 28–50.

Cauce, A.M. et al. (2002). Cultural and contextual influences in mental health help seeking: A focus on ethnic minority youth. *Journal of Consulting and Clinical Psychology*, 70(1), 44–55.

Chesla, C.A. & Chun, K.M. (2005). Accommodating type 2 diabetes in the Chinese American family. *Qualitative Health Research*, 15(2), 240–255.

Clark, M. (1969). *A short history of Australia, Revised Edition*. Signet Books, New York, NY.

Commonwealth of Australia (2002). Immigration update 2001–2002. Commonwealth of Australia, Canberra, AUS.

Davidson, N. et al. (2004). Comprehensive health assessment for newly arrived refugee children in Australia. *Journal of Paediatrics and Child Health*, 40(9–10), 562–568.

Deng, F. et al. (2013). Acculturation, dietary acceptability, and diabetes management among Chinese in North America. *Frontiers in Endocrinology*, 4, 1–6.

Department of Human Services (2000). Drugs in a multicultural community: An assessment of involvement. DHS, Melbourne, AUS.

Department of Immigration and Multicultural and Indigenous Affairs (2002). Abolition of the 'White Australia' policy. Fact sheet. Available at: http://intranet.cbhslewisham.nsw.edu.au:82/sor/supdocs/AustDeptImmigFactsSheetAbolWhiteAustPol.pdf. Accessed 2 April 2015.

Diaz-Guerrero, R. (1979). The development of coping style. *Human Development* 22(5), 320–331.

Domnich, A. et al. (2012). The "healthy immigrant" effect: Does it exist in Europe today? *Italian Journal of Public Health*, 9(3), e75321–e75327.

Dunt, D.R. (1982). Recent mortality trends in the adult Australian population and its principal ethnic groupings. *Community Health Studies*, 6(3), 217–222.

Dunt, D.R. & Parker, M.L. (1973). A computer data processing system for hospital obstetric records. Obstetric complications in non-English speaking migrants. *Medical Journal of Australia*, 2(14), 693–698.

Egger, M. et al. (1997). Language bias in randomised controlled trials published in English and German. *The Lancet*, 350(9074), 326–329.

Giorgas, D. (2008). *Transnationalism and Identity among Second Generation Greek-Australian. Ties to the Homeland: Second Generation Transnationalism*. Cambridge Scholars Publishing, Newcastle, AUS.

Glendenning, P. et al. (2003). *No Liability–tragic Results from Australia's deportations*. Edmund Rice Centre for Justice & Community Education and the Australian Catholic University, Homebush West, AUS.

Graves, A. (1993). *Cane and labour: The Political Economy of the Queensland Sugar Industry, 1862–1906*. Edinburgh University Press, Edinburgh, SCO.

Greaves, C. et al. (2008). Motivational interviewing for modifying diabetes risk: A randomised controlled trial. *British Journal of General Practice*, 58(553), 535–540.

Grove, N.J. & Zwi, A.B. (2006). Our health and theirs: Forced migration, othering, and public health. *Social Science & Amp Medicine*, 62(8), 1931–1942.

Healy, G. et al. (2004). Individualism and collectivism revisited: A study of black and minority ethnic women. *Industrial Relations Journal*, 35(5), 451–466.

Henderson, P. (1988). *Parliament and Politics in Australia: Political Institutions and Foreign Relations*. (5th edition). Heinemann Educational, Melbourne, AUS.

Johnston, V. et al. (2012). The health of newly arrived refugees to the Top End of Australia: Results of a clinical audit at the Darwin Refugee Health Service. *Australian Journal of Primary Health*, 18(3), 242–247.

Jupp, J. (1990). 'Two hundred years of immigration.' The health of immigrant Australia: A social perspective. In: J. Reid and P. Trompf (eds.), *The Health of Immigrant Australia: A Social Perspective*. Harcourt Brace Jovanovich, Sydney, AUS. pp. 11–38.

Jupp, J. (2002). *From White Australia to Woomera: The Story of Australian Immigration*. Cambridge University Press, Cambrige.

Kliewer, E. (1992). Epidemiology of diseases among migrants. *International Migration*, 30(s1), 141–165.

Kouris-Blazos, A. et al. (1999). Are the advantages of the Mediterranean diet transferable to other populations? A cohort study in Melbourne, Australia. *British Journal of Nutrition*, 82(1), 57–61.

Krupinski, J. (1984). Changing patterns of migration to Australia and their influence on the health of migrants. *Social Science & Medicine*, 18(11), 927–937.

Last, J. (1960). The health of immigrants: Some observations from general practice. *The Medical Journal of Australia*, 47, 158–162.

MacDonald, J.S. & MacDonald, I.D. (1970). Italian migration to Australia: Manifest functions of bureaucracy versus latent functions of informal networks. *Journal of Social History*, 3(3), 249–275.

Martin, J.A. & Mak, D.M. (2006). Changing faces: A review of infectious disease screening of refugees by the Migrant Health Unit, Western Australia in 2003 and 2004. *Medical Journal Australia*, 185(11–12), 607–610.

McDonald, J.T. & Kennedy, S. (2004). Insights into the 'healthy immigrant effect': Health status and health service use of immigrants to Canada. *Social Science & Medicine*, 59(8), 1613–1627.

McMichael, A. & Bonett, A. (1981). Cancer profiles of British and southern-European migrants. Exploring South Australia's cancer registry data. *Medical Journal of Australia*, 1(5), 229–232.

McMurran, M. et al. (2011). Psycho-education with problem solving (PEPS) therapy for adults with personality disorder: A pragmatic multi-site community-based randomised clinical trial. *Trials*, 12, 1–10.

Mitrou, P.N. et al. (2007). Mediterranean dietary pattern and prediction of all-cause mortality in a US population: Results from the NIH-AARP Diet and Health Study. *Archives of Internal Medicine*, 167(22), 2461–2468.

Moher, D. et al. (1996). Completeness of reporting of trials published in languages other than English: Implications for conduct and reporting of systematic reviews. *The Lancet*, 347(8998), 363–366.

Moore, C. (1999). 'Good-bye, Queensland, good-bye, white Australia; Good-bye, Christians': Australia's South Sea Islander community and deportation, 1901–1908. *The New Federalist*, 4, 22–29.

O'Neil, A. et al. (2011). A randomised, feasibility trial of a tele-health intervention for Acute Coronary Syndrome patients with depression ('MoodCare'): Study protocol. *BMC Cardiovascular Disorders*, 11(1), 8.

O'Neil, N. & Handley, R. (1994). *Retreat from Injustice: Human Rights in Australian Law*. The Federation Press, Sydney, AUS.

O'Neill, N. et al. (2004). *Retreat from Injustice: Human Rights Law in Australia*. Federation Press, Sydney, AUS.

O'Sullivan, B.G. et al. (2004). Estimates of chronic hepatitis B virus infection in Australia, 2000. *Australian and New Zealand Journal of Public Health*, 28(3), 212–216.

Pablos-Méndez, A. (1994). Mortality among Hispanics. *Journal of the American Medical Association*, 271(16), 1237–1238.

Parker, N. (1970). Accident neurosis. *Medical Journal of Australia*, 2(8), 362–365.

Petrilli, S. & Ponzio, A. (2009). Migration and hospitality: Homologies between Europe and Australia. In: R. Summo-O'Connell (ed.), *Imagined Australia: Reflections around the Reciprocal Construction of Identity Between Australia and Europe*, Peter Lang, Bern, SWI. pp. 305–331.

Pham, B. *et al.* (2005). Language of publication restrictions in systematic reviews gave different results depending on whether the intervention was conventional or complementary. *Journal of Clinical Epidemiology*, 58(8), 769–776, e762.

Proust, A.J. (1974). Proceedings: The Australian screening program for tuberculosis in prospective migrants. *Medical Journal of Australia*, 2(2), 35–37.

Razum, O. (2006). Commentary: Of salmon and time travellers — musing on the mystery of migrant mortality. *International Journal of Epidemiology*, 35(4), 919–921.

Razum, O.H. *et al.* (1998). Low overall mortality of Turkish residents in Germany persists and extends into a second generation: Merely a healthy migrant effect? *Tropical Medicine & International Health*, 3(4), 297–303.

Razum, O. *et al.* (2000). The 'healthy migrant effect'—not merely a fallacy of inaccurate denominator figures. *International Journal of Epidemiology*, 29, 191–192.

Renzaho, A. (2007). Ischaemic heart disease and Australian immigrants: The influence of birthplace and language skills on treatment and use of health services. *Health Information Management Journal*, 36(2), 26–36.

Renzaho, A.M.N. *et al.* (2011). Prevalence of vitamin D insufficiency and risk factors for type 2 diabetes and cardiovascular disease among African migrant and refugee adults in Melbourne. *Asia Pacific Journal of Clinical Nutrition*, 20(3), 397–403.

Rust, G.S. (1990). Health status of migrant farmworkers: A literature review and commentary. *American Journal of Public Health*, 80(10), 1213–1217.

Saint, E.G. (1963). The medical problems of migrants. *Medical Journal of Australia*, 50, 335–338.

Saleh, A. *et al.* (2002). The effect of migration on dietary intake, type 2 diabetes and obesity: The Ghanaian Health and Nutrition Analysis in Sydney, Australia (GHANAISA). *Ecology of Food and Nutrition*, 41, 255–270.

Schwartz, S.H. (1990). Individualism-collectivism. *Journal of Cross-Cultural Psychology*, 21(2), 139–157.

Sheikh, A. (2006). Why are ethnic minorities under-represented in US research studies? *PloS Medicine*, 3(2), 166–167.

Sofi, F. *et al.* (2008). Adherence to Mediterranean diet and health status: Meta-analysis. *BMJ*, 337, a1344.

Staszewski, J. (1972). Migrant studies in alimentary tract cancer. In: Grundmann, E. Tulinius, H. (eds.), *Current Problems in the Epidemiology of Cancer and Lymphomas*. Springer, Berlin, GER, pp. 85–97.

Stenhouse, N. & McCall, M. (1970). Differential mortality from cardiovascular disease in migrants from England and Wales, Scotland and Italy, and native-born Australians. *Journal of Chronic Diseases*, 23(5), 423–431.

Swerdlow, A.J. (1991). Mortality and cancer incidence in Vietnamese refugees in England and Wales: A follow-up study. *International Journal of Epidemiology*, 20(1), 13–19.

Tiong, A. et al. (2006). Health issues in newly arrived African refugees attending general practice clinics in Melbourne. *Medical Journal of Australia*, 185(11–12), 602–606.

Toole, M.J. & Waldman, R.J. (1997). The public health aspects of complex emergencies and refugee situations 1. *Annual Review of Public Health*, 18(1), 283–312.

Triandis, H.C. (1995). *Individualism and Collectivism*. Westview Press, Boulder, CO.

Triandis, H.C. (2000). Culture and conflict. *International Journal of Psychology*, 35, 145–152.

Trichopoulou, A. & Lagiou, P. (1997). Healthy traditional Mediterranean diet: An expression of culture, history, and lifestyle. *Nutrition Reviews*, 55(11), 383–389.

Trichopoulou, A. & Vasilopoulou, E. (2000). Mediterranean diet and longevity. *British Journal of Nutrition*, 84(S2), S205–S209.

Turra, C. & Elo, I. (2008). The impact of salmon bias on the Hispanic mortality advantage: New evidence from social security data. *Population Research and Policy Review*, 27(5), 515–530.

United Nations Office on Drugs and Crime (2004). Drug abuse prevention among youth from ethnic and indigenous minorities. United Nations, New York, NY.

Weitoft, G.R. et al. (1999). Mortality statistics in immigrant research: Method for adjusting underestimation of mortality. *International Journal of Epidemiology*, 28(4), 756–763.

Wendler, D. et al. (2006). Are racial and ethnic minorities less willing to participate in health research? *Plos Medicine*, 3(2), 201–210.

Whitlock, F. (1971). Migration and suicide. *Medical Journal of Australia*, 2(17), 840–848.

Windschuttle, K. (2004). The White Australia policy: Race and shame in the Australian history wars. Macleay Press, Paddington.

Young, C.M. (1986). *Selection and survival: Immigrant mortality in Australia*. AGPS, Canberra, AUS.

Young, C.M. (1991). Changes in the demographic behaviour of migrants in Australia and the transition between generations. *Population Studies*, 45(1), 67–89.

# Chapter 12

# The social dimensions of migration and health in China

Professor Andre M.N. Renzaho

The People's Republic of China (hereafter, China) has emerged as a dominant regional power with global influence, but such dominance can be traced back to 1949 with the arrival of the Chinese Communist Party under Mao Zedong (Mark, 2013). Since then, the Chinese economy has experienced a rapid transformation. Data from the International Monetary Fund suggest that China's annual economic growth has averaged 9.8% since 1980, making it the world's fastest-growing economy (International Monetary Fund, 2013). The United States (US) Department of State's chronology of the US–China relations from 1784 to 2000 suggests that after Mao Zedong successfully drove the Nationalists from the mainland, China formed an alliance with the Soviet Union (United States Department of State, 2014). This alliance was shaky throughout the 1950s and 1960s and the tension between China and the Soviet Union peaked in 1969 due to a long-standing dispute over the eastern border between the two countries, hence paving the way for the beginning of China's normalised relations with the USA in the 1970s (United States Department of State, 2014). By 1980, the Chinese government, under Deng's leadership, launched economic reforms, marking the beginning of China's engagement in global trade with the international community (Beatriz, 2004; Chan, 2010; Sceats and Breslin, 2012). One of the consequences of the economic reforms was the beginning of complex migration patterns. It is commonly recognised that the huge influx of population from rural to urban areas was the combined consequences of residency policy (*hukou*) system change and economic reforms. Since the acceleration of reforms and opening-up in the 1970s and the ongoing loosening of the residency control, rural–urban migration has skyrocketed due to rapid industrialisation and urbanisation, as well as marketisation. This chapter provides an overview of the migration governance and mechanisms in China. It briefly describes the types of migrants in China, their burden of disease, and finishes with the discussion of key issues surrounding policy responses to internal migration in China.

## Migration governance and mechanisms in China

### Internal migration

The legal framework and legislative measures that guide migration processes in China (migration source, transit and destination) have been developing since 1949, and have shifted from restrictive to relaxed migration laws. It is not the purpose of this chapter to review the migration policy change in China as comprehensive reviews have been adequately undertaken by other researchers (Chan and Tsui, 1992; Fang and Wang, 2008; Liu, 2009). Briefly, the policies governing migration in China relate to internal and international migration. Following the Communist Revolution, China initiated a series of policies of intensive industrialisation in 1949 (Beatriz, 2004). Such policies resulted in the development of urban areas that privileged the proletarian class in terms of infrastructure, attractive wages, and social and health benefits (Beatriz, 2004; Fang and Wang, 2008). Consequently, in order to control population migration, rural–urban labour mobility and labour resources to constrain rural farmers to their farms, the Chinese government progressively introduced a range of measures, namely the *hukou* system, which was first set up in 1951, but promulgated in 1958 (Beatriz, 2004; Fang and Wang, 2008). Since 1958, the *hukou* system has been a compulsory household registration permit based primarily on place of birth or, as it is otherwise known, a domestic or internal passport (Chan and Zhang, 1999). At its inception, people involved in non-agricultural activities in urban areas were known as the non-agricultural *hukou* population, while those from rural areas were known as the agricultural *hukou* population (Chan and Tsui, 1992; Chan and Zhang, 1999). Non-agricultural *houkou* populations had access to a range of state-subsidised social, economic and cultural incentives including free grain rations, state housing, employment and medical care. In contrast, agricultural *houkou* populations were perceived as self-sufficient, and hence did not have access to state-subsidised benefits. This system controlled place-to-place migration, as any rural–urban migration needed authorised plans by both origin and destination governments or an official agreement prior to migration, and thus led to strictly controlled transfers of labour across economic sectors, where a free labour market was not a possibility (Fang and Wang, 2008). Formal or permanent moves, which involved crossing cities, and towns and township boundaries, had to be approved by the public security authorities. From this time, Chinese citizens no longer had freedom of movement within their country and everyone received a registration status, of either "rural" or "urban", and was assigned within a specific administrative unit (Chan, 2010). However, such strict control of people's movement and regulation of the labour allowed the Chinese government to maintain and sustain a surplus of low-cost workers in various state-owned enterprises.

The *hukou* system has continued to segregate the rural and the urban populations over the past five decades. However, prior to 1978, large-scale voluntary migration in China was not prevalent. Instead, this period was characterised by involuntary migration directed by the government such as the coastal-to-inland migration of workers and families between the 1950s and the mid-1960s, and the Great Cultural Revolution during which intellectuals, cadres and entertainment workers moved from cities to rural areas (Fang, 1990). In recognition of the geographic, political and socio-economic inequalities the *hukou* system created, a series of revisions were undertaken to address some of the fundamental issues the system itself had brought about. For example, in the 1980s, the 'Household Responsibility System' was introduced as a way of addressing inequalities and of solving the long-standing incentive problem by raising the price the state paid for agricultural products (Fang and Wang, 2008). Under this system, the government gave farmers a quota of goods to produce. Framers who met the quota received compensation and there was no reward for any goods produced beyond the prescribed quota. Any surplus would be sold in the free market at unregulated prices. This reform stimulated an increase in agricultural productivity and released surplus labourers from agriculture (Fang and Wang, 2008). According to Chan and Zhang (1999), prior to 1985 long-term migration was discouraged and only people planning a short-term stay in cities were favoured. Consequently, any person with a short-term stay and who did not have local regular *hukou* was considered a temporary resident. The aim of favouring short-term stay migration was to strictly restrict migration from rural to urban areas and between urban areas.

In 1985, the Standing Committee of the National People's Congress promulgated the Residents Identification Card. All adults (>=16 years) visiting urban areas had to apply for an identification card which was valid for one year and renewable. The policy mandated identity checks, hence making the identity card not only a pass to mobility but also a pass to business transactions (Wong, 1994; Chan and Zhang, 1999). After 1992, motivated by Deng Xiaoping's speech while travelling through South China, a reform of the market-oriented economy in China gained momentum. Following the rapidly developing economy that accompanied significant foreign investments into coastal areas, there were high demands for labourers by foreign companies. The Chinese government began to play a positive role as a facilitator in rural-to-urban migration to tap into the surplus rural labour (Ling and Yue, 2011). Therefore, the internal migration in China was the combined consequence of a change in the residency policy system and economic reforms. In 2001, a new amendment was made allowing fixed domicile and legal income earners to apply for an urban *hukou* (Beijing Review, 2014). By 2013, the need to accelerate reform on the household registration system was recognised by the Third Plenary Session of the 18th National Congress of the Communist Party of China, which was actioned in 2014 (Beijing Review, 2014). That is, the State Council's publication of the 'Opinions on Further Promotion of the Reform of Household Registration System' which would remove the rural–urban divide and end the *houkou* registration system, as urban and rural residents would no longer be distinguished from one another. Such changes mean that small towns will be assigned rural residence status unconditionally, but urban cities must accept and recognise new migrants who have worked and lived in such cities for a certain period

## *International migration*

In terms of international migration, the policies relate to the control of exit and entry of citizens. From 1949 to 1978, the immigration residence and settlement was fully controlled by the state, mainly in response to China's perception of hostility towards it from Western countries (Liu, 2009). Consequently, visas for entry, internal travel and exit purposes were tightly controlled, and Chinese citizens needed to apply for exit permission to go overseas. The 1979–1985 period marked the start of reform to this restrictive migration framework, with the aim of establishing a socialist market economy, characterised by the relaxation of restrictions on international migration and recognising exiting the country as a legitimate right of Chinese citizens (Liu, 2009). These reforms guiding visas for exit and entry were officially endorsed by enacting the Law on the Control of Exit and Entry of Citizens 1985 (PRC) and the Legal recognition of Chinese right to leave and return (RLR) in 1986 (Liu, 2009). The provisions of these two laws were geared towards promoting international exchange by safeguarding the legitimate rights and interests of Chinese citizens in relation to exiting and entering China. These laws went through further revisions between 1986 and 2001, encouraging the return of the Chinese diaspora and establishing migration intermediary agencies (Liu, 2009). With China's accession to membership of the World Trade Organisation in 2001, the state recognised the need to simplify procedures and processes for obtaining a passport for Chinese citizens and protection of privacy (written permission from work units were no longer needed) (Liu, 2009). By 2012, China felt the need to overhaul the 1985 Law on the Control of Exit and Entry of Citizens. The Standing Committee of the National People's Congress passed the new Exit and Entry Administration Law, which came into force in July 2013 (Bryan Cave, 2012). The new law mirrored the migration legal frameworks of Western countries by strictly regulating foreigners' visas, residence and rights in China. The main aim was that of combatting illegal entry, safeguarding China's sovereignty, security and social order, promoting foreign exchanges, and opening China to the outside world. The main features of the new law that make it unique and distinguish it from previous legal frameworks include increasing fines and introducing new measures (Bryan Cave, 2012):

- Amendment: Linking residence certificates to employment status (previously not linked): valid for minimum of 90 days up to 5 years for work residence certificates and a minimum of 180 days up to 5 years for non-work residence certificates (Article 30).
- New: Compulsory provision of fingerprints and other biometric data (Article 30).
- New: Expected reporting of illegal foreigners to local public security bureaus, including illegal immigrants, illegal residence and illegal employment (Article 45).
- Amendment: Increased and elaborated punishments for illegal residence, with a warning for the first offence, a fine of RMB 500 per day up to a maximum of RMB 10,000 for serious offences, in some situations a detention for 5–15 days (Article 78).
- Amendment: Increased and elaborated punishments for illegal employment, with illegal foreign workers fined between RMB 5,000 and RMB 20,000; and in serious cases, the same fine plus detention for five to 15 days. Employers of illegal workers fined RMB 10,000 per foreigner, up to a maximum of RMB 100,000 and any benefits stemming from illegal employment confiscated (Article 80).
- New: Introduction of time limit for re-entry if deported: violation of the law may lead to being ordered to leave the country, and in serious situations, deported. Once deported, a ban, of a minimum of 10 years, is imposed before re-entry is allowed (Article 81).

## Dynamics and types of migration: a historical perspective

The impact of migration on economic growth and urban development in China is well documented (Fang and Wang, 2008). China has been described as a "crucial hub of the new global migration order", attracting thousands of immigrants from neighbouring Asian countries (Pieke, 2007). However, collecting reliable data on the foreign population in China proves to be a daunting task due to terminological challenges associated with the distinction between 'foreigners', 'non-Chinese foreigners', 'former Chinese nationals with foreign nationality' or Chinese nationals from Taiwan, Hong Kong, and Macao (Pieke, 2012). Notwithstanding this challenge, migrants in China can be grouped into three broad categories: rural–urban migration, immigration to China and emigration from China (Skeldon, 2012).

## *Rural–urban migration*

The complex phenomenon of population flow from rural to urban areas in post-reform China is well described by Fang and Wang (2008). Internal migration in China can be categorised into three major groups: (i) migrant with local residency rights (*hukou* migration), (ii) permanent migration with or without *hukou* change, and (iii) "floating" rural labour migrants, i.e. temporary migrants without *hukou* residency rights but are entitled to work in the urban areas with a temporary visa (Wing and Zhang, 1999). As discussed in the preceding section, the agricultural *hukou* population are often described as second-class citizens. From its inception, the non-agricultural *hukou* population was provided with food rations and grain subsidies, greater employment opportunities, and free education, medical care and old-age pensions (Chan and Zhang, 1999). In contrast, in order to retain labour in rural areas and achieve agricultural surplus, the agricultural *hukou* population was not entitled to any of these state-subsided benefits, and were seen as a means of financing national development plans through the forced sale of their agricultural produce to the state at discounted rates (Fan, 2005). Rurally-based people seeking to move to urban areas to access the non-agricultural market, activities and benefits needed permission. This required approximately six permits for which the individual had to bear the associated costs in order to secure these documents and be allowed to work outside their province of origin. The quota for permits was tightly controlled (Chan and Zhang, 1999). Agricultural *hukou* people who secured permits to work outside their authorised geographic areas were used to fill unwanted positions referred to as the 3D jobs — "dangerous, dirty, and demeaning" (Chan, 2010). As temporary contract workers, they did not qualify for state-subsidised rations, employer-supported housing or medical care (Pines *et al.*, 1998; Fan, 2008). For these reasons, the hukou system has had greater implications than simply limiting rural-to-urban migration. It has consistently widened internal migration-related inequality gaps and

Table 1: Internal rural migrant labour (in millions of people)

| | Rural migrant labour (stock) |
|---|---|
| 1988 | 26.0 |
| 1989 | 30.0 |
| 1993 | 62.0 |
| 1994 | 70.0 |
| 1995 | 75.0 |
| 1998 | 79.8 |
| 2002 | 104.7 |
| 2005 | 125.8 |
| 2008 | 140.4 |
| 2010 | 154.5 |

*Source:* Chan (2008).

the division of the Chinese society into two classes: the privileged urban class with access to social welfare and full citizenship, and the peasants tied to their land deprived of state-subsided benefits and entitlements (Pines *et al.*, 1998; Fan, 2008).

Available published data do not report the *hukou* status of migrants and tend to group all migrants together (Table 1), making it difficult to distinguish between permanent and temporary migrants (Fan, 2005). Despite this limitation, China's floating migrant population was estimated at 11 million in 1982, increasing to 56 million in 1995 and 68 million in 1996 (Liang, 2001). By 2000, the number of floating migrants was estimated at 144 million, increasing to 147 million in 2005 (Fan, 2005). The number of male floating migrants is slightly greater than that of females across all age groups, averaging 50.5%. Overall male migrants tend to be older than female migrants (Taylor, 2011) although the majority of 15- to-24-year-old floating migrants tend to be female. Despite restrictive internal migration policies, China still experiences a rapid rural exodus that could lead to the desertion of remote rural areas. Therefore, the geographic management of the population remains a key issue in China. The ongoing flow of rural workers migrating to the cities has greatly contributed to the rise in urban populations, with approximately 260 million Chinese people estimated to live away from their formally registered location, the majority being rural migrants living and

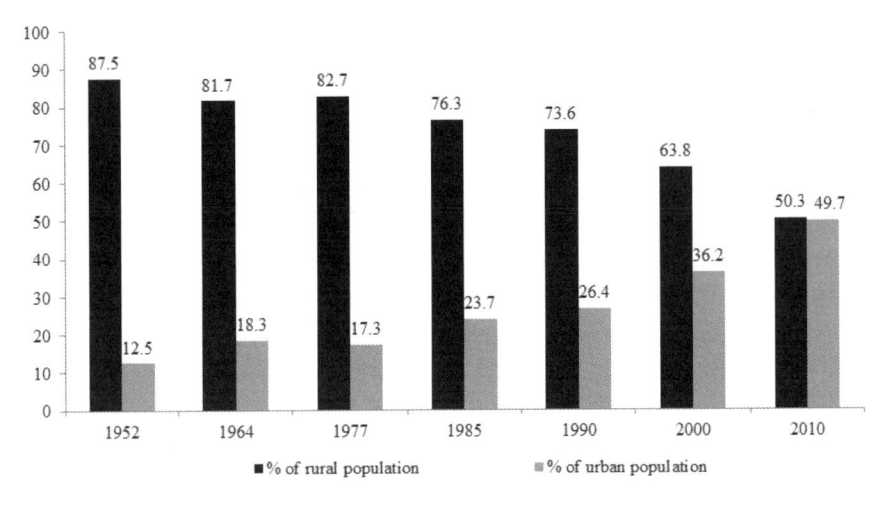

**Figure 1:** Rural vs. urban population distribution 1952–2010.
*Source:* Ratha et al. (2014).

working in urban areas but without formal urban household registration status. In around 60 years, the urban population had grown from 71.6 million in 1952 to more than 680 million in 2012, hence outnumbering the rural population for the first time. This translated into a decrease of the percentage of rural population from 87.5% in 1952 to 50.3% in 2010 and 48.7% in 2012, and an increase in the percentage of the urban population from 12.5% in 1952 to 49.7% in 2010 and 51.3% in 2012 (Figure 1), a four-fold increase in 60 years (Organisation for Economic Co-operation and Development, 2012). Another problem worth highlighting relates to the number of the so-called 'new-generation' migrant population (born after 1980) which has been increasing from 59.8 million in 2005 to 118 million in 2010. A significant number of the new generation live in cities while still holding a rural *hukou*. Consequently, they have high levels of needs not met by existing public services, including limited and unequal educational opportunities and social integration problems (National Population and Family Planning Commission of China, 2014).

As discussed earlier, the *hukou* system has created a situation where it is impossible for people to survive outside their registered *hukou* without proper documents as their daily lives are tightly connected to their work units (Chan and Zhang, 1999). The work units are watched by the police as well as the residential organisations, mainly the village or street residents' committees. The consequence of such strictly controlled registration systems has led to the 'black household' or long-term undocumented migrants (Chan and Zhang, 1999). Another social issue associated with the *hukou* system is the issue of inter-*hukou* marriage. Over the past five decades, the number of unmarried young women leaving their home towns to work in big cities without *hukou* migration (floating) and who end up marrying men they meet at work has been increasing (Ying *et al.*, 2014). Interestingly, available data suggest that nearly 10–20% of inter-*hukou* marriages are "non-laoxiangs", that is, they come from different *hukou* places (Ying *et al.*, 2014). The probability that an urban man will marry a rural woman increased by more than 5% after 1998, while it did not change for a rural man marrying an urban woman (Kang *et al.*, 2011). This pattern goes against the "laoxiang", a traditional marriage system where women are more inclined to marry men from their same home town, as they share the same registered *hukou*. In the non-laoxiangs, couples do not share the same registered *hukou*, making it difficult for an agricultural *hukou* holder to exchange it for an urban one (Ying *et al.*, 2014). Additionally, inter-*hukou* marriage does not mean that the rural women marrying a man with an urban *hukou* status is unconditionally entitled to permanent urban *hukou* status (Whyte and Parish, 1984; Wu and Treiman, 2004).

Nevertheless, today the *hukou* status is still relevant but with diminished significance in many ways. The Chinese government allows private enterprises to provide migrant workers with temporary urban resident cards, which allow them to live in cities as long as they have a job and can support themselves (Afridi *et al.*, 2015). Consequently, people can now leave their place of *hukou* registration while working elsewhere (Taylor, 2011; Afridi *et al.*, 2015) The flow of migrants is mainly directed to export or import provinces, with the three areas receiving most migrants over the past 25 years being Guangdong province, and Shanghai and Beijing municipalities (Chan, 2008). These three provinces accounted for 45% of the total net migration between 2000 and 2005 (Chan, 2008). However, it is worth noting that temporary migrants may be vulnerable to abuses as China has not signed the International Convention on the Protection of the Rights of all Migrant Workers and Members of their Families. China's ratification of core international human rights treaties and its record of participation in the Human Rights Council show its wishes to be perceived as accepting the legitimacy of the international human rights system (Table 2). Nevertheless,

Table 2: China and core international human rights treaties

| Treaty | China's status |
|---|---|
| International Convention on the Elimination of All Forms of Racial Discrimination 1965 | Party<br>Acceded 29 December 1981 |
| International Covenant on Civil and Political Rights 1966 | Non-party (applies to Hong Kong and Macau)<br>Signed on 5 October 1998 but not ratified |
| International Covenant on Economic, Social and Cultural Rights 1966 | Party<br>Signed in 1997 and ratified on 27 March 2001 |
| Convention on the Elimination of all forms of Discrimination Against Women 1979 | Party<br>Signed in 1980 and ratified on 4 November 1980 |
| UN Convention against Torture and Other Cruel, Inhuman or Degrading Treatment or Punishment 1984 | Party<br>Signed in 1986 and ratified on 4 October 1988 |
| UN Convention on the Rights of the Child 1989 | Party<br>Signed in 1990 and ratified on 2 March 1992 |
| International Convention on the Protection of the Rights of All Migrant Workers and Members of their Families 1990 | Non-party |
| Convention on the Rights of Persons with Disabilities 2006 | Party<br>Signed in 2007 and ratified on 1 August 2008 |
| International Convention for the Protection of All Persons from Enforced Disappearance 2006 | Non-party |

*Source*: Sceats and Breslin (2012, pp. 33–34).

its posture within the international human rights system remains principally defensive (Sceats and Breslin, 2012).

## *Immigration flow into China*

With China's economic reforms, it has also been a country of destination for migrants from all over the world and inflows of international immigrants remain a serious challenge for its migration policy (Chen *et al.*, 2014). China's Bureau of Exit and Entry Administration of Ministry of Public Security collect data on foreigners entering China. These data suggest that

Table 3: Foreigners entering China by year

| Year | Foreigners (millions) |
| --- | --- |
| 2000 | 10.16 |
| 2001 | 11.23 |
| 2002 | 13.44 |
| 2003 | 11.40 |
| 2004 | 16.93 |
| 2005 | 20.26 |
| 2006 | 22.21 |
| 2007 | 26.11 |
| 2008 | 24.33 |
| 2009 | 21.93 |
| 2011 | 27.11 |

Sources: Zhang et al. (2010) and Chen et al. (2014).

the number of foreigners entering China increased from 10.16 million in 2000 to 27.11 million in 2011, representing a 2.7-fold increase over 11 years (Table 3) (Zhang et al., 2010; Chen et al., 2014). Of the 27.11 million foreigners entering China in 2011, 45% were registered as international tourists, 9.9% were foreign workers and labourers, 23.4% travelled to China for business purposes, less than 1% were visiting families and friends, and 21.3% visited for other purposes. One of the most intriguing aspects of immigration to China is the increasing number of international students. China received 238,184 students in 2009 (increasing by 6.57% or 14,685 over the previous year), hence ranking third as a major destination for international students ahead of Australia and Canada (Binyi and Mwanza, 2014). International students studying in China come from all over the world, with Republic of Korea, the USA, Japan, Vietnam, Thailand, Russia, India, Indonesia, Kazakhstan and Pakistan the top 10 countries of origin.

China has had six national population censuses: 1953, 1964, 1982, 1990, 2000 and 2010 (Wu, 2014). However, the inclusion of the so-called "alien population" (including foreign citizens and residents from Hong Kong,

Table 4: The top 10 countries of foreigners residing in China

| Rank | Country | Numbers |
|---|---|---|
| 1 | Republic of Korea | 120,750 |
| 2 | USA | 71,493 |
| 3 | Japan | 66,159 |
| 4 | Myanmar | 39,776 |
| 5 | Vietnam | 36,205 |
| 6 | Canada | 19,990 |
| 7 | France | 15,087 |
| 8 | India | 15,051 |
| 9 | Germany | 14,446 |
| 10 | Australia | 13,286 |

Source: Binyi and Mwanza (2014).

Macau and Taiwan) did not occur until the sixth census in 2010 (Wu, 2014). The census estimated that 1,020,145 people of the population were from outside mainland China, of whom 234,829 were from the Hong Kong Special Administrative Region, 21,201 from the Macau Special Administrative Region, 170,283 from Taiwan and 593,832 were foreign citizens. For foreign citizens, the top 10 countries of origin are summarised in Table 4. It is worth noting that the number of foreign citizens increased from 245,700 in 1960 to 593,832 in 2010, representing a 2.4-fold increase over 50 years (Pieke, 2012).

## *Emigration from China*

Although throughout most of China's history there have been strict migration controls preventing large numbers of people from leaving the country, Chinese emigration can be traced back to 210BC (Lee, 1995). From 210BC to the end of the nineteenth century, the Chinese diaspora could be located throughout the world. However, mass emigration did not occur until the beginning of the nineteenth century to 1949, and consisted of mainly illiterate peasants and manual labourers fleeing poverty, starvation and political corruption (Heng, 2009). Migrations from China have increased in

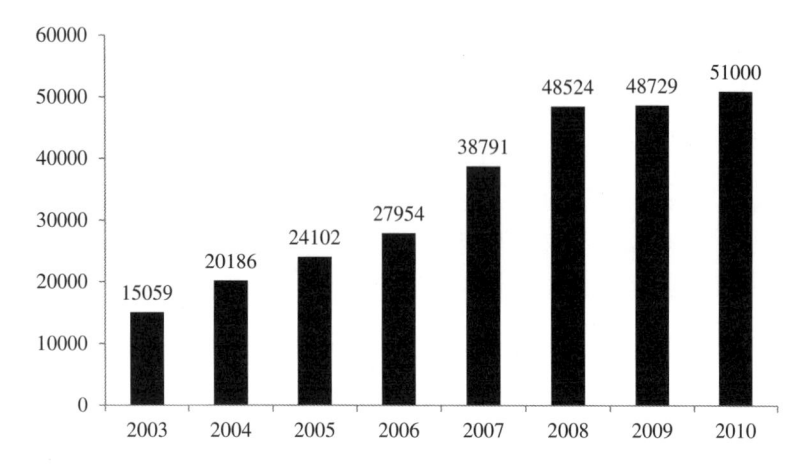

**Figure 2:** Inward remittance flows to China 2003–2010 in USD million.
*Source*: The World Bank (2011).

volume and complexity since 1979. Since the 1980s, China has remained the most important source of human movement in north-east Asia (Pieke, 2007). Mass emigration expanded with more liberalised emigration policies enacted in the 1980s. In 1982, the number of Chinese emigrants was estimated at 56,930, consisting primarily of students and for reasons of family reunion. By 1990, the number of Chinese emigrants had quadrupled to 234,000 and at the turn of the twenty-first century the 2000 Chinese Population Census estimated that the number of Chinese emigrants had more than tripled between 1995 and 2000, increasing from 236,800 in 1995 to 756,626 in 2000 (Liang and Morooka, 2004). Compared to the general population in the mainland, Chinese emigrants have a higher proportion of male (51% vs. 62%), are younger, especially between the age of 18 and 39 years (38% vs. 72%) and have higher levels of educational achievement (Liang and Morooka, 2004). Although the percentage of migrants from China remains small and represents only 0.6% of the population (Skeldon, 1996), their potential impact on their origin and destination countries is important. For example, in 2012, China was considered as the second largest recipient of migrant remittance in the world (The World Bank, 2011). In 2010, US$51 billion were sent to China through workers' remittances, employees' compensation and migrants' transfer (Figure 2) with this amount increasing to US$60 billion in 2013 (Ratha *et al.*, 2014).

## Migrants' health and burden of disease

This rapid increase in internal and international migration over the past two decades has resulted in an increase in the burden of diseases. In recent years, the burden of diseases among migrant populations in China has received greater attention. The three main categories of these include infectious disease, maternal health, occupational health conditions and injuries, non-communicable diseases such as cardiovascular diseases, and mental health.

### *Infectious diseases*

Many migrant workers in China live in environments conducive to the transmission of infectious diseases. Due to the nature of their rural *hukou* status, many of China's migrant workers are neither able to purchase an apartment nor are they entitled to one: if they are fortunate, they will receive free accommodation from their employers. It is interesting to note that by 2007, only 23–30% of all China's migrant workers working with private companies had formal labour contracts (Lee, 2007). The Chinese government introduced a series of measures to integrate migrant workers into the national social security system, starting with the Labour Contract Law which was launched in 2008, followed by the Labour Dispute Mediation and Arbitration Law promulgated in 2008, and the legislation of the Social Insurance Act that was initiated in 2009 (Chan, 2012). Despite these measures, migrant workers are prone to exploitation and increased vulnerabilities characterised by the provision of low wages, long working hours, not being paid on time (wage arrears), the lack of written contracts, short weekly rest periods, low social security coverage, and poor and overcrowded housing conditions with inadequate sanitation (Holdaway *et al.*, 2011; Chan, 2012). Such stressful work and living environment, together with increased pre-migration risk factors such as inadequate immunisation against measles and human papillomavirus virus or incomplete HBV vaccination and migrant workers' separation from families, predispose migrant workers to ill health. The most documented diseases include higher rates of malaria, hepatitis and other infectious diseases, and increase their likelihood of engaging in risky behaviours such as unsafe sex (Holdaway *et al.*, 2011; Tucker *et al.*, 2013).

For example, migrant workers have higher rates of severe acute respiratory syndrome (SARS), measles, diarrhoea, parasitic and sexually transmitted diseases, as well as tuberculosis, than non-migrant urban population and rural residents who did not migrate to cities (Hong et al., 2006; Tucker et al., 2013). In terms of sexually transmitted diseases, Zou and colleagues (2014) reported a pooled HIV infection prevalence of 0.23% (95% CI: 0.20–0.27%) among migrant workers and 0.10% (95% CI: 0.02–0.49%) among pregnant migrant women workers. In another separate review, Tucker et al. (2013) report that between 2000 and 2010, the HIV prevalence among migrant populations varied between 0% and 1.5% across 10 separate provinces with higher rates reported among migrants working in regions known to have greater intravenous drug use. As early as 1998, it was established that the HIV prevalence among rural-to-urban migrants was 1.8 times higher than that among rural residents who did not migrate to cities (Hong et al., 2006). Recently, Zou and colleagues (2014) reported that the odds of HIV infection are four times (odds ratio [OR] 4; 95% CI: 3.1–5.2) higher among migrant workers in general and eight (OR: 7.7; 95% CI: 3.4–17.4) times higher among pregnant migrant women workers than the general population. Other sexually transmitted diseases prevalent among migrant workers include syphilis, chlamydia, human papillomavirus virus and gonorrhoea (Wang et al., 2010; Tucker et al., 2013; Zou et al., 2014). In a meta-analysis of 411 studies examining whether rural-to-urban migrants are at high risk of sexually transmitted and viral hepatitis infections in China, Zou and colleagues (2014) reported the prevalence for the following sexually transmitted diseases: syphilis: 0.69% (95% CI: 0.57–0.84%), gonorrhoea: 2.18% (95% CI: 1.30–3.64%), and genital warts 1.54% (95% CI: 0.70–3.36%). Compared to the general population, the odds of syphilis, gonorrhoea and genital warts were respectively two (OR: 1.9; 95% CI: 1.1–3.0), 14 (OR: 13.6; 95% CI: 5.8–32.1) and 39 (OR: 38.5; 95% CI: 15.7–94.5) times higher than among migrant workers.

Migrant workers found to be at increased risk of sexually transmitted diseases were construction workers, long-distance truck drivers and migrant women (Zou et al., 2014). In addition, due to migrant workers' poor educational level and health literacy, they are persistently involved in high-risk sexual behaviours which will undoubtedly drive the HIV infectious rate upwards (Tucker et al., 2013). In a study examining high-risk behaviours among 17,377 migrant workers in eastern China, Pan *et al.* (2013) estimated the HIV/AIDS knowledge rate at 66.2% and found that among sexually active participants 7.5% had two or more sexual partners, 4.9% had unpaid sexual intercourse with casual partners in the previous 12 months and 3.7% had paid for sex. Worryingly, 59.4% of those who had paid for sex did not use a condom every time they had sex with their casual partner. The authors found that factors associated with high-risk sexual behaviours such as having sex with a casual or commercial sex partner without consistently using a condom were male gender, shorter duration of stay, being divorced or widowed, and working in a factory, market or in domestic service. In their analysis of HIV sentinel surveillance data in Yangquan city in 2009 ($n = 1,218$ of whom 409 were migrant workers), Jing *et al.* (2010) reported that 43% of migrant workers had had commercial sex activities in the past year, and of whom, only 40.4% used condoms each time they had casual sex with a commercial sex worker, and 47.2% had used condoms the last time they had transactional sex. The high rate of risky sexual behaviours, especially having sex with a casual or commercial sex partner without consistently using a condom, among migrant workers in China has been consistently reported by other researchers (Cai *et al.*, 2010; Wang *et al.*, 2010).

In terms of hepatitis and other viral infections, Pan *et al.* (2013) estimated that the prevalence of hepatitis C virus (HCV) infection was 0.40% (95% CI: 0.31–0.51%) among migrant workers in eastern China. In a study of the seroprevalence of HCV among 559,890 first-time volunteer blood donors at the Guangzhou Blood Centre, the prevalence of HCV infection was higher among migrant workers than non-migrant urban residents (0.30% vs. 0.40%; $p < 0.001$) (Fu *et al.*, 2010). Finally, Zou and colleagues (2014) estimated a pooled prevalence of HCV infection at 0.45% (95% CI: 0.31–3.65%). The odds of a HCV infection were four (OR: 3.8; 95% CI: 1.9–7.3) times higher among migrant workers than in the general population. Hepatitis B virus (HBV) is also more common among subsets of migrants (Heng, 2009; Liang *et al.*, 2009).

Migrant workers accounted for 7% of the 429,812 smear-positive pulmonary tuberculosis cases diagnosed in 2010 (Du *et al.*, 2011). It is possible that tuberculosis will become a serious threat among migrant workers and non-migrants for three reasons (Law *et al.*, 2008; Wong *et al.*, 2008;

Wang et al., 2011a; Wang and Wang, 2012; Tucker et al., 2013): (1) higher pre-departure burden: rural-to-urban migration from higher prevalence western and central provinces transporting and spreading the mycobacterium tuberculosis in lower prevalence eastern regions, (2) returning migrants bring back urban-acquired tuberculosis infection to villages of origin, and (3) the high risk of multi-drug-resistant tuberculosis found in temporary migrant workers.

## *Maternal and reproductive health*

Migrant women have poorer health outcomes and higher risk of reproductive health problems compared with the mainstream urban population. They have poorer reproductive outcomes, higher risks of reproductive tract infections, lower levels of health service, and poorer sexual and reproductive health knowledge than their non-migrant counterparts. For example, compared to resident urban women, postpartum haemorrhage was found to be a much more common cause of maternal death among rural–urban migrant women in Beijing (25.2% vs. 14.4% of deaths) and Shanghai (39.9% vs. 12.9% of deaths) (Shen et al., 2006; Zhu et al., 2009). In a large study involving a total of 902,807 pregnancies with live births in Shanghai covering the 1996–2005 period, Zhu and colleagues (2009) recorded 243 maternal deaths, which translated into an average maternal mortality ratio (MMR) of 26.7 per 100,000 live births. Over the study period, the MMR among Shanghai residents declined significantly by 92.9%, from 22.5 per 100,000 in 1996 to 1.6 per 100,000 live births in 2005. In contrast, the MMR among rural-urban migrant women remained significantly higher, declining only by 11.4% from a MMR of 54.7 per 100,000 to 48.5 per 100,000 live births during the same period. That is, in 2005 the MMR was only 1.6 per 100,000 live births for Shanghai residents compared to a staggering 48.5 per 100,000 live births for rural–urban migrant workers. Similarly, in the 1995–2004 period Shen and colleagues (2006) reported an average MMR of 17.9 per 100,000 live births for Beijing residents and 51.3 per 100,000 live births for rural–urban migrant workers. The main cause of maternal deaths also differed, with postpartum haemorrhage, pregnancy-induced hypertension and puerperal infection accounting respectively for 39.9%, 9.8% and 9.3% of maternal deaths in the migrating population. Among Shanghai residents the main factors contributing to maternal deaths were chronic heart and liver diseases (20.0%), postpartum haemorrhage (12.9%) and amniotic fluid embolism (12.9%) (Zhu et al., 2009). The increased risk of maternal mortality among rural–urban migrant women is due to many factors associated with inadequate access to maternity care and poor health-seeking behaviours including poor uptake of services in their destination cities, lack of health insurance, low attendance for antenatal care and delivery out of hospitals (Nielsen et al., 2005; Zhu et al., 2009; Gong et al., 2012; Zhang et al., 2014). Special initiatives have been undertaken in many cities in order to effectively address challenges associated with accessing maternity care. For example, Shanghai has undertaken pilot studies to subsidise maternity care for rural–urban migrant women in public hospitals with good outcomes (Zhan, 2002; Zhu, 2007; Zhang et al., 2014).

## *Occupational health conditions and injuries*

All available data suggest that rural–urban migrant workers in China are disproportionately affected by occupational injury, morbidity and mortality. A recent systematic review by Fitzgerald and colleagues (2013) examined occupational injury among internal migrant workers in China. A total of 19 qualitative and quantitative studies on occupational injury surveillance and prevention were included in the review. Findings identified a list of causes of injury including physical assaults by employers and management, machinery-related traumatic amputations, hazardous work-related exposure to chemicals and other poisons. The prevalence of chemical exposure varied from between 2% and 8% in shoe factories (Wang et al., 2011b) while 84% of the traumatic hand injuries at Tianjin Hospital over a one-year period occurred among internal migrant workers, 91% of which occurred at work (Fitzgerald et al., 2013). Similar results were reported at Guangdong Red Cross Hospital over a four-year period (68% of internal migrants' injuries occurred at work) (Xie et al., 2004), a hospital-based surveillance system in Shanghai (60% of injuries among internal migrant patients occurred at work vs. 30% of the Shanghai-born patients) (Perry et al., 2005). Using self-reported data, annual injury incidence rate was estimated at 20.4% in railway construction and 29% in building construction

(Fitzgerald *et al.*, 2013). The proportion of respondents reporting the history of work-related injury varied between 23% and 40.7% among internal migrants workers, compared to 16% of locally born urban workers and 10% of workers still in rural areas (Hesketh *et al.*, 2008; Zheng *et al.*, 2010; Fitzgerald *et al.*, 2013). The odds of occupational injury among internal migrant workers were higher among those with lower educational attainment (OR = 16.7), working longer weekly work hours (OR = 3.7) and without adequate job experience and training (OR = 2.1) (Fitzgerald *et al.*, 2013).

## *Non-communicable diseases*

The economic and demographic transition that China has experienced over the last 40 years means that it is experiencing an increase in the burden of lifestyle-related non-communicable diseases. However, in their systematic review of health of China's rural–urban migrant workers and their families from 2000 to 2012, Mou and colleagues (2013) found that the complex mechanisms and impacts of rural–urban migration on non-communicable chronic diseases remain less documented in China. They speculate that the reason for the scarcity of such data could be, for the most part, due to the fact that rural–urban migrant workers are still very young. As this population ages, the threat of non-communicable diseases will be unavoidable. Risk factors for non-communicable diseases such as obesity, hypertension, and diabetes are already becoming evident among rural-to-urban migrant workers. In one such rare study estimating the prevalence of obesity and hypertension among rural-to-urban migrant children aged 7–10 years ($N$ = 2457 of which 914 rural-to-urban migrant 257 workers, 795 local Shanghai subjects and 748 participants in migrants' rural areas of origin), Lu *et al.* (2015) found that the prevalence of overweight and obesity among rural-to-urban migrant children (19.0% and 2.1%, respectively) was significantly lower than that reported among city-dwellers (28.2% and 3.7%) but higher than that reported among children in rural areas of origin (0% for both overweight and obesity). This pattern was also true for hypertension, with the prevalence estimated at 1.1%, 2.0% and 0.3% among rural-to-urban migrant workers, local Shanghai subjects and rural residents in migrants' rural areas of origin, respectively. For rural-to-urban migrant children, the risk of overweight/obesity was positively associated with rice intake and family income level. While there is an inverse relationship between family income level and overweight/obesity in children in countries with advanced economies, the positive relationship between family income and obesity in rural-to-urban migrant children could be a result of increased purchasing power, compounded by culturally mediated eating habits. Despite the scarcity of data on non-communicable diseases and their risk factors in China, data from other countries experiencing rapid economic and demographic transition suggest that rural-to-urban migration is associated cardiovascular risk factors such as obesity, hypertension, and diabetes, but the risk is influenced by the age at which migration occurs (Ebrahim et al., 2010; Miranda et al., 2011). With existing evidence from China suggesting that the combined effect of rural–urban migration, population growth, and ageing will be associated with more than the doubling of cardiovascular disease events in urban areas and an increase of 27.0–45.6% in cardiovascular disease events in rural areas, rural–urban migration will continue to be a major demographic driver of the cardiovascular disease epidemic in China (Chan et al., 2012). Therefore, non-communicable diseases among rural–urban migrants in China need to be a health priority to reduce migration-related inequalities in cardiovascular disease events. This is particularly true as current estimates suggest that, from 2010 to 2030, the age-standardized coronary heart disease incidence in China will increase from 164.4 to 237.0–244.9 per 100 000 (73–81%) and that of stroke will increase from 790.1 to 801.1–830.9 per 100, 000 (Chan et al., 2012).

## Mental health

Available data indicate that rural–urban migrant workers have poorer mental health outcomes than the general Chinese population and their rural counterparts but show a small but significant advantage in mental wellbeing when compared to their city dweller counterparts (Li et al., 2014; Zhong et al., 2013). Li et al. (2007) found that rural–urban migrant workers had lower scores (52.4) for the SF-36 mental health sub-scale (suggesting poor mental health) than rural residents (60.4), but scored higher than urban residents (47.2). The difference between urban residents and migrants disappeared after adjustment for confounding factors. That is, rural–urban migrant workers had similar mental health status as their urban residents after adjusting for confounders, but still experienced worse mental health status than rural dwellers. Among rural–urban migrant workers, factors associated with better mental health status were being unmarried, migrating with a partner, higher salary, good self-reported health and good relationships with co-workers. The prevalence of mental health among rural–urban migrant workers has varied considerably across studies due to the differences and diversity of scales used. For example, Zhong *et al.* (2013) undertook a meta-analysis to estimate the pooled prevalence of psychological symptoms as measured by the Symptom Checklist-90-Revised (SCL-90-R) in Chinese rural–urban migrant workers. They found that the pooled psychological symptom scores were statistically higher among internal migrant workers than those of norms from the general Chinese population and their city-dweller counterparts on nine primary symptom dimensions of SCL-90-R (somatisation, obsessive–compulsive, interpersonal sensitivity, depression, anxiety, hostility, phobic anxiety, paranoid ideation, and psychoticism).

Using the Chinese version of Mini International Neuropsychiatric Interview, Zhong *et al.* (2015) sought to determine the prevalence of one-month and lifetime major depressive disorder among rural–urban migrant workers in Shenzhen, China (N = 3,031). The one-month and lifetime prevalence of major depressive disorders was estimated at 1.4% and 5.1%, respectively. There were no significant gender and age-group differences in the reported prevalence. Risk factors for lifetime major depression disorder were lower education, worse living conditions, poorer self-perceived physical health, migration before adulthood, infrequently calling family members, and having done lots of jobs. The authors note that of the 17 studies conducted among the general Chinese population, 10 reported a one-month (0.3–1.3%) and lifetime ((0.5–4.8%) prevalence of major depressive disorders that was lower while seven reported a prevalence (one-month: 1.5–4.3%, lifetime: 5.3–6.5%) that was higher than the 1.4% one-month and 5.1% lifetime pooled prevalence.

A number of studies have estimated the prevalence of clinically relevant depressive symptoms among rural–urban migrant workers using the Center for Epidemiologic Depression Scale (CES-D score >= 16) with contradictory results. Some of the studies have reported that the prevalence of depressive symptoms was significantly higher among rural-urban migrant workers (Lam and Johnston, 2015) while others reported a lower prevalence than that reported among their urban-non-migrant counterparts (Dai *et al.*, 2015). Qiu *et al.* (2011a) estimated the prevalence clinically relevant depressive symptoms at 23.7% among rural–urban migrant workers in Chengdu, Sichuan Province, which was higher than that reported in the general Chinese population. Lin *et al.* (2006) reported a prevalence of clinically relevant depressive symptoms at 23% among female migrant workers in Beijing. Mou *et al.* (2011) reported a prevalence of clinically relevant depressive symptoms at 21.4% among rural–urban migrant factory workers in Shenzhen, China. Using the Self-Rating Depression Scale, Chen *et al.* (2006) found that the mean score among rural–urban migrant workers was significantly higher than the norm for the general Chinese population, with the prevalence of depressive symptoms estimated at 34.2%. Poor mental health status was associated with being a minority, shorter intension of stay, working long hours, and being a casual smoker or a frequent Internet user (Mou *et al.*, 2011).

Other mental issues documented among rural–urban migrant workers include suicide ideation and deliberate self-harm. The prevalence of suicide ideation and attempts has been found to be significantly higher among rural–urban migrant workers than their rural and city dweller counterparts (Li *et al.*, 2007). While contemplation of suicide was commonest in rural–urban migrant workers, actual suicide attempts were most common among the rural population (Li *et al.*, 2007). Xiao and colleagues (2013) documented the prevalence of deliberate self-harm among rural–urban migrant workers in Zhejiang province. The study focused on cases registered in the database of Zhejiang provincial hospital-based injury surveillance system between the year 2005 and 2010 (28 hospitals from 9 counties). The prevalence of deliberate self-harm internal migrant workers was 26.8% among workers aged 15–29 years old, 44.1% among workers aged 30–44 years, and 63.6% among workers aged 45–65 years old. These results suggest that the likelihood of deliberate self-harm among internal workers increased significantly with age.

However, mental health data from the above studies need to be interpreted with caution due to many factors. Rural–urban migrant workers tend to operate in different working environments (i.e. construction vs. manufacturing vs. social services vs. real estate and housing) and the sampling and analytical framework in these studies did take into account these differences. Such working environments carry different health risks and could explain the variation in the prevalence of mental health being reported among internal migrants in China. Another issue is the operationalisation of the various scales to measure mental health disorders, especially depression. They are self-report measures, yet the prevalence of depression is being presented as clinical depression when the validation and calibration of the scales against gold standards in diagnosing depression (e.g. DSM-IV Criteria for Major Depressive Disorder) are often not reported.

## Social and health policy response

With a total population of 1.4 billion residents in 2014 and 145.3 million rural-to-urban migrants, China faces a substantial challenge in developing health care infrastructure sufficient to cover the needs of its population. The growth in GDP has been accompanied by an overall expansion in China's health care expenditure. The government expenditure has been rising rapidly since 2006 reflecting the policy change initiated with the 11$^{th}$ Plan, reaching 2.7% of the GDP in 2010 for health and nearly 8% of the GDP for social expenditures (Organisation for Economic Co-operation and Development, 2012). To address these challenges, several reforms have been initiated: generalisation of the minimum subsistence allowance to rural areas, new medical insurance schemes for people with rural registration status, and for dependants of registered urban employees and students, as well as the introduction of new pension systems for people living in rural areas and for migrant workers (Organisation for Economic Co-operation and Development, 2012). The social and health response to migrant workers' needs has been influenced by many factors. The role of external forces such as globalisation, transnational enterprises, international organisations and non-governmental organisations in China's health policy has been immeasurable. From the 1980s to the mid-2000s, internal migrant workers' health was neglected. By 2006, the government sought to address this through the universal health insurance system. It has been estimated that 96.9% of the Chinese population enjoy some type of medical insurance

Table 5: A summary of three major health insurance plans in China

| Characteristics | 1998 Urban employee-based health insurance | 2003 Rural newly cooperative medical scheme | 2007 Urban resident health insurance |
|---|---|---|---|
| Administration level | City | Country | City |
| Insured population | Urban employed residents | Rural residents | Urban non-employed residents |
| Annual premium contributions (2011) | | | |
|   Government | None | 200 Chinese Yuan | 200 Chinese Yuan |
|   Individual | 2% of wages | varied by locations | varied by locations |
|   Employer | at least 6% of wages | None | None |
| Annual maximum reimbursement cap (2011) | 6 times of disposable personal income (at least 50,000 Chinese Yuan) | at least 50,000 Chinese Yuan | 6 times of disposable personal income (at least 50,000 Chinese Yuan) |
| Inpatient and outpatient services for catastrophic illness | Yes | Yes | Yes |
| General outpatient services | Comprehensive | Limited and varied by locations | Limited and varied by locations |

Source: Fang et al. (2014).

(Zhu et al., 2014). We will summarise some of the relevant policy responses (please see Table 5 for a snapshot).

## *The 1999 Urban Employee Basic Medical Insurance*

The Urban Employee Basic Medical Insurance (UEBMI) scheme specifically covers urban residents who are still in the workforce (employees) and retirees. Cost-sharing was not part of the previous urban employees' medical insurance system (minimum cost-sharing), the consequence of which was the overutilisation of the health care services (Yip and Hsiao, 1997; Liu, 2002). A number of features were introduced into the UEBMI to contain health care service overutilisation, with cost-sharing as the main feature characterised by a combination of deductible, coinsurance and individual medical savings accounts (MSAs) (Huang and Gan, 2015). The cost-sharing was greater for outpatient care while that of inpatient care remained relatively stable (Huang and Gan, 2015). Studies evaluating the effect of the UEBMI suggest that its effect on inpatient care was small and insignificant. However, the UEBMI decreased outpatient care utilisation by 7% and outpatient expenditure by 35% (Huang and Gan, 2015). While these findings mirror those reported by similar studies (Aron-Dine *et al.*, 2012), they are not consistent with Zhou *et al.* (2014) findings. Zhou *et al.* (2014) found that, for outpatient utilisation, the UEBMI increased the pro-rich inequity, where rich people were more likely to utilise outpatient facilities than poor people. That is, by virtue of the MSAs' reimbursement structure, the more money one earns the more money goes into the outpatient account. Given that the MSAs are tied to the outpatient service (i.e. can only be used to pay for outpatient care cost), there is an incentive for high-income earners to overuse the outpatient service (Zhou *et al.*, 2014), hence widening the gap of outpatient utilisation between high-income and low-income residents (Liu *et al.*, 2002; Dong, 2008; Zhou *et al.*, 2014). For inpatient care utilisation, the UEBMI reduced the horizontal inequity index to 55.5%, suggesting that it significantly improved the equity of inpatient utilisation (Zhou *et al.*, 2014).

## *The 2003 rural New Cooperative Medical Scheme*

The New Cooperative Medical Scheme (NCMS) aimed at providing health insurance to rural citizens and to address the growing rural primary health care crisis. Locally administered and hence varying by county, the common denominator is covering a portion of inpatient expenses according to the reimbursement levels established by the local health officials. The NCMS reimbursement level and benefits are tied to designated health services and hospitals, so patients using non-designated services do not get reimbursement. By 2011, more than 95% of the rural population or 832 million farmers were covered by the new rural cooperative health insurance system (Zhu *et al.*, 2014). In their study examining whether the NCMS has affected the operation and use of village health clinics, Babiarz and colleagues

(2010) found that the scheme had increased clinic use in villages by 5%, while patients' out-of-pocket medical expenditure fell by 19%.

The scheme did not specifically target migrant workers, and holders of the rural *hukou* status are only reimbursed from the NCMS of their *hukou* registration location. This limits internal migrant workers in accessing medical and health care services in the cities of their employment. It is nevertheless worth mentioning that in the foregoing discussion we have demonstrated that the health of internal migrant workers is exacerbated by the pre-departure health burden. With a staggering 165 million people migrating from rural to urban areas in 2012, having adequate health insurance for rural populations is the key to minimising the impact of pre-departure health vulnerabilities and risk factors. In addition, there are indications the NCMS is being integrated into the urban health insurance schemes. Recently, Qiu *et al.* (2011b) conducted a study that found that among the 9,097 households and 36,720 individuals using inpatient medical services, 54.3% of migrants compared to 17.5% of non-migrants used out-of-county hospitals, many of which were not tied to the NCMS reimbursement. More than half (55.2%) of migrants as compared to 24.6% of non-migrants received no reimbursement from the NCMS. These findings suggest that although the majority of migrant workers find it difficult to receive reimbursement by undesignated providers in urban cities, 44.8% of them did. For those who did not receive reimbursement, the main reasons were (1) using medical services not designated by the NCMS, (2) lack of knowledge of NCMS policies, and (3) experiencing difficulties securing reimbursement (Qiu *et al.*, 2011b).

## The 2007 Urban Resident Basic Medical Insurance

The Urban Resident Basic Medical Insurance (URBMI) scheme has also had a role to play in promoting the equity of health service utilisation. It covers urban residents who are unemployed, children and students. The URBMI has been found to significantly increase the utilisation of formal medical services, including outpatient care and inpatient care, where increase was more pronounced for children, low-income family members and residents from poor western regions (Lin *et al.*, 2009; Liu and Zhao, 2012; Liu and Zhao, 2014). However, it did not reduce patients' total out-of-pocket health expenses (Liu and Zhao, 2012, 2014). Findings are not consistent across the board due to methodological differences and the timing of the study since the URBMI only started in 2007 and some studies may have been conducted too early to detect an effect (Liu and Zhao, 2014).

### *Some opinions to address internal migrant workers' health*

In March 2006, the State Council formulated a comprehensive guideline entitled, "Some Opinions on Resolving the Problems Faced by Migrant Workers" (Lin, 2013; Zhu et al., 2014). The government provided a number of directives geared towards tackling problems that rural–urban migrant workers are confronted with in their daily lives. These directives instructed the local governments to (i) put in place a system that regulates occupational safety and sanitation, (ii) to make industrial injury insurance coverage available to internal migrants, (iii) to ensure sickness protection for internal migrants and immunisation services to internal migrants' children are implemented, (iv) to provide birth control counselling, and (v) improve internal migrants' housing conditions (Zhu et al., 2014). Following these directives, a series of policies followed including the "Notice on Involving the Rural Migrant Workers into the Medical Insurance", outlining procedures guiding rural-urban migrant workers' access to health care services and insurance in their host cities, and the extension of contract-based migrant workers' medical health insurance coverage (Zhu et al., 2014).

## Conclusion

The demographic transition that China is experiencing is characterised by an unbalanced sex ratio due to the unnatural selection and preference for boys, and young women in rural areas migrating to cities for better opportunities and in search of men with better prospects. This means that in the long term there will be a severe bride shortage, and currently there is already increased demand for brides in rural areas. As the findings suggest that women are disproportionately affected by the health burden, it would be important that existing policies take a gender lens to reduce gender-related inequalities. Furthermore, while the literature predominantly focuses on internal migration, we have also shown that China is becoming a destination country for international migrants. The combination of this, together with rapid industrialisation, suggests China will experience issues similar to that most multicultural industrialised countries have experienced. These include, but are not limited to, occupation- and migration-related inequalities in chronic diseases such as diabetes and cardiovascular diseases, which is an area that is yet to be addressed adequately by existing health policies. International immigration will lead China to be confronted with issues related to cultural integration, as well as challenges related to religious, ethnic and race relations, and their relation to international legal and human rights' frameworks. One aspect in particular that existing policies are not addressing adequately is that of health surveillance and monitoring. Moreover, there is an urgent need for these surveillance data to be used concurrently to influence existing policies, especially in the area of communicable and chronic non-communicable diseases, and how they relate to migrant workers.

## References

Afridi, F. *et al.* (2015). Social identity and inequality: The impact of China's hukou system. *Journal of Public Economics*, 123, 17–29.

Aron-Dine, A.L. *et al.* (2012). The RAND health insurance experiment, three decades later. *Journal of Economic Perspective*, 27(1), 197–222.

Babiarz, K.S. *et al.* (2010). New evidence on the impact of China's New Rural Cooperative Medical Scheme and its implications for rural primary healthcare: Multivariate difference-in-difference analysis. *BMJ*, 341, 1–9.

Beatriz, C. (2004). Rural–urban migration in china: Temporary migrants in search of permanent settlement. *PORTAL: Journal of Multidisciplinary International Studies*, 1(2), 1–26.

Beijing Review (2014). Against the clock: Urbanization propelled as nation reforms household registration. 57(33), 1–20.

Binyi, L. & Mwanza, F.M. (2014). Social integration in public spaces & landscapes: Perceptions and experiences towards multicultural Shanghai. *Chinese Studies*, 3(1), 12–18.

Bryan Cave LLP (2012). New Entry–Exit Law Targets Illegal Foreigners in China. Asia Labour and Employment Client Service Group. Available at: http://www.bryancave.com/files/Publication/0092b976-449e-4851-a10a-a0e1a47ce127/Presentation/PublicationAttachment/13ad98ed-55b6-4a43-95c9-a7cfd8cfb86f/AsiaLaborAlert7-10-12.pdf. Accessed 21 July 2015.

Cai, Y. et al. (2010). A study of HIV/AIDS related knowledge, attitude and behaviors among female sex workers in Shanghai China. *BMC Public Health*, 10(1), 377.

Chan, F. et al (2012). Projected impact of urbanization on cardiovascular disease in China. *International Journal of Public Health*, 57(5), 849–854.

Chan, C.K.-c. (2012). Community-based organizations for migrant workers' rights: The emergence of labour NGOs in China. *Community Development Journal*, doi:10.1093/cdj/bss001. Available at: http://cdj.oxfordjournals.org/content/early/2012/03/14/cdj.bss001.full.pdf+html. Accessed 21 July 2013.

Chan, K.-w. & K.-y. Tsui (1992). "Agricultural" and "non-agricultural" Population Statistics of the People's Republic of China: Definitions, Findings and Comparisons. Occasional Paper No. 1. Department of Geography & Geology, University of Hong Kong, Hong Kong.

Chan, K.W. (2008). Internal Labour Migration in China: Trends, Geographical Distribution and Policies. Proceedings of the United Nations Expert Group Meeting on Population Distribution, Urbanization, Internal Migration and Development, 21-23 January 2008 (UN/POP/EGM-URB/2008/05). New York: United Nations Secretariat, Population Division, Department of Economic and Social Affairs.

Chan, K.W. (2010). The household registration system and migrant labor in China: Notes on a debate. *Population and Development Review*, 36(2), 357–364.

Chan, K.W. & Zhang, L. (1999). The hukou system and rural–urban migration in China: Processes and changes. *The China Quarterly*, 160, 818–855.

Chen, Y. et al. (2014). Image of China tourism and sustainability issues in Western media: An investigation of National Geographic. *International Journal of Contemporary Hospitality Management*, 26(6), 855–878.

Chen, Z. et al. (2006). Relationship between depression and self-rated health among floating population. *Chinese Journal of Health Education*, 22(10), 747–749.

Dai, J. et al. (2014). Internal migration, mental health, and suicidal behaviors in young rural Chinese. *Social Psychiatry and Psychiatric Epidemiology*, 50(4), 621–631.

Dong, W. (2008). Cost containment and access to care: The Shanghai health care financing model. *The Singapore Economic Review*, 53(1), 27–41.

Du, X., Liu, E. & Cheng, S. (2011). Characteristics of new smear positive pulmonary tuberculosis in floating population in 2010. *China Journal of Antituberculosis*, 33, 461–465.

Ebrahim, S. et al. (2010). The effect of rural-to-urban migration on obesity and diabetes in India: A cross-sectional study. *PLoS Med*, 7(4), 112.

Fan, C.C. (2005). Interprovincial migration, population redistribution, and regional development in China: 1990 and 2000 census comparisons. *The Professional Geographer*, 57(2), 295–311.

Fan, C.C. (2008). *China on the Move: Migration, the State, and the Household.* Routledge, Abingdon, UK.

Fang, S. (1990). *History of Migration in China.* Heilongjiang People's Publishing House, Harbin, PRC.

Fang, C. & Wang, D. (2008). Impacts of internal migration on economic growth and urban development in China. In: Dewind, J. & Holdaway, J. (eds.) *Migration and Development Within and Across Borders: Research and Policy Perspectives on Internal and International Migration.* J. DeWind and J. Holdaway. International Organization for Migration, Geneva, SWI.

Fang, H. *et al.* (2014). Do different health insurance plans in China create disparities in health care utilization and expenditures? *International Journal of Applied Economics,* 11(1), 1–18.

Fitzgerald, S. *et al.* (2013). Occupational injury among migrant workers in China: A systematic review. *Injury Prevention,* 19, 348–354.

Fu, Y. *et al.* (2010). The seroprevalence of hepatitis C virus (HCV) among 559,890 first-time volunteer blood donors in China reflects regional heterogeneity in HCV prevalence and changes in blood donor recruitment models. *Transfusion,* 50(7), 1505–1511.

Gong, P. *et al.* (2012). Urbanisation and health in China. *The Lancet,* 379(9818), 843–852.

Heng, D. (2009). *Sino-Malay Trade and Diplomacy from the Tenth Through the Fourteenth Century.* Ohio University Press, Athens, OH.

Hesketh, T. *et al.* (2008). Health status and access to health care of migrant workers in China. *Public Health Reports,* 123(2), 189–197.

Holdaway, J. *et al.* (2011). Migration and health in China: Challenges and responses. *Human Health and Global Environmental Change,* 1, 35–41.

Hong, Y. *et al.* (2006). Rural-to-urban migrants and the HIV epidemic in China. *AIDS and Behavior,* 10(4), 421–430.

Huang, F. & Gan, L. (2015). Impact of China's urban employee basic medical insurance on health care expenditure and health outcomes. Working Paper 20873. National Bureau of Economic Research, Cambridge, UK.

International Monetary Fund (2013). World Economic Outlook Database, Report for Selected Countries and Subjects. Available at: http://www.imf.org/external/pubs/ft/weo/2013/01/weodata/weorept.aspx?sy=1980&ey=2018&sort=country&ds=.&br=1&pr1.x=40&pr1.y=0&c=924&s=NGDP_RPCH%2CPPPPC&grp=0&a=. Accessed 22 May 2015.

Jing, L.H. *et al.* (2010). Results of HIV sentinel surveillance in Yangquan city, 2009. *Disease Surveillance,* 25(7), 554–556.

Kang, Y. *et al.* (2011). The economics of marriage in China: How hukou and migration systems leave rural China men single. *Deakin Papers on International Business Economics*, 4(2), 16–25.

Lam, K.K. & Johnston, J.M. (2015). Depression and health-seeking behaviour among migrant workers in Shenzhen. *International Journal of Social Psychiatry*, 61(4), 350–357.

Law, W. *et al.* (2008). Risk factors for multidrug-resistant tuberculosis in Hong Kong. *The International Journal of Tuberculosis and Lung Disease*, 12(9), 1065–1070.

Lee, C.K. (2007). *Against the Law. Labor Protests in China's Rustbelt and Sunbelt.* University of California Press, Berkley, CA.

Lee, K.C. (1995). *Japan: Between Myth and Reality.* World Scientific Publishing, Singapore.

Li, J. *et al.* (2014). Mental wellbeing amongst younger and older migrant workers in comparison to their urban counterparts in Guangzhou city, China: A cross-sectional study. *BMC Public Health*, 14, 1–10.

Li, L. *et al.* (2007). The mental health status of Chinese rural–urban migrant workers. *Social Psychiatry and Psychiatric Epidemiology*, 42(9), 716–722.

Liang, X. *et al.* (2009). Epidemiological serosurvey of hepatitis B in China—declining HBV prevalence due to hepatitis B vaccination. *Vaccine* 27(47), 6550–6557.

Liang, Z. (2001). The age of migration in China. *Population and Development Review*, 27(3), 499–524.

Liang, Z. & Morooka, H. (2004). Recent trends of emigration from China: 1982–2000. *International Migration*, 42(3), 145–164.

Lin, W. *et al.* (2009). The urban resident basic medical insurance: A landmark reform towards universal coverage in China. *Health Economics*, 18(S2), S83–S96.

Lin, X. (2013). *Gender, Modernity and Male Migrant Workers in China: Becoming a Modern.* Routledge Contemporary China Series. Routledge, London, UK.

Lin, D. *et al.* (2006). The relationship between mobility, depression and smoking, alcohol use among rural-to-urban female migrants in Beijing. *Chinese Journal of Clinical Psychology*, 14(6), 614–616.

Ling, L. & Yue, J. (2011). *Report on the Status Quo of Public Health of Migrants in China.* Sun Yat-sen University Press, Guangzhou, PRC.

Liu, G. (2009). Changing Chinese migration law: From restriction to relaxation. *Journal of International Migration and Integration/Revue de l'integration et de la Migration Internationale*, 10(3), 311–333.

Liu, G.G. *et al.* (2002). Equity in health care access to: Assessing the urban health insurance reform in China. *Social Science & Medicine*, 55(10), 1779–1794.

Liu, H. & Zhao, Z. (2012). *Impact of China's Urban Resident Basic Medical Insurance on Health Care Utilization and Expenditure.* Discussion Paper No. 6768. Institute for the Study of Labor, Bonn, GER.

Liu, H. & Zhao, Z. (2014). Does health insurance matter? Evidence from China's urban resident basic medical insurance. *Journal of Comparative Economics*, 42(4), 1007–1020.

Liu, Y. (2002). Reforming China's urban health insurance system. *Health Policy*, 60(2), 133–150.

Lu, J.K. *et al.* (2015). Comparison of the status of overweight/obesity among the youth of local Shanghai, young rural-to-urban migrants and immigrant origin areas. *International Journal of Clinical and Experimental Medicine*, 8(2), 2804–2814.

Mark, C.-K. (2013). *China and the World since 1945: An International History*. Routledge, New York, NY.

Miranda, J.J. *et al.* (2011). Differences in cardiovascular risk factors in rural, urban and rural-to-urban migrants in Peru. *Heart*, 97(10), 787–796.

Mou, J. *et al.* (2011). Internal migration and depressive symptoms among migrant factory workers in Shenzhen, China. *Journal of Community Psychology*, 39(2), 212–230.

Mou, J. *et al.* (2013). Health of China's rural–urban migrants and their families: A review of literature from 2000 to 2012. *British Medical Bulletin*, 106(1), 19–43.

National Population and Family Planning Commission of China (2014). Report on China's migrant population development in 2014. China Population Publishing House, Beijing.

Nielsen, I. *et al.* (2005). Which rural migrants receive social insurance in Chinese cities? Evidence from Jiangsu survey data. *Global Social Policy*, 5(3), 353–381.

Organisation for Economic Co-operation and Development (2012). China in Focus: Lessons and Challenges. OECD, Paris, FRA.

Pan, X. *et al.* (2013). Prevalence of HIV, syphilis, HCV and their high risk behaviors among migrant workers in eastern China. *PloS One*, 8(2), e57258.

Perry, M.J. *et al.* (2005). Emergency department surveillance of occupational injuries in Shanghai's Putuo District, People's Republic of China. *Annals of Epidemiology*, 15(5), 351–357.

Pieke, F.N. (2007). Editorial introduction: Community and identity in the new Chinese migration order. *Population, Space and Place*, 13(2), 81–94.

Pieke, F.N. (2012). Immigrant China. *Modern China*, 38(1), 40–77.

Pines, D. *et al.* (1998). *Topics in Public Economics: Theoretical and Applied Analysis*. Cambridge University Press, Cambridge, UK.

Qiu, P. *et al.* (2011a). Depression and associated factors in internal migrant workers in China. *Journal of Affective Disorders*, 134(1), 198–207.

Qiu, P. *et al.* (2011b). Rural-to-urban migration and its implication for new cooperative medical scheme coverage and utilization in China. *BMC Public Health*, 11(1), 520.

Ratha, D. *et al.* (2014). *Migration and Remittances: Recent Developments and Outlook*. The World Bank, Washington DC.

Sceats, S. & S. Breslin (2012). *China and the International Human Rights System*. The Royal Institute of International Affairs, Chatham House, London, UK.

Shen, R. *et al.* (2006). Study on the maternal mortality ratio from 1995 to 2004 among residential and migrant women in Beijing. *Zhonghua liu xing bing xue za zhi= Zhonghua liuxingbingxue zazhi*, 27(3), 223–225.

Skeldon, R. (1996). Migration from China. *Journal of International Affairs*, 49(2), 434–456.

Skeldon, R. (2012). China: An emerging destination for economic migration. Migration Information Source: Country Profiles. Migration Policy Institute, Washington DC.

Taylor, G. (2011). China's Floating Migrants: Updates from the 2005 1% Population Sample Survey. Migration Studies Unit, London School of Economics and Political Science, London, UK.

The World Bank (2011). Migration and remittances. Factbook 2011. World Bank, Washington DC.

Tucker, J.D., *et al.* (2013). The Influence of Migration on the Burden of and Response to Infectious Disease Threats in China. A Theoretically Informed Review. Working Paper 2013–3. The United Nations Research Institute for Social Development and the Sun Yat-sen Center for Migrant Health Policy, Geneva, SWI.

United States Department of State (2014). Chronology of U.S.–China Relations, 1784–2000. Office of the Historian, Bureau of Public Affairs. Available at: https://history.state.gov/countries/issues/china-us-relations. Accessed 31 July 2015.

Wang, L. & Wang, X. (2012). Influence of temporary migration on the transmission of infectious diseases in a migrants' home village. *Journal of Theoretical Biology*, 300, 100–109.

Wang, W. *et al.* (2010). Prevalence and risks for sexually transmitted infections among a national sample of migrants versus non-migrants in China. *International Journal of STD & AIDS*, 21(6), 410–415.

Wang, W. *et al.* (2011a). Contribution of rural-to-urban migration in the prevalence of drug resistant tuberculosis in China. *European Journal of Clinical Microbiology & Infectious Diseases*, 30(4), 581–586.

Wang, X. *et al.* (2011b). Occupational health and safety challenges in China–focusing on township-village enterprises. *Archives of Environmental & Occupational Health*, 66(1), 3–11.

Whyte, M. & Parish, W. (1984). *Urban Life in Contemporary China*. University of Chicago Press, Chicago.

Wing, C.K. & Zhang, L. (1999). The hukou system and rural–urban migration: Processes and changes. *The China Quarterly*, 49(1), 21–56.

Wong, L. (1994). China's urban migrants — The public policy challenge. *Pacific Affairs* 67(3), 335–355.

Wong, M. et al. (2008). TB surveillance in correctional institutions in Hong Kong, 1999–2005. *The International Journal of Tuberculosis and Lung Disease*, 12(1), 93–98.

Wu, X. (2014). Census Undertakings in China, 1953–2010. Report 14-833. Center for Applied Social and Economic Research, Hong Kong University of Science and Technology, Hong Kong.

Wu, X. & Treiman, D.J. (2004). The household registration system and social stratification in China: 1955–1996. *Demography*, 41(2), 363–384.

Xiao, Y. et al. (2013). Factors associated with severe deliberate self-harm among Chinese internal migrants. *PLoS One*, DOI: 10.1371/journal.pone.0080667.

Xie, Y. et al. (2004). Epidemiology of 377 patients with chemical burns in Guangdong province. *Burns*, 30(6), 569–572.

Ying, H., L. Shuzhuo. & Feldman, M.W. (2014). Trends and determinants of female marriage migration in contemporary China. Available at: http://iussp.org/sites/default/files/event_call_for_papers/IUSSP_migration_815.pdf. Accessed 1 April 2015.

Yip, W.C. & Hsiao, W.C. (1997). Medical savings accounts: Lessons from China. *Health Affairs*, 16(6), 244–251.

Zhan, S. et al. (2002). Economic transition and maternal health care for internal migrants in Shanghai, China. *Health Policy Plan*, 17(S1), 47–55.

Zhang, J. et al. (2014). Maternal deaths among rural–urban migrants in China: A case-control study. *BMC Public Health*, 14(1), 512.

Zhang, X. et al. (2010). Road traffic injuries to foreigners in the People's Republic of China, 2000–2008. *Journal of Safety Research*, 41(6), 521–523.

Zheng, S. et al. (2010). Do nutrition and health affect migrant workers' incomes? Some evidence from Beijing, China. *China & World Economy*, 18(5), 105–124.

Zhong, B. et al. (2013). Prevalence of psychological symptoms in contemporary Chinese rural-to-urban migrant workers: An exploratory meta-analysis of observational studies using the SCL-90. *Social Psychiatry and Psychiatric Epidemiology*, 48, 1569–1581.

Zhong, B.L. et al. (2015). Prevalence and correlates of major depressive disorder among rural-to-urban migrant workers in Shenzhen, China. *Journal of Affective Disorders*, 183, 1–9.

Zhou, Z. et al. (2014). The effects of China's urban basic medical insurance schemes on the equity of health service utilisation: Evidence from Shaanxi Province. *International Journal for Equity in Health*, 13(1), 23.

Zhu, L. et al. (2009). Comparison of maternal mortality between migrating population and permanent residents in Shanghai, China, 1996–2005. *BJOG: An International Journal of Obstetrics & Gynaecology*, 116(3), 401–407.

Zhu, L.P. et al. (2007). The effectiveness of pregnancy women at fixed delivery hospitals for floating population in Shanghai. *Chinese Health Resources*, 2, 89–91.

Zhu, Y., Ngok, K. & Li, W. (2014). Policy Actors and Policy Making for Better Migrant Health in China From a Policy Network Perspective. Working Paper 2014–12. United Nations Research Institute for Social Development and Sun Yat-sen Center for Migrant Health Policy, Geneva, SWI.

Zou, X. et al. (2014). Rural-to-urban migrants are at high risk of sexually transmitted and viral hepatitis infections in China: A systematic review and meta-analysis. *BMC Infectious Diseases*, 14, 1–8.

# Chapter 13

# Migration challenges and health policy in South Korea

Professor André M.N. Renzaho

Over the past four decades, South Korea (hereafter, Korea) has experienced some significant demographic transformations due to migration and changes in population patterns. It was once one of the major migrant-source countries. However, over the past three decades, Korea has become one of the major destination countries for international migrants. This chapter provides a historical perspective on the dynamics, types and process of migration in Korea. It then highlights the impact of migration on health from key perspectives such as intermarriage and labour migrants, North Korean refugees and the ageing population. It moves on to explore the implications for multiculturalism in Korea and concludes with a summary of the lessons learnt over the past four decades and their relevance in the future multicultural Korea.

## Dynamics and types of migration: a historical perspective

The push–pull factor theory provides an avenue to understand the dynamics of migration in Korea. Towards the end of the twentieth century, there was a massive influx of foreign labour from its neighbouring countries into South Korea, a process which has its roots embedded deep within Korean history. Due to its geographical location as a peninsula, Korea was faced with numerous conflicts, invasions and occupations in the past. With Japan, China and Russia as its neighbours, a power struggle over Manchuria and the Korean peninsula at the end of the nineteenth and early twentieth centuries led to the annexation of Korea to the Japanese empire in 1910 (Tanaka, 2008). At the end of World War II, following the defeat of Japan, the Korean peninsula was divided into two parts reflecting the West–East antagonism (Savada and Shaw, 1992). While the former Soviet Union was in charge of the northern territory, the USA took care of the southern territory. Following the establishment of South Korea in 1948, the country had not been exposed to a foreign culture until the 1980s. From the mid-1980s onwards, Koreans began to have closer contacts with foreigners due to the massive influx of labour migrants. Because of the Cold War, contacts between the South Korean government and ethnic Korean emigrants were extremely limited. Thus, it is only from the mid-1980s that ethnic Korean emigrants started progressively to come back when the Search Campaign for Separated Families was initiated in 1986 and later with the diplomatic normalisation between China and South Korea in 1992 (Oh *et al.*, 2012).

Over the years, Korea lost its skilled, technical and professional workforce such as academics, government officers, farmers, construction workers, miners and health professionals to Australia, the USA, Germany, south Asia and the Middle East (Han, 2003; Min, 2011). For example, push factors that led to millions of Koreans leaving the country for a new life abroad pre- and post- the 1950–1953 Korean War included lack of opportunities and economic hardship, significant increases in wages in the 1970s and 1980s that made it more difficult for small business owners to meet wage demands, the political instability that followed the Korean war and the subsequent control of people by the regime of the time, and the government's migration policies geared towards population control and stimulating the economy through earning foreign currency (Han, 2003). Korea recorded the longest weekly working hours among the Organization for Economic Cooperation and Development (OECD) countries. Various studies have reported that the average working hours per week in Korea varies between 47 and 51 among those in the workforce compared to 35.7 hours in Japan, 36.3 hours in Belgium, 36.5 hours in Germany, 37.3 hours in Norway,

38.2 hours in the United Kingdom or 39.4 hours in the USA (Park, 2004; Faggio and Nickell, 2007; Choi and Ha, 2009; Korean Ministry of Employment and Labor, 2011; OECD, 2011; Jeong et al., 2014).

Indeed, during the Japanese colonial period (1910–1945), millions of Koreans emigrated to Japan, China and Russia, in search of better job opportunities and quality of life. During the 1960s, the USA was one of the main emigrants' destinations, with thousands of South Koreans migrating for higher education and job opportunities. During the period of global economic prosperity (1970s–1980s), millions of construction workers emigrated to the Middle East as employees of South Korean contractors, with the majority returning home within a few years with substantial savings (Park, 2004; Oh et al., 2012). Nowadays, despite high living standards in Korea, there are still emigration flows of South Koreans to Asian and Anglophone countries. To better monitor the emigration of Koreans, the emigration of Korean nationals has been categorised under three types: ancestry migration (i.e. based on marriage, engagement or relative relations), non-ancestry migration (i.e. employment opportunities where Koreans emigrate through an employment contract with a foreign company), and local migration (i.e. although the intention was not to migrate overseas, the migrant acquired long-term stay or residency status in a foreign country) (Oh et al., 2012). According to government surveys of emigrants (Park, 2004), in 2003 the most popular destination countries were the USA (28.4%) mainly for family reunification, followed by China (16.8%), Japan (12.6%), Canada (10%) and Australia (5.1%). The number of permanent Korean emigrants was estimated at 5.3 million in 2010, and by 2013 the number had increased to 7 million with 84.8% of Korean emigrants living in just three countries: China, the USA and Japan (Figure 1).

As the Korean economy started to show some significant growth trajectory in the 1970s and grew significantly in the 1990s, this significant economic growth coincided with a drastic decline in the number of Korean emigrants. The Korean War, changes in the demographic profile of the Korean population and the improvements in the economic conditions were the main pull factors for the increase in inflow of foreigners into Korea (Table 1). Therefore, pull factors have included foreign brides due to low fertility rates and the new employment opportunities associated with exponential economic growth, facilitated by employment policies

**430** *Globalisation, Migration and Health*

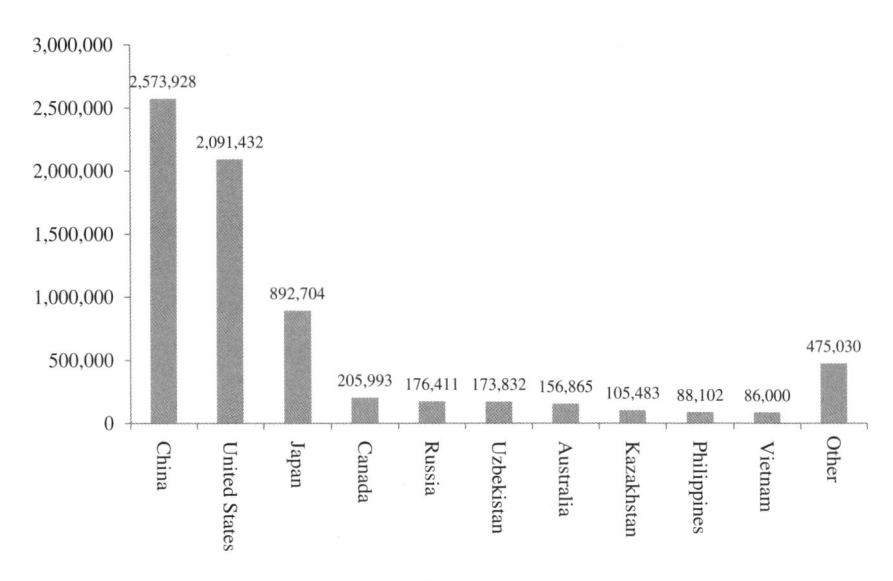

**Figure 1:** **Top 10 destination countries for Korean emigrants**
*Source*: Wikipedia (2015).

such as the Industrial Trainee Scheme (ITS), the Employment Management Scheme (EMS) and the Employment Permit System (EPS).

First, the 1950–1953 Korean War instigated the migration of 10 million North Koreans into Korea (Park, 2004). Second, employment and foreign policies and reforms instigated in the 1990s–2000s also had an impact on immigration flow. In terms of foreign policy, for example, the period between the 1950–1953 Korean War and the end of the Cold War (1991) was marked by government policies on national security. However, the Seoul Olympic Games (1988) initiated a turning point in the diplomacy of the Korean government towards other countries. Following the collapse of the Soviet Union in 1991, Korea shifted its perspective on national policies from a security to an economic one. The country moved quickly to normalise diplomatic relations with former and present communist countries, initially perceived as enemies such as Russia, China, Vietnam and eastern European countries, largely for economic objectives (Lee, 1993; Soon-Young, 1999; Oh *et al.*, 2012). This historical shift in international relations resulted in major economic implications for Korea with a majority of its current migrant workers originating from these countries.

Table 1: Recent trends in migrants' flows and stocks in South Korea

| Year | 2000 | 2001 | 2002 | 2003 | 2004 | 2005 | 2006 | 2007 | 2008 | 2009 | 2010 | 2011 | 2012 | Median annual increase | Mean annual increase |
|---|---|---|---|---|---|---|---|---|---|---|---|---|---|---|---|
| Outflows of foreign population (in 1,000s)* | | | | | | | | | | | | | | | |
| All | 89.1 | 107.2 | 114.0 | 152.3 | 148.8 | 266.7 | 183.0 | 163.6 | 215.7 | 236.4 | 196.1 | 217.7 | 290.0 | 183.0 | 183.1 |
| Inflows of foreign population (in 1,000s)** | | | | | | | | | | | | | | | |
| All | 173.1 | 163.9 | 158.9 | 168.9 | 178.5 | 253.7 | 303.0 | 300.4 | 302.2 | 232.8 | 293.1 | 307.2 | 300.2 | 253.7 | 241.2 |
| Women | 71.3 | 71.3 | 66.6 | 65.9 | 74.9 | 103.4 | 122.5 | 134.5 | 135.6 | 111.6 | 136.7 | 138.5 | 135.1 | 111.6 | 105.2 |
| Men | 101.8 | 92.6 | 92.3 | 103.0 | 103.7 | 150.3 | 180.5 | 165.9 | 166.5 | 121.3 | 156.3 | 168.7 | 165.1 | 150.3 | 136.0 |
| M:F ratio | 1.43 | 1.30 | 1.39 | 1.56 | 1.38 | 1.45 | 1.47 | 1.23 | 1.23 | 1.09 | 1.14 | 1.22 | 1.22 | 1.30 | 1.32 |
| Stock of foreign population (in 1,000s)*** | | | | | | | | | | | | | | | |
| All | 210.2 | 229.6 | 271.7 | 460.3 | 491.4 | 510.5 | 660.6 | 800.3 | 895.5 | 920.9 | 1002.7 | 982.5 | 933.0 | 660.61 | 643.78 |
| Women | 87.5 | 99.3 | 111.1 | 179.0 | 190.6 | 213.9 | 276.0 | 344.9 | 392.0 | 407.0 | 440.8 | 428.0 | 408.6 | 275.97 | 275.28 |
| Men | 122.7 | 130.4 | 160.6 | 281.3 | 300.8 | 296.6 | 384.6 | 455.4 | 503.4 | 513.8 | 561.9 | 554.5 | 524.4 | 384.63 | 368.50 |
| M:F ratio | 1.40 | 1.31 | 1.44 | 1.57 | 1.58 | 1.39 | 1.39 | 1.32 | 1.28 | 1.26 | 1.27 | 1.30 | 1.28 | 1.39 | 1.34 |

(*Continued*)

Table 1: (Continued)

| Year | 2000 | 2001 | 2002 | 2003 | 2004 | 2005 | 2006 | 2007 | 2008 | 2009 | 2010 | 2011 | 2012 | Median annual increase | Mean annual increase |
|---|---|---|---|---|---|---|---|---|---|---|---|---|---|---|---|
| Stock of foreign labour (in 1,000s)**** | | | | | | | | | | | | | | | |
| All | 123 | 129 | 137 | 415 | 298 | 198 | 317 | 499 | 538 | 555 | na | na | na | 307.5 | 320.9 |
| Women | 37 | 39 | 41 | 122 | 86 | 45 | 74 | 154 | 167 | 181 | na | na | na | 80 | 94.6 |
| Men | 86 | 90 | 96 | 293 | 212 | 153 | 243 | 345 | 371 | 374 | na | na | na | 227.5 | 226.3 |
| M:F ratio | 2.32 | 2.31 | 2.34 | 2.40 | 2.47 | 3.40 | 3.28 | 2.24 | 2.22 | 2.07 | na | na | na | 2.33 | 2.51 |

*Regulated movements of foreigners leaving Korea for a long-term period (more than 90 days) based on residence permits or other sources.
**Regulated movements of foreigners entering Korea for a long-term period (more than 90 days) based on residence permits or other sources.
***Foreigners staying in Korea more than 90 days and registered in population registers. Data have been revised since 2002 in order to include foreign nationals with Korean ancestors (called overseas Koreans) who enter with an F-4 visa and are also registered in population registers. The large increase in 2003 is mainly due to a regularisation programme for workers without permits introduced in mid-2003.
****Based on registered foreign workers, which excludes short-term (under 90 days) workers. Trainees are included.
na = not available.

*Note:* Mean and median are author's calculations based on the data. The figures may have been underestimated and may differ across studies due to different use of metrics, e.g. when population registers are used, departures tend to be less well recorded than arrivals.

*Source:* Organisation for Economic Co-operation and Development (1999).

Third, the massive exodus of Korean emigrants during the 1950s–1990s, and the static population growth, remained a serious challenge to the future Korea's economy. A recent study by the International Organisation for Migration found that the Korean population size has averaged an annual growth of less than 0.5%, increasing from 37.5 million in 1980 to 47 million in 2000 and to 49.5 million in 2014 (Oh *et al.*, 2012). The study also found that both birth rate and death rate have remained at a low level, the consequences of which have included a rapid increase in the post-working age elderly population and a significant decrease of the young working population (Oh *et al.*, 2012). To address the manpower shortage, Korea resorted to immigration policies, geared towards attracting foreign workers to fill unskilled jobs, especially the "three-D" jobs (difficult, dangerous and demeaning) shunned by the Korean population (Lim, 2003; Oh *et al.*, 2012). Finally, the decreasing female population due to low fertility rates and selective abortions of girls has attracted foreign brides leading to intercultural marriages (Chung and Kim, 2012).

These pull factors resulted in significant increases in the inflow of foreigners into Korea. The overall number of foreigners including undocumented migrants increased from just 49,500 persons in 1990 to more than 1.4 million persons in 2012, which represents an almost 30-fold increase over 22 years (Oh *et al.*, 2012). As outlined above, the migration flows in this region are predominantly composed of low-skilled workers fuelled by a surge in labour migration from neighbouring economically-disadvantaged countries, young brides and displaced people from North Korea. The shift from being a major sending to a receiving immigration country began in the 1980s. After a long period of rapid industrialisation and economic growth, the number of Koreans started to drop, while the number of immigration flows began to increase dramatically. Chung and Kim (2012) have identified three stages in Korean immigration: (1) the late 1980s immigration of unskilled and undocumented labour migrants from China, south Asia and south-east Asia; (2) the 1990s immigration of workers (predominantly males) through the 1993 Industrial Trainee Programme and the 2004 EPS and (3) the 2000s female marriage migration.

Each migration period was characterised by different precipitating factors. For example, between 1980 and 1990, the main pull factors were serious labour shortages, deceleration in the growth of the labour force due to longer periods of education, a boom in the construction industry attracting Korean workers from less-paid jobs, and increased demand for cheap and unskilled workers to fill 3D jobs. During the late 1980s, the Korean Federation of Small Businesses pressurised the government to allow entry to foreign workers on tourist visas. Because these foreign migrant workers tended to find another job at the end of their contract, hence overstaying their visa (undocumented), the request was ignored by the Korean authorities (Chung and Kim, 2012). The growing number of undocumented labour migrants soon resulted in the government developing several strategies in an attempt to control the situation.

## Types of migrants in Korea

### Employment reforms and labour migrants

Korea has experienced manpower shortages since the 1980s. In 2010, the manpower shortage was estimated at 3.2% (Table 2), an increase from 2.7% reported in 2009 (Oh *et al.*, 2012). The Korean government went through a series of employment reforms in order to meet these labour shortages through international migration. Such reforms happened in three phases: the pre-liberal economic consolidation (1987–1997), the period of economic transformation (1998–2002), and the development of liberal and ethnic immigration policies (2003–present) (Table 3 Kim, 2008). The three major schemes were the ITS, the Employment Management Scheme (EMS) and the Employment Permit Systems (EPS). Major factors that led to reforming the employment sector were the increased need for labour supply, the increase in local wages that made it difficult for local enterprises to employ domestic workers, and the globalisation of Korean firms and their products requiring training of staff at overseas branches into Korean factories and production processes (Hahn and Choi, 2006). These changes meant that the Korean government was under pressure to legalise the import of foreign workers. These developments were against the Korean immigration and emigration laws which prohibited the entrance of unskilled workers into the country for employment purposes, in part to maintain the ethnic homogeneity (Hahn and Choi, 2006). In 1991, the Industrial and Technical Training Programme (ITTP), modelled on

Table 2: Manpower shortage by industry with five regular employees or more in 2010

| Domain | Current number of employees (A) | No. of job openings (B) | No. of filled job openings (C) | No. of unfilled job openings (B–C) | % of unfilled job openings | No. of vacancies (D) | Manpower shortage (D/A) |
|---|---|---|---|---|---|---|---|
| Total | 8,380,467 | 563,341 | 459,410 | 103,931 | 18.4% | 271,009 | 3.2% |
| *Mining and quarrying* | *14,205* | *392* | *338* | *54* | *13.8%* | *233* | *1.6%* |
| Mining of non-metallic minerals except fuel | 9,586 | 371 | 318 | 53 | 14.3% | 229 | 2.4% |
| Mining of coal, crude petroleum & natural gas | 3,977 | 11 | 11 | 0 | 0.0% | 0 | 0.0% |
| Mining support service activities | 429 | 2 | 2 | 0 | 0.0% | 0 | 0.0% |
| Mining of metal ores | 212 | 8 | 7 | 1 | 12.5% | 4 | 1.9% |
| *Manufacturing* | *2,806,306* | *178,276* | *131,315* | *46,961* | *26.3%* | *119,360* | *4.3%* |
| Manufacture of |  |  |  |  |  |  |  |
| Fabricated metal products, except machinery & furniture | 274,411 | 22,737 | 15,221 | 7,516 | 33.1% | 17,732 | 6.5% |
| Rubber and plastic products | 206,540 | 15,079 | 10,416 | 4,663 | 30.9% | 11,794 | 5.7% |
| Food products | 135,862 | 10,156 | 7,612 | 2,544 | 25.0% | 6,570 | 4.8% |
| Basic metal products | 132,744 | 5,494 | 3,510 | 1,984 | 36.1% | 5,153 | 3.9% |
| Chemical products except pharmaceuticals/medicinal chemicals | 104,873 | 4,935 | 3,290 | 1,645 | 33.3% | 4,481 | 4.3% |

(*Continued*)

Table 2: (Continued)

| Domain | Current number of employees (A) | No. of job openings (B) | No. of filled job openings (C) | No. of unfilled job openings (B−C) | % of unfilled job openings | No. of vacancies (D) | Manpower shortage (D/A) |
|---|---|---|---|---|---|---|---|
| Textiles except apparel | 93,109 | 7,149 | 5,242 | 1,907 | 26.7% | 4,933 | 5.3% |
| Other non-metallic mineral products | 81,768 | 3,743 | 2,540 | 1,203 | 32.1% | 2,609 | 3.2% |
| Wearing apparel, clothing accessories and fur articles | 78,888 | 4,549 | 4,077 | 472 | 10.4% | 2,636 | 3.3% |
| Pulp, paper and paper products | 52,034 | 2,638 | 1,422 | 1,216 | 46.1% | 2,309 | 4.4% |
| Printing and reproduction of recorded media | 41,403 | 2,045 | 1,623 | 422 | 20.6% | 1,855 | 4.5% |
| Pharmaceuticals, medicinal chemicals and botanical products | 32,926 | 967 | 641 | 326 | 33.7% | 774 | 2.4% |
| Tanning and dressing of leather/luggage and footwear | 23,939 | 815 | 767 | 48 | 5.9% | 784 | 3.3% |
| Wood products of wood and cork, except furniture | 23,930 | 1,657 | 1,231 | 426 | 25.7% | 1,957 | 8.2% |
| Coke, hard-coal & lignite fuel briquettes and refine petroleum | 10,604 | 179 | 179 | 0 | 0.0% | 46 | 0.4% |
| Beverages | 9,426 | 360 | 279 | 81 | 22.5% | 277 | 2.9% |
| Tobacco products | 2,485 | 11 | 8 | 3 | 27.3% | 3 | 0.1% |

Source: Oh et al. (2012).

Table 3: Changes in immigration policies in Korea

| Phase | Period | Ethnic Koreans not from China and CIS states | Ethnic Koreans from China and CIS states | Low-skilled foreign workers |
|---|---|---|---|---|
| I | 1987–1989 | Travel documents | Travel documents | Zero-immigration policies |
|  | 1990–1991 |  | Mandating visa | Zero-immigration policies |
|  | 1992–1997 |  |  | Industrial Trainee System (D-3 visa) |
| II | 1998–2002 | Overseas Koreans Act (F-4 visa) | Mandating visa | Trainee-Employment System (D-3 & E-8) |
| III | 2003–2006 | Overseas Koreans Act (F-4 visa) | Special work permit (F-1-4 & E-9 visas) | Trainee-Employment System (E-8 visa) & EPS (E-9 visa) |
|  | 2007–2009 |  | Special work and residence permit (H-2 visa) | EPS (E-9 visa) |

Note: CIS states refer to the former Soviet Union states.
Source: Kim (2008).

the Japanese foreign labour programme yet without giving preference to ethnic Koreans, was trialled. This programme focused on inviting and training overseas staff working at overseas Korean companies for 6 months (extendable to 12 months) (Hahn and Choi, 2006; Kim, 2008; Oh and Jung, 2013). While not specifically geared towards employing them as staff in Korea, it was the first attempt to allow the entrance of skilled and unskilled workers into Korea (Oh and Jung, 2013). Therefore, by virtue of its structure and intended objectives, the scheme was not well equipped to meet the high demand for unskilled workers in Korea. The schemes' shortfalls led to many criticisms and the schemes could not address issues related to the illegal employment of foreign workers by dissatisfied small-to-medium firms. In November 1993, the ITS, an expansion of the ITTP, was introduced. That is, trainees received training for one year, a period after which they were allowed to be employed for 2 years as paid trainees.

In other words, they were viewed and treated as paid trainees and not workers (Gray, 2007; Oh and Jung, 2013).

While the ITTP catered mainly for large firms, the ITS was heralded as the policy to address the needs of small-to-medium enterprises, mainly the manufacturing and construction industry, as well as coastal fishing, and agriculture and livestock farming. Small-to-medium enterprises were given preferential treatment in the recruitment process of foreign unskilled workers, with the quota for foreign workers set at 20,000 in 1993, which increased incrementally to 30,000 in 1994, 50,000 in 1995 and to 85,500 by 2002 (Hahn and Choi, 2006). These efforts were not adequate to address the challenges of illegal unskilled workers as those who overstayed their one-year visa through paying broker fees or being transferred elsewhere by the employer did not have access to any social protection mechanisms, and were prone to exploitation and human rights abuses.

The EPS was promulgated in 2003 and fully implemented by 2004 (Gray, 2007). Prior to the EPS however, the EMS was initiated on 9 December 2002 to cater for ethnic Koreans of foreign nationality but who had relatives in Korea. Through the F-1-4 visa, ethnic Koreans of foreign nationality were allowed to be employed via the Employment Security Centre after entering Korea (Lee, 2006). The introduction of the EPS in 2004 meant that the EMS was to be operated within this new system, and by 2007 the EPS had become the sole employment system to recruit foreign unskilled workers. It incorporated the Visit and Employment Programme, which was a special programme for unskilled workers of Korean ethnicity from China and other regions (Oh and Jung, 2013). The EPS contained Acts on employment of foreign workers from only 15 countries with whom the Korean government signed a Memorandum of Understanding for labour import, with workers recognised as legal employees. The EPS excluded private recruitment agencies but expanded the labour rights of foreign workers to include a minimum wage and severance pay arrangements (Oh and Jung, 2013). Companies were allowed to hire unskilled foreign workers on a three-year visa in principle, extendable to up to four years and ten months in special cases (Roh, 2014). Quotas in terms of the number of unskilled migrants allowed per year were enforced under the EPS (Table 4). However, the scheme performed far better than the previous ITS in increasing the number of unskilled migrants (Figure 2), with a corresponding decline in the number of illegal foreign workers.

## Ethnic Korean immigrants of foreign citizenship

Ethnic Korean immigrants in Korea can be categorised into three groups: (1) those living in developed countries, (2) those from China, and (3) those from the former Soviet Union states. The number of ethnic Korean immigrants in Korea increased dramatically from the early 2000s, increasing from 127,839 in 2001 to 477,029 in 2010, and account for approximately 37.8% of total foreign residents in Korea (Oh et al., 2012). During Phase I of the policy reform (Table 3), Korean migrants and other

Table 4: Foreign quota introduction for 2007–2012

| Year | Total | Manufacturing industry | Construction industry | Service industry | Agriculture and livestock industry | Fishing industry |
|---|---|---|---|---|---|---|
| 2007 | 109,600 | 69,300 | 14,900 | 20,600 | 3,600 | 1,200 |
| 2008 | 132,000 | 76,800 | 18,000 | 31,000 | 5,000 | 1,200 |
| 2009 | 34,000 | 23,000 | 2,000 | 6,000 | 3,000 | 1,000 |
| 2010 | 34,000 | 23,000 | 2,000 | 6,000 | 3,000 | 1,000 |
| 2011 | 48,000 | 40,000 | 1,600 | 150 | 4,500 | 1,750 |
| 2012 | 57,000 | 49,000 | 1,600 | 150 | 4,500 | 1,750 |

*Source*: Roh (2014).

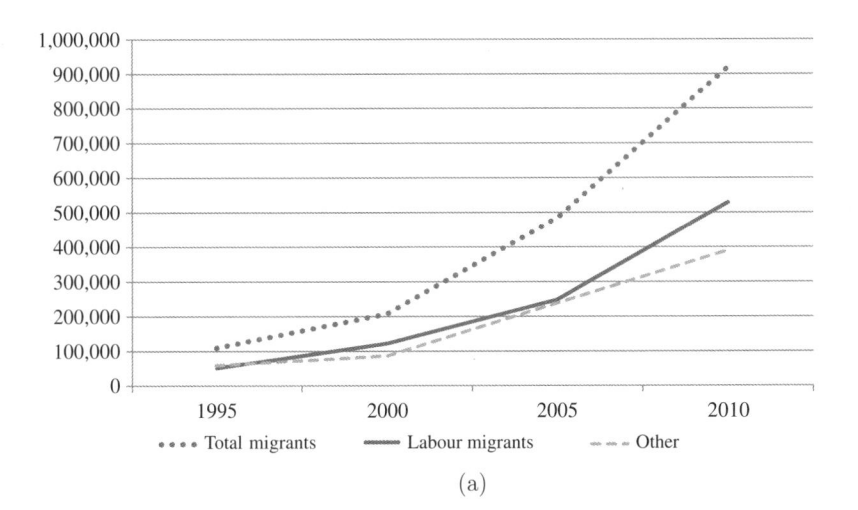

(a)

440  *Globalisation, Migration and Health*

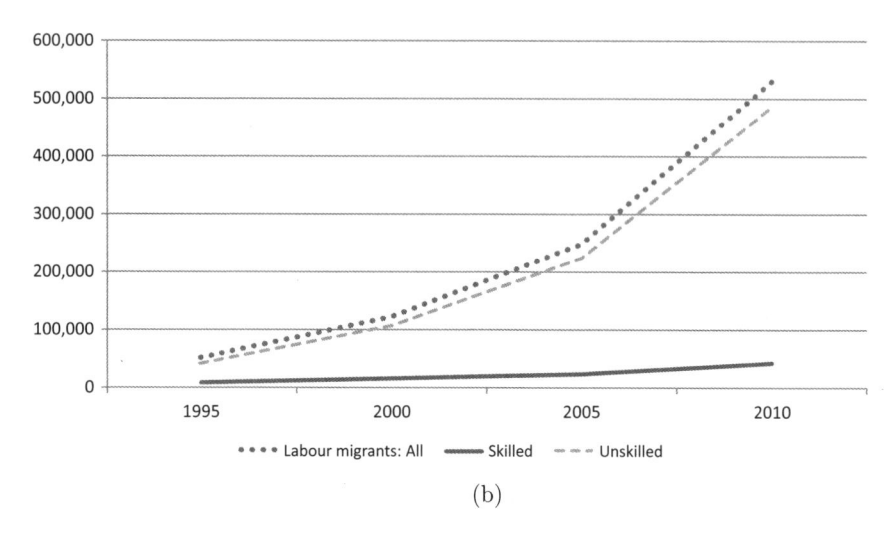

(b)

**Figure 2:** (a) **Number of migrants in South Korea (1995–2010).** (b) **Number of labour migrants in South Korea (1995–2010).**

*Note:* Based only on foreign residents staying longer than three months on any type of employment visa.
*Source:* Figures constructed by the author using data extracted from Oh and Jung (2013).

migrants entered Korea on a visiting visa and then overstayed after the visa expired to work as illegal workers. Prior to 2001, the main reason for ethnic Korean immigrants entering Korea was visiting relatives. However, ethnic Korean migrants took advantage of the economic boom in Korea by entering the country on a tourist visa and then finding jobs illegally. Their fluency in the Korean language facilitated their integration. By 2001, the proportion of undocumented ethnic Korean immigrants reached 57%. The introduction of the Visit and Employment Programme had a significant impact on ethnic Korean immigrants' migration patterns and reduced significantly the number of ethnic Korean immigrants living in Korea as illegal workers. For example, the proportion of ethnic Korean immigrants entering Korea to visit relatives dropped from 41% in 2006 to 3.3% in 2010 while those visiting for work-related reasons increased from 27% in 2006 to 65.5% in 2010 (Oh *et al.*, 2012). It is worth noting that the Korean immigration policy is characterised by a double standard. That is, low-skilled ethnic Koreans are viewed as a temporary workforce subject to government control and regulation, yet they enjoy special benefits, such as freedom of employment in service and the possibility of changing workplaces, therefore giving them more privileges than their fellow non-Korean foreign workers (Oh et al., 2012). Since they make up the majority of the migrant population, representing approximately three-quarter of immigrants, it is time for Korea to develop effective policy measures to ensure their permanent settlement and integration.

## North Korean defectors

Following the end of the Korean War (1950–1953), North Korea initiated a process of rapid industrialisation, which soon resulted in an economic downfall in the late 1970s. This downfall coupled with severe famine and floods in the 1990s prompted several thousands of North Koreans to flee their country. Refugees also fled due to politically initiated repression and persecution in their country to neighbouring countries such as China, Russia and South Korea. However, the US Committee for Human Rights in North Korea stated that around 200,000 North Koreans are still held political prisoners in their country (Tanaka, 2008). Due to the north–south Korean border being heavily guarded, most of the defectors escape via the Chinese border to reach South Korea. However, not all of them are able to arrive safely in South Korea, and an estimated 300,000 North Korean defectors are now living in China. Despite the UNHCR concern over the treatment of defectors in China, the Chinese government has failed to recognise them as refugees and has forced the repatriation of North Korean refugees. Forcibly returned refugees are subject to inhuman punishment and torture, prompting the United Nations to set up a Commission of Inquiry to investigate human rights violations in North Korea (Cohen, 2014).

In 2014, 26,483 North Korean defectors were living in South Korea, of whom 70% are female (Ministry of Unification, 2014). Following their arrival in South Korea, the North Korean defectors are not considered as refugees but as citizens of Korea since North Korea is still considered as a part of the Republic's territory (Park, 2004). The defectors are enrolled in a government operated programme known as "*Hanawon*", which offers a 12-week programme incorporating education on the Korean economy, history, vocational training, health check-up and career assistance (Cho and Kim, 2011). After this induction, the government provides them with a resettlement payment which varies according to the family size or number of household members. For example, a four-member household would receive between US$30,000 and US$57,000 in addition to "key money", a type of rental allowance approximating US$6000 (Park, 2004). However, following a law amendment in 1997, these adjustment benefits have decreased and resulted in economic difficulties for North Korean defectors, many of whom did not receive employment assistance and have resorted to small business ownerships.

## Marriage migrants: determinants and patterns

International marriage can be conceptualised as a marital union between two people of different nationalities. Historically, intermarriages occurred during and after the periods of invasion of Korea by China and Japan. Since then, international marriages in general that involve Korean women marrying foreigners have been condemned as betrayals of nationalism (Lee, 2008). Between 1910 and 1945, hundreds of Korean women served as mistresses to Japanese men. From 1945 onwards, intermarriages with soldiers from the US military occurred, resulting in Korean women marrying foreign soldiers being termed "Yanggonju" as a pejorative word to describe Korean women who marry or engage in sexual labour for foreign soldiers. The word is exclusively used to mean "Yankee whore" "Yankee wife", "GI [a noun used to describe the soldiers, airmen or marines of the United States Army or shore-bound sailors] Brides" or "a vulgar and shameful social object" (Kim, 1998; Lee, 2008). Although the term was initially used to simply describe Korean women working in militarised sex-work to provide sexual services to foreign men, it is now used to refer to women in interracial marriages (Kim, 1998). Therefore, children from the Kosian families (i.e. Korean wives with foreign husbands) experience extreme and complex forms of social prejudice and discrimination (Lee, 2003; Lee, 2008). For example, legislative frameworks that were in place between 1948 and 1998 regulated the nationality of children from international marriages along the paternal line, meaning that children of a Korean mother and a foreign father were not eligible for the Korean nationality by birth (Lee, 2003). The law was amended on 13 June 1998 to recognise "Kosian". While the term "Kosian" has strictly been used to refer to the children of Korean mothers and Asian fathers, it has now been adopted for use in describing children of Korean men and Asian "picture brides" (Lee, 2003).

The intermarriage pattern has changed and Korean men are increasingly marrying foreign women due to shortages of brides. Preference for sons over daughters has been part of the Korean culture with the number of males per 100 females estimated to be higher than 105 (Park, 1983; Das Gupta *et al.*, 2003). The discrimination against daughters occurs in four different ways: (1) before conception through the use of contraception or having more children until the number of desired sons has been reached, (2) during pregnancy through sex-selective abortion, (3) at birth through sex-selective infanticide, and (4) during early childhood through neglect as illustrated by the higher infant and childhood mortality rate among girls than boys (Das Gupta *et al.*, 2003). The reasons for preferring sons over daughters are complex but centre around economic factors and the security for old age (e.g. elderly depending on having the support of grown sons), ancestral after-life beliefs and values (e.g. without sons, grandsons and great-grandsons, one's after-life is insecure, hence leading to the mistreatment of women who fail to have sons) and family lineage (e.g. fear of losing father's lineage networks when women get married) (Das Gupta *et al.*, 2003). This discriminatory pattern against daughters has led to the shortage of brides.

The trends of international marriages in Korea displayed four significant patterns. As discussed above, the period during and after the occupation of Korea and post-war was the first period, characterised mainly by Yanggonju although their exact figures remain unknown. The pre-1990 period constitutes the second period known as the "female phenomenon". That is, international marriages involved predominantly Korean women with only a few Korean men marrying foreign women (Lee, 2008). The period between 1990 and 2005 is seen as the third period, which was characterised by a significant increase in Korean men's marrying foreign brides (Table 5A). The number of men engaged in international marriages started to increase in 1992, and by 1995 it had surpassed that of women (Lee, 2008). This shift in pattern was due to many factors including (a) rapid urbanisation in Korea, leading young women to leave rural areas in search of better education and employment opportunities, (b) disproportionate male population in rural areas engaged in farming and agriculture; and (c) sex-selective abortion in Korea (Das Gupta *et al.*, 2003; Kim, 2009a; Lee, 2012). Between 1990 and 2005, a staggering 160,000 foreign women had married Korean men, and international marriages accounted for 13.6% of

Table 5A: Number of foreign spouses of Koreans by gender and nationality, 1990–2005

|  | 1990–1999 | 2000–2005 | Total | % |
|---|---|---|---|---|
| **Foreign wives** | | | | |
| American | 3,629 | 1,719 | 5,348 | 3.3% |
| Japanese | 10,118 | 6,787 | 16,905 | 10.6% |
| Chinese | 37,171 | 70,163 | 107,334 | 67.1% |
| Filipino | 1,593 | 4,623 | 6,216 | 3.9% |
| Vietnamese | — | 10,392 | 10,392 | 6.5% |
| Thai | — | 1,727 | 1,727 | 1.1% |
| Mongolian | — | 1,773 | 1,773 | 1.1% |
| Russian | — | 1,329 | 1,329 | 0.8% |
| Other | 3,116 | 5,802 | 8,918 | 5.6% |
| **TOTAL foreign wives** | **55,627** | **104,315** | **159,942** | **100.0%** |
| **Foreign husbands** | | | | |
| American | 12,209 | 7,435 | 19,644 | 24.3% |
| Japanese | 19,266 | 15,962 | 35,228 | 43.6% |
| Chinese | 2,010 | 10,574 | 12,584 | 15.6% |
| Pakistani | — | 681a | 681 | 0.8% |
| Bangladeshi | — | 696 | 696 | 0.9% |
| Filipino | — | 121 | 121 | 0.1% |
| Nepali | — | 116 | 116 | 0.1% |
| Other | 3,951 | 7,792 | 11,743 | 14.5% |
| **TOTAL** | **37,436** | **43,377** | **80,813** | **100.0%** |

Source: Lee (2008).

all marriages in 2005 (Lee, 2008; Kim, 2009a). The post-2005 period represents the last period which has been characterised by an increase in intermarriage in rural areas, which accounts for 35.9% of marriages in rural areas (Kim, 2009a, 2009b). Rural areas have been experiencing a significant increase in the number of bachelors (Lee, 2012). This has been aggravated by the fact that even Korean women are unwilling to marry into a rural farming life or accept the traditional role of a married woman (Abelmann, 1997; Kawaguchi and Lee, 2012). Consequently, there have

Table 5B: Sex ratio of never-married population by age in rural areas 1980–2005

| Age | 1980 | 1985 | 1990 | 1995 | 2000 | 2005 |
| --- | --- | --- | --- | --- | --- | --- |
| 25–29 | 553 | 482 | 388 | 273 | 280 | 224 |
| 30–34 | 660 | 541 | 566 | 422 | 553 | 404 |
| 35–39 | 360 | 444 | 423 | 318 | 581 | 468 |
| 40–44 | 301 | 359 | 336 | 235 | 465 | 441 |
| 25–44 | 549 | 485 | 415 | 299 | 360 | 302 |

*Source*: Lee (2012).
*Note*: Sex ratio is the ratio of men per 100 women.

increased cross-border marriages to deal with the so-called the "rural bachelor's marriage problem", or the "bride famine". In rural areas, the male-to-female ratio of the never-married aged between 25 and 44 years has remained very high since the 1980s (Table 5B). For example, there were 549 men and 302 men for every 100 women in 1980 and 2005 in rural areas, respectively, which reflect a serious and a high sex ratio imbalance despite the decline (Lee, 2012).

A number of policies were put in place by the Korean government to address the crisis, including the 2006–2007 Act to Support International Marriage for Rural Bachelors, the 2007 Act regulating Marriage Brokerage Agent (Act No. 8688), and the 2008 Support for Multicultural Families Act (Act No. 8937) (Lee, 2012). Some of the initiatives which address the "bride famine" included setting up a national committee on the marriage of rural bachelors to facilitate meetings between bachelor farmers and women factory workers, and a visit to China to encourage the marriage of rural bachelors to Korean Chinese women. By 2010, cross-border marriages accounted for 10.5% of all marriages (Lee, 2012).

## Socio-demographic challenges

### *Ageing population and low fertility rate*

Despite its rapid economic growth, Korea is facing an even more rapidly ageing population which is estimated to grow in the next few decades. The population aged 65 years or older increased from 4% in 1985 to 9% in 2005 and to 12% in 2013 (World Bank, 2015). The United Nations uses the proportion of the population aged 65 and over greater than 7%, 14% and 20% to denote respectively an "ageing society", "aged society" and "super-aged society" (Kim, 2000). Based on these definitions, it is clear that Korea is rapidly becoming an aged society. For most economically established countries, it took decades to transit from being an ageing to an aged society, however, the speed of population ageing has become more rapid in Korea than other OECD countries. For example, data in Table 6 suggest that Korea is expected to reach 14% of its population aged 65 years or older in just 18 years, a process that took 115 years for France (1865–1980), 85 years for Sweden (1890–1975), 65 years for the USA (1945–2010), 40 years for Britain (1930–1970) and 45 for Germany (1930–1975).

The proportion of Koreans aged 65 years and older will increase from 12% in 2013 to 15.7% in 2020, 24.1% in 2030, 32.0% in 2040 and 37.3% in 2050 (World Bank, 2015). It reached 7% in 2000, the year that marked Korea as an ageing society. If the above projections are correct, then Korea will be an "aged society" before 2020 and a "super-aged society" before 2030. Factors accelerating this demographic transition have included a low fertility rate and increased life expectancy. For example, mean life expectancy at birth has increased from 51.1 years in 1960 to 76.2 years in 2010, and is projected to reach 82.9 years in 2050. For women, life expectancy at

Table 6: Speed of population ageing in selected developed countries

| Country | When proportion of 65+ years old reaches 7% | 14% | 20% | Years taken 7% → 14% | 14% → 20% |
|---|---|---|---|---|---|
| Korea | 2000 | 2018 | 2026 | 18 | 8 |
| USA | 1942 | 2013 | 2028 | 71 | 15 |
| Germany | 1932 | 1972 | 2012 | 40 | 40 |
| Japan | 1970 | 1994 | 2006 | 24 | 12 |
| UK | 1929 | 1976 | 2021 | 47 | 45 |
| France | 1864 | 1979 | 2020 | 115 | 41 |
| Italy | 1927 | 1988 | 2007 | 61 | 19 |
| Sweden | 1887 | 1972 | 2012 | 85 | 40 |

Source: Kim (2000).

birth has increased from 53.7 years in 1960 to 82.9 years in 2010, and is projected to reach 88.9 years in 2050 (Choi, 2015). In contrast, total fertility has dropped from 6 per 1,000 in 1960 to 4.5 in 1970, 2.8 in 1980 and 1.2 in 2003, which was the lowest level in the world and has remained steady at 1.2 since (Stephen, 2012; Howe *et al.*, 2007). This low fertility rate has slowed the population growth and is expected to lead to negative population growth rates by 2025 and a dramatic increase in the dependency ratio (by the number of persons 65+ to the number of persons aged 15–64) by 2050 (Stephen, 2012). As an illustration, in 2007, there were 7.2 Korean workers supporting each retired elder, but this number is projected to decrease to 2.5 in 2030 and 1.3 by 2050 (Howe *et al.*, 2007). Korea will have no choice but to rely on foreign labour to sustain its economy, requiring the revision and expansion of its current immigration policies to preferentially target low-skilled migrants. It could be strategic for the government to consider integrating permanent residency and immigrant citizenship into its immigration policies as part of the solutions to address national labour shortages.

## *Intermarriage and divorce*

Table 7 provides data on marriage and divorce since 2002. Statistics Korea does not provide data on divorce broken down by type of marriage. There are a number of factors that could trigger emotional stress, leading to early divorce and in some cases domestic violence due to the demographic and socioeconomic inequalities between the groom and the bride (Table 8). The majority of foreign brides tend to be younger than Korean husbands. Brides' age varies between 20 and 30 years while their husband counterparts tend to be in their 30s or 40s, leading to a 10-year age gap. Similarly, women's participation in the workforce differ considerably depending on their country of origin, with 52.4% of Korean-Chinese and 39.9% of Chinese in the workforce, while only 21.2% of Vietnamese and 12.2 % of Cambodian migrants are in the workforce. While having a child may secure migrant women's marriage and citizenship, it may also be an important factor preventing them from participating in the workforce (Lee, 2012). This could explain in part why there has been a significant increase in divorce rates in intermarriages, compared to native Korean marriages.

Table 7: Marriage and divorce statistics, 2002–2012

| Variable | 2002 | 2003 | 2004 | 2005 | 2006 | 2007 | 2008 | 2009 | 2010 | 2011 | 2012 |
|---|---|---|---|---|---|---|---|---|---|---|---|
| Number of marriages* | 304.9 | 302.5 | 308.6 | 314.3 | 330.6 | 343.6 | 327.7 | 309.8 | 326.1 | 329.1 | 327.1 |
| Marriage with a foreign spouse* | 15.2 | 24.8 | 34.6 | 42.4 | 38.8 | 37.6 | 36.2 | 33.3 | 34.2 | 29.8 | 28.3 |
| Korean males & foreign females* | 10.7 | 18.8 | 25.1 | 30.7 | 29.7 | 28.6 | 28.2 | 25.1 | 26.3 | 22.3 | 20.6 |
| Korean females & foreign males* | 4.5 | 6.0 | 9.5 | 11.6 | 9.1 | 9.0 | 8.0 | 8.2 | 8.0 | 7.5 | 7.7 |
| Number of divorces* | 144.9 | 166.6 | 138.9 | 128.0 | 124.5 | 124.1 | 116.5 | 124.0 | 116.9 | 114.3 | 114.3 |
| Crude divorce rate | 3.0 | 3.4 | 2.9 | 2.6 | 2.5 | 2.5 | 2.4 | 2.5 | 2.3 | 2.3 | 2.3 |

Compiled from Statistics Korea, available at: http://kostat.go.kr/portal/english/news/1/1/index.board?bmode=read&aSeq=287104. Accessed 28 March 2014.
*In thousands.

In 2011, Statistics Korea (2013) estimated the percentage of divorces with foreign spouses at 10.1%, an approximate four-fold increase since 2004. The percentage is more likely to be higher as the number of people who ran away from their abusive spouses or leaving a "fake marriage" are often not included in divorce rates, and such data are hard to capture. Therefore, a significant number of foreign spouses experience family dissolution (Lee, 2008).

## *Intermarriage and fake marriage*

Fake marriages occur when foreigners use international marriage for political and socioeconomic benefits (e.g. to secure a working visa) or to obtain citizenship in the host country. While the extent of the problem is hard to establish, fake marriages have become a very serious problem in Korea. The problem became so significant in the mid-1990s that the Korean government had to sign a Memorandum of Understanding with China in 1996 to make international marriages a complex and complicated process, which was later simplified in 2003 (Lee, 2008). However, Lee and

Table 8: Demographic and economic characteristics of multicultural families, 2009

| Characteristic | Variables | | |
|---|---|---|---|
| Country of origin | Korean husband & foreign wife | Korean husband & Vietnamese wife | Korean husband & Korean wife |
| Age gap | 10 years | 17 years | 2.9 years |
| Urban residence | 70.3% | 53.2% | 80.3% |
| Women's labour force participation | 36.9% | 21.1% | 49.2% |
| Child(ren) | 61.6% | 72.9% | 74.9% |
| Number of children | 0.9 | 0.9 | 1.15 |
| Living with in-laws | 27.5% | 45.5% | 4.4% |
| Registered as a person with disability within the family | 17.9% | 14.9% | 4.6% |
| Employment by life stage | % Employed | % Unemployed | % of Total ($n$) |
| Before marriage | 83.3 | 16.7 | 100 (6,723) |
| After marriage | 41.6 | 58.4 | 100 (6,723) |
| Before birth of first baby | 27.6 | 72.4 | 100 (6,199) |
| After birth of first baby | 21.8 | 78.2 | 100 (6,195) |
| Before birth of last baby | 23.5 | 76.5 | 100 (6,194) |
| After birth of last baby | 21.8 | 77.6 | 100 (6,193) |
| Before primary school enrolment of last child | 36.4 | 63.6 | 100 (4,139) |
| After primary school enrolment of last child | 41.8 | 58.2 | 100 (4,139) |

Source: Lee (2012).

colleagues (2006) argue that while women come to Korea to genuinely build a happy family, when they become dissatisfied, disappointed or experienced domestic violence, they run away. Fake marriages mostly apply to ethnic Korean women residing in China due to their easy access to employment, their command of the Korean language and their resemblance to native Koreans (Lee, 2005; 2008). Nevertheless, in some cases, fake marriages turn into a happy and real marriage when the husband is found to be sincere and generous (Lee, 2008).

## Intermarriage and domestic violence

Epidemiological studies of spousal violence are scarce in Korea in general and more so among marriages with a foreign spouse due to the difficulties in measuring violent behaviour, the lack of measurement criteria and standardised approaches to measuring spousal violence and respondents' tendency to conceal domestic violence (Kim and Cho, 1992). The few available data suggest that spouse violence has been on the rise since the 1990s. Kim and Cho (1992) reported that in 1992 the prevalence of spouse battering was 30.9% overall, 37.5% in women and 23.2% in men. The prevalence of severe spouse battering was 8.4% overall, 12.4% in women and 3.7% in men. In a paper to the United Nations' Expert Group Meeting on indicators to measure violence against women in 2007, Byun (2007) reported results from the first national survey on domestic violence in Korea that took place in 2004. The survey included 6,156 adults (male: 3,071, female: 3,085) who were or had been married in order to depict the magnitude of three indicators: spouse-violence, violence against children and violence against parents in the surveyed households. The study found that 44.6% of participants experienced at least one of the three violence-related indicators from their spouses in the year preceding the survey, while 42.1% experienced psychological violence, 15.7% experienced physical violence and 7.1% experienced sexual violence. Husband-to-wife violence was more prevalent than wife-to-husband violence. Other studies have estimated the annual incidence of husband-to-wife physical violence varies between 27.9% and 35.6%, which is higher than that reported in other industrialised countries (Kim, 1998; Byun *et al.*, 1999; Kim *et al.*, 2009). However, all these studies did not examine their data by types of marriage to establish the magnitude of spouse violence among families with foreign spouses.

Nevertheless, it is possible that spouse violence in marriages with foreign spouses is a serious problem because spouse abuse is tolerated in the Korean culture, especially high among women, and is closely linked to patriarchal and cultural values (Choi *et al.*, 2008; Hong *et al.*, 2010). Such values are well encapsulated in the Korean adage: "*a dried pollack and a wife must be beaten once every three days*" and such values that sanction wife battering are enforced to uphold "harmony" and "social order"

(Hong et al., 2010, p. 1626). Choi and colleagues (2008) note that the first reason is the teaching and beliefs within the Korean culture that maintaining family harmony at any cost and avoiding feuds within the family remain the wife's responsibilities, hence culturally institutionalising and legitimising abuse against women. The second reason relates to the socialisation and cultural acceptance of daily heavy drinking among Korean men often for the sake of business. Such a cultural acceptance of heavy drinking among men is deeply ingrained into Korean that maintains that *"it is a wife's duty to accept and obey her husband regardless of the situation and to sacrifice herself for the sake of family harmony"* (Choi et al., 2008, p. 41). The third reason is concerned with divorce being seen as bringing shame and disgrace to the wife, and any divorce is blamed on the wife regardless of the reason for divorce, making it difficult for wives to leave an abusive marriage. The last reason relates to the financial dependency whereby women tend to quit their jobs to look after the family as well as perceiving married women as inefficient at work regardless of their educational attainment, and hence making them reliant financially on their husbands. Such dependency makes wives vulnerable to exploitation and tolerant of abuses. These observations are similar to those reported by other authors (Savada and Shaw, 1992; Cho, 1998; Hong et al., 2010). Foreign wives from the Asian region marrying Korean men have also been brought up with the Confucianism modelling cultural values and practices that uphold family life harmony characterised by close family ties, where families are more valued than individuals, gender roles and hierarchy, and women's obedience and subservience (Van Tai, 1981; Ho, 1990; Jamieson, 1993; Kibria, 1993; Truong, 2001). It is worth acknowledging that the increased globalisation in Asia and legislative measures being put in place by the Korean government give the right to both men and women to divorce although the process is not as easy as one would think due to social and economic inequalities and discrimination. Difficulties with obtaining divorce can be illustrated by data in Table 7 showing that the crude divorce rate has stagnated since 2004.

Therefore, spousal violence rates in marriages with foreign spouses are more likely to be greater than the Korean averages, and such violence occurs in various forms including domestic violence, poverty and neglect, and human trafficking of foreign wives (Lee, 2008). A study commissioned by the government into problems facing migrant women in international marriages found that while more than half of the families of migrant women (53%) lived below the poverty line, only one-seventh (14%) received basic aid (Seol et al., 2005; Lee, 2008). Almost half of the families (44%) lived on income below the minimum cost of living and were unable to maintain a basic subsistence level. This could be due to their exclusion from the Korean social welfare system as a result of being ineligible or lacking knowledge of existing policies. The study found that approximately one in six foreign females (15.5%) experienced starvation due to financial stress and constraints. Given that foreign wives tend to come from economically deprived environments, together with their lack of understanding of the Korean culture and language barriers (except from ethnic Korean migrants), they are vulnerable to exploitation, mistreatment and misunderstanding, resulting in domestic violence. In a rare study looking at domestic violence and help-seeking behaviour among Vietnamese in Korea, Park (2011) reported that 18.2% of women experienced severe physical abuse by their husbands, 22.7% experienced some degree of abuse by their in-laws and 4.5% experienced severe physical abuse by both husbands and in-laws. The main reasons for physical and emotional abuse by husbands or in-laws were as follows:

- Conflict over financial matters: husbands not being employed or earning low incomes and taking away their wives' meagre wages. If the wife complains as she cannot meet financial expectations back home in country of origin, she gets beaten up.
- Demanded sexual activity: mainly sexual coercion, husbands' sexual ownership of their wives, and husbands' lack of trust in their wives, hence repeatedly accusing them of infidelity and isolating them from the wider community.
- Communication problems: wives' inability to speak and understand Korean angered their husbands or led to miscommunication, hence triggering abuses.
- Approach to parenting and housework: wives' requests that husbands help with chores were unacceptable and culturally alienating; mother-in-law differing opinion about who does household chores and how to rear children.

- Wives working outside of the home: the belief that wives should remain at home for reproduction and to undertake housework chores; if they secure any work outside home, they are accused of having extramarital affairs.
- Alcohol intoxication.

## *Intermarriage and human trafficking*

The United Nations Protocol to Prevent, Suppress and Punish Trafficking in Persons, in its Article 3, defines trafficking as

> *"the recruitment, transportation, transfer, harbouring or receipt of persons, by means of threat or use of force or other forms of coercion, of abduction, of fraud, of deception, of the abuse of power or of a position of vulnerability or of the giving or receiving of payments or benefits to achieve the consent of a person having control over another person, for the purpose of exploitation. Exploitation shall include, at a minimum, the exploitation of the prostitution of others or other forms of sexual exploitation, forced labour or services, slavery or practices similar to slavery, servitude or the removal of organs* (United Nations, 2000)."

In its 2013 Annual Report, the United States Department of State considered Korea as a "source, transit, and destination country for human trafficking of men and women subjected to forced prostitution and forced labour" (US Department of State, 2013). The report notes that Korea acts as a source by permitting the trafficking of Korean girls into the USA, Canada, Japan and Australia for forced prostitution. As a destination country, Korea receives trafficked victims from Russia, Uzbekistan, Kazakhstan, Morocco, Colombia, Mongolia, China, the Philippines, Thailand, Cambodia, North Korea, Vietnam and Japan for either forced labour or prostitution. As a transit for human trafficking, Korea is heavily involved in child sex tourism, often as a result of the high demand for sex tourism among Korean men (US Department of State, 2013). One of the consequences of the Korean War has been the ongoing presence of the US military forces in Korea as part of the policy that was initially instigated to contain communism in the region. At the height of the Cold War in the 1950s, the number of US military forces in Korea was extremely high, estimated at 326,863 in

1951 and dropping to 75,328 in 1955 two years after the Korean War. Since then the number dropped significantly, reaching 52,197 in 1970, 38,780 in 1980, 28,500 in 2010 and 29,300 in 2014 (Ahn and Lee, 2011). Such a presence of a high number of military personnel created the demand for female company and sexual service near the base (Cheng, 2004). Prior to 1996, "Yanggonju" and Korean sex workers servicing members of the US military became the Korean government's *de facto* civilian ambassadors to improve US–Korea civil–military relations. This was achieved through generous entertaining and kisaeng parties for high-ranking military personnel to smoothen US–Korea relations (Lie, 1995; Moon, 1997; Kwon, 2000).

Although the old structure of the kisaeng was composed of financially independent and intellectual women, who only chose and took men as lovers who were appealing, it declined into a structure that forced women to become mistresses of the Japanese military following colonisation (Yayori and Sharnoff, 1977), and later to serve members of the US military in Korea (Lie, 1995; Moon, 1997; Kwon, 2000). While the Korean government legalised prostitution during Japan's colonisation in 1916 (Government General Police Administration Division Ordinance No. 4), in 1948 the Korean government passed the Public Act No. 7 Abolishing the Public Prostitution Law. This led to a significant increase in the "private" prostitution business from 2,000 to 50,000 in the first nine months of the abolition (Lee, 2007). However, the Prostitution Prevention Law was re-introduced in 1961, which legally forbid prostitution. Customers, sex workers and their pimps were punishable under the law. The existence of such a law did not prevent the government setting up special districts for prostitution (104 special districts in 1962, which increased to 146 by 1964), 60% of which were meant for US soldiers and 40% for Japanese tourists and Korean men (Moon, 1997; Park, 2013). By the 1970s, there were between 30,000 and 40,000 modern kisaengs (Moon, 1997; Lee, 2007). The number remained in the 20,000s throughout the 1970s and 1980s, equating at the time to one sex worker for every two to three soldiers. The kisaengs had to meet strict requirements such as having a minimum level of junior high-school education and pass periodic health checks. They were also required to attend induction lectures on how sex workers can aid their country's economic growth through foreign exchange, and how to properly and generously behave towards and entertain foreign customers (Lie, 1995; Moon, 1997; Kwon, 2000).

With the improvement in the Korean economy, accelerated demographic transition and the stigma associated with being a "Yanggonju" or "Yankee whore", there was a shortage of women. In addition, the number of women willing to work as "Yanggonju" declined considerably as the job did not pay well. Consequently, since 1996, the Korea Special Tourism Association was established by kichich'on club owners to arrange for foreign women entertainers to work in the clubs through the E-6 visa as part of the "arts and entertainment" visa scheme. The women have to return to their country of origin once the visa expires. While the E-6 visa is a legally valid entry visa which attracted thousands of women from the region and abroad, women working in the kichich'on clubs have been identified as "victims of [sex] trafficking" (Cheng, 2004). It has been established that women are often trafficked into Korea as sex workers for US military bases and other districts in the country, which has led to a number of human rights abuses including women getting killed and living in slavery-like conditions such as forced prostitution, withholding of passports and salaries, confinement and violence (Lee, 2003).

## *Intermarriage and multiculturalism in Korea*

The growing number of intermarriages has given rise to an increase in the number of bi-racial/bi-ethnic children or Kosians. By 2006, there were approximately 50,000 Kosian children and the number is projected to reach 1.67 million or 3.3% by 2020 (Kim, 2009b) while the number of Kosian children enrolled in elementary and secondary school is projected to increase from 13,445 in 2007 to more than 870,000 or 26% by 2050 (Kim, 2009b). Increased Kosian populations are going to be a serious challenge for policymakers in Korea. As recent as 2009, in a study to establish how Koreans conceptualise "who is Korean" in the face of increased migration in a traditionally homogeneous society (Lim, 2009), a Korean, who reflected the view of many, noted: *"I have always believed that Korea is a single-race country — And I'm proud of that. Somehow, Korea becoming a multiracial society doesn't sound right"* (p. 1). When trying to explain why migrants as well as ethnic Korean migrants from China, Russia, Japan, the

USA and other countries throughout the world have failed to fit into Korean society, the authors found: "*to be 'truly' Korean, one must not only have Korean blood, but must also embody the values, the mores, and the mind-set of Korean society... At the same time, those who lack a 'pure blood' relationship, no matter how acculturated they may be, have also been rejected as outsiders*" (p. 1).

These findings reflect the difficulties ahead in making Korea a true multicultural society. The increase in migration has signalled the end of the so-called "homogenous society" in Korea, but is the country ready to address challenges that multiculturalism brings with it? There is already evidence of discrimination against Amerasians at personal and institutional levels. They are subjected to extreme and pervasive interpersonal and social abuse, while at the same time they are being denied the right to mandatorily serve in the Korean military like any other Korean male, which is a prerequisite for accessing citizen rights (Lim, 2009). The law was amended in 2006 to allow for voluntary enlisting of Kosians. This level of institutional discrimination could have some debilitating effects on Korea's social and economic fabric. Some of the challenges include (1) how to promote a whole-school approach to address the need of culturally diverse migrants' cohorts, (2) how to ensure that government and public systems are culturally competent in harnessing human resources in the most productive way and reduce socioeconomic and health inequities and inequalities, and (3) how to develop and implement policies that are geared towards promoting both the toleration of difference and engagement across differences. This may require the Korean government to establish a national multicultural agenda that is couched in international human rights and migration laws, and is adequate enough to cater for the cultural and religious diversity unfolding in Korea. However, as Nye (2007) cautions, multiculturalism is a process which is contextual to particular places and cultural experiences, so what has worked in other countries like Australia, Canada and other multicultural countries may be of little use to Korea. Therefore, the need to contextualise multiculturalism may limit the amount of lessons Korea can extract from these countries to inform its multicultural agenda. Nye also notes that the dynamics between groups and people within a multicultural context are subject to change and development. In this sense, the author conceptualises multiculturalism as a process that is temporary and liable to change, and such dynamic change could lead to positive (e.g. peaceful and respectful relationships) or negative (e.g. conflicts and ethnic hatred) outcomes. These outcomes may be dependent on the state management and governance of difference. Hence, in order to manage and govern difference adequately, Korea may need to train all its workforces in human rights, build protection of human rights into its legislation, and develop policies to protect the rights of the minority and oppressed.

## Health of migrants in Korea

### *Trafficked women and commercial sex workers*

The health of migrants in Korea differs according to their migration status. Trafficked women for commercial sex are at increased risk of sexually transmitted diseases, sexual trauma and psychological burdens of rape and their consequences. Korea has a long history of mandatory health screening for all registered sex workers. The country has been successful in implementing effective sexual health programmes (Beyrer and Stachowiak, 2003). For example, the government has moved quickly to ensure free health check-ups are available to both legal and illegal sex workers while free condoms are available, and distributed HIV/AIDS pamphlets have been translated into foreign languages (Cheng, 2004). These measures may have halted the increase in the transmission of sexually transmitted diseases. The prevalence of positive antibodies to the Hepatitis C virus has varied between 1.4% and 10.3% (Kim et al., 2003; Kweon et al., 2006). However, in a large community-based sero-epidemiologic study of 1,527 female commercial sex workers, Kweon and colleagues (2006) found the prevalence of syphilis was 2.7% and there were no cases of HIV among study participants. Other studies have reported that the prevalence of HIV/AIDS among commercial sex workers is 0.02%, which is comparable to the national average (UNAIDS/UNICEF/WHO, 2004). The prevalence of human papillomavirus among sex workers has been estimated at 47% (Choi et al., 2003). Trafficked women who end up working as commercial sex workers are also vulnerable to sexual exploitation and rape. They may experience the emotional burden of rape and sexual violence, and the associated health complications such as shame, suicide, depression and drug addiction.

They are also at increased risk of unsafe abortions, unwanted pregnancies and ectopic pregnancy (Beyrer and Stachowiak, 2003).

## Migrant workers

There are several upstream and downstream factors influencing the health status of migrant workers. The downstream factors mainly operate in those employed in 3D jobs and include low income, poor housing, lack of knowledge on workplace safety, language barriers leading to poor health service utilisation, unfamiliarity with workers' rights and accident-prone work environments (Lee et al., 2008). The upstream factors include lack of proper health insurance benefits for unskilled migrant workers, poor living conditions, racism and discrimination. In addition, poorer health literacy, longer working hours and lower income compared with native Korean workers equally contribute to upstream factors influencing migrant health (Hong et al., 2000). As indicated earlier, migrant workers are commonly employed in the construction and manufacturing industries, in addition to agriculture, fisheries and restaurants. This means that occupational health conditions and health insurance are the biggest health challenges. In a study examining the status and characteristics of industrial accidents of migrant workers and native workers, Lee and colleagues (2008) found a higher industrial accident rate among migrant workers than native workers. The injury death rate was found to be 2.2 times higher among migrant workers than their native counterparts.

Prior to 2000, outbreaks of occupational diseases among migrant workers could be grouped into two categories depending on their causes: chemical agents, and physical and biological agents (Table 9). Diseases caused by poisonous chemicals included heavy metal poisoning, solvent poisoning, and occupational asthma or pneumoconiosis (Kang and Kim, 2010). For example, reproductive problems such as pancytopenia, azoospermia, oligospermia, reduced sperm motility, bone marrow effects and ovarian failure were reported among workers exposed to 2-bromopropane (Kim et al., 1996), while toxic hepatitis and liver dysfunction were prevalent among workers exposed to dimethylformamide in the synthetic fibre and leather industry (Kang et al., 1991). Similarly, mercury poisoning in the thermometer and fluorescent lamp manufacturing industry (Cha et al.,

Table 9: Compensated occupational diseases by specific year

| Year | Total Total | Occupational diseases Sub-total | Pneu | ARD | NIHL | Vib | PA | HM | OS | CH | OCH | Inf | Derm | Others | Work-related disease Sub-total | CVD | MSD | Back | Others |
|---|---|---|---|---|---|---|---|---|---|---|---|---|---|---|---|---|---|---|---|
| 1972 | 195 | | | | | | | | | | | | | | | | | | |
| 1991 | 1,537 | 1,537 | 1,228 | | 178 | | | 61 | 60 | 0 | | | | 10 | | | | | |
| 1996 | 1,529 | 771 | 366 | | 163 | | | 26 | 121 | 35 | | | | 60 | 758 | 252 | 345 | 161 | 0 |
| 1998 | 1,838 | 1,040 | 595 | | 232 | | | 30 | 97 | 24 | | 0 | | 62 | 798 | 674 | 73 | 51 | 0 |
| 2003 | 9,130 | 1,905 | 1,320 | | 314 | | | 19 | 33 | 58 | | 127 | | 34 | 7,225 | 2,358 | 2,906 | 1,626 | 335 |
| 2006 | 10,235 | 2,174 | 1,620 | 10 | 272 | 9 | 18 | 8 | 17 | 12 | 41 | 131 | 29 | 7 | 8,061 | 1,607 | 1,615 | 4,618 | 221 |
| 2007 | 11,472 | 2,098 | 1,422 | 21 | 237 | 16 | 32 | 6 | 26 | 14 | 86 | 188 | 50 | 0 | 9,374 | 1,493 | 1,390 | 6,333 | 158 |
| 2008 | 9,721 | 1,653 | 1,145 | 21 | 220 | 7 | 15 | 11 | 14 | 44 | 0 | 134 | 37 | 5 | 8,068 | 1,207 | 1,471 | 5,232 | 158 |
| 2009 | 8,765 | 1,746 | 1,003 | 31 | 205 | 9 | 7 | 3 | 14 | 23 | 0 | 427 | 20 | 4 | 7,019 | 639 | 1,343 | 4,879 | 158 |

Pneu, pneumoconiosis; ARD, asbestos-related cancer, NIHL, noise-induced hearing loss; Vib, vibration; PA, physical agents; HM, heavy metals; OS, organic solvents; CH, specific chemicals; OCH, other chemicals; Inf, infection; CVD, cerebro-cardiovascular disease; Derm, dermatitis, MSD, musculoskeletal disorder. Back: neck pain.
Source: Kang and Kim (2010).

1992) and lead poisoning with subsequent anaemia, neurologic diseases, neurobehavioural changes and renal dysfunction (Lee, 1982; Kim et al., 1995; Weaver et al., 2003; Schwartz et al., 2005) were all common among migrant workers. Among plating workers, the prevalence of nasal septal perforation and ulceration of mucosa was 31.7% and 10.5%, respectively (Park et al., 1989), however these diseases were later documented among welders exposed to hexavalent chromium (Lee et al., 2002). Other chemical-related occupational diseases documented among migrant workers included proteinuria and interstitial fibrosis, found among workers in the cadmium smelting and battery recycling factory (Cho et al., 2001), Parkinson syndrome related to manganese exposure among welders (Kim et al., 1999; Park et al., 2004), and carbon disulfide poisoning with subsequent retinal microaneurysm, renal glomerulosclerosis, multiple cerebral infarction, peripheral neuropathy, ischaemic heart disease, mental diseases and impotence (Choi and Jang, 1991; Park et al., 1992; Kim et al., 1993; Yum et al., 1994; Lee and Kim, 1998).

In terms of diseases caused by physical and biological agents, noise-induced hearing loss was one of the leading disease burdens among migrant workers (Kim et al., 1998). However, heat-related stroke (Park et al., 1999), tuberculosis infectious (Ahn and Lim, 2008), musculoskeletal disorders (Cho et al., 1989), stress-related mental disorder (Choi et al., 2002), and cancers (Cho et al., 1998; Kim et al., 1999; Kang et al., 2001) have also been documented among migrant workers. A study on medical utilisation and health status among migrant workers found that the most common complaints included longer working hours (Hong et al., 2000). Recent data by 2014 (Amnesty International) indicate that migrant workers in Korea typically work between 250 and 364 hours a month, averaging more than 10 hours a day or around 50 hours per month more than stated in their contract. These figures compare unfavourably with the mandated 8 hours per day for Korean workers. Migrant workers also have poorer health than their Korean counterparts and the most common symptoms for clinical encounters were respiratory (21.2%), musculoskeletal (20.6%), digestive (15.8%) and cardiovascular (12.5%) (Hong et al., 2000). The turn of the twenty-first century was characterised by the rise in the number of workers' unions and civil movements for democracy, who demanded that the government and employers implement policies to improve the work environment and ensure the wellbeing of employees. Consequently, by the end of the 1990s, there was a rapid decline in chemical-related diseases and pneumoconiosis (Kang and Kim, 2010). A new pattern of diseases emerged. Since then, job stress or work overload-related diseases such as cerebro-cardiovascular and mental diseases, musculoskeletal and infectious diseases, and occupational cancers have all become the leading causes of disease burden (Kang and Kim, 2010).

## *North Korean refugees*

North Korean defectors are vulnerable to poor health due to exposure to traumatic conditions during three phases of their lives, namely the pre-migration life in North Korea, transit through China and neighbouring countries, and finally during the settlement phase in Korea. Defectors experience health issues unique to each phase. Prior to the migration process, defectors experience torture, starvation, forced labour and large-scale massacres. During the transit phase, they are faced with malnutrition, exposure to physical injuries, diseases and hostage situations (Lee *et al.*, 2001; Jeon *et al.*, 2005; Lee *et al.*, 2009; Choi *et al.*, 2011). Available data suggest that North Korean defectors living in Japan have higher levels of depression and poorer quality of life than Korean migrant and Japanese workers (Lee *et al.*, 2009). In addition, the prevalence of depression and anxiety among North Korean defectors in Korea was estimated at 36.1% and 53.7%, respectively. Their poor mental health is associated with lower quality of life (Choi *et al.*, 2011). While the prevalence of anxiety was significantly higher than the Korean national average, the prevalence of depression was comparable to that of Korea. The high prevalence of anxiety could be related to earlier traumas, but depression could be closely linked to settlement-related challenges such as racism, discrimination and social exclusion.

## *Intermarriage migrants*

Foreign female immigrants face a double-barrelled stressor when they engage in intermarriages — first, when coping with the stress of a married life and second, when coping with the shock of living in a new culture. The severe culture shock and language difficulties faced by migrant women often result in a lack of accurate knowledge on pregnancy and childbirth, leading to negative physical health consequences for both the mother and child (Jeong et al., 2009; Kim et al., 2013; Chang and Wallace, 2014). Factors that affect the health of intermarriage migrants can be grouped into nine major categories: conjugality, inconvenience in communication, conflict, lack of understanding, cultural difference, worry, effort, desire and support (Kim et al., 2013). For example, migrant women experience higher frequency of birth problems compared to native Korean women with 21.4% of pregnant women not receiving antenatal care, 14.5% of pregnancy considered as high risk and 39.7% receiving no support (Jeong et al., 2009). Factors associated with poorer health outcomes in intermarriage migrants include length of stay in Korea, level of social interaction with Koreans and pre-migration socioeconomic status. In a study examining migration processes and self-rated health among marriage migrants, Chang and Wallace (2014) found that Korean–Chinese had the poorest health when compared with Vietnamese and Han Chinese. However, the post-migration socioeconomic status and social integration were associated with health in all three groups. That is, good health was associated with having more social relationships with Koreans, while poor health was associated with having more social relationships with co-ethnic groups. Perception of a better social status in their natal and marital families was a better predictor of health than traditional measures of socioeconomic status such as education attainment of the wives and their Korean husbands. The health of Korean-Chinese, Han Chinese, and Vietnamese decline in linear fashion after marriage. These findings indicate that the health of marriage migrants' erodes after arrival regardless of their age and marriage channel; while those from higher pre-migration socioeconomic status and greater social integration in Korea had better health outcomes (Chang and Wallace, 2014).

Intermarried migrant women in Korea have a higher prevalence of anxiety compared to native Korean women, while their children have a higher incidence of behavioural and emotional problems compared with native Korean children. This therefore supports the "migration morbidity" hypothesis which stipulates that migration-related stress may contribute to mental health problems in immigrants (Lee et al., 2014). Furthermore, immigrant women differ in their perception of parenting and expect their

Korean spouses to share childrearing tasks. These expectations are often not met by the patriarchal Korean husbands, which result in marital conflicts (Park, 2011). Frequent conflicts negatively impact the coping skills of migrant women, making them more vulnerable to stress and mental ill-health. The prevalence of depression among migrant women varies between 26.5% and 40.6%, which compare unfavourably with the prevalence of 19% reported among their native counterparts (Yang and Kim, 2007).

## *Policy response*

While this chapter does not intend to review all Korean migration policies, four important areas stand out: (1) managing and controlling immigration, (2) international marriages, citizenship and legal status, (3) multiculturalism, and (4) the health of migrants.

## Managing and controlling immigration

The review of policies related to the management and control of immigration suggests that the Korean modern immigration policy was enacted during the US military occupation in 1946 and was known as "Regulation for Entry and Departure Movement Control and Record of South Korea". Three years' later, after the establishment of Korea, it was replaced by the "Foreign Entry, Departure and Registration Law" (Oh et al., 2012). This piece of legislation had serious limitations. While it was geared towards regulating foreign entry, departure and registration, it did not address the migration of nationals and transportation business operators (departure and entry), temporary landing, and port of entry and departure (the captains of ships and landing permission of crew members) (Oh et al., 2012; Ministry of Legislation, 2015). Consequently, it was replaced by the "Immigration Control law" under the Act No. 1289 in 1963 to incorporate the movements, employment, stay and residence restrictions for immigrants in South Korea (Oh et al., 2012; Ministry of Legislation, 2015).

The Act went through a series of amendments (wholly Amended by Dec. 8, 1992 Act No. 4522; Amended by Dec. 10, 1993 Act No. 4592; Dec. 22, 1994 Act No. 4796; Dec. 12, 1996 Act No. 5176; Dec. 13, 1997

Act No. 5434; Feb. 5, 1999 Act No. 5755; Dec. 29, 2001 Act No. 6540; and Dec. 5, 2002 Act No. 6745) over the years to address the following deficiencies: entry and departure of all Korean nationals and foreigners including the control of foreigners' sojourn, procedures for recognition of refugees, measures to deal with foreigners failing to meet the entry requirements through the granting of a provisional permission for entry, entry and exit regulations of North Korean defectors and foreigners travelling between South and North Koreas, migration regulations to address and tackle the labour shortage through the protection of foreign industrial trainees, the lawful employment of foreigners and the prevention of unlawful employment of foreigners (Ministry of Legislation, 2015). Migration measures related to the employment of foreigners have been discussed earlier in this chapter.

## International marriages and citizenship and legal status

As Korea becomes a multicultural society through international marriages, the country faces a number of challenges related to the meaning of Korean nationhood and citizenship. A historical analysis of issues related to international marriages and citizenship, and legal status in Korea, is provided by Lee (2008). The author remarks that before the 1998 revision of Nationality Law, existing laws discriminated against Korean women who married foreign men. For example, the pre-1998 Nationality Law was patrilineal and gender-biased, permitting the nationalities of children to follow those of their fathers only. The consequence of such laws meant that children of Korean mothers and foreign fathers were denied Korean nationality by birth. In contrast, foreign women marrying Korean men were allowed the Korean nationality after their marriage, while foreign men marrying Korean women had to wait 2 years as well as meet certain eligibility requirements before they could apply for citizenship. Although the 1998 revision of the nationality law was to prevent fake marriages, it addressed many of the issues above, except the legal status of foreign spouses. The legislation regulated foreign spouses to first obtain a visiting and joining visa (F-1), which prohibited them to work in Korea, and therefore created severe financial and economic hardships especially for foreign husbands. Further amendments were made in 2002 allowing foreign spouses to get residence (F-2) visas which allowed them to work.

These improvements in the Nationality Law and F-visa did not eliminate all the problems that foreign spouses experienced. In the case of divorce, matters became complicated because there were some cases where foreign wives chose not to be naturalised, making it difficult for them post-divorce. Those who did not get naturalised had no access to Korean resident cards given to migrants who became Korean citizens. Without having such a card meant that there were some restrictions that limited their quality of life, including not being able to open a bank account or to get a driving licence. Between 2002 and 2005, Korea established the denizenship, first for Chinese residents and investors in Korea (2002), then extending it to foreign spouses who had been in the country for more than 2 years (2005). Finally, foreign wives wanting to divorce their husbands within 2 years of marriage were mandated to leave their children and return to their country of origin. In 2003 and later in 2007, the revision to the Nationality Law was made, allowing a divorced wife to apply for naturalisation as long as she met the following criteria: her husband was dead or missing, she did not live with her husband, the divorce was due to her husband's imputation or she was claiming the custody of the children (2003–2007). Essentially, the woman had to prove that she was a victim of her husband's imputation first before any mitigation could be done (2007). The 2010 Nationality Law reform allowed foreign spouses from intermarriages to gain permanent residency and citizenship (Chung and Kim, 2012).

## Multiculturalism

It has been acknowledged that the increase in the rate of international marriages and Kosian children have posed serious multicultural-related challenges to Korean society (Lee, 2010). In order to incorporate foreigners in Korea, the government embarked on policies promoting social integration which started in 2006 (Lee, 2010; Ministry of Justice, 2012). As a result, the Korean immigration policies have slowly shifted from immigration control to the integration of immigrants. As a positive step towards mitigating these risks, the Korean government established the "Grand Plan" in April 2006, a comprehensive policy targeting the social integration of female marriage migrants. The Plan's primary objectives centred on reducing discrimination against international marriage migrants and mix-raced people, as well as raising social awareness of multicultural issues (Lee, 2008; Chung and Kim, 2012). The Ministry of Gender Equality and Family was appointed as the major coordinator of the Grand Plan, with participation from the Ministry of Justice, Labour, Social Welfare and Health, and local and central government departments (Chung and Kim, 2012). The Grand Plan covered seven domains: (1) the regulation of international marriage agencies as well as the protection of foreign wives before entry into Korea, (2) legislations supporting victims of domestic violence, (3) programmes supporting and orientating foreign wives on arrival including Korean language and culture classes, (4) the provision of support for children of international marriages in schools, (5) foreign wives' access to social welfare, (6) creating social awareness of multicultural issues, and (7) putting in place the establishment of a comprehensive support system to make Korea a leader in embracing foreigners (Lee, 2008; Lee, 2010). The Grand Plan led to the opening and operation of 21 International Marriage Immigrants Support Centres nationwide, which were later named the Multicultural Family Support Centres. The number of these centres had increased to 80 by 2008 and addressed various issues including Korean language programmes, vocation training and counselling for family-related issues (Lee, 2010).

In order to provide support for the increasing number of foreign brides, the "Support for Multicultural Families Act" was established in 2008 and aimed to improve the integrity and quality of life of intermarriage and multicultural families living in South Korea (Oh et al., 2012). Therefore, the first Basic Plan for Immigration Policy (2008–2012) outlined three principles which guided the policies on foreigners: (1) the protection of foreigners' human rights, (2) attracting high-skilled foreign workers while limiting low-skilled workers in order to enhance national competitiveness, and (3) promoting multicultural and social integration (Lee, 2010). The Ministry of Gender Equality and Family responsible for this Act enforced the conducting of multicultural research, development of anti-racism, educational and childcare policies, and regulation of intermarriage brokerage. In 2011, this ministry implemented 23 initiatives, including child-nurturing support and protection for female migrants who were experiencing domestic violence (Oh et al., 2012). However, these initiatives were discriminatory towards low-skilled workers in many ways. The Grand

Plan did not address issues related to marriages between low-skilled workers and their offspring. Low-skilled migrants are on a rotational system whereby they are expected to return to their country of origin at the expiration of their visa period (Gray, 2007; Lee, 2010). The consequence of such a system is the isolation of children from marriages among low-skilled workers, as they are prevented from enjoying basic education during their stay in Korea. Similarly, low-skilled migrants are treated as temporary sojourners, meaning they are not included in social integration policies. In addition, the first Basic Plan created confusion over what the government meant by multiculturalism, with various government departments applying different terminologies such as "immigration policy", "multicultural policy", "multilateral family policy" and "immigrant spouse policy", therefore leading to overlapping and uncoordinated policies (Ministry of Justice, 2012).

The second Basic Plan for Immigration Policy whose vision is "a vibrant Korea growing with immigrants" addressed some of the deficiencies in the first Basic plans. It has five goals and 19 action plans (Ministry of Justice, 2012; Lee, 2013): (1) openness (i.e. support economic vitalisation and attract global talents), (2) social integration (i.e. integrate immigrants and pursue common Korean values), (3) human rights (i.e. prevent discrimination and foster greater appreciation of cultural diversity), (4) public safety (e.g. foster a safe and orderly society for nationals and non-nationals), and (5) cooperation (i.e. prosper with countries of origin through international cooperation). This plan has introduced a layered approach to gaining citizenship. It included an introduction of a system requiring permanent residence as a prerequisite for nationality (except those who qualify for "Special Naturalization"), the addition of a reading comprehension test and the Korea Immigration Naturalization Aptitude Test, the introduction of the Refugees Seeking Resettlement programme, and the integration of various services into a simplified programme so immigrants could easily submit applications for citizenship (Ministry of Justice, 2012). The advantages of the second Basic Plan comprise a whole-of-government approach and streamlining programmes among ministries, including the respect for diversity, strengthening the foundation of the multicultural family, the support for employment of marriage immigrants and the education of their offspring. By 2014, there were 217 multicultural family support centres nationwide providing education of Korean culture (tradition, custom and cuisine) and language, a number of counselling and information services for daily life and occupational training for multicultural families. Services for children of multicultural families also included after-school tutoring and Korean language classes (Yang, 2015). However, critics maintain that these policies continue to be excessively led by the central government and its bureaucracy, and are not initiated at the grassroots level. They lack unity and standardisation of basic philosophy of multicultural policy, policy infrastructure, and laws and regulations for action plans (Yang, 2015). The policies fail to meet the demands of local government areas with different types of immigrants.

## *Health of migrants*

The most common challenge facing the government, in terms of providing equitable health care to all levels of the society is the barrier associated with culture and language. In 2007, the Korean government established 38 Multicultural Family Centres which later increased to 171 centres by 2010. These centres provide maternal and child health services to immigrant families (Ahn, 2012). However, achieving cultural competence in the Korean health system remains one of the biggest challenges for the government. Training alone, without commensurate policies, may not be sufficient. Despite the training provided to its workforce, available data suggest that nurses lack cultural competence in the delivery of care to multicultural families, especially in public health centres (Ahn, 2012). In order to achieve cultural competence Ahn (2012) has proposed policy directions: (1) the integration of the health care system with language, culture and health literacy, (2) the development of national standards regarding culturally and linguistically appropriate services and in-service education on culturally competent health care for nurses, (3) the development of an assessment instrument for high-risk immigrant women and provision of individualised intervention programmes, and (4) vitalising functions of health centres.

Apart from cultural competence, another issue relates to the gap in occupational health and safety. While the Korean government has put in place programmes to address and strengthen safety and health management for foreign workers, a report by Amnesty International suggested that injuries among migrant workers increased by 32% between 2007 and 2008, including a 34% increase in injury-related deaths (Amnesty International, 2009). The same report noted that industrial accidents were much higher among migrant workers than Korean-born workers, with approximately 1,060 accidents per 100,000 reported among migrant workers, compared to only 770 accidents per 100,000 among Korean-born workers. Existing policies make it difficult for migrant workers to change jobs easily. Consequently, they are prone to workplace harassment, poor wages and working conditions. These factors force them to work under inhuman conditions and substandard workplace safety, predisposing them to ill-health. Therefore, the proportion of work-related injuries among the labour migrant population is expected to rise exponentially. Unless the Korean government develops clear guidelines for preventing and controlling fatal and non-fatal work-related injuries among migrants, the country will face economic losses in terms of increased health expenditure as well as loss of productivity.

## Conclusion

In the recent past, Korea has dealt with issues such as low fertility rates, an ageing population and labour shortages, factors which have encouraged intermarriages and contributed to an influx of foreign labour. As a result, the Korean government has managed to regulate and monitor the migration flow by developing work permit systems, and immigration and multicultural family policies. While the civic and religious organisations have actively promoted, defended and advocated for labour rights and legal protection of migrants, there are more multicultural-related challenges that need to be addressed in order to effectively carry the voice of migrants into the political debate in Korea. This may require the government to develop a more structured and streamlined approach. This could include consolidating the various programmes which are currently fragmented across several departments, in order to both adequately meet the needs of migrants in Korea and their integration into society. In terms of international migration, the social acceptance of immigrants into the mainstream Korean population will ultimately reduce social isolation and discrimination, and improve the health and wellbeing of migrants. These objectives will only be achieved if the Korean government moves away from the top-down approach to immigration policies and frames its international immigration policy from the grassroots level. Given that Korea is dependent on foreign brides to improve its population growth, it is mandatory for the government to implement adequate and accessible programmes to lessen pregnancy-related stress and anxiety among new mothers.

# References

Abelmann, N. (1997). Women's class mobility and identities in South Korea a gendered, transnational, narrative approach. *The Journal of Asian Studies,* 56(2), 398–420.

Ahn, C. & Lee, H. (2011). Number of US Troops in South Korea. Available at: https://sites.google.com/site/nzdprksociety/number-of-us-troops-in-rok-by-year. Accessed 2 May 2015.

Ahn, Y.-H. (2012). Immigrated, interculturally-married women in South Korea: Mental health status, health care utilization, and suggested policy directions. *World Cultural Psychiatry Research Review,* 7, 21–24.

Ahn, Y.-S. & Lim, H.S. (2008). Occupational infectious diseases among Korean health care workers compensated with industrial accident compensation insurance from 1998 to 2004. *Industrial Health,* 46(5), 448–454.

Amnesty International (2009). Republic of Korea: Briefing to the UN Committee on Economic, Social and Cultural rights. ASA 25/011/2009. Amnesty International Publications, London, UK.

Amnesty International Australia (2014). South Korea: End rampant abuse of migrant farm workers. Amnesty International, Chippendale, AUS. Report. Available at: https://www.amnesty.org/en/latest/news/2014/10/south-korea-end-rampant-abuse-migrant-farm-workers/ Accessed 3 August 2015.

Beyrer, C. & Stachowiak, J. (2003). Health consequences of trafficking of women and girls in Southeast Asia. *Brown Journal of World Affairs,* 10(1), 105–117.

Byun, W. (2007). Violence against women in Korea and its indicators. Working Paper 10. United Nations Economic Commission for Europe, United Nations Division for the Advancement of Women, and United Nations Statistics Division, Geneva, SWI.

Byun, W.S. *et al.* (1999). A study on gender-consciousness and violence against women in Korea. Korean Women's Development Institute, Seoul, KOR.

Cha, C.W. *et al.* (1992). A study on the mercury contamination sources and risk for occupational mercury poisoning of mercury exposed workers in Korea. *Korean Journal of Occupational and Environmental Medicine,* 4(1), 92–104.

Chang, H. & Wallace, S.P. (2014). *Ethnicity and Health*, 3, 1–19.
Cheng, S. (2004). Interrogating the absence of HIV/AIDS interventions for migrant sex workers in South Korea. *Health and Human Rights*, 7(2), 193–204.
Cho, D. & Kim, Y. (2011). A study on settlement service for North Korean defectors. *Journal of Korean Public Police and Security Studies*, 8(2), 25–50.
Cho, H. (1998). Male dominance and mother power: The two sides of Confucian patriarchy in Korea. In: Slote, W.H. & DeVos, G.A. (eds.), *Confucianism and the Family*, University of New York Press, Albany, NY, pp. 187–207.
Cho, K.H. et al. (1989). Cervicobrachial disorders of female international telephone operators II. muscle tenderness and neurological tests. *Korean Journal of Occupational and Environmental Medicine*, 1(2), 151–159.
Cho, S. et al. (2001). Cadmium intoxication and its effects on kidney function. *Korean Journal of Nephrology*, 20(6), 1004–1013.
Cho, S.-H. et al. (1998). Estimates of occupational cancer in Korea. *Occupational Health and Industrial Medicine*, 4(38), 166.
Choi, B.S. et al. (2003). Genital human papillomavirus genotyping by HPV oligonucleotide microarray in Korean commercial sex workers. *Journal of Medical Virology*, 71(3), 440–445.
Choi, E.S. & Ha, Y. (2009). Work-related stress and risk factors among Korean employees. *Journal of Korean Academy of Nursing*, 39(4), 549–561.
Choi, J.W. & Jang, S.H. (1991). A review of the carbon disulfide poisoning experiences in Korea. *Korean Journal of Occupational and Environmental Medicine*, 3(1), 11–20.
Choi, K.S. et al. (2002). Posttraumatic stress disorder among occupational accident patients. *Journal of Korean Neuropsychiatric Association*, 41(3), 461–471.
Choi, M. et al. (2008). Construct validity of the Korean Women's Abuse Intolerance scale. *Nursing Research*, 57(1), 40–50.
Choi, S.J. (2015). Active ageing in South Korea. In: Walker, A. & Aspalter, C. (eds.), *Active Ageing in Asia*. Routledge, New York, NY, pp. 57–75.
Choi, S.K. et al. (2011). Anxiety and depression among North Korean young defectors in South Korea and their association with health-related quality of life. *Yonsei Medical Journal*, 52(3), 502–509.
Chung, E.A. & Kim, D. (2012). Citizenship and marriage in a globalizing world: Multicultural families and monocultural nationality laws in Korea and Japan. *Indiana Journal of Global Legal Studies*, 19(1), 195–219.
Cohen, R. (2014). China's Forced Repatriation of North Korean Refugees Incurs United Nations Censure." *International Journal of Korean Studies*. Available at: http://www.brookings.edu/research/opinions/2014/07/northkorea-human-rights-un-cohen. Accessed 20 April 2015.

Das Gupta, M. *et al.* (2003). Why is son preference so persistent in East and South Asia? A cross-country study of China, India and the Republic of Korea. *The Journal of Development Studies,* 40(2), 153–187.

Faggio, G. & Nickell, S. (2007). Patterns of work across the OECD. *Economic Journal,* 117(521), 416–440.

Gray, K. (2007). From human to workers' rights: The emergence of a migrant workers' union movement in Korea. *Global Society,* 21(2), 297–315.

Hahn, C.H. and Y.S. Choi (2006). The Effects of Temporary Foreign Worker Program in Korea: Overview and Empirical Assessment. Paper presented at the Korea and the World Economy Conference, Seoul, KOR, July 7–8, 2006. Available at: http://faculty.washington.edu/karyiu/confer/seoul06/papers/hahn-choi.pdf. Accessed 3 January 2015.

Han, G. (2003). The pathways of Korean migration to Australia. *Korean Social Science Journal,* 30(1), 31–52.

Ho, C.K. (1990). An analysis of domestic violence in Asian American communities: A multicultural approach to counseling. *Women & Therapy,* 9(1–2), 129–150.

Hong, J.S. *et al.* (2010). Wife battering in South Korea: An ecological systems analysis. *Children and Youth Services Review,* 32(12), 1623–1630.

Hong, S.K. *et al.* (2000). A study of medical utilization and health status for migrant workers in Korea. *Journal of the Korean Academy of Family Medicine,* 21(8), 1053–1064.

Howe, N., Jackson, R. & Nakashima, K. (2007). *The Aging of Korea: Demographics and Retirement Policy in the Land of the Morning Calm.* Global Aging Initiative. Center for Strategic and International Studies and MetLife, Washington DC.

Jamieson, N. (1993). *Understanding Vietnam.* University of California Press, Berkeley, CA.

Jeon, W. *et al.* (2005). Correlation between traumatic events and posttraumatic stress disorder among North Korean defectors in South Korea. *Journal of Traumatic Stress,* 18(2), 147–154.

Jeong, G.H. *et al.* (2009). A survey on health management of during pregnancy, childbirth, and the postpartum of immigrant women in a multi-cultural family. *Korean Journal of Women Health Nursing,* 15(4), 261–269.

Jeong, I. *et al.* (2014). Working hours and cardiovascular disease in Korean workers: A case-control study. *Journal of Occupational Health,* 55(5), 385–391.

Kang, S.-K. & Kim, E.A. (2010). Occupational diseases in Korea. *Journal of Korean Medical Science,* 25(Suppl), S4–S12.

Kang, S.K. *et al.* (1991). A study on the liver dysfunction due to dimethylformamide. *Korean Journal of Occupational and Environmental Medicine,* 3(1), 58–64.

Kang, S.K. *et al.* (2001). Occupational cancer in Korea in the 1990s. *Korean Journal of Occupational and Environmental Medicine,* 13(4), 351–359.

Kawaguchi, D. & Lee, H. (2012). Brides for sale: Cross-border marriages and female immigration. Working paper Working Paper 12-082, Harvard Business School. Available at: http://www.hbs.edu/faculty/Publication%20Files/12-082.pdf. Accessed 3 March 2015.

Kibria, N. (1993). *Family tightrope: The changing lives of Vietnamese Americans.* Princeton University Press, Princeton, NJ.

Kim, A.E. (2009a). Demography, migration and multiculturalism in South Korea. *The Asia-Pacific Journal,* 6(2), 1–33.

Kim, A.E. (2009b). Global migration and South Korea: Foreign workers, foreign brides and the making of a multicultural society. *Ethnic and Racial Studies,* 32(1), 70–92.

Kim, C.S. *et al.* (1993). 2 cases of chronic renal failure resulted from carbon disulfide intoxication. *Korean Journal of Nephrology,* 12(3), 452–458.

Kim, H.S. (1998). Yanggongju as an Allegory of the Nation: The Representation of Working-Class Women in Popular and Radical Texts. In: Kim, E.H. & Choi, C. (eds.), *Dangerous Women: Gender and Korean Nationalism.* Routledge, New York, NY. pp. 175–202.

Kim, J. *et al.* (2009). The incidence and impact of family violence on mental health among South Korean women: Results of a national survey. *Journal of Family Violence,* 24(3), 193–202.

Kim, J.Y. (1998). Conjugal violence in Korean elderly couples: An analysis with socio-economic status. *Journal of the Korea Gerontological Society,* 18(1), 170–183.

Kim, K. and Y. Cho (1992). Epidemiological survey of spousal abuse in Korea. In: E. Viano (ed.), *Intimate Violence: Interdisciplinary Perspectives.* Hemisphere Publishing Corp., Washington, DC, pp. 277–282.

Kim, K.S. *et al.* (1998). Sudden sensorineural hearing loss caused by noise exposure to intense sound. *Korean Journal of Occupational and Environmental Medicine,* 10(4), 618–626.

Kim, N.H.J. (2008). Korean immigration policy changes and the political liberals' dilemma 1. *International Migration Review,* 42(3): 576–596.

Kim, O. *et al.* (2003). Seroprevalence of sexually transmitted viruses in Korean populations including HIV-seropositive individuals. *International Journal of STD & AIDS,* 14(1), 46–49.

Kim, S. (2000). The Challenge of Rapid Ageing and Low Fertility in Korea. Department of Economics University of Wisconsin, Milwaukee, WI.

Kim, S.A. *et al.* (1999). Bladder cancer with exposure to benzidine-based dyes of dyer. *Korean Journal of Occupational and Environmental Medicine,* 11(2), 304–312.

Kim, S.R. *et al.* (1995). Multiple brain calcification in chronic lead poisoning. *Korean Journal of Preventive Medicine,* 28(2), 398–405.

Kim, Y. et al. (1999). Increase in signal intensities on T1-weighted magnetic resonance images in asymptomatic manganese-exposed workers. *Neurotoxicology*, 20(6), 901–907.

Kim, Y. et al. (1996). Hematopoietic and reproductive hazards of Korean electronic workers exposed to solvents containing 2-bromopropane. *Scandinavian Journal of Work, Environment & Health*, 22(5), 387–391.

Kim, Y.M. et al. (2013). Cultural transition and well-being experience of immigrant women married to Korean men in South Korea. *Advanced Science and Technology Letters*, 40, 19–23.

Korean Ministry of Employment and Labor (2011). Survey Report on Labor Conditions by Employment Type. Labor Market Analysis Division, Employment Policy Bureau, Ministry of Employment and Labor, Seoul, KOR.

Kweon, S.-S. et al. (2006). Seroprevalence and risk factors for hepatitis C virus infection among female commercial sex workers in South Korea who are not intravenous drug users. *The American Journal of Tropical Medicine and Hygiene*, 74(6), 1117–1121.

Kwon, I. (2000). A feminist exploration of military conscription: The gendering of the connections between nationalism, militarism and citizenship in South Korea. *International Feminist Journal of Politics*, 3(1), 26–54.

Lee, B. (1982). Occupational lead exposure of storage battery workers in Korea. *British Journal of Industrial Medicine*, 39(3), 283–289.

Lee, B. (2010). Incorporating foreigners in Korea: The politics of differentiated membership. *Journal of Multicultural Society*, 1(2), 35–64.

Lee, C.R. et al. (2002). Nasal septum perforation of welders. *Industrial Health*, 40(3), 286–289.

Lee, C.-H. et al. (2009). Mental health and quality of life of North Korean defectors living in Japan. *Asian Journal of Psychiatry*, 2(3), 95–99.

Lee, E. & Kim, M.-H. (1998). Cerebral vasoreactivity by transcranial Doppler in carbon disulfide poisoning cases in Korea. *Journal of Korean Medical Science*, 13, 645–651.

Lee, H. (2012). Political economy of cross-border marriage: Economic development and social reproduction in Korea. *Feminist Economics*, 18(2), 177–200.

Lee, H.-K. (2003). Gender, migration and civil activism in South Korea. *Asian and Pacific Migration Journal*, 12(1–2), 127–153.

Lee, H.-K. (2005). Marriage migration to South Korea: Issues, problems, and responses. *Korean Journal of Population Studies*, 28, 73–106.

Lee, H.-K. (2006). Migrant domestic workers in Korea: The effects of global householding on Korean-Chinese domestic workers. *International Development Planning Review*, 28(4), 499–514.

Lee, H.-K. (2008). International marriage and the state in South Korea: Focusing on governmental policy. *Citizenship Studies*, 12(1), 107–123.

Lee, H.-K. et al. (2006). Feminization of migration and transnational families of Korean-Chinese migrants in South Korea. *Korean Journal of Sociology*, 40(5), 258–298.

Lee, H.Y. (1993). South Korea in 1992: A turning point in democratization. *Asian Survey*, 33(1), 32–42.

Lee, J. (2013). Migration policy development in the Republic of Korea: A brief review of the Second Basic Plan for Immigration Policy (2013–2017). International Organization for Migration, Geneva, SWI.

Lee, N.Y. (2007). The construction of military prostitution in South Korea during the US military rule, 1945–1948. *Feminist Studies*, 33(3), 453–481.

Lee, S.H. et al. (2014). Mental health of intermarried immigrant women and their children in South Korea. *Journal of Immigrant and Minority Health*, 16(1), 77–85.

Lee, S.W. et al. (2008). The status and characteristics of industrial accidents for migrant workers in Korea compared with native workers. *Korean Journal of Occupational and Environmental Medicine*, 20(4), 351–361.

Lee, Y. et al. (2001). Trauma experience of North Korean refugees in China. *American Journal of Preventive Medicine*, 20(3), 225–229.

Lie, J. (1995). The transformation of sexual work in twentieth-century Korea. *Gender and Society*, 9, 310–327.

Lim, T. (2009). Who is Korean? Migration, immigration, and the challenge of multiculturalism in homogeneous societies. *The Asia-Pacific Journal*, 30 (1). Available at: http://www.asia-studies.com/asia/JPFocus/3192.pdf. Accessed 3 August 2015.

Lim, T.C. (2003). Racing from the bottom in South Korea?: The nexus between civil society and transnational migrants. *Asian Survey*, 43(3), 423–442.

Min, P.G. (2011). The immigration of Koreans to the United States: A review of 45 year (1965–2009) trends. *Development and Society*, 40, 195–224.

Ministry of Justice (2012). The 2nd Basic Plan for Immigration Policy 2013–2017. Vibrant Korea growing with immigrants Immigration Policy Commission, Korea Immigration Service, Ministry of Justice, Seoul, KOR.

Ministry of Legislation (2015). Immigration Control Act (Republic of Korea). Available at: http://unpan1.un.org/intradoc/groups/public/documents/APCITY/UNPAN011498.pdf. Accessed 19 May 2015.

Ministry of Unification (2014). Ministry of Unification: Data and Statistics. Available at: http://eng.unikorea.go.kr/content.do?cmsid=1822. Accessed 30 March 2015.

Moon, K.H. (1997). *Sex among allies: Military prostitution in US–Korea relations.* Columbia University Press, New York, NY.

Nye, M. (2007). The challenges of multiculturalism. *Culture and Religion,* 8(2), 109–123.

Oh, J.A. & Jung, J. (2013). Determinants of international labor migration to Korea. KIEP Working Paper 13-08. Korea Institute for International Economic Policy, Seoul, KOR.

Oh, J.-E. et al. (2012). Migration profile of the Republic of Korea. IOM MRTC Research Report Series No. 2011-01. Migration Research and Training Centre, International Organization for Migration, Goyang-si, KOR.

Organisation for Economic Co-operation and Development (1999). Evaluation and aid effectiveness. Evaluating country programmes. Vienna Workshop, 1999. Development Assistance Committee, OECD.

Organisation for Economic Co-operation and Development (2011). OECD Factbook 2011–2012. OECD Publishing, Paris, FRA.

Park, C.B. (1983). Preference for sons, family size, and sex ratio: An empirical study in Korea. *Demography,* 20(3), 333–352.

Park, H.C. et al. (1992). The analysis of impotence in workers exposed to carbon disulfide. *Journal of Korean Andrological Society,* 10(1), 55–59.

Park, J. et al. (2004). Occupations and Parkinson's disease: A case-control study in South Korea. *Industrial Health,* 42(3), 352–358.

Park, J.G. et al. (1989). Health hazards of plating workers. *Korean Journal of Occupational and Environmental Medicine,* 1(2), 218–227.

Park, J.-M. (2013). Paradoxes of gendering strategy in prostitution policies: South Korea's "toleration-regulation regime", 1961–1979. *Women's Studies International Forum,* 37, 73–84.

Park, S. (2011). Domestic violence and help seeking behaviour among Vietnamese in Korea. Doctorate thesis. Michigan State University, East Lansing, MI.

Park, S.H. et al. (1992). A clinical study on chronic carbon disulfide (CS2) intoxication. *Journal of the Korean Neurological Association,* 10(2), 136–142.

Park, S.W. et al. (1999). A case of heat stroke in an aluminium utensil plant. *Korean Journal of Occupational and Environmental Medicine,* 11(2), 293–303.

Park, Y.-b. (2004). South Korea: Balancing Labor Demand with Strict Controls. Migration Information Source. Available at: www.migrationinformation.org. Accessed 28 May 2013.

Roh, J. (2014). Korea's employment permit system and wage development of foreign workers. *Public Policy and Administration,* 2(3), 41–63.

Savada, A.M. & Shaw, W. (1992). Area handbook series. South Korea: A country study. Library of Congress, Federal Research Division, Washington, DC.

Schwartz, B.S. et al. (2005). Occupational lead exposure and longitudinal decline in neurobehavioral test scores. *Epidemiology,* 16(1), 106–113.

Soon-Young, H. (1999). Thawing Korea's cold war: The path to peace on the Korean peninsula. *Foreign Affairs*, 78(3), 8–12.

Statistics Korea (2013). Marriage and Divorce Statistics 2012. Available at: http://kostat.go.kr/portal/english/news/1/1/index.board?bmode=read&aSeq=287104. Accessed 28 May 2015.

Stephen, E.H. (2012). Bracing for low fertility and a large elderly population in South Korea. Korean Economic Institute, Washington D.C.

Tanaka, H. (2008). North Korea: Understanding Migration to and from a Closed Country. Migration Information Source. Available at: http://www.migrationinformation.org. Accessed 28 May 2013.

Truong, T.T. (2001). Hmong and Vietnamese women's perception of domestic violence: An exploratory study. Thesis (M.S.W.), California State University, Fresno, CA.

UNAIDS/UNICEF/WHO (2004). Republic of Korea, 2004 Update. Epidemiological Fact Sheets on HIV/AIDS and Sexually Transmitted Infections. World Health Organization, Geneva, SWI.

United Nations (2000). Protocol to Prevent, Suppress and Punish Trafficking in Persons, Especially Women and Children, Supplementing the United Nations Convention on Transnational Organized Crime. Available at: http://www.osce.org/odihr/19223?download=true.

US Department of State (2013). Trafficking in Persons Report 2013 — Republic of Korea. Available at: http://www.ecoi.net/local_link/250872/361758_en.html. Accessed 23 June 2014.

Van Tai, T. (1981). The status of women in traditional Vietnam: A comparison of the code of the Le dynasty (1428–1788) with the Chinese codes. *Journal of Asian History*, 15(2), 97–145.

Weaver, V. et al. (2003). Associations of lead biomarkers with renal function in Korean lead workers. *Occupational and Environmental Medicine*, 60(8), 551–562.

Wikipedia (2015). Korean diaspora. Available at: http://en.wikipedia.org/wiki/Korean_diaspora#cite_ref-MOFAT_1-21. Accessed 12 April 2015.

World Bank (2015). Population ages 65 and above (% of total). World Development Indicators. United Nations Population Division's World Population Prospects. World Bank, Washington, D.C. Available at: http://data.worldbank.org/indicator/SP.POP.65UP.TO.ZS. Accessed 12 April 2015.

Yang, K.H. (2015). A Critique of Government-Driven Multicultural Policy in Korea: Towards Local Government-Centered Policies. Available at: http://asj.upd.edu.ph/mediabox/archive/ASJ-49-2-2013/Yang.pdf. Accessed 12 April 2015.

Yang, O.K. & Kim, Y.S. (2007). A study on the effects of depressiveness among foreign wives through marriage migration. *Mental Health & Social Work*, 26(26), 79–110.

Yayori, M. & Sharnoff, L. (1977). Sexual slavery in Korea. *Frontiers: A Journal of Women Studies*, 2(1), 22–30.

Yum, Y. *et al.* (1994). Study on the progression of biological effects of workers following termination of CS2 exposure: In cases of peripheral polyneuritis and retinal change. *Korean Journal of Occupational and Environmental Medicine*, 6(2), 348–363.

## Chapter 14

# Migrant health in the workplace: a multi-country comparison

Dr Lata Satyen, Professor John W Toumbourou,
Professor David Mellor, Dr Ilmiye Secer
and Dr Matin Ghayour-Minaie

The decision to migrate is often filled with uncertainty. Migrants make their life-changing decisions with limited knowledge of life in the new country. Despite the uncertainty, increasing millions of people across the world migrate each year. In recent decades, the net international migration (i.e. the difference between the number of people who immigrate and emigrate) to developed nations has increased from 2.5 million people per year between 1990 and 2000 to 3.5 million people per year between 2000 and 2010 (United Nations Department of Economic and Social Affairs/Population Division, 2013). The developed nations of Canada, Australia, New Zealand and the USA gained the highest numbers of migrants, while countries in the developing nations of Bangladesh, China and India experienced the highest net emigration.

Whether one relocates internally or internationally, alone or with family, temporarily or permanently, voluntarily or forced, it is necessary to consider the aspirations for migration. Individuals may choose to relocate for reasons associated with economic opportunities, social and family enrichment, career development, exploration, personal growth and safety.

Free-market policies value economic migration as a workforce stimulus to host countries that can advance economic prospects for migrants and their families. Critics of these policies raise concerns that economic migration may undermine developed labour markets, entrench inequality by increasing brain drain from developing nations, and adversely impact migrant health. In what follows we provide a contemporary overview of migrant health in the workplace. We compare health indicators for migrants in five major host countries against indicators in migrant source nations.

## Migrant health interventions within free-market policies

Migrant health in the international workplace is heavily influenced by national economic migration policies. There are tensions in the political debates that underlie economic migration policies. Those that argue in favour of international free markets have their roots in neoliberal and laissez-faire (Harvey, 2005) economic philosophies. Such philosophies argue that there are benefits in encouraging the liberalisation of economic markets and trade, and that there are inherent flaws in government centralised and planned economies. The underlying perspective of these philosophies can be traced back to the Enlightenment intellectual movement in Europe in the late seventeenth and eighteenth centuries where reason and individualism were argued to be more important than tradition. This movement associated market freedom with the quest for liberty from monarchs, kings and religious rulers who had traditionally owned all resources. Market freedom was conceived as a means of allowing human potential for innovation and creative adaptation to be more fully realised in economic pursuits. Since the 1980s, these varied philosophies have become more narrowly centred on arguments for reductions in government spending in order to increase opportunities for the development of a strong private sector (Fried, 2009).

Critics of laissez-faire economic philosophies have pointed out that market freedom is itself underpinned by systems of justice and principles of social organisation that protect rights and economic resources required for the successful operation of economic markets (Fried, 2009). A number of examples exist where migrants have been exploited by being deliberately sourced for undesirable jobs with wages below national minimum rates (Fried, 2009). Such examples have led to resistance to laissez-faire approaches to economic migration. Arguments to set limits on migration are also based in nationalism and the desire to protect national and local culture, identity and self-determination.

Within the present chapter, we consider migrant health in the international workplace from the perspective of public health and human development approaches. These approaches seek to use scientific approaches to reduce and alleviate harm that may arise in the processes of adjustment required in economic migration transitions.

International human development approaches imply the need for international migration to encourage skill-building, economic development and human rights. Sachs (2005) has been influential within the United Nations human development programme in arguing that student and economic migration and free-market approaches benefit international development and efforts to alleviate extreme poverty. Sachs has argued for policies such as international student exchange and migration to ensure educational and human development outcomes in developing nations. Sachs argues that without basic assistance, many poor nations are unable to address underlying disadvantages in health and social disorganisation, and hence are prevented from entering and gaining benefits from the international market economy. The tensions between encouraging international free markets and the rights of individuals and nations to self-determine their destiny remain a key issue in international development.

## Factors influencing the health of migrant workers

Fundamental to evaluating whether migration offers overall benefits is the question of whether migrants maintain good health within their new nation. The health of migrants in the workplace is influenced by three interrelated factors: successful adaptation, social support, and the threat of discrimination.

**Adaptation:** Upon resettlement in a host country, migrants experience a cultural transition known as acculturation. Berry's (1997) influential model of acculturation identifies four different ways in which a migrant could adapt to a host society: assimilation, integration, separation and marginalisation. Although acculturation is a necessary part of the transition, this can become a source of stress where cultural values, norms and rules differ markedly between the host nation and the country of origin. Hence, acculturation challenges need to be considered in understanding the process of adaptation.

A key dimension that influences acculturation is the nature of the relation between the group and the individual explained along an individualism–collectivism dimension (Hofstede, 1984; Triandis, 1994). Individualism refers to an emphasis on the self (e.g. workplace self-direction), and is common in Western countries such as Australia and the USA (Hofstede, 1984). In contrast, collectivism refers to an emphasis on the group (e.g. workplace obedience), and is common in Eastern countries such as those in Asia (Hofstede, 1984). These dimensions have implications for workplace acculturation: for example, value discrepancies may undermine job satisfaction (Locke, 1976). Luijters et al. (2006) argue that acculturation to workplace satisfaction is less likely where migrants place high value on maintaining their collectivist cultural traditions. However, outcomes may be mitigated where workplaces value teams. Retaining collectivist cultural values may not have any adverse effects on work relationships and indeed, may benefit cultural diversity within organisations (Jian, 2012).

**Social support:** The workplace is a significant avenue for migrants to develop social networks that can assist their adjustment. Such networks can assist in obtaining information regarding job vacancies and economic opportunities (Garcia-Ramirez et al., 2005) and may also enhance mental health (Tsai and Thompson, 2013). For example, emotional social support from family and friends can be protective against psychosocial distress and substance use (Tsai and Thompson, 2013). Improved mental health for male migrant workers has been associated with instrumental support in the form of help during difficult times and, for females, with perceived esteem support (Wong and Leung, 2008). Language barriers and discrimination are domains that have been found to reduce managers' support for migrant workers (Amason et al., 1999).

**Discrimination:** Discrimination can undermine migrant health in the workplace. Workplace discrimination refers to:

> "behaviours, decisions, and actions that involve different or inferior treatment of individuals on the basis of their race, skin colour, ethnic origin, or any other grounds that are not related to their occupational merit" (Forstenlechner and Al-Wagfi, 2010, p. 769).

Migrant groups often report experiences of racial discrimination such as verbal abuse and bullying in the workplace (Agudelo-Suarez *et al.*, 2009; Forstenlechner and Al-Wagfi, 2010; Laer and Janssens, 2011; Syed and Pio, 2010). Furthermore, negative stereotypes towards certain migrant groups impact on their employment prospects when applying for high-paying jobs and those that require a high level of interpersonal skills (Baltes and Rudolph, 2008; Krings and Olivares, 2007). As one example, highly qualified migrants have been found to be rated less suitable for managerial roles than members of the host country who are equally qualified (Baltes and Rudolph, 2008). Discrimination may reduce migrants' job satisfaction and wellbeing in the workplace.

Workplace values, migrants' adaptation to the workplace, the level of available support and the resulting occupational health and safety differ across countries. In the sections that follow, the workplace health of migrants will be examined in Australia, Canada, the USA, Europe, South America and the developing nations to provide a broad picture of migrant health across a diverse range of host countries.

## *Immigrant worker experiences in Australia*

Australia's first fleet brought with it radical economic and social changes that was destined to have long-term repercussions for the fledgling nation and for the Indigenous population. The initial convict transportations and free settler migrations from England were followed by more diverse settlement inspired by the gold rush, including the migration of Chinese labourers. From the post-war years, depending on the mood of the nation, migrants were sought to tackle the economics of nation-building and on occasions were received as refugees. Although the influence of migration has been met with ambivalence and at times resistance by the settlers from earlier migrations, it has played an important role in shaping Australia into a culturally and linguistically diverse society (Rowland et al., 2003) and is a significant contributor to the Australian economy and workforce.

After the post-war period, to meet the demands for semi-skilled and unskilled labour, Australia accepted migrants from European countries such as Italy, Greece, the former Yugoslavia and Turkey (Colic-Peisker, 2011). In later years, the end of the White Australia policy introduced Asian and African (e.g. Chinese, Indian, Pakistani and Somali) migrants to seek settlement and employment in Australia in larger numbers (Hibbins, 2005). Shortages of professionals in the health and education sectors further led to the recruitment of permanent skilled migrant workers and temporary skilled migrant workers (Hugo, 2006; Khoo et al., 2004), mainly from the Indian subcontinent (e.g. India, Pakistan and Bangladesh) while migrants from Middle-Eastern countries entered Australia under the humanitarian visa category. They all, however, are not employed in a profession relevant to their skill, leading to the issue of underemployment where they have been unable to obtain employment at their skill level. Australia is currently a multicultural society and employs skilled and unskilled migrant workers from several cultural groups that include Chinese, Indian, Anglo-Saxon, Middle-Eastern, European and African migrants, along with temporary workers from other nations as well.

The Department of Immigration and Border Protection (2013) reports that of the 6.5 million overseas-born residents, 61.9% participate in the Australia labour force. Persons born overseas have markedly better health than people born in Australia on measures of mortality, disability, and on health behaviour risk factors (Singh and de Looper, 2002). In 1999, mortality rates were lower at 520:100,000 for non-Australians compared to Australians 610:100,000 (Singh and de Looper, 2002). Rates of disability and health behaviour risk factors of alcohol, sedentary behaviour and obesity are lower for non-Australian born residents relative to Australian-born (Singh and de Looper, 2002). However, rates of mortality are generally lower per 1,000 people in Australia (6.5 deaths) than the main migrant source nations of the United Kingdom (8.8), China (7.1), India (7.1), Pakistan (7.3), New Zealand (6.7) and Italy (9.7).

Despite broad evidence that migrants enjoy relative health advantages in Australia, there is some evidence that migrants may be at greater risk for workplace injury. To date only a few studies (Corvalan *et al.*, 1994; Reid *et al.*, 2014; Trajkovski and Loosemore., 2006) have examined the incidence of work-related injuries among migrants in Australia. As part of a larger study, Corvalan *et al.* (1994) examined work-related fatalities in Australia during 1982–1984 for Australian-born and overseas-born workers. Using census data from the 1981 and 1986 national censuses adjusted according to the annual labour force survey, 1,211 workers were identified with a known country of birth, of which 333 were born outside of Australia. Results from this study showed that migrant workers from non-English-speaking countries working in manufacturing and construction industries had significantly higher rates of fatality than Australian-born workers. Similarly, Trajkovski and Loosemore (2006) conducted a survey on 400 migrants working at construction sites in Sydney to examine the role of language diversity in occupational health and safety risks, and found that migrant workers had higher levels of health and safety risks than Australian-born workers. They attributed these problems to migrants' low knowledge of workplace safety procedures.

In a more recent study, Reid *et al.* (2014) used the Australian national Multi-Purpose Household Survey and found lower work-related injuries reported by non-Australian-born workers in the previous 12 months during the years of 2005–2006 and 2009–2010. Increased awareness regarding occupational health and safety among employees in Australia was one explanation offered to account for the decrease in migrant worker injuries and fatalities. An increase in the number of skilled migrant workers in Australia was a further factor offered to account for these trends. However, injuries incurred by migrant workers may also be underreported. As Reid *et al.* (2014) found, migrant workers with fewer educational qualifications and limited English skills had greater difficulty recognising potential hazards and reporting work safety incidents. Well-educated and skilled migrant workers were also resistant to reporting health and safety issues out of fear that discrimination could threaten their jobs.

The extant literature revealed only a handful of studies that have assessed migrants' psychological wellbeing at work. One cross-national study (Olgiati *et al.*, 2013) assessed the relationship between income, subjective wellbeing and immigration status in 16 countries, including Australia. Using data from the Gallup World Poll, which represents 95% of the world's adult population, between the years 2006 and 2011, the study reported income to be positively associated with the life satisfaction of migrant workers in Australia. Another large study (Kifle and Kler, 2008) that used data from the Household, Income and Labour Dynamics in Australia (HILDA) Survey (between 2001 and 2005) examined the employment status of 820 African migrants and found that unemployment was negatively associated with the financial satisfaction of African migrants. A qualitative study by Ogunsiji *et al.* (2012) also examined the experiences of 21 African migrant women living in Sydney and found that unemployment significantly contributed to their mental health problems.

Psychological wellbeing in the workplace is further influenced by acculturation and adaptation to the host country. Omer and Atkins (2002) examined the workplace experiences of five migrant nurses from non-English speaking countries using a descriptive study design and found that migrant nurses reported feelings of unhappiness, loneliness and being unsupported. Other studies (Collins and Reid, 2012; Limpangog, 2013) that used the survey method showed that migrant workers experience workplace discrimination and bullying, while female migrant workers particularly felt shame and discomfort working in a male-dominated environment because of the differences in cultural norms.

A major factor associated with migrants' workplace injury is the lack of English skills. Trajkovski and Loosemore (2006) observed that migrant workers from non-English speaking countries who used their native language in the workplace were less likely to develop English language competence and this was associated with higher injury risks. They suggested that in workplaces with restricted opportunities for English competence, occupational health and safety training should be provided in multiple languages. To protect workers in these contexts, Trajkovski and Loosemore argued that safety signage and equipment manuals be translated to images rather than words to enhance their comprehension.

There are a range of findings from studies adopting different study designs that have attempted to examine Australian migrants' health in the workplace. Although descriptive studies provide valuable insight into the workplace experiences of migrants, larger representative studies are needed to obtain a comprehensive picture of migrants' occupational health and mental wellbeing. Further research is needed to assess the health of migrant workers and better understand the role of demographic, economic and linguistic factors that may influence their physical health and psychological wellbeing.

## *Migrant worker experiences in Canada*

Like Australia, Canada is a prosperous and developed country that continuously attracts skilled economic migrants. The migration trend to Canada started in 1896 when a large number of people from the United Kingdom, Europe and the USA moved to Canada to take advantage of the offer of free land, and it continued until 1905 after which there was a decrease in the flow of people in 1914 because of World War I. Then, in the 1940s, during and after World War II, approximately 48,000 war brides and their 22,000 children went to Canada, followed by half a million migrants from Europe in the 1950s. Following this period, Canada accepted 37,500 Hungarian refugees in 1956. Since then Czechoslovakian, Ugandans, Asians, Chilean, Indochinese, Vietnamese, Cambodians, Laotian and Kosovars have all settled in Canada. In 2012, the main source countries of migration were Asia-Pacific, followed by Africa and the Middle-East (Citizenship and Immigration Canada, 2012).

With the large migrant intake (more than 225,000 on average per year), many of whom joined the labour force, it is vital to understand the health risks and issues among migrant workers (Citizenship and Immigration Canada, 2005). Smith and Mustard (2007) used the secondary data from the 2003 and 2005 Canadian Community Health Surveys on work-related injury involving nearly 100,000 people and examined the risk of self-reported activity-limiting work-related injuries among migrants. They found that the proportion of work-related injuries among the most recent migrants was significantly higher than Canadian-born participants (90% vs. 65%) but declined for migrant men who had lived in Canada for 6–10 years, illustrating with increased time and workplace experience, occupational injuries decline. Another study based on the results of the Canadian Community Health Survey (CCHS) that also compared injury rates among migrants and Canadian-born residents showed that recent male migrants had higher rates of work-related injuries requiring medical attention (Schenker, 2008). Premji and Smith (2013) also examined the risk that migrants faced based on the mismatch between their education and job using the same CCHS and found that the risk of a work injury requiring medical attention was five times higher for migrant men with low education who had resided in Canada for less than 5 years compared to non-recent migrants.

While examining the ripple effects of non-recognition of overseas qualifications, studies (e.g. Baker and Benjamin, 1994; Bauder, 2003; Li, 2001; Reitz, 2001; 2007) have suggested that the market value of migrant qualifications is generally less than for native-born Canadians and this results in excluding migrant workers from the higher sectors of the labour market, leading to a change in their careers and experiencing a loss of social status (Bauder, 2003). Consequently, underemployment leads to a decline in migrants' mental health (Beiser, 2005). There are other barriers that exist for migrant workers. Similar to migrants in other countries, several professional associations and the state try to exclude migrants from the most in-demand occupations and instead employ Canadian-born and Canadian-educated workers (Bauder, 2003).

Migrants' ethnicity and country of origin also play a role in their employment success rate in Canada (Picot and Sweetman, 2005; Reitz, 2007). It is seen that migrants from visible minorities such as African and Asian countries earn less than their counterparts from European origins or native-born Canadian workers (e.g. Baker and Benjamin, 1994; Boyd, 1992; Canadian Council on Social Development, 2000; Christofides and Swidinsky, 1994; Reitz, 2007). They have also been found to earn less regardless of their education level and their legal status (Picot and Sweetman, 2005; Reitz, 2007). This could be one reason for the existing intergroup tensions (Reitz, 2005) and racial prejudice and employment discrepancies in Canada (Baker and Benjamin, 1994; Boyd, 1992; Christofides and Swidinsky, 1994; Reitz, 2007).

Syed (2013) found work-related musculoskeletal conditions, workplace violence, mental health issues due to overt discrimination and profiling, as well as exposures to second hand-tobacco smoke as issues of concern among migrant workers. Examining workplace conditions, a World Health Organisation report (WHO, 2007) found that several workplaces do not provide basic occupational health services to their employees, especially migrant workers, and that only a few migrants might be aware of, and use, national social security compensation or rehabilitation schemes for occupational illness or injury. Overall, the WHO report indicates that migrants are more vulnerable to health risks and potential hazards as a result of high stress arising from displacement and insertion into new environments. These studies suggest that there are stark differences in the workplace health of Canadian migrants compared to their non-migrant counterparts. As such, workplaces should enhance their workplace policies and ensure that migrants are provided with the opportunity to utilise their skills and reduce their job-related injuries.

**Immigrant worker experiences in the USA:** The USA is a cultural mosaic of migrants from all over the world. According to the Office of Immigration Statistics (2013), 1,031,631 people were granted permanent residence (e.g., family and employment categories) for the fiscal year, 2011–2012. The main countries these people came to the USA from were Europe, Asia, central and south America, Africa, and Oceania. A further 58,179 people entered the USA as refugees, while 11,978 persons were granted asylum. Furthermore, 65,500,000 persons entered the USA in the same fiscal period as non-migrants of which 3,049,419 were temporary workers and families, 717,893 intracompany transfers, 386,472 traders and investors, 1,653,576 students, 475,232 exchange visitors, 365,779 diplomats, 42,025,488 temporary visitors for pleasure and 5,705,106 temporary visitors for business. These figures illustrate not only the large numbers of migrants entering the country but also the broad range of visitors who are likely to be impacted by USA employment experiences.

Migrants from European countries such as Germany, Ireland, Italy and Poland have traditionally been granted entry to work as farmers, construction labourers, tailors or shop owners (Mass, 2014). On the other hand, skilled and unskilled migrants from Asia, the Indian sub-continent and Latin America work in agriculture, construction, cleaning, community services, the medical sector and in information technology industries. It is clear that migrants contribute a significant proportion of the American workforce, which warrants an examination of their workplace health profile. Compared to other countries, extensive research has been carried out in the USA in this area and can be classified into occupational injuries, mental health and unfavourable working conditions.

In spite of occupational health and safety training, three medium- to large-scale qualitative studies found that migrants working in low-skill and low-wage jobs experienced greater occupational health hazards including an exposure to loud noise and chemicals, inhalation of fumes and dust, poor living conditions, lack of protective safety equipment (e.g. masks, gloves, safety glasses) and absence of health insurance compared to native-born Americans (Castro *et al.*, 2006; Eggerth *et al.*, 2012; Magana and Hovey, 2003). In another qualitative study, Tsai (2009) conducted focus groups with Chinese migrant restaurant workers and found that they experience greater cuts and burns as a result of common injuries. Similarly, Brunette (2004) in his review found Hispanic migrants working in construction to be involved in a greater number of falls from lifts, motor vehicle crashes and being struck by falling objects. Other reviews (Das *et al.*, 2001; Hansen and Donohoe, 2003; Mobed *et al.*, 1992) have concluded the health risks for agricultural workers include pesticide-related infections and poisoning, cancer, and musculoskeletal and soft tissue problems. All these studies illustrate that migrants in the USA face serious health threats.

Stressful work experiences further lead to a number of mental health risks. Migrant farmworkers, who report long working hours, isolation and no access to transportation or a telephone to call family members, have been found to experience significantly reduced mental health that includes mood disorders, depression and suicidal ideation, increased levels of anxiety, drug and substance use, and alcohol dependence (Alderete *et al.*, 2000; Arcury *et al.*, 2015; Grzywacz *et al.*, 2006; Hiott *et al.*, 2008; Magana and Hovey, 2003). It is therefore essential that occupational health and safety practices are reinforced to improve the working conditions and mental health of migrant workers.

Policies that target improving migrants' level of English and adjustment to the USA are also important as a lack of English language proficiency limits migrants' ability to interact and communicate with colleagues in the workplace and can lead to feelings of frustration, dissatisfaction and discomfort (Liou and Cheng, 2011). Furthermore, discrimination and sexual harassment in the workplace are additional issues that impinge upon psychological wellbeing (e.g. psychological distress, happiness and life satisfaction) of migrants (Castro *et al.*, 2006; Williams *et al.*, 2003). Although policies in the USA exist to protect employees from harassment, most migrants are not aware of their rights and do not complain out of fear of losing their jobs. Disseminating information regarding workers' rights in English and other languages could assist with the process of improving occupational health.

## *Immigrant worker experiences in Europe*

Although immigration into and across Europe has a long history, since the Second World War there has been a dramatic increase in the extent and nature of immigration. Indeed over the past 50 years, Europe has become a migrant continent with citizens of former colonies moving to their colonisers' homelands. Refugees and asylum seekers arriving via sanctioned and unsanctioned means, and the 1989 Schengen Agreement allow citizens of member states to live and work anywhere within the European Union (EU). This has led to both legal and illegal work engagements. The complexity of immigration within and into Europe presents a challenge for any analysis of the health of immigrant workers in this context. As Wren and Boyle (2001) noted the term "migrant" encompasses:

> "a very diverse range of people in terms of their origins and reasons for migrating, from the highly skilled migrants operating within an increasingly integrated EU labour market, to non-EU citizens from prospective EU member states, and forced migrants and refugees, who often face the greatest difficulty in re-establishing their working lives" (p. 5).

In addition, within any particular nation state, there is likely to be a mix of migrant populations. For example, France has significant populations of migrants from Algeria, Morocco, Portugal, Italy Spain, Turkey and Tunisia. Each of these populations is likely to have a different level of engagement with the employment market. Italy, on the other hand, has significant populations of Romanians, Albanians and Moroccans, as well as people from eastern European states, and again there is a range of engagement in the workforce.

Given the complexity of European migration and the diverse nature of host and immigrant countries, it is difficult to generalise about immigrant health and the work environment. However, studies in various locations in Europe suggest that a recurring experience of immigrant workers is discrimination, bullying and harassment from supervisors/managers, colleagues and co-workers, and even from clients, patients or others to whom service is provided (European Agency for Safety and Health, EASH, 2007). Some groups, such as Asians are more likely to be bullied. A related feature of this discrimination is social marginalisation, especially among those workers who are forced to forego their private and social lives due to the demands of their employers.

As the EASH report (2007) points out, while there have been studies in Europe on immigrant health, there are few studies of work-related health. These studies suggest that immigrants are prone, for example, to develop allergies in Italy (Tedeschi *et al.*, 2003), musculoskeletal disorders in Austria (European Foundation for the Improvement of Living and Working Conditions, 2007) and premature ageing in Switzerland (Weiss, 2003). Studies that look more specifically at work-related health suggest that immigrant workers may have elevated levels of hearing loss, scoliosis, tenosynovitis, asbestosis and skin disease (Becher *et al.*, 1997; Erdogan and Schneider, 2000). This elevated risk can be attributed to the workers being employed in workplaces with high health risks and heavy manual tasks, or lack of vocational training which leads them to being allocated high-risk roles. Other contributing factors are poor language skills which are associated with inability to access occupational health and safety (OHS) services or medical services until it is too late, and diseases which could have been treated earlier before they became chronic (Pochobradsky *et al.*, 2002). They may not even be aware of OHS services because they do not exist in their home country (Kamphuis *et al.*, 2003).

Among other studies that have looked specifically at work-related health, Wren and Boyle (2002) investigated the links between migration, employment and health using psychological questionnaires and in-depth interviews in Britain, Italy and Sweden with: (1) intra-EU migrants, (2) migrants from Poland, which in 2002 was not an EU member state, and (3) Bosnian refugees. While the study methodology was not consistent across contexts, the analyses of both qualitative and quantitative data indicated that the most significant work-related health problems reported were musculoskeletal and sleeping problems. A number of other migration-related factors associated with health were identified in the various contexts but these were generally not work-related. For example, discrimination was a common experience in the labour market in Sweden, and in general in Italy for Bosnians, while mental health was generally a problem for illegal and older migrants.

A particularly vulnerable group of workers in Europe are domestic workers. The International Labour Organisation (2013) reported that in 2010, there were approximately 52.6 million immigrant domestic workers around the world. Research shows that in Europe, female migrant workers contribute strongly to the domestic workforce. For example, 36% of all female migrant workers in Spain find work as domestic workers, while in Italy, 27.9% work as domestics in private households. In France, the figure is 21.1% (Oso Casas and Garson, 2005), the majority of whom were women, and working in Spain, France and Italy. Those in Spain were mainly from Latin America, those in Italy from eastern Europe, and those in France from Algeria, Morocco and Tunisia. Because these workers are often in the informal sector and the households remain largely unregulated, unscrutinised and almost invisible to the public, they are particularly vulnerable to the risk of hazards and work-related diseases (Salih, 2013).

Ahonen *et al.* (2010) conducted a study to investigate the work-related health of female migrant domestic workers in Spain. Through focus groups with 46 women who worked in domestic roles, they identified that they were exposed to a number of environmental, ergonomic and psychosocial hazards that were associated with physical and psychological health effects. The hazards included ongoing exposure to respiratory and skin irritants such as ammonia and bleach, repetitive movements which were associated with chronic pain and compounded by an inability to take time off work, long working hours when the worker lived in the household, and associated fatigue, and heavy workloads associated with anxiety and stress. These hazards and outcomes were consistent whether the worker was formal (documented) or not, and in a context in which there are laws governing domestic work since the 1990s (ILO, 2013).

Overall, it is evident that it is very complex to summarise a general picture for the whole of Europe. There are limited overviews available for the workplace health of migrants in all of Europe, given the diversity of the population and the immigrants. Therefore, the available evidence has to be considered in sections based on the source countries of migrant workers.

## *Immigrant worker experiences in South America*

In South American countries, there is little data available on the health of immigrants. However, reports from the International Organization for Migration (IOM, 2013) indicate that immigrant workers are prone to many factors that are likely to have negative impacts on their health. Among these are that they are often engaged in manual work or highly demanding domestic work. These jobs leave workers and their families trapped in poverty and with little prospect of socioeconomic advancement. They often live in poor-quality housing and are subjected to discrimination, xenophobia and stigmatisation (Nicolao, 2011) that extends to health services that are not culturally relevant. In essence, there is a lack of fulfilment of the basic needs of many immigrant workers.

The above synopsis should be considered in the context of immigration to and within South America. There have been few well-conducted studies in this continent and hence we report mostly the available descriptive evidence. Cabieses Valdes (2011) points out that most Latin American countries remain non-developed with relatively small local economies. Thus, while immigration into these countries was largely from Europe in the nineteenth and first half of the twentieth centuries, recent trends have seen immigration to be intra-regional. The United Nations Educational, Scientific and Cultural Organization (UNESCO, 1999) noted that various political events associated with dictatorships, and subsequent liberation and stability may have played a role in this recent pattern. In addition, recent economic growth in some countries (e.g. Argentina, Brazil, Chile and Uruguay) has created employment opportunities for migrants within the region (Texido and Warn, 2013). Thus, the majority of the migrant workforce comes from within Latin America. Chile is a good example of this. Its economy has shown accelerated growth for more than a decade, mostly due to copper mining and higher demand for this commodity. It has become a new country of destination for migrants who are mostly young, and coming mostly from other Latin American countries to Santiago, the capital (Doña-Reveco and Levinson, 2012). There is thus considerable change to a new economy in much of South America.

Texido and Warn (2013) point out that despite the increased movement of people across regional borders, opportunities for migrant workers in South America still tend to be constricted to low-skilled employment such as in agriculture, construction and domestic work (IOM, 2012). For example, more than 60% of South American migrants in Argentina are employed in construction, trade and domestic work, and the textile, clothing and footwear industries, similar to those in other developed nations such as the USA. However, within the workplace, these workers are likely to experience discrimination, a contention that is supported by studies in Argentina (Pizarro, 2012) and Chile (Pavez Soto, 2012), where Bolivian and Peruvian migrant workers, respectively, are most at risk.

Given that data on the experiences of migrants in Latin America is scarce, for the purposes of this chapter, the focus will be on Chile. The Department of Foreigners and Migration (Departamento de Extranjeria y Migracion, 2007) reported that one of the major immigrant groups coming to Chile are low-income Latin American women who come to work in domestic service roles, usually as nannies. Many of them come from neighbouring Peru (IOM, 2002), and Peruvians are now the second largest immigrant community in Chile after Argentineans (Núñez and Holper, 2011). As reported above, when migrant domestic workers in Europe were discussed, these female migrant workers were vulnerable due to their possible occupational and living conditions. They may be required to be "on duty" for 24 hours a day, but are lowly paid, often working for the minimum salary or less, and perform duties well beyond their role, similar to their Nepalese counterparts in North America. Living away from their families and without social support they are exploited to the point of being responsible for the entire running of the household, including working for the extended family for no extra pay. They have no respite because they live with their employing family, and may be restricted in their movements outside the home. This results in feelings of loneliness and imprisonment (Núñez and Holper, 2011) similar to those found among migrants in Australia, Canada and the USA.

## Immigrant worker experiences in developing nations

When examining internal and external movements in developing nations, it is clear that there are few extensive studies and mostly descriptive studies available. Several developing nations face a problem of a different kind as a result of external migration. This is known as the "brain drain" where most of their skilled workers emigrate to developed countries to seek better employment opportunities and an enhanced earning capacity. This leads to a shortage of professionals internally, especially in the education and health care systems (Kuehn, 2007; Stilwell *et al.*, 2004). This is especially seen among skilled educational and medical professionals in India (Raveesh, 2013) and the African countries (Naicker *et al.*, 2009).

Along with emigration, there is internal migration or migration to neighbouring countries in search of better economic conditions. Limited employment opportunities and poor living conditions force many individuals to seek better employment in developing countries such as China, India, Turkey, Indonesia, Zimbabwe, Kenya, the Philippines, Qatar and others. These migrants undertake labour work in cleaning services, construction, farming or textile industries. Harsh working conditions, harassment and abuse are the major workplace experiences of migrant workers in developing countries, and these lead to a range of negative health outcomes. Although several newspaper articles and anecdotal reports publicising such effects exist, there is limited research available in relation to the specific health of migrant workers in many developing nations. However, the available data suggest that migrants face more serious workplace threats in these countries.

Among migrants in developing countries, a recurrent experience of people employed in labour jobs is the exploitive work conditions. These conditions include hard physical labour, long work hours, low wages, inadequate rest breaks and holidays, job insecurity, limited opportunities for socialisation with other workers, and inadequate medical and social security insurance (Bhattacharyya and Korinek, 2007; Dedeoglu, 2011a; 2011b; Rao and Mitra, 2013; Sharma, 2013; Wong *et al.*, 2008). For example, young women who migrate to India to work at construction sites report the physically draining work conditions which require them to dig soil and carry bricks (Bhattacharyya and Korinek, 2007). Likewise, young Indian men who migrate internally to Western Uttar Pradesh to work on the farms indicate the hard manual work that is required of them. This work usually comprises cleaning the courtyards, feeding and washing the cattle, preparing the fields for cultivation, and doing agricultural and non-agricultural tasks assigned by the employer and household members (Rao and Mitra, 2013). Working under these conditions leads to a negative impact on migrants' health. For example, construction and domestic workers regularly experience body aches, sunstroke, skin irritations, weakness, and fatigue (Bhattacharyya and Korinek, 2007; Sharma, 2013) while factory workers have mental health problems such as obsessions and compulsions, hostility, depression and anxiety (Wong et al., 2008). There is little opportunity for such workers to seek different employment due to their low educational attainment and limited employment opportunities. Consequently, a fear of losing one's jobs precludes migrants from accessing improved work conditions (Bhattacharyya and Korinek, 2007; Wong et al., 2008) which could lead to better health.

Migrant workers in developing countries also regularly report harassment and abuse at the workplace (Bhattacharyya and Korinek, 2007; Dedeoglu, 2011a; Gulcur and Ilkkaracan, 2002), all leading to poorer physical and mental health. For example, female workers report harassment in the form of gestures, remarks and unwanted touching from either male co-workers or supervisors and yet they do not complain for fear of losing their jobs (Bhattacharyya and Korinek, 2007). Migrant workers from Azerbaijan who work in Turkey also report abuse in the workplace. It was found that migrants working in the textile industry are frequently physically abused by their employers (Dedeoglu, 2011a; 2011b). Similarly, migrant men from Bulgaria reported verbal abuse in spite of their hard work (Nichols et al., 2010).

There are a few positive workplace experiences that have also been reported. Young men working on farms in India maintain a psychological sense of security because food, clothing and shelter are usually provided by the employers. Further, some financial assistance is also provided if a family member back home is faced with ill-health or any other difficulty (Rao and Mitra, 2013). A sense of community and security has also been reported by migrants working on construction sites in India who feel secure because a few contractors recruit workers from the same village to protect female workers from harassment (Bhattacharyya and Korinek, 2007). This demonstrates that workplaces can employ a range of procedures to improve the psychological wellbeing of migrant workers. However, the extent to which this is occurring across countries and industries is limited. Extensive research is required to further examine the health of migrant workers within developing nations. Although these countries account for the largest populations in the world, the amount of information available regarding their occupational health is exceptionally limited.

## Enhancing migrant health in the workplace through evidence-based practices and policies

In order to improve occupational health outcomes, we need to examine which practices and policies would be effective. In the ensuing section, a brief summary of a range of migrant health programmes that have been subject to evaluation is provided.

An important challenge in migrant health remains the tension between valuing cultural diversity, including traditional health practices, vs. ensuring the benefits of modernisation including adaptation to evidence-based health practices. The importance of providing specialist assistance to workplaces seeking to support migrant adjustment and adaptation is emphasised in the World Health Organisation (WHO), that has developed a series of resources for workplace health promotion.

The workplace has been established by the WHO as among the priority settings for health promotion due to its potential to assist large and diverse populations. The concept of the health promoting workplace (HPW) is increasingly recognised as an important means of coordinating evidence-based actions that can reduce work accidents, absenteeism and occupational health claims, while also increasing productivity. Workers' lifestyles and health behaviours are known to have important impacts on occupational workplace health and safety and productivity as migrant workers tend to have increased negative health outcomes such as higher rates of type-2 diabetes (Attridge et al., 2014) and sexually transmitted diseases (STDs) (Ojo et al., 2011).

Attridge et al. (2014) noted that ethnic minority groups in upper-middle-income and high-income countries tend to be socioeconomically disadvantaged and tend to have a higher prevalence of type-2 diabetes than is seen in the majority population. This review searched for high-quality evaluation designs evaluating culturally appropriate health education for the management of type-2 diabetes and identified 33 studies. From the review of these studies, the authors concluded that culturally appropriate health education has short- to medium-term effects on glycaemic control and on knowledge of diabetes and healthy lifestyles. They recommended long-term follow-up within standardised, multi-centre randomised control trials (RCTs) to compare different types and intensities of culturally appropriate health education within defined ethnic minority groups.

In another review, Ojo et al. (2011) noted that migrant workers who leave their spouses to work abroad are vulnerable to contracting STDs. Workplace interventions targeting workers to prevent STDs may reduce risky sexual behaviour. No randomised trials were found in a comprehensive search of interventions, hence trials of such interventions with target groups such as migrant workers were recommended (Ojo et al., 2011).

Horvat et al. (2014) evaluated cultural competence education for health professionals. This form of education aims to ensure all people receive equitable, effective health care, particularly those from culturally and linguistically diverse (CALD) backgrounds. The strategy has been developed in high-income English-speaking countries in response to evidence of health disparities, structural inequalities, and poorer quality health care and outcomes among people from minority CALD backgrounds. Based on high-quality evaluation design criteria, the study included five RCTs involving 337 health care professionals and 8,400 patients; at least 3,463 (41%) of which were from CALD backgrounds.

An overview of the trials comparing the effects of cultural competence training for health professionals with no training show some promising effects on health service usage, although longer follow-up across a wider range of measures may be important in providing more definitive conclusions on other health impacts. There have been two studies that have reported that cultural competence training may improve migrant access to health services. In a US study (Wade and Bernstein, 1991) that included a racially diverse population, client attendance at health services and evaluations of health professionals improved significantly among intervention participants compared with controls. A study in the Netherlands (Harmsen *et al.*, 2005) found that involvement in care by "non-Western" patients (described as "mainly Turkish, Moroccan, Cape Verdean and Surinamese patients") with largely "Western" doctors improved in terms of mutual understanding. Two trials (Sequist *et al.*, 2010; Thom *et al.*, 2006) comparing cultural competence training with no training found no evidence of effect for treatment outcomes, including the proportion of patients with diabetes achieving cholesterol control targets or weight loss.

Overall, it is evident that there are increasing rates of economic migration internationally. Free-market policies hold the hope that economic migration will boost host country economies while also improving the wealth and health of migrants and their families. Our review is unable to provide a definitive evaluation of the extent to which this ideal is being achieved. What is clear is that progress is uneven and varies across nations. Progressive policies and evidence-based practices are emerging to ensure migrant health in the workplace. One step in the right direction for the future is to place a greater priority on disseminating effective policies and practices. Further research is needed across most of the developing and developed countries to examine the state of migrant health in the workplace in both the short and long terms. With millions of people moving across countries each year, the challenges that arise with a new labour force and new workplaces must be recognised and managed to improve their health and wellbeing, and fulfil their aspirations.

## References

Agudelo-Suarez, A.G.-G. *et al.* (2009). Discrimination, work, and health in immigrant populations in Spain. *Social Science and Medicine*, 68, 1866–1874.

Ahonen, E. *et al.* (2009). Invisible work, unseen hazards: The health of women immigrant household service workers in Spain. *American Journal of Industrial Medicine*, 2009; 53(4), 405–416.

Alderete, E.V. *et al.* (2000). Lifetime prevalence of and risk factors for psychiatric disorders among Mexican migrant farmworkers in California. *American Journal of Public Health*, 90, 608–614.

Amason, P.A. *et al.* (1999). Social support and acculturative stress in the multicultural workplace. *Journal of Applied Communication Research*, 27, 310–334.

Arcury, T.A. *et al.* (2015). Job characteristics and work safety climate among North Carolina farmworkers with H-2a visas. Journal of agromedicine, 20(1), 64–76.

Attridge, M.C. et al. (2014). Culturally appropriate health education for people in ethnic minority groups with type 2 diabetes mellitus. Cochrane Database Systematic Review. 4,9, CD006424. doi: 10.1002/14651858.CD006424.pub3.

Baker, M.B. & Benjamin, D. (1994). The performance of immigrants in the Canadian labour market. *Journal of Labor Economics*, 12, 369–405.

Baltes, B.B.R. & Rudolph C.W. (2008). Examining the effect of negative Turkish stereotypes on evaluative workplace outcomes in Germany. *Journal of Managerial Psychology*, 25, 148–158.

Bauder, H. (2003). *"Brain Abuse", or the Devaluation of Immigrant Labour in Canada*. Blackwell Publishing, Oxford, UK.

Becher, S.S. et al. (1997). Ausländische Arbeitnehmer in der BRD — eine Auswertung von betriebsärztlich untersuchten Gastarbeitern zur Feststellung vonGesundheitsstörungen. *Gesundheitswesen*, 59, 174–180.

Beiser, M. (2005). The health of immigrants and refugees in Canada. *Canadian Journal of Public Health*, 96, S30–S44.

Berry, J.W. (1997). Immigration, acculturation, and adaptation. *Applied Psychology: An International Review*, 46, 5–68.

Bhattacharyya, S.K. & Korinek, K. (2007). Opportunities and vulnerabilities of female migrants in construction work in India. *Asian and Pacific Migration Journal*, 16, 511–531.

Boyd, M. (1992). Gender, visible minority and immigrant earnings inequality: Reassessing an employment equity premise. In: Satzewich, V. (ed.), *Deconstructing a Nation: Immigration, Multiculturalism and Racism in the 1990s Canada*, Garamond Press, Toronto, CAN.

Brunette, M.J. (2004). Construction safety research in the United States: Targeting the Hispanic workforce. *Injury Prevention*, 10, 244–248.

Citizenship and Immigration Canada (2005). Facts and figures — immigration overview: Permanent and temporary residents. Ottawa, CAN.

Citizenship and Immigration Canada (2012). Facts and figures — immigration overview: Permanent and temporary residents. Ottawa, CAN.

Canadian Council on Social Development (2000). Unequal access: A Canadian profile of racial differences in education, employment and income. Canadian Race Relations Foundation, Toronto, CAN.

Cabieses Valdes, B.B. (2011). The living conditions and health status of international immigrants in Chile: Comparisons among international immigrants, and between them and the Chilean-born. PhD thesis, The University of York, Department of Health Sciences, York, UK.

Castro, A.B. et al. (2006). How immigrant workers experience workplace problems: A qualitative study. *Archives of Environmental and Occupational Health*, 61, 249–258.

Christofides, L.N.S. & Swidinsky, R. (1994). Wage determination by gender and visible minority status: Evidence from the 1989 LMAS. *Canadian Public Policy*, 2, 34–51.

Colic-Peisker, V. (2011). A new era in Australian multiculturalism? From working-class 'ethnics' to a 'multicultural middle-class'. *International Migration Review*, 45, 562–587.

Collins, J.R. & Reid, C. (2012). Immigrant teachers in Australia. *Cosmopolitan Civil Societies Journal*, 4, 38–61.

Corvalan, C.F. et al. (1994). Role of migrant factors in work-related fatalities in Australia. *Scandinavian Journal of Work, Environment & Health*, 20, 364–370.

Das, R.S., Baron, A. Beckman, S.J. & Harrison, R. 2001. Pesticide-related illness among migrant farm workers in the United States. *International Journal of Occupational and Environmental Health*, 7, 303–312.

Dedeoglu, S. (2011a). Survival of the excluded: Azerbaijani immigrant women's survival strategies and industrial work in Istanbul. *Migration Letters*, 8, 26–33.

Dedeoglu, S. (2011b). Garment ateliers and women workers in Istanbul: Wives, daughters, and Azerbaijani immigrants. *Middle Eastern Studies*, 47, 663–674.

Departamento de Extranjería y Migración (2007). Desarrollo del fenómeno de las migraciones en Chile. Evolución de la gestión gubernamental desde 1990.

Department of Immigration and Border Protection (2013). Australia's Migration Trends 2012–13. Available from: http://www.immi.gov.au/pub-res/Documents/statistics/migration-trends-2012-13.pdf. Accessed 24 April 2015.

Doña-Reveco, C. & Levinson, A. (2012). Chile: A growing destination country in search of a coherent approach to migration. Country Profiles. Migration Policy Institute, Washington, DC. Available at: http://www.migrationinformation.org/USfocus/display.cfm. Accessed 20 January 2015.

Eggerth, D.E.D. et al. (2012). Work experiences of Latina immigrants: A qualitative study. *Journal of Career Development*, 39, 13–30.

Erdogan, M.S.S. & Schneider, J. (2000). Berufskrankheiten türkischer arbeitnehmer in Deutschland. *Arbeitsmedizin*, 50, 326–334.

European Agency for Safety and Health. (2007). Literature study on migrant workers. Available at: https://osha.europa.eu/en/tools-and-publications/publications/literature_reviews/migrant_workers/view. Accessed 25 May 2015.

European Foundation for the Improvement of Living and Working Conditions (2007). Employment and working conditions of migrant workers. Available at: http://www.eurofound.europa.eu/docs/ewco/tn0701038s/tn0701038s.pdf. Accessed 1 August 2015.

Forstenlechner, I. & Al-Waqfi, M.A. (2010). "A job interview for Mo, but none for Mohammed" Religious discrimination against immigrants in Austria and Germany. *Personnel Review*, 39(6), 767–784.

Fried, B. (2009). *The Progressive Assault on Laissez Faire: Robert Hale and the First Law and Economics Movement.* Harvard University Press, Cambridge, MA.

Garcia-Ramirez, M.M. et al. (2005). Psychosocial empowerment and social support factors associated with the employment status of immigrant welfare recipients. *Journal of Community Psychology,* 33, 673–690.

Gulcur, L.I. & Ilkkaracan P. (2002). The 'Natasha' experience: Migrant sex workers from the former Soviet Union and Eastern Europe in Turkey. *Women's Studies International Forum,* 25, 411–421.

Hansen, E.D. & Donohue M. (2003). Health issues of migrant and seasonal farmworkers. *Journal of Health Care for the Poor and Underserved,* 14, 153–164.

Harmsen, H.B.R. et al. (2005). The effect of educational intervention on intercultural communication: Results of a randomised controlled trial. *British Journal of General Practice,* 55, 343–350.

Harvey, D. (2005). *A Brief History of Neoliberalism.* Oxford University Press, Oxford, UK.

Hibbins, R. (2005). Migration and gender identity among Chinese skilled male migrants in Australia. *Geoforum,* 36, 167–180.

Hiott, A.E.G. et al. (2008). Migrant farmworker stress: Mental health implications. *The Journal of Rural Health,* 24, 32–39.

Hofstede, G. (1984). *Cultures Consequences: International Differences in Work-Related Values.* Sage, Beverly Hills, CA.

Horvat, L.H. et al. (2014). Cultural competence education for health professionals. Cochrane Database of Systematic Reviews, Issue 5. Art. No.: CD009405.

Hugo, G. (2006). Temporary migration and the labour market in Australia. *Australian Geographer,* 37, 211–231.

International Labour Organisation (2013). *Domestic Workers Across the World: Global and Regional Statistics and the Extent of Legal Protection.* International Labour Office, Geneva, SWI.

International Organization for Migration (2012). Panorama Migratorio de América del Sur. International Organization for Migration, Buenos Aires, ARG.

Jian, G. (2012). Does culture matter? An examination of the association of immigrants' acculturation with workplace relationship quality. *Management Communication Quarterly,* 26, 295–321.

Kamphuis, E.A. (2003). *Arbozorg voor Allochtone Werknemers.* Tilburg/Utrecht, NED.

Khoo, S. et al. (2004). Temporary skilled migration to Australia: Employers' perspective. 12th Biennial Conference of the Australian Population Association. Canberra, Australia.

Kifle, T.K. & Kler, P. (2008). The financial satisfaction of African immigrants in Australia. *Australasian Review of African Studies,* 29, 66–77.

Krings, F.O. & Olivares, J. (2007). At the doorstep to employment: Discrimination against immigrants as a function of applicant ethnicity, job type, and raters' prejudice. *International Journal of Psychology*, 42, 406–417.

Kuehn, M.B. (2007). Global shortage of health workers, brain drain stress in developing countries. *Journal of the American Medical Association*, 298, 1853.

Laer, K.J. & Janssens, M. (2011). Ethnic minority professionals' experiences with subtle discrimination in the workplace. *Human Relations*, 64(9), 1–25.

Li, P.S. (2001). The market worth of immigrants' educational credentials. *Canadian Public Policy*, 27, 23–38.

Limpangog, C.P. (2013). Racialized and gendered workplace discrimination: The case of skilled Filipina immigrants in Melbourne, Australia. *Journal of Workplace Rights*, 17, 191–218.

Liou, S.C. & Cheng, C. (2011). Experiences of a Taiwanese nurse in the United States. *Nursing Forum*, 46, 102–109.

Locke, E.A. (1976). The nature and causes of job satisfaction. In: Dunnette, M. D. (ed.), *Handbook of Industrial and Organizational Psychology*. Rand McNally, Chicago, IL.

Luijters, K. et al. (2006). Acculturation strategies among ethnic minority workers and the role of intercultural personality traits. *Groups Processes and Intergroup Relations*, 9, 561–575.

Magana, C.G.H. & Hovey J.D. (2003). Psychosocial stressors associated with Mexican migrant farmworkers in the Midwest United States. *Journal of Immigrant Health*, 5, 75–86.

Mass, W. (2014). Our fascinating immigrant experience. *The New American*, January 6, 37–39.

Mobed, K.G., Gold, E.B. & Schenker, M.B. (1992). Occupational health problems among migrant and seasonal farm workers. *Western Journal of Medicine*, 157, 367–373.

Naicker, S.P.-R. et al. (2009). Shortage of healthcare workers in developing countries — Africa. *Ethnicity and Disease*, 19, S1–S60.

Nicolao, J. (2011). *Migraciones Intrarregionales en Sudamérica (ARI)*. Real Instituto Elcano, Madrid, SPA.

Núñez, L.H. & Holper, D. (2011). In Peru nobody dies of hunger weight loss and food practices among Peruvian domestic workers in Chile. In: Vysma, M. T. M. (ed.), *Roads & Boundaries. Travels in Search of (Re)connection*. AMB Diemen, Cambridge, UK.

Office of Immigration Statistics (2013). *Yearbook of 2012 Immigration Statistics*. U.S. Department of Homeland Security, Washington, DC.

Ogunsiji, O. et al. (2012). Beginning again: West African women's experiences of being migrants in Australia. *Journal of Transcultural Nursing*, 23(2), 279–286. Ojo, O.V., J.H.

Olgiati, A.C. et al. (2013). Are migrants going up a blind alley? Economic migration and life satisfaction around the world: Cross-national evidence from Europe, North America, and Australia. *Social Indicators Research,* 114, 383–404.

Omer, A.A. & Atkins, K. (2002). Lived experiences of immigrant nurses in New South Wales, Australia: Searching for meaning. *International Journal of Nursing Studies,* 39, 495–505.

Oso Casas, L.G. & Garson, J.P. (2005). The feminisation of international migration. "Migrant women and the labour market: Diversity and challenges". OECD and European Commission seminar, Brussels, BEL.

Pavez Soto, I. (2012). Chile — Las otras discriminaciones: Niñas y niños peruanos inmigrantes. *Alterinfos America Latina.* 01 July 2012. Available at: http://www.elquintopoder.cl/sociedad/las-otras-discriminaciones-ninas-y-ninos-peruanos-inmigrantes-en-chile/. Accessed 25 August 2015.

Picot, G.S. & Sweetman, A. (2005). *The deteriorating economic welfare of immigrants and possible causes.* Analytical Studies Branch Research Paper Series, Statistics Canada, Update 2005, No. 262.

Pizarro, C. (2012). El racismo en los discursos de los patrones Argentinos sobre inmigrantes laborales Bolivianos: Estudio de caso en un lugar de trabajo en Córdoba, Argentina. *Revista de Ciencias Sociales,* 19, 255–285.

Pochobradsky, E.H. et al. (2002). *Soziale Ungleichheit und Gesundheit. [Social inequality and health].* Österreichisches Bundesinstitut für Gesundheitswesen, Vienna.

Premji, S. & Smith, P. (2013). Education-to-job mismatch and the risk of work injury. *Injury Prevention,* 19(2), 106–111.

Rao, N.M. & Mitra, A. (2013). Migration, representations, and social relations: Experiences of Jharkhand labor to Western Uttar Pradesh. *The Journal of Developmental Studies,* 49, 846–860.

Rasanen, K. et al. (2011). Interventions to reduce risky sexual behaviour for preventing HIV infection in workers in occupational settings. Available at: The Cochrane Library, doi: 10.1002/14651858. CD005274.pub3. Accessed 25 August 2015.

Raveesh, S. (2013). Brain drain: Socio-economic impact on Indian society. *International Journal of Humanities and Social Science Invention,* 2, 12–17.

Reid, A.L. et al. (2014). Taking risks and survival jobs: Foreign-born workers and work-related injuries in Australia. *Safety Science,* 70, 78–386.

Reitz, J.G. (2001). Immigrant skill utilization in the Canadian labour market: Implications of human capital research. *Journal of International Migration and Integration,* 2, 347–378.

Reitz, J.G. (2005). Tapping immigrant's skills: New directions for Canadian immigration policy in knowledge economy. *IRPP Choices,* 11(1), 1–18.

Reitz, J.G. (2007). Immigrant employment success in Canada, part i: Individual and contextual causes. *Springer Science,* 8, 11–36.

Rowland, B.T. et al. (2003). Preventing Drug Related Harm in Communities Characterised by Cultural and Linguistic Diversity. Technical Report 8. Australian Drug Foundation, Melbourne, AUS.

Sachs, J.D. (2005). *The End of Poverty: Economic Possibilities for Our Time.* Penguin Books, New York, NY.

Salih, I.I. (2013). Dissecting domestic workers' problems: Domestic or international way out-which way forward? Available at: Social Science Research Network. http://papers.ssrn.com/sol3/papers.cfm?abstract_id=2365753. Accessed 2 August 2015.

Schenker, M. (2008). Work-related injuries among immigrants: A growing global health disparity. *Occupational and Environmental Medicine,* 65(11), 717–718.

Sequist, T.D. et al. (2010). Cultural competency training and performance reports to improve diabetes care for black patients: A cluster randomized, controlled trial. *Annals of Internal Medicine,* 152, 40–46.

Sharma, J.R. (2013). Marginal but modern: Young Nepali labor migrants in India. *Young,* 21, 347–362.

Singh, M.D.L. & de Looper, M. (2002). Australian health inequalities: Birthplace. Australian Insititue of Health and Welfare, Canberra, AUS.

Smith, P.M. & Mustard, C.A. (2007). Comparing the risk of work-related injuries between immigrants to Canada and Canadian-born labour market participants. *Occupational and Environmental Medicine,* 66, 361–367. doi:10.1136/oem.2007.038646.

Stilwell, B.D. et al. (2004). Migration of health-care workers from developing countries: Strategic approaches to its management. World Health Organanization.

Syed, I.U. (2013). Occupational health of newcomers and immigrants to Canada. Third Cross-Cultural Health Care Conference: Collaborative and Multidisciplinary Interventions. *Hawai'i Journal of Medicine and Public Health,* 72(8), S3, 27.

Syed, J.P. & Pio, E. (2010). Veiled diversity? Workplace experiences of Muslim women in Australia. *Asia Pacific Journal of Management,* 27, 115–137.

Tedeschi, A.B. et al. (2000). Onset of allergy and asthma symptoms in extra-European immigrants to Milan, Italy: Possible role of environmental factors. *Clinical and Experimental Allergy,* 33(4), 449–454.

Texido, E.W. & Warn, E. (2013). Migrant well-being and development: South America. International Organization for Migration, Geneva, SWI.

Thom, D.H. et al. (2006). Development and evaluation of a cultural competency training curriculum. *BMC Medical Education,* 6, 1–9. doi:10.1186/1472-6920-6-38.

Trajkovski, S.L. & Loosemore, M. 2006. Safety implications of low-English proficiency among migrant construction site operatives. *International Journal of Project Management,* 24, 446–452.

Triandis, H.C. (1994). Theoretical and methodological approaches to the study of collectivism and individualism. In: Kim, U. Triandis, C. Kagitcibasi, C. Choi, S. &

Yoon, G. (eds.), *Individualism and Collectivism: Theory, Method and Applications*. Sage, Thousand Oaks, CA.

Tsai, J.H. (2009). Chinese immigrant restaurant workers' injury and illness experiences. *Archives of Environmental and Occupational Health*, 64, 107–114.

Tsai, J.H. & Thompson, E.A. (2013). Impact of social discrimination, job concerns, and social support on Filipino immigrant worker mental health and substance use. *American Journal of Industrial Medicine*, 56, 1082–1094.

United Nations Educational, Scientific and Cultural Organisation (1999). Globalisation and international migration in Latin America and the Caribbean: Trends and prospects for the 21st century. Migration Studies Network for Latin America and the Caribbean. UNESCO, Paris, FRA.

United Nations Department of Economic and Social Affairs/Population Division (2013). Net international migration. International Migration Report. United Nations, New York, NY.

Wade, P. & Bernstein, B. (1991). Culture sensitivity training and counselor's race: Effects on black female clients' perceptions and attrition. *Journal of Counseling Psychology*, 38, 9–15.

Weiss, R. (2003). Macht Migration krank? Eine transdisziplinäre Analyse der Gesundheit von Migrantinnen und Migranten, [Does migration cause diseases? A transdisciplinary analysis of the health of migrants] Zürich, SWI.

Williams, D.R.N. et al. (2003). Racial/ethnic discrimination and health: Findings from community studies. *American Journal of Public Health*, 93, 200–208.

Wong, D.F. et al. (2008). Mental health of migrant workers in China: Prevalence and correlates. *Social Psychiatry and Psychiatric Epidemiology*, 43(6), 483–89.

Wong, D.F. & Leung, G. (2008). The functions of social support in the mental health of male and female migrant workers in China. *Health and Social Work*, 33, 275–285.

World Health Organization (2007). Health of migrants, Executive board EB 122/11, 122nd Session, 20 December 2007, Provisional agenda item 4.8. Retrieved from http://www.who.int/hac/techguidance/health_of_migrants/B122_11-en.pdf. Accessed 5 February 2015.

Wren, K.B. & Boyle, P. (2002). Migration and work-related health in Europe. National Institute for Working Life, Stockholm, SWE.

# Chapter 15

# The morbid effects associated with racism experienced by immigrants: findings from Australia

Professor Kevin Dunn, Professor Yin Paradies, Ms Rosalie Atie and Dr Naomi Priest

Racism can be defined as the avoidable and unfair inequalities in power, resources, capacities and opportunities across racial or ethnic groups, occurring through stereotypes, prejudices, violence or discrimination that range from racial slurs to deeply embedded inequities in social systems and structures (Berman and Paradies, 2010). In the context of increasing globalisation and unprecedented migration flows across the world, racism remains a social problem of worldwide significance (United Nations, 2009). Survey evidence from around the globe indicates that racism is on the rise in Europe (Brika et al., 1997; Semyonov et al., 2006), the USA (Gallup Poll, 2014), the UK (The Guardian, 2014) and Australia (Markus, 2014).

Racism has been found to be associated with a series of morbidities and socioeconomic malaise. Global research has made a consistent link between mental ill-health and the ongoing and cumulative experience of racism (Pascoe and Richman, 2009; Williams and Mohammed, 2009;

Brondolo et al., 2011; Conklin and Hokulea, 2011; Goto et al., 2013; Schmitt et al., 2014; Paradies, 2006). There is also evidence that racism is associated with economic costs (Paradies et al., 2015) within workplaces such as labour turnover, absenteeism and the regulatory costs associated with complaint resolution (Triana, Jayasinghe and Pieper, in press). Racism is also linked to political instability, giving rise to public disorder and widespread civil disturbance (Noble, 2009). Racism can also undermine sense of belonging among target minority groups, undermining social cohesion and collective citizenship (Nelson et al., 2011). Research has also shown that migration are often more exposed, in general, to racism than non-migrants (Dunn et al., 2004). This is particularly the case where there has been substantial migration into a country from relatively new sources, and in circumstances where the official reception and settlement support of immigrants is not propitious. The diversity associated with migration is likely to be poorly received by a large part of the population if there is no widespread consent to a broad and inclusive definition of citizenship (Forrest and Dunn, 2010).

Racism has morbidities not only upon targets but also upon the associates of targets and upon the witnesses of those acts. Research has also shown that families and friends are negatively affected by vicarious racism (Tran, 2014; Priest et al., 2012; Halim et al., 2013; Chrobot-Mason et al., 2013). Vicarious racism is defined as hearing about or seeing another person's experience of racism (Harrell, 2000) as well as carers or close family members, including children and adolescents, experiencing discrimination that may or may not be witnessed by them (Priest et al., 2012; 2013).

In this chapter, we report Australian data on the impacts of vicarious racism for non-relative or peer witnesses of racism. The experience of racism can be stressful for a witness, and we report in this chapter on negative emotions that are felt in such circumstances, such as stress or anger, as well as physical effects (pounding hearts, headache). Witnesses of racism also face a pro-social challenge — to speak up or stay silent. There are of course many responses and actions to racism with various typologies developed (Paradies, 2006; Girndt, 2010; Lamont et al., 2012) and a growing body of empirical research on the best approaches to "coping" with or combating racism in its aftermath (Brondolo *et al.*, 2009; Seaton *et al.*, 2014; Miller *et al.*, 2013; Benjamins, 2013; Paradies and Cunningham, 2012a; Paradies and Cunningham, 2012b; Lee and Ahn, 2012). This work predominantly focuses on coping strategies of targets rather than witnesses. Complete or unsatisfactory inaction may be linked to regret and other phenomena that can lead to ill-health, in and of themselves, such as rumination (Utsey *et al.*, 2013; Borders and Liang, 2011) and vigilance (Karlsen and Nazroo, 2004; Lindstrom, 2008; LaVeist, Thorpe Jr and Pierre, 2014; Himmelstein *et al.*, 2015; Hicken *et al.*, 2013; 2014). Previous studies suggest that passive coping tends to worsen the detrimental impacts of racism on health while active coping can reduce these morbidities (Krieger, 1990; Noh and Kaspar, 2003; Tull *et al.*, 2005; Wei *et al.*, 2008; Alvarez and Juang; 2010; Cardarelli *et al.*, 2010; West *et al.*, 2010; Krieger and Sidney, 1996; Paradies and Cunningham, 2012a; 2012b; Sanchez *et al.*, in press).

In this chapter, first we report on the uneven experience of racism in Australia across ethnic groups and aim to reveal the burden of racism upon migrants. Second, we outline the extent to which morbidities are associated with those experiences of racism. Third, we analyse the differential impacts of racism on targets and witnesses. Finally, we explore how these effects play out within the new media world of online interaction, including social media.

In presenting these data, we acknowledge that the categorisation of "race", "ethnicity", "culture" and "language" in data collection, public policy, and within everyday vernacular, is predominantly driven by historical and contextual circumstances and politics, and that these "categories" are often combined and conflated (Nobles, 2000). As a result, quality data on the health of migrants, and on their experiences of racism, is currently limited in Australia, where country of birth and/or language spoken at home are used as proxies rather than self-reported ethnicity or race (Sevoyan and Hugo, 2013). These proxies are often collapsed into binary "English speaking/non-English speaking" or "Overseas born/Australian born" categories. Doing so creates highly heterogeneous groupings across multiple characteristics, such as nativity, migration experience and ethnicity, leading to considerable potential for misinterpretation of findings and conflation of differences between distinctive sub-groups of ethnic minorities. Notwithstanding these data limitations, it remains important to report data using these categories to illuminate uneven patterns of experiences and outcomes, while at the same time advocating for a more nuanced collection of ethnicity and migration status.

In this context, here we use language spoken at home as an indicator of non-Anglo and non-majority group status with speaking a language other than English (LOTE) at home considered a proxy for "migrant". In doing so, we acknowledge that not all migrants come from non-English speaking source countries, and English-only migrants are assumed not to face the same level racism burden. Using LOTE also includes those whose parents were born overseas, that is, the children of migrants.

## Method and sources

This chapter draws upon three surveys carried out by the Australian-based Challenging Racism Project team. Challenging Racism: the Anti-Racism Research Project team perceived a lack of comprehensive data on the nature of racism in Australian society. Their emphasis was to collect defensible empirics on the extent and variation of racist attitudes and experiences to inform anti-racism. Large-scale telephone and online surveys were conducted. A telephone survey used here collected detail on the experiences of racism by Australians, including the forms of racist experience (name-calling, exclusion, violent incitement, discrimination). The survey was carried out by the Hunter Valley Research Foundation between January and March 2006, among residents of all states and territories, excluding Tasmania. It achieved a completed sample of 4,020.

The Bystander Survey was conducted online in March 2014. Over the eight-day survey period, 3,920 online panellists were emailed the survey link and 1,068 (or 27%) indicated that they had witnessed an incident that they thought involved racism in the previous 12 months. The sample generation was contracted to a commercial online provider, MyOpinion. Data were collected on the respondents' actions and feelings after witnessing racism.

To obtain insight into racism and morbid effects in the online world, we used data from The Cyber Racism Survey. This online survey used the same categories of racism as in the telephone survey, but adapted those for Internet platforms like Facebook, Twitter, YouTube and, more broadly, on

Internet forums. The survey also examined the extent of the morbid effects of such encounters (sense of wellbeing, belonging, etc.), and the actions taken by respondents (report, formal complaint, ignore, engage with, etc.). MyOpinion provided two online panels: one reflecting the demographics of the Australian population aged 15–54 as at the 2011 Census (mirroring the ethnic diversity of Australia), the other being drawn from groups significantly at risk of racism, including Australians from the following groups: Indigenous Australians ($n = 58$), Australians of North African and Middle Eastern background ($n = 34$), Australians of south-east Asian background ($n = 192$), Australians from north-east Asian background ($n = 266$) and Australians from southern and central Asian background ($n = 142$). Panel participants self-nominated to participate in the survey. The data were collected in December 2013 and the total number of respondents was 2,141. The age range of respondents in the three surveys were spread fairly evenly across most age brackets (excluding those under 18 years of age) and roughly half the respondents were male and half female.

## Experiences of racism

Table 1 outlines the rates of exposure to racism in Australia. Almost one-in-five (19%) respondents reported that they had experienced racist talk, such as verbal abuse, name-calling, racist slur or ridicule, based on their cultural background. The rates of experiences in the form of exclusion was the next most prevalent (11%) followed by discriminatory treatment on the basis of ethnicity (7%) and then physical attack or threat (6%). Table 1 also shows dramatic variation across those who do and do not speak a LOTE at home. The LOTE variable is a proxy for migrants in this chapter. Table 1 shows that among the LOTE respondents the experience of race hate talk was shared by over one-third of respondents (36%), whereas this was only the case for 15% of non-LOTE respondents. We also tested for variations across ancestry, and 45% of those respondents with a north African and Middle-Eastern ancestry had been a focus of race hate talk. The percentage rates of exposure to exclusionary racism (which includes being made to feel like you don't belong or are inferior, people avoiding you, etc.) were four times those for non-LOTE Australians, and the same was true for unfair treatment (discrimination in accessing scarce resources,

Table 1: Experience of racism, migrants and non-migrants, Australia, 2006

|  |  | LOTE n | LOTE % | No LOTE n | No LOTE % | Total n | Total % |
|---|---|---|---|---|---|---|---|
| Racist talk | Yes | 273 | 35.8 | 486 | 14.9 | 759 | 18.9 |
|  | No | 489 | 64.2 | 2,771 | 85.1 | 3,260 | 81.1 |
|  | Total | 762 | 100 | 3,257 | 100 | 4,019 | 100 |
| Exclusion | Yes | 193 | 25.3 | 245 | 7.5 | 438 | 10.9 |
|  | No | 570 | 74.7 | 3,012 | 92.5 | 3,582 | 89.1 |
|  | Total | 763 | 100 | 3,257 | 100 | 4,020 | 100 |
| Unfair treatment | Yes | 143 | 18.7 | 141 | 4.3 | 284 | 7.1 |
|  | No | 620 | 81.3 | 3,116 | 95.7 | 3,736 | 92.9 |
|  | Total | 763 | 100 | 3,257 | 100 | 4,020 | 100 |
| Attack | Yes | 63 | 8.3 | 165 | 5.1 | 228 | 5.7 |
|  | No | 700 | 91.7 | 3,092 | 94.9 | 3,792 | 94.3 |
|  | Total | 763 | 100 | 3,257 | 100 | 4,020 | 100 |

Source: The Experiences of Racism Survey, Challenging Racism: the Anti-Racism Research Project, url: http://www.uws.edu.au/__data/assets/pdf_file/0020/37037/DunnQuestionnaire.pdf.

goods and services or unfair scrutiny, etc.). Rates of attack (threats and violence towards self or property) were smaller for all Australians though the LOTE rates were still higher at 8% compared to 5%.

Table 2 examines effects from the experiences outlined in Table 1. One-fifth of those respondents who had experienced racism reported that it had weakened their sense of belonging, and the same proportion reported becoming bitter and cynical. One-third regretted a lack of action following the experience, raising the potential of rumination. However, not all targets reported these morbid effects, and 65% stated that they felt stronger as a result of the experience. Respondents who spoke a LOTE at home (our proxy for migrancy) were especially vulnerable to regret and especially a weakened sense of belonging. They were also more likely to report being toughened through the process. Research in the USA has found members of minority groups who are a focus of racism are socialised for dealing with that experience (Forsyth and Carter, 2012). Minorities are pre-armed by peers and family to be ready for the racism

Table 2: Attitudes and feelings in response to racist incidents*, migrants and non-migrants, Australia, 2006

|  |  | Agree** | Neither | Disagree*** | Total | p |
|---|---|---|---|---|---|---|
| Sense of belonging weakened | LOTE% | 28.9 | 8.3 | 62.8 | 100 ($n = 349$) | **0.000** |
|  | No LOTE% | 16.8 | 6.1 | 77.1 | 100 ($n = 590$) |  |
|  | Total% | 21.3 | 6.9 | 71.8 | 100 ($n = 939$) |  |
| Stronger as a result | LOTE% | 71.8 | 16 | 12.3 | 100 ($n = 351$) | **0.003** |
|  | No LOTE% | 61.7 | 18.8 | 19.5 | 100 ($n = 590$) |  |
|  | Total% | 65.5 | 17.7 | 16.8 | 100 ($n = 941$) |  |
| Bitter and cynical as a result | LOTE% | 22.1 | 7.4 | 70.5 | 100 ($n = 349$) | 0.917 |
|  | No LOTE% | 22.5 | 8.1 | 69.4 | 100 ($n = 592$) |  |
|  | Total% | 22.3 | 7.9 | 69.8 | 100 ($n = 941$) |  |
| Regret times I didn't act | LOTE% | 34 | 14.2 | 51.8 | 100 ($n = 338$) | **0.045** |
|  | No LOTE% | 26.3 | 15.5 | 58.2 | 100 ($n = 582$) |  |
|  | Total% | 29.1 | 15 | 55.9 | 100 ($n = 920$) |  |

Source: The Experiences of Racism Survey, Challenging Racism: the Anti-Racism Research Project, url: http://www.uws.edu.au/__data/assets/pdf_file/0020/37037/DunnQuestionnaire.pdf.
*Question wording: "How did you feel after experiencing the racist incidents we discussed?";
**Includes response options: agree and strongly agree; ***Includes response options: disagree and strongly disagree.

they are likely to experience, whereas this is not a form of training that members of privileged groups learn.

## Racist encounters as witnesses

Just over 27% ($n = 1,068$) of respondents to the 2014 Bystander Survey (total $n = 3,917$) said that they had witnessed a racist incident within the past 12 months. Of those 1,068 witnesses, 21.9% indicated that they spoke a LOTE ($n = 234$) while 77.2% indicated that they did not ($n = 825$). Those respondents were then asked about the positive and negative outcomes from their experience of the racist incident. These data suggest that witnessing a racist event can have morbid effects. However, the likelihood of such effect is not as strong as it pertains for the targets of racism, as discussed in the previous section. In the next section, we directly compare morbid effects for witnesses and targets in the online world using a unique dataset that allows for such comparisons. Table 3 does still show that the

Table 3: Negative outcomes of racist experiences, migrants and non-migrants, Australia, 2014

|  |  | Yes | No | Total | p |
|---|---|---|---|---|---|
| Effects on interpersonal relationships | LOTE% | 7.5 | 92.5 | 100 ($n = 241$) | **0.031** |
|  | No LOTE% | 4.1 | 95.9 | 100 ($n = 833$) |  |
|  | Total% | 4.8 | 95.2 | 100 ($n = 1,074$) |  |
| Targeted by perpetrator | LOTE% | 12.9 | 87.1 | 100 ($n = 255$) | 0.083 |
|  | No LOTE% | 9.2 | 90.8 | 100 ($n = 836$) |  |
|  | Total% | 10.1 | 89.9 | 100 ($n = 1,091$) |  |
| Guilt or shame | LOTE% | 3.3 | 96.7 | 100 ($n = 248$) | 0.377 |
|  | No LOTE% | 4.7 | 95.3 | 100 ($n = 838$) |  |
|  | Total% | 4.4 | 95.6 | 100 ($n = 1,086$) |  |
| Negative perception of certain groups | LOTE% | 3.4 | 96.6 | 100 ($n = 235$) | 0.581 |
|  | No LOTE% | 4.2 | 95.8 | 100 ($n = 832$) |  |
|  | Total% | 4 | 96 | 100 ($n = 1,067$) |  |
| Reputational damage | LOTE% | 7.9 | 92.1 | 100 ($n = 241$) | 0.179 |
|  | No LOTE% | 5.5 | 94.5 | 100 ($n = 831$) |  |
|  | Total% | 6.1 | 93.9 | 100 ($n = 1,072$) |  |
| Hostility or conflict | LOTE% | 3 | 97 | 100 ($n = 235$) | 0.902 |
|  | No LOTE% | 3.1 | 96.9 | 100 ($n = 829$) |  |
|  | Total% | 3.1 | 96.9 | 100 ($n = 1,064$) |  |
| Fight occurred | LOTE% | 5 | 95 | 100 ($n = 214$) | **0.001** |
|  | No LOTE% | 1.4 | 98.6 | 100 ($n = 829$) |  |
|  | Total% | 2.2 | 97.8 | 100 ($n = 1,070$) |  |

Source: Bystander Survey.

vicarious experience of racism did make one in 10 witnesses feel that they were targeted, and that one in 20 felt that it caused them reputational damage or threatened their interpersonal relationships. The latter was a negative outcome that was strongly felt by witnesses who spoke a LOTE at home. Only 2% of respondents witnessed a physical altercation as a consequence of this racist event. However, this was much more likely for those with a LOTE, affecting 5% of such witnesses (Table 3).

The National Bystander Survey in Australia also asked respondents for their feelings following the racist event they witnessed. These provide further insight into some morbid effects from racism, and we use the variable of LOTE to indicate the migrant experience from witnessing racism. Anger and annoyance (34%) and sadness and being upset (27%) were prominent among the negative feelings of witnesses (Table 4). Shame and humiliation (13%) and disgust (13%) were felt by just over one in 10 witnesses. Those witnesses who spoke a LOTE at home were statistically more likely to report feelings of sadness/upset, alienation, violation and anxiety. These are quite morbid effects. For example, 37% of LOTE witnesses reported feeling sad or upset, whereas this was reported by only 27% of non-LOTE witnesses. The rates of reported alienation and violation among LOTE witnesses were three times the rates for non-LOTE, and for anxiety, the rate was almost double (Table 4). Non-LOTE (our proxy for non-migrant) had a significantly higher reported rate of shame/humiliation than LOTE witnesses. LOTE Australians are more likely to be targets of racism, and so the relatively privileged groups of non-LOTE witnesses could be expected to feel a heightened level of shame for the events they witness.

## Racism and effect in the online world

When asked about online encounters of racism, 5% ($n = 103$) indicated that they had been targets of racist content online while 35% ($n = 744$) indicated that they had witnessed racist content online. This unique dataset shows us that the vicarious experience of racism online is seven times the experience as a target. Of those who spoke a LOTE at home ($n = 624$), 5% indicated that they had been a target of racist content online ($n = 31$), while 40% ($n = 238$) said that they had witnessed racist content online.

**Table 4:** Bystanders' feelings after racist encounter,** migrants and non-migrants, Australia, 2014

| | | Yes | No | Total | p |
|---|---|---|---|---|---|
| Guilty | LOTE% | 1.3 | 98.7 | 100 (n = 236) | **0.042*** |
| | No LOTE% | 0.2 | 99.8 | 100 (n = 826) | |
| | Total% | 0.5 | 99.5 | 100 (n = 1,062) | |
| Ashamed, humiliated or embarrassed | LOTE% | 6.4 | 93.6 | 100 (n = 236) | **0.000** |
| | No LOTE% | 15.4 | 84.6 | 100 (n = 837) | |
| | Total% | 13.4 | 86.6 | 100 (n = 1,073) | |
| Amused or happy | LOTE% | 1.7 | 98.3 | 100 (n = 235) | 0.254* |
| | No LOTE% | 0.8 | 99.2 | 100 (n = 826) | |
| | Total% | 1 | 99 | 100 (n = 1,061) | |
| Angry, annoyed or frustrated | LOTE% | 38 | 62 | 100 (n = 274) | 0.155 |
| | No LOTE% | 33.3 | 66.7 | 100 (n = 895) | |
| | Total% | 34.4 | 65.6 | 100 (n = 1,169) | |
| Anxious, fearful, intimidated or unsafe | LOTE% | 11 | 89 | 100 (n = 245) | **0.007** |
| | No LOTE% | 6 | 94 | 100 (n = 838) | |
| | Total% | 7.1 | 92.9 | 100 (n = 1,083) | |
| Sympathy or empathy for perpetrator | LOTE% | 10.6 | 89.4 | 100 (n = 245) | **0.017** |
| | No LOTE% | 6.1 | 93.9 | 100 (n = 831) | |
| | Total% | 7.2 | 92.8 | 100 (n = 1,076) | |
| Disgusted | LOTE% | 11.5 | 88.5 | 100 (n = 243) | 0.513 |
| | No LOTE% | 13.1 | 86.9 | 100 (n = 839) | |
| | Total% | 12.8 | 87.2 | 100 (n = 1,082) | |
| Powerless, hopeless or depressed | LOTE% | 3.4 | 96.6 | 100 (n = 237) | 0.228 |
| | No LOTE% | 2 | 98 | 100 (n = 835) | |
| | Total% | 2.3 | 97.7 | 100 (n = 1,072) | |
| Headache, upset stomach, tense, pounding heart or sweaty | LOTE% | 2.5 | 97.5 | 100 (n = 237) | 0.991 |
| | No LOTE% | 2.5 | 97.5 | 100 (n = 825) | |
| | Total% | 2.5 | 97.5 | 100 (n = 1,062) | |

(*Continued*)

## The Morbid Effects Associated with Racism Experienced by Immigrants 519

**Table 4:** (*Continued*)

| | | Yes | No | Total | p |
|---|---|---|---|---|---|
| Shocked or surprised | LOTE% | 7.1 | 92.9 | 100 ($n = 240$) | 0.162 |
| | No LOTE% | 4.8 | 95.2 | 100 ($n = 835$) | |
| | Total% | 5.3 | 94.7 | 100 ($n = 1,075$) | |
| Awkward or uncomfortable | LOTE% | 13 | 87 | 100 ($n = 247$) | 0.591 |
| | No LOTE% | 14.3 | 85.7 | 100 ($n = 100$) | |
| | Total% | 14 | 86 | 100 ($n = 1,107$) | |
| Sad, upset or hurt | LOTE% | 37 | 63 | 100 ($n = 265$) | **0.000** |
| | No LOTE% | 23.7 | 76.3 | 100 ($n = 855$) | |
| | Total% | 26.9 | 73.1 | 100 ($n = 1,120$) | |
| Alienated, invisible or loss of confidence | LOTE% | **6.2** | 93.8 | 100 ($n = 243$) | **0.000*** |
| | No LOTE% | 0.6 | 99.4 | 100 ($n = 827$) | |
| | Total% | 1.9 | 98.1 | 100 ($n = 1,070$) | |
| Disappointed | LOTE% | 5.4 | 94.6 | 100 ($n = 239$) | 0.628 |
| | No LOTE% | 4.7 | 95.3 | 100 ($n = 834$) | |
| | Total% | 4.8 | 95.2 | 100 ($n = 1,073$) | |
| Indifferent or disinterested | LOTE% | 4.6 | 95.4 | 100 ($n = 237$) | 0.184 |
| | No LOTE% | 7.1 | 92.9 | 100 ($n = 836$) | |
| | Total% | 6.5 | 93.5 | 100 ($n = 1,073$) | |
| Concerned | LOTE% | 2.1 | 97.9 | 100 ($n = 236$) | 0.575 |
| | No LOTE% | 2.8 | 97.2 | 100 ($n = 827$) | |
| | Total% | 2.6 | 97.4 | 100 ($n = 1,063$) | |
| Violated, offended or insulted | LOTE% | **7.4** | 92.6 | 100 ($n = 243$) | **0.000** |
| | No LOTE% | 1.4 | 98.6 | 100 ($n = 830$) | |
| | Total% | 2.8 | 97.2 | 100 ($n = 1,073$) | |
| Confused | LOTE% | 1.7 | 98.3 | 100 ($n = 236$) | 0.253* |
| | No LOTE% | 0.8 | 99.2 | 100 ($n = 830$) | |
| | Total% | 1 | 99 | 100 ($n = 1,066$) | |

*Source*: Bystander Survey.

*Notes*: *1 or more cells have an expected count of less than 5; **These data come from coded qualitative responses.

Of those who did not speak a LOTE at home ($n = 1,508$), 5% indicated that they had been a target of racist content online ($n = 72$), while one-third ($n = 506$) said that they had witnessed racist content online. Migrants would therefore be equally likely to experience racism as a target online as non-migrants, but would be much more likely to witness racism. The difference in terms of witnesses was statistically significant ($x^2 = 3.964$, $df = 1$, $p = 0.046$).

Table 5 reveals the stress associated with being either a target of racism online or from witnessing racism online, for both LOTE and non-LOTE respondents to the Cyber Racism Survey. Three-quarters of targets reported feeling stress from the encounter, whereas only 68% of witnesses reported such stress. For respondents who spoke a LOTE at home, the likelihood of stress from being a target was much higher than for non-LOTE speakers, and this was also true when witnessing racism. These

Table 5: Stressfulness of racist encounter, migrants and non-migrants, Australia, 2013

|  |  | LOTE spoken at home |  |  |  |
|---|---|---|---|---|---|
|  |  | Yes% | No% | Total% | p |
| TARGET | Stressful* | 83.9 | 70.4 | 74.5 | 0.152 |
|  | Not stressful | 16.1 | 29.6 | 25.5 |  |
|  | Total | 100 ($n = 31$) | 100 ($n = 71$) | 100 ($n = 102$) |  |
| WITNESS | Stressful* | 74.3 | 65.1 | 68 | **0.012** |
|  | Not stressful | 25.7 | 34.9 | 32 |  |
|  | Total | 100 ($n = 237$) | 100 ($n = 501$) | 100 ($n = 738$) |  |
| ALL | Worried** | 81.5 | 58.8 | 65.8 | **0.000** |
|  | Not worried | 18.5 | 41.2 | 34.2 |  |
|  | Total | 100 ($n = 557$) | 100 ($n = 1,246$) | 100 ($n = 1,803$) |  |

Source: The Cyber Racism and Community Resilience project, Available at: https://www.facebook.com/pages/Cyber-Racism-and-Community-Resilience/1488582398063427.

*Question wording: "How stressful was this racist encounter?" Stressful includes the following response options: a little stressful, somewhat stressful, very stressful and extremely stressful; **Question wording: "I worry about experiencing racism while online". Worried includes response options: Very often, often, sometimes, hardly ever. Targets and witnesses were not distinguished for this question, it was asked of the entire sample. Those who indicated that this question was not applicable have been excluded.

variations were significant, indicating that migrants are hit much harder by the experience of racism, and vicarious racism online. Similarly, Table 5 shows that worry about experiencing racism while online was much more likely among LOTE respondents (82%) than non-LOTE (59%). This indicates a substantial morbid burden for migrants online, and corresponds with North American work that indicated minorities have much higher rates of experience of racism online, and with negative consequences (Tynes *et al.*, 2013).

The data in Table 6 reflect the earlier findings from the Bystander Survey insofar as attitudes and feelings following an encounter with racism (Table 4). Feelings of shame and regret were expressed by one-third of those who experienced or witnessed racism online. About one-fifth reported weakened sense of belonging or bitterness as a result. It was the LOTE respondents who were especially so affected on sense of belonging (33% versus 19% for non-LOTE) and regretfulness about inaction (40% versus 32% for non-LOTE). LOTE respondents were also more likely to feel "ashamed to be Australian" as a result of the racism they had encountered online, which was a reverse of the data from the Bystander Survey, where non-LOTE were more likely to report shame/humiliation/embarrassment. The online experiences survey specifically attached shame to nationality (ashamed to be Australian), and the Bystander Survey added embarrassment to the question, and these together may explain the varied outcomes on shame between Tables 4 and 6. The variations between LOTE and non-LOTE on belonging, bitterness, shame at being Australian and regret were statistically significant. They indicate that migrants would report a stronger emotional load and burden from their experience of racism online. However, as with earlier findings from the non-online world, respondents speaking a LOTE at home were more likely to express a feeling of being stronger as a result of the encounter.

In Tables 7 and 8, we can compare witness and target feelings following their racist encounters. Anger and disgust were the feelings that were most prominent among those who had witnessed or been targets of racism online. Half of the targets and two-fifths of the witnesses felt anger or annoyance as a result of their racist encounter (Tables 7 and 8). Half of the witnesses and two-thirds of targets felt disgust. Interestingly, these two dominant effects were reversed as the leading and second most common

Table 6: Attitudes as a result of racist encounters online*, migrants and non-migrants, Australia, 2013

|  |  | Agree** | Neither | Disagree*** | Total**** | p |
|---|---|---|---|---|---|---|
| Sense of belonging weakened | LOTE% | 32.9 | 33.8 | 33.3 | 100 ($n = 538$) | **0.000** |
|  | No LOTE% | 18.7 | 32.2 | 49.1 | 100 ($n = 1,116$) |  |
|  | Total% | 23.3 | 32.7 | 44 | 100 ($n = 1,654$) |  |
| Ashamed to be Australian | LOTE% | 38.8 | 36.3 | 25 | 100 ($n = 521$) | **0.000** |
|  | No LOTE% | 29 | 34.6 | 36.4 | 100 ($n = 1,166$) |  |
|  | Total% | 32 | 35.1 | 32.9 | 100 ($n = 1,687$) |  |
| Negatively impacted my life | LOTE% | 23.1 | 40.7 | 36.2 | 100 ($n = 464$) | **0.000** |
|  | No LOTE% | 10.4 | 39.1 | 50.5 | 100 ($n = 924$) |  |
|  | Total% | 14.6 | 39.6 | 45.7 | 100 ($n = 1,388$) |  |
| Bitter and cynical as a result | LOTE% | 25.4 | 39.6 | 35 | 100 ($n = 512$) | **0.000** |
|  | No LOTE% | 14.3 | 35.1 | 50.6 | 100 ($n = 1,087$) |  |
|  | Total% | 17.8 | 36.6 | 45.6 | 100 ($n = 1,599$) |  |
| Regret times I did not act | LOTE% | 40.4 | 43.4 | 16.2 | 100 ($n = 493$) | **0.000** |
|  | No LOTE% | 31.5 | 44.3 | 24.2 | 100 ($n = 1,016$) |  |
|  | Total% | 34.4 | 44 | 21.6 | 100 ($n = 1,509$) |  |
| Stronger as a result | LOTE% | 43.4 | 44.7 | 11.9 | 100 ($n = 523$) | **0.000** |
|  | No LOTE% | 29.4 | 56.5 | 14.2 | 100 ($n = 1,031$) |  |
|  | Total% | 34.1 | 52.5 | 13.4 | 100 ($n = 1,554$) |  |

*Source*: The Cyber Racism and Community Resilience project, Available at: https://www.facebook.com/pages/Cyber-Racism-and-Community-Resilience/1488582398063427.

*These statements were posed to the entire sample. Those who indicated that the statements were not applicable to them have been excluded; **Includes response options: agree and strongly agree; ***Includes response options: disagree and strongly disagree; ****Only those who encountered racist content online as targets or witnesses are included here.

feelings across targets and witnesses. A feeling of powerlessness, anxiety or physical effects like a headache or pounding heart were less frequent. Nonetheless, 18% of targets and 15% of witnesses felt powerlessness. Anxiety was reported by 9% of targets and 5% of witnesses. One in 10 of

Table 7: Targets' feelings after racist encounter, migrants and non-migrants, Australia, 2013

|  |  | Yes | No | Total | p |
|---|---|---|---|---|---|
| Guilty | LOTE% | 16.1 | 83.9 | 100 (n = 31) | 0.149* |
|  | No LOTE% | 6.9 | 93.1 | 100 (n = 72) |  |
|  | Total% | 9.7 | 90.3 | 100 (n = 103) |  |
| Ashamed or humiliated | LOTE% | 22.6 | 77.4 | 100 (n = 31) | 0.081* |
|  | No LOTE% | 9.7 | 90.3 | 100 (n = 72) |  |
|  | Total% | 13.6 | 86.4 | 100 (n = 103) |  |
| Amused | LOTE% | 25.8 | 74.2 | 100 (n = 31) | 0.931 |
|  | No LOTE% | 18 | 54 | 100 (n = 72) |  |
|  | Total% | 25.2 | 74.8 | 100 (n = 103) |  |
| Angry, annoyed or frustrated | LOTE% | 54.8 | 45.2 | 100 (n = 31) | 0.402 |
|  | No LOTE% | 45.8 | 54.2 | 100 (n = 72) |  |
|  | Total% | 48.5 | 51.5 | 100 (n = 103) |  |
| Anxious or fearful | LOTE% | 16.1 | 83.9 | 100 (n = 31) | 0.081* |
|  | No LOTE% | 5.6 | 94.4 | 100 (n = 72) |  |
|  | Total% | 8.7 | 91.3 | 100 (n = 103) |  |
| Sympathy or empathy for perpetrator | LOTE% | 16.1 | 83.9 | 100 (n = 31) | 0.353 |
|  | No LOTE% | 9.7 | 90.3 | 100 (n = 72) |  |
|  | Total% | 11.7 | 88.3 | 100 (n = 103) |  |
| Disgusted | LOTE% | 35.5 | 64.5 | 100 (n = 31) | 0.744 |
|  | No LOTE% | 38.9 | 61.1 | 100 (n = 72) |  |
|  | Total% | 37.9 | 62.1 | 100 (n = 103) |  |
| Powerless, hopeless or depressed | LOTE% | 32.3 | 67.7 | 100 (n = 31) | **0.010** |
|  | No LOTE% | 11.1 | 88.9 | 100 (n = 72) |  |
|  | Total% | 17.5 | 82.5 | 100 (n = 103) |  |
| Headache, upset stomach, tense, pounding heart or sweaty | LOTE% | 9.7 | 90.3 | 100 (n = 31) | 0.994 |
|  | No LOTE% | 9.7 | 90.3 | 100 (n = 72) |  |
|  | Total% | 9.7 | 90.3 | 100 (n = 103) |  |

*Source*: The Cyber Racism and Community Resilience project, Available at: https://www.facebook.com/pages/Cyber-Racism-and-Community-Resilience/1488582398063427.*1 cell has expected count less than 5.

Table 8: Witness' feelings after racist encounter, migrants and non-migrants, Australia, 2013

|  |  | Yes | No | Total | p |
|---|---|---|---|---|---|
| Guilty | LOTE% | 4.2 | 95.8 | 100 ($n = 238$) | 0.230 |
|  | No LOTE% | 2.6 | 94.4 | 100 ($n = 506$) |  |
|  | Total% | 3.1 | 96.9 | 100 ($n = 744$) |  |
| Ashamed or humiliated | LOTE% | 14.3 | 85.7 | 100 ($n = 238$) | 0.077 |
|  | No LOTE% | 9.9 | 90.1 | 100 ($n = 506$) |  |
|  | Total% | 11.3 | 660 | 100 ($n = 744$) |  |
| Amused | LOTE% | 10.9 | 89.1 | 100 ($n = 238$) | 0.484 |
|  | No LOTE% | 9.3 | 90.7 | 100 ($n = 506$) |  |
|  | Total% | 9.8 | 90.2 | 100 ($n = 744$) |  |
| Angry, annoyed or frustrated | LOTE% | 48.7 | 51.3 | 100 ($n = 238$) | **0.007** |
|  | No LOTE% | 38.3 | 61.7 | 100 ($n = 506$) |  |
|  | Total% | 41.7 | 58.3 | 100 ($n = 744$) |  |
| Anxious or fearful | LOTE% | 7.6 | 92.4 | 100 ($n = 238$) | **0.012** |
|  | No LOTE% | 3.4 | 96.6 | 100 ($n = 506$) |  |
|  | Total% | 4.7 | 95.3 | 100 ($n = 744$) |  |
| Sympathy or empathy for perpetrator | LOTE% | 14.3 | 85.7 | 100 ($n = 238$) | 0.209 |
|  | No LOTE% | 11.1 | 88.9 | 100 ($n = 506$) |  |
|  | Total% | 12.1 | 87.9 | 100 ($n = 744$) |  |
| Disgusted | LOTE% | 48.7 | 51.3 | 100 ($n = 238$) | 0.945 |
|  | No LOTE% | 49 | 51 | 100 ($n = 506$) |  |
|  | Total% | 48.9 | 51.1 | 100 ($n = 744$) |  |
| Powerless, hopeless or depressed | LOTE% | 17.2 | 82.8 | 100 ($n = 238$) | 0.129 |
|  | No LOTE% | 13 | 87 | 100 ($n = 506$) |  |
|  | Total% | 14.4 | 85.6 | 100 ($n = 744$) |  |
| Headache, upset stomach, tense, pounding heart or sweaty | LOTE% | 5.5 | 94.5 | 100 ($n = 238$) | 0.095 |
|  | No LOTE% | 3 | 97 | 100 ($n = 506$) |  |
|  | Total% | 3.8 | 96.2 | 100 ($n = 744$) |  |

*Source*: The Cyber Racism and Community Resilience project, Available at: https://www.facebook.com/pages/Cyber-Racism-and-Community-Resilience/1488582398063427.

those who had been targets of racism online, and 4% for witnesses had experienced the physical effects (headache, upset stomach, tense, pounding heart or sweaty). There are clearly some morbid effects upon many people who encounter racism online, and it is worse for targets than witnesses.

Tables 7 and 8 also show the statistically significant variations in effect between LOTE and non-LOTE speakers. Disgust did not vary significantly across the two groups, however anger was more likely among LOTE respondents, especially those who had been witnesses to racism online. Powerlessness was felt more strongly by targets who were LOTE-speaking, at three times the rate (32% for LOTE and 11% for non-LOTE). There is evidence here that migrants bear a greater exposure to negative effect from the racism they experience online.

## Discussion

The nationwide Challenging Racism Surveys in Australia have shown that almost one-in-five Australians report having experienced racist talk. One-in-10 have experienced exclusion on the basis of an ethnicity and 7% have suffered unfair treatment or discrimination. Almost 6% had been the focus of racist violence, and 5% reported that they had been the target of racism online. Fifty per cent of respondents told us they had witnessed racism online. The data demonstrate that racism is a substantial social problem in Australia.

Those respondents who spoke a LOTE at home were consistently more likely to experience racism. Unfair treatment was four and a half times more likely for LOTE speakers, and exclusion was three and a half times more likely. The experience of racist talk was more than double for LOTE speakers, reaching 36%. In the online world, LOTE speakers were more likely to report that they had witnessed racism (38% vs. 34%) although LOTE and non-LOTE speakers reported the same rate of being a target of racism online. The encounter with racism is culturally uneven in Australia, and minority groups are more exposed.

Some of the concerning outcomes of racism, as recorded in the surveys, included the impact on the sense of belonging of respondents. Regret was also a strongly felt outcome, especially where there had been non-action in response to an encounter with racism. These were both more strongly felt by LOTE speakers, both in general and when online. Anger and disgust were prominent emotions among those who had been targets of racism and also those who had witnessed racism. Anger was stronger for LOTE speakers. Awkwardness was also a prominent feeling, but alongside disgust it was shared across LOTE and non-LOTE speakers who had witnessed racism. Disgust and awkwardness are shared negative effects that could be efficaciously focused on if attempting to mobilise broad support for anti-racism interventions. Negative effects included sadness, being upset and feeling alienated. This was much more so for the LOTE-speaking respondents. In general, the data show that respondents who spoke a LOTE felt more guilty, anxious/fearful, sad/upset/hurt, alienated and violated/offended than non-LOTE speakers. These are inner-directed disempowered effective responses (Paradies, 2006) that are associated with worse health outcomes for targets of racism. Given this high prevalence, it is particularly notable that one-third of LOTE respondents are upset by witnessing racism compared to only one-quarter of non-LOTE. Stress was reported by three-quarters of those who had been a target of racism online, and for 68% of those who had witnessed such racism. The stress impact on LOTE speakers was significantly higher (84% for targets and 74% for witnesses). The negative emotional impact was reflected in the uneven levels of worry, where the 82% of LOTE speakers worried about experiencing racism online, and only 59% of non-LOTE speakers did so.

There are also some lessons and resources perceptible in the findings. LOTE speakers felt more sympathy/empathy. As outward-directed empowered emotions (Paradies, 2006), these have been found to ameliorate the impacts of racism on the health for targets (Paradies and Cunningham, 2012a). Interestingly, non-LOTE respondents were more than twice as likely to feel ashamed, humiliated or embarrassed after witnessing racism (15%) compared to LOTE respondents (6%). It is unclear why this has occurred, but perhaps greater familiarity with experiences of racism (both as witnesses and targets) among LOTE respondents reduces such feelings over the long term. Finally, in two of the surveys there were findings that showed how LOTE speakers consider themselves stronger or toughened as a consequence of the encounters with racism. Nonetheless, it is not clear what the personal benefits of this toughening are, as there has been little empirical investigation of this in Australia. And the social effects of having minorities "hardened" to the experience of racism are not really known. Forsyth and Carter's (2012) work on minorities in the USA suggest that members of minority groups are being socialised to "put up" with racism, whereas members of privileged groups are not receiving such instruction. There is an uneven expectation of forbearance and an unfair dispensation of privileged ignorance.

## Conclusion

The three surveys used in this analysis provide a sense of the uneven impact of racism in a Western society like Australia. We have outlined the uneven experience of racism, and the impacts of that include negative emotions, as well as some physical effects. We deployed the oft-used LOTE variable to identify the generalised experience and feelings of a large component of Australian minorities. This served as an indicator of migrant status. This chapter reveals that those who speak a LOTE are more exposed to racism, both as targets and witnesses, and to the negative effects of that experience. This suggests that migrants, especially those from other than Anglo backgrounds, are exposed to a morbidity burden that is not endured by non-migrants.

## References

Alvarez, A.N. & Juang, L.P. (2010). Filipino Americans and racism: A multiple mediation model of coping. *Journal of Counseling Psychology* 57(2), 167–178.

Benjamins, M.R. (2013). Comparing measures of racial/ethnic discrimination, coping, and associations with health-related outcomes in a diverse sample. *Journal of Urban Health*, 90(5), 832–848.

Berman, G. & Paradies, Y. (2010). Racism, disadvantage and multiculturalism: Towards effective anti-racist praxis. *Ethnic & Racial Studies*, 33(2), 214–232.

Borders, A. & Liang, T.H. (2011). Rumination partially mediates the associations between perceived ethnic discrimination, emotional distress, and aggression. *Cultural Diversity & Ethnic Minority Psychology*, 17(2), 125–133.

Brika, J.G. & Jackson, J. (1997). Racism and xenophobia in Europe, Eurobarometer opinion poll no. 47.1. Employment, Industrial Relations and Social Affairs Directorate (DGV), the European Commission.

Brondolo, E. et al. (2009). Coping with racism: A selective review of the literature and a theoretical and methodological critique. *Journal of Behavioral Medicine*, 32(1), 64–84.

Brondolo, E. et al. (2011). Racism as a Psychosocial Stressor. In: Baum, A. & Contrada, R. (eds), *Handbook of Stress Science*, Springer, New York, NY, pp. 167–184.

Cardarelli, R. et al. (2010). Self-reported racial discrimination, response to unfair treatment, and coronary calcification in asymptomatic adults — the North Texas Healthy Heart study. *BMC Public Health*, 10(1), 285.

Chrobot-Mason, D. et al. (2013). Second hand smoke: Ambient racial harassment at work. *Journal of Managerial Psychology*, 28(5), 470–491.

Conklin, Hokulea H.D. (2011). Perceived Racism and Mental Health: A Meta-Analytic Review. Doctor of Philosophy, Brigham Young University, Provo, UT.

The Cyber-Racism and Community Resilience Project, https://www.facebook.com/pages/Cyber-Racism-and-Community-Resilience/1488582398063427. Accessed 1 August 2015.

Dunn, K.M. et al. (2004). Constructing racism in Australia. *Australian Journal of Social Issues*, 39(4), 409–430.

Forrest, J. & Dunn, K.M. (2010), Attitudes to multicultural values in diverse spaces in Australia's immigrant cities, Sydney and Melbourne. *Space and Polity*, 14(1), 81–102.

Forsyth, J. & Carter, R.T. (2012). The relationship between racial identity status attitudes, racism-related coping, and mental health among Black Americans. *Cultural Diversity and Ethnic Minority Psychology*, 18(2), 128–140.

Gallup Poll (2014). Race relations. Available at: http://www.gallup.com/poll/1687/race-relations.aspx. Accessed 2 April 2015.

Girndt, M. (2010). Responses to racial and ethnic discrimination: A study examining Indigenous people in Australia and Chile. PhD, University of Bielefeld, Bielefeld, GER.

Goto, J.B. et al. (2013). Systematic review of epidemiological studies on interpersonal discrimination and mental health. *Cadernos De Saude Publica*, 29(3), 445–459.

Halim, M.L. et al. (2013). Cross-generational effects of discrimination among immigrant mothers: Perceived discrimination predicts child's healthcare visits for illness. *Health Psychology*, 32(2), 203–211.

Hicken, M.T. et al. (2013). "Every Shut Eye, Ain't Sleep": The role of racism-related vigilance in racial/ethnic disparities in sleep difficulty. *Race and Social Problems*, 5(2), 100–112.

Hicken, M.T. et al. (2014). Racial/ethnic disparities in hypertension prevalence: Reconsidering the role of chronic stress. *American Journal of Public Health*, 104, 117–123.

Himmelstein, M.S. (2015). Vigilance in the discrimination-stress model for Black Americans. *Psychology and Health*, 30(3), 253–267.

Karlsen, S. & Nazroo, J. (2004). Fear of racism and health. *Journal of Epidemiology and Community Health*, 58, 1017–1018.

Krieger, N. (1990). Racial and gender discrimination: Risk factors for high blood pressure? *Social Science and Medicine*, 30(12), 1273–1281.

Krieger, N. & Sidney, S. (1996). Racial discrimination and blood pressure: The CARDIA Study of young black and white adults. *American Journal of Public Health*, 86(10), 1370–1378.

Lamont, M. et al. (2012). Varieties of responses to stigmatization: Macro, meso, and micro dimensions. *Du Bois Review: Social Science Research On Race*, 9(1), 43–49.

LaVeist, T.A. et al. (2011). Estimating the economic burden of racial health inequalities in the United States. *International Journal of Health Services*, 41(2), 231–238.

LaVeist, T.A. et al. (2014). The relationships among vigilant coping style, race, and depression. *Journal of Social Issues*, 70(2), 241–255.

Lee, D.L. & Ahn, S. (2012). Discrimination against Latina/os: A meta-analysis of individual-level resources and outcomes. *The Counseling Psychologist*, 40(1), 28–65.

Lindstrom, M. (2008). Social capital, anticipated ethnic discrimination and self-reported psychological health: A population-based study. *Social Science and Medicine*, 66(1), 1–13.

Markus, A. (2014). Mapping Social Cohesion: The Scanlon Foundation surveys 2014. Caulfield East: Australian Centre for Jewish Civilization.

Miller, B. et al. (2013). Coping with racial discrimination: Assessing the vulnerability of african americans and the mediated moderation of psychosocial resources. *Society and Mental Health*, 3(2), 133–150.

Nelson, J. et al. (2011). Australian racism and anti-racism: Links to morbidity and belonging. In: Mansouri, F. & Lobo, M. (eds.), *Migration, Intercultural Relations and Social Inclusion*, Ashgate Publishing, Surrey, UK, pp. 159–175.

Noble, G. (2009). *Lines in the Sand: The Cronulla Riots, Multiculturalism and National Belonging*. Institute of Criminology Press, Sydney, AUS.

Nobles, M. (2000). *Shades of Citizenship: Race and the Census in Modern Politics*. Stanford University Press, Stanford, CA.

Noh, S. & Kaspar, V. (2003). Perceived discrimination and depression: Moderating effects of coping, acculturation, and ethnic support. *American Journal of Public Health*, 93(2), 232–238.

Paradies, Y. & Cunningham, J. (2012a). The DRUID study: Exploring mediating pathways between racism and depressive symptoms among Indigenous Australians. *Social Psychiatry and Psychiatric Epidemiology*, 47, 165–173.

Paradies, Y. & Cunningham, J. (2012b). The DRUID study: Racism and self-assessed health status in an indigenous population. *BMC Public Health*, 12(131), 1–12.

Paradies, Y. (2006). Defining, conceptualizing and characterizing racism in health research. *Critical Public Health*, 16(2), 143–157.

Paradies, Y. Ben, J. Denson, N. Elias, A. Priest, N. Pieterse, A. Gupta, A. Kelaher, M. & Gee, G. (2015). Racism as a determinant of health: A systematic review and meta-analysis. *PLOS ONE*, 10(9) e0138511.

Pascoe, E.A. & Richman, L.S. (2009). Perceived discrimination and health: A meta-analytic review. *Psychological Bulletin*, 135(4), 531–554.

Priest, N. et al. (2012). Exploring relationships between racism, housing and child illness in remote Aboriginal communities. *Journal of Epidemiology and Community Health*, 66(5), 440–447.

Priest, N. et al. (2013). A systematic review of studies examining the relationship between reported racism and health and wellbeing for children and young people. *Social Science & Medicine*, 95(5), 115–127.

Sanchez, D.T. et al. (in press) Confronting as autonomy promotion: Speaking up against discrimination and psychological well-being in racial minorities. *Journal of Health Psychology*, in press.

Schmitt, M.T. et al. (2014). The consequences of perceived discrimination for psychological well-being: A meta-analytic review. *Psychological Bulletin*, 140(4), 921–948.

Seaton, E.K. et al. (2014). A moderated mediation model: Racial discrimination, coping strategies, and racial identity among black adolescents. *Child Development*, 85(3), 882–890.

Semyonov, M. et al. (2006). The rise of anti-foreigner sentiment in European societies, 1988–2000. *American Sociological Review*, 71(3), 426–449.

Sevoyan, A. & Hugo, G. (2013). Exploring Migrant Health in Australia. XXVII IUSSP International Population Conference, Busan, Korea.

The Guardian (2014). Racism on the rise in Britain. Available at: http://www.theguardian.com/uk-news/2014/may/27/-sp-racism-on-rise-in-britain. Accessed 2 April 2015.

Tran, A.G.T.T. (2014). Family contexts: Parental experiences of discrimination and child mental health. *American Journal Of Community Psychology*, 53(1–2), 37–46. doi: 10.1007/s10464-013-9607-1.

Triana, M.C. et al., Perceived workplace racial discrimination and its correlates: A meta-analysis. *Journal of Organizational Behavior*, 36(4), 491–513.

Tull, E.S. et al. (2005). Relationships between perceived stress, coping behavior and cortisol secretion in women with high and low levels of internalized racism. *Journal of the National Medical Association*, 97(2), 206–212.

Tynes, B. et al. (2013). Extending campus life to the internet: Social media, discrimination, and perceptions of racial climate. *Journal of Diversity in Higher Education*, 6(2), 102–114.

United Nations (2009). World Conference against Racism, Racial Discrimination, Xenophobia and Related Intolerance: Declaration and Programmeme of Action.

Utsey, S.O. et al. (2013). Development and validation of the prolonged activation and anticipatory race-related stress scale. *Journal of Black Psychology*, 39(6), 532–559.

Wei, M. et al. (2008). Moderating effects of three coping strategies and self-esteem on perceived discrimination and depressive symptoms: A minority stress model for Asian international students. *Journal of Counseling Psychology*, 55(4), 451–462.

West, L.M. et al. (2010). Coping with racism: What works and doesn't work for black women?" *Journal of Black Psychology*, 36(3), 331–349.

Williams, D.R. & Mohammed, S.A. (2009). Discrimination and racial disparities in health: Evidence and needed research. *Journal of Behavioral Medicine*, 32(1), 20–47.

# Section 3: Conclusion

# Chapter 16

# Globalisation and migration: reflections, policy directions and conclusion

Professor André M.N. Renzaho

Globalisation and international migration are two concepts that will continue to divide opinions depending on which side of the fence one is sitting on. People in remote villages with almost no roads and without any infrastructures can communicate with the rest of the world through mobile phones and the internet. They have access to the global market through the diffusion, adoption and use of information and communication technologies (ICTs) and ICT-based goods and services such as e-agricultures, mobile banking, borderless business-to-consumer electronic commerce, e-health solutions, and mobile agricultural services (Dermish *et al.*, 2011; Medhi *et al.*, 2009; Nabareseh and Osakwe, 2014; Ngugi *et al.*, 2010; Ruxwana *et al.*, 2010; Sharma, 2012). These few examples suggest that the manifestation of globalisation is being felt in remote human settlements of the developing nations and affecting how people interact with each other and their ecological environment. Remote communities' access to the global market is no longer dependent on new roads or rails or ports, it is occurring through migrant social and global technology networks.

Proponents of globalisation can point to the following benefits: greater free trade and associated reduction in trade and investment barriers, greater movement of labour which provides access to more and better-paying jobs, integrated regional trades, increased access to an abundance and diversity of goods and services for the consumer and associated lowered prices brought about by competition, increased capital flows, and increased access to and affordability of health care and associated improvements in health and overall living standards (Davis, 2006; Dunning, 1998; International Monetary Funds, 2008; Munck, 2010). Some policymakers have claimed that globalisation and expanded global markers could harm developing economies, increase individualism and consumerism and associated competition for resources with serious environmental costs, as well as the labour drain (Haque *et al.*, 2015; Ibarra and Carlos, 2015; Zoomers, 2010). However, the International Monetary Fund (2008) has noted that arguments of globalisation downwarding pressure on wages, causing the world's multinational corporations to scour the globe in search of the lowest-paid labourers, being able to deliver economic growth on its own, and shrinking states, are simply myths. Therefore, the lure of the expanded global markets and its benefits means that globalisation and international migration are here to stay and unavoidable, and will continue to dominate the international policy agenda for many years to come. Rather than focusing on challenges and risks arising from globalisation and international migration, there is an urgent need to celebrate the many benefits they bring with them.

While labour migration will continue to dominate the discussion around globalisation and people movements, research by the Organisation for Economic Co-operation and Development (OECD) on the impact of globalisation on the environment suggests that globalisation impacts the whole migration spectrum (Huwart and Verdier, 2013). Globalisation impacts directly and indirectly on people movement in various ways: by increasing greenhouse gas emissions; impoverishing biodiversity; by creating uneven political efforts; and creating capitalistic and democratic political systems that foster trade and cross-border mobility. Emerging evidence suggests that globalisation promotes $CO_2$ emissions from transport and increased industrial transformation, encourages deforestation and logging, reduces stocks of fish due to overfishing, and leads to uneven political efforts unable to take pro-environmental measures to prevent or repair the environmental damage due to the increased power and influence of multinational corporate organisations (Huwart and Verdier, 2013). Similarly, there is a direct relationship between globalisation and militarism. That is, globalisation promotes inequality, and economic inequalities are associated with more conflicts and civil wars (Staples, 2000). It has been hypothesised that the world economic system associated with globalisation promotes military economies over civilian economies, hence fuelling the means to wage war (Gencer, 2013; Staples, 2000).

Globalisation and its various aspects lead to the integration of the global workforce, which, in turn, facilitates voluntary migration through labour market mobility and the flow of skilled migrants from low- and middle-income countries to developed nations. In addition, the environmental consequences of globalisation could include natural and man-made disasters, which are responsible for forced migration. Therefore, there are some lessons that can be learnt from forced and voluntary migration to inform international social, economic and cultural policy agendas.

## Lesson 1: Prevention and management of forced migration

There has been a number of non-legally and legally binding frameworks put forward to better meet the needs of IDPs. Indeed, over the past 20 years, there has been notable and significant progress in the development of priorities and strategies related to the protection and assistance of and durable solutions for IDPs. This progress has been a result of the adoption and ratification of soft and hard laws, supported by implementation frameworks. It is also encouraging to see that the United Nations High Commissioner for Refugees (UNHCR) has developed guidelines on applicable criteria and standards relating to the detention of asylum seekers and undocumented migrants. Similarly, the UNHCR Handbook for Emergencies and the Sphere Humanitarian Charter and Minimum Standards have transformed how the international community responds to emergencies.

Due to the above guidelines, there have been improvements in emergency preparedness, response and management. Despite these successes, there is a long way to go in order to successfully alleviate suffering among forced migrants. First, the coordination and integration of non-legally and legally binding in response to the needs of IDPs at various levels of displacements remains very difficult. Due to competing national priorities and economic interests, and lack of political will and commitment, it is difficult to coordinate and integrate policies geared towards addressing the needs of IDPs. Second, there has been an increase in the number of asylum seekers and undocumented migrants locked up indefinitely in immigration detention facilities. Despite the UHNCR's guideline on detention and the existence of international human rights instruments, asylum seekers and undocumented migrants in immigration detention facilities continue to live in appalling conditions and to experience human rights abuses. Finally, forced migration and displacement remain a global phenomenon that threatens the effectiveness of development initiatives and the political stability of fragile states, and is a significant burden to the international community. There is no doubt that forced migration is a product of failed economic and political systems as well as social and cultural vulnerabilities to environmental hazards. The prevention and effective management of forced migration and its consequences may require a combination of political solutions, policies addressing the root causes of displacement, and human rights and advocacy frameworks. While apolitical humanitarianism has, to some extent, reduced the suffering of forced migrants through targeted programmes, it does not necessarily address causes of displacements.

## Lesson 2: Voluntary migration is unavoidable and is here to stay: myths vs. realities

### International migration and skilled labour shortages

Most developed countries have been experiencing labour shortages. Factors influencing the demand for skills in developed nations are summarised in Table 1. According to Cameron (2011) and Shah and Burke (2003), skill labour shortages can fall into three main rubrics: (1) *labour shortage*, which occurs when the supply of qualified workers who are available and willing to work under existing market conditions is far lower than the demand for workers for a particular occupation, (2) *skill gap*, which

Table 1: Factors influencing the demand for skills and level of shortages

| Demand for skills | |
|---|---|
| Domain | Factors |
| Participation | • Demographic change.<br>• Worker attraction and retention.<br>• Employment arrangements. |
| Market pressures | • Globalisation.<br>• Market expansion.<br>• Customer and consumer service demands.<br>• Competitiveness and productivity demands. |
| Technological change | • Technological advancement.<br>• E-Business. |
| Regulatory compliance | • Regulatory compliance.<br>• Health and safety issues.<br>• Insurance. |
| **Levels of shortage** | |
| Level 1 shortage | • Few people have the essential technical skills, but are not already using them. It may take a long training time to develop the skills and build human capital. |
| Level 2 shortage | • Few people have the essential technical skills but are not already using them. It may take a short training time to develop the skills and build human capital.<br>• Skills mismatch: A significant and sufficient number of people have the essential technical skills, but are not already using them. They are not willing to use the needed skills by applying for vacancies under current conditions.<br>• Quality gap: A significant and sufficient number of people have the essential technical skills, but are not already using them. They are willing to use the needed skills by applying for vacancies under current conditions but do not have some important qualities that employers are after. |

*Source*: Summarised from Cameron (2011), Richardson (2007) and Shah and Burke (2003).

occurs when employers cannot find adequately skilled people for available positions and fill such positions with under-skilled workers relative to the desired level, and (3) *recruitment difficulties*, a situation which occurs when employers are unable to fill vacancies even when the supply of workers is adequate either due to low remuneration, poor working conditions, reputation of the industry, and inflexible or unsatisfactory working arrangements. The level of skill labour shortage will depend on many factors including the characteristics and dimensions of employer demand, characteristics of and segmentations in labour supply, and immigration and labour demand (Anderson and Ruhs, 2009).

The characteristics and dimensions of employer demand for skill labour are complex and multifaceted, and are influenced by the demographic profile of the workforces, the socioeconomic conditions of the labour force and overall investment in skills development. For example, there has been a significant growth in female employment and prime age (25–54 years) male inactivity in most developed countries (Anderson and Ruhs, 2009). Prime age male inactivity in the United Kingdom has increased by more than five times since the early 1970s with unemployment rates remaining much the same (Faggio and Nickell, 2005). That is, there have been more inactive people of working age in the UK than unemployed. Prime age male inactivity refers to males classified as neither employed nor unemployed (without work and not looking for a job). They usually fall into one of the four categories: full-time students, looking after family, people who are sick or with disability, early retires (Faggio and Nickell, 2005). Labour market participation statistics by the European Statistics System of the European Commission indicate that in 2013 people outside the labour market across the European Union was 36.6% among people who had attained a low educational level (i.e. less than lower secondary), 20.5% among people with a medium educational level (at least lower secondary level, but less than tertiary) and 11.4% among people persons with a high educational level (Eurostat, 2015). That is, poorly educated people are more than three times more likely to be out of the labour market than for highly educated people. However, when examined by age group, the data reveal a more serious picture. The proportion of inactive people averaged 57.7% for persons aged 15–24 years (ranging from 30% in the Netherlands and 38.3% in Denmark, to 73.7% in Luxembourg and 72.8% in both Hungary and Italy, mainly due to education-related commitments), 37.3% for men and 53.6% for women aged 55–64 years (mainly due to early retirement, illness or disability, and personal or family responsibilities), and 8.6% for men and 20.8% of women aged 25–54 years (mainly due to family responsibilities).

The consequence of very high inactivity rates for young and old people means that there is a high demand for both unskilled and skilled labour, and international migration is one of the priority measures available to address such a shortage. Nonetheless, well-educated migrants find it very difficult to utilise their educational training due to issues related to overseas qualifications and skills recognition, local labour conditions, discriminatory practices and lack of proficiency in the language of the host country. They end up taking low-level work. Consequently, migrants find themselves in jobs for which they are overqualified. As can be seen from Table 2, in 13 out of 20 OECD countries (65%), the proportion of migrants in jobs for which they overqualified was greater than or equal to 50% higher than native-born workers (Fauth and Brinkley, 2006). The top 10 countries with a high ratio for foreign-to-native-born workers in overqualified jobs were Greece (39.3% vs. 9.0%), Italy (23.5% vs. 7.0%), Sweden (16.1% vs. 6.5%), Norway (20.3% vs. 8.4%), Canada (13.2% vs. 7.2%), Portugal (16.8% vs. 7.9%), Austria (21.1% vs. 10.3%), Czech Republic (10% vs. 5.2%), Spain (42.9% vs. 24.2%) and Germany (20.3% vs. 11.4%). With the majority of OECD countries experiencing a shift in the demand for labour against the unskilled since the 1980s (Faggio and Nickell, 2005), which has coincided with rampant economic growth in the Middle East and Asia, a significant number of highly qualified migrants have found themselves performing the so-called 3D jobs — "dangerous, dirty, and demeaning" jobs that inactive people in the host country are unwilling to fill. These jobs include the transport industry (e.g. taxis), construction work, and the agricultural, mining and health care sector (Czapka, 2012; Thomson, 2014). This pattern occurs due to factors such as the mismatch between migrants' skills and job expectations, discrimination and stereotypes in recruitment and selection practices, clashes in social and cultural values related to work ethic and productivity, and differing emphasis of recruitment channels such as migrant networks vs. recruitment agencies (Anderson and Ruhs, 2009).

## *Immigration impacts on government expenditures and revenues*

The question related to the costs and benefits of immigration will continue to polarise opinions in the international communities. The argument that

Table 2: Overqualification rates across the OECD, 2003–2004

|  | Total % | Native-born (A) % | Foreign-born (B) % | Ratio (B/A) |
|---|---|---|---|---|
| Greece | 11.3 | 9.0 | 39.3 | 4.4 |
| Italy | 7.0 | 7.0 | 23.5 | 3.6 |
| Sweden | 7.6 | 6.5 | 16.1 | 2.5 |
| Norway | 9.2 | 8.4 | 20.3 | 2.4 |
| Canada | 7.2 | 7.2 | 13.2 | 2.2 |
| Portugal | 9.0 | 7.9 | 16.8 | 2.1 |
| Austria | 11.5 | 10.3 | 21.1 | 2.0 |
| Czech Republic | 5.2 | 5.2 | 10.0 | 1.9 |
| Spain | 25.5 | 24.2 | 42.9 | 1.8 |
| Germany | 12.3 | 11.4 | 20.3 | 1.8 |
| Denmark | 10.9 | 10.4 | 18.6 | 1.8 |
| Ireland | 16.6 | 15.7 | 23.8 | 1.5 |
| Hungary | 6.4 | 6.4 | 9.7 | 1.5 |
| Belgium | 16.2 | 15.6 | 21.6 | 1.4 |
| USA | 14.0 | 13.4 | 18.1 | 1.4 |
| France | 11.6 | 11.2 | 15.5 | 1.4 |
| Australia | 20.4 | 19.0 | 24.6 | 1.3 |
| Finland | 14.4 | 14.3 | 19.2 | 1.3 |
| Switzerland | 10.5 | 10.0 | 12.5 | 1.3 |
| UK | 15.5 | 15.3 | 17.8 | 1.2 |

*Source*: Extracted from Fauth and Brinkley (2006).

immigration impacts on government expenditures though additional load on social welfare, education and health systems is tenuous. In reviewing the literature and analysing multi-country data from OECD countries, Liebig and Mo (2013) found that the fiscal impact of cumulative waves of migration over the years is around zero, averaging ±0.5% of GDP. Migrants' net positive contributions to the public purse as the proportion of the GDP averaged 0.3–0.7% in the UK, 0.5% in southern European countries, 0.8% in France, 1% in Germany, and about 2% in New Zealand, Switzerland and Luxembourg. They also found no difference between migrants and the native population in the take-up of social benefits while the average sums of social assistance, unemployment aid and pension paid out to recipient migrant households were significantly lower than those paid to native-born households. It has been estimated that migrants' fiscal contributions through employment-related taxes and social contributions through national insurance contributions are far greater than what they receive in benefits (OECD, 2014).

Data presented in this book suggest that immigration benefits both the sending and the receiving countries through five different channels: emigration, wages and economic adjustment; brain drain and labour markets effects of remittances on labour markets; diaspora networks and labour markets; and return migration and employment (Dayton-Johnson and Schwinn, 2009). On the one hand, as extensively discussed in Chapter 4, sending countries can immensely benefit from the emigration of skilled workers, provided adequate policies are in place to harness those benefits. Such benefits include the positive fiscal and social effects of remittances; increased social, human and financial capital through direct foreign investment and trade; transitional networks; brain circulation; and harnessing the diaspora, and technological, knowledge and skill transfer that can be facilitated by effective policies geared towards turning brain drain into brain gain. On the other hand, skilled migration schemes can have a positive impact on labour markets, tax revenues and overall economic growth in the receiving countries. First, skilled migration schemes allow receiving nations to provide targeted solutions to specific skill shortages (Cameron, 2011). For example, migrants account for a significant share of the workforce in OECD countries to fill important labour niches in targeted sectors of the economy, ranging from 47% of the workforce in the USA to 70% in Europe (OECD, 2014). Second, not only does the skilled migration scheme contribute to human capital development and technological progress in receiving countries, it also allows such countries to boost their declining working-age population, hence impacting positively on their economic growth (OECD, 2014). Finally, most rural areas in OECD countries are experiencing financial strain, social isolation, and depopulation associated with declining birth rate and mass out-migration of young people to urban areas, (OECD, 2010). The skilled migration provides governments with considerable discretion to formulate incentivised policies to influence the size, mix and promotion of migration to rural areas (Cameron, 2011).

Therefore, by contributing significantly to labour-market flexibility and filling strategic positions in important sectors of the economy, migrants contribute significantly to the public purse. However, it is worth acknowledging that efforts to compute migrants' net fiscal contribution remain complex and inconsistent. As Anderson and Ruhs (2009) point out, the results from studies estimating migrants' net fiscal contribution in receiving countries depend very much on the adopted methodology, the timeframe being considered and migrants' length of stay in receiving countries, the assumptions on inclusions and exclusions, specifications of which public services are pure public goods, choices of the discounting approach and the demographic unit of analysis (individuals or households). These differing methodological approaches make comparison across studies and between nations very difficult. Nevertheless, while approaches differ, the majority of studies have attempted to quantify migrants' net contribution and migration effects on government outlays from a welfare-spending perspective with consistent findings. That is, compared to native-born with similar characteristics, migrants are less likely to receive public assistance, and for those receiving social security and welfare benefits, they do obtain lower levels of transfers (Anderson and Ruhs, 2009).

## *Demographic transition in advanced and transition economies and international migration*

Most advanced and transition economies are experiencing serious demographic transitions. In most OECD countries, the demographic transition is characterised by a dramatic decline in birth rates, an increasingly ageing population, and a projected significant decline of the working age population and associated increase in the demographic dependency ratios. In transition economies and middle-income countries, the demographic transitions are mainly characterised by the influx of rural populations to urban areas, imbalanced gender ratio (especially in Asia due to the one-child policy in China and the preference for boys over girls in Asian cultures), an ageing population, and the continuing decline of the ratio of the prime working age to those less than 24 years and older than 55 years. The impacts of these demographic transitions are enormous, including their negative impact on economic growth. International migration has provided an avenue to counteract the negative effects of such demographic transitions in most advanced and transition economies. The various chapters presented in this book illustrate that the demand for migrants to address issues related to demographic transitions in receiving countries has led to various forms of migration, including direct labour migration, marriage migration, family reunion, and refugees and humanitarian entrants. Each form of migration brings with it some challenges and the need for immigration reforms in receiving countries. For example, the increased multiculturalism that accompanies migration requires reforms to put in place culturally competent policies to address issues related to migrants' cultural integration and issues related to racism. There are issues related to labour migration and occupation, and migration-related inequalities. The unbalanced sex ratio and unnatural selection and preference for boys over girls in Asian countries result in an increased demand for brides. However, marriage migration brings with it a range of serious challenges including intermarriage and domestic violence, intermarriage and fake marriage, intermarriage and human trafficking, international marriage and citizenship and legal status, and intermarriage and multiculturalism.

## Some policy recommendations

This section does not intend to be exhaustive in terms of policy options related to international migration. The chapters included in this book have been comprehensive in summarising region- and country-specific policies. In this section we focus on some of the policies with universal applicability that would maximise the social and economic benefits of internal and international migration. There is no doubt that international migration can be harnessed to promote productive investments that can transform the economic, social, political and cultural landscapes of both sending and receiving countries through partnership and policy reforms. Policy reforms should embrace tested cost-effective approaches that incorporate a combination of compensation-based policies (especially for permanent migrants), the diaspora option, the return of and retaining talents, and migration reforms.

## Restrictive migration policies are undesirable

Given that most advanced economies have developed and put in place legislative measures to facilitate the entry of skilled migrants to address labour shortage, policies geared towards restricting international mobility should be discouraged as they negatively impact on the economy. Restrictive migration policies discourage migrants with competitive alternatives while at the same time indirectly attracting older and lower-skilled migrants. Similarly, most countries have options for bonds to regulate migration flow. Under these options, applicants will need to deposit a bond, which is refundable if the migrant has not breached visa conditions (e.g. successful return to the country of origin within a specified timeframe as per visa conditions). Any breach of the visa conditions means that the bond would be subject to forfeiture. The problems with a bond-based restrictive migration policy include the fact that the push factors that force people to emigrate are not addressed. Such a policy favours only those who can afford to raise the required amount of money for the bond.

Those who aspire to emigrate to work abroad but cannot afford the cost of the bond are left demotivated and dissatisfied, hence affecting their work productivity and they could engage in corrupt and nepotistic practices as the last resort in order to achieve their dream of moving abroad. In contrast, those who can afford the bond may choose to forfeit it in order to avoid returning home because such an opportunity to work abroad may be a once-in-a-lifetime opportunity. Within the context of international migration and human rights, restricting people's freedom of movement may constitute human rights violations

## Remittance markets and diaspora savings for development

Remittances can have a significant impact on social, human and financial capital in sending countries. However, to maximise the impact of remittances, policy reforms need to address some of the legislative and economic barriers that impede the economic impact of remittances. Such policies should focus on smart remittance price reduction interventions, promoting direct investments from diaspora savings, and monitoring and reducing the use of remittances for the purpose of money laundering and terrorism-financing risks. However, assessing the size of remittances and the diaspora savings may require the sending countries to implement best practices related to emigration of skilled migrants including maintaining up-to-date migration databases (monitoring emigration and returnees) and recruitment databases through which employers can access, identify and recruit professional and skilled migrants; creating and maintaining socially and economically viable professional associations and networks to facilitate skill transfers; and effective taxation and financial services that minimise informal channels of remittance transfer such as hand deliveries.

## *Reverse brain drain by promoting the return of migrants and brain circulation*

Such policy reform should focus on effective and incentivised strategies supporting and promoting the return of international students who have graduated abroad, an effective engagement with the diaspora to return as expatriates and entrepreneurs, the physical return of the diaspora after training and work experience in industrialised nations through the promotion of dual nationality and flexible residential rights to facilitate technology and knowledge transfer, and the movement of highly skilled people between countries other than their country of origin.

## *Transnational diaspora option*

The diaspora is an important asset for economic development in sending countries. Apart from the technology and knowledge transfer and remittances summarised above, the diaspora has extensive international networks that can create links with the international trade and facilitate direct foreign investments. It is also possible that the impact of the diaspora option can be maximised through the recovery of economic losses in sending countries by imposing an effective taxation system on the diaspora saving and remittances in receiving countries. This money can be deposited as a national fund in the sending country to support the development of human resources, to create assets that promote employment such as firms, and to support technology transfer.

## Addressing inactivity

There are a number of options to address the consequence of inactivity. The first option would include policies that increase workforce participation, especially those that promote greater participation of young people and low-skilled workers through attractive professional development initiatives and incentives to lure young people into the workforce. Expanding and enhancing the lure of certain occupations traditionally neglected and poorly paid- such as respite care, attendant care, personal care or home care- to create more demand for an entry job could increase workforce participation among those who are inactive. Increasing the retirement age and the age at which pension is entitled is another option. Policies geared towards boosting the prime working age through strategic migration schemes should be a priority. Such policies need to build on migrants' resilience and adaptability to encompass programmes that promote their integration into the workforce and offer further training opportunities. However, refugees and humanitarian entrants are also an asset in receiving countries in the long run as long as there are policies promoting and supporting their integration and addressing their training needs. The successful integration of skilled migrants as well as refugees and humanitarian entrants requires a multifaceted package of policies to (1) address barriers related the recognition of overseas skills and qualification, (2) ensure jobs' requirements are commensurate with migrants' skills and qualifications, (3) put in place programmes addressing the social and cultural needs of migrants' families (e.g. network opportunities to address isolation or education opportunities for children), (4) embed cultural competence in all aspects of work policies in order to promote cultural pluralism and eliminate discrimination, and (5) implement employment and language support (e.g. assistance with job search for skilled migrants' partners or further language courses).

## Bridging the rural–urban divide

Most low- and middle-income countries (LMICs) have experienced an astounding proliferation of national and international NGOs. The significant increase in the number of NGOs brings with it the demand for highly qualified professionals and skilled individuals. To sustain such demand,

NGOs rely on poaching staff from government departments as they can offer higher salaries and further training opportunities than what the government provides. Therefore, the presence of NGOs in LMICs has translated into scarcity of staff for the public sector. NGOs' hiring of specialised staff from the public system on very high salaries means that governments have been deprived of a much needed workforce, hence leading to the deteriorating conditions of the public system. In addition, poverty, lack of opportunities, and neglect force rural-based professionals and skilled individuals to relocate to urban areas to fill vacant positions in the public sector resulting from aggressive NGO recruitments, and in search of better opportunities, and advanced facilities.

In order to address the rural–urban divide, there are a number of policy options. The obvious one is to promote and monitor the NGO voluntary code of practice and put in place administrative and legislative measures that govern NGO recruitment practices including salary capping. Another policy option is to facilitate rural–urban linkages through structural adjustments and economic reforms to promote the economic development of rural areas and knowledge exchange between rural and urban areas. The economic reforms should consider creating incentivised job opportunities (e.g. tax concessions, extra pay, subsidised accommodation, specialised professional development and training, point-based incentivised professional registrations or migration schemes) to lure professional and skilled people back to rural areas.

## Conclusion

The argument that migration is bad for the economy remains a myth. What is clear from the various chapters in this book is that migration is good for the economy, provided that adequate and tested policies are put in place to govern the immigration system and border protection. The demand for highly skilled international migrants will continue to increase over the years as the ageing population in most developed countries continue to increase in tandem with low fertility rates. A package of policies addressing push factors such as the promotion of conflict prevention and work safety and security in sending countries, maximising brain circulation and harnessing the diaspora, would represent a viable option over restrictive migration policies.

# References

Anderson, B. & Ruhs, M. (2009). Who needs migrant workers? Introduction to the analysis of staff shortages, immigration and public policy. Centre on Migration, Policy and Society, University of Oxford, Oxford, UK.

Cameron, R. (2011). Responding to Australia's Regional Skill Shortages Through Regional Skilled Migration. *Journal of Economic and Social Policy*, 14(3), Article 4. Available at: http://epubs.scu.edu.au/jesp/vol14/iss3/. Accessed 28 April 2015.

Czapka, E. (2012). The health of new labour migrants: Polish migrants in Norway. In: Ingleby, D., Krasnik, A., Lorant, V. & Razum, O. (eds.), *Health Inequalities and Risk Factors among Migrants and Ethnic Minorities*, Garant Publishers, Antwerp, BEL. pp.150–163.

Davis, M. (2006). Planet of slums. *New Perspectives Quarterly*, 23(2), 6–11.

Dayton-Johnson, J. & Schwinn, J. (2009). Migration and employment. In: *Organisation for Economic Cooperation and Development, Promoting Pro-Poor Growth: Employment*. OECD, Paris, FRA. pp. 149–177.

Dermish, A. et al. (2011). Branchless and mobile banking solutions for the poor: A survey of the literature. *Innovations*, 6(4), 81–98.

Dunning, J.H. (1998). Location and the multinational enterprise: A neglected factor? *Journal of International Business Studies*, 29, 45–66.

Eurostat (2015). People outside the labour market. Available at: http://ec.europa.eu/eurostat/statistics-explained/index.php/People_outside_the_labour_market. Accessed 28 April 2015.

Faggio, G. & Nickell, S. (2005). Inactivity among prime age men in the UK. Centre for Economic Performance. London School of Economics and Political Science, London, UK.

Fauth, R. & Brinkley, I. (2006). Efficiency and labour market polarisation: Knowledge economy programme report. Work Foundation, London, UK.

Gencer, E.A. (2013). The Impact of Globalization on Disaster Risk Trends: A Macro- and Urban-Scale Analysis. Background Paper prepared for the Global Assessment Report on Disaster Risk Reduction. United Nations International Strategy for Disaster Reduction, Geneva, SWI.

Haque, M.Z. et al. (2015). Corporate social responsibility, economic globalization and developing countries: A case study of the ready made garments industry in Bangladesh. *Sustainability Accounting, Management and Policy Journal*, 6, 166–189.

Huwart, J. & Verdier, L. (2013). What is the impact of globalisation on the environment? In: Huwart, J & Verdier, L. (eds.), *Economic Globalisation: Origins and Consequences*, OECD Publishing, Paris, FRA, pp. 108–125. Available at: http://dx.doi.org/10.1787/9789264111905-8-en. Accessed 10 November 2014.

Ibarra, A. & Carlos, A. (2015). Mexican mass labor migration in a not-so changing political economy. *Ethnicities* 15, 211–233.

International Monetary Fund (2008). Globalization: A Brief Overview. Issue Brief 02/08. IMF Publication Services, Washington, D.C.

Liebig, T. & Mo, J. (2013). The Fiscal Impact of Immigration in OECD Countries. OECD, International Migration Outlook 2013, OECD Publishing, Paris, FRA. pp. 125–184. Available at: http://dx.doi.org/10.1787/migr_outlook-2013-6-en. Accessed 10 November 2014.

Medhi, I. *et al.* (2009). Mobile-banking adoption and usage by low-literate, low-income users in the developing world. *Lecture Notes in Computer Science* 5623, 485–494.

Munck, R. (2010). Globalization and the labour movement: Challenges and responses. *Global Labour Journal,* 1(2), 218–232.

Nabareseh, S. & Osakwe, C.N. (2014). Can business-to-consumer electronic commerce be a game-changer in Anglophone West African countries? Insights from secondary data and consumers' perspectives. *World Applied Sciences Journal,* 30(11), 1515–1525.

Ngugi, B. *et al.* (2010). M-PESA: A case study of the critical earlyadopters' role in the rapid adoption of mobile money banking in Kenya. *The Electronic Journal on Information Systems in Developing Countries (EJISDC),* 43(3), 1–16.

OECD (2010). OECD Rural Policy reviews: Québec, Canada. OECD, Paris, FRA.

OECD (2014). Is migration good for the economy? Migration policy debates. Available at: http://www.oecd.org/migration/mig/OECD%20Migration%20Policy%20Debates%20Numero%202.pdf. Accessed 2 January 2015.

Richardson, S. (2007). What is a skill shortage? National Centre for Vocational Education Research (NCVER), Adelaide, AUS.

Ruxwana, N.L. *et al.* (2010). ICT applications as e-health solutions in rural healthcare in the Eastern Cape province of South Africa. *Health Information Management Journal,* 39(1), 17–29.

Shah, C. & Burke, G. (2003). Skilled shortages: Concepts measurement and implications, Working Paper No. 52, November 2003, Centre for the Economics of Education and Training, Monash University, AUS. Available at: http://monash.edu/education/non-cms/centres/ceet/docs/workingpapers/wp52nov03shah.pdf. Accessed 10 June 2015.

Sharma, S.K. (ed.) (2012). E-Adoption and Technologies for Empowering Developing Countries: Global Advances. Information Science Refence, IGI Global, Hershey, PA.

Staples, S. (2000). The relationship between globalization and militarism. *Social Justice,* 27(4), 18–22.

Thomson, L. (2014). Migrant Employment Patterns in Australia: Post-Second World War to the present. Adult Migrant English Service, Melbourne, AUS.

Zoomers, A. (2010). Globalisation and the foreignisation of space: Seven processes driving the current global land grab. *The Journal of Peasant Studies*, 37, 429–447.

# Index

## A

Abandonment, 55
Abdominal Obesity, 91
Abolition of Slavery, 311
Abusive, 223, 246, 448, 451
Accident Litigations, 392
Accountability, 51, 58, 339
Account-to-Account, 178
Acculturation
    acculturating groups, 17
    acculturation theory, 16–17
    acculturative family distancing, 20
    Bi-Directional or Bi-Dimensional Model (*see also* BDM), 17, 19
    psychological acculturation, 17
Acute Food and Livelihood Crisis, 92
Acute Malnutrition, 43, 49–50, 89, 91, 93
Acute Phase of an Emergency, 84
Acute Respiration Infections (*see also* ARI), 47, 84
    Prevalence of ARIs, 84

Adaptation, 19–20, 98, 480–483, 486, 498
Adaptive Capacity, 87
Adequate Livelihood Assets, 92
Administrative and Legislative Measures, 549
Administrative Detention of Children, 227
Afghan Refugees, 108, 210, 313
Afghanistan Urban Refugees, 90
Africa
    1981 African Charter on Human and Peoples' Rights, 51
    2009 Kampala Convention, 59
    Africa's colonisation, 76
    African continent, 77, 139, 143, 186
    African countries, 60, 74, 76, 144–145, 153, 155, 186, 294, 496
    Africa Diaspora Initiative, 176
    Africa diaspora programme in 2010, 176

**554** *Index*

Intra-African emigration, 148
African Institute for Remittances, 176
African Refugee Convention, 99–100, 109
African states, 52, 100
African Union (*see also* AU), 52–53, 59, 99, 174, 176
Central and Eastern African regions, 77
decolonisation of Africa, 76
Eastern Africa, 77, 79, 93, 132
independent African countries, 76
Middle Africa, 79
Migration for Development in Africa (*see also* MIDA), 166, 175
Northern Africa, 79, 131
Organisation of the African Unity (*see also* OAU), 80, 100
1969 OAU Convention, 80
refugee protection in Africa, 100
Return of Qualified African Nationals (*see also* RQAN), 166, 175
Southern Africa, 79, 93, 95, 148–150
Sub-Saharan Africa (*see also* SSA), 34, 38–56, 86–90, 124–126, 144–148, 150–152, 157–160, 174–175, 178–180, 188, 371
Western Africa, 45, 79, 93, 149
Aged Society, 446
Ageing Population, 15, 139, 188, 427, 445, 469, 544, 549
Agreement on Trade-Related Aspects of Intellectual Property Rights (*see also* TRIPS), 185
Agricultural Hukou, 393, 397, 400
Agricultural Injury, 136
Agricultural Workers, 136, 144, 490

Alcohol and Drug Abuse, 87
All-Cancer Mortality, 132
Alternatives to Detention (*see also* ATD), 209, 230, 231–235, 246, 248, 297–299
American Convention on Human Rights, 105–106
Amnesty International (*see also* AI), 239–240, 468
Anaemia, 93–94, 96, 135, 137, 460
Anglo-Saxon, 366, 484
Anti-Money Laundering, 178
Anti-Racist Legislation, 225
Anxiety, 20–21, 98, 223–224, 265, 268–270, 272, 412, 461–462, 470, 490, 493, 497, 517, 522
Apolitical Humanitarianism, 538
Appeals Committee, 228
Arab Socialist Baathists, 103
Armed Conflict, 33–34, 55, 59–60, 107, 237, 293
Armed Forces, 103
Armed Insurrections, 77
Arteriosclerotic and Degenerative Diseases, 369–370
Arthritis, 129, 222
Artificial Cultural Homogenisation, 3
Ashkenazic Jews, 306
Asia
  Asian region, 77, 451
  Asia's refugees, 77
  Central Asia, 35, 79, 179, 258, 513
  Eastern Asia, 79
  Southeast Asian Nations, 184
  South-Eastern Asia, 79, 183
  Southern Asia, 79, 133
  Western Asia, 79, 132
Association for the Social Support of Youth (*see also* ARSIS), 241, 243, 245
Asthma, 129, 134–135, 221, 271, 458

Asylum
  asylum applications, 212–213, 220, 228, 230, 246, 293
  asylum claim, 229–230, 232, 283
  asylum committees, 228
  asylum policy, 212, 246
  asylum service, 225, 228, 230
  asylum system, 210, 226, 228–230, 239, 244
  asylum training, 230
  asylum-seeking procedure, 229
  community-based asylum seekers, 265, 267, 269
  detained asylum seekers, 210
  homeless asylum seekers, 224
  individual asylum claim, 232
  medical screening of asylum seekers, 221
  permits for asylum seekers, 228
  restrictive asylum policy, 212
  south–north asylum seekers, 24
  temporary asylum, 110
  tolerated asylum seekers, 228
  transfer of asylum seekers, 229, 260
  unauthorised asylum, 262–264
  vulnerable asylum seekers, 227
Attack Rate, 46, 85
Attractive Salary Packages, 165
Australia
  Australian Council of Social Service, 282
  Australian data, 510
  Australian Human Rights Commission (*see also* AHRC), 270–271
  Australian minorities, 527
  Australian services, 278
  Australia's refugee and humanitarian, 371
  challenging racism surveys in Australia, 525
  high court of Australia, 261, 264
  migrants in Australia, 372, 378, 485
  restrictive policy in Australia, 269
  Royal Australian College, 273
  the detention environment in Australia, 270
  White Australia Policy, 364–367, 484

## B

Bail or Bond, 231, 233
Bali Process, 103–105
Baseline, 47, 82–83, 127, 129
Basic Care, 90
Basic Health Services, 41
Basic Occupational Health, 489
Bearers, 55, 63
Beriberi, 93–94, 96
Bhutanese Refugees, 94, 96, 111
Biafran War in Nigeria, 76
Bi-Cultural Orientation, 18
Bilateral Agreement, 180, 184, 260
Bilateral Oedema, 91
Birth Rates, 15, 188, 347, 544
Birthweight, 314–315, 317, 346–348
Blood Pressure, 224, 316–317, 319, 324, 353, 373, 375
Boat Arrivals, 212, 258, 261
Boat Loads, 103–104
Body Fat, 316, 318
Body Mass Index, 316, 318, 375
Border
  border control, 172, 211, 264, 292, 295
  border crossings, 211
  border protection, 124, 171, 212, 259, 261, 382, 484, 549
Bosnian War, 99

Brain Drain
   brain drain and labour, 543
   brain drain circulation, 164
   brain drain into brain gain, 188, 543
   brain drain/gain, 123
   internal brain drain, 153, 181–183
   reverse brain drain (*see also* RBD), 162–165, 170, 547
   south–north brain drain, 139, 182
   south–south brain drain, 148
   transnational brain drain, 153
Brain Gain, 22, 154, 158, 164, 176, 183, 188–189, 543
Brain Return, 168
Breakdown of Authority, 77
Breast-Feeding, 96
Bride Famine, 445
Bridging Visas, 261, 274
Britain
   1905 British Aliens Act, 73
   British Focus, 367
Bronchial Responsiveness, 135
Brown Adipose Tissue, 130
Building Houses, 159
Burden of Communicable Diseases, 84
Burden of Disease, 23, 31, 48, 63, 81, 89, 125, 135, 143, 157, 224, 381, 392, 405
Burden of Malaria, 86–87
Burden of Mental Health, 86
Bureau of Aliens, 108
Burmese
   Burmese refugee women, 95
   Burmese refugees, 94, 97
   Burmese urban refugees, 90

# C

Cambodia
   Cambodian migrants, 447
   Cambodian refugees, 81, 85, 90, 95–97, 367
Canada
   Canadian Doctors for Refugee Care (*see also* CDRC), 338
   Canadian immigrant health guidelines, 331
   Canadian tax incentives, 166
Cancer
   bladder and nasopharyngeal cancers, 132
   breast cancers, 132, 373
   cancer incidence, 369, 378
   cancer mortality patterns, 132
   cancer of the digestive system and the urinary tract, 132
   cancer of the genital organs, 132
   cancer of the intestinal track, 369
   cancer registries, 132
   cancer screening, 132
   cancers of the respiratory system, lymphoid, hematopoietic and related tissue, 132
   colon, prostate, lung and breast cancers, 132, 373
   skin cancer, 132
   stomach cancer, 369
   testicular, gynaecological, ovarian and cervical cancers, 132
Capacity-Building, 63, 177
Capital Markets, 2
Capital, Goods, and Services, 22
Capital, Trade, Investment, Knowledge and Technology Transfers, 161
Caracas, 107
Cardio-Vascular Diseases, 89–90
Cardiovascular Health, 320
Cardiovascular Mortality, 131
Cardiovascular Outcomes, 318–319
Cardiovascular Risk Factors, 316, 320, 373, 411

Case Fatality Rate, 49, 85–86, 88
Case Management, 232–233
Cash-to-Account Transfer, 178
Central America, 79, 292, 351
Central Expenditures, 35
Centre for Justice and International Law (*see also* CEJIL), 105, 107
Certified Victims of Torture, 227
Chad, 36, 39, 47, 50, 77, 81–82, 101, 149
Challenging Racism Project, 512
Charter, 52–53, 74, 338
Child
   child alienation, 20
   children of immigrants, 348
   child labour, 226, 236
   children maladjustment, 20
   childhood populations, 314
   childhood mortality, 314, 443
   child pornography, 226
   child prostitution, 226
   child survival, 161
China
   Chinese citizens, 393, 395
   Chinese Communist Party, 167, 391
Cholera, 45, 49, 84
Chronic Diseases, 43, 89, 129, 222, 266, 368–369, 371, 373, 377, 410, 419
Chronic Obstructive Pulmonary Diseases (*see also* COPD), 135
Civil Wars, 34, 76, 107, 537
Clean Water, 41
$CO_2$ Emissions, 536
Coast Guard Detention Facility, 218
Collapse, 77, 100, 186, 256, 430, 511
Collective Identity, 1
Collectivism–Individualism Continuum, 382
Collectivist Communities, 383
Colonial Heritage, 320
Combat, 45, 87, 104, 263, 395, 511
Commodities, 1, 16, 93
Common Opinion, 308–309, 312–313
Common Wealth Code, 180
Communicable Diseases, 43, 81, 84, 89, 97–98, 126, 238, 273
Community Assessment and Placement (*see also* CAP), 234, 298
Community Condition, 298
Community Detention, 259–260, 262, 272, 275
Community Health Workers, 97
Community Leaders, 59
Community Service Learning, 334–335, 339
Community Stabilization, 62
Community Supervision, 232
Compensating Counter-Current, 5
Compensation and Reform, 172
Compensation Schemes, 183
Complex Humanitarian Emergencies (*see also* CHE), 73, 75–78, 81, 84–91, 93–95, 99–100, 111
Complex Emergencies, 41, 76, 94, 97–98
Compliance, 53, 88, 106, 211, 232, 246, 298, 383, 539
Composite International Diagnostic Interview, 98
Comprehensive Plan of Action (*see also* CPA), 103–104
Conflict Resolution, 76
Conflicts, 8, 20, 34–36, 40–44, 49–54, 56–59, 76–77, 100–101, 105, 150, 175, 367, 378, 428, 463, 537
Congenital Anomalies, 315–316, 323
Congenital Malformations, 137

Congo
    Congolese refugees, 86
    Democratic Republic of Congo (*see also* DRC), 34, 39, 40, 44, 45, 48–50, 93, 140, 150, 174, 177
    DR Congo, 77, 81, 91, 101
Consanguineous Partner, 315
Consanguinity, 315–316, 323
Consequence of Inactivity, 548
Consolidated Refugee Convention, 74
Convention against Torture and other Cruel, 240, 247, 256–257, 401
Convention on the Rights of the Child, 247, 256, 260, 296, 338, 401
Convicts, 365–366
Coolies, 366
Coronary Heart Disease, 130, 411
Corrupt System, 173
Corruption, 8, 178, 182, 403
Cost–Benefit Analysis, 12
Costs and Benefits, 14, 138, 541
Counselling, 234, 237–238, 240, 242, 244–245, 273, 418, 466, 468
Country of Refugee, 82–83
Credit Markets, 14
Crimes against Humanity, 58, 101
Criminalisation, 234
Criminality, 8
Crises, 76, 101, 299
Crisis Intervention, 99
Critical Shortage, 139, 174
Cross-Border Marriages, 445
Cross-Border Surveillance, 211
Crossed Boundaries, 306
Crowded Conditions, 45
Crude Mortality Rates (*see also* CMR), 38–43, 82–83, 92, 376–377
"Cultural Buffering" Effect, 376
Cultural Competence, 278, 331, 468, 499–500, 548
Cultural Exchange, 3, 16, 171
Cultural Incorporation, 18
Culture Shock Stage Theory, 20–21
Cultural Shift, 18
Cultural Transition, 17, 481
Cultural Values and Beliefs, 348, 355
Culturally Competent Practices, 248
Culturally Sensitive, 236, 380
Culturally Validated Screening Instruments, 98
Culture of the Home Country, 354
Culture Shock, 20–21, 461
Cyber Racism, 512, 520

# D

Dadaab Refugee, 87
Dangerous Jobs, 136
Dar Es Salaam Summit, 56
Decolonised Countries, 77
Deemed Ineligible, 104
Deficiencies, 91, 93, 96, 129, 134–135, 238, 263, 266, 274, 464, 467
Defilement, 45
Definite Law, 5
Degree of Integration, 364
Degree of Severity, 91
Deleterious Health, 228, 246
Demands for Labourers, 394
Dementia, 95
Democracy, 3, 56–57, 106, 180, 460
Democratisation, 3, 107
Demographic Transitions, 544–545
Demographic Trends, 139
Dental Care, 238, 266, 277, 333
Dental Disease, 266, 333
Dental Problems, 221, 266–267

Dependence on Foreign, 155
Depopulation, 5, 543
Deposit of Identity, 231
Depression, 49–51, 98, 223–224, 269–270, 412–414, 461, 463, 493, 497
Depressive Illness, 371
Dermatitis, 95, 459
Dermatological, 221, 267
Destination by Stages, 5
Detained and Deported, 225
Detainees, 216, 219–234, 241, 259, 267–274, 286, 297–298
Detainees and Detention Centre Staff, 220
Detention Centre Staff, 220, 224
Detention Centres, 208–210, 216–228, 236–238, 246–247, 259–260, 264–270, 296
Detention Inmates, 217, 221, 234
Detention of Children, 225, 227, 235–236, 246, 248, 271, 296, 299
Detention of Vulnerable Persons, 227, 236
Detention Policies, 208–209
Detention Strategy 2014–2019, 299
Deterrence Framework, 264
Developed Countries, 2, 124, 139, 148, 163, 180, 189, 246, 380, 439, 446, 496, 500, 538, 540, 549
Development Challenge, 61
Development Marketplace for African Diaspora in Europe (*see also* D-MADE), 176–177
Development Marketplace for African Diaspora Action (*see also* DMADA), 177
Development of the Assets, 164
Development Projects, 6, 33, 35, 164, 172, 177–178

Development-Related Benefits, 154
Deworming, 93
Diabetes
    diabetes management, 134
    diabetes-related complications, 134
    diabetes-related mortality, 133
    diabetic nephropathy, 134
    type-2 diabetes, 130, 133, 369, 498–499
Diagnostic and Statistical Manual, 49, 98
Diagnostic Procedures, 185
Diarrhea, 43, 45–46, 84, 88, 95
Diaspora
    diaspora bond, 179, 180
    diaspora networks, 158, 164, 543
    diaspora options, 158, 162, 163
    diaspora savings, 177–179, 546–547
    medical diaspora, 187
Differences in Lifestyle, 317, 369
Dignity, 108, 224, 283, 300
Direct Business Model, 162
Direct Effect, 4, 154–155
Direct Investment, 158, 162, 173
Direct Recruitment, 189
Directed Residence, 231
Disabilities, 224, 227, 242, 247, 401
Disadvantaged Persons, 339
Disbursement, 72
Distribution of Insecticide-Treated Bednets, 47
Discrimination against Women, 247, 401
Discriminatory, 171, 209, 297, 443, 466, 513, 541
Disease Burden, 84, 143, 221, 460–461

Disease of the Respiratory System, 134
Disease Outbreaks, 92, 247
Disgust and Awkwardness, 526
Disintegration of socioeconomic structures, 77
Dispersion, 5
Displaced People, 8, 33, 40, 101, 255, 293, 379, 433
Dispute Resolution, 58
Distribution of Non-Food, 237
Diversity of Income, 14
Doctor Shortfall, 143, 148
Doctor–Patient Interaction, 185
Doctors of World/Médecins, 244
Domestic Law, 55, 58, 61, 106, 108, 246
Domestic or Internal Passport, 392
Domestic Violence, 335, 447, 449–452, 466
Domiciles, 108
Dominant Group, 17, 21
Department of Refugee Affairs (*see also* DRA), 109
Drinking Habits, 369
Drugs, 89, 97, 380
Dual Citizenship, 165
Dual Labour Market Theory, 14–15
Dual Nationality, 109, 162, 547
Dublin II Regulation, 229, 247
Durable Peace, 57
Durable Solutions, 51, 56, 58, 61–64, 166, 301, 537
Dutch Antilleans, 314
Dutch Citizens, 310
Dyslipidaemia, 91, 130

# E

Early Integration Barriers, 336
Early Intervention, 98, 281
Early Marriages, 44

Earthquake, 290
Europe
 Eastern Europe, 80, 134, 157, 217, 306, 334, 357, 371, 430, 491, 493
 European Union (*see also* EU), 56, 127–129, 169, 208, 210–211, 213–214, 296–297, 339, 491, 540
  EU Law, 231
  EU member states, 208, 211, 213, 227, 229–230, 233, 491
  EU Returns Directive, 214
 European Commission, 105, 176, 208, 244, 540
 European Council on Refugees, 236–237, 239
 European Court of Human Rights, 230
 European Human Rights, 230
 European irregular migrant, 296
 European Refugee Fund (ERF), 240, 243–244
 European Social Fund (ESF), 243
 detention in Europe, 297
 Northern Europe, 339
 seeking asylum in Europe, 210
 Southern Europe, 80, 133
 wars in Europe, 75
 Western Europe, 80, 134, 306, 314
Ebola Crisis, 291
Economic Considerations, 7
Economic Crisis, 309, 310, 312–313
Economic Development, 13, 16, 35, 57, 163–164, 170, 176–177, 301, 481, 547, 549
Economic Growth, 22, 138, 154–159, 163, 391, 396, 429, 433, 445, 454, 494, 536, 541, 543, 545
Economic Means, 14

*Index* **561**

Economic Opportunity, 95
Economic Recovery, 63
Economic Reforms, 391–392, 394, 401, 549
Economic Transformation (1998–2002), 434
Economic, Social and Cultural Rights, 52, 103, 247, 256, 300, 401
Ecumenical Refugee Programme, 244
Edict of Nantes, 75
Educational Attainment, 12, 154, 161, 410, 451, 497
Educational Level, 151, 315, 406, 540
Effect of Distance, 5
Effective Response, 62, 526
Effective Sexual Health Programmes, 457
Effects of Cultural Competence, 499
Efficiency, 3, 175
Efforts of Recruitment Officers, 308
Electronic Media, 1
Electronic Monitoring, 233, 298
Electronic Tagging, 232
Emergency Affairs, 101
Emergency Care, 222, 235
Emergency Human Resource, 180
Emergency Response Priorities, 95
Emergency Situations, 95, 235
Emergency Thresholds, 36, 41–43, 98
Emergency Transit Agreement, 103, 105
Emigration Flows, 307, 429
Emigration Rates, 139–140
Emotional Abuse, 224, 452
Employment Management Scheme (*see also* EMS), 430, 434, 438
Employment Opportunities, 3, 15, 429, 443, 494, 496–497

Employment Permit Systems (*see also* EPS), 434, 437–438
Employment Reforms, 434
Endemic Infectious Diseases, 89
Ending Displacement, 56, 62–63
Endothelial Dysfunction, 131
Enforcement Officials, 225, 236, 239–240
Entrepreneurs, 155, 164, 167, 547
Environmental Factors, 62, 86
Environmental Inequalities, 317–318
Epidemics, 97, 237
Epidemiological Paradox, 345–347, 349, 351–357
Epilepsy, 222
Equality, 55, 107, 243, 366, 466
Eradication, 101
Ethical Code of Practice, 181
Ethical Principles, 180
Ethical Recruitment, 180
Ethiopia, 77–96, 109, 144–151, 156–160, 174, 176–177
Ethnic Conflicts, 8, 35, 40, 51, 150, 378
Ethnic Differences, 131, 313–314, 317–320, 322–324
Ethnic Disparities, 318, 324
Ethnic Disparities in Ischaemic Stroke, 318
Ethnic Inequalities, 322
Ethnic Profiling, 215–216, 246
Ethnically Homogeneous Neighbourhoods, 323
Ethnicity, 129, 131, 193, 215, 318–319, 322, 356, 438, 488, 511–513, 527
Etiological Factors, 315
Evidence-Based Approaches, 330
Evidence-Based Guidelines, 93, 329–330

Evidence-Based Programming, 62
Evidence-Based Science, 330, 340
Excess Morbidity, 89
Excessive Bleeding, 137
Exorbitant Prices, 89
Expanded Market Economy, 4
Expatriates, 155, 163–164, 166, 547,
Expectancy Estimates, 354
Experience of Racism, 509–511, 514, 517, 521, 527
Exploitation, 3, 171, 226, 297, 405, 438, 451–453, 457
Exploitative Work, 226
Extended Family, 14, 495
Extensive Violence, 77
External Conflict, 77
External Forces, 13, 53, 414
Extreme Distress, 272

## F

Factor Price Equalisation, 12
Failed Political Systems, 111
Fake Marriage, 448–449, 464, 545
Falangists, 76
Family Conflicts, 20
Family Link, 226
Family Members, 8, 10–11, 22, 229, 265, 281, 363, 412, 417, 490, 510
Family Reunification, 8, 61, 240, 429
Family Reunion, 8, 263, 363, 378, 404, 545
Family Tracing and Reunification, 248
Family-Related Factors, 165
Famine, 7, 85, 256, 441, 445
Fast Track Process, 264
Fastest-Growing Economy, 391
Fatalities, 94, 136, 293, 485
Fatality Incidence, 136
Fatality Rates, 85

Federal Laws, 108
Federal Parliament, 364
Federation in 1901, 364
Feedback Effect, 154, 158
Financial Capital, 162, 176, 543, 546
Financial Insecurity, 269
Financial Trades and Flows, 1
Financial Transactions, 1
First Basic Plan, 466–467
First Cousin Relationships, 316
First Reception Service (*see also* FRS), 228, 230
Five Country Initiative, 339
Five Regular Employees, 435
Fleeing Conflicts, 76, 367
Fleeing Phase, 51, 57
Fleeing War, 210, 295
Flexible Residential Rights, 162, 547
Foetal Growth, 314
Foetal Life, 314
Food Aid, 93–94
Food Fortification, 94–95
Food Insecure, 92
Food Shortages, 91
Forced Crossings, 293
Forced Internal Displacement, 32
Forced Mass Displacements, 81
Forced Repatriation, 101, 104, 224
Forced Returns, 229
Forcibly Displaced People, 293
Foreign Aid, 1, 22, 177
Foreign Companies, 394
Foreign Direct Investment, 158
Foreign Entry, Departure and Registration Law, 463
Foreign Exchanges, 395
Foreign Immigrant Affairs, 108
Foreign Investment, 1, 2, 164, 187, 394, 543, 547

Foreign Ownership, 187
Foreign Workers, 15, 163, 396, 402, 432–434, 437–438, 441, 466, 468
Foreign-Born Hispanic Immigrants, 357
Foreigners Order, 108
Formal Financial System, 172
Formal Labour Contracts, 405
Fortified Food Rations, 95
France
　French occupation, 307
　French protestant minorities, 75
　The 1793 French Constitution, 73
Free Grain Rations, 393
Free Health Care, 110, 275
Free Movement, 4, 149, 172, 211, 231
Free Trade Agreement, 16, 184–185, 296
Freedom of Movement, 58, 209, 231, 307, 393, 546
FRONTEX, 211
Functioning Banking Systems, 178
Functioning Impairment, 98

# G

Gang Rape, 45
Gastarbeiders, 309
Gastrointestinal, 221, 267–268,
Gaza Strip, 99
Gross Domestic Product (*see also* GDP), 2, 157–158, 177–179, 414, 542
Gender-Based Violence, 8, 45
General Agreement on Tariffs and Trade (*see also* GATT), 2, 185
General Agreement on Trade in Services (*see also* GATS), 23, 185, 188–189
General Food Distribution, 92
General Health Service, 276
Generalised Violence, 33–34

Generation Minorities, 320
Genetic Diseases, 168, 323
Geneva Convention, 247
Genocide, 58, 101
Germany
　1648 Peace Treaty of Westphalia, 75
　German Academic International Network (*see also* GAIN), 168
　German Jews, 308
Giardia Intestinalis, 373
Global Acute Malnutrition, 91, 93
Global Capitalism, 3
Global Code of Practice, 181
Global Financial System, 22
Global Health Canmeds Competency Model, 335
Global Integration, 1
Global Interchange, 1
Global Refugees, 81
Global Strategy, 234–235
Global Voluntary Code of Practice, 180, 182
Goal-Striving Stress, 21–22
Golden Century, 305
Good Jobs, 15
Good Sanitation, 84
Governance Structures, 61, 178
Government
　government-assisted refugee (*see also* GAR), 338
　government-sponsored social welfare, 171
　government bonds, 165
　government expenditures, 188, 541–542
　government income, 188
　government institutions, 77, 381
　government ministries, 57, 248

**564** *Index*

Grand Plan, 465–466
Great Cultural Revolution, 393
Great Lakes Protocol, 56, 58–59, 63–64
Greece
    Greek Action Plan on Asylum and Migration Management, 219
    Greek asylum system, 229–230
    Greek authorities, 211, 214, 225, 235–236, 239–240, 246
    Greek Council For Refugees (*see also* GCR), 236–237, 244
    Greek detention centres, 220, 224
    Greek forum of refugees, 239
    Greek government, 225, 228, 234, 237–238, 240, 246–248
    Greek Law, 214, 216, 227
    Greek legal council, 214
    Greek legal system, 241
    Greek–Turkish border, 211, 237
    impact on the Greek economy, 230
Gsorm Gala Studenilor, 168
Guarantor/Surety, 231
Guest Workers, 6, 309, 312–313
Guidelines for Detention, 208, 234
Gvahim, 168

# H

Hallmark, 76
Hanawon, 441
Hard Law, 57, 60, 64, 537
Harmonising Skills Evaluation, 149
Harsh Working Conditions, 137, 496
Harvard Trauma Questionnaire, 98
Hassle-Free Travel, 149
Haven Enterprise Visas, 263
Healthy Lifestyle Factors, 320
Health Advantage, 131, 353, 356–357, 377–378, 485
Health And Safety Risks, 124, 226, 485
Health Burden, 35, 81, 90, 94, 123–124, 323, 364, 417–418
Health Care
    health care benefits, 235
    health care infrastructure, 89, 414
    health care utilisation and medication, 235
Health Conditions, 23, 25, 220, 223, 266, 274, 331–332, 405, 409, 458
Health Disadvantage, 322
Health Disorders, 97–98, 129, 272, 414
Health Education, 37, 241, 246, 339, 499
Health Equity Impact Assessment Movement, 339
Health Equity Methods, 330
Health Expenditure, 125, 223, 469
Health Gaps, 281
Health in Childhood, 314
Health Insurance, 187, 307, 354, 409, 414–418, 458, 490
Health Literacy, 277, 280, 379, 406, 458, 468
Health of Hispanic Immigrants in The USA, 345
Health of Migrants, 22, 210, 220, 238, 368, 378, 384, 457, 463, 468, 481, 483, 494, 500, 511
Health Outcomes, 22, 35–36, 95, 138, 227–228, 264, 270, 275, 284, 323, 331, 346, 348, 351–353, 379, 408, 411, 462, 496, 498, 526
Health Package, 180
Health Policy Response, 107, 256, 261, 414
Health Problems, 221, 236, 272, 277, 279, 281, 294–295, 305, 314, 323, 329, 408, 462, 486, 493, 497

Health Screening, 124, 221, 227, 266, 274, 339, 368, 371, 376, 382, 457
Health Services Utilisation, 322
Health Status and Mortality, 355
Health Systems, 7, 181–184, 269, 281, 291, 299–301, 324, 329–330, 355, 542
Health Threats, 81, 490
Health Tourism, 185, 186
Health Transition, 376
Health Workers, 6, 8, 88, 97, 143, 150, 155–157, 174, 180–181, 183, 189, 280, 337
Health Workforce, 155–157, 174
Height-For-Age (*see also* HFA), 91
Hellenic Coast Guards, 211, 216
Hellenic Red Cross (*see also* HRC), 240, 244–245
Hepatitis, 126, 128
Hepatitis B, 128, 220, 371, 373, 407
Hepatitis C, 129, 242, 333, 407, 457
Heterogeneity, 91, 95, 97, 298, 322
Hezbollah, 103
High Frequency, 127, 316
High Human Development Index, 149
High Incidences, 89
High Risk Families, 323
High Risk of Depression, 322
High Transmission, 86
High-Case Fatality, 85, 93
High-Density Lipoprotein Dysfunction, 131
High-Income Countries, 12, 15, 89, 126, 132, 138–139, 498
Highly Educated, 136, 138, 140–142, 154, 163, 313, 540
Highly Qualified Professionals, 139, 548
Highly Skilled and Business Migrants, 6

High-Risk, 92, 322, 406–407, 468, 498
High-Technology Clusters, 165
Hindustani, 311, 314
Hiring Policies, 183
Hispanic Epidemiological Paradox, 346, 350–352, 354, 356–357
Hispanic Immigrants, 345, 347, 351, 353–357
Hispanic Mortality Advantage, 351
Hispanic Paradox, 346–347, 351–352, 356
Hispanic/Latino Immigrants, 345, 351–352
HIV
    health promotion on HIV, 241
    HIV and hepatitis, 220, 241–242
    HIV epidemic, 48
    HIV infection, 8, 48, 127–128, 406
    HIV/AIDS, 43, 87, 126–158, 150, 157, 235, 407, 457
    mandatory HIV testing, 88
    mass HIV/AIDS interventions, 87
Holding Cells, 216
Holding Centres, 209
Holding Facilities, 218
Home Care, 322, 548
Home Countries, 6, 9, 13, 75–76, 164, 176–177, 210, 215, 233, 306, 308–309, 356, 358
Home Curfew, 232, 298
Homecoming Revolution, 166
Homelands, 73, 101, 166, 471
Homelessness, 220, 262, 280
Homicide Deaths, 134
Homogeneity, 3, 97
Hookworms, 373
Hopkins Symptom Checklist-25, 98
Hospital Discharge, 137
Hospitalisation, 130, 137, 373

Host Communities, 35–36, 51, 58, 108
Host Countries, 89, 111, 128, 184, 227, 275, 293, 299, 353–354, 379, 453, 480
Household Registration, 392, 394, 399
Household Workers, 144
Housing Assistance, 242
Hub, 149, 396
Huguenots, 306
Hukou Migration, 397, 400
Hukou Status, 398, 400, 405, 417
Human Capital Return, 12
Human Capital Transfer, 162
Human Control, 3
Human Resources, 97, 162, 164, 181, 184, 219, 248
Human Rights
　human right abuses, 51, 207
　human right treaties, 247
　human right violations, 236
　human rights and health, 298
　human rights challenge, 61
　human rights conventions, 256–257
　Human Rights Law, 55, 59, 61, 225, 236, 284
　human rights victims, 107
　human rights violations, 441, 546, 33–34, 36, 100–101, 106–107, 239, 247
　International Human Rights, 400–401, 456, 538
　International Human Rights Law, 58–59, 61, 225
　member states human rights records, 106–107
　monitor human rights, 106
　numerous acts of human rights, 239
　physicians for human rights, 181
　public on human rights, 239
Human Trafficking, 33, 104, 211, 227, 240, 379, 452–453, 545
Humanitarian
　humanitarian catastrophe, 92
　humanitarian emergency, 76, 92
　humanitarian agencies, 95
　humanitarian aid delivery, 88
　humanitarian and social issues, 57
　humanitarian assistance, 55, 99, 102–103, 107, 109
　humanitarian challenge, 61
　humanitarian industry, 76
　humanitarian interventions, 90
　humanitarian law, 55, 57–61
　humanitarian organisations, 40–41, 216
　humanitarian programme, 257, 363
　humanitarian relief, 77
　humanitarian response, 77, 107, 111
　international humanitarian law, 57–61
　medical humanitarian NGO, 242
　refugee and humanitarian entrants, 371
Hungarian Revolution, 76
Hunger, 78, 270
Hygiene Education, 46, 84
Hypertension, 89–91, 131, 350, 352, 374, 408, 410–411

# I

Identification Centres, 216–217
Illegal Arrivals, 207, 210, 212, 216, 224, 228
Illegal Departures, 104

Illegal Entry, 210, 212, 215, 395
Illegal Movement, 105
Ill-Health, 220, 463, 469, 497, 509, 511
Ill-Treatment, 225, 239, 295, 297
Imbalanced Economic Relations, 16
Immigrants
    families and children in
        immigration detention, 271
    illegal immigrants, 215, 232, 396
    illegal immigration, 215
    immigrant health, 331–332, 345, 492
    immigrant paradox, 348–350, 355
    immigrant populations, 350
    immigration control law, 463
    immigration detention, 207–210, 216, 219, 227, 235–236, 248, 259, 261, 267–274, 282–283, 296, 298, 538
    immigration flows, 307–308, 433
    immigration history, 314, 365
    immigration policy response, 238
    immigration procedures, 233
    immigration process, 259, 268
    immigration restriction act, 365–366
    mental health impact of immigration detention, 270
    operation of immigration detention facilities, 219
    second basic plan for immigration policy, 467
Immunisation, 46, 405, 418
Impact of Event Scale, 98
Impaired Fasting Glucose, 133
Impaired Health Environment, 91
Imperialism, 3
Implementation Frameworks, 64, 537
Imported Diseases, 368

Impoverished Urban Areas, 89
Improved and Expanded Transport and Communication, 22
Improved PTSD Symptoms, 98
Inadequate Access to Food, 41
Inadequate Treatment, 279, 324
Incentives, 12, 154, 162, 166, 176, 336, 393, 548
Incest, 45
Incidence of Stroke, 131
Income Maximisation, 12–13
Incomplete Vaccination, 220
Increased Cost of Health Care, 155
Increased Risk, 50, 127, 130, 133
Indefinite Detention, 209, 248, 283
Indefinite Period, 312–313
Infrastructures and Technologies, 22
Independence, 51, 53, 100–101, 383
Indigenous, 100, 364, 366, 483, 513
Indirect Effect, 4
Individual Rational Choice, 12
Individualised Assessment, 298
Individualism, 13, 382–383, 480, 482, 536
Individualistic Communities, 383
Indochinese Refugees, 103
Indonesia, 82, 98, 103–105, 258, 266, 308, 320, 366, 402, 496
Induced Abortions, 137, 267
Induced Effect, 154
Industrial and Technical Training Programme (*see also* ITTP), 434, 437–438
Industrial Development, 6
Industrial Trainee Scheme (*see also* ITS), 430, 434, 437–438
Inequalities, 17, 129, 134, 187, 189, 317–324, 364, 382, 393, 411, 418–419, 447, 451, 456, 499, 509, 537, 545

Infant Death, 316
Infant Mortality, 37, 95, 161, 314–316, 346–348
Infantile Beriberi, 96
Infectious Diseases
  infectious and communicable diseases, 81
  infectious disease transmission, 221
  infectious diseases treatment, 235
Inflammatory Risk Factors, 130
Inflation, 7
Influx, 20, 81, 104, 108–110, 214, 237, 392, 427–428, 469, 544
Informal Channels, 159, 547
Information and Communication Technologies (*see also* ICT), 535,
Infrastructure, 3, 22, 35, 89, 173, 176, 179, 212, 234, 392, 414, 468, 535
Inhuman or Degrading Treatment or Punishment (*see also* CAT), 217, 240, 247, 257, 401
Insecticide-Treated Bednets, 47
Insecurity, 8, 41, 85, 108, 269–270, 496
Insomnia or Sleeplessness, 223
Inspection, 209
Institutional Accommodation, 95
Institutionalisation of Knowledge, 155
Instrumentations Diagnostic Criteria, 91
Insurance, 354, 405, 409, 414–418
Integrated Interventions, 87
Integrated World Trade, 4
Integration of Refugees, 244
Integration of Returnees, 162
Intellectual Stimulation, 7
Intergenerational Changes, 320
Intergenerational Discrepancy Theory, 20

Inter-American Commission on Human Rights, 105–106
Inter-American Court of Human Rights, 106
Inter-Hukou Marriages, 400
Interim Federal Health Programme (*see also* IFHP), 337
Interim Health Schemes, 235
Internal Conflicts, 51
Internal Displacement, 33, 42, 54, 56–59, 64, 94, 294
Internal Displacement Monitoring Centre (*see also* IDMC), 34–35
Internal Labour Markets, 6
Internally Displaced Persons (*see also* IDPs), 23, 33–36, 40–52, 55–64, 75–76, 101, 537–538
International and Domestic Laws, 55
International Borders, 4, 9, 33, 87
International Capital Flows, 2, 22
International Committee of the Red Cross, 59–60
  1967–1970 humanitarian emergency response, 76
International Community, 40–41, 54, 391, 537–538
International Convention on the Protection Rights of Migrant Workers and Members of their Families, 247, 400–401
International Covenant on Civil and Political Rights, 231, 247, 256–257, 401
International Detention Coalition (*see also* IDC), 234, 236, 239, 298
International Donor Community, 104
International Donors, 53
International Exchange, 395
International Intervention, 64

International Marriage, 442–443, 445, 448, 452, 463–466, 545
International Movement, 2
International NGOs, 53, 153, 175, 181–183, 208, 548
International Obligations, 111, 257
International Protection, 207, 215, 229, 242, 247–248, 255
International Refugee Organisation (*see also* IRO), 74, 76, 367
International Response, 77
International Standards, 54, 104, 208–209, 235, 299
International Students, 164, 402, 547
International Trade and Markets, 22
International Treaty, 54
Internet-Based Training, 185
Interpretation Services, 221, 244
Interpreter, 220, 270, 277–278, 280–281
Intervention Strategies, 86
Intestinal Parasites, 226, 332
Intracerebral Haemorrhage, 318, 320–321
Intra-Regional Migration, 494
Intrinsic Demand, 15
Involuntary Migration, 393
Iodine Deficiency, 93
Iran
　　Iranians, 313
　　Islamic Republic of Iran, 34, 77, 108, 293
Iraq
　　Iraqi Refugees, 90–91
　　Iraqis, 313
Iridimi, 39, 82
Irish Christmas Recruitment, 166
Irregular Arrivals, 211
Irregular Migrants, 207, 210–211, 213–215, 220, 225, 228–233, 237, 240, 242, 291–296, 299–301, 339
Ischaemic Heart Disease, 130, 460
Ischaemic Stroke, 318, 320–321
Islamic Bonds, 180

## J

Japanese Colonial Period (1910–1945), 429
Jewish Holocaust, 76
Job Opportunities, 7, 165, 429, 549
Job Security, 7, 15, 165
Job Vacancies, 482
Jordan, 34, 83–84, 90, 93, 96, 98, 293–294
Judicial Capacity, 53
Judiciary, 101
Jurisdictional Court, 106–107

## K

Kampala Declaration, 181
Kanakas, 364
Katale, 82, 91
Kenya, 52, 56, 77, 83–91, 101, 103, 109, 121, 140, 144, 149–151, 157–160, 294, 496
Khao-I-Dang, 82
Kibumba, 82, 91
Kingdom of the Netherlands, 307, 311
Kisaeng Parties, 454
Knowledge and Skill Transfer, 173, 187, 543
Knowledge-Sharing and Transfer, 176
Korea
　　2006–2007 Act to Support International Marriage for Rural Bachelors, 445
　　2010 Nationality Law Reform, 465
　　annexation of Korea, 428

destination countries for Korean emigrants, 430
ethnic Korean emigrants, 428
exodus of Korean emigrants, 433
emigration of Koreans, 429
homogenous society in Korea, 456
immigration policies in Korea, 437
Korea immigration naturalization aptitude test, 467
Korean adage, 450
Korean defectors, 441–442, 461, 464
Korean Immigrants in Korea, 439
Korean immigration policies, 465
Korean nationality, 442, 464
Korean nationhood and citizenship, 464
Korean social welfare system, 452
Korean War, 428–430, 441, 453–454
Korean-Chinese, 447, 462
migration in Korea, 427
North Korean refugees, 91, 427, 441, 461
period between the 1950–1953 Korean War, 430
South Korea, 146, 168, 170, 427–435, 440–445, 449, 463–470
truly Korean, 456
Kosian Families, 442
Kounoungo, 82
Kule, 83

# L

1919 League of Nations Charter, 74
Labour Contract Law, 405
Labour Dispute Mediation, 405
Labour Dynamics, 13, 82, 486
Labour Market, 6, 12–15, 22, 138, 165, 171, 175, 240, 245, 393, 480, 488, 491, 493, 537, 540, 543, 544
Labour Shortages, 172, 188, 433–434, 447, 469, 538
Lack of Funding, 7, 89
Lack of Hygiene, 221
Lack of Information, 89–90, 297
Land Arrests, 211
Language Barriers, 246, 269, 277, 452, 458, 482
Language Competence, 322, 486
Language Inability, 324
Language other than English (*see also* LOTE), 381, 512–527
  LOTE Speakers, 525–526
Large Ethnic Differences, 313, 324
Law Enforcement, 225, 236, 239–240
Law of Lagos, 52
Law Standards, 60
League of Nations, 73–74
Lebanon, 34, 77, 81, 84, 89–93, 98, 110, 293–294, 367, 374
Left-Wing Citizens, 308
Legal Aid, 63, 244, 296–297
Legal Assistance, 233, 237, 241, 244, 262, 283
Legal Counselling, 242, 245
Legal Documents, 89, 171–172
Legal Framework, 51, 54, 57–58, 61, 108, 208, 231, 256, 297, 392, 395–396
Legal Income Earners, 394
Legal Instruments, 56, 64
Legal Representation, 244
Legal Status, 6, 33, 147, 215, 238, 345, 463–464, 488
Legal Support, 238, 240–241

*Index* **571**

Legally and Non-Legally Binding, 23
Legally Binding, 59, 60, 182
Length of Detention, 214, 224
Length of Residence, 369, 372, 375, 377
Lesser Visa Restrictions, 189
Levels of Industrial Revolution, 5
Liberal Capitalism, 4
Liberalisation, 2, 22, 480
Lifesaving Interventions, 88
Life-Threatening, 86, 129
Lijan Sha'biyya, 102
Limited Studies, 90
Linear or Unidirectional Model
    (*see also* UDM), 17
Lipid Levels and Insulin, 317, 319
Lipoprotein-Cholesterol Levels, 316
Lisungwe Camp, 82
Literacy Rate, 37
Livelihood, 61, 92, 109
Living Conditions, 7, 85, 102, 110,
    216, 218, 220–221, 223, 236–238,
    244, 246, 267, 271, 331, 458, 490,
    495–496
Local Legislations, 99
Local Residency Rights, 397
Location Tracking, 233
Long Working Hours, 405, 490, 493
Loss of Beneficial Health, 320
Loss of Life, 77
Low And Middle-Income Countries
    (LMICs), 3, 4, 13, 98, 123–125, 133,
    154, 157–159, 164, 179, 182–183,
    189, 208, 375, 537, 548–549
Low Birthweight, 315, 317, 347–348
Low Class, 15
Low Gestational Weight Gain, 315
Low Skilled and Low Social Status
    Jobs, 136
Low Social Security, 405

Lower Physical Activity, 318
Low-Paid Semi-Skilled, 136

## M

Macro Theory, 11
Macronutrient, 91
Macrostructure, 9
Maize-Based Rations, 95
Major Minority Groups, 310–311
Malaria
    malaria control policies, 86
    malaria elimination, 87
    malaria incidence, 86
    malaria outbreaks, 86
    malaria-endemic areas, 86
Malnutrition, 91–93
Management Tool, 210, 213–214
Mandate or Capacity, 77
Mandatory Detention, 208–209, 260
Manpower, 187, 433
Mantoux Test, 333, 371
Marginalisation, 19, 51, 60, 77, 482, 492
Market Failures, 14
Market Freedom, 480
Markets Realities, 13
Maronites, 103
Mass Immunisation, 46, 85
Massive Displacements, 77
Mastery, 20, 355
Material and Non-Material Incentives,
    162
Maternal Death, 137–138, 408–409
Maternal Mortality, 37, 409
Maturity Periods, 179
Mauritius Grand Bay Declaration
    and Plan of Action, 101
Meakong Countries, 103
Measles and Diarrheal Diseases, 88
Measles Case Fatality Rates, 85

Measles Fatality, 46
Measles Immunisation, 46, 85, 93–94
Measles Mortality, 46, 85
Médecins Du Monde-Greece, 242
Médecins Sans Frontières (*see also* MSF), 76, 89, 222, 295
Mediation, 241, 245
Medical and Pharmaceutical Coverage, 242
Medical Assistance, 235, 237–238, 245
Medical Conditions, 222, 245, 276, 300
Medical Education Partnership Initiative (*see also* MEPI), 173
Medical Follow-Up, 237
Medical Personnel, 221, 223
Medical Schools, 143–145, 173–174, 335
Medical Services, 337, 417
Medical Treatment, 222, 234, 276
Medicare, 263, 274, 276–279, 282
Medication and Social Services, 243
Mediterranean Diet, 320
Mediterranean Workers, 308
Melenasia, 80
Melting Pot Theory, 18
Memberships, 11, 383
Memoranda of Understanding, 282
Mental Health
  mental health care interventions, 99
  mental health conditions, 223, 266, 274, 331
  mental health differences, 322
  mental health disorders, 97–98, 129, 227, 234, 272, 414
  mental health screening, 274
  mental health services, 274, 278
  mental illness, 22, 220, 224, 272
Meso-Structure, 10
Metabolic Syndrome, 91, 133, 316
Methodological Equilibration, 13
Methodological Instrumentalism, 13
Mexican Immigrant Children, 349
Mexican Student Loan Forgiveness, 166
Micro Theory, 12
Micronesia, 80
Micronutrient Deficiencies, 91, 93, 96
Microstructure, 9
Middle Eastern Region, 91, 94, 100, 102
Migrants
  deterrence of migrants, 298
  economic migrants, 134, 306–307, 487
  evidence-based migrant health guidelines, 300, 331, 335
  exhausted migrant effect, 376
  first generation of migrants, 21, 310, 313, 356
  floating migrant population, 398
  forced migrants, 23, 95, 134, 378, 491, 538
  healthy migrant effect, 23–24, 205, 320, 346, 353, 361, 375–387
  housing of migrants, 309
  internal migrants, 294, 409–410, 414, 418
  long-distance migrants, 6
  migrant communities, 309, 330
  migrant groups, 17, 131, 333
  migrant health, 300, 345, 380, 455, 479–499
  migrants fiscal contributions, 543
  migrated workers, 309
  migratory flows, 295
  'new-generation' migrant population, 399

Index 573

non-western migrants, 313
reasons for migrants, 306
registered migrants, 147, 235
residency of the migrants, 309
return migrants, 8
rural labour migrants, 397
second-generation migrants, 322
short-journey migrants, 5
skilled migrant workers, 458, 485
skilled economic migrants, 487
south–north migrants, 24, 126
south–north migration, 23, 123, 139, 183
south–south migration, 123, 139, 148–149
temporary labour migrants, 6
undocumented migrants, 172, 225, 227, 246, 382, 400, 433, 537–538
unsafe migrant corridors, 292
vulnerable migrants, 227

Migration
circular migration, 162
coastal-to-inland migration, 393
continuous migration, 314
cumulative causation of migration, 10
equilibrium model of migration, 12
female migration, 5
forced migration, 6, 33, 123, 266, 294, 378–379, 538
growth of migration, 312
history of migration, 305
labour migration, 12, 149–150, 433, 536, 545
laws of migration, 4–5
mass migration, 307

migration act 1958, 258
migration amendment (complementary protection) act, 256
migration by stages, 5
migration capital, 11
migration control policies, 295
migration flows, 124, 210, 307–308, 312–313, 509
migration for economic motives, 6
migration governance, 255, 392
migration health policy, 235
migration inflows, 230
migration management tool, 210, 213–214
migration movements, 305
migration phenomenon, 4
migration self-selection, 369
migration source, 148, 392
migration status, 260, 332, 350, 384, 512
migration stream dynamics, 5
migration stress, 294
migration systems theory, 9–10
migration theories, 4, 123
migration trends, 104, 144, 293
net labour migration, 12
north–north migration, 123
north–south migration, 123
out-migration, 11, 543
permanent general skilled migration, 171
permanent migration, 376, 397
place-to-place migration, 393
restrictive migration framework, 395
restrictive migration policies, 546, 549

**574** *Index*

  restrictive to relaxed migration laws, 392
  return migration and employment, 543
  reverse migration, 346, 353–354
  selective migration theory, 19
  strategic migration schemes, 548
  substantial migration, 510
  third wave of migration, 367
  transnational migration theory, 9
  volume of migration, 5
  wave of migration, 364–367
Militarisation, 103
Military Constraints, 77
Military Dictatorship, 77, 311
Militias, 102
Ministerial Conference, 101
Ministers of Foreign Affairs, 105
Ministry of Health & Welfare, 235
Minority Groups, 310–312, 325
Minors and Victims of Trafficking, 241
Miscarriages, 137, 271
Mobile Medical Units, 242
Mobile School, 245
Mobile Units, 228, 241, 244
Mobility, 280, 306, 392, 537–538
Modern State, 75
Monetary Compensation, 162
Money Transfer Companies, 178
Monitoring Requirements, 231
Moral Sanction, 106
Morbid Effects, 510–527
Morbidities, 111, 509, 511
Morbidity and Mortality, 47, 84, 86–89, 137, 352
Morocco
  Moroccans, 308, 311, 313, 320, 491
  Moroccan government, 313
  Moroccan migrants, 131, 322
  Moroccan minority group, 312
Mortality
  mortality advantage, 346, 351–355, 376, 379
  mortality and morbidity, 64, 84, 299
  mortality attributable, 84
  mortality rates, 42, 82, 353–356, 372, 376–378
  mortality ratios, 136, 374–375
  mortality surveys, 41–43
Motivational Problems, 15
Mozambican Children, 85
Mugunga, 93
Multi-Causal, 76
Multiculturalism, 365, 427, 455–456, 467, 545
Multidimensional Model, 19
Multilateral Agreements, 2
Multilateral Organisations, 2
Multinational Firms, 2
Musculoskeletal Disease, 90
Musculoskeletal Problems, 221
Myocardial Infarction, 320

**N**

Naming and Shaming, 106
National Health Care System, 237, 246
National Health Interview Survey, 351
National Legislation, 57–59, 99
National Sovereignty, 124
Nationalists, 391
Nationality Law, 464–466
Native Dutch, 131–132, 320
Natural Disasters, 8, 49, 77, 378
Natural or Environmental, 33
Natural Processes of the Environment, 81
Nazi Germany, 76

Negative Emotional Impact, 526
Negative Growth, 143
Neoclassical Economics Theory, 11–12
Neocolonial Governments, 16
Neonatal, 227, 315, 335
Nepal, 86, 94, 96, 111, 291, 444, 495
Nepotism, 178
Net Capital Flows, 12
Netherlands, 127, 131–141, 176, 245, 305–324, 367, 371, 374, 499, 540
Network of Champions, 239
Network Theory, 10
'New Britannia' Policy, 366
New Cooperative Medical Scheme (*see also* NCMS), 416–417
New Directions in Detention Policy, 259
New Globalisers, 2
New Natural Resources, 15
New Low-Cost Labour, 15
New Outlets, 15
New Wave of Refugees, 76
Niacin, 93, 95
"No Advantage" Principle, 263
No Language Requirements, 309
Non-Agricultural Hukou Population, 393
Non-British Immigrant, 366
Non-Combatants, 45
Non-Communicable Diseases (*see also* NCDs), 89, 93, 134, 405, 410–411
Non-European, 110
Non-Government Organisations (*see also* NGO), 24, 182–184, 243
　NGO Code of Conduct, 182–184
　NGO Initiatives, 243
Non-Indigenous, 309
Non-LOTE Respondents, 513, 520, 526
Non-Policy, 309

Non-Refugee Populations, 87, 90
Non-Signatories, 55
Non-State Actors, 54, 100–102
Non-White Refugees, 366
Normal Historical Phenomenon, 306
Normlessness, 21
Numerator, 356
Nurses, 133–134, 139, 143, 147, 150, 156–157, 187, 277, 312, 330, 468
Nursing Education Partnership Initiative (*see also* NEPI), 173–174
Nutrition Deficiencies, 129, 134
Nutritional Services, 242

# O

Obesity, 91, 129–130, 316–318, 348, 352, 360, 374, 410–411, 484
Obstetrical Interventions, 137
Occupation Specifications, 137
Occupational Accidents, 137
Occupational Diseases, 126, 135, 368–369, 458–460
Occupational Health, 405, 409, 458, 468, 483, 485, 487, 489, 490–491
Occupational Injury, 136, 137, 410
Occupational Standards, 149
Oceania, 142, 373
Official Development Aid, 155
Offshore Detention Centres, 268, 273
Old Age Dependency Ratio, 188
Open Access App, 332
Open Centres, 231–233
Open Reception Centres, 228
Operation Aspida (Shield), 211
Operation Sovereign Borders, 264
Operation Xenios Zeus, 215–216
Oppressive Regimes, 77, 105
Organisation of American States (*see also* OAS), 105–106

Organisation for Economic Co-Operation and Development (*see also* OECD), 8, 124, 126, 129, 131–144, 147–152, 187, 429, 446, 536, 541–543
Outpatient Attendance, 47
Outpatient Clinics, 47
Overcrowded Cells, 217
Overcrowding, 46, 85, 217, 221, 271, 298
Overseas Contract Workers, 6
Overseas Qualifications, 135, 188, 488, 541
Overweight, 316–318, 411
Overwhelmed, 76, 81, 111

# P

Pacific Island Labourers Act, 264
Pacific Islanders, 364, 366
Pacific Solution, 260
Pact of San José, 106
Palestinians
    1948 mass displacement of palestinians, 102
    Palestinian refugee camps, 100
    Palestinian refugees, 80, 103
Passport for Emigration, 154
Patient Compliance, 88
Patras, 242–244
Peace Agreements, 58
Peace and Security, 57
Peace Treaty, 39, 42, 75
Peace-Building, 61, 63
Peacekeeping, 76
Peer Discussion Groups, 323
Pellagra, 95–96
Pension, 7, 397, 414, 543, 548
People Smugglers, 10, 104, 258
People Smuggling, 103–105, 263–264

Per Capita Income Gap, 2
Perinatal and Infant Mortality, 315
Perinatal Death, 137
Perinatal Health, 227
Peripheral Countries, 16
Periphery Societies, 16
Permanent Solutions, 108
Permanent Urban Hukou Status, 400
Perpetrators, 240
Perpetual Movement, 11
Perpetuation, 9
Persecuted People, 307
Persecution, 6, 8, 34, 73, 75–76, 230, 284, 367, 378
Personal Hygiene Kits, 237
Physical Abuse, 226, 452
Physical and Psychological Risks, 137
Physical Capital, 159
Physical Disabilities, 227
Physical Effects, 510, 522, 525
Physical Health Conditions, 220, 266
Physical Injuries, 44, 224, 461
Physical Security, 8
Physical Violence, 224, 450
Physician Advocacy, 329, 331, 337
Physician Coverage, 144
Physician-to-Patient Ratio, 143
Picture Brides, 442
Pioneer Brazilian Law, 107
Plantations, 311, 364–366
Pneumonia, 49
Police Authorities, 211, 238, 240
Police Officers, 211, 222, 225–226
Police Stations, 215–216, 218
Policies of Deterrence, 259
Policy Advocacy, 183
Policy Options, 23–24, 162, 545, 549
Policy Recommendations, 210, 246, 545

Policy Response, 23, 31, 33, 51, 123, 163, 210, 228, 256, 281, 392, 414–415, 463
Policymakers, 138, 324, 378, 455, 536
Political Aspects, 1, 6
Political Barriers, 275
Political Considerations, 8
Political Democratisation, 3
Political Instability, 35, 64, 175, 180, 292, 428, 510
Political Mismanagement, 77
Political Obstruction, 55
Political Restrictions, 102
Political Risk, 102
Political Solutions, 76, 111, 538
Political Violence, 98
Politically Induced Disasters, 77
Politically Turbulent, 110
Politically Volatile, 100, 102
Polyclinics, 237, 241–243
Pooled Cross-Sectional Data, 377
Poor Ante and Post-Natal Care, 137
Poor Camp Conditions, 87
Poor Camp Organisation, 88
Poor Economic Growth, 155
Poor Health Literacy, 277, 280, 379
Poor Living conditions, 41, 102, 220, 375, 490
Poor Mental Health, 25, 50, 95, 411
Poorest Countries, 35, 81
Population Growth, 124, 347, 433, 447, 470
Poseidon Land, 211
Poseidon Sea Joint Operations, 211
Positive Growth, 143
Positive Participation, 309
Positive Skilled Emigration, 154
Possess Legal Documentation, 235
Post-Detention, 223, 247

Post-Displacement, 95
Post-Emergency Camps, 86
Post-Emergency Sites, 87
Postpartum Depression, 137
Postpartum Sterilisation, 137
Post-Traumatic Stress Disorder (*see also* PTSD), 50–51, 97–99, 224, 265, 268–269, 335
Poverty and Social Instability, 87
Power Struggle, 35, 428
PRAKSIS, 242–245
Preconception Testing, 323
Pre-Departure, 297, 334, 379, 381, 408
Pre-Eclampsia, 137
Pregnancy Outcomes, 315, 348
Pregnancy-Related Morbidity, 137
Prejudiced Attitudes, 323
Pre-Liberal Economic Consolidation (1987–1997), 434
Pre-Migration, 126–129, 221, 226
Pre-Migration Environment, 363
Pre-Migration Examination, 127
Pre-Migration Factors, 266
Pre-Migration Health Risks, 221
Pre-Refugee Shelter Training, 336
Pre-Removal Detention, 216–219
Presidential Decree 114/2010, 214
Presidential Decree 668, 235
Pressure on Politicians, 312
Preterm Birth, 315, 317
Prevalence
    allergic diseases, 134–135
    atopy, 135
    cardiovascular disease (*see also* CVD), 90, 129–131, 316, 318, 320, 352, 373–376, 405, 411, 419, 459
    chemical exposure, 409

clinically relevant depressive symptoms, 412–413
high blood pressure, 224, 373
human papillomavirus, 405–406, 457
inflammatory risk factors, 130
major depressive disorders, 412
malarial parasitaemia, 46–47
mental disorders, 49, 98, 350, 368
mortality patterns, 36, 42, 135
nasal septal perforation, 460
Pellagra outbreak, 95
positive antibodies, 457
psychological symptoms, 412
Salmonella, 373
seroprevalence, 407
sexual abuse, 45, 265
sexually transmitted diseases, 406, 457, 498
spouse battering, 450
ulceration of mucosa, 460
vitamin D deficiency, 135
war-related and non-war-related sexual assault against women, 45
wasting, 91–92
Preventable Blindness, 93
Primary Health Care, 98, 100, 173, 237, 242–245, 291, 330
Principles of Refugee Protection, 100, 102
Private Sector, 110, 157, 163, 175, 188, 480
Privatisation, 187, 189
Pro-Bono, 107, 274–278
Procedural Requirements, 188
Production and Exchange, 16
Productivity, 329, 394, 469, 498, 539, 541

Professional Licensing, 188
Professional Mobility, 158
Profile of Refugees, 239
Programme Exchange, 173
Proletarian Class, 392
Promotion, 241, 348, 389, 394, 498
Proper Legal Documents, 89
Property Rights, 185
Proportional Morbidity, 47
Proportional Mortality Rates, 46
Prosecutors Act, 226
Prostitution, 44, 226, 453–454
Protection of Privacy, 60
Protection on Return, 58
Protein-Energy Malnutrition, 91
Protracted Refugee, 108, 111
Provision of Health Care, 24, 108, 275
Psychiatric Disorders, 270, 371, 374
Psychiatric Morbidity, 49
Psychiatric Services, 238, 274
Psychological Assessment, 272
Psychological Assistance, 238
Psychological Counselling, 234
Psychological Distress, 224, 491
Psychological Health, 493
Psychological Illness, 223
Psychological Morbidity, 277
Psychological Services, 238
Psychological Stress, 21
Psychological Support, 242, 274
Psychological Wellbeing, 486–491, 498
Psychosocial Adaptation, 98
Psychosocial Stressors, 315
Psychosocial Support, 237–241, 244
Psychotherapy, 98
Public Health Burden, 81
Public Information Sites, 185
Public Policies, 35
Public Services, 189, 235, 399, 544

## Index 579

Public Transportation, 279
Pull Factors, 7–8, 429, 433
Pull–Push Factors, 5
Push Factors, 5–8, 111, 189, 428, 548
Push–Pull Theory, 6

## Q

Quality of Care, 7, 138
Quality of Life, 7, 154, 215, 429, 465

## R

Racial Discrimination, 247, 483
Racism, 224, 458, 461, 466, 509–525, 545
Racist Colonial Legislation, 366
Racist Crime, 236, 239, 244
Racist Incident, 515–516
Racist Violence, 224–225, 239, 244, 525
Rallying Point, 76
Randomised Controlled Trials, 99, 380
Randomised Trial, 98, 499
Rape, 44–45, 92, 97, 220, 457
Rapid Assessment, 97
Rapid Industrialisation, 392, 419, 441
Rapid Influx, 81
Rapporteur, 101, 296–297
Rate of Smoking, 320
Rates of Overweight, 316
Ratification, 58, 64, 108, 240, 400, 537
Rational Choices, 12
Real-World Markets, 13
Reception Accommodations, 220
Reception Centres, 228, 236
Reception Conditions, 212, 229
Reception Facilities, 225–226, 241
Reception Mobile, 244
Reciprocity, 9
Reconciliation, 58, 63
Reconstruction Challenge, 61

Recruitment Agreement, 312–313
Recruitment Difficulties, 539
Recruitment Efforts, 308
Red Cross EU Office, 240
Reduced Competitiveness, 155
Reduced Mortalities, 111
Referrals, 222, 228, 241, 243, 245
Reforms, 180–181, 230, 391–392, 401, 545
Refoulement, 101, 103, 105
Refugee
    refugee act, 109
    refugee affairs, 76, 105
    refugee burden, 81, 100–103
    refugee camps, 84–88, 93, 100, 265, 276, 378
    refugee children, 91, 93, 99
    refugee claims, 210, 260, 263
    refugee conditions, 111
    refugee disease, 221
    refugee governance, 99–100
    refugee health nurses, 277
    refugee law, 55, 110
    refugee legislation, 110
    refugee lives at sea, 104
    refugee morbidity, 87
    refugee mortality, 81
    refugee mortality and morbidity, 87
    refugee movements, 108
    refugee population, 82–90, 94–96, 270
    refugee processing, 103
    refugee registration, 89
    refugee sites, 86
    refugee status, 105, 109, 255, 382
    refugees and global health e-learning program, 334
    refugees and non-refugee populations, 90

refugees basic rights, 88
refugees fleeing violence, 102
refugees' health, 81, 105, 109
refugees' welfare, 102
Regional Boundaries, 306
Regional Mechanisms, 105–107
Regional Resettlement Arrangement, 263, 283
Regional Screening, 104
Registration Centres, 89
Registration Status, 393, 399, 414
Regulations, 163, 182, 464, 468
Re-Integration, 51, 58, 65, 229, 245
Related Transnational Crime, 103–104
Relief Response, 51
Religious Factions, 102
Relocation Expenses, 367
Remittance Flows, 22, 161, 404
Remittance Markets and Diaspora Savings for Development, 177, 546
Remittances, 6–7, 11, 22–23, 123, 138, 158–162, 176–178, 188–190, 543, 546
Remote Areas, 4–5, 242
Removal Process, 216
Remuneration, 7, 153, 175, 539
Renal Disease, 90
Repatriation, 101, 104, 108, 242
Repressive Regimes, 103
Reproductive Health, 126, 138, 408
Resentment, 103
Resettlement, 55, 57, 104, 108, 110, 256, 261, 263, 283, 339, 441, 481
Residence Permits, 309, 432
Residency Policy System, 394
Residents Identification Card, 394
Resilience, 92, 323, 355–356, 520–524
Resourcing, 162–163
Respiratory Tract Infections, 43, 47, 221
Responses and Policies, 76

Responsibility, 15, 55, 57, 184
Restriction of International Mobility, 163, 169
Retention, 162–163, 167, 173–174, 182, 539
Retinopathy, 134
Re-Traumatisation, 223, 265
Retrospective Mortality, 40–43
Return Houses, 233
Return of and Retaining Talents, 175, 545
Return Option, 158, 162
Return to Bavaria, 167
Returning Phase, 51, 65
Reunify with their Families, 309
Revolutions, 76
Right to Development, 52
Rights and Freedoms, 55, 106, 338
Risk Factor, 85, 131, 134, 224, 265–266, 315–316, 320, 355, 373–375, 410–411
Risk of Absconding, 216, 233, 297
Risk of Obesity, 316
Rohingya Refugees, 105
Role Displacement, 21
Role Instability, 21
Rule of Law, 61, 63, 101, 338
Rural Regions, 5, 312
Rural/Urban, 153
Rural–Urban Labour Mobility, 392
Rural–Urban Linkages, 549
Russian Revolution, 76
Rwanda
    Rwandan refugee children, 93
    Rwandese refugee crisis, 81, 84
    Rwandese refugees, 88

## S

Safe Haven, 263, 308
Safe Water, 84

# Index

Safety Nets, 92
Salaries, 7, 153, 172, 181–183, 307, 455, 549
Salmon Bias, 23–24, 354, 375, 379–382
Sanitary Conditions, 41, 159
Sanitation, 45–46, 71, 84, 97, 217, 221
Scabies, 221, 238, 299
Scale-Up, 86, 323
Schengen Agreement, 211, 491
Schengen Area, 211
Schengen Borders Code, 211
Schengen Convention, 211
Schistosomiasis, 126, 332, 373
Schizophrenia and Sleeping Disorders, 322
School-Based Group Intervention, 98
Schooling Rate, 154
Science without Borders, 167
Scientific Outputs, 155
Screening Prior to Resettlement, 90
Scurvy, 93–96
Sea Arrests, 212
Second World War, 2, 109, 366, 491
Secondary Care, 228
Second-Generations Minorities, 320
Security Conditions, 41
Security Council, 101
Security Risks, 63, 77
Segmented Labour Market, 14
Segregated Districts, 309
Seizure of Power, 311
Selective Preference, 109
Self-Classification of Ethnicity, 322
Self-Determination, 52, 383, 481
Self-Sufficient, 393
Sending and Receiving Countries, 12, 23, 169, 172, 188, 545
Seoul Olympic Games (1988), 430
Separation of Families, 229

Service Utilisation, 279, 287, 458
Settlements, 43, 535
Severe Acute Malnutrition, 93
Severity of Malnutrition, 92
Sexual Coercion, 45, 452
Sexual Exploitation, 226, 453, 457
Sexual Slavery, 45
Sexual Torture, 44
Sexual Violence, 44–45, 87, 299, 329, 450, 457
Shelters, 241, 243
Shigella Dysentery, 84
Shortage of Unskilled Workers, 308
Signatories, 55, 109, 183, 256
Significant Barriers, 177, 277
Significant Burden, 81, 89, 538
Single Men, 220, 308
Single Mothers, 315, 323
Single-Continuum Model, 17
Skill Gap, 538
Skill Stream, 363
Skill Transfers, 132, 168, 547
Skilled Labour Market Shortages, 165
Skilled Recognised Graduate, 171
Skills Set For Advocacy, 336
Skin Diseases, 221, 267
Skin Lesion, 95
Slave Trade, 311
Slavery, 33, 453, 455
Slaves, 311
Sleeping Disorder, 322
Smoking, 129, 135, 315, 320, 348
Smuggling People, 33
Social Accountability, 339
Social and Recreational Events, 241
Social Cohesion, 63, 510
Social Counselling, 244
Social Institutions, 11

Social Insurance, 235, 246, 405
Social Integration Problems, 399
Social Isolation, 223, 269–270, 469, 543
Social Justice, 101, 106
Social Media, 511
Social Networks, 10, 17
Social Protection, 63, 111
Social Security Data, 354
Social Security System, 405
Social Services, 81, 242–243, 295, 301, 331, 414
Social Structures, 87, 354
Social Support, 237, 241–245, 262, 279, 355
Sociocultural Context, 185, 300
Sociocultural Factors, 279, 354
Socioeconomic Position, 315
Socioeconomic Status, 313, 315, 317–318, 322, 346–355, 462
Socioeconomic Structures, 77
Soft Commitment, 161
Soft Law, 55, 60, 64, 182
Soft Policies, 161
Somalia
    Somali refugees, 88
    Somalians, 313–314
South America, 79, 97, 185, 314, 347, 351, 483, 489, 494–495
Sovereignty, 51, 64, 124, 395
Soviet Union, 76, 391, 428, 430, 437, 439
Spanish Civil War, 76
Special Eligibility, 363
Special Naturalisation, 467
Specialised Scabies, 238
Specialist Medical, 247
Specific Administrative Unit, 393
Sphere Emergency, 83
Sphere Guidelines, 98, 217

Sports, 147, 248, 343
Spousal Violence, 450–451
Square Demonstration, 367
Sri Lanka, 78, 141, 147–148, 264, 292, 365
Staff Retention, 182
Staffing, 248
Standard Deviations, 91, 95
Standard of Living, 61, 257, 306
Standard Treatment, 88
Standardisation, 89, 102, 468
Standing Committee, 56, 61, 91, 93, 101, 394
Start-Up Chile, 167
Starvation, 403, 452
State Housing, 393
State Responsibility, 62
State Sovereignty, 51, 64
State-Orchestrated, 107
Status of Refugees, 6, 23, 74–75, 93, 256
Statutory Refugees, 109
STEGI Plus, 245
Stigma, 98, 299, 495
Stillbirth, 227
Street-Work, 245
Strengthening of Institutions, 173
Stress Impact on LOTE Speakers, 526
Stress Lead, 221, 447
Stress-Related Psycho-Somatic Problems, 98
Stroke Mortality, 131
Strongyloidiasis, 332
Stunting, 91
Subarachnoid Haemorrhage Incidence, 318
Subsist On Rice, 94
Substandard Living Conditions, 216, 246
Substantial Burden of Disability, 376

Index 583

Sub-Tropical Regions, 86
Sudan
　Eastern Sudan, 88
　Sudanese refugee children, 99
　Sudanese refugee settlement, 87
Suffer Violence, 224
Suicidal Ideation, 51, 269, 272, 490
Suicide Attempts, 51, 413
Super-Aged Society, 446
Supplementary Feeding Program (*see also* SFP), 92
Supplementation, 85, 94
Support for Multicultural Families Act, 445–446
Supporting the Declaration, 367
Surgery, 185–186
Surveillance, 85, 95, 97, 247, 407, 409, 419
Surveys, 40–43, 159, 380–382, 513, 523–526
Survival Sex, 44
Sustainable Return, 60
Sweep Operations, 239, 246
Syphilis, 371, 373, 406
Syria
　Syrian refugees, 81, 89–90, 93, 98
Systematic Monitoring, 247
Systemic Barriers, 275–276
System-Wide, 76

## T

Tax Breaks, 165
Taxation System, 173, 547
Taxation-Based Method, 178
Taxes, 162–163, 172, 543
TB Infection Reactivation, 127
Teachers, 52, 144, 147, 149, 349
Technical Assistance, 155, 177, 340
Technological Disasters, 81

Technological Revolution, 1
Technology Transfer, 158, 161–164, 547
Teenage Pregnancies, 315, 323
Teenage Pregnancy Problems, 323
Telecommunication, 3, 179
Telemedicine or E-Health, 185
Temporary and Unskilled Workers, 308
Temporary or Permanent Return, 162
Temporary Protection Visas, 263, 283
Temporary Urban Resident, 400
Temporary Work, 137, 171–172, 440, 484, 489
Termination of Pregnancy, 323
Terrorism, 178, 547
Testing Methods, 373
Thai–Myanmar Border, 87
Therapeutic Feeding Program, 92
Therapeutic Protocols, 97
Thiamin Deficiency, 93
Thiamine Deficiency, 94–95
Third Countries, 104–105, 294
Third Reich, 76
Third-Country National, 208, 221, 297
Thousand Talent Program, 165
Three-D Jobs, 433
Thresholds, 36, 41–43, 82–83
Tiananmen Square, 367
Togo, 90, 145, 152, 158
Tolerant Attitude, 306
Torture and Trauma, 273, 278
Touloum, 39, 82
Trade Agreement, 16, 183–188, 296
Trade and Investment Flows, 2
Trade Liberalisation, 2
Trade Practices, 11
Trade-Related Aspects of Intellectual Property Rights (*see also* TRIPS), 2, 185

Traficked, 226, 240, 457
  trafficked women and commercial sex workers, 457
  trafficking, 103–104, 226
Training and Support, 183–184
Traitors, 108
Transactional Sex, 87, 128
Transfer Centres, 218
Transfers of Labour, 393
Transit and Destination, 392, 453
Transit Point, 110
Transitional Measures, 169
Transitional Settlement, 51
Transitions, 76, 481, 544–545
Transnational Communities, 9
Transnational Corporations, 6
Transnational Crime, 103–104
Transparent and Healthy Policies, 178
Transportation, 2–6, 22, 275, 279, 332, 453, 483, 490
Trauma-Processing Activities, 98
Traumatic Idioms, 98
Travel Documents, 108–109, 257, 437
Trend Analysis, 212
Trends, 23, 87, 104, 144, 210–213, 293, 352, 431, 443
Tryptophan Deficiency, 95
Tuberculosis, 43, 48–49, 88, 126, 220, 227, 333, 368–369, 406–408, 460
Turkey
  the migration flows from Turkey, 312
  Turkish migrants, 131, 312, 376–377
  Turkish minority group, 312
  Turkish natives, 110
  Turks, 305, 308, 310–312
Two-Culture Matrix Model, 17
Typology, 77–78

## U

U5MR, 38–43, 82–83
United Nations (*see also* UN)
  1998 United Nations Guiding Principles on Internal Displacement, 54, 59
  United Nations Economic and Social Council, 54–55, 74
  United Nations High Commissioner for Refugees (*see also* UNHCR), 34, 59, 65, 74–76, 80, 83–86, 90, 98–110, 208–220, 230–246, 255–258, 292–300, 338–339, 537
    1951 UN Convention, 80
    1967 Protocol, 6, 75, 80, 99–100, 103, 109–110, 256
  United Nations Protocol to Prevent, Suppress and Punish Trafficking, 453
  United Nations Relief and Works Agency (*see also* UNRWA), 34, 100, 102
  United Nations System Standing Committee on Nutrition, 91, 93
  UN agencies, 99, 340
  UN Committee, 225, 259
  UN country program, 77
  UN General Assembly, 56, 102, 298
  UN Special Rapporteur on Torture, 54, 102
Unaccompanied Minors (*see also* UAMS), 218, 225–227, 237, 240–245, 260, 262, 271, 283
Unaccompanied Children, 229, 241–242
Unbalanced Sex Ratio, 418, 545
Uncontrolled Migratory, 295
Underemployment, 488
  Under-Five Mortality Rate, 36, 83, 92

underweight, 91
undesirables, 291, 294
undocumented arrivals, 207, 246
undocumented migration flows, 210
Unemployment, 175, 294, 308, 312, 323, 486, 540
Unfilled Vacancies, 157
Unhealthy Behaviours, 320, 353
Unintended Consequences, 173
Union of Soviet Socialist Republics, 76
Unique Detention Guidelines, 299
Universal Definition, 74
Unskilled Jobs, 136, 433
Unskilled Workers, 308–313, 433, 438
Uproot Millions of Refugees, 101
Upstream and Downstream Factors Influencing the Health, 458
Urban Employee Basic Medical Insurance (see also UEBMI), 458
Urban Refugees, 90–91
Urban–Rural Divide, 5
Use of Health Services, 135
Use of Land, 4
US Committee for Human Rights, 441
US-Born Hispanics, 351, 353
US–Korea Civil–Military Relations, 454
Utilisation of Health Systems, 324
Utilisation of Primary Health Care, 98

# V

Vacancies, 157, 435–436, 482, 539
Vacancy Rates, 157
Vaccination, 46, 85, 97, 203, 220, 246, 332–333, 405
Varicella, 333
Ventilation or Sunlight, 217
Vertical Trauma, 95

Vietnam War, 258, 367
Violations, 33–36, 53, 58, 100, 101–107, 236, 239, 441, 546
Violence Against Women, 45, 107, 450
Violent Penetrative Sexual Acts, 45
Visceral Adipose Tissue, 318
Visit and Employment Programme, 440
Vitamin A Deficiency, 85, 93–94, 96
Vitamin A Distribution, 93
Vitamin A Supplementation, 85, 94
Vitamin C, 93–94
Vocational Counselling, 237
Voluntary Repatriation, 242, 245, 263
Voluntary Return, 214, 229, 298
Vulnerability, 87, 220, 269, 297, 323, 366, 453
Vulnerable Detainees, 228

# W

Wage Arrears, 405
Wages, 12, 15, 392, 405, 415, 428, 452, 469, 480, 492, 496, 536, 543
Waist Circumference, 316
War or Violence-Related Injuries, 43–44
War-Traumatised, 98
Wasting Chronic Malnutrition, 91
Water Supply, 45–46
Water, Health, Soaps, 92
Waves of Refugees, 100
Weak Comprador Governments, Systems and Structures, 76
Weapon, 44
Weight-for-Age, 91
Weight-for-Height, 91
Well-Functioning Alternatives, 233
Wilson, Thomas Woodrow, 74
Win–Win, 183, 301

Work Permits, 235
Workplace
　　health in the workplace, 479–480
　　workplace acculturation, 482
　　workplace health, 483, 489, 492
　　workplace integration, 137
　　workplace policies, 489
Work Placement, 173
Work Related Disability, 136
Work Rotation, 137
Workforce, 15, 147, 150, 153–157, 163, 174–175, 182, 428, 440, 447, 457, 468, 480, 484, 489, 491, 493–494, 537, 540, 543, 548
Working Conditions, 7, 136–137, 469, 490, 492, 539
Working Holiday Programme, 171
Working-Age Population, 139, 543
Work-Related Fatalities, 136, 485
World Bank, 1–2, 159, 161, 176, 178, 404, 445–446

World Economy, 1
World Health Organisation (*see also* WHO), 24, 41, 43–44, 46–48, 85–86, 110, 188, 199, 498
　　WHO classification, 92
　　WHO European Region, 127–128
　　WHO-Led Resilient Health System, 300
World Systems Theory, 15–16
World Trade Organization, 2, 185
World War I, 307–308, 366, 487
World War II, 308, 367, 486–487

# X

Xenophobia, 224, 494
Xerophthalmia, 96

# Y

Yanggonju, 442–443, 454–455
Youth, 177, 241, 349